BIG BOOK OF
Apple
Hacks

First Edition

Chris Seibold

O'REILLY

BEIJING · CAMBRIDGE · FARNHAM · KÖLN · SEBASTOPOL · TAIPEI · TOKYO

BIG BOOK OF APPLE HACKS

by Chris Seibold

Published by Make:Books, an imprint of Maker Media, a division of O'Reilly Media, Inc.,
1005 Gravenstein Highway North, Sebastopol, CA 95472.

O'Reilly books may be purchased for educational, business, or sales promotional use.
For more information, contact our corporate/institutional sales department:
800-998-9938 or *corporate@oreilly.com*.

Print History

April 2008: First Edition

Publisher: Dale Dougherty
Associate Publisher: Dan Woods
Executive Editor: Brian Jepson
Editor: Tom Sgouros
Creative Director: Daniel Carter
Designers: Susan Brown and Jen Jackowitz
Production Manager: Terry Bronson
Copy Editor: Mary Anne Mayo
Indexer: Patti Schiendelman
Cover Photograph from Peter Belanger Stock
(http://stock.peterbelanger.com)

ISBN: 978-0-596-52982-6

CONTENTS

PREFACE

Ostensibly, you buy a computer or gadget to get something done. The something might be as simple as listening to MP3s you've ripped from your CD collection or as challenging as creating a full-length feature film. Apple is happy to sell you products to meet your needs. The trouble is your needs aren't exactly the needs of the next guy, and that's where hacking comes in. With a little (or sometimes a lot) of effort, you can make your Apple gadgets and software perform in the manner you wish them to. Apple stuff that does things exactly the way you want makes the Apple experience that much better.

There are over 100 hacks in this book and a passel of quick tips and tricks. Some are simple enough—you've probably already pulled them off—while others are a bit more challenging. All, to the right person, can be fun and useful.

So what can you expect? There is a wide range of hacks here. If you've got an iPhone, you can learn how to take your hard drive with you when you go. Tired of the look of OS X? Discover ways to tweak interface elements. Want to watch your Apple TV on yesterday's television set? You'll learn how. Worried about your Mac's security? You're covered.

This book covers Mac OS X, the iLife Suite of programs, the iPod, the iPhone, and Apple TV. Any particular part of the Apple universe you carry in your pocket is in here.

How to Use This Book

This is a book about hacking, so deciding how to use this book is completely up to you. You could, if the inclination hits you, use the pages for interesting origami projects. If you want to use the book in a more traditional manner, just start reading, it doesn't matter where. Each hack is as self-contained as possible (and points to other hacks when not) so there isn't any reason not to crack open the book at random and start reading. Chapter 1 contains some hacks that provide background for a lot of the other hacks in the book, so many will find that a useful place to start. Others might leap to the specific chapter that seems most interesting. A lot of the hacks depend on the command-line interface available via the Terminal program, so Chapter 4 is a good place to start if you haven't used that in a while.

How This Book Is Organized

While you can start reading anywhere in the book, it isn't a jumble of unrelated hacks. If you have a specific interest, this is a good place to decide where to begin.

Chapter 1, Before You Hack

Any time you're hacking Mac OS X, you run a risk of accidentally losing data. This chapter will help you minimize the risk by showing you how to create a solid backup and an emergency boot drive. This chapter also introduces some of the hacker's favorite tools, such as Xcode and PLIST files.

Chapter 2, Hacks for the Net

Everyone uses the Internet, but that doesn't mean you have to use the Internet in the Apple-recommended way. Learn how (and why) to use an alternative browser, enable Safari's Debug menu, build your own web server. You'll also learn how to reset Safari, how to avoid sending data you'd rather keep private when you're sending files, and how to automate web retrieval. You can even discover a great method for keeping files you create on the Internet for your eyes only.

Chapter 3, Hacking Mac OS X

Mac OS X has a lot going on, and you might not like all of it. Grown tired of Dashboard? You'll learn how to kill it. Love a particular Dashboard widget? You can move it to the Desktop. If that isn't enough, discover how to display a constantly changing picture on your Desktop, displaying information you want to know. Maybe you want to lose the Desktop altogether? No problem: you'll discover how to quit the Finder. You'll also be introduced to the wonder of OS X automation: Automator. Here you'll find a way to make disks targeted for specific Macs available to any Mac you choose, and so much more.

Chapter 4, Command-Line Fun

There is a lot of power in the command line, but the interface scares away some people who would love to harness its power. This chapter will ease your fears and then show some very cool things you can do with the Terminal. Want to batch process images? A few commands typed into the Terminal, and you're done! Want to run programs from the world of Linux? You'll learn how. You'll find how to use shell scripts to make life easier and even discover how to use virtually any storage space on the Internet as a virtual hard drive.

Chapter 5, Customizing the OS X Look and Feel

Sometimes you just want your Mac to look different than the guy's machine next to you at Starbucks. You can start by changing the login window, move forward by making Safari's error page look the way you want it to, and make Mail play the sounds you want it to. If that isn't enough, discover how to make custom screensavers and your own icons. There's more; by the time you're done, your Mac will look just like you want it to.

Chapter 6, Network and Security Hacks

Your computer is hooked to a giant network every time you hop on the Internet. Controlling the data that enters and leaves your computer is crucial. Learn how to monitor the data flowing out of your Mac (there is more than you think), learn how to protect your Mac from those with physical access, how to keep your traffic private and tricks to lock down (or share) your wireless network.

Chapter 7, Hacking the iPod

Everyone loves the iPod—well, there may be a few holdouts. If you are one of the millions of iPod owners out there, this chapter has something for you. You can learn how to lose the scratches and how to prevent them from happening in the first place for two cents. You'll discover a nifty way to get Wikipedia pages into your iPod and how to use your iPod to transport your Home folder. Taking your Home folder with you not enough? Discover a way to boot your Mac from your iPod. There's even more, so if you're an iPod fan, don't miss this chapter.

Chapter 8, Maximize Your Mac with Multiple Operating Systems

This book is focused on Apple, and hence Mac OS X. But a lot of the wider world uses Windows. With this chapter, you won't be left out of the Windows party. You can learn how install Windows on your Mac, how to get your data painlessly from one machine to another, and how to remove Windows when you just can't stand it any more. Not interested in Windows? There's more. Discover how to cleanly partition your hard drive prior to the Leopard upgrade and how to run Classic Mac OS on your Intel machine. For the intrepid hackers out there, a method to build your own screaming fast (and cheap) Mac is included.

Chapter 9, Hacking the iLife

The iLife suite is one of the best things about owning a Mac. But being one of the best things doesn't mean you won't want to hack it! Discover how to fix those messed up tags in iTunes, how to get your buddies chatting to a chatbot in iChat, how to print pictures from iPhoto the way you want, how to build a custom music visualizer, how to get more out of iWeb, and much more.

Chapter 10, Hack the Apple TV

The Apple TV is an under-rated piece of Apple hardware. With this chapter, you can turn your Apple TV into a web-browsing machine, discover a method to use it with older TVs, find out how to upgrade the hard drive, and learn how to manipulate the files on the AppleTV remotely. If you've got an Apple TV, you won't want to miss these hacks.

Chapter 11, Hack the Latest and Greatest: Leopard

Leopard is the latest (and likely greatest) release of Mac OS X. But Leopard isn't so perfect you shouldn't touch it. Make Leopard bow to your will by designing your own stationery for Mail, get more out of Spotlight searches with Boolean operators, and discover a method to get Time Machine to back up where, what, and when you want it to. Here, you'll gain control over widget creations with three simple tricks, make Leopard more visually appealing.

Chapter 12, Hack the iPhone

The iPhone Software Development Kit (SDK) is finally here, but that doesn't mean there aren't any reasons to hack the iPhone. In this chapter, you can find ways to make password management easier, install third-party applications, jailbreak your iPhone, bypass activation, blog with your iPhone, and access the media on your Mac while you're on the go with your iPhone.

Chapter 13, Hacks for Laps

Laptops have gone from expensive luxury to everyday computers in the last few years. That means you want more control over your MacBook. Learn how to disable the iSight, how to soup up that old iBook, build a custom laptop cooler for your machine, install dual drives in your MacBook Pro, or just swap the current drive out for a larger one. If that isn't enough, there is also a method to have your MacBook respond to being slapped.

Chapter 14, Multimedia Hacks

One of the most useful things about a Mac is how effortlessly you can use the machine to store, sort, and play multimedia files. In this chapter, you'll gain even more control over your media by learning how to get your TiVo and Mac to play together, where to find sources for free and legal music, a method of playing music without bothering with iTunes, and how to use MacMame to turn your Mac into a classic arcade machine. If multimedia is your thing, this is your chapter.

Chapter 15, Hack Some Hardware

Hardware hacks are my favorite kind of hack; if they are your favorite, this is the chapter for you. Want a Mac in your car? Learn how to install one. Got a scratched DVD? It isn't necessarily a coaster: fix it up with stuff you have lying around the house. Into the weather? With a few tools you can turn your Mac into a weather-monitoring beast. Tired of losing the Internet when the power goes out? Run your modem off batteries! That isn't all: this chapter also covers integrating a Mac into your home, custom video cable production, and more.

Conventions Used in This Book

This book uses the following typographical conventions:

Italic

Used to indicate new terms, URLs, filenames, file extensions, directories, and folders.

`Constant width`

Used to show code examples, verbatim searches and commands, the contents of files, and the output from commands.

Gray

Used in examples and tables to show commands or other text that should be typed literally.

`Constant width gray`

Used in examples, tables, and commands to show text that should be replaced with user-supplied values.

Pay special attention to notes set apart from the text with the following icons:

 This icon indicates a tip, suggestion, or general note. It contains useful supplementary information or an observation about the topic at hand.

This icon indicates a warning or note of caution.

The slider icons, found next to each hack, indicate the relative complexity of the hack:

Easy:

Intermediate:

Expert:

$, #

The $ symbol is used in some examples to show the user prompt for the bash shell; the hash mark (#) is the prompt for the root user

Using Code Examples

This book is here to help you get your job done. In general, you may use the code in this book in your programs and documentation. You do not need to contact us for permission unless you're reproducing a significant portion of the code. For example, writing a program that uses several chunks of code from this book does not require permission. Selling or distributing a CDROM of examples from O'Reilly books does require permission. Answering a question by citing this book and quoting example code does not require permission. Incorporating a significant amount of example code from this book into your product's documentation does require permission.

We appreciate, but do not require, attribution. An attribution usually includes the title, author, publisher, and ISBN. For example: "Big Book of Apple Hacks, by Chris Seibold. Copyright 2008 O'Reilly Media, Inc., 978-0-596-52982-6."

If you feel your use of code examples falls outside fair use or the permission given above, feel free to contact us at permissions@oreilly.com

Acknowledgments

First of all, I want to thank my wife, Gina, for supporting me through this process. She puts up with a lot just being married to me and putting up with the production of this book was above and beyond the call of duty.

I'd also like to thank my editors. Brian Jepson put up with all of my silly questions and Tom Sgouros put up with all of my silly writing. Without the help of Tom and Brian this book would be both impossible to read and the hacks would be impossible to implement. I'd also like to thank Rich Rosen who performed a time-crunched bit of heroic editing. Anything you read in this book that strikes you as good is likely due to the outstanding work by Brian, Tom, and Rich.

On a more personal note, I'd like to thank a few people who told me I could do this. First is Dr. Catherine Higgs, an excellent teacher who encouraged me to write more often. I'd also like to thank Hadley Stern who believed I could actually write a book for O'Reilly, and Chuck Toporek who told me, "You can definitely do this" after seeing some sample hacks.

I'd also like to thank my dad, Steve Seibold, mostly because he gave me $50 to get his name in the book somehow.

We'd Like to Hear from You

Please address comments and questions concerning this book to the publisher:

O'Reilly Media, Inc.

1005 Gravenstein Highway North

Sebastopol, CA 95472

(800) 998-9938 (in the United States or Canada)

(707) 829-0515 (international or local)

(707) 829-0104 (fax)

We have a web page for this book that lists errata, examples, and any additional information. You can access this page at: http://www.makezine.com/go/applehacks.

To comment or ask technical questions about this book, send email to *bookquestions@oreilly.com*.

Maker Media is a division of O'Reilly Media devoted entirely to the growing community of resourceful people who believe that if you can imagine it, you can make it. Consisting of Make Magazine, Craft Magazine, Maker Faire, as well as the Hacks, Make:Projects, and DIY Science book series, Maker Media encourages the Do-It-Yourself mentality by providing creative inspiration and instruction.

For more information about Maker Media, visit us online:

MAKE: www.makezine.com

CRAFT: www.craftzine.com

Maker Faire: www.makerfaire.com

Hacks: www.hackszine.com

BIG BOOK OF
Apple
Hacks

First Edition

Chris Seibold

1

BEFORE YOU HACK

When you get a new computer, iPhone, or iPod, the device comes preconfigured in the way Apple feels will be of most use to the greatest number of their customers. Apple usually gets the out-of-the-box experience just right, thus Apple products are quickly set up and easy to use with the factory-set defaults. The problem is that you're not a faceless average Apple user, you're an individual, and you likely want to make your Apple product conform to your wishes rather than conforming to the way Apple intended you to use the product. This is the essence of hacking: getting your stuff to do what you want in the manner you want. Fortunately, tech stuff tends to be near infinitely hackable, customizable, and extensible, which means that you can truly be the unbending overlord of all your Apple gadgets. That said, there are a few initial steps that will make your forays easier and safer. The hacks in this chapter are where to begin.

HACK 01: Back Up Now with Disk Utility

When it comes to backing up your data, the options are bountiful. This hack reveals how to make an exact copy of your hard drive using Apple's free Disk Utility.

There's an old joke that says it isn't a question of "if" your hard drive will crash, it is a question of "when." Which is undoubtedly true: given enough time, everything will fail. This is a certainty that many of us have avoided either by dumb luck or buying a new machine every couple of years. That means that the people who haven't suffered a computer catastrophe feel immune to the possibility of massive data loss and behave accordingly. If you're one of the smug folks thinking unintended data destruction will never happen to you, please note that in your hands you are holding *The Big Book of Apple Hacks* and realize that things are different now. Once you start hacking, you're implicitly taking a chance that something could go wrong.

So back up your files. If you're running Leopard, you can let Time Machine do the heavy lifting; if you're running an older version of OS X or if you don't like Time Machine for some reason, you can try one of these strategies.

Backing Up with Disk Utility

There are a lot of options when it comes to backing up your files. A backup could be as simple as a copy of your data on the same hard drive or as complex as a secure hard drive stored in a fireproof and waterproof box with full-time security guards. This hack covers a middle ground of sorts: your data stored on a separate hard drive but a hard drive you can still use on a day-to-day basis. What no-cost, included-on-every-Mac application can be used to make an all-inclusive backup? Why, the aptly named Disk Utility! (see Figure 1-1.)

Figure 1-1.
It's hard to tell by looking but Disk Utility is a powerful backup tool

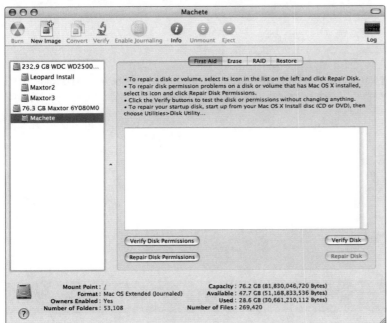

The confusing thing for some is Disk Utility's terminology. Instead of calling the process something recognizable to the average guy, Disk Utility calls the copies it creates *images*. These images are much more useful than a simple drag-and-drop copy. Disk Utility manages to maintain permissions, hidden Unix files and a plethora of other unseen, but very important, data throughout the process. The upshot of all this careful copying is that the copy is, when restored, **exactly** like the original.

First things first: to use Disk Utility to copy your startup drive, you'll have to start up from an alternate source. The source could be an OS X installation disk, another Mac in FireWire disk mode, or even another partition.

Figure 1-2 >>
You can't duplicate your current start up disk!

QUICK TIP

YOU CAN DO MORE THAN INSTALL FROM YOUR OS X INSTALL DVD

If you boot up from an installation DVD, you don't have to install OS X. Wait until your Mac is up and running, and access Disk Utility from the drop-down Applications menu. From here, you can repair permissions, erase and partition entire drives, set up a Redundant Array of Independent/ Inexpensive Drives (RAID) scheme, format drives in a variety of formats, and duplicate your main hard drive (see Figure 1-2). If you're using Leopard and Time Machine, starting up from an install disk is the recommended way to restore your disk if something very icky has happened. Be aware that running a Mac from a DVD is much slower than from a hard drive so be prepared to wait.

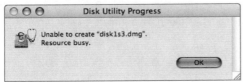

Once your Mac has been restarted from an alternate source, you can go about the business of copying your hard drive. Select the drive you want to back up, and click the `New Image` button. Once the selection is made, you'll get a chance to name the image and select where you want the image to live (Figure 1-3).

Figure 1-3.
This is your big chance to name the image and decide where the backup will reside

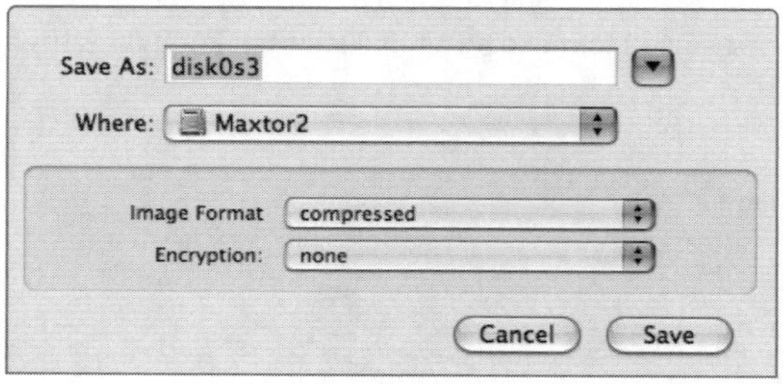

You're also presented with some other options. Clicking the arrows next to the Image Format label gives you some exclusionary options. You can pick one of the following:

- Read-only

- Compressed

- Read/write

- CD/DVD master

QUICK TIP ✕

AVOID CD/DVD CONFUSION

If you want your backup to go to a CD or DVD, you don't have to choose the CD/DVD master option to burn the image. That option exists to make a duplicate of CDs and DVDs. Backing up your complete hard drive to a DVD will be quite a trick since it likely consumes far more data than a DVD can hold. If you're determined to use DVDs as a backup option, you'll have to devise a method to systematically store all your data on DVDs. Reserve one DVD for the System, one for your media files, etc.

Incidentally, here's a useful trick, now that you've been introduced to Disk Utility. You can use the CD/DVD master option to create a copy of a CD or DVD that is required to be in your optical drive when a particular program is running (games do this all the time). Simply create the image, and park it on your regular disk drive. Once mounted, said image will likely fool the onerous program into thinking the required disk is present. The benefits are obvious: you can save the actual disk, the annoying noise from your optical drive will be gone, and your hard drive is much faster than an optical drive. There are limits, though. This sounds great for movie DVDs right? Not so fast. While you can create the necessary copy, trying to get OS X to play the movie from your hard drive won't work because of copyright restrictions.

Your choices come down to *read only*, *compressed*, or *read/write*. Since we are backing up an entire disk for archival reasons, the two best choices are either read-only or compressed. Choose **read-only** if you have copious amounts of backup space and want the process to go a little faster; choose **compressed** to save some precious hard drive space.

> *Read-only* and *compressed* make sense but what about *read/write*? Creating a disk image with read/write generates an image that, when mounted, can be manipulated. It's a very useful feature if you want to add files at a later date or trouble-shoot a software problem, but since you're after a rock-solid immutable backup, it's not the ideal option in this instance.

Finally, you can chose between an encrypted image and one that anyone can use. Choosing AES-128 (Advanced Encryption Standard) encryption results in Disk Utility asking for a password and requiring said password before you can get at the stored data. With that in mind, either go unencrypted or take pains to make sure the password is not lost. Saving the password in the Keychain is the default option, but this is one case where that isn't enough. You'll need this image in case of catastrophic failure and that means you might not be able access Keychain. Hence, if you choose to password-protect your data, write your password down somewhere safe. A backup you can't access is exactly as useful as no backup at all.

Once all the choices have been made, click Save, and Disk Utility will create a disk image containing all of your valuable data (see Figure 1-4).

Figure 1-4.
Protecting your data from prying eyes

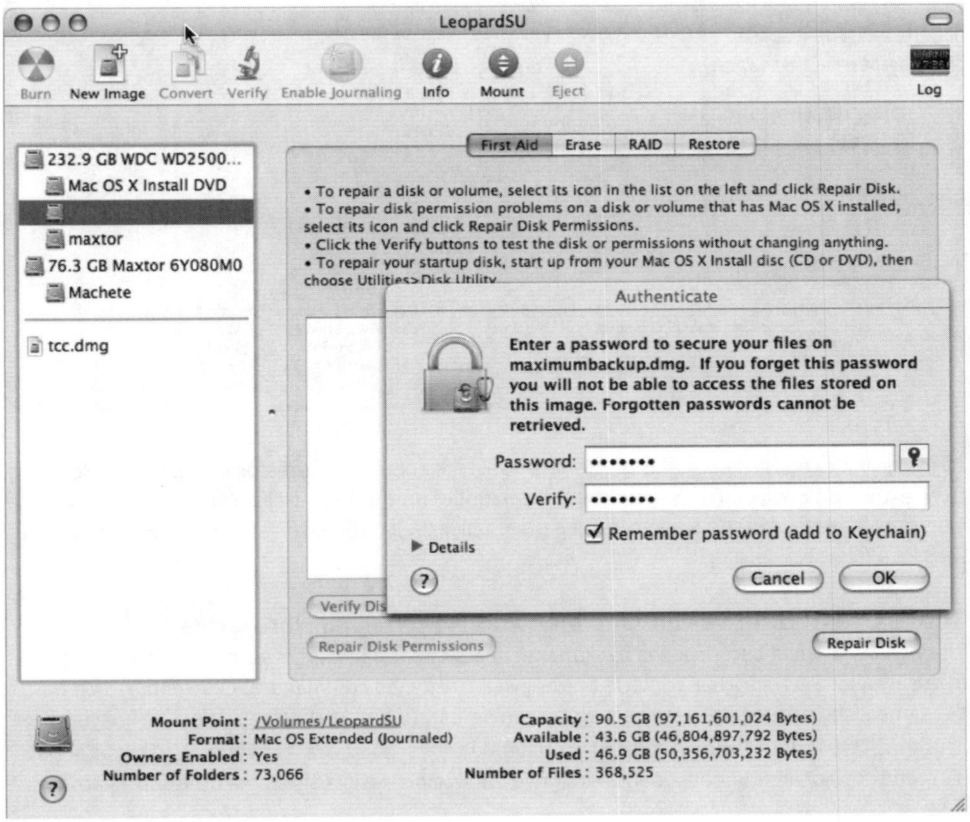

LEOPARD IS EVEN MORE SECURE

Leopard takes security up another level by adding AES-256 encryption. The encryption is tougher to crack (your password choice will be the weak link) but takes significantly longer to encode.

Now that you've done all this work, you're ready for the worst, or at least a sudden complete hard-drive failure. Once that happens, you'll want to know how to get your precious data back in a usable format. The process is deliciously simple: open up Disk Utility, click on the Restore option, and drag the disk image you want to use as your source to the Source field. Choose the drive you want the disk to be restored to, and drag it to the (predictable) Restore field. There is a bit of oddness about Disk Utility in Tiger that isn't present on Leopard. In Tiger, for some unknown reason, in some instances you can only drag the disk to the Restore field from the Disk Utility window (see Figure 1-5).

Figure 1-5.
Disk Utility oddity

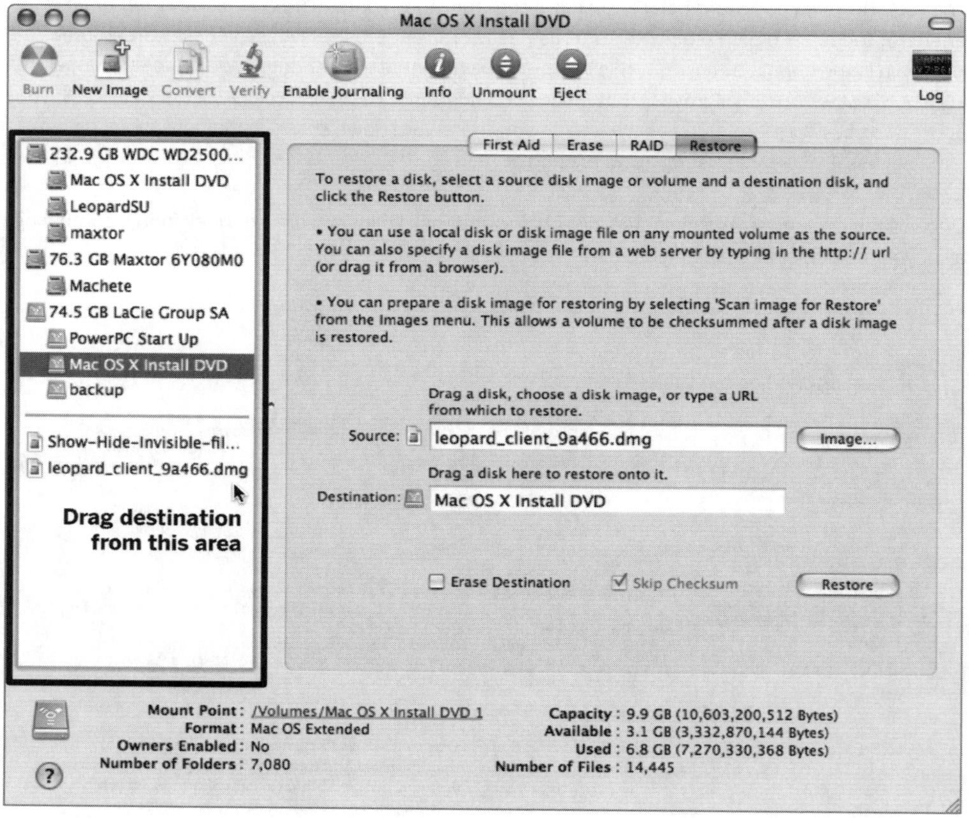

All that is left to do is sit back and wait for Disk Utility to complete the restoration process. Be aware that restoring a drive can take a substantial amount of time, and you'll lose any changes since you've created the disk image, so restoring from a Disk Image should be only attempted after other repair methods have failed.

That's Great, But I've Got One Mac and No External Hard Drive!

The weakest form of backup is the backup that exists on the same drive as the rest of your data. In the event of a physical hard drive failure or even a mistyped command, backup data stored on the same disk as the one you are backing up can be lost. That said, the duplication of information provides some level of security, and if your options are limited and your hard drive is spacious enough, a second copy of all your data on the hard drive is a worthwhile investment of time and gigabytes.

QUICK HACK

SELECTIVELY BACK UP WITH DISK UTILITY

While this hack reveals a method for backing up the entire drive, it might occur to you that creating images of individual files or folders instead of the entire drive might be very useful. Disk Utility won't copy any file until it is ensconced in a folder, so once your file or files are *folderized,* choose File→New→Disk Image from folder from the Disk Utility pull-down menu, and create images with reckless abandon.

Unfortunately you can't create an image of the disk and store it on the disk with Disk Utility because, while Disk Utility is attempting to image the disk, it will also be attempting to image the image that is imaging the disk. Another tactic is needed. First, you'll need to create at least two partitions on your hard drive and then copy the partition where your precious data resides to the newly created partition following the steps outlined earlier. For information on nondestructive partitioning, see [Hack #66].

Figure 1-6.
A very quick backup

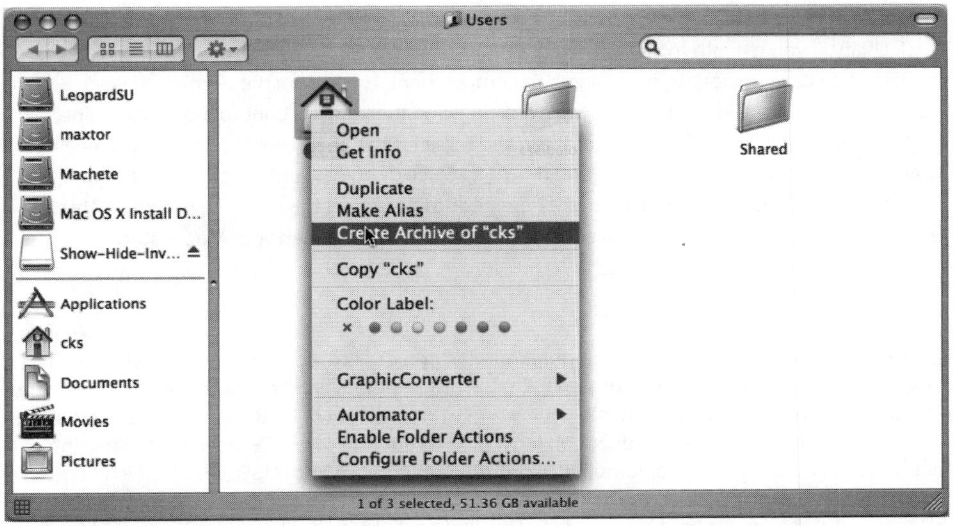

QUICK TIP

ONLY BACK UP THE HOME FOLDER

This hack describes ways to back up your entire hard drive, but with the way OS X is laid out, most of the information that is important to you resides in your Home folder. If you've dutifully saved your various install disks, you can get by with only duplicating your Home folder (and the Home folders of other users of the computer). Backing up only the Home folder isn't as comprehensive, but offers the benefits of being much quicker and easier to implement. Using Disk Utility, simply right-click the home folder (or any folder you want to back up for that matter), and select Create Archive (see Figure 1-6).

HACK 02: Create an Emergency Bootable Flash Drive

A full reinstall of a backup isn't necessary every time something goes wrong; often problems can be fixed with your favorite Disk Utility or a copy of free software found on the Web. This hack shows you how to create an emergency boot volume with the fix-it applications of your choice.

It would be nice to be able to burn a startup Mac OS X DVD with repair tools of your choice on the disk, but that is a very tricky thing to do. Some high-level Apple developers have the tools to pull it off, but those without access to the tools, you can't create a bootable DVD. Since creating a bootable DVD is out of the question, it is time to think of a second option. How about flash memory? Flash memory is ideal for this hack because it is not volatile (the contents don't change if the chip is powered down), can be found everywhere (thumb drives, iPod nanos, and camera cards all employ flash), and is relatively cheap. (A 4 GB thumb drive sufficient for our purposes retailed for $20.44 on Amazon at the time of writing.) Flash also has one important advantage over a DVD in this case, it can be written to during the boot process, which is the primary sticking point about creating a bootable DVD.

Before getting started, it is important to note that this process is much easier with Intel-based Macs. USB thumb drives are everywhere. USB flash drive readers can be found as cheap as $5, and you probably already have one built into your printer. This ubiquity of USB flash devices is great if you have an Intel Mac but doesn't do much for you if you have a PowerPC-based Mac. While Intel Macs can boot off of USB with aplomb, PowerPC Macs can't boot from USB. Well, that isn't strictly true. By meddling with the firmware, it is possible to boot at least some PowerPC-based Macs from USB drives, but the results are far from ideal. The cheapest way to boot a PowerPC-based Mac from flash is to obtain a FireWire card reader. While much pricier than USB card readers, you'll not only be able to boot your PowerPC-based Mac from flash, you'll be able to transfer pictures in record time. One option for a FireWire card reader is produced by Lexar (www.lexar.com), though there are undoubtedly others.

Creating a Bootable Disk

The goal is clear: devise a method to slim down the system folder from a bloated all-inclusive mess to a svelte, useful copyable size. There are obstacles in the way, though. As mentioned before, just dragging and dropping isn't going to cut it. Not only will that method not maintain symbolic links and permissions, it will also fail to catch invisible files and folders. To perform this hack, we'll need a few things:

- A partitioned drive or flash media with at least 4 GB of space

- A willingness to use SuperDuper! or Terminal and `rsync`.

⚡ Don't try to pull off this hack using your current startup disk as a guinea pig (i.e., erasing huge chunks of your drive). The best-case scenario is that you'll still be able to boot your computer with a loss of functionality; the worst-case scenario is that you'll have a machine that won't boot and no emergency boot disc.

Time to get started creating something bootable. If you use SuperDuper!, you'll note that you have only one option if you want your system to end up on the target disk. That is, you'll have to clone the entire drive. If you have the space, the replication doesn't matter, you'll be deleting files as soon as the process is over. Think of it as a momentary inconvenience.

You aren't left out if you simply don't have the space to clone your drive: `rsync` can come to the rescue. While SuperDuper! insists on cloning the whole drive, `rsync` can selectively clone folders. It is a little more work in the Terminal but the process is less drive space-intensive.

> You can use scripts with SuperDuper!, so a script to clone just selected parts of the drive is possible. By the time you wrote the script, if you were so inclined, you could have accomplished the task with `rsync`. If you find yourself repetitively using SuperDuper!, it is well worth your time to write a script to free you from repetitive tasks.

Before going further, take this moment to inspect your target disks to ensure they are ready for the process. The things to be aware of are the partitioning scheme used and the Ownership and Permissions settings. For the partition scheme, you'll want to choose the appropriate scheme for your particular Mac. For Power PC-based Macs, the choice is Apple Partition Map (APM), while Intel-based Macs prefer the Globally Unique Identifier (GUID) partition scheme. Determine which partition schemes your disk is using, and change them if necessary using Disk Utility.

Just one more step to fully prepare for this hack: checking the Permissions for the target disk. By default, OS X ignores ownership on disks connected through FireWire and USB but that isn't an option for a bootable drive. Right-click the disk(s) you'll copy to and choose Get Info. Finally, uncheck the box next to "Ignore ownership on this volume" (see Figure 1-7).

Figure 1-7.
In this case, ignoring ownership is a bad idea

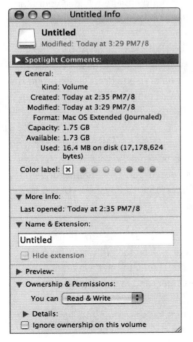

QUICK TIP

HEY, IT'S THE TERMINAL

If you've used the Terminal before, `rsync` will exhibit the behavior you expect. If you haven't used it before, the commands, options, and bleakness of the interface might leave you a little confused. The Terminal has too much in it to fit in a little sidebar, so check out Chapter 4 for a more detailed discussion of the Terminal and how to use it.

QUICK HACK

JUST STICK WITH APM

While Intel Macs "officially" require a GUID-partitioned drive, reality differs quite a bit from Apple's position. Intel Macs have no problems booting from the more venerable APM scheme. That inclusive behavior might change with a future software update or OS release, so the safest route to take is the one recommended by Apple. On the other hand, changing a disk's partitioning scheme requires partitioning the disk, something you might not want to do, so don't be afraid to stick with APM.

If you're using SuperDuper! for this hack, the first step is easy: fire up SuperDuper!, and choose the drive to copy and the destination you want the copy to occupy (see Figure 1-8).

Figure 1-8.
SuperDuper! gets to work

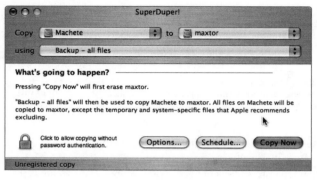

Once the copying process is complete, you really ought to remove any unnecessary (for booting) files. This can seem an impossible task. Sorting through all your files and culling the superfluous would be impossible even if you were blessed with an uncanny ability to tell what each file did simply by looking at the filename.

As fate (or Apple programmers) would have it, it turns out that only a few folders and files are necessary to boot your Mac. It further turns out that these files and folders are invisible. So the chances of deleting the bin folder accidentally are zero. All that means is that once you've copied your drive with SuperDuper!, you can delete everything but the System folder, and the drive will boot your Mac. Be aware that if you just wantonly pitch everything but the System folder, your Mac will boot, but you won't be able to do much. After all, all the applications are gone.

The easiest thing to do is to pitch everything but the System folder, but recreate an Applications folder on the bootable drive and place copies of the applications you wish to use in case of sudden nastiness there. This will work flawlessly for programs you install via drag and drop. Other programs rely on more invasive installs; the likelihood that these programs will continue to function without complaint is small.

Now that your system is sufficiently slim to fit on 4 GB of flash media, it is time to put the system on the flash drive. Select the drive, and choose Get Info. Ensure the box is not checked next to Ignore Ownership on this volume, and use SuperDuper! to copy your slimmed-down emergency drive with your hand-selected applications to the flash drive. Once SuperDuper! is finished, you are in possession of a bootable flash drive suitable for dire situations.

Using SuperDuper! is a great option if you have the required drive space and the time to fiddle with multiple copies. If you don't, then `rsync` is the answer you're looking for. With `rsync`, you can specify which folders to copy or exclude, and write everything directly to the flash drive. The downside is that you'll have forgo the easy-to-use GUI of SuperDuper! and rely on the Terminal.

The tempting thing to think is that you can simply copy the System folder with `rsync` and be done with the problem. That isn't the case; necessary folders like *usr* and *bin* don't actually reside in the System folder as you might expect. Instead, the required folders reside at the root level of your directory. You just can't see them because they are invisible. Hence a more encompassing approach is needed. The solution is to tell `rsync` to copy the entire disk except the folders that aren't needed.

If you've been playing along, you know that the only folder you need that you can actually see is the System folder. On a typical Mac, at the root level, you'll have just a few folders. My machine looks like Figure 1-9.

Figure 1-9.
A semi-typical Mac folder system

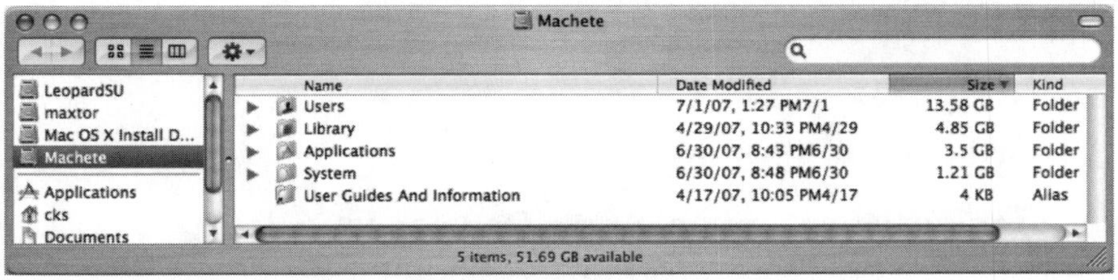

There are three directories we want to exclude from the copying. By default, `rsync` copies everything. To exclude specific directories (folders), `rsync` has to be made aware of your wishes. A typical `rsync` command to complete the operation will look something like:

```
$ sudo rsync -av --exclude /Users/ --exclude /Applications/ \
    --exclude /Library/ / /Volumes/Emerboot
```

The command is a little cryptic to the average user, so a look at what each bit of instruction is doing is required.

The `sudo` command authenticates the user to make sure you have sufficient privileges to run the process (`rsync` needs to run as root). Leave this step out, and you'll get a ton of messages telling you about insufficient privileges.

The `rsync` part of the command line invokes the program. It might not a have a GUI interface but `rsync` is still a powerful program.

Right after `rsync` are a collection of "flags" that indicate various options involved in running `rsync`. The `-av` you see is really two flags mashed together for ease of typing. The `-a` tells `rsync` to copy the directories recursively and preserve things like symbolic links. The `-v` notifies `rsync` that you want some feedback while it is doing the job. This isn't strictly necessary to get the job done, but at least you'll see what files are being copied.

A little further out the line, the single slash, `/`, indicates the root of your filesystem, while the `/Volumes/Emerboot` identifies the target you want to copy to. Mac OS X puts all its disks and disk images into the */Volumes* directory, which is a little confusing because that's under the root level. Just think of it as a way to keep track of the things in the upper left corner of your Finder windows. The `rsync` program won't try to copy in that directory, so you don't really have to worry about it.

Finally the three `--exclude` declarations tell `rsync` what not to copy, a critical factor when you're trying to save space. In this case, you are telling `rsync` to leave the */Users*, */Applications* and */Library* folders alone.

Hit return, and let `rsync` do all the hard work of duplicating bits and bytes, and when the process is complete, you'll have a destination disk with the necessary files for booting your Mac. Create an Applications folder (File→New folder) on your new boot drive, drop the applications you want to use when things go wrong into your new emergency drive, and you're ready to go!

Using the Emergency Boot Disk

With all that work behind you, you now have a bootable flash disk. When booting off this disk, some disconcerting things will happen. The Dock will be full of transparent question marks (remember, you didn't copy all the space-hogging programs when you were making the disk), and your Mac will launch into the Setup Assistant. Ignore the Setup Assistant (you can delete *Setup Assistant.app* from your system folder if you don't want to deal with it) or use the Finder to force quit if necessary. Navigate to wherever you chose to store your emergency repair programs, and run them until your Mac's built-in drive is returned to a working state.

HACK 03: Install Developer Tools

Every Mac ships with a copy of Apple Developer Tools; install these free tools for maximum hacking fun.

It wasn't that long ago that if you wanted to use Apple Developers Tools, you had to steel yourself for a wallet-lightening experience. That changed when Panther shipped, and every copy of the system came bundled with a full copy of Apple Developers Tools.

Developer Tools might seem like a waste of disk space if you're not planning to develop any software for Macs, but the free Developers Tools aren't useful only to clever caffeine-fueled programmers. The programs included with Apple Developer Tools can be useful to just about anyone who owns a Mac.

What You'll Get

The Xcode installer installs a suite of programs. Each one does something different, and together they can generate powerful applications for OS X. We're not concerned with all the programs that come with an Xcode install but a few programs are valuable hacking tools referenced later in this book. The programs that are particularly useful for the hacks in this book are:

- Property List Editor (great for editing *.plist* files)

- Interface Builder (for giving applications a face lift)

- Icon Composer (for making your art into icons)

Installing Xcode

Xcode uses an installer program, so installing it isn't much of a trick. There aren't an abundance of customization options, so just click the installer, and let it go. You can minimize even that step by installing Xcode when you're installing OS X.

While the install is easy, finding Xcode can be a chore. You know you've installed Xcode, but it isn't in the Applications folder where the tools you use every day usually reside. This can cause more than a little confusion; after recommending a friend install Xcode, he later confided he tried to install the suite again and again. He could tell something was happening because the free space on his hard drive shrank with every install (a standard Xcode install requires 2.8 GB of hard drive space), but he couldn't find Xcode.

Instead of being installed in the *Applications* folder (where you'd expect), Xcode is installed at the root level of your hard drive, under *Developers* (where developers expect it). To get at Xcode, use the Finder and have fun exploring.

HACK 04: Understand Your User Account

Before Mac OS X was released, there wasn't really a concept of a user or account in the Macintosh environment. This hack introduces you to what it means to have an account and what this business of a Home directory is all about.

When Mac OS X first appeared, a lot of old-school Mac users were aghast at the concept of user accounts, especially when they were the only ones using their computer. "Why go through all the hassle when I'm the only one who uses my computer?" they asked. The complaints only intensified as users were asked to enter an administrator password for access to certain files, sometimes even denied access to settings and files on their very own computers—the gall of it!

The reasoning is twofold: to protect you from yourself and to support Mac OS X's multiuser environment.

The concept of protecting you from yourself might at first blush appear intrusive, but we've all had an instance in which we've deleted an innocent file from our OS 9 System folder, only to discover our idiocy when our system didn't reboot, our printer didn't print, or our modem didn't sizzle. In this regard, OS X has your back; crucial files necessary for everyday operation are protected from overzealous removal.

The multiuser environment of OS X is based on technology that's been around for a while in the Unix world: a system of checks and balances that stop your kid sister from gleefully deleting that Photoshop file you've been working on all weekend. Whether you're the only user isn't a concern; protection from the inside (yourself or your kid sister) and protection from the outside (malicious crackers, viruses, and Trojans) becomes paramount.

While a determined user can delete any file on his OS X machine with enough effort, Apple has wisely made it difficult to do so through Mac OS X.

What's in a Name?

When creating an account (System Preferences→Accounts→New User), either the initial account upon installing Mac OS X, or an additional account—you're prompted for both your Name (e.g., John Jacob Jingleheimer Schmidt) and something called a Short Name, as shown in Figure 1-10.

Figure 1-10.
Selecting a Name and Short Name

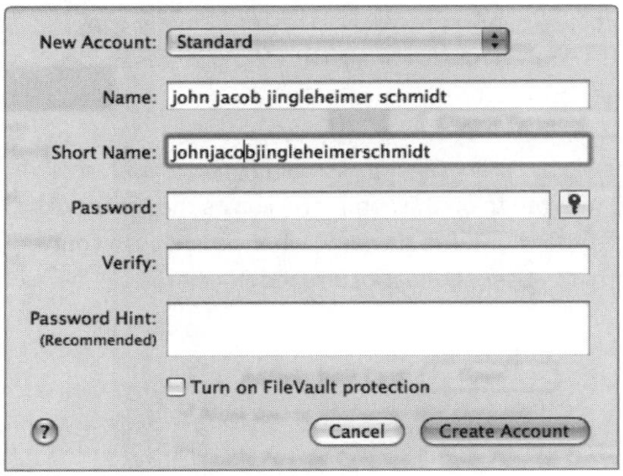

QUICK TIP

KEEP XCODE UP TO DATE

If you've installed the Xcode that came on your original install disks, you should have few, if any, problems using it. However, if you've upgraded from one version of Mac OS X to another, you need to upgrade Xcode separately, or you won't be able to access all of the functionality that Xcode provides. The safest thing to do is to stay up to date with the Xcode releases on ADC.

Your Short Name is your actual username, or login name, the name by which your computer knows you. It is usually three to eight characters long, composed of letters or numbers. While Mac OS X attempts to choose a Short Name for you based upon what you entered as your Name, it doesn't do a particularly good job if your name isn't as simple as Sam Smith. And, trust me, you don't want to spend your days being known by your computer as johnjacobjingleheimerschmidt. Choose something short and quick to type, like john, johnj, or schmidt. Here's why. …

Your Home Directory

Your home directory, shown in Figure 1-11, is where you'll be keeping all your stuff. In it you'll find special directories for your documents, pictures, movies, and settings (that's what the Library is). Of course, you're not forced to organize your stuff this way, but it is a good convention. Feel free to settle in, create new folders, and shuffle things about. It's generally a good idea not to throw out the special folders because the operating system and its applications often use them and expect them to be there. In particular, don't touch your Library folder; it's the home of your preferences, settings, and other pieces used by particular applications.

Figure 1-11.
Finder view of a typical home directory

If you chose john as your Short Name, your home directory is Macintosh HD→Users→john. By creating a central place for all your important data, Mac OS X ensures easy backup or deployment on other machines. Instead of having to single out your favorite control panels or extensions from OS 9, you can simply back up your home directory. When you're ready to restore, simply copy it over to the same location, and your environment (iTunes music library, Desktop pictures, added software tweaks, etc.) takes effect the next time you log in.

From the command line's point of view, your home directory (again, assuming your Short Name is john) is */Users/john*. You'll sometimes see it referred to on the command line as the ~ symbol. That's a shortcut that saves you from having to type your full login name when you refer to your home directory. So, *~/Documents* actually refers to */Users/john/Documents* (Macintosh HD→ Users→john→Documents in the Finder).

Who's the Boss?

As the primary user of your computer (or at least as the user you created when you installed the system), you're automatically afforded administrative privileges, which means you can install just about any software, modify settings that affect how Mac OS X functions, and create and delete other accounts. Needless to say, if you don't want that kid sister messing up your computer, you shouldn't make her an administrative user. Give administrative access only to those people (read: accounts) that truly need it.

Deleting an Account

Deleting an account under Mac OS X is easy using the Accounts System Preferences pane (System Preferences→Accounts→Delete User). This removes the account and disables the associated home directory.

Deleted accounts, however, do not have to be completely forgotten. If you take a moment to actually read the confirmation dialog shown in Figure 1-12, you can specify the fate of the soon-to-be-deleted account's home directory.

Figure 1-12.
Options for deletion

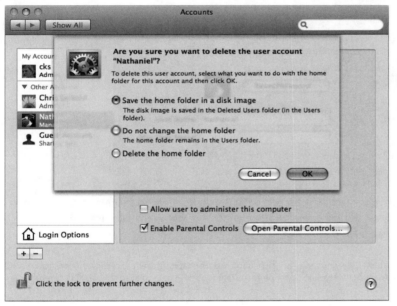

 Become an Administrator for a Moment

Your Mac does its best to protect you from yourself and your family by requiring authentication, both in the GUI and on the command line, when you're about to do something potentially problematic.

OS X, being a multiuser Unix system at its heart, tries to prevent you (or your family) from doing anything that might adversely affect your Mac. It does so by denying access to particular files that keep your system running and disallowing actions that it considers potentially harmful. Every now and again, however, you need to install a piece of software or touch a vital Unix configuration file to get something done. Before it lets you do so, Mac OS X requires that you authenticate yourself as an administrative user, known in Unix parlance as root.

Desktop Root

While most applications can be installed simply by dragging them into the Applications folder, some require a little more tomfoolery. Application and package installers often need to create folders, drop files into place, and adjust configuration settings in restricted parts of the operating system.

At these times, you're either not allowed to continue if you're not listed as an administrative user of the system (take a look at the System Preferences Users pane) or prompted for your password if you are. Figure 1-13 shows a typical Authenticate dialog.

Figure 1-13.
The Authenticate dialog

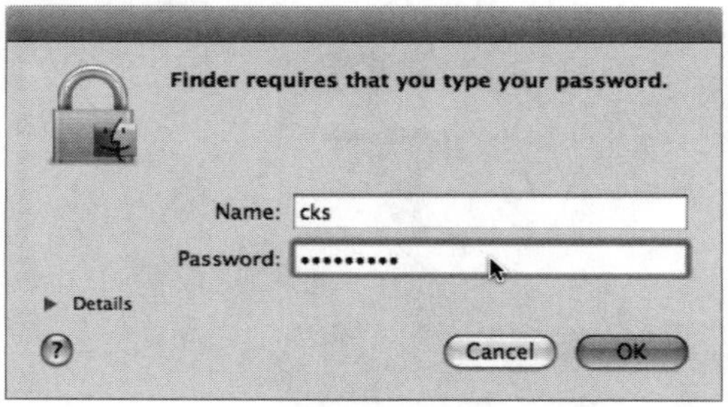

You'll notice that there is a Details arrow button in the window. Clicking this will let you see exactly which application is requesting the use of the password.

After you type in your password, the Installer continues. In effect, you've become an administrator with full power over your system, if only for a moment. You've then granted the Installer similar power to do what it needs to do.

> Whenever you authenticate yourself to an application, realize that it's going to fiddle with your system, and make sure you have some idea what it's trying to do. Read the notices displayed by installers carefully.

You'll also encounter times when you need to authenticate yourself to make a configuration change in System Preferences or the like. If you're unable to change some settings that seem as if they should be editable, look around the window for a little lock icon. If it's locked (see Figure 1-14), you might need to unlock it (click on the lock icon) and authenticate yourself.

Figure 1-14.
Locked settings

If you feel the need to lock the settings again when you're done, click the lock again.

Command-Line Root

On the command line, there is no fancy dialog for authenticating you as the root user. The **sudo** utility (the name is a shortened form of substitute-user do) allows you to gain temporary root privileges on a per-command basis. To use **sudo**, simply preface the command you want to run as root with **sudo** and a space; **sudo** prompts you for your (not root's) password. If you have administrator privileges, entering your password runs the **sudoed** command as if the root user were doing it.

Use **sudo** with care. You can easily make mistakes with **sudo** that could require a complete reinstallation of the OS to get going again. If that thought makes you queasy, you're better off avoiding it.

Typical **sudo** use looks like this:

```
$ sudo apachectl restart
```

> The Terminal is discussed with much more detail in Chapter 4, but for now, remember that the $ represents the Terminal prompt; don't type the $.

Here are a few notes about **sudo**:

- The first time you run **sudo**, you'll see another reminder to use sudo with care.

- You need to enter your password only when you haven't already used **sudo** within the last five minutes.

- It's not necessary to activate the root account or do anything else special to start using **sudo**.

- If you need to execute several commands as root in a row and don't want to type **sudo** continually, you can get a shell as the root user by using the following command:

  ```
  $ sudo -s
  Password: *****
  #
  ```

  The prompt changes to # to indicate that every command typed will run as the root user.

> Even though it takes more work, you can and should avoid opening root shells using the **sudo** command. By making the extra effort, you are less likely to make a horrific mistake and hose your system.

If you want to run a particular shell as root, say **bash**, you can also use the following command:

```
$ sudo bash
```

Enabling the Root Account

Some people really want to be able to log into their system as root. For some reason, having administrative privileges and the ability to execute any command by using **sudo** isn't enough. If you are one of these people, you can enable the root user so that you can log into either the GUI or the command line and have unfettered and unmonitored access to your system. We don't recommend you do this, but if you insist, here's how:

For Leopard:

1. Launch Directory Utility (*/Applications/Utilities*).

2. Unlock the Lock icon.

3. Select Enable Root User from the Edit menu.

4. Give the root user a password that is as secure as you would give any administrator of the system.

For Tiger:

1. Launch NetInfo Manager (*/Applications/Utilities*).

2. Authenticate yourself using the SecurityAuthenticate menu.

3. Enable the root user using the SecurityEnable Root menu.

4. Give the root user a password that is as secure as you would give any administrator of the system.

If you follow this procedure, you will have a fully functional root user.

Logging in as root
Log in as root just as you would log in as a user. The only difference is that root won't appear in the list of users and their associated cute icons. Click Other, enter root as the Name, and enter the password you assigned to the root account as Password.

— Chris Stone and Rael Dornfest

HACK 06: Behold the Power of PLIST

PLIST files are strewn all over your Mac, but chances are you never see them. That's too bad: PLIST files offer one of the most direct ways to hack your machine. Spend a few moments with this hack, and discover techniques to conquer those PLIST files.

PLIST is short for "property list," and the files are the main method used by Mac OS X (and some other operating systems) to organize data so that is accessible by programs and structured enough that you can generate your own if need be. That very brief explanation doesn't really say much, but the explanation of what PLIST files actually do is a little dense. If you're really interested in the functionality of PLIST files, check out http://developer.apple.com/documentation/Darwin/Reference/ManPages/man5/plist.5.html or type `man plist` into the Terminal.

PLIST Files for Hackers

When you are bending your machine to your will, the most frequent PLIST files you'll be mucking with are the ones that store the default values of parameters for various programs. These can range from default colors to default behaviors. These files are typically found in the Library→Preferences folder of your Home directory. Tweaking these files can yield unexpected functionality and is mostly harmless. If you screw one up, you can always just drag the PLIST file to the trash, and a new one will be generated. Of course you'll lose your preference set for that program, so the better way (as with all hacking when possible) is to back up the file so you'll have a ready-made replacement.

There is more than one way to access PLIST files. The quickest is the Terminal, via the *default* command. An example will help. Some programs can be made to display a Debug menu (most can't), and iCal is one of these. For most of us, an iCal Debug menu is just a distraction, but for heavy iCal users, a Debug menu can be very useful. Time to add the Debug menu:

1. Quit iCal if necessary.

2. Fire up Terminal (Applications→Utilities→Terminal).

3. At the $ prompt, type: **defaults write com.apple.iCal IncludeDebugMenu 1**

4. Relaunch iCal.

Like magic, iCal has a brand new Debug menu (see Figure 1-15).

Figure 1-15.
Some may find this list useful

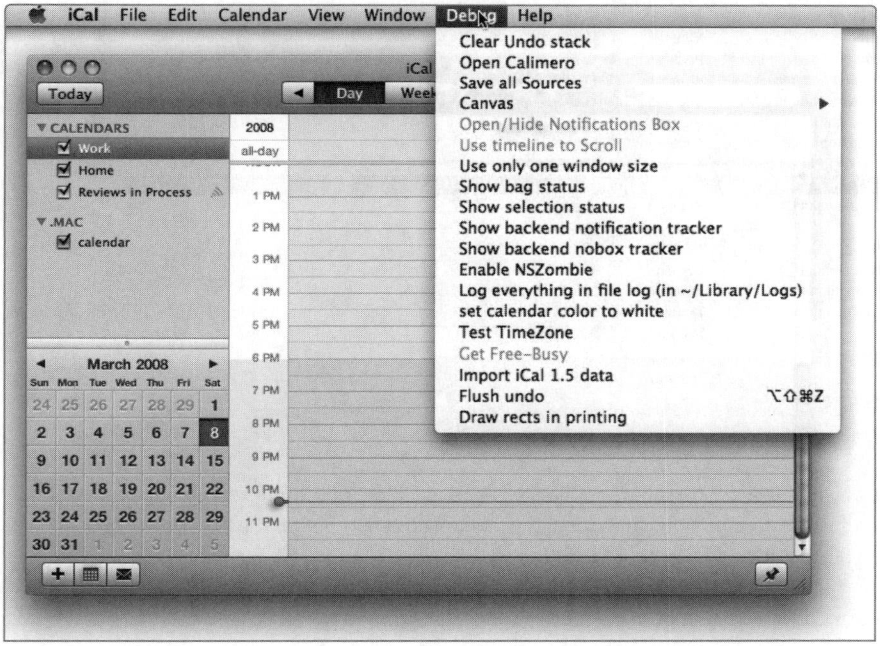

The Terminal is great when you know specifically what you want to change, but not so useful if you just want to know what you can change. For this, you need the property list. As mentioned in the beginning of this section, you'll usually find the PLIST files you want to hack in the Library folder of your home directory. The specific path for the iCal property list I'm using for an example is ~/Library/Preferences/com.apple.ical.plist. Once you've navigated to the file, open it with a property list editor. If you've worked through [Hack #3], you have a powerful PLIST editor installed on your Mac already. It is called (without much originality) Property List Editor. You can find it under /Developer/Applications, or just double-click on the PLIST file to open it, and see all your options (see Figure 1-16).

Figure 1-16.
That is a bunch of choices

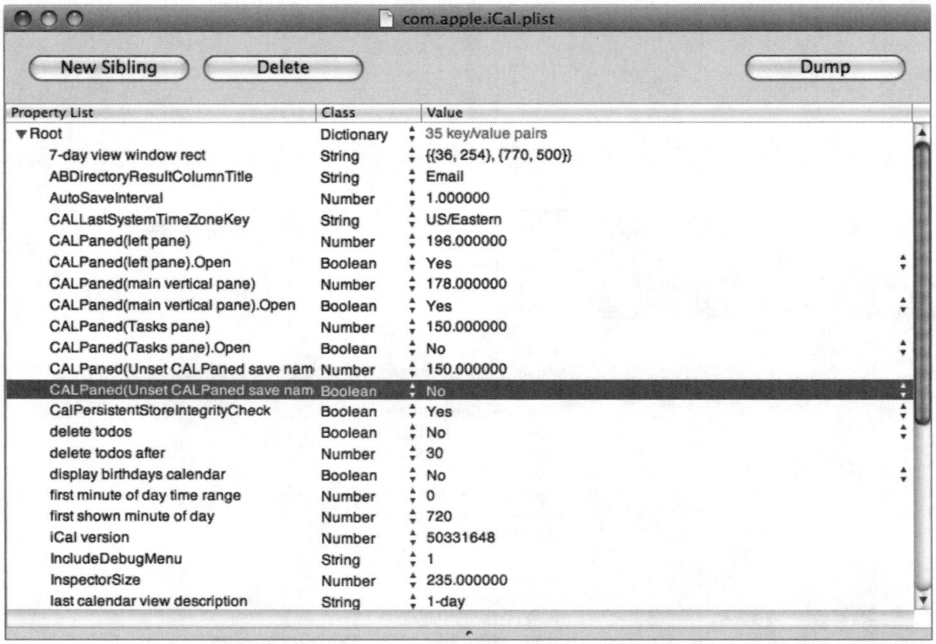

You can change any of the lines you see when the file is opened. Most of the lines don't mean much to you (or me), but some have obvious functionality. Changing the number on the line "delete todos after" from 30 to 60 tells iCal to keep your todos for 60 days.

So now you are armed with a command-line method and a program to tweak PLIST files. It turns out you can also touch up PLIST files with a text editor. In the days before Tiger rolled out, you could just open a PLIST file with a text editor directly, but now the files are stored in binary format. To open a PLIST in a text editor, you'll have to convert it first. The easiest way to convert said PLIST file? The Terminal. iCal's PLIST has been abused enough for now, so try poking around in Safari's bookmarks. The location of this file is ~/Library/Safari/Bookmarks.plist. Since it is smart to work off a copy, right-click the file, and choose Duplicate from the contextual menu. Convert the file with the command line:

```
$ plutil -convert xml1 ~/Library/Safari/Bookmarks\ copy.plist
```

Here the plutil command invokes the property list utility, -convert xml1 (that's the letters "x-m-l" followed by the number "1") tells plutil to convert the property list to XML, and the rest is just the path to the file. Once the command has run, navigate to the location of the file with Finder, right-click and choose Open With→Other, and pick Text Edit. The formerly unreadable PLIST is now easily understandable (see Figure 1-17).

Figure 1-17.
A human-readable bookmarks PLIST

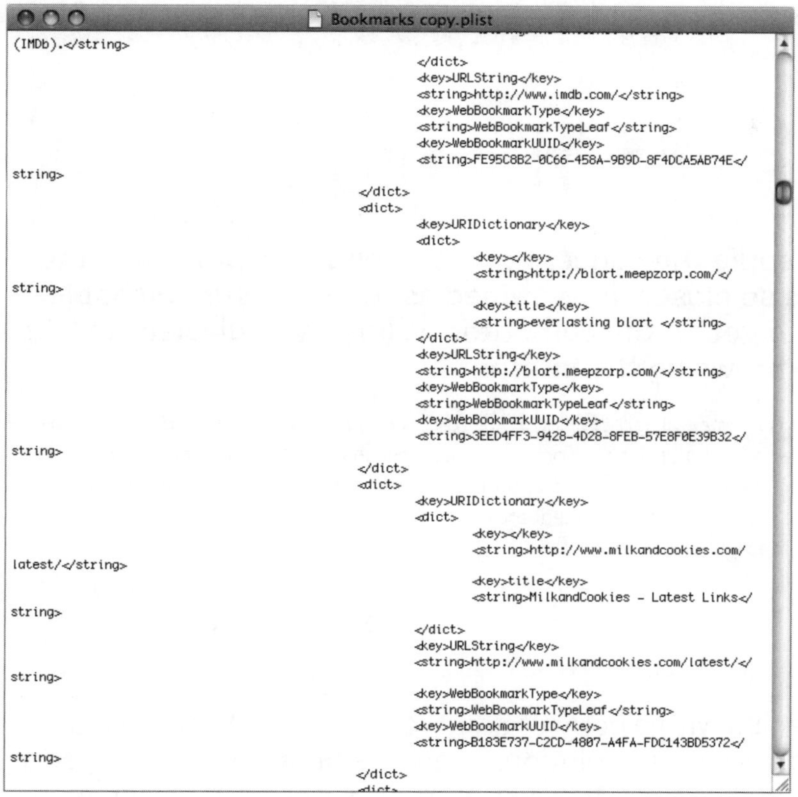

```
(IMDb).</string>
                                    </dict>
                                    <key>URLString</key>
                                    <string>http://www.imdb.com/</string>
                                    <key>WebBookmarkType</key>
                                    <string>WebBookmarkTypeLeaf</string>
                                    <key>WebBookmarkUUID</key>
                                    <string>FE95C8B2-0C66-458A-9B9D-8F4DCA5AB74E</
string>
                            </dict>
                            <dict>
                                    <key>URIDictionary</key>
                                    <dict>
                                            <key></key>
                                            <string>http://blort.meepzorp.com/</
string>
                                            <key>title</key>
                                            <string>everlasting blort </string>
                                    </dict>
                                    <key>URLString</key>
                                    <string>http://blort.meepzorp.com/</string>
                                    <key>WebBookmarkType</key>
                                    <string>WebBookmarkTypeLeaf</string>
                                    <key>WebBookmarkUUID</key>
                                    <string>3EED4FF3-9428-4D28-8FEB-57E8F0E39B32</
string>
                            </dict>
                            <dict>
                                    <key>URIDictionary</key>
                                    <dict>
                                            <key></key>
                                            <string>http://www.milkandcookies.com/
latest/</string>
                                            <key>title</key>
                                            <string>MilkandCookies - Latest Links</
string>
                                    </dict>
                                    <key>URLString</key>
                                    <string>http://www.milkandcookies.com/latest/</
string>
                                    <key>WebBookmarkType</key>
                                    <string>WebBookmarkTypeLeaf</string>
                                    <key>WebBookmarkUUID</key>
                                    <string>B183E737-C2CD-4807-A4FA-FDC143BD5372</
string>
                            </dict>
                            <dict>
```

There's much more to learn about PLIST files, but these tidbits should get you comfortable enough to start PLIST hacking adventures and let you know what is going on when the things get abused throughout the rest of this book.

2

HACKS FOR THE NET

For many people the concept of a personal computer and the Internet are so closely intertwined as to be indistinguishable. "I'm going to get on the computer" is largely equivalent to "I'm going to be browsing the Internet."

Since the Internet is an integral part of using a Mac (or any computer) for most of us, hacks, tips, and tricks to enhance the experience are only natural. In this chapter, ways to get more from your browsers, get data off the Web into your computer, use a computer to host your own web site and even going completely browser-independent are discussed. There's a lot of fun to be had hacking your way through Mac OS X's net applications.

HACK 07: Change Your Browser

Every Mac ships with a copy of Safari but don't feel compelled to use the Apple-supplied solution. There are other browsers offering features Safari doesn't. Discover other browser options and learn what these alternatives can do for you.

Apple ships its zippy Safari with a strong suite of features that integrate well with other applications, but it isn't the only game for browsing the Web with a Mac. Firefox's selling point is its strong community and plethora of add-ons. Opera is unique, and Shiira offers Safari-rendering speeds with added extensibility. Of course, no good Mac browser would be complete without a few hacks that can bend it to a user's desire, so I'm going to show you both popular and unsung plug-ins, tricks, and tips for getting the most from a few of the Mac's best alternative browsers.

Firefox

Why not start with the alternative browser of choice. Firefox, as you've undoubtedly at least heard of, is Mozilla Corporation's open source browser. With add-ons as far as the eye can see and the second-largest browser market share, Firefox (see Figure 2-1) is a good choice for those who want extra tools and plug-ins that can make their browser work better with all sorts of sites and services.

Figure 2-1.
The very popular Firefox browser

Google Browser Sync

If you're one of the many who work (and browse) across multiple computers—be it for work, school, or other reasons—Google's Browser Sync add-on is a killer way to save time with keeping one computer's records in step with another. Compatible with Firefox 1.5 or later and any OS that will run Firefox, Browser Sync can keep your bookmarks, history, active cookies, and saved passwords synchronized between each of your computers, even if they're powered by Windows or Linux.

As icing on the cake, Browser Sync can even synchronize your open tabs between sessions and computers. If you have five tabs open on your PC at work when you restart after an update, Google Browser Sync can reopen them when you start it up again. As of Version 2.0, Firefox does basic session saving on its own, but Browser Sync goes one step further by synchronizing your sessions between computers. To illustrate: in our previous example, let's say you shut down for the day after that update and head home. Once you log in and start up Firefox on your personal Mac, it will ask if you want to reopen those same five tabs from Firefox on your PC at work. These syncing features of Browser Sync add a whole new layer to living the mobile, multicomputing lifestyle.

Google Browser Sync is a free download from http://www.google.com/tools/firefox/browsersync and is currently compatible with Firefox 1.5 and up.

LIKE SHOCKWAVE? GOT AN INTEL MAC? YOU'LL WANT TWO BROWSERS

There are still quite a few games that rely on Adobe's Shockwave Player to run. This is bad news for Intel Mac owners because even though the Intel Macs have been around since January 2006, Shockwave won't run natively. Shockwave will run under Rosetta so the workaround is obvious: force a browser to run using Rosetta emulation (the browser will have to be Universal). To pull this off select the browser you want to use for Shockwave, use the Get Info command (Command-I), and select the checkbox next to "Open using Rosetta." You can also use the Duplicate command (select the application you want duplicated and hit Command-D or File→ Duplicate) and have one copy open natively while the duplicated version uses Rosetta.

Greasemonkey

Since the dawn of the graphical Web, surfers have more or less been forced to use a web site the way its designers intended—take it or leave it. But what if you could take the reins and customize a web site to your wishes? Enter Greasemonkey, an open-source Firefox add-on that allows users to manipulate the look and even functionality of web sites through the use of powerful Javascript files. Thanks to the flourishing popularity of web technologies such as CSS and Ajax, these Javascript files can virtually redesign a site for your use, and even add (or remove) features. Users are encouraged to write their own scripts or to download them from communities. Popular examples of these scripts in action include adding more keyboard shortcuts to Gmail, editing Facebook's colors and banner to match a favorite sports team, and even adding a pop-up menu when browsing Amazon to reveal prices from competing stores.

Greasemonkey enables a lot of power for its users, so head over to Mozilla's add-on page (http://addons.mozilla.org) to grab a copy. Then visit UserScripts.org (http://userscripts.org) and find nearly 9,000 scripts already written for many of the sites Greasemonkey can alter.

Trim Firefox's fat on Intel Macs

Universal binary (UB) applications that work across both PowerPC and Intel-based Macs are certainly handy in their own right, but they have a significant downside for anyone concerned with conserving hard-drive storage or running at optimum speeds. Because these UB applications contain the code necessary to run on both processors, they contain code you might never use if you've gone Intel and don't plan to look back. Now for some applications, this extra, unused code could amount to not much more than a few hundred kilobytes, but in Firefox's case, a version that runs specifically on Intel Macs can shave over 20 megabytes from the application (as you might guess, this means other larger applications can shave even more space; check out **[Hack #24]** and generally speed up overall performance.

Unfortunately, unless you like Camino, Mozilla doesn't provide these leaner, meaner versions of Firefox itself, but Neil Lee at the BeatnikPad (www.beatnikpad.com) provides Intel-native copies for free. (I've tried, but so far I can't find a donation link anywhere.) Lee does a pretty good job of keeping his Intel-native Firefox builds current too, releasing a new one even for Mozilla's .0.0.x security and bug fix editions. The only catch with this version is that, due to its unofficial status (that is, it isn't coming from the horse's mouth), Lee isn't allowed to brand or name his custom build with the official Firefox name and icon. Instead, Lee simply sticks with Firefox 2.0's code name of "BonEcho," using the blue earth part of the actual Firefox logo for his icon. Your friends might not recognize that icon in your Dock, but Lee's version of Firefox is otherwise identical to the original, aside from some noticeable boosts in startup and general speed, of course (see Figure 2-2).

Figure 2-2.
It doesn't look like Firefox in the dock, but BonEcho acts like Firefox in use

Opera

A long-standing competitor to Internet Explorer on Windows, Opera (see Figure 2-3) has been doing the browser thing for quite a while now. While the company once charged for its desktop browser (or forced users to view banner ads right underneath the toolbar), they listened to user feedback and went free in 2005. The company now makes money through search-based ad affiliate programs and charges for versions of its client that run on various alternative platforms, such as mobile phones and even the Nintendo Wii. With an experience and feature set all its own, Opera is arguably in a league of its own on the Mac for its decidedly unique UI and occasional innovations to the web-surfing experience.

Figure 2-3.
Opera's Speed Dial option

Search your history—every last word of it

Opera (http://www.opera.com), like most browsers, keeps track of the URLs you visit for easy recall later on. Begin typing an address, and Opera can usually auto-fill it for you. A new 9.5 version, however, brings a full text search of your history into the address bar as well. In addition to simple URLs, Opera can now search every word on web sites stored in your history (hint: adjust your history preferences if this sounds appealing). Remember a few choice words or phrases from an article you read, but don't remember where you read it? Opera's address bar can now help you search for the site's URL, or simply find the URL based on what text you remember from the site. It's a whole new way to cut down on those forgetful moments.

Shiira: A WebKit-Based Safari Alternative

Shiira is a little-known browser based on Apple's home-grown, open source WebKit engine that the company uses in Safari (see Figure 2-4). (WebKit is also what most other third-party applications use if they offer any kind of web-browsing features.) This means that Shiira shares Safari's nimble page-rendering speeds, but it aims to offer a beefed-up set of features for users who want a little more out of their web-surfing experience.

Figure 2-4.
The unique interface of Shiira

With floating palettes for things like history, RSS articles, and bookmarks, as well as a thumbnail-based tab bar (with the option for "regular" tabs), Shiira offers some handy features at first glance (see Figure 2-5). Under the hood, however, there's even more.

Figure 2-5.
Shiira is better looking than most browsers

All your bookmarks belong to Shiira

Shiira recognizes that it probably isn't your first (and possibly not your only) browser, so it offers a preference for viewing bookmarks from Safari and Firefox within Shiira's own bookmarks menu.

You can even specify the use of a different bookmarks bar in place of Shiira's own. Unfortunately, this doesn't mean Shiira can edit or update bookmarks from these other browsers, so anything you bookmark in Shiira stays in Shiira; there is no syncing relationship with Safari or Firefox (see Figure 2-6).

Figure 2-6.
If you've got a bookmark in another browser, you've got a bookmark in Shiira

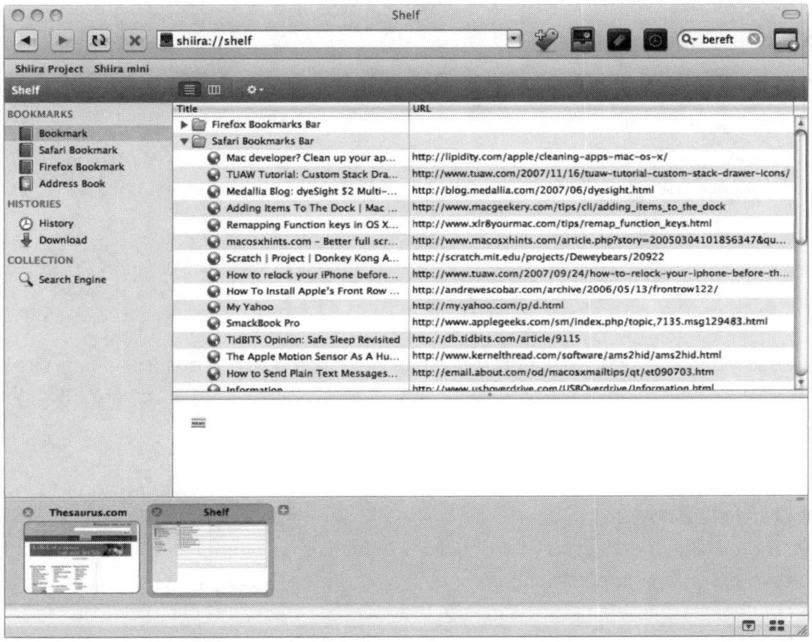

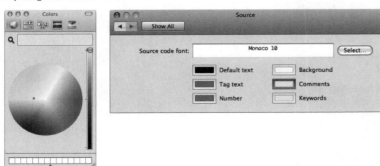

Better options for viewing page source

Web designers have always enjoyed the ability to view a web page's source code with virtually every graphical browser since the dawn of dancing GIFs. Even today though, many browsers offer a bare-bones set of features when it comes to viewing a page's source, neglecting even the basic necessity of colorizing code. Shiira, fortunately, can change all that with another preference pane (Shiira→ Preferences→Source: see Figure 2-7).

Figure 2-7.
Adjusting code colors in Shiira

Shiira doesn't stop with source code coloring; when you check out a page with Shiira, you get a lot of options broken down in convenient categories. Interested in the images on the page? One click, and you can see all the images the page uses and the URLs for said images. Clicking the cookies reveals the cookies a site sends to your machine. It really is a much more understandable way to view the source of a page (see Figure 2-8).

Figure 2-8.
Safari compared to Shiira viewing the source of a page

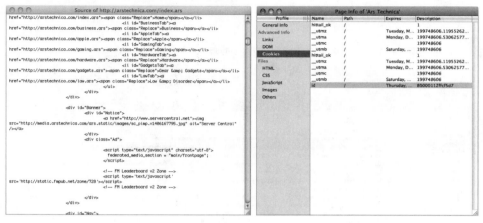

Of course, this probably can't stack up to your HTML editor of choice, but for a quick peek at a site, these simple options sure beat most of the browsing competition.

Shiira is a free download from the Shiira Project web site at http://shiira.jp/en.php.

Change Your Default Browser

So you've seen your browsing options, and you're thinking of making a switch. Thing is, the switch won't truly be complete; you won't be able to call yourself a hard-core Opera user until you make your new browser of choice your default browser—the browser that opens up links clicked in Mail or other programs. To get that new browser feeling throughout your Mac, you need to find somewhere to change the default browser setting. In bygone days this was handled in Internet preferences but since Internet preferences have gone the way of the smiling Mac icon, you'll have to find another way to change the default browser. Most browsers feature a preference to change the default browser, but the most familiar way to complete this is action is with Safari's preferences. Head to Safari→Preferences→General, and select your (new) browser of choice from the pop-up menu.

Figure 2-9.
Defaulting to Opera with some help from Safari

— David Chartier

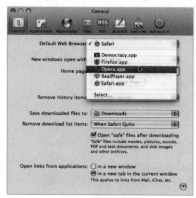

HACK 08: Safari: More Than Meets the Eye

Safari may not share Firefox's reputation for being infinitely extendable through add-ons, but it has a respectable share of popular and powerful plug-ins and tricks, as well as a healthy community behind them. Maximize your Safari experience with these add-ons and tips.

If you've got a Mac, there is a better than even chance that the program you spend the most time with is Safari. Actually, that isn't much of a surprise. Safari is the default browser on the Mac, and with the Internet pervading every corner of daily life, the chances that you spend more time using a web browser than anything else are pretty good.

Since you're spending copious amounts of time in Safari, you are undoubtedly interested in anything that will make the experience more efficient, safer, or simply more fun. And you should; it is one thing to claim that Safari is the best browser in the world (as Apple does), but it doesn't necessarily follow that the default Safari set-up is the pinnacle of web browsing for your personal web habits.

Safari Tricks

Safari is a straight-ahead browser. You can use it all day long, and the program will function how you probably expect it to function. But Safari has more to offer than is apparent on the first pass. Safari has tricks.

Retroactive private browsing

Let us not be shy here: let's admit our foibles and embrace our weaknesses as human beings. We are all tempted by things we shouldn't be. Because we all have base instincts, Apple has included a feature with Safari called *private browsing*. Private browsing prevents others from viewing your web history, your searches, and other compromising info by not adding anything to Safari's history. The allure of private browsing is easy to understand: imagine you are surfing around the Internet looking at stuff you'd rather people not know you were looking at. If you have private browsing turned on, once you close Safari's window, every identifying bit of info Safari usually stores (cookies, history, Activity) are all deleted (see Figure 2-10).

Figure 2-10.
With private browsing, no one ever has to know...

QUICK HACK ✕

TURN OFF SAFARI 3 WARNINGS WHEN CLOSING WINDOW WITH MULTIPLE TABS OPEN

If you've been using Safari for a while, Safari 3 has an unpleasant surprise for you: the annoying message warning you that you are about to close a window with multiple tabs open. Old schoolers are aware of this and have long since adjusted their browsing habits accordingly. To get back to the warning-free days of Safari 2 and earlier, fire up the Terminal and type (all on one line):

```
defaults write
com.apple.Safari
ConfirmClosingMultiplePages 0
```

You won't be bothered by warnings anymore. To unhack this change, repeat the command and change 0 to 1.

Private browsing works okay as long as you remember to enable it before you end up at at a URL you'd be embarrassed to share. If you end up at a site of questionable taste before you enable private browsing, you can reset Safari, but that nukes everything from your history to your cookies to your passwords. It's not the best solution because most users want to view their history for later reference, they want the cookies sent from web sites saved so they don't specify their location every time they are trying to get the weather, and they want their passwords entered automatically. In the end, if you want your browsing to remain private on occasion, and you want your web history to be available to you the rest the time, you have to make a conscious decision to turn private browsing on before you begin surfing web sites you'd rather others not know you visit. Too much to ask!

Why not go private retroactively? The first step is obvious: delete your Google searches (see Figure 2-11).

Figure 2-11.
No more revealing searches

The searches are gone, but what about the web history? Anyone that comes along can hit the history button and see exactly where you've been: not a good situation. With Safari ,you can delete items selectively from your history. One way to pull this off is to choose "Show All History" from Safari's history menu. Select the sites you'd like to purge, and click the delete button on your keyboard (see Figure 2-12). Unless you're dealing with someone very determined to find out where you've been, you've effectively made your browsing privately retroactively.

Figure 2-12.
Delete the embarrassing past

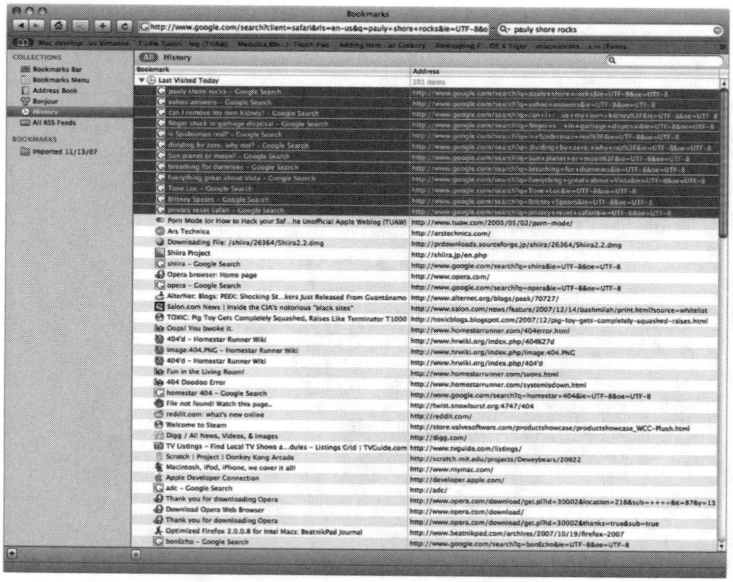

QUICK TIP

PRIVATE BROWSING WON'T COVER EVERYTHING

If you use private browsing, you need to be aware that it doesn't mean that nobody can tell what you've been doing. Obviously your ISP knows where you've been surfing, but a clever user can probably get the same information from your home router if it is set to log activity, and they have your router's password. If you really want privacy in your home setup, either disable logging for your router or protect the router from inspection by others with a strong password.

Put your Activity to work

Safari's Activity pane (available from Window→Activity) offers an unassuming list of every little bit and piece of a web site that you download. Images, Flash files, QuickTime movies, JavaScript files: they're all on the menu. Unfortunately, Safari's cache system (located in *~/Library/Caches/Safari/*) doesn't make these files very easy to find if you want to take a close look at them, but there's a way around this shortcoming using the Activity pane (see Figure 2-13).

Figure 2-13.
Accessing the only the stuff you want with the Activity pane

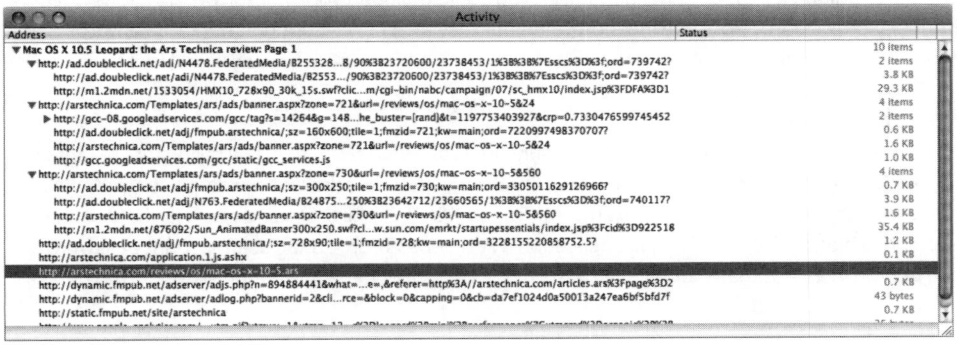

Simply double-clicking any item in the Activity pane will open it in a Safari window for your perusing pleasure. Images open with their specific URL in the address bar, while even text files such as CSS and Javascripts will open for your study, copy, and pasting needs. Flash files can sometimes be a bit more tricky, depending on how the author built the site and whether they want to keep prying eyes out, but other media such as QuickTime files are often readily accessible here. Simply using a Command-S keyboard shortcut or dragging and dropping out of this window will allow you to save these files in a location of your preference.

Of course, with great power over every bit and byte you download in Safari comes great responsibility. As a writer who relies heavily on the content I create for Ars Technica to feed my family, I must advise you to please be kind and obey the copyright rules that web sites and content owners apply to their work. While it's a general rule of thumb that anything on the Web can be downloaded and studied by curious users like you and I, reusing some content is prohibited by copyright law and is simply a shady and disingenuous thing to do.

Safari Add On: Saft—The Do-It-All Sidekick

Probably the most popular Safari plug-in, Saft's feature list could have an entire chapter dedicated to it. In short, Saft is a Swiss army knife, offering features across the board such as ad blocking, a full-screen mode, tab thumbnails (à la Shiira), undo support for closing tabs, URL shortcuts (for example, type "am" and hit enter to visit http://www.apple.com/macosx/), auto-hiding the Downloads window when downloads finish, a sidebar scratchpad for saving links and snippets, and much, much more.

As a happy owner of this plug-in for a few years now, I can personally attest to Saft's usefulness. Its developer, Hao Li, is also well-known for updating almost immediately with each Safari update Apple publishes, ensuring that users don't have to go long without updating Safari or Saft.

Saft is a commercial download costing $12, available from http://haoli.dnsalias.com/Saft/index.html.

— David Chartier and Chris Seibold

Don't become a slave to a single browser: expand your choices by accessing your bookmarks and password from any computer with any browser.

In the idealized world of standards-compliant browsers, which browser you use shouldn't really matter. So why let one browser define your web habits? In fact, getting rid of the browser isn't enough. Wouldn't it be a better experience if you could maintain your web-browsing habits not only from any browser but from any location? Find out how to access your bookmarks, passwords and even engage in a little social fun while unchaining yourself from both browsers and locations.

Portable Passwords
Mac OS X's built-in Keychain application (found in *Applications/Utilities*) is a solid storage bin for login and password information. Many Mac OS X apps and a handful of browsers use the Keychain to store information. To cite a few examples: Transmit's FTP addresses and passwords, MarsEdit and ecto's blog and login info, mail application's server passwords, Mac user account passwords.... You get the idea. But that's about all Keychain does: it stores this information securely and recalls it for use when required.

For those who need a little more out of a secure information hub, Agile Web Solution's 1Password (http://1passwd.com) might fit the bill. While 1Password also stores its login and password information in a secure keychain that you can in fact read with Keychain (and subsequently sync via .Mac), the similarities stop there. 1Password goes way above and beyond by also acting as a one-stop shop for secure identity management on the Web. Users can create multiple profiles with different addresses, standard forum information (your web site, IM name, and occupation, for example) and even credit-card numbers for one click auto-filling when shopping or registering for virtually any site on the Web.

Another significant benefit of 1Password is that it can integrate with some browsers and other popular applications that can surf the Web but do not support or directly interact with the Keychain by default. These supported applications include Firefox (Firefox eschews Keychain because it features its own built-in password manager), DEVONagent, and even NetNewsWire.

Last but not least, as of Version 2.5 (released late October 2007), 1Password can also create a bookmarklet for the iPhone that stores a list of all your passwords and identity information. Protected with 448-bit Blowfish with Cipher Block Chaining (CBC) and randomized salt encryption, the bookmarklet itself requires a password before displaying any of your information. It's an impressive feature and a handy way to bring all this stuff on the go in a tiny, touchy-feely package.

A demo of 1Password is available at http://1passwd.com. A single license costs $29.95, while bundles of three or more are also available.

Liberate Your Bookmarks
Most of us work in one, maybe two, browsers throughout the day depending on our needs. This means that your bookmarks are most likely locked away in one browser, possibly on a single computer if you aren't using .Mac bookmark syncing with Safari or a solution such as Google Browser Sync add-on for Firefox. This easily leads to plenty of "oh, I saved it on that other computer" moments right when you needed a key bookmark. Wouldn't it be nice to give all those URLs some wings and access from the virtually any device, browser, and location that can get on the Web?

If you haven't hopped on the trend of "social bookmarking" yet, it more or less entails cataloging bookmarks in a web service instead of your browser. While this might sound clunky at first, there are a few utilities and tricks that not only make these services easy to use from any computer, but you can also subsequently use your bookmarks in any browser, on any computer or even mobile device that can access these social bookmarking sites and services. All you need is an app or two.

There are a lot of options in this realm but, for the sake of our sanity, we're going to stick with one of the most popular social bookmarking sites: del.icio.us, which can be found at—yep, you guessed it—http://del.icio.us. There is quite a bit to the "social" aspect of social bookmarking—like seeing what sites others are bookmarking, which sites are popular, and how many people bookmarked the same site you just did; however, here we'll focus primarily on how to use these sites as personal bookmarking liberators.

Make your mark

The catch with using social bookmarking sites such as del.icio.us is that you need to use something other than your browser's bookmarks menu to actually save your bookmarks to the site. For the actual act of saving bookmarks, virtually every one of these sites offers a "bookmarklet"—a pseudo-bookmark you install on your browser's bookmarks bar (usually just by dragging it there), but it isn't a traditional bookmark. These bookmarklets are actually small bundles of JavaScript that do something instead of take you somewhere. Del.icio.us has its own bookmarklet that opens an actual input window that allows you to: name the bookmark (if you don't like the name automatically pulled from the page you're bookmarking), edit the URL (just in case), add a description and tags to help categorize it, and even set a bookmark as private so no one but you can see it listed in your account (and only when you're logged in).

If you're wondering how to get all your current bookmarks into del.icio.us, the site had the foresight to list some instructions in its help section on how to export a copy of your bookmarks for easy importing. The process is pretty straightforward—custom tailored for most popular browsers. Because the instructions vary from browser to browser, you're better off getting the information straight from del.icio.us. The point, after all, is that you don't have to lose any bookmarks or spend time rebookmarking sites just to start using del.icio.us.

Make a better mark

Now these bookmarklets are pretty useful and very cross platform-friendly, but as usual, web technologies are easily trumped by good desktop software. If you'd like a more powerful way to both create del.icio.us bookmarks from your browsers (and even RSS newsreaders) and access your bookmarks, look no further than Code Sorcery Workshop's Pukka, available at http://codesorcery.net/pukka. As a $12.95 piece of shareware (demo available), Pukka packs two specific punches that justify the cash outlay.

First, Pukka lets you install its own bookmarklet in your browsers, which calls it up and harvests the current site you're on. If you aren't impressed yet, I don't blame you, because this is more or less what a del.icio.us bookmarklet does (albeit as desktop software, Pukka is a bit snappier). Pukka's worth as a bookmarking utility comes in many layers, from its ability to warn you if you've already bookmarked something (and give you the option to edit that previous bookmark) to its support for multiple accounts and even compatibility with various newsreaders such as NetNewsWire.

The second punch Pukka brings to the ring is a menu-bar item that acts as a bookmarks menu for your del.icio.us bookmarks. This menu organizes all your del.icio.us bookmarks into folders (including your private 'marks) based on the tags you use when you create them. This menu also has a very significant and positive side effect of allowing you to use any browser you want or even swap between them throughout your daily routine. When these bookmarks are clicked, they'll open in whatever browser you currently have set as the default, finally allowing you to spread your wings and stop being shackled to one browser or another simply because all your bookmarks are in it.

Another bookmark menu option

If you simply need to view all your del.icio.us bookmarks in your menu bar, Shiny Frog's delibar (available at http://www.shinyfrog.net/it/software/delibar) might fit the bill a little better. It's a donationware utility that, like Pukka, lists all your bookmarks in folders according to the tags you use. It doesn't do any bookmarking itself though, so you're on your own for that end of the del.icio.us equation. That said, the price is right, and delibar is fun to use.

Add all these options together and you've got a very nice recipe for comfortable browsing anywhere you go. You've got bookmarks and passwords at your beck and call from every machine you touch. While these might seem like solutions to a nonexistent problem for people who use the same machines day after day, it can make for a much better surfing experience for those who are constantly using a different computer.

HACK 10: Enable Safari Debug Menu

You know that you can extend Safari's abilities with third-party add-ons and use some clever tricks to make the surfing experience more enjoyable [Hack #8]. The fun doesn't have to stop there. You can access options in Safari usually reserved for developers by typing a single line in the Terminal and discover a world of options ranging from the incomprehensible to the indispensable.

While you're hacking your way through the Apple product line, you'll note that with many hacks there is a tradeoff. You can jailbreak your phone but later software updates might not work. You can keep your home folder on your iPod but then you're tethered to your iPod every time you feel like using your computer. Those are just two specific examples, but the general rule of thumb is that the more work a hack is, the bigger the payoff. To illustrate: you can do awesome things with the Terminal but to truly master the command line, you'll need to learn a bevy of commands.

Enabling the Safari Debug Menu is one hack that breaks the rule. Enabling the Debug menu is dead simple, the payoff is huge and there is no loss of functionality. A win, win, win situation as far as a hacker is concerned. With no shortcomings, there isn't a reason not to jump right in and hack. As mentioned before, the hack is deliciously simple. Fire up the Terminal application and type:

```
defaults write com.apple.Safari IncludeDebugMenu 1
```

Nothing happens in the Terminal when you run the command and, if you left Safari running, nothing much seems to happen to Safari. For the changes to take effect, you'll have to restart Safari. Once Safari has been relaunched, you'll see the ever useful Safari Debug menu (see Figure 2-14).

Figure 2-14.
The fun begins with your new Safari Debug menu

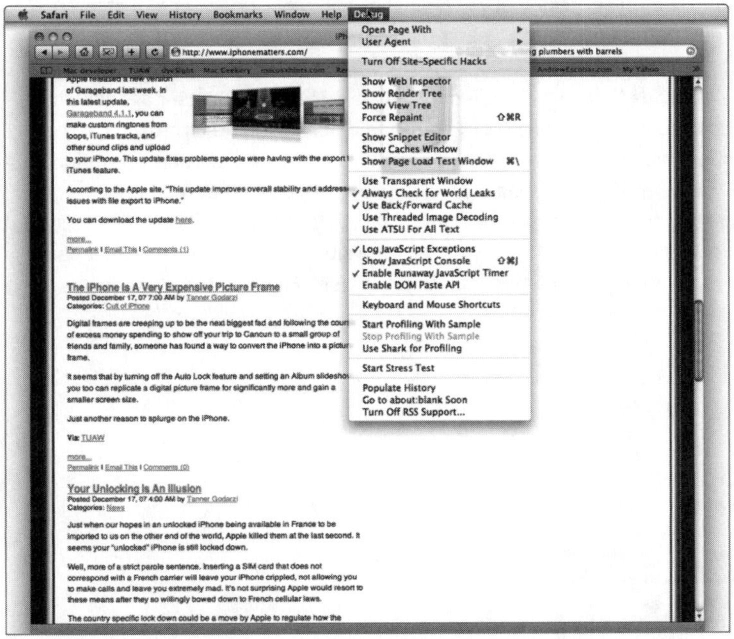

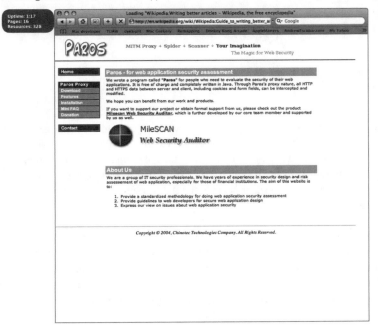

Once you enable the Debug menu, you'll find that you suddenly have many more options for Safari. Most of the options are only of interest to developers or those working on Safari in Cupertino. Some are actually very fun. Want to see how much surfing Safari can take? The Stress test is just the ticket (Debug→Start Stress Test). Safari contacts del.icio.us and begins loading page after page, keeping count of just how much surfing has been done (see Figure 2-15).

Figure 2-15.
Stressing Safari, the readout in the upper left corner reveals how much abuse you're passing out

It isn't only a way to see how much Safari can handle. For the lazy among us who can't be bothered to find interesting web pages, Safari's Stress Test will almost always yield a page or two of interest. To quit the Stress Test once it is running, hit the Debug menu again, and choose Stop Stress Test.

More useful but not quite as fun as Safari's Stress Test is the ability to choose a user agent with the Debug menu. This lets you use Safari while telling the servers it is some other browser. If the functionality seems questionable at first (why would you want Safari to masquerade as a different browser? You're a proud Mac user after all!), wait until you run across a site that requires Internet Explorer. If you're broadcasting the fact that you're using Safari, you'll be straight out of luck. By having Safari tell the server it is actually Windows MSIE 6.0, the site will let you in because it has been tricked into believing you are one of the Windows brethren (see Figure 2-16).

Figure 2-16.
Safari can masquerade as a variety of browsers

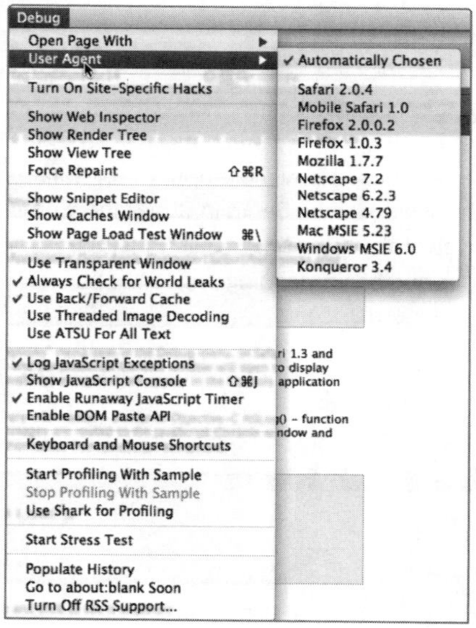

That doesn't magically make the site work properly in Safari however. If the site uses ActiveX, Safari won't be able to use the site no matter how well the application fibs about its identity. However, there are plenty of sites that are Internet Explorer (IE)-only because of laziness or sloppy coding. It isn't that Safari can't render and interact with the sites properly, it's that the webmasters decided it was easier to only support IE. Changing the user agent in the Debug menu gets you into those formerly inaccessible sites.

There's more fun to be had with user agent. If you're after faster browsing, telling servers you're using Mobile Safari 1.0 is telling them that you're using an iPhone. Some pages will only open for Mobile Safari (the classic example being http://reader.mac.com/), and many other sites automatically shuffle Mobile Safari users to lower bandwidth pages. Amazon, for example, sends Mobile Safari users to a page that is much less bandwidth intensive and easier on the eyes (see Figure 2-17).

Figure 2-17.
The Amazon web page for Mobile Safari

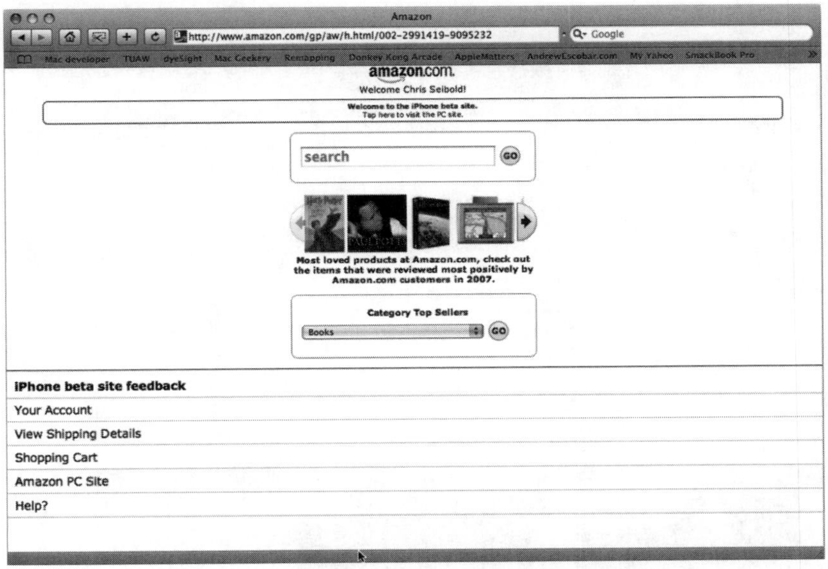

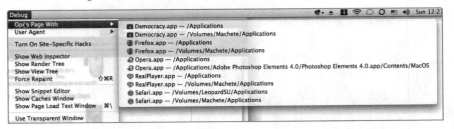

If no amount of user-agent trickery will get you the results you need, the Debug menu saves you from scrambling through your Applications folder looking for a compatible browser. As long as you're on the troublesome site simply choose Debug→Open Page With... and pick the right browser for the job (see Figure 2-18).

Figure 2-18.
Don't hunt for the right browser—let Safari find it for you

The utility of the Debug menu doesn't stop with user-agent tricks. When you enable the Debug menu, you also get a surprisingly adept site inspector tool. This is a tool that can inspect any element of a page you find of interest, fully nested and color coded for easy deciphering. Invoking the Web Inspector for an entire page involves a trip to the menu bar (Debug→Show Web Inspector), but if you're interested in a specific element of a page, a right-click→Inspect Element will take you right to the part of the page you want to examine (see Figure 2-19).

Figure 2-19.
Web Inspector reveals all

There is more to the Debug menu. You can turn off RSS support if you use Mail or a standalone RSS reader such as NetNewsWire. The Debug menu will also let you turn Safari's window transparent, an interesting visual if nothing else (see Figure 2-20).

Figure 2-20.
That is hard to read!

There are many more options of interest to developers more than anyone else (World Leaks, Profiling, etc.), but one of the most useful things found in the Debug menu is the big list of Safari Shortcuts. There are keyboard shortcuts listed in this file that few are aware of, but they can be great time savers when you're doing heavy browsing (see Figure 2-21).

Figure 2-21.
Wow, that is a lot of shortcuts

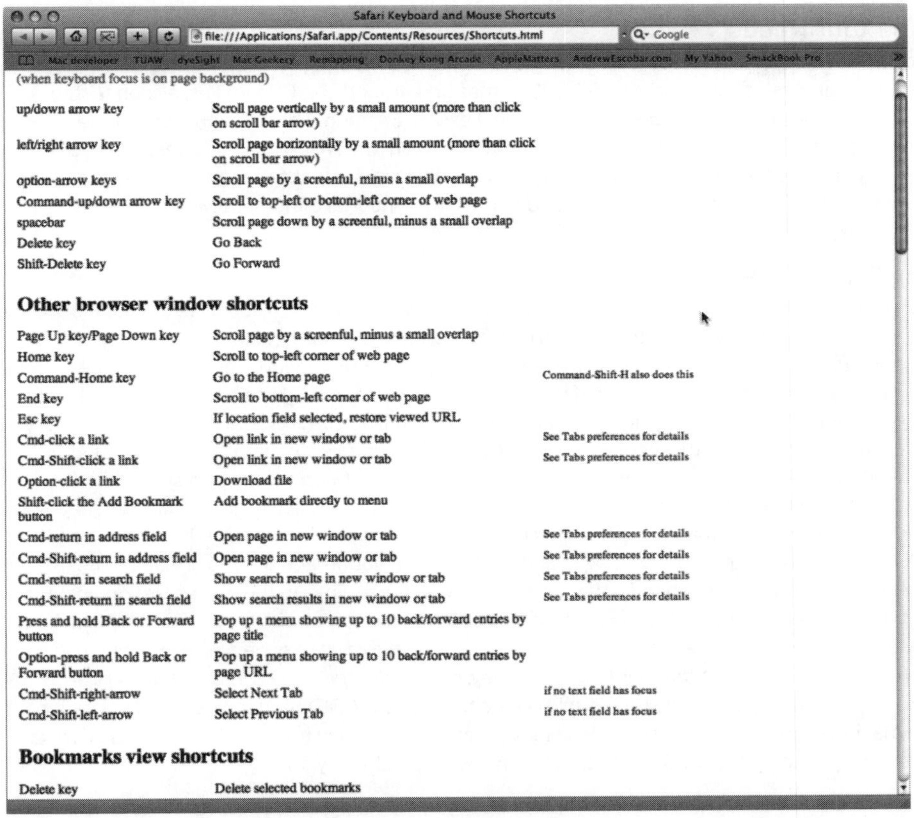

If you don't feel like enabling the Debug menu but still want access to all the nifty shortcuts, just point your browser to *file:///Applications/Safari.app/Contents/Resources/Shortcuts.html*, and bookmark the list. It's a local file stored in Safari's package but it is much easier to access through your browser than to spend your time drilling through folders and opening packages hunting for the information you want.

Now that the Debug menu has been revealed, it is natural to wonder if every Apple-created application has this hidden feature. It would be a lot of fun after all if you could muck about with any application you wanted in developer fashion. Unfortunately not all applications have a hidden Debug menu—but a few do. Try this trick out with iCal to find another application with a less-fun Debug menu. If you ever get tired of having the Debug menu around, turning it off is as simple as launching the Terminal and typing:

```
defaults write com.apple.Safari IncludeDebugMenu 0
```

It is doubtful that anyone is actively developing viruses or much else for OS 9; the most recent metric of usage by W3 Counter gives pre-OS X versions of Mac OS a .03% share of the OS market. That number likely isn't accurate because of the way the data is collected, but the message remains: not many people are bothering with OS 9 anymore. Does the lack of interest mean that your web server running OS 9 is safe? Steve Wozniak, cofounder of Apple, argued that it did during a speech at a college in 2003 saying:

"If you wanted to have servers and not be subjected to viruses, I have one suggestion: Macintosh Mac OS 9. I run all my servers and keep them on Mac OS 9. I have never had a firewall, and I have never been hit in all these years, even though I appear on TV shows with other hackers and the like. I'd be a prime target, and they have not hit any of my machines."

HACK 11: Roll Your Own Web Server

If you maintain a site with predictable and moderate traffic needs, paying for hosting is a waste of money. Learn how to host a site from the comfort of your own home using cheap hardware with this very useful hack.

I've been running a web server from my house for about seven years now. I started with a PowerMac 6100 (pizza box), and later moved up to an el-cheapo hamfest special ($10) PowerMac 7500. I later upgraded that with a Sonnnet G3 processor, and now am using a 1.25 GHz G4 Mac mini.

Define Your Needs

What kind of web site is ideal for this? The one I host is a genealogically oriented site with a searchable database containing over 30,000 names and around 10,000 families, all connected to our progenitors, Matthew and Rose Greenell of Lexden, England. That is quite a bit of data; the printed book that will be derived from this database will run upwards of 1,500 pages, or at least that's the current estimate. But the amount of data isn't as important to a web server as the amount of traffic. The site I host doesn't require massive amounts of horsepower.

Using Pre-OS X Macs

First, let's look at hardware. Please plan on running your web server on a separate machine from your regular home machine(s). The reasons include performance and most of all, security. You really need to keep your web server isolated from the rest of your network, for reasons more completely explained later in the hack. If you want to use a Mac, the first thing you need to decide upon is old(er) hardware or new(er) hardware. Like I said at the start, my site initially ran on a very elderly PowerMac 6100. With a genteel 66 MHz 601 processor, this kind of machine won't get out of its own way for most normal uses, but as a small home-based web server with static HTML pages, if you don't plan on huge numbers of hits per day, it will really do an amazingly adequate job. Consider this: most broadband hookups can only provide between 128 and 256 Kb/second on the uplink (when people request HTML pages and content from your machine, you are uploading to the Net), so it won't take much to fill that pipe. Other great machines in the older category include the highly reliable PowerMac 7500/8500/9500 family. These can be easily upgraded for less than $100 to a 500 MHz G3 processor from Sonnet and others. Storage may be a problem because SCSI hard disks are getting tougher to find, but hey, how about the early G3 (beige) towers and desktops? They use more easily obtainable (and cheaper) ATA (IDE) hard drives. Used prices for those machines are low, so you're not looking at a large cash outlay to get the web-server hardware you desire. You can put 768 MB of RAM into them relatively cheaply, too.

Any of these machines will work well with Mac OS 9.2, which comes with a combination extension and control panel, Personal Web Sharing (PWS). It's easy to set up, too. What I don't know is how "hackable" this software is—that is, I don't know if is it sufficiently secure in this modern day and age. Remember, PWS was written in the mid to late 90s when security wasn't the concern it is now. All I can say is you should have all your web server data backed up to a separate drive if you use this (or any) solution. That caution aside, PWS is a great way to cheaply throw together a web server with an old and otherwise unwanted Mac.

Using OS X Hardware

Want to use more modern hardware with OS X? The good news is that Mac OS X comes with the best web server software on the planet, and it's free, too! Apache Web Server is used pretty much anywhere that Microsoft's Internet Information Services (IIS) is not (and the places where Apache Web Server is used vastly outnumber the places where IIs is used). Open source, extensible, customizable, and supported heavily by the volunteers who wrote it, Apache is the bees' knees of web serving.

This is a terrific solution for simple, static sites, and it's scalable to enterprise-class web sites (though I wouldn't run a huge site from home unless I had a bunch o' bandwidth). It is tightly integrated with two additional web-standard applications: PHP and MySQL.

Suffice it to say, any Mac truly capable of running OS X will make a great web server. This means that bargain G4 and early G5 towers will do the trick, as will any Macintosh mini, or iMac (generally I suggest running Mac OS 9.2 on G3 iMacs, OS X on G4 and newer iMacs). Heck, there are people out there using PowerBooks as web servers.

Getting Your Domain

Once you've decided on the hardware you've got to keep your Internet service provider (ISP) in mind. Most ISPs don't like the idea of your running a web site from your home. They don't like to see lots of uploads from your site to the Net and could impose bandwidth limitations or other restrictions if the site is too heavily trafficked. That said, with the popularity of BitTorrent [Hack #114], the chances of your ISP noticing you're running a low-volume web site are minimal.

First, you will need to determine if you can get a static Internet protocol (IP) address from your current ISP. While it is possible to run a web site with an ever-changing IP address as controlled by your provider's Dynamic Host Configuration Protocol (DHCP) server and getting additional services from folks [Hack #48], it's just easier if your IP address never changes. Most ISPs will provide this service for an additional fee. Some may try to put you into a business plan and thus charge a large additional fee. If they do, shop around for another provider using the databases on www. dslreports.com or another resource. One major ISP local to my area is so hostile to anyone really taking advantage of an "always on" DSL connection that they renew IP addresses of people they believe to be "hogging resources" as often as every 10 to 15 minutes! This is entirely legal, and for a typical casual Internet surfer, totally transparent. Suffice it to say, renewing an IP address every few minutes does terrible things to a secure virtual private network connection between your computer and your employer's network. Two of my coworkers were faced with this problem that was only corrected by paying extra for a static IP address. That was all the ISP wanted—to make users pay for bandwidth they were otherwise guaranteed they would have available. An always-on connection isn't necessarily an always-on connection.

Once you have a static IP address from your ISP, the next step is to register your domain name. I use www.register.com, but there are scads of domain registration services out there; a Google search will help you determine the right registrar for your needs. Plan on spending anywhere from $6.95/year (introductory rate) to $30 per year or more. The domain registration service is needed not only to protect your domain name, but also is used to translate your domain name (www.mywebsite.com) to an IP address. Once registered, as long as your site is not violating copyright, obscenity, or other laws, no one else can take that domain name or take your site down. Setting up your account with a registration service can be different from service to service. You will need to find out if the name you want is even available. Most of these services offer free domain searches from their home page. You will need to decide if your site is a *.com* (commercial), *.net*, *.org* (nonprofit), *.biz*, or *.info*, among many other options.

When you have identified and registered your domain name, you will need to locate the page that you use to translate your domain name to the static IP address assigned by your ISP. This is necessary because you and I work with names—much easier to remember. The Internet, however, works with IP addresses, which are a lot harder to remember. Domain name servers (DNS) store this lookup information and perform the translation from name to address. Also, domain name servers talk to other domain servers, so your address translation information is stored on multiple machines around the world, speeding the translation process, and thereby speeding the connection to the desired server. Most domain registration companies provide domain name services. You will have to locate those services on your domain registration company's web site.

When you have done this, you are almost ready to go online! It can actually take a few days for your new domain name to propagate throughout all the DNS servers across the globe, so people might not be able to see your site right away. This gives you time to start setting up your router to permit outsiders to see your web server and only your web server.

Opening Your Router So Your Web Server Can Peek Out

This is probably the hardest part of the hack. You will have to do a fair amount of research and maybe will need more than one conversation with your ISP to make sure you have all the information to set up your router and network computers correctly.

I strongly suggest the use of a router, whether you have one computer or many. Routers have built-in security features that make it more difficult for folks on the Internet to peek inside your network. Most routers also have features to open themselves up to individual machines, and this is what I will discuss momentarily.

First, the web server computer will need to have its own static IP address. Get back with your ISP to make sure you have not only your static IP address, but also your subnet mask, DNS server addresses, and search domain information.

If you haven't already set up your router for your new static IP address, you should do so now.

Your ISP will provide the following information to you:

IP address
The static IP address your ISP assigned to you.

DNS address
You should get this from your ISP. If there are two addresses, copy them both.

Gateway address
Your ISP provides this number.

Subnet mask
You should get this from your ISP.

Search domains
Some "domain.com" address.

Next, you will need to assign a static IP address to the computer you're using as a web server and complete its configuration.

In your Network Systems Preference (OS X) or the Networks control panel (OS 9), you will need to create a custom network configuration for your Macintosh. It should look something, but not exactly like the following list. Just plug those numbers into the assigned fields.

- DNS: bbb.bbb.bbb.bbb (if there are two addresses, copy down both numbers)
- Gateway: 192.168.2.1 (usually the IP address of your router)
- Subnet mask: 255.255.255.255
- Search domains: somethingorother.com

Your router will usually assign IP addresses in the ranges of:
- 192.168.0.n (where n is a number from 2 to 254)
- 192.168.1.n (where n is a number from 2 to 254)
- 192.168.2.n (where n is a number from 2 to 254)
- 192.168.3.n (where n is a number from 2 to 254)

In this example, it's IP: 192.168.2.5.

Your remaining computers can use regular DHCP connectivity settings (where the router assigns IP addresses).

You will need to make sure your router's DHCP server does not automatically assign IP addresses in the range where you will be assigning your static IP address. For example, if you want to assign your web server an internal IP address like 192.168.2.5, make sure your router begins assigning addresses at 192.168.2.10.

Some more explaining is needed here. You are actually working with different kinds of IP addresses. Your router automatically translates (or routes) addresses from the outside (the Internet) to your internal network. This is a function known as Network Address Translation (NAT), which actually helps hide your network from the Internet and is your primary mode of protection. On the Internet side of your router, there's only one IP address (the static IP address your ISP assigned to you). On the other side of your router is your internal network, for which your router either assigns IP addresses from its own DHCP server,or permits devices with static IP addresses to operate as long as they fall within the correct range of addresses (like your web server). So, on your internal network side, there's your web server with the IP address of 192.168.2.5, and you may have dozens of additional computers using the DHCP server that automatically assigns IP addresses beginning with (in this example) 192.168.2.10, all the way up to 192.168.2.254. With only one IP address on the Internet side, you can theoretically have hundreds of computers sharing that single outside IP address. Your internal network computers can communicate with each other without going outside, but if they need to go to a web page on the Internet, the router automatically translates the address to the Internet (along with all the rest of the users on your internal network). Whew! A cautionary note: don't try to run a business with hundreds of computers on your side of the network. Your ISP will certainly make note of a high level of traffic at all times, and will likely object and will probably insist on you upgrading your account to a higher traffic business account.

This said, there are two ways in which consumer routers can be configured to let your web server work correctly. The most common method is the DMZ (demilitarized zone). This places a computer with a designated IP address on the "other side" of the firewall; it receives no protection from the NAT server or firewall. This may be less of an issue with a Mac but is still an issue nonetheless. The DMZ and virtual server methods (described next) are also used by computer gamers, who need to open specific ports on their routers so they can share data with other gamers.

The other method, offered on my Belkin router and probably others, is what they call a virtual server. What this does is open only specific ports on the router for a designated computer to connect to the Internet. For example, if you are using a standard web server, you would only need to open up port 80, which is the Internet standard for HTTP servers. If you wish to move files back and forth from the Internet using File Transfer Protocol (FTP), you need to open up port 25 on the virtual server. As always, RTFM (Read The Fine Manual—the clean version—I learned it differently!). There are so many variations based upon platform, manufacturer, etc., there's no way I can describe in detail every possible way to set up a router.

With either of these two configurations, your web server and the rest of the computers on your internal network should be able to access the Internet and function properly.

If you are using a wireless router on your network, make absolutely sure you have secured the wireless functions in multiple ways. Do not broadcast your SSID, and use WPA-PSK security [Hack #54]. No sense in securing your web server from the wired Internet only to leave it and the rest of your network vulnerable to wireless attacks. Read the documentation that came with your router, as well as the router's online help (most have it) for more detailed instructions.

Setting Up Your Web Server on Older PowerPC Equipment

If you have an older PowerPC or G3/G4 Mac, running Personal WebSharing (PWS) under Mac OS 9 is a viable option, and worthy of your consideration. Running simple static, low-traffic web sites requires very little in the area of RAM or processor speed.

PWS under Mac OS 9 is incredibly easy to use (actually, for simple web sites, Apache under Mac OS X is real easy, too). This could be a great application for an older machine.

First, boot your Mac OS 9-based Mac (we are presuming you already have installed the operating system and are ready to load the web server software), and load the Mac OS 9.x installer CD. Double-click the Software Installers folder. Then, double-click the Personal WebSharing folder. Read the "About Personal Web Sharing" SimpleText document for any special news or issues you may need to know about. If you are ready to install, double-click the Installer icon. Agree to the software license, and make sure the Easy Install shows in the upper left of the "webscript" window. Install on your default hard drive.

Let's configure your new web server

In MacOS 9, go to the Apple menu, and select Control Panels. Launch Personal WebSharing. You are greeted by a menu (shown in Figure 2-22) to get you started on the path to running your own web server.

Figure 2-22.
The first step to configuring your web server

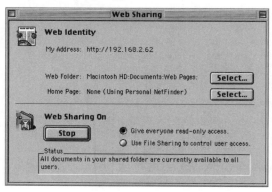

The Web Folder location is shown (next to the first "Select..." button). This folder is where you will put all your HTML and graphics files. It is also where Apple has placed several excellent tutorials (*About Personal WebSharing.htm* and *Using Personal WebSharing.htm*), as well as a default web page you can use to verify the server is working (more in a moment).

One of the most important security settings is next to the Start/Stop button on the PWS control panel window. There are two radio buttons: give everyone read-only access, and Use File Sharing to control user access. If you want a wide open web site that anyone can access, use the first choice. If you want to set up access permissions (beyond the scope of this article), use the second choice.

For PWS to function properly, you will need to tell it what your default home page will be. This is usually a file named something like *index.html*, *default.html*, or something similar. To do so, click the Home Page button (the lower of the two "Select..." buttons). This brings up a new window. Select the file (for this test, use default.html) and click the Select button (see Figure 2-23).

Figure 2-23.
Getting ready to test your server

If you want, you can go to the Edit→Preferences menu item and look around. You probably won't need to do anything here, unless you want to have PWS generate a logfile of everything that goes on (possibly useful), to change the default port (don't do it!), allow Aliases to open items outside the web folder (probably not a good idea for security reasons), or allow guests with write access permissions to replace files in the web folder (also not a good idea). MIME Types tab? Leave it alone. Actions tab? Leave it alone. If you have made any changes, click the Save button. Otherwise, click the close button at the upper left of the window (see Figure 2-24).

Figure 2-24.
Your computer is ready to serve

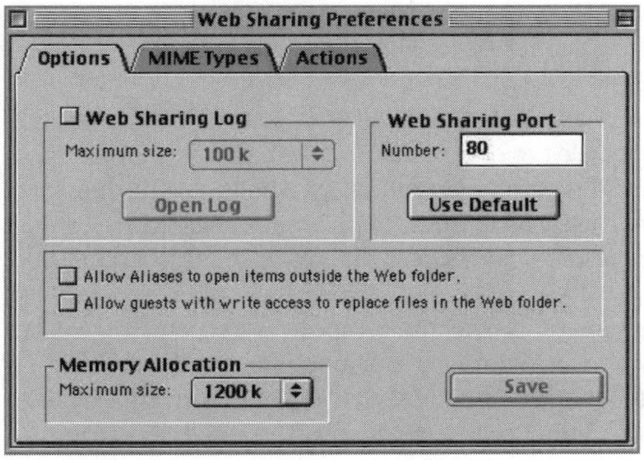

To start the web server, click the Start button on the main PWS control panel. To test it, open your web browser and type `http://localhost`. If you get the Apple file named *default.html*, you got it right.

Obviously, you don't want to broadcast a web site with just Apple's *default.html* file as your content. You want to create your own. Hopefully, you were working on that long before you began planning on the hardware/software equation. You will need to write your web pages in HTML. You can do so with a number of excellent commercial tools, including iWeb **[Hack #81]**, Dreamweaver, GoLive, Freeway, PageSpinner, and more. There are also plenty of freeware, open source, and shareware products out there. Check out www.versiontracker.com to discover and try out a bevy of programs and then pick the one you like best.

Pulling It Off with OS X

Personal Web Sharing in Mac OS X is "personal" in name only. As mentioned earlier, the built-in web server that comes with every copy of Mac OS X is the industrial-strength open source product, Apache. Apache runs on more web servers than just about any other product out there. It is scalable, extensible, and works with virtually every web scripting language out there, including HTML, PHP, Perl, Javascript, Ruby on Rails, Ajax, Python, and many more, but that's waaaaay beyond the scope of this hack.

Setup couldn't be easier. To activate Apache, go to System Preferences→Sharing. Make sure the Services tab is selected. Click the checkbox for Personal Web Sharing. You will be prompted to enter your administrator's password. In a moment, Apache will be up and running (see Figure 2-25).

Figure 2-25.
Turning Personal Web Sharing on

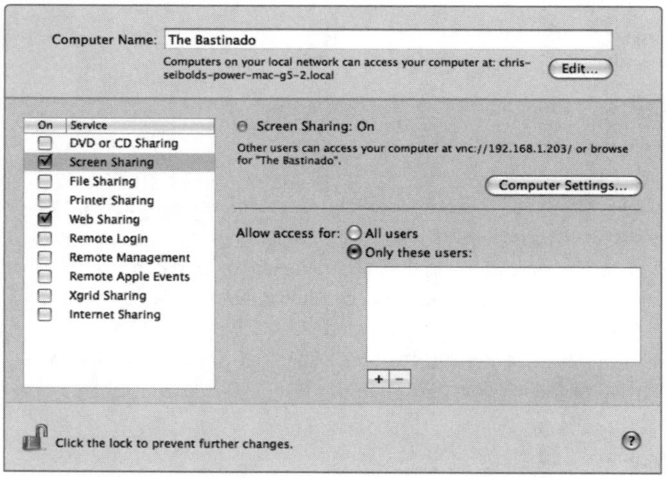

Your web server is now running! Wasn't that easy? Now, what do you do with it, and where do you put your files? Let's move back a bit, and we'll turn the web server off while we do some simple setup.

At the top level of your hard drive (by default, it's named Macintosh HD, but you could have named it something else), open the */Library/Web server/Documents* folder. Your web site normally is placed in the Documents folder at this location. Alternately, you can set up what's called a "personal web site" within your Sites folder, at path */Users/username/Sites* (for example, *Macintosh HD/Users/LarryGrinnell/Sites*). The difference is how you would access the site from the Internet.

Using the first example (the Documents folder), also known as the computer's web site, you would use the URL http://192.168.2.2/, while the second example (your personal web site) would be http://192.168.2.2/~LarryGrinnell/. Please note that the IP address and user account are examples only. When you activate PWS in the Services tab of the Sharing window, you will see the exact addresses for both options toward the bottom of the window. Clicking the first example link in the Services tab of the Sharing window, you will be taken to an Apache home page. Clicking the second example takes you to a PWS home page. Either link shows the server is functioning.

To set your web site up for outside use (why else would you be setting one up?), use the first example—the computer's web site. Obviously, you don't want to broadcast a web site with just the Apache demo page as your content. You want to create your own content. Hopefully, you were working on that long before you began planning on the hardware/software equation.

Because OS X is using Apache, and has a whole library of tools preinstalled for your use, including PHP, MySQL, Perl, and such, with mostly free open source software, you can create very powerful and professional web sites. You can create your own blog site with software like WordPress, Movable

Type, and so many more. You can also build a complete web content management system that includes user forums, photo galleries, news, articles, download areas, and more. Check out http://en.wikipedia.org/wiki/Content_management_system to learn about content management systems (CMSs). For my own web site, I use an open source CMS called PHP-Fusion (http://php-fusion.co.uk/news.php) that offers all I need to support a family genealogy society. I am also using another specialized package, The Next Generation of Geneology SiteBuilding (http://lythgoes.net/genealogy/software.php) that permits me to publish the complete linked Grinnell family genealogy, containing the names and data of some 30,000 individuals, and 10,000 families—all on a rather modest 1.25 GHz G4 Macintosh mini with only 512 MB of RAM.

These are but a few examples of what you can do with your own web site running on your own Macintosh at your own home. It's fun and can be very rewarding.

— Larry Grinnell

HACK 12: Two Ways to Reset Safari

Remember the awe and wonder you had when you first launched Safari? The Apple-supplied browser rendered pages with incredible speed and felt positively zippy. As time passed, you undoubtably noticed Safari lost some of its zippiness. Get Safari's missing speed back with this nifty hack.

Everyone wants a faster web browsing experience and ISPs are always trying to boost bandwidth to get an advantage over the competition. Sometimes the slowdown in your browsing experience isn't the fault of the service provider; sometimes the slowdown is due to the browser.

Most Safari users have experienced these slowdowns. As Safari is used, the caches get bloated, favicons get out of control, and cookies run amok. If Safari was slowing down prior to Safari 3.0, you had the option to Reset Safari (Safari→Reset Safari), but you lost all the passwords and information used by autofill. Once the operation was complete, Safari was faster but any speed gain was more than offset by the maddening process of reentering passwords and rebuilding autofill information. As previously mentioned, Safari 3 alleviates this problem by allowing users to select what information they would like reset. To take advantage of the Safari's new-found ability, use "Reset Safari...", found under the Safari menu bar item.

Once you've selected "Reset Safari...", you'll be presented with a window full of options (see Figure 2-26).

Figure 2-26.
A bevy of reset choices

Most of the choices are self-explanatory, and the truth is you probably won't miss any of the data if you choose to reset the cache and web site icons (favicons), and clear the download window. Choosing to clear out the cookies will result in unexpected behavior when you visit a site you're normally logged into (you'll have to log back in), and opting to reset passwords and AutoFill text can be a maddening prospect (completely resetting Safari does offer some security but using a Guest Account is a safer and easier method to protect your sensitive Safari information).

In all likelihood, you'll find yourself using the "Reset Safari…" option quite frequently. Often enough that it would be nicer if you had an Apple Script to do the job instead of having to make conscious decisions each time about what to reset and what to leave. There is a script to do just that:

```
try
  tell application "Finder"
    -- Let's get the name of the current user
    set myUserName to (do shell script "whoami")

    -- Is Safari running?
    set safariIsRunning to false
    if (do shell script "ps -U " & myUserName) contains "Safari.app/Contents/MacOS/
Safari" then set safariIsRunning to true

    -- Let's quit Safari or the cleaning will not take effect
    if safariIsRunning then tell application "Safari" to quit

    -- Let's delete the application's cookies
    try
      set deleteCookies to 1
      do shell script "rm -r /Users/" & myUserName & "/Library/Cookies/"
    on error
      set deleteCookies to 0
    end try

    -- Let's delete the application's caches
    try
      set deleteCaches to 1
      do shell script "rm -r /Users/" & myUserName & "/Library/Caches/Safari/"
    on error
      set deleteCaches to 0
    end try

    -- Let's delete the application's icons
    try
      set deleteIcons to 1
      do shell script "rm -r /Users/" & myUserName & "/Library/Safari/Icons/"
    on error
      set deleteIcons to 0
    end try

    -- Let's delete the application's history
    try
      set deleteHistory to 1
      do shell script "rm -r /Users/" & myUserName & "/Library/Safari/History.
plist"
    on error
        set deleteHistory to 0
    end try

    -- Let's delete the application's downloads folder
    try
      set deleteDownloads to 1
      do shell script "rm -r /Users/" & myUserName & "/Library/Safari/Downloads.
plist"
```

```
    on error
      set deleteDownloads to 0
    end try

    -- Let's reopen Safari if it was running when the script was called
    -- Note: this does not always work! Eeek!
    if safariIsRunning then tell application "Safari" to activate

    -- Let's conclude by letting the user know everything is OK
  end tell
  if safariIsRunning then
    tell application "Safari" to display alert "Safari has now been cleaned up."
message "You can now resume using the application." as informational buttons "OK"
default button 1 giving up after 2
  else
      tell application "Finder" to display alert "Safari has now been cleaned up."
message "Changes have already taken effect and will be retained the next time you
launch the application." as informational buttons "OK" default button 1
  end if

on error TheError
  tell application "Finder" to display alert "Safari could not be cleaned because
of a script error." message "Below is the error returned by Apple Script, which may
assist you in troubleshooting this issue:" & return & return & TheError buttons
"OK" default button 1 as warning
end try
```

The script is nifty: it quits Safari and then proceeds to delete cookies, caches, icons history, and downloads. Of course, if you had to type that in every time you wanted to partially reset Safari, you'd be much better off using Safari's built-in methods mentioned earlier in this hack. So let's make the script more convenient to use. Launch the Apple-supplied Script Editor application (Applications→Apple Script→Script Editor.app), and a blank window opens ready to receive the Safari-cleaning Apple script. At this point you can manually transpose the script from the book or you could visit http://www.oreillynet.com/mac/blog/2005/08/homebrew_safari_updated.html, and copy and paste the required code.

If you're bold, you'll just compile the script, but it's probably a better idea to run it the script at least once to check for transcription or copying errors. Click the run button. and the Script Editor will run through the tasks assigned, reformatting the text and providing you with the outcome of the actions (see Figure 2-27).

Figure 2-27.

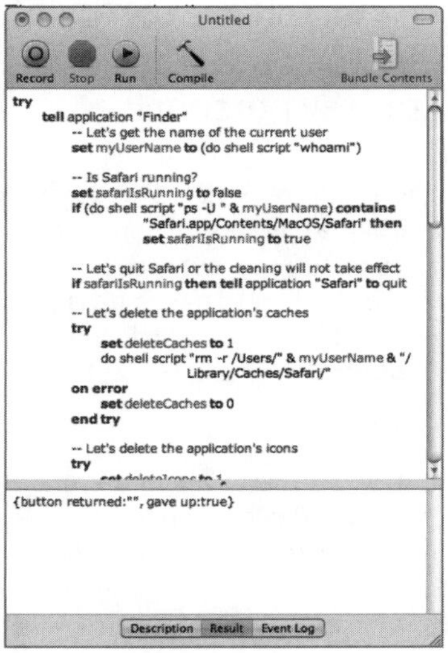

If you're satisfied the script worked, you'll want to turn the script into something a bit more accessible for frequent use. Choose "Save As..." from the File menu, choose Application, give your new application a good name, and you'll be ready to reset Safari with a click of the mouse any time you wish (see Figure 2-28).

— FJ de Kermadec

Figure 2-28.
You've got a new, very useful app

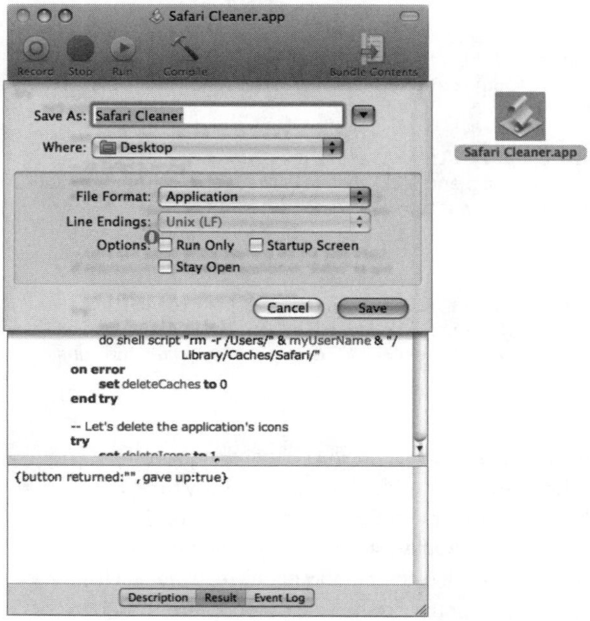

HACK 13: Ditch That Hidden Data

If you're using the Internet, there is a good chance you aren't just interested in downloading files; you're probably interested in uploading files for others to see. The trouble is that uploading files for others to see can often reveal more information than you intend to share. Take control of the amount of information others can gain from the files you post by understanding where the data hides and how to keep from sharing the data you want to stay personal.

There is data associated with your files that you are probably not aware of. This is data that doesn't appear in the files but is useful for revisions, generating thumbnails, or making life easier in general, and it's often referred to as *metadata*. Metadata is data about your data. The concept seems redundant, but metadata makes your computing life much easier. The idea behind metadata is pretty simple; data about data can provide useful information that wouldn't generally be found within the file. The simplest metadata is just the file suffix, which indicates whether a file contains a GIF image, a PDF document, an MP3, or something else.

Metadata can be much more complicated than that. For example, metadata associated with your digital photos and stored within the files, reveals the camera you used and the focal length at the time of the shot. Metadata associated with documents reveals the creator of the file and the program used to generate the file. This metadata is indexed by Spotlight and is used to generate the lightning fast and pinpoint accurate searches Mac users have come to know and love.

As long as the files are on your computer away from prying eyes, hidden data and metadata is no problem. When you start flinging files around a network or the Internet, metadata can become a serious problem. One is reminded of the case of Cat Schwartz who had some interesting pictures taken for her blog and posted said pictures. They were cropped in unusual dimensions, and it didn't take long for folks to grab the image, examine the photos in Photoshop, and note that Cat wasn't wearing a shirt when the photos were taken thanks to inclusion of thumbnails in the hidden data associated with the pictures.

The oversight by Cat Schwartz was merely embarrassing (or titillating, depending on your point of view), but other instances of not knowing what data is associated with the file when shunting the file to others haven't been as innocuous. There have been multiple instances of regrettable information leaking out because the people didn't realize what information they were posting when they uploaded files generated by Word or PDFs to the Internet. In one telling example, the Balco steroid trial names were inadvertently released when a PDF was released with names blacked out on the document, names readily accessible via the metadata.

Luckily, there are ways to ensure that when you're sharing a sensitive file over a network, you're just sharing the information you want to share. But before you can decide what information you want to share you should know what information is there.

Viewing Metadata

The amount and format of a file's metadata is dependent on the format of that file. Some file formats offer tremendous opportunities for metadata, and for others, it's limited to a comment or two. Depending on the file type, OS X offers several ways to have a look at your metadata with varying levels of completeness. The most obvious method is invoking the Get Info (single-click the file in question and hit Command-I, or simply right-click and select Get Info). Using the Get Info command on an image, you're treated to the standard information such as creation and modification dates, but you also get a bevy of information about your camera (see Figure 2-29).

Figure 2-29.
The more you know...

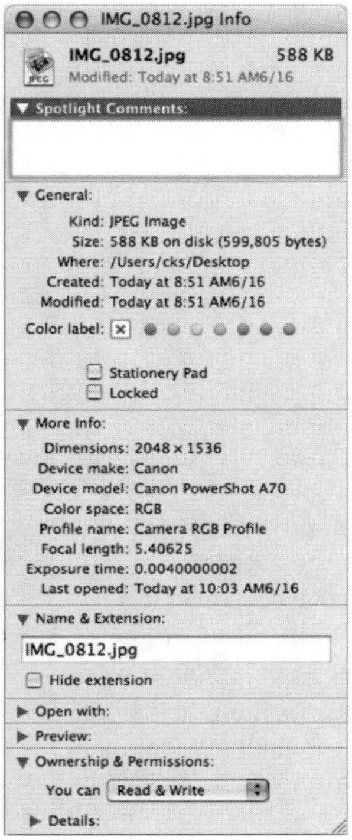

While using the Get Info command provides a method to view some of the metadata and the ability to add some more data about your data, it is not a complete solution because you're not seeing all of the metadata. In the case of a PDF file, the complete text is also included in the metadata, but Get Info doesn't reveal the text. For a more complete picture of the metadata associated with a file a quick trip to the Terminal is in order. Here's the necessary command:

```
$ mdimport -d2 filename
```

The `mdimport` program imports the metadata while the `-d` flag stands for debug. Debug sounds like some scary programming thing, but in this instance the `-d` option followed by 1-4 merely specifies the level of detail revealed. By specifying `-d2`, you'll see all the metadata relevant to you (see Figure 2-30). Feel free to adjust the level though; the information returned can be fun to look at.

Figure 2-30.
The metadata returned from a PDF file

Ditching the Metadata

Now that you know the metadata is there, it's time to get rid of the information you don't want to share with others. If you're wondering when it might be useful to get rid of metadata, picture a scenario where you tracked changes in a Word document, and you're sending that document to a client. Turns out that with a little investigation, the client can see the changes; so if you had written a parenthetical comment along the lines of "How stupid is this guy?" after a request to generate a web site in mauve and puce, a clever client might see it. Not the best idea. The easiest way to get around this is to save any document generated in Word, Excel, etc. as a PDF. That strips out the comments and most of the other stuff you might not want the recipient to see.

Figure 2-31
Saving a text document as a PDF

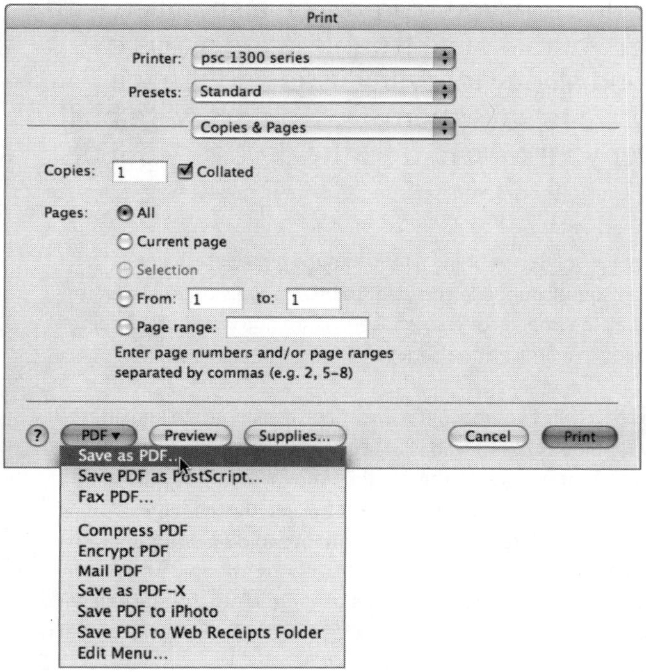

QUICK HACK ✕

SAVE FILES AS PDFS

You hear a lot about saving files as PDFs on your Mac, but the process isn't as straightforward as it could be. The intuitive way to save files as PDFs would be to add a PDF option to the "Save As..." dialog. No luck. To save files as a PDF on the Mac, select Print and from that dialog, choose "Save as PDF" (see Figure 2-31).

For photos, you might want to lose the Exchangeable Image File Format (Exif) information. If you're using a variant of Photoshop, the procedure is very simple: just choose "Save for web...". That doesn't do you much good if you're not using Photoshop, so be aware that not all image formats allow Exif data to be stored with the image file. For example, the PNG format has no facility for containing Exif data, so if you want to lose the Exif data, convert the image to PNG and post away. If you really want to use JPEG, convert back to .JPEG, and the Exif data will be lost in the process.

While these steps will strip away most of the embarrassing data about any files you share, there will still be information left. Inspecting the file will still reveal the creator, the time the file was created, and other seemingly harmless information. Of course, if you're stuck in a repressive society and trying to foment a rebellion, even the generally innocuous information can be too much. You want to cover your tracks with a maximum of obfuscation? There's no easy straightforward method to get rid of all the metadata associated with a file or even a good way to see all of the information. So, if you're creating a manifesto that will bring down a totalitarian regime, paste the text anonymously into an online editor and save away. Coupled with TOR [Hack #49], that method should keep the jackboots at bay for a little while.

HACK 14: Scrape the Web for Images

You're surfing around the Net, and you stumble on a site filled with lots of images you want for yourself. The trouble is the site is big, and you don't want to spend all day following links and dragging the images to your hard drive to save them. Computers were built for the repetitive: empower your Mac to take the drudgery out of collecting images.

One of the suggested hacks for this book involved grabbing all the images off a web site with minimal user intervention. The idea was sound: suppose you want to be a professional stalker; it would certainly behoove you to collect all the images of your chosen victim automatically, freeing you to print the images and stick them up in a little shrine dedicated to the chosen celebrity.

That may be an extreme example. Few of us will ever reach the level of professional stalker, after all. On the other hand, many of us have stumbled across a web album or a Flickr page of images that have some personal meaning to us. You might not want to spend the time manually downloading every picture from your nephew's birthday party, but you might want to keep those images around for reference to embarrass the child at a future date. When you talk about avoiding drudgery with a Mac, the most common solution is to use Automator, and it turns out enough people want to scrape the Web for images that you can find a simple version of this built right into the starting page of Automator.

To get to the example workflow, launch Automator (Applications→Automator), and click the Photos and Images starting point. Select "the Web" and "Use links on Safari web page when workflow runs." (See Figure 2-32.)

Figure 2-32.
The built-in workflow

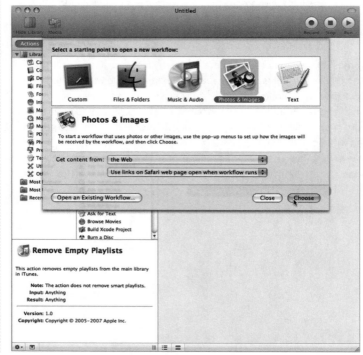

You might be tempted to think that the workflow would work as advertised, but it doesn't. Running that workflow doesn't result in images, it results in a slew of HTML pages, which isn't what you want. Tweaking the workflow is necessary. In this case, the goal is ending up with images, so we need to limit the results to images only. Click Internet→Get Image URLs from Webpages from Automator's library and add that to the workflow after the Get Link URLs from Webpages action. As you can see in Figure 2-33, the workflow will yield what you want.

Figure 2-33.
The corrected workflow

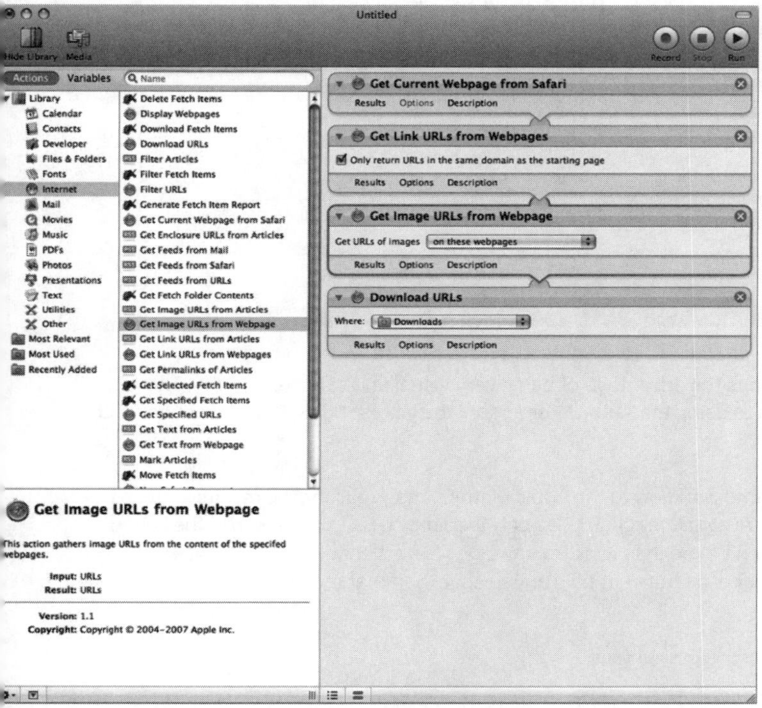

The tweaked script runs nicely, running through a web site and downloading all the images it happens across. If you were to run the script with a Think secret gallery as the frontmost page in Safari, the results would be an impressive array of JPEGs and GIFs (see Figure 2-34).

Figure 2-34.
A lot of pictures

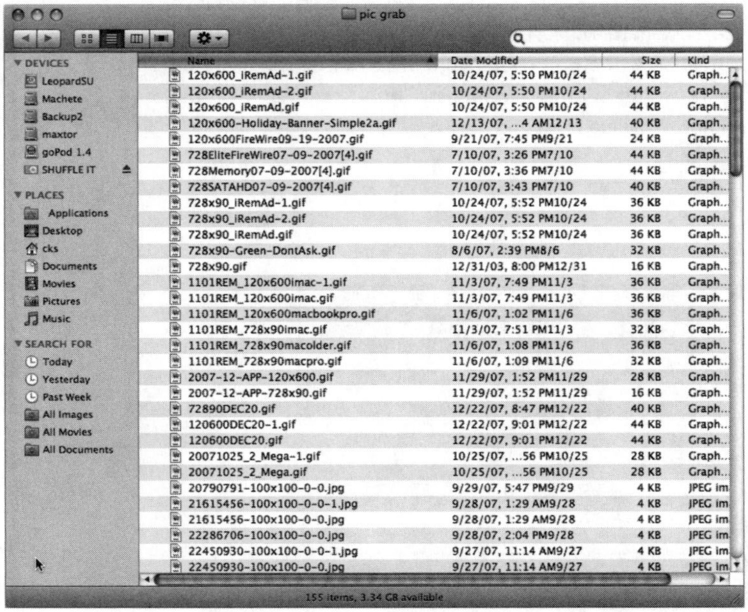

Using Automator for this task has the advantage of being very visual and self-explanatory. There are, however, some downsides to using the Automator action, the largest being that the action isn't very flexible.

For example, if you apply the same workflow to the Apple Matters image gallery, the results aren't as desirable. The reason is that the Automator action looks only two links deep. In other words, the action works as long as the pictures aren't more than two clicks away, so the action will get the images linked from pages linked to the starting page but won't dig any deeper than that (see Figure 2-35).

Figure 2-35.
The action got the thumbnails but not the full size images

You can tweak Automator to search ever deeper for images but there is an easier, more general solution for grabbing images (or any particular type of file) from web sites. The solution to this problem is a command-line application called **wget**. The **wget** program simplifies scraping the Web for the stuff (in this case) images you want. Unfortunately, **wget** is not part of the OS X install, so you'll have to do a little preparation before you can join in the web-scraping fun,

Once you've decided to install **wget**, you've got some choices to make. You can download the latest version and build the program yourself, which is an interesting experience but for the purposes of grabbing images, an older version of **wget** works just as well as the latest and greatest. So if you're after a prebuilt Mac OS X version of **wget**, point your browser to http://www.statusq.org/images/wget.zip, and download the program.

 You can also get **wget** via Fink or MacPorts **[Hack #31]**. For many users, this will be the easiest way, and it will open up some new doors to command-line hacks.

Once you've got the *.zip* file expand it, you'll find four files. Since **wget** is a command-line application, these files need to go in specific folders. Trouble is that the folders where the files need to live are invisible, so you can't just do the standard OS X drag-and-drop methodology.

The following commands will get the files where they need to be, assuming the downloads have ended up in your download folder:

```
$ sudo cp /Users/cks/Downloads/wget/wget /usr/local/bin
$ sudo cp /Users/cks/Downloads/wget/wget.1 / usr/local/man/man1
$ sudo cp /Users/cks/Downloads/wget/wget rc // usr/local/etc
```

You will be prompted for your password; be sure you're logged on with an administrator's account.

Now that **wget** is installed where it needs to be, you can start downloading images using your brand-new application. **wget** is quite powerful and supports a variety of powerful downloading options (type **man wget** at the Terminal prompt for more information), but for the purposes of downloading images from a web site, the usage is very simple. All **wget** really needs is a URL and a file type (see Figure 2-36). If you wanted all the JPEGs from BrandonBird.com, the command might looks like the following:

```
wget -r -l5 --no-parent -A.jpg http://www.brandonbird.com/paintings.html
```

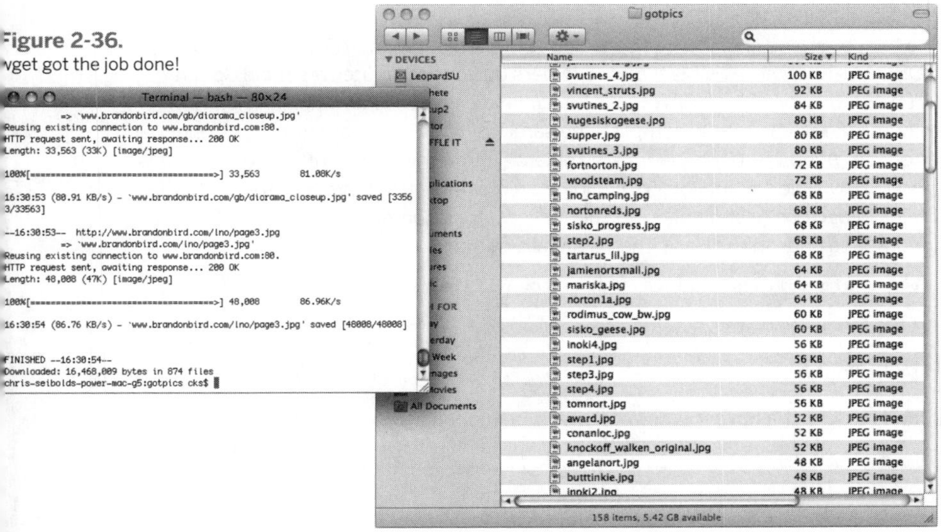

Figure 2-36.
wget got the job done!

Here are the relevant options in this case:

`-r`
Tells `wget` to copy recursively.

`-l5`
Tells `wget` how many levels deep you want to go. If you want `wget` to follow only links from the starting page one level deep, use `-l1`.

`--no-parent`
Tells `wget` to not to go back to the starting page when downloading recursively.

`-A.jpg`
Tells `wget` to grab only files ending in *.jpg*, if you were after MP3s, using `-A.mp3` would result in `wget` retrieving only files ending in *.mp3*.

`wget` downloads the files to your current directory, so it is probably a good idea to change the directory you're in to someplace you want the files stored. If, for example, you'd like the files to end up in a folder on your Desktop called *gotpics*, you'd want to change your current directory to that folder via the terminal. For this example, the command would be:

```
$ cd /Users/cks/Desktop/gotpics
```

Downloading particular file types is just one small sample of what you can do with `wget`, reading the `wget` manpage will reveal methods of downloading entire web sites and reconstructing them on your computer, among other very useful and interesting uses. So now that `wget` is on your machine play around with it, there is a lot of fun to be had.

QUICK HACK ✕

SEE THE INVISIBLE FILES IN OS X

Your Mac relies heavily on files you can't see in directories you can't alter using the GUI. This has the advantage of making it more difficult for novice users to really mess things up but has the disadvantage of forcing those who are fairly comfortable with their machines to use the command line to add programs like `wget`.

If you loathe the command line, you can still use the familiar drag-and-drop methodology by forcing OS X to reveal the invisible files and folders on your computer. A simple Google search for "show OS X invisibles" will reveal a lots of utilities that will turn the invisibility of files and folders off. You can also accomplish the same thing using Automator with a one-step Automator action (Actions→Library→Files & Folders→Show Invisibles). After the action has run, the formerly invisible file and folders can be manipulated via the familiar GUI methods. To turn invisibility back on (a good idea: accidentally deleting some of those hidden folders will render your Mac unusable), fire up the Terminal and type:

```
$ defaults write com.apple.finder AppleShowAllFiles NO
```

Now restart the Finder using this:

```
$ killall Finder
```

Or log out and back in: the formerly visible files will be hidden again.

HACK 15: User-Initiated Privacy for Web Applications

If you're one of the many who are starting to use online tools instead of the traditional computer-based applications, security should be a concern. Your code, your writing, your spreadsheets (with financial data) are always accessible to the service you're using, even when it is protected from other users. Protect your information using this valuable hack.

Web-based applications are becoming increasingly popular, offering a variety of compelling advantages over desktop-based applications, both to developers and to users. These applications are platform-independent, accessible from any Internet-connected computer, offer offsite data storage, and often provide integrated tools for collaboration and sharing. One major tradeoff, however, is a loss of privacy. As users adopt web-based applications, their personal data (emails, address books, calendars, to-do lists, and so on) slowly migrates from the privacy of their computer to live instead on various web-app providers' servers scattered across the Internet. While some of these web applications allow a user to tag certain data as private, (Google Calendars, to cite one example), this is a very limited notion of privacy, referring only to whether the web-application provider will share user data with other parties (such as other users.) Virtually by definition, the user's data is always accessible (not private) to the company or individuals providing the web application. This is a step back from the level of privacy afforded by desktop-based applications and should be recognized as such. But this doesn't mean that we need to give up on privacy (or give up on web applications.) We just need to think more creatively.

After reading Peter Wayner's book, *Translucent Databases*, on Jon Udell's recommendation, I saw that translucent database designs could directly address this issue. Unfortunately, many (most?) web-application databases are not being designed translucently. But if your web-application's database wasn't designed for translucency, is this a lost cause? I'm going to argue that it isn't, and will show how **you**, the user of web applications, can initiate database translucency yourself, and thereby protect the privacy of your hosted personal data whenever you desire.

What do I mean by *user-initiated database translucency*? Think of it as BYOC: Bring Your Own Crypto. The idea here is for you, the user, to encrypt your personal data before it finds its way onto the web-application server. As long as the encrypted data is considered valid by the application (i.e., doesn't violate string-length or legal-character limitations), the application will continue to work as it did before, but the personal data will remain private. Later, when you need to view some of this data, the decryption and viewing can be done offline. If you do this right, your data will remain usable to you in the context of the web application without ever being visible (unencrypted) to the web-application provider.

I'll describe one approach to implementing this idea, which you can download and test out. Many others approaches are possible, and I'll throw out a few ideas to get things started.

Page Axe (http://www.cs.brandeis.edu/~ari/scripts/PageAxe/PageAxe.dmg) is a Mac OS X (i.e., offline) application that I wrote to demonstrate this idea. Upon running for the first time, Page Axe generates and saves a randomly-generated 256-byte key (via `openssl rand -base64 -out /path/to/key 256`). After that, any text typed into the Page Axe text box is encrypted with this key using the AES-CBC cipher algorithm (via `openssl enc -aes-256-cbc -a -salt -pass file:/path/to/key`). This encrypted text is copied to the clipboard, ready to be pasted into a text field in your web application. Page Axe also allows you to view this encrypted data. Copy and paste the encrypted text from the web application to Page Axe, and the text is decrypted (via `openssl` `enc -d -aes-256-cbc -a -pass file:/path/to/key`) and displayed for you to read again. At its core, Page Axe is simply moving text between trusted desktop-land and untrusted browser-land in a way that guarantees data privacy is maintained.

This, however, leaves a lot to be desired in terms of usability, so I added a few extra features:

Context for decrypted text
Select a block of text from the web application that includes encrypted private data, and Page Axe will locate, decrypt, and display the private data in the context of the entire text block (using Growl, if installed).

Easy in, easy out
Page Axe encryption and decryption can be accessed via Quicksilver triggers.

Mobile application
Just drag the app and your key onto your portable USB drive, and access your private data from any computer (um… any Mac.)

To get a real handle on what Page Axe can do, you need to see it in action: check out Figures 2-37, 2-38, 2-39, and 2-40.

Figure 2-37.
Simple interface for decrypting text

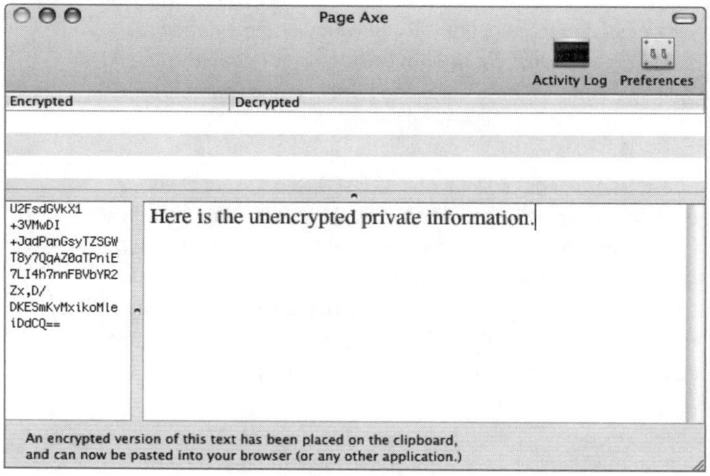

Figure 2-38.
Encrypted text is pasted into a web application

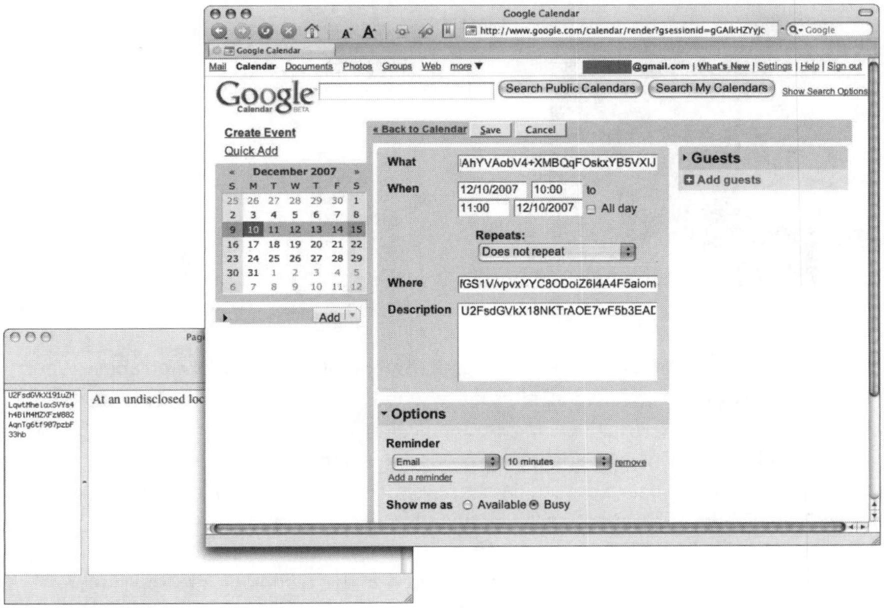

Figure 2-39.
The encrypted text can then be decrypted offline

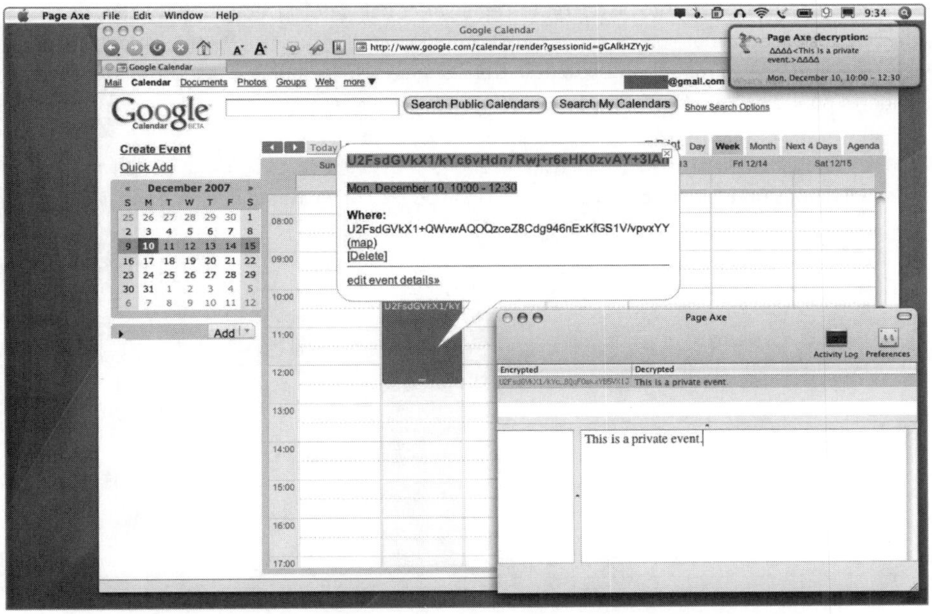

Figure 2-40.
Alternative UI hooks are possible, such as this Quicksilver trigger

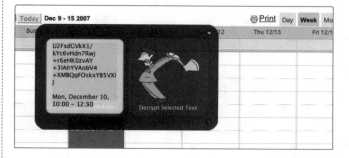

Page Axe is only one implementation of this concept of user-initiated privacy for web applications, written as a full-blown desktop application. Alternatively, one might figure out how to implement this as a Firefox extension, a bookmarklet, an InputManager hack (on Mac OS X), an offline browser, a platform-independent Java application for use on a portable USB flash drive, or perhaps something else. As long as the user's private data is never accessible through the DOM to the "untrusted" web application, you've got a valid implementation.

I think one fascinating possibility here would be to incorporate this technique into applications designed to automatically sync offline and online data. Consider, for example, Spanning Sync (http://spanningsync.com), an application designed to provide two-way syncing between Apple's iCal desktop application and Google's web-based Calendar application. Imagine a new "Keep data private" checkbox, which causes offline data to be encrypted before being uploaded to Google's servers and causes online data to be decrypted again after being downloaded. (For access to Google's web application data on-the-go, a mobile implementation such as Page Axe would provide access.) This example shows how data translucency can be initiated post-hoc via the web application's published API! Many interesting possibilities exist here.

In summary, the move towards web-based applications comes at the expense of our privacy, but with the techniques outlined here, you can reclaim the privacy of your data any time you like!

— Ari Bader-Natal

3 HACKING MAC OS X

The default behavior of Mac OS X isn't for everyone. There are undoubtedly things you can't stand about Mac OS X or times you find yourself wondering why you can't do something that seems like it should be easily done. Of course, Apple designs its software to appeal to the largest number of its users, and any time a person or company tries to appeal to the broadest number of users, there is a risk of pandering to the lowest common denominator. While Apple largely avoids this trap with Mac OS X, there are still bound to be times when you wished Mac OS X was tailored a little more closely to your personal preferences.

There is good news: Mac OS X is highly hackable. You can move Widgets to your Desktop, add a quit option to the Finder, or adopt a variety of fun, interesting, and productivity-enhancing hacks. This chapter covers everything from changing the default file type of screenshots to getting things done with Automator. Your customized, enhanced version of Mac OS X is just a few hacks away...

HACK 18: Know Your Cats

Mac OS X has gone through seven distinct iterations. Find the differences (and your hacking capabilities) with this guide.

You can always hit "About This Mac..." in the Apple menu (see Figure 3-1) to find which version of Mac OS X you're running, but that won't tell you its cat name or what features you can expect.

If you're hacking your way through your Mac, this can be a problem. Just what version is Tiger? Did Jaguar have Exposé? When did iChat come along? Why isn't my shell prompt a $? A brief rundown of the versions of Mac OS X will clarify matters:

Mac OS X Beta
Mac OS X Beta was beta in every way imaginable. Slow, unstable and full of bugs, but it was a serious alternative to OS 9. Mac OS X Beta did manage to introduce the Dock and the Aqua interface to Mac users.

Mac OS X 10.0 —Cheetah—March 24, 2001
If you're enjoying a usable version of Mac OS X, you're not using Cheetah. The first true release of Mac OS X, Cheetah was more stable than the Beta but still left a lot to be desired, though Cheetah did bring back the Apple menu that was missing in the Beta version. Stability and speed still needed attention, too.

Figure 3-1.
Quick information about your Mac

Mac OS X 10.1—Puma—September 25, 2001
Puma was released free to Cheetah users and introduced Image Capture (to get images off of digital cameras) and DVD playback. Puma was the first version of Mac OS X to be used as the default operating system on new Macs, though you could choose to boot your Mac into OS 9.

Mac OS X 10.2—Jaguar—August 23, 2002
This is where things started to get interesting. Jaguar introduced iChat, Inkwell, Address Book, Bonjour (called Rendezvous in Jaguar, it's zero configuration networking, which Apple TV relies on to network with your computer), Quartz Extreme, and a journaled filesystem.

Mac OS X 10.3—Panther—October 24, 2003
Panther brought a lot to the table including: Fast User Switching, Exposé, FileVault, iChat AV (adding video and audio conferencing), and Safari.

Of supreme interest to those using the Terminal is that Panther changed the default shell of Mac OS X from *tcsh* to *bash*. If you're using a version of Mac OS X before Panther, you might find that while all the Terminal lines in this book start with $, your Terminal shows %. There are nontrivial differences between *bash* and *tcsh*, but basic commands work exactly as you'd expect.

Mac OS X 10.4—Tiger—April 29, 2005
If you have an Intel-based Mac, you're using Tiger or Leopard. New features in Tiger include Dashboard, Spotlight, Automator, Boot Camp, Dictionary, and Quartz Composer.

Mac OS X 10.5—Leopard—October 26, 2007
Leopard adds Time Machine, Spaces, Quick Look, among a host of other less obvious improvements.

Kill Dashboard

Don't like the Dashboard? Make it go away. Sure, you'll be killing one of 10.4's most hyped features but it is a completely reversible process, and there isn't a reason to run Dashboard all the time if you never use it.

As great as Dashboard is, some folks just don't like it. And if you don't like it, there's no legitimate reason to keep it around taking up Dock space, using a valuable function key (to learn how to remap the function keys see **[Hack #71]**), and gobbling up valuable system resources. So the only question left is: just how much do you love Dashboard?

You'd think that quitting Dashboard would be an easy thing, but you would be wrong. Removing the Dashboard icon from the Dock seems to be a possible fix, but that will only free a little more Dock space and still leave Dashboard running in the background. To truly kill Dashboard and to keep the program from restarting every time the computer is restarted, it is time for a trip to the Terminal **[Hack #30]**.

1. Open a Terminal window and enter the following command:

    ```
    $ defaults write com.apple.dashboard mcx-disabled -boolean YES
    ```

    As always spelling, spacing, and capitalization all count.

2. Hit Return

You would think that would be enough to get rid of Dashboard, but you would be wrong again. At this point, you've set the stage for killing it (it is at the gallows so to speak), but you haven't pulled the lever. To fully rid yourself of the Dashboard, you're going to have to restart the Dock. There are a lot of ways to do this. You could log out and back in, you could restart the machine, or you could go to the basement and flip the breaker that controls the circuit your machine is using. All of these are much more trouble than the optimal method: typing the following into a Terminal window:

```
$ killall Dock
```

The Dock restarts and, if you investigate by looking at the Activity Monitor or repeatedly hitting the Dashboard key (F12 on older Apple keyboards, F4 on newer ones), you won't be able to tell that the Dashboard ever existed.

✉ If you've moved widgets to your Desktop **[Hack #18]**, these widgets will also vanish.

Unhacking the Hack

At some point you're going to hear about a great new widget and want full Dashboard functionality back. Don't fret: all the steps are easily undoable. To get Dashboard running again, open a Terminal window, and enter the following command:

```
$ defaults write com.apple.dashboard mcx-disabled -boolean NO
```

Naturally you'll need to follow that command up with:

```
$ killall Dock
```

Dashboard returns to whatever state it was in when you killed the process. That is to say the widgets you were running will be running again, and widgets you moved to your Desktop will reappear.

To put the Dashboard icon back on the Dock, all you need to do is open up the Applications folder in a Finder window, locate the Dashboard application, and then drag Dashboard's icon back to the Dock.

HACK 18: Move a Widget to the Desktop

Tired of switching to Dashboard just to get the latest stock prices or check the weather? Move that much-loved widget to the Desktop.

Dashboard was one of the most hyped, and consequently, anticipated features of Tiger. In this case, both the hype and the anticipation were accurate; Dashboard really is a fairly great addition to Mac OS X. It is even better in Leopard [Hack #93]. The biggest problem with Dashboard is that some of the widgets are a little too good. Take, for example, the Stock widget. This nifty widget, which shipped with Tiger, beautifully and informatively displays the current price of your financial holdings. With money on the line, stock prices are something that people like to check with obsessive frequency. Sure, watching shares of the company you own skyrocket and plummet can be nerve-racking, but it's information you want to know.

The most obvious thing to do is constantly hit the Dashboard key or mash the scroll ball on the Mighty Mouse. However, constantly invoking Dashboard can get a little repetitive. What we need is a method to move the widget from the Dashboard to the Desktop. You've got an option here, you can search the Web for a program to do just that for you, or you can save time and money (plus feel a little hackerish) by firing up the Terminal and doing it yourself:

1. Open a new Terminal window.

2. At the prompt (shown here by a dollar sign; on your machine it may be slightly different) type the following (and remember the Terminal isn't your wacky ninth grade English teacher; spelling and spacing counts here):

   ```
   $ defaults write com.apple.Dashboard devmode YES
   ```

3. Hit Return.

You're probably wondering why nothing seems to have changed. The truth is that plenty has changed, just nothing you can see. You're about to enter Dashboard's developer mode—a convenient way to test and tweak widgets without invoking Dashboard. There is one more thing you need to do before you can get that wonderful widget onto your Desktop: you need to kill the Dock in one manner or another. The most obvious way is to log out and log back in, but that has the disadvantage of killing any other applications that are running. Since you used the Terminal to enable developer mode, why not use it to terminate the Dock? Here's the simple one-line instruction:

```
$ killall Dock
```

Your windows might jump around a little, but the Dock is the only process that suffers. Once you're back, the protocol to get a widget onto the Desktop is fairly simple even if it does take the slightest bit of manual dexterity.

Fire up Dashboard using the method of your choice (the Dashboard key, Dashboard icon in Dock, Mighty Mouse scroll ball), then click and begin dragging the widget you want to move to the Desktop. Time for the inner video gamer to come out: while you're dragging said widget, press the Dashboard key, then release the mouse button. The Dashboard disappears, and the widget now resides on your Desktop (see Figure 3-2). Repeat for as many widgets as you like or as many as your screen will hold. You can reverse the process by starting to drag the widget from the Desktop, pressing the Dashboard key, and releasing the mouse button.

Figure 3-2.
A widget that never goes away

Naturally there are some downsides to having widgets running all over your Desktop. The first thing you'll notice immediately is that the widget "floats" above all the other windows. Not a big deal if it is a small widget or if you own a 30-inch monitor, but you give up a certain amount of screen real estate until you close the widget. Another ramification of widgets floating on the Desktop is that they are constantly using your computer's resources. Ideally, Dashboard widgets only suck the computing power down when Dashboard is running (there have been reports to the contrary in the case of some poorly design widgets), but if the widget is always running, it is always affecting system performance.

Later

You moved a widget to the Desktop and have now become bored with it. You'll want to know just how to get it back off your Desktop. If you want to take the widgets off of the Desktop piecemeal, the answer is less than intuitive, but it is very simple to do. Simply press the Option key while hovering your mouse in the general vicinity of the widget. A bubble with a white X in the center appears at the upper left corner of the widget. Banish the widget by clicking the white X (works in Dashboard as well); see Figure 3-3.

Figure3-3.
Banish that widget back to the Dashboard

Killing the widget in this manner also removes it from Dashboard, so the next time you want to use the widget in Dashboard, you'll have to find it among the available-but-uninstalled widgets and drag it back onto the Dashboard playing field. If you wish to return the system back to the state in which Apple shipped it to you (remove all the widgets from the Desktop and back to the Dashboard), simply repeat the procedure for entering Developer mode outlined earlier, but change YES to NO, like this:

```
$ defaults write com.apple.Dashboard devmode NO
```

HACK 19: Turn Your Desktop into a Font of Useful Information

The Desktop is generally reserved for displaying beautiful Apple-supplied images or pictures from your iPhoto library. Learn how to display useful information on your Desktop using GeekTool.

Your Desktop is slacking. While your other applications are off collecting pertinent information and displaying interesting results (even your screensaver can display your RSS feeds), the Desktop just sits there, rarely changing and providing no contribution to your daily computing life.

What would be great would be a way to have your Desktop display something useful and something timely. This concept harkens back to one of the earliest Mac OS X hacks: running a movie as your Desktop background. While interesting, those who actually ran movies as their Desktop quickly found that not only was the hack processor-intensive, it was also very distracting. With this lesson in mind, it is obvious that choosing the information the Desktop displays is almost as important as getting the Desktop to tell you a little something about what is going on in the world. The ideal Desktop information for Desktop residence would be something that is updated relatively infrequently, is not of crucial importance (if you have a bunch of windows open, you won't see it), and can impart a vast amount of information at glance.

What fits all the above criteria? Traffic, of course. A quick snap of the route (or routes) you take to and from work will tell you volumes about what you're likely to face on the commute. Sure, you can't personally do anything to speed up the traffic flow, but you can change your travel plan if one path looks intractably tangled.

First things first: you have to find a traffic cam that displays the trouble spot you're after. In my case, I-40 at Lovell Road is potential trouble spot for those traveling east or west around the Knoxville area. A quick Google search reveals that there is a traffic cam devoted to that particular spot (no surprise here). Turns out that the image I'm after is on a page with a few other images. I need to isolate the one I want. That is easily accomplished with a right-click of your mouse (Control-click for those in the single button camp) and selecting "Open image in new tab" or "Copy Image Location." This provides the exact URL of the continuously updated image I wish to use.

> Some traffic cams don't play well with this approach; if the script that generates the camera feed is designed to thwart deep-linking, you may get an error when you try to load the image outside the traffic cam's web page.

Once I am assured that the traffic cam I need is available, it is time to go about getting said image to the Desktop. There are a variety ways to do this, but installing one piece of free software not only makes the process simpler, it also makes it much more adaptable as cravings for an information-packed Desktop grow. A quick visit to http://projects.tynsoe.org/en/geektool/ yields a link to download GeekTool.

You might read the description provided and wonder what a Preference Pane designed to display console logs and processor loads on your Desktop has to do with traffic. Well, this is a hack, after all!

Once GeekTool is downloaded, it is time for the install. The process is as smooth as cold milk on a July afternoon. Just double-click the installer, and the let the program do the heavy lifting. You get the option of installing for a single user or for the entire system, in case you want everyone to have access to GeekTool.

With all the tools assembled, the moment of pulling this hack together (and the payoff) is close at hand. Thing is, you can't tell it by looking, as shown in Figure 3-4. You can get back to this preference pane later by opening System Preferences and choosing GeekTool.

QUICK HACK ✕

LOSE UNWANTED PREFERENCE PANES

GeekTool installs yet another preference pane, something your computer may be becoming overburdened with if you try every hack in this book. You might find yourself wanting to get rid of the extraneous preference panes. Usually selecting the offending preference pane with a right-click→Remove will get rid of the no-longer-desired preference pane but when that fails, take a trip to the Library (*/Library/ PreferencePanes* for global installs, */Users/ username/Library/ PreferencePanes* for single user installs) and delete the preference pane manually.

Figure 3-4.
This will make your Desktop better

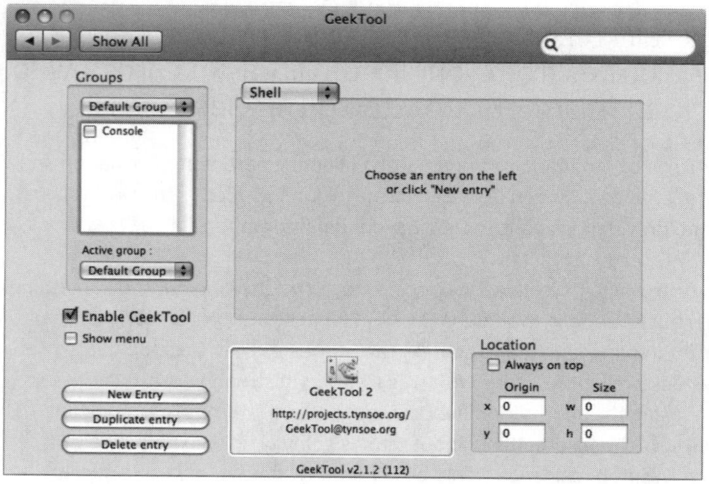

GeekTool

Show All

Groups

Default Group

☐ Console

Active group :

Default Group

☑ Enable GeekTool
☐ Show menu

Shell

Choose an entry on the left
or click "New entry"

New Entry

Duplicate entry

Delete entry

GeekTool 2
http://projects.tynsoe.org/
GeekTool@tynsoe.org

Location
☐ Always on top

Origin   Size
x 0   w 0

y 0   h 0

GeekTool v2.1.2 (112)

First, make sure the "Enable Geek tool" box is checked, hit the New Entry button, and change the topmost menu (it may be labeled File or Shell) to Picture. Under the Source tab, provide GeekTool with the URL you discovered earlier. Click the Style tab: the only thing you need to worry about there is the Opacity setting; make sure it isn't 0. If you're worried about placement and size, it turns out you can take care of that with the mouse. Move System Preferences (and whatever other windows might be open) out of the way so you can see the Desktop, and drag the image wherever you wish it to sit on your Desktop. Then drag its corner to set the image size, as shown in Figure 3-5.

Figure 3-5.
By dragging the entire picture you can choose placement; by grabbing
the (sometimes hard to see) handle, you can resize the image to your liking

Click and drag to
scale the picture

Once you've got all the settings just the way you like them, GeekTool will constantly update the picture without any user intervention. You'll be able to master your traffic routes or keep up with your favorite webcam by merely glancing at your Desktop, as shown in Figure 3-6.

Figure 3-6.
No traffic today

Of course, GeekTool isn't just for displaying interesting images. The tool is set up to spew any amount of text and other information to your Desktop. That functionality is useful for some, but for the rest of us a constantly updating picture on the Desktop can be a really spiffy thing.

QUICK HACK ✕

A MORE INFORMATIVE DOCK

Like the visual feedback of GeekTool? You might like to get other information at a glance as well. For example, everyone seemingly has multiple email accounts. Some aren't as important as others but the red number displayed by mail doesn't tell you if the reason Mail just went bing! was because a Google news alert arrived or because your boss just sent you an email notifying you of a promotion. Hey, you don't want to miss a second of executive washroom-key goodness do you?

Dockstar (Figure 3-7) takes care of that. By using different symbols and colors for up to five inboxes you can tell. with just a glance, which inboxes are vying for your attention, and you can use different sounds for different mailboxes.

Wait, there's more. Concerned about how much of *X* your computer is using at any given time (where *X* is disk access, RAM, etc)? Apple is happy to provide visual feedback about the current state of your Mac right in the Dock. Fire up Activity Monitor (found in */Applications/ Utilities*), right-click the Dock icon that appears, and you'll find a multitude of choices for displaying information about your Mac, as shown in Figure 3-8.

Figure 3-7.
You've got mail... in more than one mailbox

Figure 3-8.
Activity Monitor in the dock

HACK 20: Tame the Finder

The Finder is just another program, so why run it if you're not using it? If you're using the Dock, Spotlight, or a third party launcher as the primary method of navigation and launching files, the Finder isn't doing you much good. Don't be frustrated by the lack of control over the Finder—add an option to quit.

The Finder in Mac OS X is likely both the most-used Mac OS X program and the most loathed. The Finder seems perpetually stuck halfway between behaving like the Finder in Classic Mac and behaving like a web browser. Fortunately, there are many options to use instead of the Finder: users who like raw speed can rely on Quicksilver (http://quicksilver.blacktree.com/), those in love with Spotlight are more than happy to launch all their applications via everyone's favorite magnifying glass, and, finally, those inclined to use the Terminal don't ever have to use the Finder [Hack #27].

If you're one of the people who use an alternative to Finder, you're probably wondering why your Mac is burdened with the overhead of the Finder when it is a program (and the Finder is just a program) that you don't use on a regular basis. A good question, and the simplest answer is: "because the Finder is a hassle to turn off." Sure, you could always kill the Finder via the Terminal, but if you're not already using Terminal, that can be big hassle, too. It would be better and easier if the Finder had a quit option in the File menu. So let's add one.

> When working on *.plist* files with the Terminal, it's a good idea to back the file up first.

To add a quit option to the Finder menu, you need to edit the Finder's *.plist* (Property List) file found at the following location:

> /Users/**username**/Library/Preferences/com.apple.finder.plist

That is the file named *com.apple.finder.plist* in the Preferences folder found in the home Library folder (see Figure 3-9). Back up the file by making a copy of it before you proceed.

Figure 3-9.
Finding the Finder's .plist

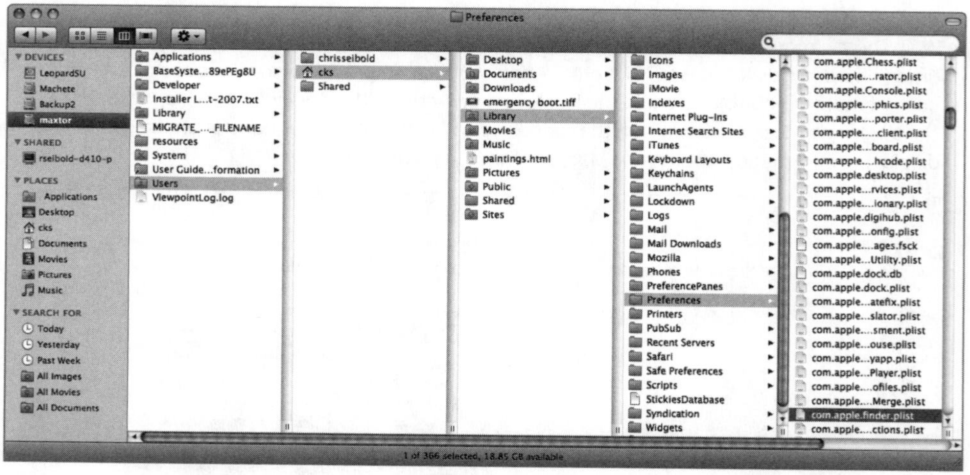

With the file located and backed up, you can now make the change. Since you've got a backup of the file, you can safely work on it while it is in residence in your Preferences folder. Open the *com. apple.finder.plist* file using a Property List editor. A Property List editor is an application specifically designed to edit *.plist* files. If you've installed Apple's free Developer Tools [Hack #3], you have Apple's *.plist* editor (called Property List Editor) already installed. If you need a *.plist* editor, a quick search on http://www.versiontracker.com will yield a variety of options.

After you've opened the file, look for the line that reads `QuitMenuItem`. Change NO to YES, and you're on your way to quitting the Finder (see Figure 3-10).

Figure 3-10.
Enabling the Quit option

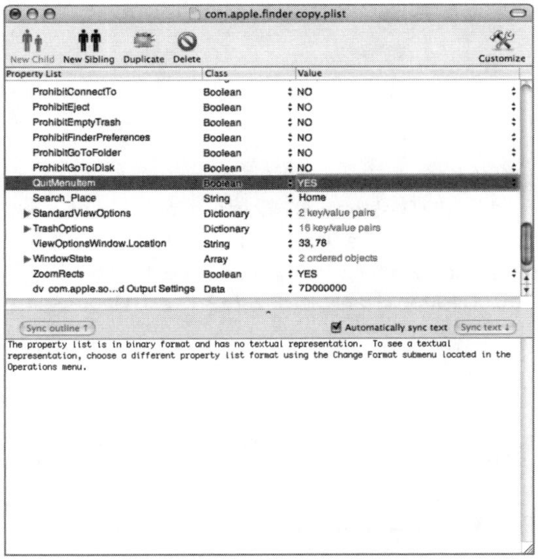

Once the change has been made, you need to save the *.plist* file. In Figure 3-11, I am using PlistEdit Pro (http://www.fatcatsoftware.com/plisteditpro), so I choose Save To, make sure File Format is set to Property List, and save it in the Preferences folder.

Figure 3-11.
Saving the change

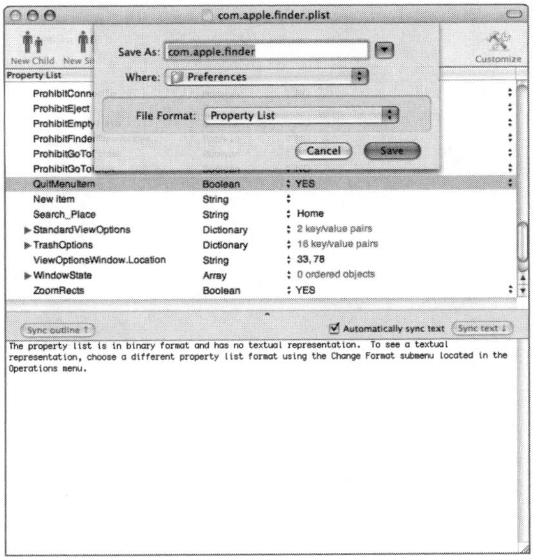

QUICK HACK

MORE THAN ONE WAY TO WRITE A .PLIST FILE

In this hack, the method used to change a *.plist* file involves locating the file and manually changing the value of an entry. In the case of the Finder, the *.plist* file is interesting to look at and there is fun stuff to play with, but digging through folders and scanning for *.plist* files isn't strictly necessary. You can accomplish the same task using the Terminal. In this case the command looks like the following (it's followed by the Return key):

```
defaults write
com.apple.finder
QuitMenuItem YES
```

That's it; you're done. To see the change, you'll need to log out of your account and log back in. Open the Finder menu, and notice the Quit option shown in Figure 3-12.

Figure 3-12.
Wow, a new choice in the Finder menu

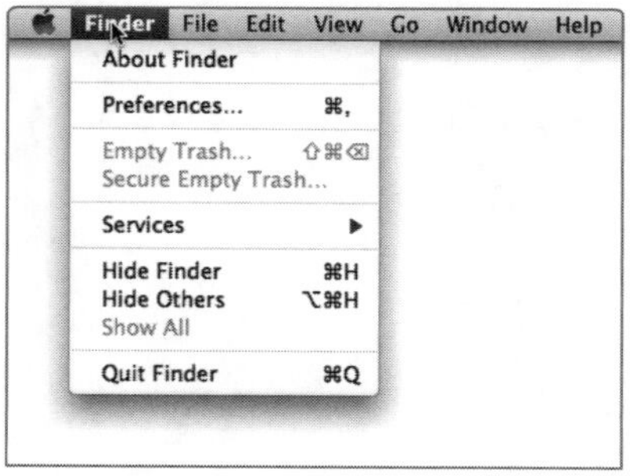

After using your newly added quit option, you'll see the usual menu bar at the top of the screen and the Dock at the bottom, but the area once reserved for the Desktop and Finder windows is completely blank except for a Desktop background. Which isn't a surprise: the Desktop is controlled by the Finder, and each icon you see on the Desktop is, in reality, another window your Mac is forced to render so even if you don't quit the Finder, keep that Desktop clean! (see Figure 3-13 and Figure 3-14.)

Figure 3-13.
That is one ugly, cluttered Desktop; maybe if I quit the Finder...

Figure 3-14.
A pristine Desktop means you're Finder free

When performing this hack, many people get suddenly scared because all their files and drive icons disappear from the Desktop without warning. Don't worry: nothing has been deleted. You just can't see them because the Finder is no longer running. Think of it as an instant Desktop cleanup for those of us who have too many files lying around.

There are going to be times when you need the Finder. Spotlight is great for finding files if you know what you're looking for, but if you just want to randomly wander through your file hierarchy, Spotlight isn't going to do the trick. To get the Finder up and running again, just click the Finder tile in the Dock, and the Finder will spring to life ready to serve until you quit it again.

Undoing the Hack

If you decide that you can't live without an always-on Finder, you can easily return the Finder back to the original state. You can retrace the earlier steps finding the proper *.plist* and changing YES to NO. As before, you can use the Terminal instead of a Property List editor:

```
defaults write com.apple.finder QuitMenuItem NO
```

Once you hit return, the *.plist* file is changed but to see the Quit option disappear from the Finder's menu, you'll have to wait until you log out or restart.

Use That Software Restore Disk on (Almost) Any Mac

The situation is a familiar one: you have a software restore disk but no restore disk for the Mac you want the software on. Learn how to get the apps off your software restore disk to the destination Mac of your choice.

Have you ever wondered: "How does an installation work under Mac OS X?"

Most of the time when you download an application from the Internet, you simply drag it to the Applications folder and double-click it to start using it.

Sometimes, though, applications come with an installer. This is because the application needs to place some files here and there (for instance, */Users/**username**/Library/Application Support/ Name of the App/*) to work properly.

Installers appear to the user as guided procedures that ask a few questions (agree to a license, choose installation disk, provide administrator password, and so forth) and then install all the needed files. They look a lot like a peculiar piece of software whose aim is to install other software.

However, this is just an illusion. Installers are (usually) not applications. Instead, they are just files, called packages (see Figure 2-15), which, when double-clicked, are opened by an application provided by Apple. This application, Installer, is found in */System/Library/CoreServices*. Installer analyzes the package file, shows the user only the options that are meaningful, eventually asks for a password, and then copies all the files to the correct places (see Figure 3-16).

Figure 3-15.
What packages and metapackages look like in the Finder

QTSSPublisher.pkg   ServerAdministrationSoftwa
                              re.mpkg

Figure 3-16.
An example of the standard installer

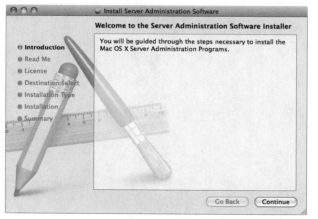

Packages can be described as atomic installation units (e.g., the iCal or iChat applications), which can themselves be gathered in metapackages. These are not real packages but are simply the combination of packages that might be installed together. (Think of iMovie, iWeb, iDVD etc., which, together, form the iLife suite.)

How can you discern between packages and metapackages? They differ in the extension: packages end with *.pkg*, while metapackages end with *.mpkg*. That tidbit of knowledge will help you out when using the DVDs that come with every Mac, which can be used to restore Mac OS X, perform hardware tests, and install extra software (for instance, Xcode).

On such DVDs, software is organized, as you expect, in packages and metapackages; this means that the installation of Mac OS X involves installing many packages and meta-packages.

At this point you might ask: "Can I use one Mac's DVDs to install software on another Mac?"

The answer is: yes, yes, and yes, because there are three different ways to do that.

As an example of when you might need this, I'll tell you one instance that happened to me a few months ago: I was on the train, and I wanted to try out iLife 06, which I had bought a few days before. Unfortunately I had forgotten the DVD at home. I really wanted to install the latest version of the famous Apple suite on my PowerBook, but I had with me only my brand-new MacBook's DVDs, so I figured out a way to extract the iLife packages and installed them.

You may be wondering: "Couldn't you simply insert your MacBook's DVDs into your PowerBook and install the software you wanted?" This would work for the Developer Tools (Xcode, Interface builder) and all the Optional installs (extra fonts printer drivers, Safari, Dictionary, iCal, iChat, iTunes, X11, Address Book)—see Figure 3-17 and Figure 3-18. The same isn't true for the so-called "bundled software" (such as iPhoto, iMovie, iDVD and many others) and, of course, the operating system. If you try to install MacBook's DVD bundled software on the PowerBook, you will get an unfortunate, seemingly intractable, error (see Figure 3-19). The next sections will show you what to do about that.

Figure 3-17.
Optional and Xcode installs

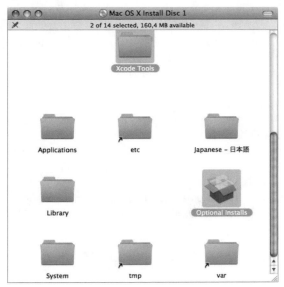

Figure 3-18.
Xcode tools and optional installs can be cross installed without hacking

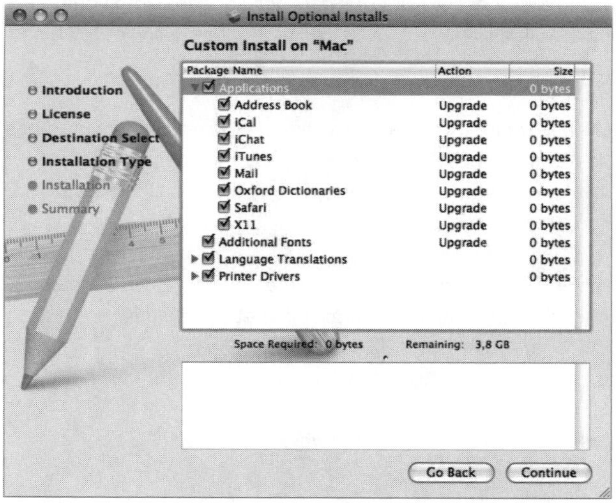

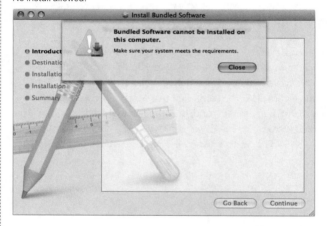

Figure 3-19.
No install allowed!

This hack has been tested with a MacBook, its DVDs, a PowerBook, and an iMac G4; it shouldn't be much different on similar systems.

To be more general, I'll refer to my MacBook as NewMac, my PowerBook OldMac, and the iMac G4 AnotherOldMac.

Please use this hack only if you have a license for the software you're installing.

Target-Disk Mode Approach (Not 100% Safe)

This is the easiest way to avoid the "cannot be installed on this computer" error seen earlier. Simply start the installer on NewMac and then choose, as the destination disk, OldMac's hard drive.

This is possible thanks to Target Disk mode, which turns OldMac into an external hard drive that can be accessed by any FireWire-equipped Mac (that is, more or less, any Mac bought after 1997). Figure 2-20 shows Target Disk mode.

Figure 3-20.
Restarting in Target Disk Mode

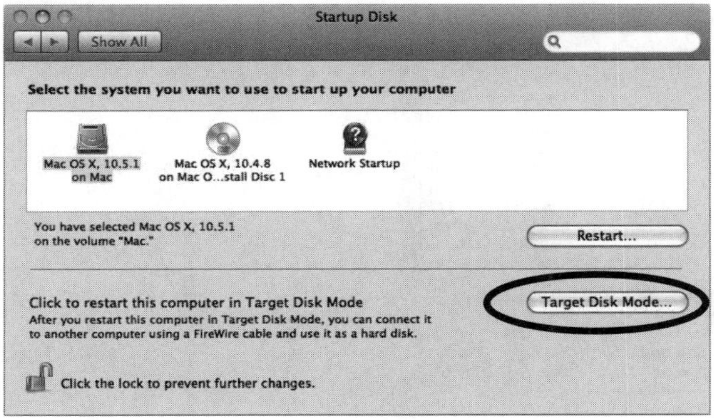

If you want to install NewMac's bundled software on OldMac, follow these steps:

1. Connect your two Macs (OldMac and NewMac) with a FireWire cable (you will need a 6-pin to 6-pin cable).

2. Put OldMac in Target Disk Mode:

    a. Click on the Apple Menu (top-left corner), choose System Preferences, and click on Startup Disk.

    b. Click on the button "Target disk mode..." and hit Restart.

    c. A big FireWire logo will appear on OldMac.

3. On your NewMac's Desktop, you will see a new icon named after your OldMac's hard drive (usually "Macintosh HD").

Your machines are now linked, and you can insert NewMac's first DVD into NewMac and start the installer.

Install bundled software

Double-click on "Install Bundled Software Only" if you want to install iPhoto, iDVD, iMovie, GarageBand, iWeb, iWork Trial, Front Row, Photo Booth, Comic Life, OmniOutliner, or any of the other software titles that is bundled with releases of Mac OS X. (The bundled software slightly varies among different Macs.)

> Many newer Macs, particularly those released after Mac OS X 10.4 Tiger was released, include a drop-in DVD that contains the iLife installer. That DVD should not require modification to use.

Installing operating system

If you want to install a newer version of the operating system on the older machine, follow these steps. Open a Finder window, hit Command-Shift-G (or select Go→Go to Folder), and type:

```
$ /Volumes/Mac OS X Install Disc 1/System/Installation/Packages/
```

Note that the name of the disc may vary. For example, with an install DVD, it's named */Volumes/ Mac OS X Install DVD/System/Installation/Packages*.

Double-click on *OSInstall.mpkg*, follow the steps and, when asked for a destination, select OldMac's hard drive (see Figure 3-21).

Figure 3-21.
Cross-installing bundled software

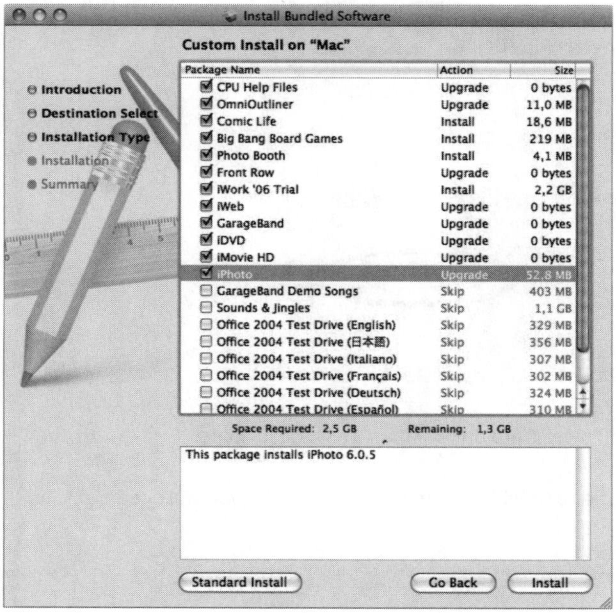

Why isn't this procedure 100% safe?

This procedure isn't 100% safe because the installer might make certain assumptions based on the hardware on which the Installer is executed (in this case, NewMac), while the operating system is installed on different hardware. This actually worked for me and many others, but depending on your particular setup, it might not work for you. Consider yourself warned.

Two old machines

But what if you don't have a NewMac and instead have two older Macs, neither of which meet the requirements of the restore disk? Is the situation hopeless? Absolutely not, but you will have to do a little hacking.

Unfortunately, this procedure does not work on Mac OS X 10.5 Leopard because the format of the package files has changed since Mac OS X 10.4 Tiger.

Here's the procedure:

1. Connect OldMac and AnotherOldMac with a FireWire cable as described earlier.

2. Put OldMac in Target-Disk mode as described earlier.

3. Insert NewMac's first DVD into the AnotherOldMac drive.

4. Open a Finder window and go to (as described earlier) the folder */Volumes/Mac OS X Install Disc 1/System/Installation/Packages/* or */Volumes/Mac OS X Install DVD/System/Installation/Packages/*.

5. Copy the package *OSInstall.mpkg* onto your Desktop.

6. Right-click (or Ctrl-click) on it, and select "Show package contents"; a new window will open.

7. Browse to the Contents folder (see Figure 3-22).

Figure 3-22.
Locating *OSInstall.dist*

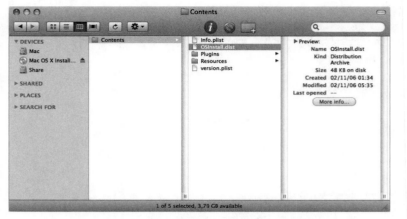

8.   Next, you need to make the Installer skip the hardware check.

Open *OSInstall.dist* in your favorite editor: right-click the file, choose File→Open with→other, and then choose TextEdit (or any other editor you like). The file will open up in your editor, as shown in Figure 3-23.

Figure 3-23.
The file in TextEdit

```
<?xml version="1.0"?>
<installer-gui-script minSpecVersion="1">

        <options mpkg="com.apple.mpkg.OSInstall.UserDVD" eraseOptionAvailable="true"/>

        <title>MacOSX_Title</title>
        <license file="License.rtf"/>
        <welcome file="Welcome.rtfd"/>

        <script>

        function checkSupportedMachine(machineType){
                // Fail on G3
                if (1 != system.sysctl('hw.vectorunit') ) {
                        return false;
                }
                var badMachines = ['iMac','PowerBook1,1','PowerBook2,1', 'AAPL,Gossamer',
'AAPL,PowerMac G3', 'AAPL,PowerBook1998', 'AAPL,PowerBook1999'];

                try{
                        var cpuFreq = system.sysctl('hw.cpufrequency');
                } catch(e) {
                        system.log('checkSupportedMachine threw exception ' + e);
                }

                if(machineType){
                        var length = badMachines.length;

                        // Fail if any of the compatible values match the list of badMachines
                        for( var j = 0; j &lt; length; j++ ){
                                if(machineType == badMachines[j]){
                                        return false;
                                }
                        }

                }

                // if we can't find it, assume it's supported
                return true;
        }
```

9. Search for `hwbe_machine_message`; you should get only one result, shown in Figure 3-24.

Figure 3-24.
The text requiring modification

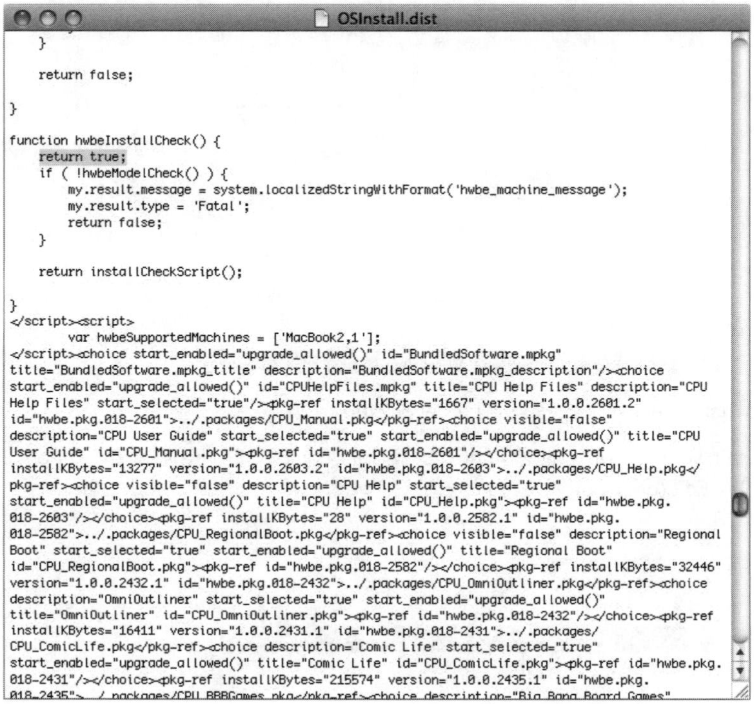
OSInstall.dist

```
    }

    return false;

}

function hwbeInstallCheck() {
    return true;
    if ( !hwbeModelCheck() ) {
        my.result.message = system.localizedStringWithFormat('hwbe_machine_message');
        my.result.type = 'Fatal';
        return false;
    }

    return installCheckScript();

}
</script><script>
        var hwbeSupportedMachines = ['MacBook2,1'];
</script><choice start_enabled="upgrade_allowed()" id="BundledSoftware.mpkg"
title="BundledSoftware.mpkg_title" description="BundledSoftware.mpkg_description"/><choice
start_enabled="upgrade_allowed()" id="CPUHelpFiles.mpkg" title="CPU Help Files" description="CPU
Help Files" start_selected="true"/><pkg-ref installKBytes="1667" version="1.0.0.2601.2"
id="hwbe.pkg.018-2601">../packages/CPU_Manual.pkg</pkg-ref><choice visible="false"
description="CPU User Guide" start_selected="true" start_enabled="upgrade_allowed()" title="CPU
User Guide" id="CPU_Manual.pkg"><pkg-ref id="hwbe.pkg.018-2601"/></choice><pkg-ref
installKBytes="13277" version="1.0.0.2603.2" id="hwbe.pkg.018-2603">../packages/CPU_Help.pkg</
pkg-ref><choice visible="false" description="CPU Help" start_selected="true"
start_enabled="upgrade_allowed()" title="CPU Help" id="CPU_Help.pkg"><pkg-ref id="hwbe.pkg.
018-2603"/></choice><pkg-ref installKBytes="28" version="1.0.0.2582.1" id="hwbe.pkg.
018-2582">../packages/CPU_RegionalBoot.pkg</pkg-ref><choice visible="false" description="Regional
Boot" start_selected="true" start_enabled="upgrade_allowed()" title="Regional Boot"
id="CPU_RegionalBoot.pkg"><pkg-ref id="hwbe.pkg.018-2582"/></choice><pkg-ref installKBytes="32446"
version="1.0.0.2432.1" id="hwbe.pkg.018-2432">../packages/CPU_OmniOutliner.pkg</pkg-ref><choice
description="OmniOutliner" start_selected="true" start_enabled="upgrade_allowed()"
title="OmniOutliner" id="CPU_OmniOutliner.pkg"><pkg-ref id="hwbe.pkg.018-2432"/></choice><pkg-ref
installKBytes="16411" version="1.0.0.2431.1" id="hwbe.pkg.018-2431">../packages/
CPU_ComicLife.pkg</pkg-ref><choice description="Comic Life" start_selected="true"
start_enabled="upgrade_allowed()" title="Comic Life" id="CPU_ComicLife.pkg"><pkg-ref id="hwbe.pkg.
018-2431"/></choice><pkg-ref installKBytes="215574" version="1.0.0.2435.1" id="hwbe.pkg.
018-2435">../packages/CPU_BBBGames.pkg</pkg-ref><choice description="Big Bang Board Games"
```

You should see a piece of text similar to the following:

```
function hwbeInstallCheck() {
  if ( !hwbeModelCheck() ) {
    my.result.message =
      system.localizedStringWithFormat('hwbe_machine_message');
    my.result.type = 'Fatal';
    return false;
  }
```

10. Edit the code to match:

```
function hwbeInstallCheck() {
  return true;
  if ( !hwbeModelCheck() ) {
    my.result.message =
      system.localizedStringWithFormat('hwbe_machine_message');
    my.result.type = 'Fatal';
    return false;
  }
```

11. Save the file and close it.

12. Now you have to edit one more file inside the package:

    a. Open *Info.plist* in your favorite editor. You'll find this file in the same folder as the *OSInstall.dist* file you just edited.

    b. Search for `component`; you should get only one result.

c. Locate the following:

```
<key>IFPkgFlagComponentDirectory</key>
<string>..</string>
```

d. Edit that bit of information to read as follows (replace "Disc 1" with "DVD" if you are using an installation DVD):

```
<key>IFPkgFlagComponentDirectory</key>
<string>/Volumes/Mac OS X Install Disc
    1/System/Installation/Packages</string>
```

13. Save the file and close it.

Now you have the package set up to install in your specific situation. Basically, you've changed the set up instructions to include the specific computer you want to install software on. Double-click on *OSInstall.mpkg* and follow the steps; when asked for a destination, select the correct hard drive. Figure 3-25 shows the installer.

Figure 3-25.
You're ready to install the software

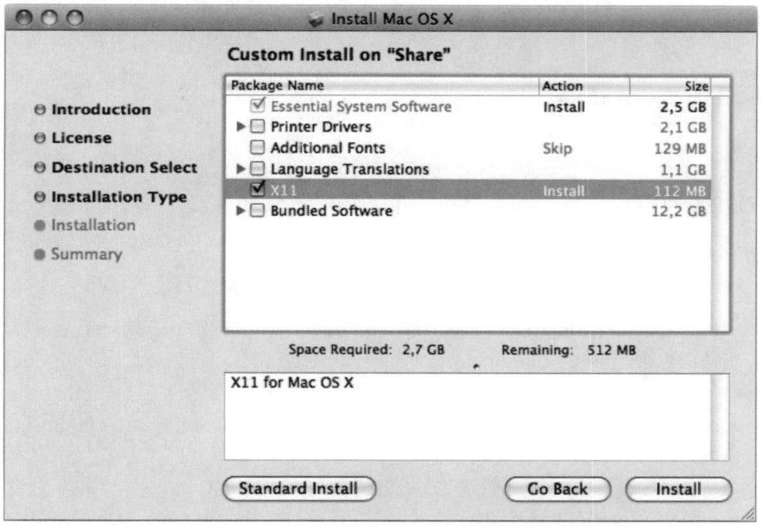

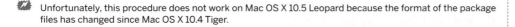

Installation of Single Packages (Safe but Complicated)

This approach is more complicated than the others, but it will help you understand something more about how packages work. This approach can also be useful if you have only a single Mac and a noncompliant restore disk because, as you'll discover later, you can work directly on OldMac using NewMac's DVDs.

If you are interested in installing only one particular application (iPhoto will be taken as an example), you can look for the package *iPhoto.pkg* or *iPhoto.mpkg* and install the software directly.

> Unfortunately, this procedure does not work on Mac OS X 10.5 Leopard because the format of the package files has changed since Mac OS X 10.4 Tiger.

Finding the package on a CD
Go to the folder */Volumes/Mac OS X Install Disc 1/System/Installation/Packages/.packages/* and—you've found it!

But not so fast: as you might have noticed, its size is only 1.4MB. It is not the whole iPhoto install; in fact, this package is only a placeholder for a bigger package that resides on Mac OS X Install Disc 2.

Insert Disc #2 in your drive and go to the folder */Volumes/Mac OS X Install Disc 2/Packages* where you'll see a different *iPhoto.mpkg* that weighs in at a more data-intensive 500 MB.

Finding the package on a DVD
Go to the folder */Volumes/Mac OS X Install DVD/System/Installation/Packages/.packages/* and—you've found it! (I'm not kidding this time!)

Double-click it and—another error! This package can only be installed along with the other bundled applications.

Copy it to the Desktop (it may take a few moments), right-click on it, choose "Show package contents", and browse to the Contents folder. Find and open *iPhoto.dist* in your favorite editor and edit:

```
function installationCheck()
{
  // yes, this is secure
  if (system.files.fileExistsAtPath('/tmp/com.apple.mpkg.iLife'))
```

To match:

```
function installationCheck()
{
  // yes, this is secure
  // if (system.files.fileExistsAtPath('/tmp/com.apple.mpkg.iLife'))
```

See the extra slashes in the fourth line? It doesn't seem like much, but this little change will avoid the last error.

Save it, and double-click on *iPhoto.mpkg* (the one that now resides on your Desktop): everything should work fine.

For those of you familiar with the Terminal, and with the operating system installer on CD, there is a quicker way you could have performed this operation. Instead of copying the whole *iPhoto.mpkg* from Disc #2, you could have copied the one from Disc #1, edited *iPhoto.dist* as explained earlier, and created symbolic links to the Installers on Disc #2.

Here are the commands (the first command, **cd**, returns you to your Home folder):

```
cd
ln -s /Volumes/Mac\ OS\ X\ Install\ Disc\
      2/Packages/iPhoto.mpkg/Contents/Installers/* \
      Desktop/iPhoto.mpkg/Contents/Installers/
```

Change the Requirements (Safe)

The third way is actually the most elegant of the three methods to install bundled software, and also does not require Target Disk mode (the installation can be performed right on OldMac).

The idea behind the third approach is to edit the requirements of the package, which in my case are "installation allowed only if this is a particular kind of MacBook."

Being that most packages (at least until now) are independent of the Mac on which they are installed, this limitation has no technological reasons but it is, indeed, part of Apple's antipiracy policy.

Before starting, you should know that every model of Mac is distinguished by a name and two numbers. Here are some common examples:

- The iMac G3 SE was "called" PowerMac2,1
- The last iMac G5: PowerMac12,1
- The iMac aluminum (intel): iMac7,1
- The first PowerMac G5: PowerMac7,2
- The last iBook G4: PowerBook6,7
- The first MacBook: MacBook1,1
- The first MacBook Pro: MacBookPro1,1

If you have one of those machines, you're covered. But where can you read the name of your Mac? Simply go to the Apple menu, choose About This Mac→More Info; the System Profiler application (located in */Applications/Utilities*) will open and show you the Model Identifier.

Here's an example of information returned by System Profiler:

```
Hardware Overview:
Model Name: PowerBook G4 12"
Model Identifier: PowerBook6,8
Processor Name: PowerPC G4 (1.5)
Processor Speed: 1.5 GHz
Number Of CPUs: 1
L2 Cache (per CPU): 512 KB
Memory: 1,25 GB
Bus Speed: 167 MHz
Boot ROM Version: 4.9.0f0
Serial Number: --------------------
Sudden Motion Sensor:
State: Enabled
Version: 1.0
```

After you have retrieved your Model Identifier, you can insert NewMac's first DVD into OldMac's drive and follow these steps:

1. Select the Install Bundled Software Only icon and hit Command-R (or choose File → Show Original).

2. Copy *Bundled Software.mpkg* to the Desktop.

3. Right-click on it, and select Show Package Contents.

4. Browse to the Contents folder and open *Info.plist* in your favorite text editor.

5. Change the following:

   ```
   <key>TestObject</key>
   <string>MacBook2,1</string>
   ```
   to:
   ```
   <key>TestObject</key>
   <string>PowerBook6,8</string>
   ```

I've written PowerBook6,8 because that's the Mac on which I want to install "Bundled Software". You will have to type your own model identifier.

6. Change the following:

```
<key>IFPkgFlagComponentDirectory</key>
<string>../.packages</string>
```

to:

```
<key>IFPkgFlagComponentDirectory</key>
<string>/Volumes/Mac OS X Install Disc 1/
    System/Installation/Packages/.packages</string>
```

to make the installer find all the packages (if you are using an installation DVD, you'll need to change "Disc 1" to "DVD").

7. Save this file and double-click on *Bundled Software.mpkg*. Everything should work just fine (see Figure 3-26).

Figure 3-26.
Your software is ready to install

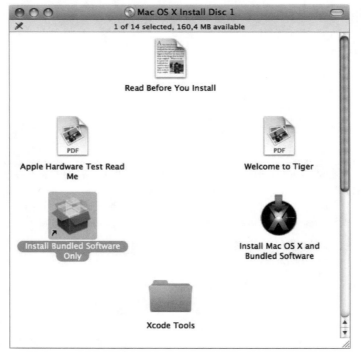

This hack is the result of my curiosity about how packages and metapackages work and how they can be manipulated. In the future, Apple might change it or might make the removal of restrictions (such as the Model Identifier check) more complicated. That's when you should start being curious and find out how things work under the hood with a little investigation of your own.

— Marco Triverio

HACK 22: Get Things Done with Automator

Automator uses the familiar drag-and-drop features of most applications to create "workflows" that will let you ditch the tedious and repetitive tasks you find yourself doing with your Mac.

With Automator, you don't need to know a special coded language to create workflow actions; if you are loath to write shell scripts, or are shy around the Terminal, Automator is the answer to creating programs you want to use. All you have to do is figure what you want done and see if Automator has the events and actions to help you get it done. If you want to, for example, rename, resize, or email a set of photo files, an Automator workflow can do it for you. If you want to have a folder backed up each time you add something new to it, Automator can help. Or say you just want to quit all your open applications from your Dock, Automator has a workflow just for you. While these are basic tasks, you can get more advanced with some knowledge of Apple's classic AppleScript program and advanced Automator events and actions.

In this hack, I'll show you how to develop a few simple workflows designed to introduce you to the program and develop solutions tailored to your own particular needs. Several Automator-related web sites also exist where you can learn more about the program and even download workflows developed by other Automator users. These web sites include:

- Apple's Mac 101: Automator tutorial (http://docs.info.apple.com/article. html?artnum=304759).
- Automator World (http://automatorworld.com), which features a good collection of workflows, hints, tips, and news items about the application.
- Apple also provides free action downloads on its site: http://www.apple.com/downloads/ macosx/automator.

Quit All Applications Workflow

To introduce Automator 2.0, which comes installed with Leopard, let's create a simple one-click workflow that will close all your running applications except the Finder.

✉ If you don't want to see the list of Automator starting points each time you start it up, click Automator in the left side of the menu bar, and select Disable Starting Points.

1. You will find Automator, represented by the Otto icon, in your Applications folder (Otto is the robot's name). When you open the application, you're presented with a starting point for creating workflows, shown in Figure 3-27. This starting point is not very useful if you've never used the program, so select Custom, and then click the Choose button.

Figure 3-27.
Getting started with Automator

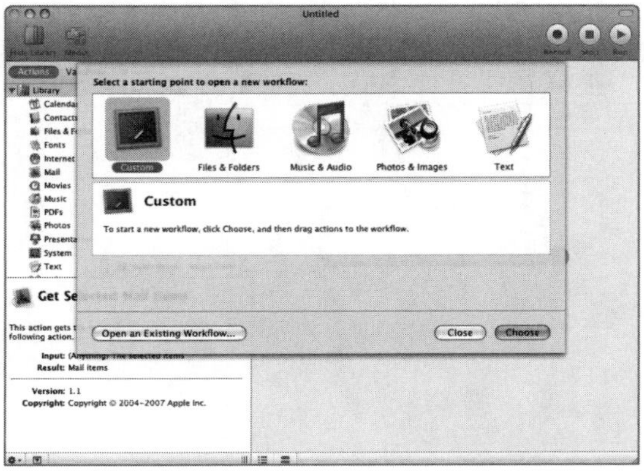

QUICK TIP

IT'S TIME TO REVISIT AUTOMATOR

If you used (or are using) the earlier version of Automator (Version 1.0 shipped with Tiger), you might have found the process to be a little less than clear. You could create great workflow but if something went wrong in the workflow, the thing wouldn't run, and users were left frustrated by not knowing where the process failed. Things are much improved in Automator 2.0 and later. Now, every step of the workflow can be inspected to see what results are returned—a true boon to those who desire to automate repetitive tasks.

2. At this this point, you're presented with an interface consisting of five parts. Starting with the left column, you get a list of applications, Finder functions, and utilities that have actions and events installed for them. In the same column, you will find *smart groups* or *folders*, which help you organize your actions and workflows.

   In the middle column, you get a list of all the available actions and events that can be found by doing a search or clicking on an item in the first column. In the box below the first two columns, you get a brief description of selected actions. The last box contains copyright information for each action.

   The larger pane on the right is used for assembling your workflow, which simply entails dragging and dropping actions and events from the middle column to build a workflow. Some workflows will require only one action or event while more complex workflows will require additional input. Actions and events have to be ordered in a particular way in order to run successfully. For example, some actions will require identifying the input of one or more files in which will be passed onto subsequent actions and events.

   Above all three columns in the toolbar are five buttons. The one on the far left is for hiding the first two columns. The media button provides you access to all the audio files stored in iTunes or created with GarageBand, your photos stored in iPhoto and Aperture, and the movies stored in iMovie '08, iPhoto, iTunes, and your Movies folder. You can use your media to create workflows.

   The Record button is for recording actions. This is a new feature in Automator 2.0, which will be briefly explored later in the "Watch Me Do" section of this hack.

   The Run button is used to try out your workflow to see if and how it works. And of course, the Stop button cancels the execution of a workflow in progress.

3. In the Library pane, scroll down and click on the Utilities actions. In the next column, scroll down and click on Quit All Applications. Drag that action into the workflow pane, and the Automator window will look like Figure 3-28. At this point, if you like, you can simply hit the Run button and watch the action close down all your applications, including Automator, if you have it open.

Figure 3-28.
Building the Quit all Applications workflow

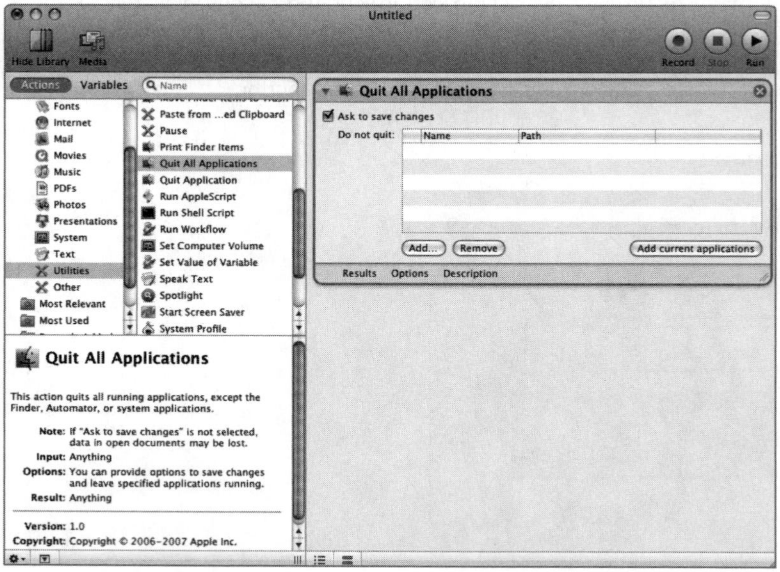

4. Leave the "Ask to Save Changes" button clicked if you want to be asked about unsaved files in running applications. If there are particular applications you don't want to quit, add them using the Add button.

   At the button of the action, you will find three additional features. When you run a workflow or action, you can click the Results button to find out whether or not the action ran successfully. If not, it will provide you some idea of why not.

   Clicking Options will provide some choices you can make before or while a workflow or action is running. In this particular action, if you check the "Show this action when the workflow runs," you will be given the opportunity to cancel the action before it runs or to add or remove listed applications from the workflow (see Figure 3-29).

   The Descriptions button (of course) provides some additional information about how the workflow will run and what the results will be. It also gives you some guidance about action or events that might proceed it.

5. After the workflow is complete, you need a way to run it without requiring that Automator be open. To do this, save the workflow as an application. Go to File→Save. Choose the place you want to save the workflow; you'll probably want to save this workflow in your personal Applications folder or a special folder where you keep all your application workflows. Now click on the File Format button, and select Application. You can also save as Workflow, but if you select that option, it will save the workflow as is, and when you click on it, it will open up in Automator. By saving the workflow as an application, it will perform independently like any other application on your computer (see Figure 3-30).

Figure 3-29.
The ever-useful Options, uh, option

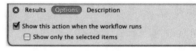

Figure 3-30.
Saving your first workflow

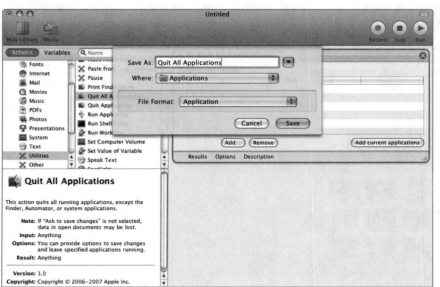

You can also save a workflow as a plug-in (File→Save As Plug-in) and access it in various ways throughout Mac OS X. If you save it as a Finder plug-in, you can Ctrl-click or right-click your mouse and choose More→ Automator→Get My Photos from the context menu. You could save as a Script plug-in where it will be saved and accessed in your Scripts menu that you can set up in your computer's menu bar (run/Applications/ AppleScript/AppleScript Utility and choose "Show Script menu in menu bar").

After saving the workflow as an application, you can locate it where you saved it and drag its icon to the Dock so that it sits next to the Finder icon. With the last step out of the way, you now you have a quick way to close all running applications without quitting them all individually.

Access the Media Browser

If you're an experienced user of iLife programs such as iMovie and iDVD, or iWork programs such as Keynote and Pages, you know that each of these applications includes a media browser for choosing and using images from your iPhoto Photo Library (or Aperture 1.5 if you have it installed).

But suppose you want to access your iPhoto or Aperture photos while working in applications that don't feature the nifty media browser? Well, again, Apple's Automator comes to the rescue. Using Automator, you can easily create a photo media or even an audio media browser that you can access anywhere in the Finder.

Here are the steps:

1. Open up Automator 2.0. Choose Custom.

2. In left column of Automator's browser, choose Photos under Library. Next, in the middle column, select Ask for Photos. (If you'd rather create a similar browser for music files stored in your iTunes and GarageBand libraries, click on Music Actions under the Automator Library and then Ask for Songs in the middle column.)

3. Drag the Ask for Photos workflow into the main window of Automator.

4. Under "Prompt", type something instructive: "Get My Photos" or whatever you like.

5. Now go to File→Save As and save the workflow as an application. You will probably want to save the workflow in your Applications folder, and then drag it to your Dock for easy access.

6. Now simply click on your new application's icon in the Dock, and the action will run, bringing up a browser of your photos from iPhoto and Aperture, if you have one or both of them installed (see Figure 3-31). You can click and drag one of the photos from the browser into an application, and you'll get the full resolution size to use as you wish.

Figure 3-31.
Access your photos without bothering with iPhoto

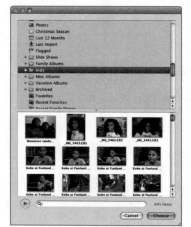

QUICK TIP

QUIT SELECTIVELY

You can also create a similar workflow that quits only selected applications. Simply drag and drop the Quit Application action (directly under the Quit All Applications action) for each application you want closed down, and save the entire workflow as an application.

Watch Me Do

The more you explore Automator and see what it has to offer, the better you can address your own particular automation needs. In addition, if you learn how to use Apple's classic automation program, AppleScript, you can make even more advanced automation workflows. However, if a programming language is too foreign for you, you still may be able to use Automator to record keyboard and mouse actions that perform in applications that don't have the Automator events you're looking for. Using Watch Me Do, Automator can record actions and produce a custom workflow. In order for this record feature to work, you must open the Universal Access preference pane (System Preferences→ Universal Access) and enable access for assistive devices. Be aware that the recording actions do not work in all cases, but when they work, they can very useful.

Before you try this out, create a folder on your Desktop called WatchMe and put some files you don't care about into it. Next, drag the folder to your Dock so you can access it from there.

1. Open Automator and select Custom workflow.

2. Click on the red Record button in the Automator menu. The interface of Automator will be replaced with a small black box that indicates that cursor movements and keyboard actions you perform you on your computer will be recorded until you click the stop button.

3. For this example, while Automator is doing the recording, Command-click on the WatchMe folder in your dock. When the folder opens up on your Desktop, press Command-A. Then click the Delete button. All the items will go into your trash. Do not empty the trash. Now click the stop button on the recorder. You can press Command-Z to put everything back into your WatchMe folder.

4. Now take a look at the resulting "Watch Me Do" workflow that reflects all the actions in the previous step (see Figure 3-32). Click the run button in the toolbar. You will see Automator execute the exact same cursor movements and keyboard inputs you made in the previous step. After the workflow is completed, simply press Command-Z in the Finder to undo the action of dumping files in your trash.

5. If you like, you can run the action again, but this time change the Playback Speed (found on the right side of the workflow) to 10x to see the action run faster than the default setting.

Figure 3-32.
Watch Me Do has watched and is now doing

Locating Your Workflows

After creating and saving workflows, you can open your Home folder and go to Library→Workflow→ Application. There, you will see folders for actions you have saved as Finder, Folder, or iCal workflows.

You can also save your workflows for further development or changes. To do this, with a workflow opened in Automator, choose File→Save or Save As and select Workflow as the file format. Save the workflow wherever you like. When you next open the saved workflow, Automator will automatically launch, and you'll be able to continue developing the workflow to your heart's content.

Obviously there is a lot more to Automator, but this hack gives you a good idea of where to start. Where you want to end, and how easy you want to make your computing life is up to you but spending just a little time in the friendly confines of Automator can result in a huge time savings after your workflows are complete.

— Bakari Chavanu

HACK 23: A Context Menu for Moving Files

Make moving files easier with a context menu addition.

Moving files with a Mac can get complicated. You can make it dead simple with a little help from Automator [Hack #22]. Using the mouse, Mac OS X provides only one way in the Finder to move files: drag and drop, and if the source and destination are on the same drive, it defaults to move. If you'd rather the Finder copied the files and left the old ones where they were, hold the Option key down while dragging. Want to do it if you are moving the files to a different drive? Then hold the Command key down while dragging, and the files will move. These are useful tips, but there are times when drag and drop is not convenient or might not suit the way you work.

Sure you can cut and paste, but who wants to use the keyboard? If you want to move files via the context menu (the menu that pops up when you Ctrl-click or right-click a file, shown in Figure 2-33) instead of copying them, you are out of luck.

Figure 3-33.
The default context menu

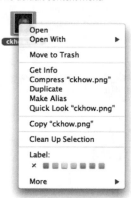

This is a challenge you can overcome by writing a simple Automator script:

1. Fire up Automator.

2. Select Files and Folders in the Actions Library.

3. Select the Move Finder Items action and drag it onto the right-side pane.

4. Click the Options button in the newly created Step 1 of the workflow.

5. Check the box labeled "Show this action when the workflow runs."

6. Make sure "Show only the selected items" is unchecked.

And that's it! The easiest Automator workflow you'll ever develop (see Figure 3-34).

Figure 3-34.
Your completed workflow; it really is that simple

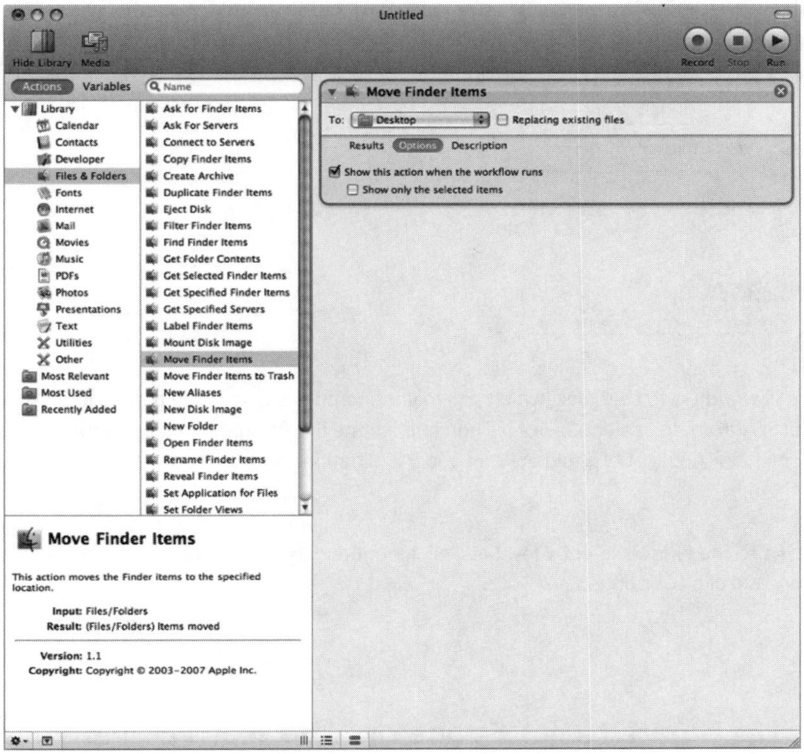

Now to use it: first save it in a folder in your Documents folder where you keep your Automator workflow source code. Give it a clear name, such as Move Files.

Then save it again but this time select "Save As Plug-in" from Automator's File menu (see Figure 3-35). Give it a name you'd like displayed on the context menu, such as "Move Files." Select Finder as the "Plug-in for." Then click Save.

Figure 3-35.
Creating a plug-in

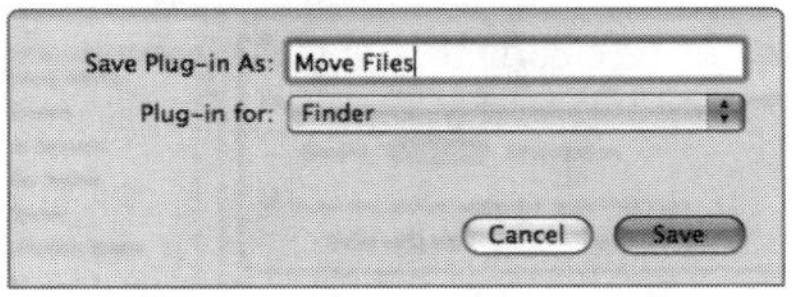

Now to test it out, go to the Finder, select a few files. Ctrl-click (or right-click) on them to bring up the context menu. Select More→Automator, then the workflow you just created.

At this point, a small dialog will appear prompting you to select where to move the files to, as shown in Figure 2-36. Select a destination, and click Continue. The files will then be moved.

Figure 3-36.
Choose your destination

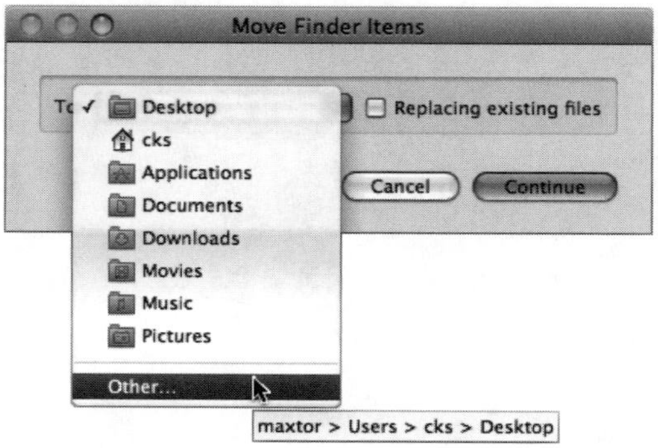

You can also add this workflow to the Dock, which you might find an easier method to use. To do so, from the File menu in Automator, select Save As. Then change the File Format to Application, give it a name, and save it in your Applications folder. From your Applications folder, drag and drop it onto your Dock.

Now to test it out, go to the Finder, select a few files, click on the icon you created on the Dock, select a destination, and click Continue.

— Chris Howard

HACK 24: Free Up Gigabytes of Space on Your Hard Drive (and Never Miss the Data)

Hard drives are getting ever larger, but libraries seem to be outpacing even the rapid expansion of hard drive space. Discover ways to shave gigabytes off your hard by deleting data you don't use.

Hard drives keep getting bigger, but no one ever seems to have enough space. The phenomenon isn't new. We have all heard stories about someone getting a new hard drive and wondering how they would ever fill up the seemingly endless space. In one telling example, I installed a (then) seemingly massive 4 GB hard drive on a friend's computer, which he clearly thought was overkill. The next week he discovered peer-to-peer file sharing and wanted yet another hard drive installed.

The good news is that you can get rid of gigabytes of data on your Mac and probably never miss a single byte of it. It would be possible, for example, to examine each application's contents, delve into the Resources folder, and delete the superfluous foreign language *.lproj* files. That would be a project for Sisyphus, and the payoff would be very slow. You can instruct Mac OS X not to install the foreign languages when you're installing Mac OS X by choosing Custom Install (a great idea), but chances are you simply fired up your Mac and transferred settings from your previous machine, or just used Mac OS X as it came out of the box.

Figure 3-37.
Do the work for me, Get Info... option!

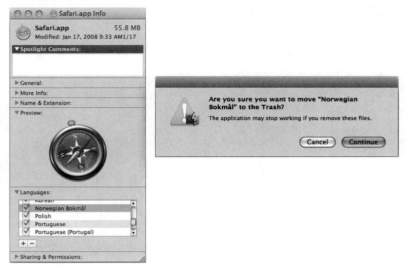

Depending on your preferred language, the *.lproj* files that seem useless to you will change. The one *.lproj* folder that you shouldn't get rid of is the *English.lproj* folder even if you refuse to speak or read anything but Esperanto. The reason is that the other *.lproj* folders folders often contain links to crucial files in the *English.lproj* folder. Hence removing the *English.lproj* is likely to remove files required for the application's continued functionality.

Of course, foreign-language files aren't the only things on your Mac that take up space. iPhoto saves the previous state of edited photos, and depending on how heavily you use the editing features, this can grow from a manageable size to truly epic proportions. Finally, Mac OS X installs printer drivers for just about every printer imaginable and while each particular driver is small, the sheer number of them adds up to a lot of wasted space.

Older versions of GarageBand installed an incredible number of loops that you can get rid of if you don't plan to use them. To figure out where the loops are hiding, check out this Apple support page: http://support.apple.com/kb/HT1045

Removing Unneeded Language Files
You could remove the language files you don't want using the command line but since that process is error-prone, it's better to leave the hard work to a program. Head to http://monolingual.sourceforge.net/, and download the Monolingual application. Install as usual, and get ready to save some space.

Select the languages you want removed—remembering, as noted earlier, that removing English would be a very bad idea. Then click Remove, as shown in Figure 3-38. After warning you that you're about to do something dangerous and asking for your password, Monolingual races through your hard drive removing all traces of the languages you've decided you no longer want, and reports how much space it freed (Figure 3-39).

Figure 3-38.
Removing unwanted languages

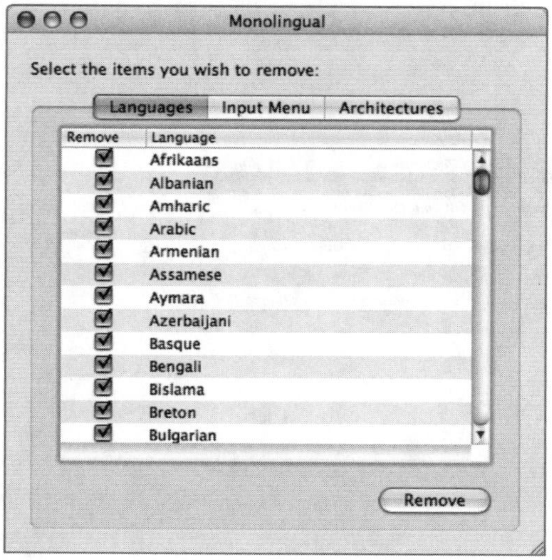

Figure 3-39.
Monolingual reports the space freed by the process

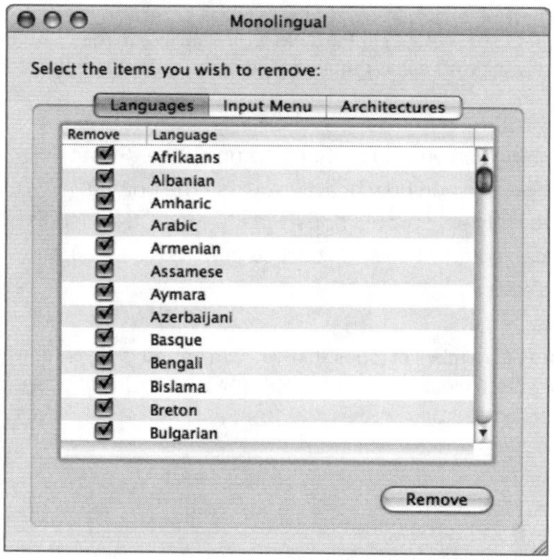

You might be tempted to continue saving space by removing unwanted keyboard layouts via Monolingual's Input Menu button, but the space savings are negligible (24 MB, in my case) and not really worth the effort.

> If you're tempted to try save even more space by removing items under the Architecture button the best advice is: don't do it. Removing the seemingly useless PowerPC architectures if you have an Intel-based Mac renders Rosetta (and any nonuniversal) applications unusable.

Getting Rid of Unneeded Printer Drivers

Removing printer drivers is another trick that you can use to save space; the files add up to over a gigabyte with a typical Leopard install, and chances are that you only use a single printer. The printer drivers are stored in the */Library/Printers* folder.

 If you're using any variety of MacBook or PowerBook, you probably don't want to delete any of the printer drivers. You never know what printer you'll want to print to when you're out and about! If you do end up short a printer while on the go, point your computer to http://localhost:631/ and try using Common Unix Printing System (CUPS).

There are two ways to go about removing the printer drivers: the safe and not very efficient way, and the efficient but not as safe way. The safe way is to drill down into the folder where your printer driver resides, carefully put aside the driver for your printer, delete all the remaining printer drivers, and then restoring yours. The more efficient method is simply to delete all the printer drivers and head to the Web to download the driver for the printer you actually use. Not only is this method quicker than manually hunting down your printer driver; there is every chance your driver has been updated since it was first installed. You might as well use the latest version (see Figure 3-40). Of course, if you never installed any drivers—that is, if your printer is supported natively by Mac OS X—then you should be careful to only remove printer drivers you know you won't use.

Figure 3-40.
Headed for the trash

Slimming Down iPhoto

iPhoto doesn't start out as a troublemaker, but the application can quickly become a hard-drive hog. The problem isn't serious if you don't use iPhoto often or don't use iPhoto to edit images, but if you do, the space consumed by your photos can spiral out of control.

The problem doesn't involve the photos themselves; the problem has to do with the previous versions of the pictures iPhoto saves so that you can undo earlier edits with ease. For example, if you crop a photo, iPhoto not only saves the resulting image, but the earlier version of the image as well. While this is a feature I'm willing to trade gigabytes of space to use, some people may never want to see those old versions again. If you're completely sure you want to get rid of earlier edits to save space, then all you need do is a little digging and a little deleting.

 Remember, once you delete the file, you can't revert to the photo before you edited the image!

If you're satisfied with the current state of the photos in your iPhoto library, you can get rid of the previous versions iPhoto is saving by navigating to */Users/username/Pictures/iPhoto Library/ Modified* (Figure 3-41) and deleting the contents of said folder. The amount of space saved is completely dependent on how frequently you modify images with iPhoto.

Figure 3-41.
Old versions of your photos

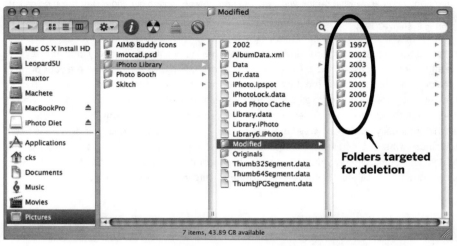

There is probably no end to all the ways you can save copious amounts of space on your hard drive, but these tips typically return the most bang for the buck without the smallest impact on day-to-day usability.

HACK 25: Create an Encrypted USB Drive

As the capacity of flash disks increase, and the price plummets, it is becoming ever more tempting to transport significant chunks of data on an easy-to-lose USB drive. Learn how to keep your data safe with a few simple steps.

While it is very convenient to carry files from computer to computer on some form of rewritable portable media, the convenience comes with a security cost. Portable media has become expansive in terms of memory, but it has also become diminutive in physical size. The small size means, for many, that the device is easy to lose. Once you lose your USB drive, not only have you lost the physical asset, but you've also exposed your data to a wider world.

Truth be told, most people aren't interested in your data, and the average person who finds your mobile miracle of memory won't be interested in the files; they will be interested in the device as a place to store their files. Even if they are mildly interested in what is on your memory stick, they're likely stick it in a Windows machine, and there be prompted to reformat the drive. On the other hand, if you're around a Mac a lot, then there is every chance that you'll lose the USB drive near a Mac, and your data will be laid open for anyone who shoves the device into a Mac to use as they will.

That isn't a pleasant scenario, but simply planning not to lose your USB drive with your precious data ensconced within the circuitry isn't a workable plan for protection. After all, losing something (with the exception of weight) isn't usually a conscious decision. The obvious solution would be applying a password-protection scheme. By invoking the functions of Disk Utility, you can do just that.

Getting Started

The first decision you have to make is how much room on your USB drive you want to devote to password-protected data. Generally "all" is good. If that is the case, back up your USB drive to the Desktop (drag and drop all of its files into a folder) because you're about to wipe it out. Next, reformat the drive using Disk Utility (it's located in */Applications/Utilities*). Once the drive is wiped, Mac OS X automatically creates a new volume called "Untitled". You can leave the drive with that lame name or change it to something meaningful.

Let's now encrypt the drive. What you'll do next is create an encrypted *.dmg* file on the USB drive so it will end up looking like a drive stored on a drive (it can get a little confusing). Head back to Disk Utility, and click New Image.

Once you click New Image, youre presented with various options for the *.dmg* file that you are about to create. The first thing that needs to be taken care of is the location of your soon-to-be-birthed *.dmg* file. You can create the file on the Desktop and then copy it to your USB drive, but why not skip the middleman and create the file directly on the target drive?

Once the location of the *.dmg* file is set, it is time to choose the size. While Disk Utility includes a bunch of easy-to-choose predefined sizes that corresponding to common forms of storage (CDs, DVDs, etc.), there is a good chance that there isn't a predefined size appropriate for your USB drive. Select Custom from the Size pop-up menu. Obviously your chosen size will need to be less than the capacity of the drive, but you'll have to allow for the overhead of the drive's formatting as well. On a 2 GB drive, the maximum file size, I was able to get was 1.7 GB.

Once the location and size are set, you need to specify the type of image you want to create. In this case, you'll want an image you can both read and write and, so as not to render this entire hack moot, one that is encrypted. Figure 3-42 shows how all these options appear in the dialog.

Figure 3-42.
All the decisions are made

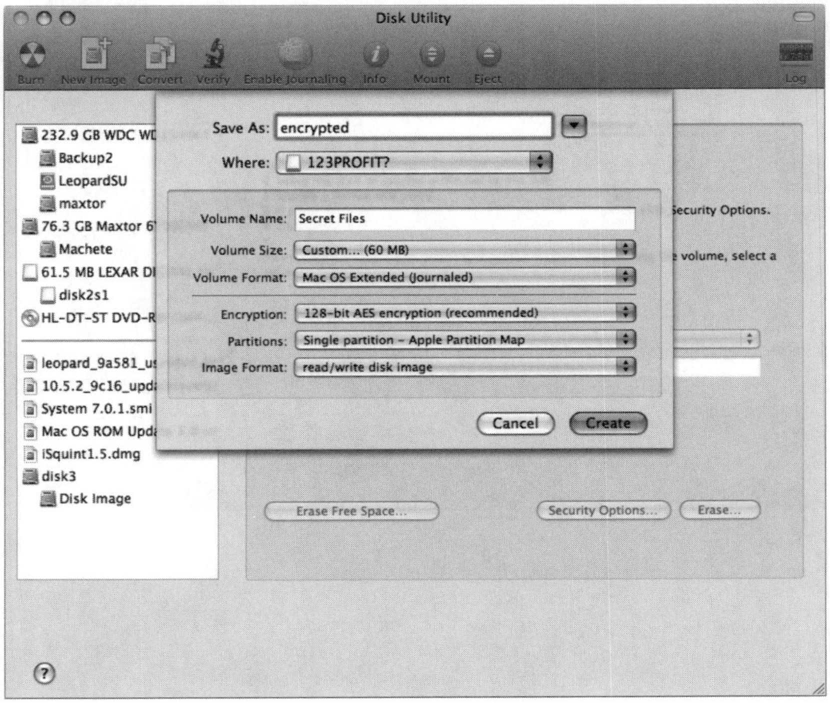

> **QUICK TIP**
>
> **SAVE SOME CONFUSION**
>
> When you're attempting this hack, make sure that none of the disks are selected when you click New Image. If any disks are selected, Disk Utility will attempt to image the selected disk instead of creating a new untouched image. If you do make this mistake, nothing bad will happen except that you'll likely get a Resource Busy error.

Click Create, and you're almost done. Mac OS X will demand you supply a password twice, and when you've supplied the same password twice, your Mac will create a brand-new encrypted disk image on your USB drive.

Figure 3-43.
Mac OS X knows how to help with passwords

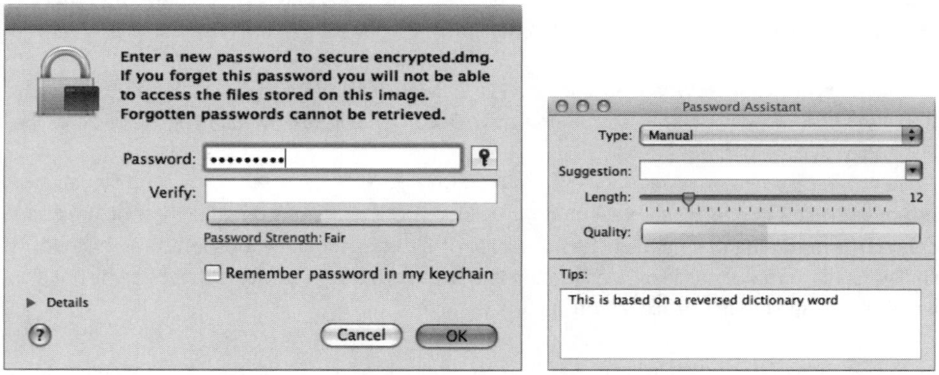

Using Your New Image

All the the work is a thing of the past at this point, and all that is left to do is to start using your newly encrypted USB drive. Your *.dmg* file is contained within the USB drive (in this case, Potion X is inside of Pizza Box), but they will appear as separate volumes on your Desktop. Drag and drop the file you want to take with you onto the encrypted portion of the drive, and you're ready to travel safely with your data. When you get to your destination, simply plug the USB drive in, open the *.dmg* found inside, supply the password (see Figure 3-44), and you're working on encrypted files.

Figure 3-44.
Keep your hands off my data

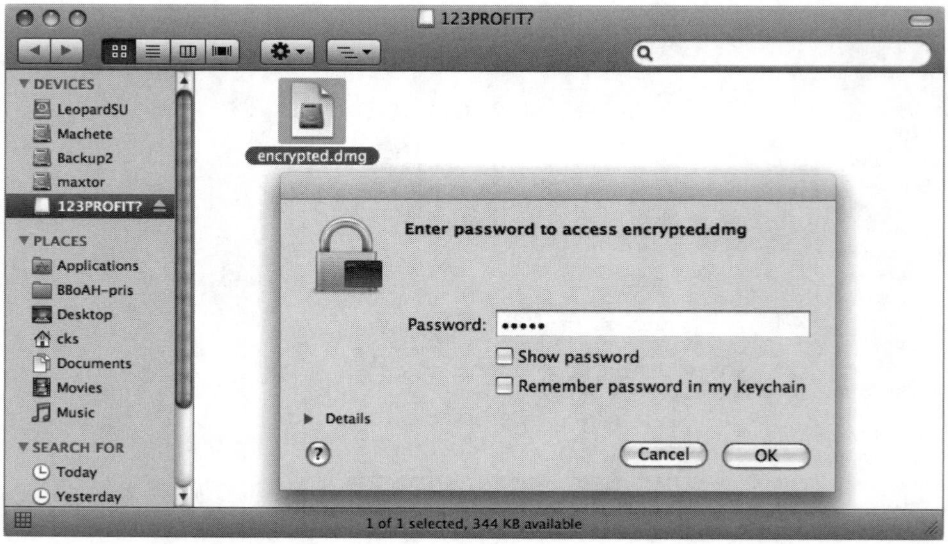

QUICK HACK

LET MAC OS X HELP YOU CHOOSE PASSWORDS

Mac OS X comes with a handy utility for generating passwords—the Password Assistant shown in Figure 3-43. Not only can Mac OS X rate the password you supply, it will happily provide you with passwords of varying degrees of crackability. Just click the key icon next to any Password field, and Mac OS X will go about the business of rating your password. Clicking on the Type pop-up menu in Password Assistant reveals several different options for Mac OS X-supplied passwords.

Capture That Screen

Save the content on your Mac's screen, the way you want it saved.

If you're using a PC and want to capture the screen, life is easy: simply hit the Print Screen button, and you're set. If you're using Mac OS X, things aren't quite as cozy. There's no PrntScrn button on Apple-supplied keyboards, and even if you have a PC keyboard plugged in to your Mac, the PrntScrn key won't snap that screen.

Apple knows users occasionally need to take screenshots and built the functionality into Mac OS X. While there isn't a simple print-screen button, a few keystrokes will give you the screenshots you crave.

Capturing the Whole Screen

If you want to capture the whole screen, Apple has you covered; you can do it straight from the keyboard with the key combination Command-Shift-3.

There are times when you don't want a snap of the entire screen; you just want to share a window with someone. Typing Command-Shift-4, followed by pressing the Space bar (do not try just mashing the keyboard with your elbow; unless you have great aim, it won't work) turns the familiar mouse pointer into a camera and highlights the window you're about to capture with a gentle blue hue, as shown in Figure 3-45.

Figure 3-45.
Capturing a single window

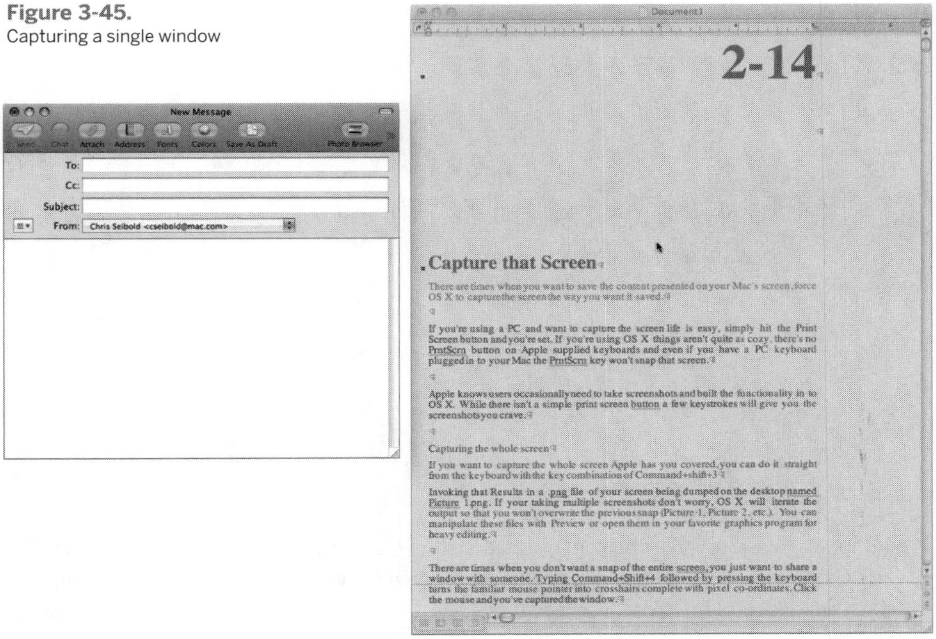

If you're ever desperate to snap a picture of the Dock, you can use the same command to capture the entire Dock. Simply click when the camera is over any blank space on the Dock.

Capturing a Portion of the Screen

Sometimes you want more than one window without the entire screen. If you want a section of the screen, Command-Shift-4 turns the mouse pointer into crosshairs complete with pixel coordinates. Drag this over the portion of the screen you want to capture and, like magic, you've got your sectional screen snap.

Invoking any of the previous methods results in a *.png* file of your screen named *Picture 1.png* being dumped on the Desktop. If you are taking multiple screenshots, don't worry. Mac OS X will increment the output name so that you won't overwrite the previous snap (Picture 1, Picture 2, and so on). You can manipulate these files with Preview or open them in your favorite graphics program for heavy editing. Finally, if you start taking a screenshot and change your mind, the Esc key (predictably) kills the process.

You'll note all the snaps taken in this fashion results in a *.png* file that might or might not be your preferred file type. You can change this behavior with a quick trip to the Terminal. The following command lets you specify the type of image you want Mac OS X built-in screen-capture abilities to output:

```
defaults write com.apple.screencapture type image_format
```

Where *image_format* is the type of output you desire. Supported types include **pdf**, **gif**, **jpg**, **bmp**, **pict,** and **tiff**. Changing the default behavior can be a time saver if, for example, you want your screen shots formatted as JPEG files for posting to your blog.

Keyboard commands can be a little tough to remember if you don't use them all the time, so Apple includes a screenshot utility with every copy of Mac OS X called Grab. Likely you're used to seeing Grab in the Services menu where the options to use Grab are usually grayed out, as shown in Figure 3-46.

Figure 3-46.
You call that service?

So if you want to use Grab, you'll find it in Applications→Utilities. And there is every chance you will want to use Grab. Grab lets you take timed screenshots (see Figure 3-47), which can be essential if you want to take a snap of the screen while you're doing something besides messing with capturing the screen.

Figure 3-47.
The timed-screen option

Additionally Grab copies the capture image to the clipboard rather instantly generating a file on your Desktop. You get a chance to review the image before you decide if you want to keep it.

You can also click Preferences from the Grab menu to choose whether to include a mouse pointer, and which pointer to use, in the resulting screenshot.

The Next Level in Screenshots

If you take a ton of screenshots, the tools included with Mac OS X aren't going to be enough: you'll want a more robust solution. You have a lot of choices, but if you want to streamline your workflow, I think no choice is better than Skitch. As of this writing, Skitch is still in beta, but you can sign up to be a tester, just navigate to http://plasq.com/skitch and request an invite.

Once you're invited, and have your copy of Skitch, you'll find the tool invaluable. Skitch doesn't follow the standard paradigm of screen-capturing utilities. It offers not only a streamlined way to take screenshots, but also an easy way to get said screen captures to their final destination with very little user intervention. On top of that, Skitch does everything in a graphically interesting, fun, and usable manner.

Skitch features most the options you'd expect for screenshots, as shown in Figure 3-48. You can take a timed snap of a section of a screen (an improvement over Grab), the entire screen, or even a snapshot with your iSight. Skitch doesn't stop there; you can also choose what format you want to save the graphic in.

Figure 3-48.
Adjusting the image settings with Skitch

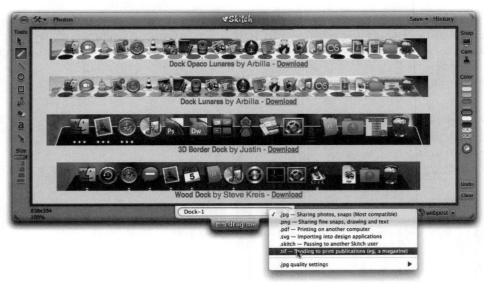

Saving an image is no problem. Instead of showing up on the Desktop like images generated with Mac OS X's built-in screen capture, you simply drag the image to whatever destination you desire. There's more to Skitch, including simple editing capabilities. Adding text to Skitch-generated images is no problem (see Figure 3-49), which is very useful if you're, say, writing a book or generating visual instructions.

Figure 3-49.
Adding text and arrows with Skitch

You can also set Skitch to post images to your online accounts and use the tool to edit the photos found in your iPhoto library, among a myriad of other services. None of the settings are obtuse or difficult to change. You can click the Hammer/Wrench icon in Skitch's upper left corner and choose Preferences from the menu that appears, or you can select Skitch→Preferences to get to Skitch's preferences (which gives you a veritable laundry list of options, shown in Figure 3-50).

Figure 3-50.
Skitch preferences

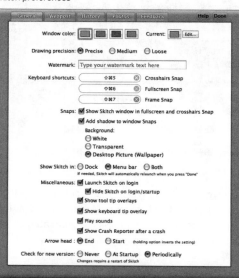

There is a ton you can do with Skitch—far too much to cover in one hack—but the best thing about Skitch isn't what it does as much as what it doesn't do. What Skitch doesn't do is get in the way. Once you're done saving, mailing, or posting your screen snap, press the minus (-) icon in the upper left corner, and Skitch floats back to the menu bar using the genie effect, waiting until you need its goodness once again.

HACK 27: Launch in a Different Way

There's more than one way to run a program.

Mac OS X offers a solid set of tools for working with your files and applications right out of the box. The Finder is a good, flexible file browser, and its Column view offers a unique way to quickly surf through folders but still preview many file types before opening them. The icon-rich Dock allows applications to display quick at-a-glance feedback, and the menu bar offers extended functionality for third-party applications. Of course, we can't forget Spotlight. Apple's revolutionary systemwide search engine can peek inside most files and even serves as a halfway decent keyboard-centric application launcher. In Mac OS X 10.5 (Leopard), all these features received some significant updates, such as Cover Flow and Quick Look for viewing rich previews of many documents and media types right in the Finder before opening them.

That said, Apple's file-manipulation tools are by no means the only ones on the block. For years, plenty of third parties have offered their own tools for interacting with Mac OS X, allowing you to manipulate files, launch applications, play and organize media, and simply get around your Mac faster. Some of these tools focus on using the keyboard as a navigation tool, while others offer a more visual perspective of your stuff. I'll highlight a few of these most popular tools, and while they are typically referred to as "file launchers," some offer a staggering amount of power to do so much more.

LaunchBar

Objective Development Software bills its LaunchBar as a:

> Productivity utility that provides instant access to your applications, documents, contacts, and bookmarks, to your iTunes library, to search engines and more, just by entering short abbreviations of the searched item's name

Offering perhaps the most familiar interface and easiest learning curve for new users, LaunchBar looks and acts a lot like Apple's own Spotlight but offers a lot more functionality, as shown in Figure 3-51.

Figure 3-51.
The basic LaunchBar interface

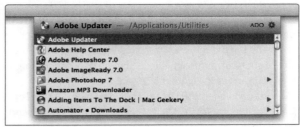

Like Spotlight, LaunchBar is also invoked via a customizable keyboard shortcut, and users are presented with a simple box in which to type the first letters or abbreviation of something to find. You can find many typical things such as bookmarks, files, iTunes songs, and contacts, but LaunchBar's power comes from all the things it allows you to do with what you find. Instead of simply opening an item in its default application as does Spotlight, LaunchBar allows you to, for example, send a file to Mail which creates a new blank message with the file attached—no shuffling through Finder windows, no mousing or drag-and-dropping. Bookmarks can be opened in alternative browsers, iTunes libraries can be searched (even if iTunes isn't open), AppleScripts can be run or edited, and searches can even be sent out to the Web.

In a way, LaunchBar is more or less a command center for your computing, allowing you to perform most operations that typically involve a lot of mousing, digging, and clicking, with the power and speed of the keyboard. If you aren't used to working this way, LaunchBar will likely require some getting used to, so be sure to give yourself some time to explore its features and everything you can do with it. A LaunchBar demo is available from http://www.obdev.at, and single, family, and business licenses start at $19.95.

Quicksilver

Offering similar "find something, then do something with it" functionality to LaunchBar, Quicksilver is a favorite across the Mac community for its unparalleled extensibility, open-source nature, and free price. While a minor drawback to Quicksilver is a slightly higher learning curve due to its vast power, users who are looking for the ultimate in file launching and manipulating utilities are rarely disappointed. Figure 3-52 shows QuickSilver.

Figure 3-52.
The two-paned window of Quicksilver

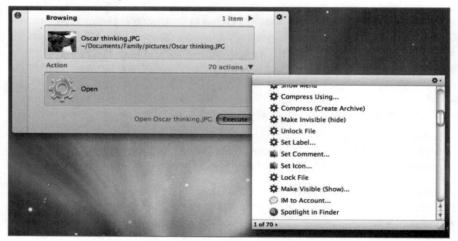

By default, Quicksilver covers much of the same territory as LaunchBar, except Quicksilver is powered by a very enthusiastic plug-in community. Upon opening Quicksilver for the first time, you're prompted to download plug-ins for many fundamental applications such as Address Book, Mail, and iTunes. Instead of a Spotlight-like menu bar though, users are presented with a two-paned window when invoking Quicksilver's keyboard shortcut, enforcing the distinction between *finding something*, then *doing something* with it. As you can see in Figure 3-52, I searched for a photo buried in my Documents folder, and the Actions pane offered 70 things I could do with it. I can Get Info on that photo, open it with Photoshop, send it to the Trash, IM it to a friend online, or even send it to third-party applications such as VoodooPad or transmit for uploading to a web site via FTP. Of course, if you don't use some of these applications or actions, you can turn them off in Quicksilver's preferences, but even the Actions menu is searchable via keyboard shortcuts to help keep your hands flying across the keyboard instead of stumbling with a mouse.

I've mentioned a few times that Quicksilver is highly extensible, and Figure 3-53 shows a great example. Here, I've replaced Quicksilver's default user interface with my preferred, built-in alternative. In the first pane on the left, I typed some basic text that displays "Write about Quicksilver." In the second pane, where an action is chosen, I have selected, in "create Task In…", Remember The Milk—a popular web-based todo list manager whose employees might or might not have ever heard of Quicksilver (it's predominantly a Mac shop though, so I bet they have). Thanks to Remember The Milk's open system of APIs (Application Programming Interfaces, a way to allow outside parties to interact with one's services), a member of the Quicksilver community put together this plug-in, which enables you to create a task and send it to one todo list or another—all without ever opening the Remember The Milk web site or even moving the mouse.

Figure 3-53.
A customized Quicksilver menu

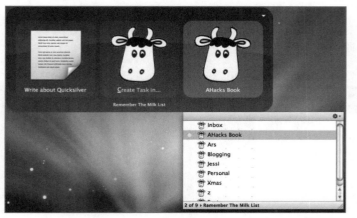

This kind of extensibility is indeed one of the most appealing aspects of Quicksilver, but again, it can sometimes make for a rocky ride when you're learning it. Quicksilver and its plug-in development is powered in part by a Wiki and support forums, and some plug-ins and features are sometimes poorly documented, if they are documented at all. Quicksilver's preferences pane houses a robust set of features for browsing many of its plug-ins and tweaking its available actions, but to get something working the way you want, you might be at the mercy of your own ingenuity or the support forums. Sticklers for stability should also be warned, because Quicksilver can sometimes be a good example of what happens when you add too many bells and whistles. Download too many plug-ins and tweak the app too much, and you can sometimes find Quicksilver crashing a little too often for your tastes.

Still, for most of its users, Quicksilver's benefits far outweigh its minor drawbacks. With support for setting systemwide keyboard triggers for just about any file and action combo Quicksilver offers, selecting and manipulating multiple files at once, a multi-item clipboard, and the largest catalog of third-party applications on the block, Quicksilver is one of those rare Swiss army knife applications that arguably excels at almost everything it's capable of.

Learning curves, a crash or two, and the occasional DIY aspects aside though, Quicksilver has remained my favorite among the Mac OS X file launchers. Its unmatched plug-in base makes it the only launcher that allows me to use the many third-party applications and web services I depend on, all from the comforts of my keyboard. Like LaunchBar though, you'll almost definitely need some time to get used to the productive doors that Quicksilver opens, and there is no shortage of tutorials, screencasts, and walkthroughs on the Web from users who can no longer work without it. Since Quicksilver is provided for free from http://www.blacktree.com (you'll even find a link to the source code on the site), you only stand to lose a little bit of time while learning how to save countless hours working on your Mac.

Spotlight

Of course, Spotlight itself is more or less designed to be a basic file and application launcher. The ability to search inside most documents—including things like the author of a document or even the name of a Photoshop layer—is incredibly useful in and of itself, and it's something LaunchBar, Quicksilver, and most similar applications actually don't do very well.

In Mac OS X 10.5 Leopard, Apple made some changes to the way Spotlight returns search results based on the observation that users like an easy way to find and open applications. First, Spotlight now returns applications immediately, before any other type of file. This makes it more appealing as a simple application launcher (see Figure 3-54) because that is one of the fundamental features most users look for in any kind of file launcher utility.

Figure 3-54.
Spotlight as a very basic launcher

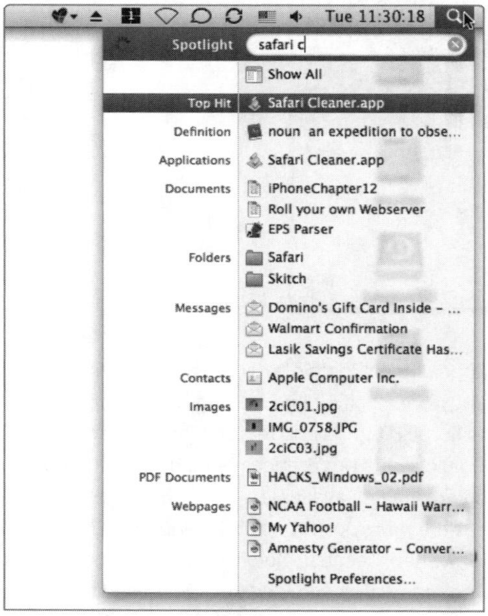

A second change Apple made to Spotlight involved a way to search Macs across your network (another feature most other file launchers don't have). For home and small business users, this can make it easier to keep a central repository of documents with which everyone can work. You can also have a central collection of applications that multiple users can run over the network (instead of managing and constantly updating the same apps across multiple machines), though I wouldn't recommend doing this with really large applications such as Microsoft Office, Adobe Creative Suite, or Apple's iLife applications.

Plenty More Where That Came From

Earlier, I said there was no shortage of file launcher applications for the Mac, and I meant it. Without writing a bible for every one of these programs, I'll list a few more that certainly deserve a mention.

Butler

Butler from Many Tricks offers much of the same functionality as LaunchBar and Quicksilver, but it is much more focused on providing GUI tools such as customizable menu bar items and extra mini docks for accomplishing your tasks. If you prefer icons and drop-down menus to a keyboard-heavy command line-like interface, Butler is a powerful option backed by a successful Mac software company.

Surprisingly, Butler is provided as donationware, and you can grab a copy from http://www.manytricks.com/butler/. If Butler fits your work style, be sure to show Many Tricks some appreciation with a donation for the company's hard work.

Overflow

Resembling the new Leopard Stacks feature for years before Stacks arrived, Overflow is perhaps best described as an extension for the Dock. Clicking on Overflow (or calling it via a keyboard shortcut) presents a pop-up window containing any variation of applications and documents you choose. While Leopard's Stacks works only when dragging a folder to the Dock (and not a manual selection of files), Overflow allows you to create multiple categories and organize exactly which applications and files you need at the click of a mouse or keyboard shortcut.

A demo of Overflow is available from http://StuntSoftware.com/Overflow, and a license costs $14.95.

Valet

Valet is a unique application that combines some of the most useful features of Spotlight, Quicksilver, and Overflow, but includes its own special sauce. While it is mostly an application and file launcher, Valet presents itself as a full-screen pop up over your Desktop when you call it via keyboard shortcut or—surprisingly—by voice control. Valet sits in the background and keeps track of the applications you use the most, presenting them first for easy access.

Besides voice control though, Valet's unique claim to fame is its ability to present applications from Microsoft Windows running in Parallels—the popular virtualization software that allows you to run Windows inside Mac OS X on Intel Macs. Valet can display Windows applications right alongside your Mac OS X applications, further blurring the line of computing if you live in both Mac and PC worlds.

A demo of Valet is available from http://94-west.com/Valet/Valet.html, and a license costs $25.

— David Chartier

**Meet the Dictionary:
Your Hidden Wikipedia Browser**

Hiding in Leopard's Dictionary is a specialized browser, a browser built with Wikipedia in mind.

Mac OS X features a fantastic built-in dictionary. Most of us only use it when we're typing a word and are alerted that our spelling isn't as fantastic as we thought it was. We're typing along when a little, red, dashed line suddenly appears, alerting us to the fact that we are about to abuse the accepted spellings in our language of choice. A Control-click or right-click on the offending word brings up a slew of options, shown in Figure 3-55, all of which are self-explanatory.

Figure 3-55.
The Dictionary in action

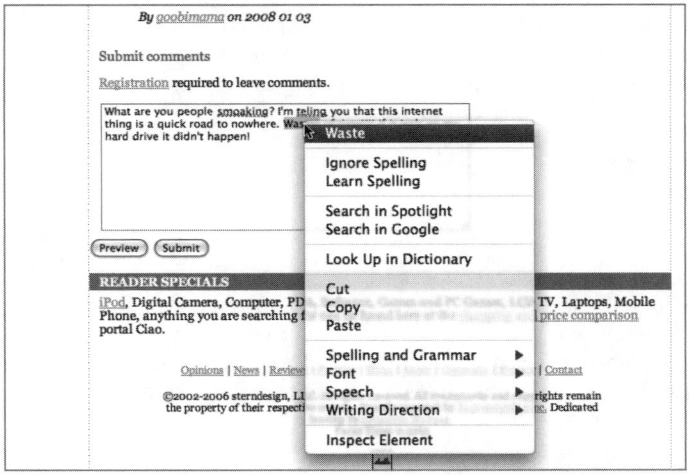

Of course, a dictionary isn't just a spell checker. Even the most stripped-down Scrabble-oriented dictionary that's used only to discover a two-letter word that includes Q provides terse definitions (the answer is Qi by the way). It's the same with the Mac OS X dictionary: it doesn't just offer proper spelling references—typing an enigmatic word into Spotlight reveals the definition as shown in Figure 3-56.

Figure 3-56.
Spotlight knows more than just where your files are

Of course, retyping or copying and pasting a troublesome word into Spotlight seems like a little too much work to be useful. Spotlight is obviously getting that information from somewhere; you'd think it would be easy to skip the transcription. It is easy to get around the transcription problem, but it requires a little finger work. Hover over the word you're wondering about, and press Command-Control-D, and the definition will float over the document you're interested in, as shown in Figure 3-57. In fact, as long as you keep the key combo pressed, the definitions will spew forth as you roll over any word on the page.

Figure 3-57.
The definition is revealed

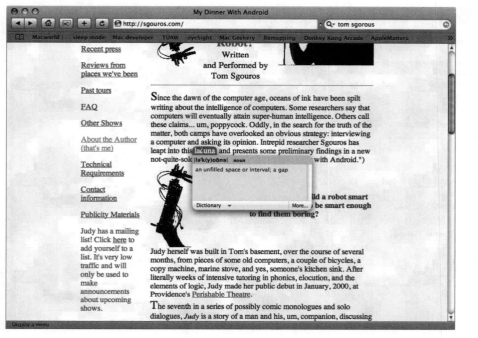

You'll see two options on the floating definition window. You can switch to a thesaurus, or you can opt for "More." Who doesn't want more? Selecting the More option does something unexpected: it launches the Dictionary application. Who knew that there was an entire application devoted to correcting your spelling mistakes and discovering synonyms, antonyms, and definitions lurking in Mac OS X?

These tricks won't work with all applications. For example, Microsoft Office uses the Carbon software development frameworks, which were designed to make it easier for applications to make the transition from Mac OS 9 to Mac OS X. Applications based on Cocoa (such as iWork) will work just fine with these tricks.

Anyone who paid careful attention to the Applications folder wasn't surprised, but even people with eidetic memories would be surprised by the utility found by poking around in the Dictionary application. Once the application is running, you've got some interesting things going on that most people wouldn't notice on initial inspection.

A quick trip to the preference panel (Dictionary→Preferences) is all that is needed to get the Dictionary application behaving in the fashion most conducive to your personal tastes (see Figure 3-58).

Figure 3-58.
Choose your sources

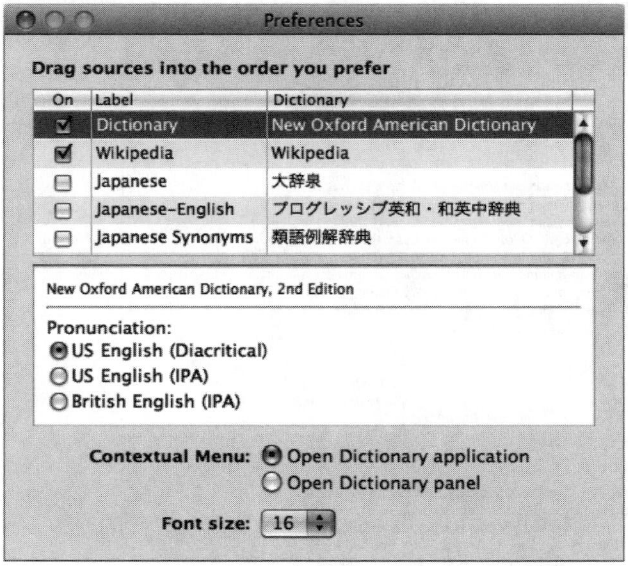

Once you've invoked the Preferences menu, you'll see your choices. If you've got a strong feelings about the sources for your definitions, you are allowed to pick the ones you like and reject the ones you don't. Think the New Oxford American Dictionary is a heretical tome? Uncheck the box. There are other options: you can change the default pronunciation display and change the order in which information is returned.

The most interesting thing in the Dictionary application isn't the dictionaries you can choose, the size of the font, or even whether to go with the Diacritical pronunciation style or the IPA pronunciation style. (And what relationship hasn't gone through the harsh words on that debate?) No, the best thing about the Dictionary is that it's actually web-based, and all the words are linked. That means you can use the Dictionary as a pretty svelte Wikipedia browser. Type anything into the search box in the upper left corner, and you can find the Wikipedia entry on that subject, as shown in Figure 3-59.

Figure 3-59.
A very cool Wikipedia browser

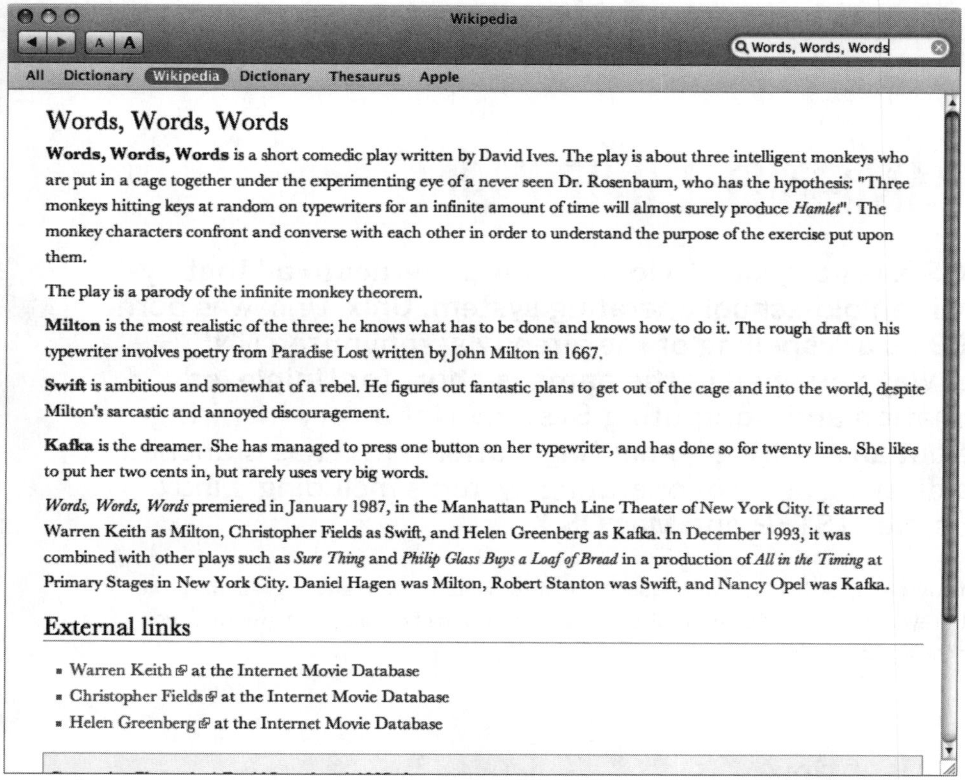

The Dictionary application takes Wikipedia one step farther than most browsers: instead of displaying only the links intended by the authors, every single word is linked. Moving your mouse over a word turns the word blue. and subsequent clicking brings up all the associated Wikipedia topics.

4. COMMAND-LINE FUN

Mac OS X is gorgeous to look at but underneath all that eye candy is an old-school operating system: Unix. Unix was born in 1969 as a respelling of the already acronymized UNICS. Either way you spell it, the name is short for Uniplexed Information and Computing System. Not a very inspiring name but an inspiring computing platform that has branched into a dizzying array of operating systems including: Linux, Solaris, NeXTSTEP, and Mac OS X.

While the Unix roots of Mac OS X are hidden from the casual user, you can still get at the power behind the eye candy using the Terminal. Discover a new world of computing power when you discover the world of Unix.

HACK 29: Meet Unix

This hack reveals some information about the power behind Mac OS X Unix and details a powerful way to kill unruly programs and processes.

Unix was originally intended to be used from a text-only terminal console, and many of its features are still accessed via typed commands. To access the command line, users of Mac OS X fire up the Terminal. Mac OS X users never have to use the Terminal to get everyday work done. (At least not anymore; in early versions of Mac OS X, firing up the Terminal was sometimes required to empty Trash.) So the question is, why would anyone want to be bothered with something as mundane as the command line?

For hard-core hackers, the answer is obvious: to harness the power of the underlying system. But the command line isn't just for the geekiest among us: the command line is a useful tool for everyone. Not only can otherwise unchangeable parts of Mac OS X be modified via the command line [Hack #37], but in certain situations, the command line can be a superior tool to the graphical user interface.

The easiest way to get to the command line is via an application called Terminal (you can find it in your Mac's Applications→Utilities folder). After Terminal is running, you are presented with a *shell*, Unix-speak for a program that waits for your commands and executes them, sort of analogous to Mac OS X's Finder. It is in this shell that you can navigate, copy files, create directories, and modify files in a nongraphical, generally non-intuitive, completely unMac-like, but powerful way.

Almost all Unix features are configurable (which is how Apple engineers managed to shoehorn it into Mac OS X), so you actually have some choices when it comes to the shell. The default shell is `bash` (Bourne Again Shell), but there are plenty of choices. For most people, it is wise to stick with `bash` to ensure compatibility with the scripts you'll see throughout the book and with scripts you'll find online.

Figure 4-1.
Changing the login shell

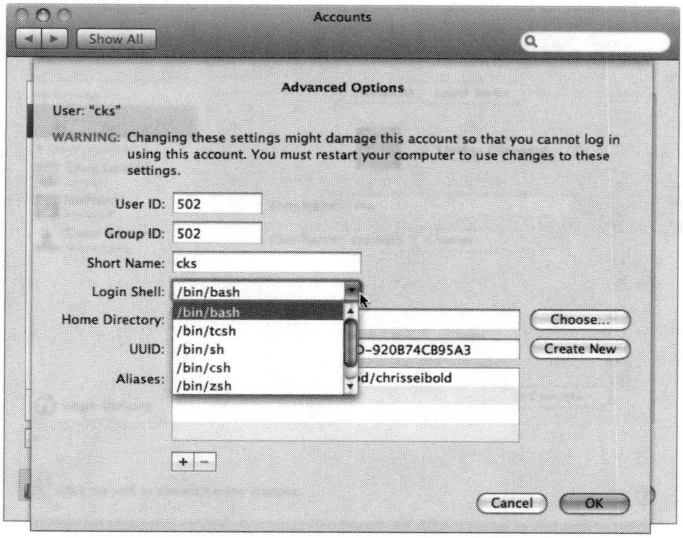

Time to get up and running with Unix. Launch the Terminal (Applications→Utilities→Terminal). Once the Terminal launches, you'll see something along the lines of:

```
computer:~:username$
```

Where ***`computer`*** is the name of your Mac, and ***`username`*** is your login name. (The prompt is endlessly configurable. In this book, we'll just use $ to indicate the command prompt.)

What you see is a Unix representation of the current directory (directory being the Unix way to say "folder"). The tilde (~) tells you that you're in your home directory, and the $ represents the command prompt. You can prove this by typing:

```
$ ls
```

and hitting return. Wow, that list exactly mirrors your Home folder.

The $ represents Terminal's command line prompt; don't type the $ you see in the examples.

See the difference (and the similarity) between the Unix way and the Mac way in Figure 4-2 and Figure 4-3.

QUICK HACK

CHANGING YOUR SHELL

If you've steadily upgraded from earlier versions of OS X, you may find that the default shell when Terminal is invoked is `tcsh`. Don't be surprised: `tcsh` was the default shell until Panther was released, and the preferences were saved as you upgraded. To change the default shell in Leopard to `bash` (or to switch from `bash` to another shell), head to System Preferences and select Accounts. After clicking the Lock icon to authenticate, right-click or Ctrl-click on the account name in the left side of the pane where the accounts are listed. A menu with a single option, Advanced Options, will appear. Click it, and a dialog window appears, as shown in Figure 4-1. You can change the login shell by clicking on the down arrow next to the Login Shell field.

YOUR NEW FRIEND TILDE

The ~ can cause a lot of confusion to those new to the Terminal. The standard way of explaining ~ is to say that it represents your home directory. That explanation is accurate but can still be confusing if you're not sure where (or what) your home directory is. An alternative way of thinking about ~ is that it is the same as typing **/Users/*username*** in the Terminal.

Figure 4-2.
The directory contents as displayed by the Terminal

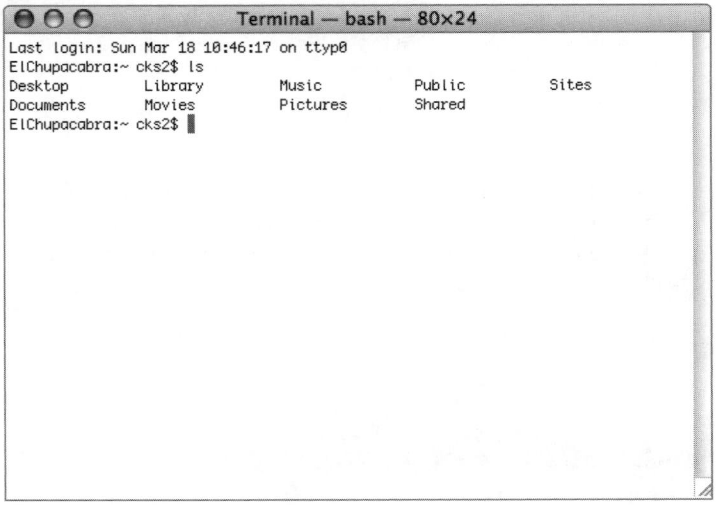

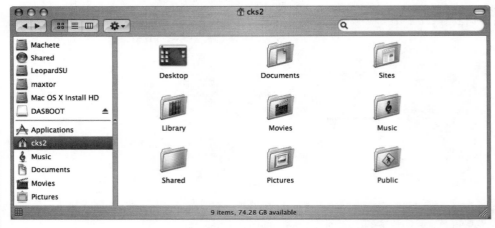

Figure 4-3.
The directory contents as displayed by the Finder

EASY HELP FROM THE TERMINAL

If you're using the Terminal you might be wondering where the Help option lives. For the Terminal as a program, it is where you expect, at the top of the Finder window. That doesn't do you much good if you want to know about the application you're using within the Terminal. For example, if you want to know about `grep`, the seemingly all powerful search utility, you won't find helpful information with the Help menu of the Terminal All is not lost, programs you launch via the Terminal (`cp`, `grep`, `imaemagick`, etc.) all include *manual pages*, or *manpages*. Manual pages are instructions telling you how to use the program. To read the manpage, type $ **man *programname***. For example, $ **man rm** will bring up a page telling you all about the `rm` program, with examples.

Now that the Terminal is running, it's time for a few modifications to make things a little better. First thing to note is that Terminal supports multiple windows and multiple tabs (the tab feature is similar to Safari's, but is only available in Leopard). This is a feature you'll want to take advantage of because while Terminal can do many different things at once, the amount of information you get back is seriously limited. If you're working in a terminal window writing a Perl script and suddenly (but predictably) want to access a man page (see sidebar), you're in trouble, because there is no easy way to take care of all your needs in a single window. The solution is to use tabs or multiple windows. A typical (and the term is used loosely) setup might be to have one tab running a command-line text editor, another tab devoted to manpages, yet another tab for testing Perl scripts, and still another tab watching your network traffic.

✉ If you're using a pre-Leopard version of Mac OS X, Terminal tabs aren't an option. You'll have to rely on multiple windows. That is, unless you give the free iTerm a try. It's a tab-enabled Terminal replacement you can download from http://iterm.sourceforge.net.

Now that Terminal is a bit more familiar, time to find a way to exploit it!

It's likely you've had a program hang before and used the Force Quit option found in the Apple menu to kill off a misbehaving application. The trouble is that there are a lot more processes running on your Mac than are revealed in the Force Quit application window. You can see all the running processes using the **top** command. To invoke **top**, type **top** at the ⅄ prompt, and hit return (Figure 4-4).

Figure 4-4.
The result of the top command

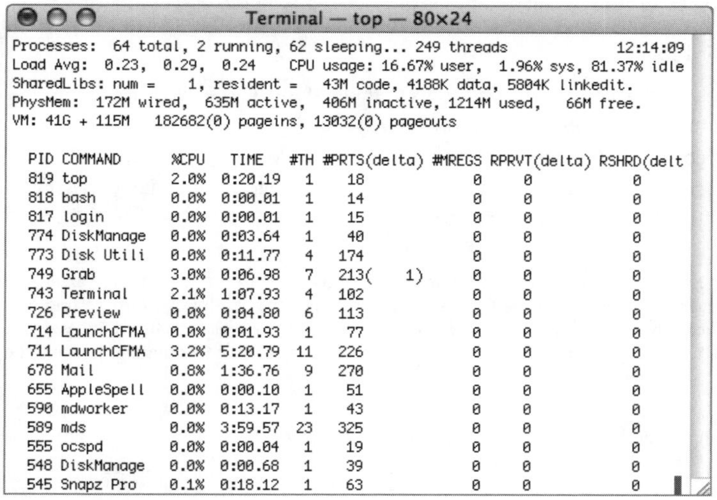

```
000                 Terminal — top — 80x24
Processes:  64 total, 2 running, 62 sleeping... 249 threads      12:14:09
Load Avg:  0.23,  0.29,  0.24     CPU usage: 16.67% user,  1.96% sys, 81.37% idle
SharedLibs: num =    1, resident =   43M code, 4188K data, 5804K linkedit.
PhysMem:  172M wired,  635M active,  406M inactive, 1214M used,   66M free.
VM: 41G + 115M   182682(0) pageins, 13032(0) pageouts

PID COMMAND      %CPU   TIME    #TH #PRTS(delta) #MREGS RPRVT(delta) RSHRD(delt
819 top          2.0%  0:20.19  1    18              0     0             0
818 bash         0.0%  0:00.01  1    14              0     0             0
817 login        0.0%  0:00.01  1    15              0     0             0
774 DiskManage   0.0%  0:03.64  1    40              0     0             0
773 Disk Utili   0.0%  0:11.77  4   174              0     0             0
749 Grab         3.0%  0:06.98  7   213(     1)     0     0             0
743 Terminal     2.1%  1:07.93  4   102              0     0             0
726 Preview      0.0%  0:04.80  6   113              0     0             0
714 LaunchCFMA   0.0%  0:01.93  1    77              0     0             0
711 LaunchCFMA   3.2%  5:20.79 11   226              0     0             0
678 Mail         0.8%  1:36.76  9   270              0     0             0
655 AppleSpell   0.0%  0:00.10  1    51              0     0             0
590 mdworker     0.0%  0:13.17  1    43              0     0             0
589 mds          0.0%  3:59.57 23   325              0     0             0
555 ocspd        0.0%  0:00.04  1    19              0     0             0
548 DiskManage   0.0%  0:00.68  1    39              0     0             0
545 Snapz Pro    0.1%  0:18.12  1    63              0     0             0
```

If you open up a Force Quit window and compare it to the output of **top**, you'll note that **top** reveals many more processes than Force Quit. If something isn't behaving properly, or if you just want to kill off a process that Force Quit won't let you get at, it's the Terminal to the rescue. Note the PID number of the process you want to quit and either hit Q (to quit **top**) or open a different tab in the Terminal (a new tab is much more useful if you plan on halting multiple processes), and type **kill** followed by the PID number. In this example, if you wanted to kill off Snapz Pro (it doesn't show up in the Force Quit menu) simply type: **kill 545** and hit return (note that this number is likely to be different on your computer and will probably be different each time you run whatever application you're trying to shut down). Snapz Pro is no longer running. Now that you're armed with the **kill** command and a way to watch things in the Terminal, you can track down those pesky performance drainers and banish them to the digital ether!

QUICK TIP ✕

ACTIVITY MONITOR IS TOP WITH GRAPHICS

What is that you say? You love the idea and functionality of **top** but loathe the very notion of firing up the Terminal? Today is your lucky day: Every Mac ships with a cool GUI version of **top** called Activity Monitor. Just dig into Applications→Utilities and fire it up. All the goodness of **top** with pretty icons everywhere. Here's a fun experiment: fire up **top** and Activity Monitor at the same time and see which one requires more from the CPU. On my machine, Activity Monitor requires roughly four times the resources of **top**.

The command line is the path to the power behind Mac OS X. Investigate how to tap that power with this hack.

Killing processes with the command line is great fun and empowering [Hack #29] but that example doesn't even begin to hint at all the abilities of the command line. The first order of business is deciding how to move around using the command line. It isn't as intuitive as the GUI of OS X, but the process is straightforward. Try:

```
$ cd Documents
```

The command changes the *working directory* to the documents folder of your home folder. Your working directory is the one you're "in" at the moment. You can think of it as analogous to the active Finder window. You can see the results of the move by typing:

```
$ pwd
```

The output displays the path to the current destination: */Users/username/documents*.

To get back to the home directory, type:

```
$ cd
```

Which is a lot like Dorothy's red slippers inasmuch as it takes you back to your home directory no matter where you are in Unix space. You can, naturally, string things together. If you wanted to get to your iPhoto library, just keep extending the pathname of where you want to end up. To wit:

```
$ cd Pictures/iPhoto\ Library
```

There are a couple of things to note here. If you want Unix to understand where you want to go, you can't skip ahead and type only *iPhoto\ Library*; you'll have to follow the path from the directory where you currently sit. Secondly, if your destination contains a space, you'll have to replace the space with "\ " (forward slash and a space). It is enough to make you want to use underscores! For your iPhoto Library the path is: $ **cd Pictures/iPhoto\.**

 It is easy to forget that names don't always translate from the Finder to Unix. In Unix, the file extension is visible even if you saved a file with the Hide Extension option. It is possible, though rare, to find files without extensions. It probably won't happen to you but, if it does, you've been warned.. If you find yourself wondering why you can't copy a file that is clearly present in the Finder, use the `ls` command to see if the name you're typing matches the name the command line is looking for.

Navigating backwards a single level is easy enough: two dots tell Unix to move up to the parent directory:

```
$ cd ..
```

If you're not a big fan of moving about using the command line, you can always use a nifty OS X feature that automatically completes the path. Simply type **cd** at the command prompt, followed by a space, then drag a folder from a nearby Finder window over to your Terminal window. The path will be automatically completed. Typing **cd**, space, and then dragging the iPhoto Library folder onto the Terminal window results in (on my Mac, anyhow) the following:

```
ElChupacabra:everything cks2$ cd /Users/cks2/Pictures/iPhoto\ Library
```

Hitting return takes me to the desired directory:

```
ElChupacabra:iPhoto Library cks2$
```

With the fundamentals of traveling about using the command line covered, we can move on to creating directories. The command to create a directory (folder) is `mkdir`. On it's own, `mkdir` won't do anything; it needs the name of the new directory. Type:

```
$ mkdir bigbook
```

Whatever directory you were in before now has a new folder in it called *bigbook*. Does this mean you can only create directories in wherever you're in at that moment in time? Of course not; using the navigation method we used before replaces `cd` with `mkdir`, and the new directory can be created in the place of your choosing. This command, for example:

```
$ mkdir ~/Documents/bigbook
```

Results in a folder called *bigbook* in the Documents folder.

What good is a directory without files in it? None at all. Moving files in Unix is accomplished using the `mv` command. Here's what to do if you wish to move a file into the newly created *bigbook* folder:

```
$ mv monk.tif bigbook/
```

The command moves the specified file (in this case *monk.tif*) into the *bigbook* folder. You can also use `mv` to rename a file:

```
$ mv monk.tif bigbook/monknew.tif
```

That changes the name of *monk.tif* to *monknew.tif* and also moves the file to the *bigbook* folder. But you could just as well have kept it in the same location with:

```
$ mv monk.tif monknew.tif
```

Of course, you don't always want to move a file; sometimes you want to copy a file. In Unix, the command for copying a file is `cp`. You have to specify the name of the file and the name of the copy:

```
$ cp monk.tif monkcopy.tif
```

This results in the original file and an identical file called *monkcopy.tif* residing in the working directory. It's great, but most of the time, you want the file copied to some other location. No problem:

```
$ cp monk.tif bigbook/monkcopy.tif
```

You've generated a directory and some superfluous files. But who wants a bunch of worthless files lying around? Time to get rid of them!

> We are about to invoke the `rm` command. This is the time to remember that in Unix spelling, spacing and capitalization all count.

Before using the `rm` command, it is a good idea to make sure you know where you are and what you're about to remove. Until you feel very confident in your skills, use the `ls` command before the `rm` command, and you'll see what files are in the directory before you banish them for eternity.

```
$ rm monkcopy.tif
```

Bam, *monkcopy.tif* is gone! And I mean gone. Don't look for it in the Trash, because it's not there.

You can extend the `rm` command by specifying multiple files for deletion. Put a space between the filenames. For example, the following:

```
$ rm monk.tif monkcopy.tif
```

QUICK HACK ✕

MAKE THE TERMINAL WARN YOU

The `cp`, `mv`, and `rm` commands are the stuff that give people new to the Terminal pause. They are two letter commands, but they can be incredibly destructive. `cp` and `mv` will overwrite any files with the same names in the target directory without warning. This can be a real problem when you're moving files to a backup location; your old backups will be overwritten without a peep from the Terminal. The `rm` command can be even more worrisome because those two letters are the Unix equivalent of saying goodbye forever. The good news is that all three commands support the `-i` option, which will prompt you (in the case of `cp` and `mv`) if any files are going to be overwritten and (in the case of `rm`) which file is about to be deleted. Type `rm -i filename` to use this feature. Some users will set an alias like this: `alias cp='cp -i'` [Hack #32].

deletes both files. You can add as many files as you wish, and they will all be gone as soon as you hit return.

Moving files and creating directories is useful, but it is time to step things up a notch using the command line. It turns out that there is more power in these commands than is apparent from the way you've been using them. In general, commands have arguments and options. Arguments are usually the file you want the command to act upon (in the example of `rm monkcopy.tif`, the argument would be *monkcopy.tif*), and options are ways to specify how the command should work. The options vary from command to command. You can find a list of the options for any particular command by typing **man** followed by the command you are interested in. For example, typing **man ls** returns a list of the various options you can invoke when using the `ls` command (see Figure 4-5).

Figure 4-5.
The manpage for ls

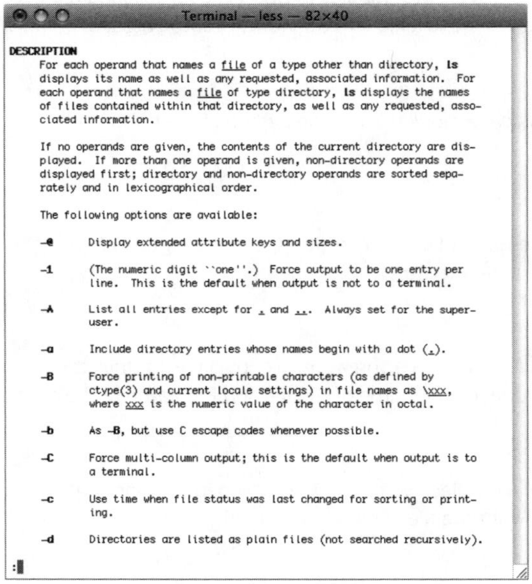

It is one thing to read the list of the options; it is another to actually use them. Try stringing together a command, an option, and an argument. Pick a folder (I'll use Music) and type:

```
$ ls -F /usr/libexec/
```

You've specified a command (`ls`) an option (`-F`), and a folder to inspect. Thanks to the option you supplied, `ls` won't just return a list; `ls` now returns a list in which directories are identified with a trailing /; executables are identified with an *. Here's the partial output of that command:

```
ApplicationFirewall/      gdb/             rexecd*
CCLEngine*                getNAME*         rlogind*
InternetSharing*          getty*           rpc.rquotad*
MiniTerm.app/             gnurmt*          rpc.yppasswdd*
```

The `-F` option modifies the behavior of the `ls` command. But there is more to adding options and arguments. You can string them together like so:

```
$ ls -F -a ~/Desktop/Chapter_4 ~/Desktop/bboah_bu
```

In my case, that command roots through a folder called *Chapter_4* and a folder called *bboah_bu* on my Desktop return the results according to the `-F` `-a` options of the `ls` command.

Finally, it turns out that there are a lot of hidden programs on your Mac. The Finder won't reveal them but you can run them from the command line. One program included on the Mac is Emacs. Type:

```
emacs
```

What happens is that a useful built-in text editor opens. Emacs is a funny animal. It's a text editor, but it's programmable, and over the years, lots of people have written lots of programs for it that have nothing to do with editing. Try hitting the escape key, then X. You'll see an odd kind of prompt at the very bottom of the screen. Try typing:

```
doctor
```

If that's not weird enough for you, press Escape-X again, then type:

```
tetris
```

or:

```
snake
```

or:

```
dunnet
```

and let the fun begin!

If you want to learn about how to use Emacs to do useful work, type Ctrl-H, then T, and you'll be led through a tutorial, including a set of editing exercises.

Naturally there is a lot more Unix can do. Libraries of books have been written about the subject, but this is enough to get started on a hacking adventure.

HACK 31: Get More Out of Your Mac with Fink and MacPorts

There is a lot of software written explicitly for the Mac, but there is another world of software you can discover with a few tools and a little bit of planning. Expand your software library with this useful guide.

One of the smartest moves Apple made in the metamorphosis that was Mac OS X was to base it on BSD, a free Unix derivative almost as old as the personal computer. This new operating system, called Darwin, allowed Apple to tap into the preexisting developer community of the Unix/Linux world and expand their user base to include engineers of all stripes. Consequently, applications that are available to BSD or Linux users are available to you as well.

Fink and MacPorts are two projects that unleash the beast that is BSD Unix from underneath the gorgeous shell of Mac OS X. They are free and open source software (FOSS) projects that provide modified Unix software that compiles and runs on Mac OS X. They also provide a tool for easy installation and management of installed packages.

There are many good reasons to use Fink and MacPorts:

- To update the open source software that came with your Mac, such as Perl and Python, to their latest available versions.

- To install programs that don't have equivalents on the Mac, such as Gnucash and ImageMagick.

- To install free and open source alternatives to Mac applications such as Amarok instead of iTunes or Gimp instead of Photoshop.

- To install tools, interpreters, and libraries to develop software for the Unix and Mac platform.

- To have the opportunity to use software that is free as in "free beer" and free as in "free speech."

The thing to keep in mind is to choose Fink or MacPorts, and stick with it. Open source software comes with many dependencies. Installing one piece of software may require the installation of many other pieces. It is best to leave these details in the hands of a capable package manager, which is what these programs are. Hence the choice of either Fink or MacPorts will keep things consistent. There is a lot of debate in the community about the benefits of one system over the other, but both MacPorts and Fink have their strengths. In most cases, the same person maintains the software in both projects. Their goal is to bring more open source software to the Mac OS X. They tweak, massage, and mold open source Unix software to behave on Mac OS X while providing a relatively simple method for users to obtain the software.

Before you install Fink or MacPorts, you need to prepare your computer. Your copy of OS X needs to be installed with the BSD Subsystem (automatically installed in Leopard). You will also need the Xcode development environment, which is available from the Apple Developer Connection (ADC) web site (http://developer.apple.com) or can be found on the discs that came with your machine. You will have to register on the ADC site in order to download the Xcode installation, but this is free and mostly painless. Xcode provides your Mac with the basic tools needed to compile and run most open source software. Finally, you will also need X11 (you won't see the .app extension in Finder, but you'll need to include it when you're using the Terminal), which is included in the "Optional Installs" package on the Mac OS X install disk for older versions of OS X. If you're using Leopard, this step is taken care of for you.

It would be useful at this point to familiarize yourself with Terminal [Hack #30] and X11, if you are not already. Terminal will be your window in to the world of command-line software. Fire it up, and try simple commands such as `ls` to list the contents of a directory or `wc` to show the number of lines, words, and characters in a text file.

X11.app provides a windowing system for GUI applications in the world of Unix and Linux. In order to launch the GUI of many open source applications, you need to have X11 running (or let it launch automatically in Leopard when you run an X11 program from the Terminal). You can find *X11.app* in your */Applications/Utilities* directory.

Getting Started with Fink

Download Fink (http://fink.sourceforge.net) and install it. Towards the end of the installation, you will be asked for some system information. If you are comfortable using the command-line interface (Terminal), then run the following to get started:

```
$ fink scanpackages; fink index
```

To install any package, type the following:

```
$ fink install package_name
```

For example, `fink install gaim` will install the popular open source instant messaging client Gaim, including all the packages that Gaim depends on to run. To run Gaim, you would type `gaim` at the Mac OS X Terminal. Fink installs all of its software in the */sw* directory by default, and the executable programs are installed in */sw/bin*. This keeps the software installed through Fink separate from that which comes with Mac OS X and makes uninstalling all Fink packages a matter of simply deleting the */sw* directory.

If you cringe at the thought of using the command line, there is a graphical alternative. The FinkCommander (http://finkcommander.sourceforge.net) is an open source GUI frontend to Fink. You can list, maintain, install, and update packages from this graphical interface. Download and install FinkCommander the way you would install any other OS X application. On first run, it will attempt a "self-repair" and then allow you to select packages to install.

FinkCommander will present you with a list of available packages for installation. This is just a graphical representation of the Fink command `fink list`. In Fink, you have the option of installing packages from binaries (prebuilt programs) or source (programs built on and for your system). Fink has literally thousands of packages to choose from. To install any one, select it from the list or search in the search box in the upper-right corner. To install from source, click on Source→ Install from the menu. For binary, click on Binary→Install. For beginners, the binary installations are usually fine. Installing from the source allows you to build programs tailored to your system and may provide a slightly newer version of the software you're installing. Fink will prompt you for your administrator password every time you need to install software if it has not asked you recently. Also, the bottom pane of the FinkCommander window displays the progress of the installation.

When new versions of the packages are available, you will want that to be reflected in Fink's table. To refresh the Fink database, click Source→Selfupdate from the menu. This will update the list of packages so that you can see if any of your installed packages are outdated. You can find a lot more usage information in the Fink user guide, the Fink FAQ on its web site or by typing **man fink** on the command line.

MacPorts

MacPorts is similar to Fink in many respects. It also provides a large variety of open source packages for installation and a straightforward way to manage them. Once you have downloaded and installed it (http://www.macports.org), typing the following at the command line will install the package of your choice:

```
$ sudo port install packagename
```

Just as Fink has FinkCommander, MacPorts has PortAuthority, a GUI frontend for MacPorts. PortAuthority has a well-designed and self-explanatory interface for the installation and management of your packages. Of course, the repository for MacPorts is separate from that of Fink and is installed in the */opt/local* directory. It is a good idea to pick either Fink or MacPorts as your package manager of choice to maintain consistency and ensure that software is not unnecessarily duplicated.

Example: Three Ways to Install Gimp

Let's take the open source image-editing powerhouse, Gimp, as an example. The easiest method of doing so is to install it as you would any other OS X application—from a DMG (http://gimp-app. sourceforge.net). Many popular open source applications are available as OS X *.app* files, and Gimp is one of them. Gimp requires *X11.app*.

However, to practice the skills you learned here, you can install the same application as follows under MacPorts:

```
$ sudo port install gimp-app
```

If you decided to go with Fink, you can install Gimp with the command:

```
$ fink install gimp2
```

The last method mentioned, using Fink, does not create a *.app* file (*.app*s are really semihidden folders containing lots of resources) in your Applications directory. It creates a binary in */sw/bin* that can be executed from Terminal by typing:

```
$ gimp
```

If an open source package is not available in Fink or MacPorts, it may still be possible to install it in OS X. The package may be available directly from some web site, sometimes as compiled binaries, and sometimes as source code that needs to be compiled.

Software available as source code is usually compressed as a compressed archive (*.tar.gz*) file. The procedure for installation has become fairly standard. First, decompress the file like this:

```
$ tar -zxf packagename.tar.gz
```

This command usually creates a directory called *filename* that contains the source of the package. It may also include a *README* file or *INSTALL* (or both), containing instructions on installation and other useful information. If not, the most common way to install open source software on Unix-like systems is the following series of commands:

```
$ cd packagename
$ ./configure
$ make
$ sudo make install
```

Usually, the *configure* script will bring potential issues with installation to light. If you do not see any errors in these three commands, the software should be ready to use.

The community of developers working on ports for Mac OS X helps Macs remain a viable alternative not only to Windows but also to common forms of Unix and Linux. Having said that, there are some problems with Fink and MacPorts the way they exist today. There are issues with stability (the consensus as of this writing is that MacPorts is much better than Fink under Leopard, but this isn't a static situation) and the ease of use for new users. They have improved a lot over time and can only get better as the Mac OS X user base grows, making now the perfect time to add one of them to your computing quiver.

— Devanshu Mehta

Make Life Easy With Shell Scripts

A Unix shell isn't just a way to tell your Mac what to do. It's actually a simple programming language that can automate almost any task you need to repeat.

After learning about the shell, you might wonder why anyone still uses such an archaic method to order their computer around. Haven't those Unix users heard about graphical user interfaces? Well here's what keeps people typing: wildcards, scripting, and automation.

Wildcards are simple. Want to look at all the JPEG files in some folder? Type this in your Pictures folder at the Terminal prompt:

```
$ ls -l *.jpg
```

The `*.jpg` expands to the list of all the files that end with *.jpg*, and sure enough, you'll get a listing of the sizes of any such files that are sitting in your current directory.

In the folder that contains chapters from this book, I typed this:

```
$ grep Devanshu *.doc
```

And got this list of the chapters that contain hacks contributed by Devanshu Mehta;

```
Binary file BBoAH-04-Commandline.doc matches
Binary file BBoAH-06-Network-file.doc matches
Binary file BBoAH-14-Multimedia.doc matches
```

The program works on binary files, as you can see, but it works even better on plain text, including HTML and XML files, where it will show you the line that matches the pattern.

`grep` is a program that searches through a file for a pattern. It actually has a sophisticated way to describe the pattern, called a *regular expression*. Using a regular expression, you can match patterns that involve alternate letters, and classes of letters and numbers. For example, `[sS]hell` matches both "shell" and "Shell," and `[a-z]+` matches any sequence of one or more lowercase letters. Type **man grep** to learn more.

Used in conjunction with the `find` program, it's sort of like using Spotlight, with the disadvantage that it really is best used on text files, and the advantage that it can look for much more complicated patterns. Here's a `find` command that will come up with a list of all the files in a directory (including in the subdirectories) that contain mention of any ISO standard:

```
$ find . -type f -exec grep "ISO [0-9]+" {} \; -print
```

The `find` program sorts through the directories, checking out files, and feeding them to `grep`, which looks for the letters "ISO" followed by one or more digits. Looks like a mess, doesn't it? I use this all the time, but I never type it. Read on to find out how.

Variables and Aliases

A shell has a couple of ways to remember stuff for you: aliases and variables. An alias is a simple way to abbreviate some command you use all the time. For example, I keep the folders of books I'm working on in directories sorted by year. This is convenient, but it makes it annoying to type *~/ tech/08/oreilly/applehacks/draft* repeatedly, and clicking in windows gets old, too. So I can do this:

```
$ alias ah='cd ~/tech/08/oreilly/applehacks/draft'
```

Now, if I type **ah** at the command prompt, I move to that directory immediately. Better yet, I can put that line (not counting the $ which is the command prompt) into a special startup file called *.bash_profile* in my home directory, and the alias will be created whenever Terminal or any other program that runs the Bourne Again Shell starts up.

Shells also have variables you can define. These can substitute for any part of a command. The alias is a nice trick, but it's a little limiting. For something more flexible, I could have done this:

```
$ export WORK=~/tech/08/oreilly/applehacks/draft
$ alias work='cd $WORK'
```

Now when I type:

```
$ work
```

I go right to the directory I want to work in. The $ tells the shell that what follows is a variable name, and that what I want is that variable's value, substituted right here. I can keep the $WORK variable updated, and then typing **work** gets me to where I left off, wherever that was.

Shells define a number of environment variables that make the system work. For example, $HOME is the same as ~, your home directory, usually something like */Users/username*. Your current working directory is defined by a variable called $PWD. When you use the **cd** command, you're changing only the value of that variable. The $PATH variable is an important one, too. It lists a bunch of directories in which the system looks for commands you type. Try this:

```
$ echo $PATH
```

The collection of variables in use at any time is called your *environment*. You can see the whole collection by typing this at the command prompt:

```
$ env
```

There are a lot of possibilities here, limited mostly by your imagination and your desire to spend a little time hacking for convenience's sake.

Avoid Drudgery with Shell Scripting

I'm lazy. Remember that mess of a **find** command a few pages back? Who wants to type that? Not me. Well you don't need to, either. Make a two-line text file that looks like this:

```
#!/bin/bash
find . -type f -exec grep $1 \{\} \; -print
```

Call your new file something like *findfile* and type the following, to tell the shell that it's OK to execute the commands in this file:

```
$ chmod +x findfile
```

Now you can do this:

```
$ ./findfile "ISO [0-9]+"
```

The shell will open up the file, but not before defining a variable called $1 to be equal to ISO [0-9]+. The first line of the file tells the shell to use **bash** to interpret the rest of it. (The default is to use the original Bourne shell, so it might work, but the Bourne Again Shell, **bash**, is much better.) The second line of the script gives the **find** command to execute, including the variable to substitute.

But what's the "./" at the beginning? This has to do with the $PATH variable, a colon-separated list of directories in which the shell looks for commands you type. If a command you type isn't

obviously a pathname, the shell will look through the directories listed in that variable. The ./
business looks enough like a pathname that the shell skips the $PATH and executes the file
straightaway. (In Unixland, the period means the current directory.) By default, the current
directory is not in that list for security reasons. If you have a command you want to use regularly,
you can put it in /usr/local/bin or make a bin directory in your home directory. I did that, and told
the shell to search there for commands by putting this in my .bash_profile startup file:

```
export PATH=~/bin:$PATH
```

I parked my findfile program there, and now I can just type:

```
$ findfile "ISO [0-9]+"
```

Doing Real Work with Loops and Ifs

The cool thing about shell scripts is that the shell is a real programming language, complete with
the control features you expect from any programming language. You've already seen how you can
create variables. Now here are a couple of the missing pieces.

Suppose I want to rename all the Word files in a directory, by sticking "-old" on the end of them all. I
could do this:

```
$ for file in *.doc; do mv $file $file-old; done
```

This loops through all the files found with the ls *.doc command, and uses mv to change their
name by putting −old on the end. Now all the .doc files end in .doc-old. There is a way to sneak
the −old before the .doc part, but you'll have to look it up in the bash manpage. I seldom type
something like this at the command line; I'd more likely put it into a file, where the formatting can
be a little freer.

Recently, I was writing something for a company that changed its name. I had to edit a bunch of
XML files to change a name that appeared a couple of times in each file. There were about 120 of
these files, and the idea of doing them all by hand was appalling. So I wrote a shell script like this:

```
#!/bin/bash
for file in *.xml; do
    mv $file $file.bak;
    sed -e s/OldName/NewName/g $file.bak >$file;
done
```

This loops through all the files, applying the sed command to each one. sed, or "stream edit" is
another astonishingly useful Unix program you didn't know about. It's a text editor that operates
entirely from the command line. Here, it's being used to execute a single substitute command,
changing all occurrences of OldName to NewName.

sed doesn't change the original file, so I changed the name of the original file to add the .bak to the
end, and then sent the output from sed to the original filename. This way I got to pretend to spend
the entire day working on this laborious name change, but in fact it took about three minutes of
work, and I spent the rest of the day napping.

Incidentally, I could have done it this way:

```
#!/bin/bash
for file in *.xml; do
    if (grep −q OldName $file); then
        mv $file $file.bak;
        sed -e s/OldName/NewName/g $file.bak >$file;
    fi;
done
```

This operates only on the files in which `grep` found the `OldName` string inside. Now when I'm done, I've only edited the files that needed editing.

So now you have a scripting language with variables, loops, and conditional statements—everything you need to make scripts to do exactly what you want them to do. This little introduction barely scratches the surface of what's possible within `bash`. There are whole books about `bash` alone, and other books about other shells and other, more elaborate, scripting languages, such as Perl and Python. If you want your scripts to do more, they probably can.

Hacking the Hack

The real power of scripting is getting the computer to do something for you while you do something you really enjoy, like napping or eating. Now that you know how to write a script, how about arranging for it to be run automatically? Mac OS X provides four different ways to do this: two old-fashioned Unix-ish ways and two newfangled Mac ways.

Old-fashioned ways

If you want your program to run at some future time, just once, use the `at` program. Make up a script and name it *test.sh*. (Don't name it "test," because that's a built-in name used by the shell. You'll only make yourself miserable trying to figure out why your program isn't running.) If you can't think of one, use this:

```
#!/bin/bash
echo "hello" >>trash.txt
```

Don't forget to run `chmod +x` on it. When you run the program, it will add a line to the file *trash.txt* that says "hello."

Try typing:

```
$ at -f test.sh 1735
```

Now wait until 5:35 in the afternoon, and look at the *trash.txt* file.

Would you like your script to be run routinely? Use `cron`. The `cron` program looks at a file called *crontab*, which specifies what to do at a particular time. To set up `cron`, you have to create a *crontab* file. To do that, try this at the Terminal prompt:

```
$ export EDITOR=/usr/bin/nano
$ crontab -e
```

This opens up a `nano` editor session, probably on a blank screen. Look at the bottom of the screen for a list of the commands you can use with `nano`. The ^ indicates the Control key, so ^G means to press Ctrl-G.

A *crontab* file contains a time specification and a command. Try this, or something like it:

```
15 * * * * $HOME/test.sh
30 12 * * * $HOME/test.sh
35 12 1 * * $HOME/test.sh
40 12 * * 1-5 $HOME/test.sh
```

The first line tells `cron` to run your job 15 minutes after each hour. The second line tells `cron` to run it at 12:30, every day. The third line says to run it at 12:35 on the first of every month, and the fourth line will run it at 12:40 on weekdays. Type Ctrl-X to exit `nano`, and answer "Yes" when it asks you whether you want to save this work. Each time the job runs, it will add another line to the output file, so you can watch its progress that way.

As you can see, `cron` is pretty flexible about its specifications. It's a little confusing, too. At the Terminal prompt, you can type:

```
$ man 5 crontab
```

This will get you a complete explanation of `cron` files.

New-fangled ways

The problem with `cron` is that your computer probably isn't always on. A program run via `cron` won't be run if the computer is off at that time.

What if you have some job to do but you want it done at a specific time if the computer is on, but you still want it done eventually if the computer is off? (Backups come to mind here.) There are two ways.

First, you can just put your script into one of the directories in */etc/periodic*. There are three: *daily*, *weekly*, and *monthly*. (You will need to be an administrator of your machine to do this. In fact, if you're not an administrator, you should stick to the old-fashioned ways.) These will be run automatically at intervals you can probably guess at. (To be more specific, the daily jobs run at 3:15 in the morning, the weekly jobs run at 3:15 a.m. on Saturday, and the monthly jobs run at 5:30 a.m. on the first of every month.) The scripts in each directory are run in alphabetic order, so if you want one script to be run before another, make sure they are named properly.

If you find this schedule too confining, try checking out `launchd`. This is the modern way to run jobs at whatever intervals you care to specify, but it is way beyond the scope of a hack like this. Type this to read more:

```
$ man launchd
$ man launchd.plist
```

You'll find examples of `launchd` property lists in */System/Library/LaunchDaemons*.

— Tom Sgouros

HACK 33: Fun with MacFUSE, or Mount Nearly Everything as a Virtual Hard Drive

Use Google Mail as your personal storage bin or soup up Spotlight by extending your filesystem to include all sorts of unusual data sources.

A filesystem is a method for storing and organizing computer files to facilitate finding and using them. Many popular filesystems provide a way to access files by maintaining the physical location of the files. This includes Hierarchical File System (HFS+), the preferred filesystem of Mac OS X, in addition to NT File System (NTFS) and (File Allocation Table (FAT32). Filesystems may also be simply act as clients for a network protocol, allowing access to files on a server (e.g., NFS). Finally, there are "virtual" filesystems that provide a way to access data. For example, *procfs* under Unix provides information about processes in a directory-like structure.

MacFUSE makes it possible to implement a fully functional filesystem in a "user-space" program on Mac OS X. This means that the implemented filesystem code can be created and run by nonprivileged users without the need to write kernel code. The File System in Userspace (FUSE) module provides a bridge to the actual kernel. It attempts to be compliant with the original FUSE mechanism that originated on Linux. This allows users to compile and use many popular FUSE filesystems that have been developed on other platforms in addition to new ones built specifically for Mac OS X. This also enables developers to build filesystem definitions that will work on any platform as long as they meet the FUSE specifications.

MacFUSE was developed by Amit Singh, Manager of Macintosh Engineering at Google and is available on the MacFUSE web site hosted by Google Code (http://code.google.com/p/macfuse). MacFUSE requires Mac OS 10.4 Tiger or higher. To install it, download and open the MacFUSE Core package available on the web site. Once the installation is complete, your computer should be ready for some of the available FUSE filesystems. To install some of them, however, you may need the open source packages `pkg-config`, `gettext`, and especially `glib`. These packages can be installed using Fink, MacPorts, or the instructions provided in the *HOWTO* on the MacFUSE web site (http://code.google.com/p/macfuse/wiki/HOWTO).

FTPFS and SSHFS are FUSE filesystems that allow you to mount remote systems accessible using File Transfer Protocol (FTP) or Secure Shell (SSH) on your system. These will seamlessly appear as mounted drives that you can easily drag and drop files from. FTP is a common network protocol used to transfer files; SSH allows for encrypted communication with remote machines. SSHFS will allow you to securely mount a remote filesystem (such as the one on a file server at work, school, or the one hosting your web site) to transfer or access files using the SSH protocol. SSHFS is available on the MacFUSE web site and is easy to use with a fairly basic graphical user interface.

Normally, under Mac OS X, drives formatted with NTFS are read-only. NTFS is the favored format for modern Windows systems (including Macs running Boot Camp) and may be one that you come across quite often. The ntfs-3g FUSE file system allows you to read from and write to an NTFS drive.

Use Gmail for File Storage

> If you're a heavy user with lots of items to transfer, don't use Gmail for file storage. Storing files on Google is one of the behaviors that will get your account flagged, and you'll lose access for up to 24 hours.

There are also some very interesting virtual filesystems such as WikipediaFS and GmailFS. WikipediaFS allows you to virtually mount Wikipedia on your computer so that you can browse to different articles or edit them as if they were files on your computer. So, instead of browsing to http://en.wikipedia.org/wiki/Apple and clicking edit, you could simply open */Volumes/ WikipediaFS/Apple* in your favorite text editor and have the changes appear on the Wikipedia. GmailFS allows you to store files in your Gmail storage. Similarly, filesystems for many online services such as PicasaWeb, Flickr, RSS feeds, and Google docs have been created.

To prepare your system for the GmailFS (and many other popular FUSE filesystems), you need to install the following, in addition to MacFUSE:

Python 2.4 or higher
This can be installed using MacPorts or Fink.

Python-FUSE bindings
Also available in MacPorts (install *fuse-bindings-python*) and Fink (install *fuse-py24* or *fuse-py25*).

libgmail
Available through MacPorts (install *py-libgmail*) and Fink (install *libgmail-py24* or *libgmail-py25*).

GmailFS

Available through Fink and directly from the developer's web site (http://richard.jones.name/
google-hacks/gmail-filesystem/gmail-filesystem.html).

Since all of these components are available through Fink, that would be the easiest way to install
GmailFS. If you already use MacPorts and are comfortable with it, you may install everything up
to `libgmail` using MacPorts. After that, you can download the latest version of GmailFS from the
developer's web site.

If you have installed GmailFS using Fink, you can skip these instructions. Once you have
downloaded it from the web site, you will have to open it and move the source files from the
command line in Terminal as follows:

```
$ tar -zxvf  gmailfs-0.8.0.tar.gz
$ cd gmailfs-0.8.0/
```

The number 0.8.0 represents the version of GmailFS, which may change in the future. The following
commands may prompt you for your OS X password:

```
$ sudo mv gmailfs.py /usr/local/bin/gmailfs.py
$ sudo mv mount.gmailfs /sbin/mount_gmail
```

Now you should have a working GmailFS installation, except for one last thing. In the *gmailfs-0.8.0*
directory, there will be a file called *gmailfs.conf*. Edit this file in your favorite text editor to change
these lines:

```
[account]
username = gmailusername
password = gmailpassword
```

Set **gmailusername** to your actual Gmail username and **gmailpassword** to your Gmail password.
Then save this file in the */private/etc* directory of your computer (you'll need to use **sudo**). It is
time to try moving files to the storage space of your Gmail account. In Terminal, enter the following
commands:

```
$ mkdir ~/gmailfs
$ mount -ovolname=bla -o username=gmailuser -o password=gmailpass \
  -o fsname=z0lRRa -t gmailfs /usr/local/bin/gmailfs.py ~/gmailfs
```

This mounts your Gmail account in your home directory at */Users/yourosxusername/gmailfs*. (On
the command line, ~ stands for your home directory.)

Now, if the last command was successful, any files you move to the *~/gmailfs/* directory will be
stored in your Gmail account. You can access this through Finder, where your Gmail space should
also appear as a mounted drive or through the command line.

The files you store on your Gmail drive will appear as strange emails in your Inbox. This is normal
but may not be the desired effect. To make sure these emails do not show up in your Inbox, you can
create a filter in Gmail to send every email that matches the search string z0lRRa directly to your
archived email. The string z0lRRa is what is used in the **mount** command above as your filesystem
name and can be replaced with any other word of your choice.

To install WikipediaFS, you will also need Python 2.4 or higher and the Python-FUSE bindings. As
described above, these can be installed using Fink, MacPorts, or directly from the source, if you are
so inclined.

WikipediaFS is not currently available through Fink or MacPorts, and so needs to be installed manually. The package is available at the developer's web site (http://wikipediafs.sourceforge.net/) along with instructions for its use.

Get More Out of Spotlight

SpotlightFS is one of the more interesting FUSE filesystems developed for Mac OS X. It is also one of the first that was made available. SpotlightFS creates true Spotlight-driven smart folders, in which the contents of the folders are generated on the fly. These are more powerful than the built-in Mac OS X smart folders because they are actual folders. In Mac OS X, the smart folders are actually XML files that run your Spotlight query when opened. The advantage of having actual folders is that they can be used from any other application, including the command line. SpotlightFS can be obtained from the Downloads section of the MacFUSE web site. Once the disk image is installed, you should be able to use it immediately by launching *SpotlightFS.app*.

There are two fundamental ways to use SpotlightFS. The easiest is to use *SmarterFolders*, which, as the name suggests, are smarter than the smart folders that Mac OS X provides. These are folders that do not need to be created, just accessed, in order to view their contents. Once you are running SpotlightFS, click on Go→Open Folder in Finder and type in */Volumes/SpotlightFS/SmarterFolder/apple*. This will bring you to a virtual folder that contains all the files returned by the Spotlight query "apple". This allows you to use smart folders ad hoc, without creating them in advance and to use them in a variety of applications. From the command line, you can type:

```
$ ls -lrt /Volumes/SpotlightFS/SmarterFolder/apple
```

This lists all the files returned by the Spotlight query "apple". If you are fluent with the command line, you can come up with many ways to perform bulk operations on similar files using SpotlightFS.

The second way to use SpotlightFS is to actually create a directory under */Volumes/SpotlightFS* with the search string you are interested in. For example, you can create a directory called *Apple Hacks*, which will behave similarly to smart folders in Mac OS X, but as a real folder. At the command line, you can type:

```
$ mkdir /Volumes/SpotlightFS/Apple\ Hacks/
$ ls -lrt /Volumes/SpotlightFS/Apple\ Hacks/
```

FUSE provides many ways to make data more useful and accessible, in addition to providing implementations to filesystems that have historically not been supported under Mac OS X. While experimenting with virtual file systems is fairly harmless, make sure you have backed up your data and read the instructions carefully before you use fully functional filesystems such as `ntfs-3g`.

— Devanshu Mehta

HACK 34: Starting and Stopping Unix Daemons

If you're used to the Unix and Linux way of starting up and stopping daemons, you are probably wondering why Mac OS X has nothing resembling an *init.d* directory.

Although Mac OS X 10.4 introduced a great facility, `launchd`, for starting and stopping daemons, there are some good reasons to use the approach used in Mac OS X 10.3 and earlier: `StartupItems`. This is because many of the Unix programs you are likely to find in the wild (or write yourself) do things the old-school Unix way, which is likely to annoy `launchd`. For example, the *launchd.plist(5)* manpage specifically warns against using `launchd` with applications that call `daemon` (a Unix utility that spawns a program that runs without a user) or act like it (by spawning a sub-program and exiting, for example).

What's more, `launchd` would prefer that you don't do any of these things:

- Setup the user ID or group ID.

- Setup the working directory.

- chroot(2).

- setsid(2).

- Close "stray" file descriptors.

- Change stdio(3) to /dev/null.

- Setup resource limits with setrusage(2).

- Setup priority with setpriority(2).

- Ignore the SIGTERM signal.

It's possible to modify many Unix daemons to behave themselves under `launchd`. If you peruse the Darwin source code at http://www.opensource.apple.com/darwinsource/, you'll find `launchd`-specific patches for many of the Unix daemons, such as OpenSSH and `cron`. For example, Apple's source code for `cron.c` contains this little snippet to make everything `launchd`-safe:

```
#ifdef __APPLE__
/* Don't daemonize when run by launchd */
   if (getppid() != 1 && daemon(1, 0) == -1) {
#else
   if (daemon(1, 0) == -1) {
#endif
```

As time goes on, you'll probably find that very popular open source packages will incorporate Apple's patches into their official code releases. So if you've read the *launchd(8)* and *launchd. plist(5)* manpages, and are certain that your daemon will play by Apple's rules, then by all means, use `launchd`. For more information on `launchd`, see "Creating launchd Daemons and Agents" at: http://tinyurl.com/27l9mg.

However, there's one more advantage of using `StartupItems`: although `launchd` knows how to kill a process, you can't specify an explicit shutdown routine to be triggered when you're powering the system down. However, `StartupItems` can handle it.

Consider the MySQL database server: to start it up, you use a program called `mysqld_safe`, which in turn starts the MySQL database server. However, to shut it down, you issue the command `mysqladmin shutdown`. If you use `launchd` to manage starting up and shutting down MySQL, it's going to kill the MySQL server in a less-than-graceful manner. If you use `StartupItems`, you can define how the process gets shut down.

A startup item is controlled by three things: a folder (such as */Library/StartupItems/MyItem*), a shell script with the same name as the directory (such as *MyItem*), and a property list named *StartupParameters.plist*. The shell script and the property list must appear at the top level of the startup item's folder. You can also create a *Resources* directory to hold localized resources, but this is not mandatory.

To set up a MySQL startup item, create the directory */Library/StartupItems/MySQL* as root [Hack #5] Then, create two files in that directory: the startup script *MySQL* and the property list *StartupParameters.plist*. The *MySQL* file must be an executable because it is a shell script:

```
$ sudo mkdir /Library/StartupItems/MySQL
$ sudo touch /Library/StartupItems/MySQL/MySQL
$ sudo touch /Library/StartupItems/MySQL/StartupParameters.plist
$ sudo chmod +x /Library/StartupItems/MySQL/MySQL
```

After you put the right information into these two files as directed in the following sections, MySQL is launched at each boot. Use your favorite text-only editor to edit these files and put the information into them. Because the files are owned by root, you will have to authenticate to use them. Smultron and TextMate are two editors that will allow you to authenticate in order to edit them; if you use vi at the Terminal, you can run it under sudo, as in **sudo vi /Library/ StartupItems/MySQL/MySQL**.

The Startup Script

The startup script should be a shell script with StartService(), StopService(), and RestartService() functions. The contents of */Library/StartupItems/MySQL/MySQL* are shown in the next listing. The function call at the bottom of the script invokes the RunService() function from */etc/rc.common* (this is a file that is part of Mac OS X), which in turn invokes StartService(), StopService(), or RestartService(), depending on whether the script was invoked with an argument of start, stop, or restart.

```
#!/bin/sh

# Source common setup, including hostconfig.
#
. /etc/rc.common

StartService()
{
  # Don't start unless MySQL is enabled in /etc/hostconfig
  if [ "${MYSQL:=-NO-}" = "-YES-" ]; then
    ConsoleMessage "Starting MySQL"
    /usr/local/mysql/bin/mysqld_safe --user=mysql &
  fi
}

StopService()
{
  ConsoleMessage "Stopping MySQL"
  # If you've set a root password within mysql, you may
  # need to add --password=password on the next line.
  /usr/local/mysql/bin/mysqladmin shutdown
}

RestartService()
{
  # Don't restart unless MySQL is enabled in /etc/hostconfig
  if [ "${MYSQL:=-NO-}" = "-YES-" ]; then
    ConsoleMessage "Restarting MySQL"
    StopService
    StartService
  else
```

```
      StopService
   fi
}


  RunService "$1"
```

Because it consults the settings of the $MYSQL environment variable, the startup script won't do anything unless you've enabled MySQL in the */etc/hostconfig* file. To do this, edit */etc/hostconfig* in a text editor, and add this line:

```
SQL=-YES-
```

Mac OS X does not recognize any special connections between *hostconfig* entries and startup scripts. Instead, the startup script sources the */etc/rc.common* file, which in turn sources *hostconfig*. The directives in *hostconfig* are merely environment variables, and the startup script checks the value of the variables that control its behavior (in this case, $MYSQL).

The Property List

The property list (*StartupParameters.plist*) can be in XML or NeXT format, and the list contains attributes that describe the item and determine its place in the startup sequence. The NeXT format uses NeXTSTEP-style property lists, as shown in the following example:

```
{
  Description = "MySQL";
  Provides = ("MySQL");
  Requires = ("Network");
  OrderPreference = "Late";
}
```

The XML format adheres to the *PropertyList.dtd* Document Type Definition (DTD). You can use your favorite text editor or the Property List Editor (*/Developer/Applications/Utilities*) to create your own property list. Here is the property list in XML:

```
<?xml version="1.0" encoding="UTF-8"?>
<!DOCTYPE plist
SYSTEM "file://localhost/System/Library/DTDs/PropertyList.dtd">
<plist version="0.9">
  <dict>
  <key>Description</key>
  <string>MySQL</string>
  <key>Provides</key>
  <array>
    <string>MySQL</string>
  </array>
  <key>Requires</key>
  <array>
    <string>Network</string>
  </array>
  <key>OrderPreference</key>
  <string>Late</string>
  </dict>
</plist>
```

The following list describes the various keys you can use in a startup parameters property list:

Description
This is a phrase that describes the item.

Provides

This is an array of services that the item provides (e.g., Apache provides Web Server). These services should be globally unique. In the event that SystemStarter finds two items that provide the same service, it starts the first one it finds.

Requires

This is an array of services that the item depends on. It should correspond to another item's `Provides` attribute. If a required service cannot be started, the system won't start the item.

Uses

This is similar to `Requires`, but it is a weaker association. If SystemStarter can find a matching service, it will start it. If it can't, the dependent item still starts.

OrderPreference

The `Requires` and `Uses` attributes imply a particular order, in that dependent items will be started after the services they depend on. You can specify `First`, `Early`, `None` (the default), `Late`, or `Last` here. SystemStarter does its best to satisfy this preference, but dependency orders prevail.

You can now manually start, restart, and stop MySQL by invoking SystemStarter from the command line:

```
$ sudo SystemStarter start MySQL
$ sudo SystemStarter restart MySQL
$ sudo SystemStarter stop MySQL
```

— Brian Jepson

HACK 35: Image Management with ImageMagick

Bulk process, transform, and otherwise manage your images with this extremely useful batch image-processing tool.

ImageMagick is an extraordinarily powerful open source package that contains many different utilities to edit and create images. With a single typed command, you can rotate, resize, merge, convert, and subtitle an entire collection of images in precisely consistent ways. You can get started right away—once you've installed ImageMagick—with fairly simple commands, such as the first `convert` example below. But once you get comfortable with it, it could even replace your trusty (bloated!) image editor.

To install ImageMagick, you will need either Fink, MacPorts [Hack #31] or install the Mac OS X Binary available on the ImageMagick web site (http://www.imagemagick.org).

Each of these commands needs to be run on the command line in an application like Terminal. To explore any command in detail, you can either use `man` (e.g., `man convert`) on the command line or visit the extensive ImageMagick help documents on the web site.

Converting File Formats

With ImageMagick, converting the file format is as simple as giving it a new file extension:

```
$ convert flower.jpg flower.png
```

Replace png with gif or the extension for any other supported image format (there are around a hundred) to convert it to that format.

Create Thumbnails in an Instant

Creating thumbnails of images in most image editors requires a few clicks, and editing them in bulk is harder than pulling each hair out of your scalp individually.

With ImageMagick, it is much simpler:

```
$ convert flower.jpg -resize 50% flower50.jpg
```

That changes the image *flower.jpg* to 50% its original size and names the newly created file *flower50.jpg*. The convert command always creates a new image file, and the last argument supplied to it is the new filename:

```
$ convert flower.jpg -resize 50x50 flower5050.jpg
```

The previous command creates a 50 x 50 thumbnail version of *flower.jpg*. You can combine different ImageMagick options, for example, to resize and convert the image format:

```
$ convert flower.jpg -resize 50% flower50.png
```

Rotate a Set of Images

Rotating an image is just as simple. The following example (also see Figure 4-6) will rotate *flower. jpg* 30 degrees in the clockwise direction. The output image will be larger than the input, so that it can contain the entire original image, rotated.

```
$ convert flower.jpg -rotate 30 flower30r.jpg
```

Figure 4-6.
Rotated 30 degrees via the command line

Of course, it is more likely that you will want to rotate your photograph by 90 or 270 degrees, but no one is stopping you from being quirky.

To Add a Subtitle or Text Caption

Sometimes you just want to add a little text to your image. This can be done with most GUI image editing tools, but not quite as simply as with ImageMagick—especially if you want to add the same text to many images. Examples of such a situation would be a watermark with the source of the image, a subtitle with the album name or a copyright notice.

```
$ convert flower.jpg -draw 'text 10,10 "Nifty Text!"' flowerNifty.jpg
```

This command adds the text "Nifty Text!" to the image *flower.jpg* at the coordinates (10,10), which are calculated from the top-left corner. You can even specify font and point size to make your text more or less pronounced (see Figure 4-7).

```
$ convert flower.jpg  -font Courier-Regular -pointsize 35 \
-stroke white -draw 'text 40,40 "Nifty Text!"'  flowerNifty.jpg
```

Figure 4-7.
Add text to your image

With practice, you will be able to combine all of these tools without giving it much thought.

Create a Text Banner

Creating a banner in ImageMagick is also fairly simple. You can use the `convert` command without an actual source file to make one. The command synthesizes the banner on its own (see Figure 4-8).

```
$ convert -size 200x40 xc:transparent -font Courier-Regular \
  -pointsize 20 -channel RGBA -gaussian 0x6 -fill darkred \
  -stroke magenta -draw 'text 10,30 "My Nifty Banner!' \
  nifty-magick.png
```

Figure 4-8.
Generate a banner

This example will create a new transparent image sized 200 x 40, and type the magenta text "My Nifty Banner!" at coordinates (10,30). You can see how far you can get with a few options, and the `convert` command has many more.

Create a Montage

ImageMagick also comes with the `montage` command, which allows you to create—you guessed it—a montage of all the images you specify. In addition to simply creating a montage, you can give it a background, border and each image a caption (Figure 4-9).

```
$ montage -background gray -border 1 -label %f *.jpg montage.jpg
```

Figure 4-9.
Everyone loves a montage

This command is almost self-explanatory, but in case you don't agree, it creates a montage of every image that ends with *.jpg* in the current directory (`*jpg`), with a gray background and calls it *montage.jpg*. The `-label %f` gives each image a label with its filename, and `-border 1` gives each image a thin border.

Get Information About an Image

Simply type the following to get some basic information about an image:

```
$ identify flower.jpg
```

This gives you basic information such as:

```
flower.jpg JPEG 1024x859 1024x859+0+0 DirectClass 8-bit 347.061kb
```

To get a really large amount of information, including EXIF data from your digital camera, try the following:

```
$ identify -verbose flower.jpg
```

You can even pull out individual pieces of information from the file:

```
$ identify -format "%f %wx%h\n" *.jpg
```

This command displays only the information we requested (%f is the filename, %w width, %h height) in the format specified. The output would be as follows:

```
flower.jpg 1024x859
flower270r.jpg 859x1024
flower30r.jpg 1316x1255
flower50.jpg 512x430
flower5050.jpg 50x42
flower90r.jpg 859x1024
flowerNifty.jpg 512x430
montage.jpg 520x288
```

Bulk Actions on Image Files

In many cases, the *.jpg type wildcard will suffice to perform actions on a large number of files. For example:

```
$ mogrify -resize 200x200 *.jpg
```

This resizes every single JPEG image in the directory to a 200 x 200 size and retain their name. The mogrify command is similar to convert, except that it overwrites the original image, so be careful. If you want to create a new file, you can use the convert command mentioned earlier, but in order to use convert on a large number of files, you will have to script a bit:

```
for image in *.jpg
do
  convert $image -resize 200x200 size200-$image
done
```

This should be easy to read if you have written a shell script before [Hack #32]. Basically, it takes every JPEG file in the current directory, resizes it to 200 x 200 and renames it with the prefix size200-. Edit it and test it on some images you can afford to mangle. This is great for creating thumbnails for a web site or smaller sized images to email.

Once you become more familiar with scripting languages, you can easily use ImageMagick as part of a much larger program or repeatable script to automate actions tedious processes.

— Devanshu Mehta

The Unix and Mac OS X worlds are not so far apart as you might imagine. You can bridge them easily if you know the correct incantations.

Mac OS X and Unix seem like an odd pairing at first. Mac OS X is slick, intuitive, and for the most part, pretty friendly. Unix is, at least at first, looks gritty, counterintuitive (you want me to `grep` my what?), and surly at times. But just because they have really different personalities doesn't mean they can't cooperate nicely. Here are a few tricks you can use from the command line to bridge the two.

AppleScript

Mac OS X has a couple of spiffy new ways to automate things in Mac OS X: Automator and Quartz Composer. While both are fantastic, AppleScript has been with Mac OS since before the days of Mac OS X, and many applications support AppleScript automation. Apple made it really easy to issue AppleScript commands from the Terminal with the `osascript` command. Just give `osascript` the name of a script file, or use the `-e` option to run an AppleScript one-liner:

```
$ osascript -e 'say "Hello world"'
```

You can use - and a special shell quoting style called the "here-doc" to pump a short script into `osascript` (the - tells `osascript` to read a script from the shell's standard input, and everything between <<EOF; and EOF is treated as that input):

```
$ osascript - <<EOF;
tell application "Finder"
  activate
  open folder "Applications" of startup disk
end tell
EOF
```

Clipboard

If you're doing a lot of work at the command line, you might eventually produce some output you need to paste into another program, such as a spreadsheet or an email message. You can highlight output in the Terminal window and use the usual copy/paste shortcuts, but you could also pipe the output into the clipboard. For example, you could put a list of all processes running on your Mac into the clipboard with this command:

```
$ ps -ef | pbcopy
```

Similarly, if you want to send the contents of your clipboard into a Unix command, you can use `pbpaste`. This would search the contents of the clipboard for any lines that contain numbers of the form `nn:nn` (such as timestamps like 08:30):

```
$ pbpaste | grep '[0-9][0-9]:[0-9][0-9]'
```

Some applications, such as Microsoft Word, store their text in the clipboard in a Unix-unfriendly format (using the old classic Mac OS line endings of a single carriage return). You can fix this with a trip through Perl (behaving here a lot like the `sed` utility and replacing `\r`, the carriage return with `\n`, the linefeed):

```
$ pbpaste | perl -pe 's/\r/\n/g' | grep '[0-9][0-9]:[0-9][0-9]'
```

Open

Want to open something? How about a file or folder? This will open it in the Finder:

```
$ open ~/Music
```

You can open applications with the -a switch:

```
$ open -a iTunes
```

open has a bunch of cool options, so be sure to check out its manpage by typing **man open** at the Terminal.

QuickLook

You can pop QuickLook up from the Terminal, too. To display a file:

```
$ qlmanage -p flower.jpg
```

You can also display a group of files:

```
$ qlmanage -p *jpg
```

Spotlight

You can perform Spotlight searches from the shell. To search for a term:

```
$ mdfind N95
```

If you know where you want to search, use the -onlyin option (try changing N95 to the model of camera or camera phone you use):

```
$ mdfind -onlyin ~/Pictures N95
```

You can also use Spotlight's keywords:

```
$ mdfind "kMDItemComposer == '*Garcia*'"
```

Here's how to inspect a file's Spotlight metadata:

```
$ mdls ~/Pictures/iChat\ Icons/Planets/Pluto\ and\ Charon.gif
```

Take a Screenshot from the Command Line

You can take a screenshot with the screencapture utility. Provide the filename you want, and it will be created:

```
$ screencapture cap.png
```

You can even invoke screencapture remotely, when you're not logged into the computer. [Hack #37] explains how.

— Brian Jepson

5

CUSTOMIZING THE OS X LOOK AND FEEL

Customizing the Macintosh operating system has been one of the most enjoyable hacking experiences for Mac users since the earliest days of the Macintosh. This isn't a surprise. By and large Mac users don't follow the herd (they'd use Windows if they did), and they put a premium on individuality. This chapter explores ways to personalize your Mac. For bonus points, it turns out that some of these touches of personalization also make your Mac more useful.

HACK 37: Customize the Login Window

It's your computer; you should be able to personalize the machine in any particular manner you wish. Here's how to use the Terminal, Nano, and Interface Builder to add an entire new level of customization to your set up.

One thing that classic Mac operating systems had over Mac OS X was the ability (with a little manipulation of a *resource fork*) to change the startup screen. Some may argue that losing the ability to easily change the startup screen is a small price to pay for protected memory and a delicious GUI, but the old-school users among us still yearn for the days when a black-and-white representation of Cyndi Lauper was displayed as our faithful compact Macs booted to life. While you can't change the startup screen as easily in Mac OS X, you can modify the login window until that feeling of calm contentment returns.

Let's begin by adding a bit of text to the login window. The text can be anything you like (within reason, the login window is only so big), but for this hack I'm just going to use the text "This User Has Too Much Free Time" Deciding on text was easy, now to modify the login window. Start up the Terminal program (it's located in the Utilities folder underneath the Applications folder).

The first file you'll need to muck with is *com.apple.loginwindow.plist*, but before you do, you need to make a backup of that file. A good place to store the backup (temporarily) is the Desktop, but any place will do. If you decide to go with the Desktop, the command would look something like:

```
$ cp /Library/Preferences/com.apple.loginwindow.plist ~/Desktop
```

The $ represents the Terminal prompt; don't type the $.

What is going on in this command is pretty simple. You're telling the Terminal to copy (**cp**) the file at */Library/Preferences/com.apple.loginwindow.plist* to a new destination: */Users/username/*

Desktop ("~" is a Unix shortcut that equals *Users/yourusername/* and saves a copious amount of typing when you're using the Terminal). In my case, the username would be `cks`; in your case it will likely be something different (unless you're named Chuck Kevin Simpson or something). In any event, you'll know the backup was successfully created when a new item shows up on your Desktop named *com.apple.loginwindow.plist*.

Once you have the backup safely ensconced, you can get serious about tweaking the original. You can't just open the file with any text editor and change it because, for one thing, the file is binary. That means it's time to turn back to our good friend the Terminal. The next thing you'll need to do is translate the file to something you can edit. The Terminal can do the heavy lifting for you with the aid of the `plutil` command:

```
$ sudo plutil -convert xml1 /Library/Preferences/com.apple.loginwindow.plist
```

Since you're prefixing the command with `sudo` (this gives you the elevated privileges needed to modify the file), you'll be asked for your password and given a bit of a warning, as shown in Figure 5-1 (this warning only appears the first time you run `sudo`; you won't see it again).

Figure 5-1.
Has someone been watching Spider Man?

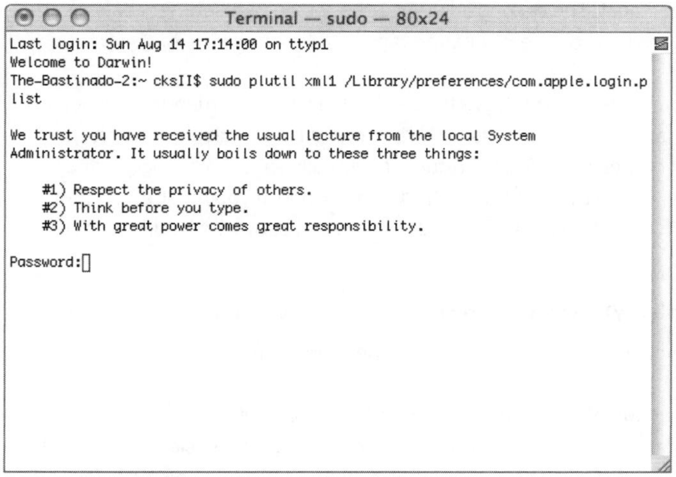

```
● ○ ○                Terminal — sudo — 80x24
Last login: Sun Aug 14 17:14:00 on ttyp1
Welcome to Darwin!
The-Bastinado-2:~ cksII$ sudo plutil xml1 /Library/preferences/com.apple.login.p
list

We trust you have received the usual lecture from the local System
Administrator. It usually boils down to these three things:

    #1) Respect the privacy of others.
    #2) Think before you type.
    #3) With great power comes great responsibility.

Password:[]
```

The file is now readable by Nano, a Unix text editor that you use from the Terminal's command line. To open the file with Nano, enter the following command:

```
$ sudo nano /Library/Preferences/com.apple.loginwindow.plist
```

✉ Nano used to be Pico, and you can still start Nano by typing `pico` at the $ prompt.

This is seemingly a
monumentally useless
hack for anyone but
someone writing a book
or putting together an
instruction manual.
That said, I've received
plenty of questions
about how to snap
pictures of the login
window. It is a good
question, since none
of the usual options
(command keys, Grab
or Skitch) work when
you're logging in. You'll
need two Macs to
pull this off, and if you
want to do it the easy
way, both need to be
running Leopard. If your
machines are Leopard-
endowed, enable screen
sharing (go to System
Preferences→Sharing,
check the box next to
Screen Sharing), select
the computer's screen
you want to share from
the Finder window
sidebar, and the Finder
window will change a
little. You'll see a "Share
Screen..." button in the
upper right corner. Click
the "Share Screen..."
button, authenticate,
and a new window
will open showing you
exactly what is on the
remote computer's
screen. This isn't just
voyeurism; you'll also
get a lot of control over
the remote computer
when you share the
screen.

*Continued on next
page...*

The Terminal now looks something like that shown in Figure 5-2.

Figure 5-2.
If your screen looks like the screenshot, you are ready to add a bit of personal text to the login window

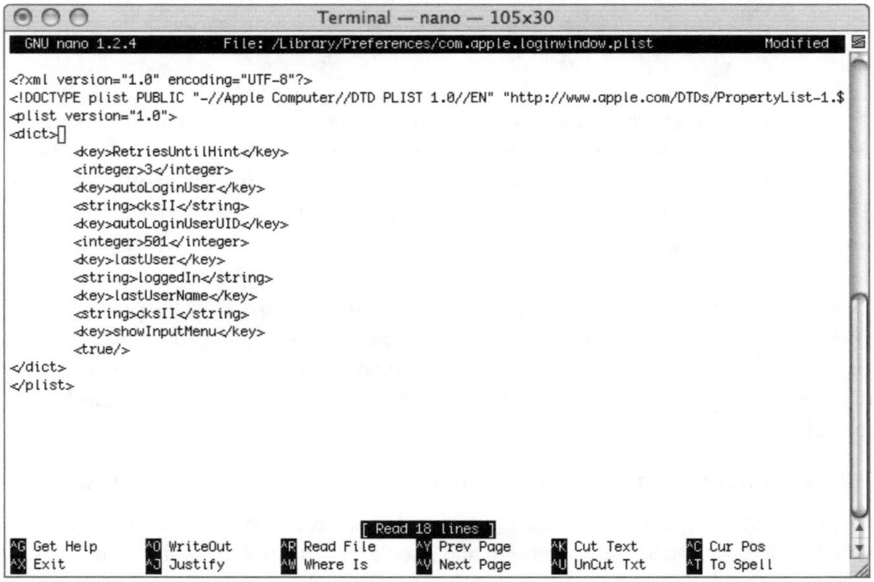

Move the cursor so that it's positioned after **<dict>** (move the cursor around with the arrow keys in Pico), and hit return. Now type the following:

```
<key>LoginwindowText</key>
<string> This User Has Too Much Free Time</string>
```

Note that the first line (**<key>**) is not negotiable; it has to be there because that's what the system looks for to see what it should do next. The second line is your opportunity to let the real you come through! Well, as long as you keep it inside the **<string>** tags.

With those two lines added, your next step is to save the file. In Nano, the commands are invoked by pressing the Control key (that is what "^" means at the bottom of Nano's display), so hit Ctrl-O to save (or "WriteOut" in Nano-speak) the file. Hit return (to actually save the changes), and the modded file is now in place. Follow this by hitting Ctrl-X to exit Nano. If you recall earlier, you converted the file from binary form with **plutil**. If you'd like, you can convert it back with **plutil**, with the following command:

```
$ sudo plutil -convert binary1 /Library/Preferences/com.apple.loginwindow.plist
```

Now, the next time you log in, you'll see something like that shown in Figure 5-4.

If you're using a pre-Leopard version of Mac OS X, the method is similar but more cumbersome. The trick is to set up a SSH connection **[Hack #53]** between the machines. The easiest way to do this is to check the box next to Remote Login in the System Preferences→Sharing pane (see Figure 5-3). Once you've told the remote Mac you want to enable remote login, the pane will display the information you need to type in the Terminal to log in. Just so you know, you'll also need the password for the user account.

Figure 5-3.
The Sharing Pane will tell you how to log in via the Terminal

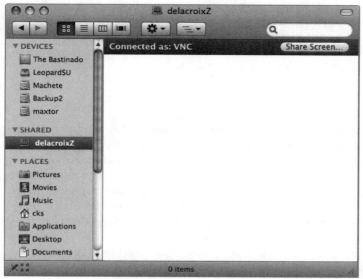

Continued from previous page...

To get a snap of the login window, log out of the account if someone is logged in (yes, you can log out on the remote computer via screen sharing). You'll get a lost connection message from *Screen Sharing.app* but the connection will be restored automatically, so don't worry. Once the login screen appears, snap the login screen with your favorite utility.

Once that is done, use the command-line screen capture utility to capture the screen of the target Mac. A typical command might look like this:

```
$ sudo screencapture -tjpg logwindow.jpg
```

The `sudo` program elevates the permissions of the command (`screencapture`, a utility that takes a snapshot of the screen) that follows it. The `-t` option sets the format for the image (I've chosen a JPG format), and `logwindow.jpg` instructs `screencapture` about how to name the resulting image file. And where will that image end up? The image shows up on the remote computer in whatever directory you were in when you issued the command to capture the screen (likely your Home folder). Because you had to run the `screencapture` command using `sudo`, the file will be owned by the root user, so you can use this command to make it yours:

```
$ sudo chown yourusername logwindow.jpg
```

Figure 5-4.
The text you added appears in the login window

Unhacking the Hack

If you've grown tired of your custom verbiage in the login window, undoing the change is no problem. Just locate the backup you made of the file at the beginning of this hack and move it to the Preferences folder found in your Library folder. Easy stuff! Wait, you didn't bother to actually make a backup? No problem. Repeat the process exactly as before, but instead of adding text with Nano, delete the `<key>` and `<string>` lines you added. Save the file as described, and you're back to login window boredom.

Hacking the Hack

Somehow a custom banner just doesn't seem like enough. You're using a Mac, so you probably appreciate the visual aspect of Mac OS X. So let's take this hack to the next level and add some visual customization to the login window. This is going to be a serious hack, so first you need to do a little prehack preparation. Create or choose a TIFF that is 90 × 90 pixels with a resolution of 72 dpi. In the example, I am using a picture of my son that goes with the text I added earlier, but any image you find pleasing will, of course, do. Name the image something that won't conflict with any of the filenames already used in the folder, and move your newly chosen file to the Resources folder. If you're thinking "Hey, just how do I know what files are already in the Resource folder?", you're thinking ahead. You're not going to get into trouble using an obscure name, but you don't want to overwrite any of the existing files right? You could dig through the folder hierarchy, but the answer comes more quickly with a trip to the Terminal. First get to the target directory with (make sure you don't put any spaces in the name of the target directory; you need to type this all on one line):

```
$ cd /System/Library/CoreServices/SecurityAgentPlugins/loginwindow.bundle
/Contents/Resources
```

Follow that up with the ever useful:

```
$ ls
```

This shows you the list of filenames to avoid (see Figure 5-5).

Figure 5-5.
Avoid replacing a file: know the names!

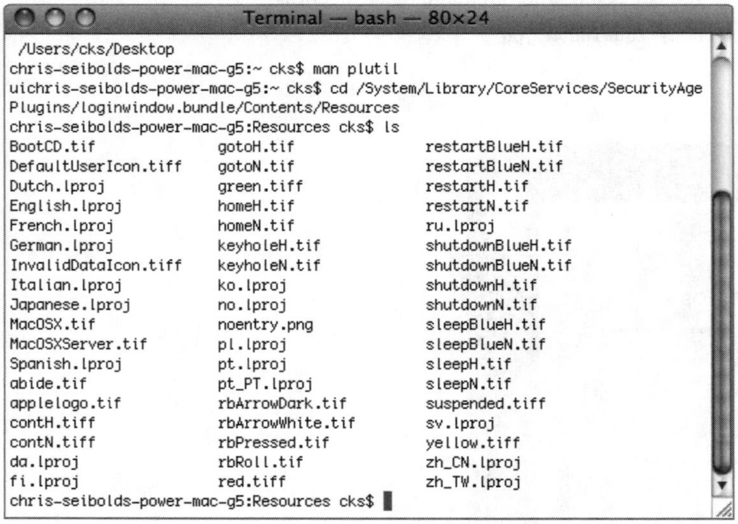

Well you probably wouldn't have picked *rbPressed.tif* out of the thin air, but if you're a big ColdPlay fan, *yellow.tiff* might have been a reasonable (but unfortunate) choice. Now that you know the names to avoid it is time to create your new image. Remember, 90 × 90 TIFF format; use your image editor of choice. If you don't have an image editor of choice one viable option comes built-in to Leopard: an application named Preview. Just open up the file you want to use in Preview, and edit away. The same rules still apply.

With the new image created, everything is in place. Put the new image in the proper location. Here you can burrow through folders and packages, or you can use the Terminal. The Terminal is much quicker. Using the Terminal, the drill is as follows. First, save the TIFF file on your Desktop; then (type this all on one line with no space between `SecurityAgentPlugins/` and `loginwindow.bundle`):

```
$ sudo cp ~/Desktop/abide.tif /System/Library/CoreServices/SecurityAgentPlugins/
loginwindow.bundle/Contents/Resources/
```

Where *abide.tif* is the source file. Everything after that is the destination folder.

Next, you'll need to modify the *LoginWindowUI.nib* file, which contains the layout of the login window. First, you need to create a working copy of this file and also back it up. The command to make the copy is as follows (type the command all on one line, and don't put a space between `loginwindow.bundle` and `Contents`):

```
$ cp -R /System/Library/CoreServices/SecurityAgentPlugins/loginwindow.bundle/
Contents/Resources/English.lproj/LoginWindowUI.nib ~/Desktop
```

After you hit return, you'll note that there is a new .*nib* file on your desktop named *LoginWindowUI. nib*. Now make a backup copy of this file, and place it somewhere it can remain untouched by hacking hands. Now double-click on the Desktop copy of *LoginWindowUI.nib*, and Interface Builder will open the file (make sure you've installed Xcode as described in **[Hack #3]** before you do this). You'll see a couple of unintuitive windows, as shown in Figure 5-6.

Figure 5-6.
The default windows of Interface Builder

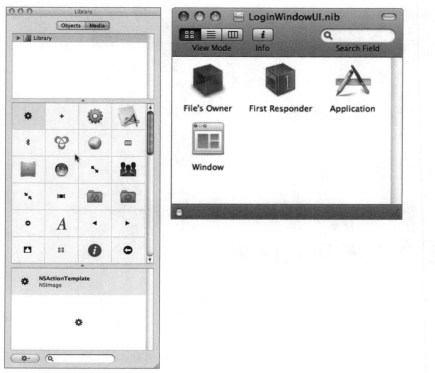

Here things get a little tricky. Double-click the Window icon, and a window will pop open (see Figure 5-7).

Figure 5-7.
Editing the login window

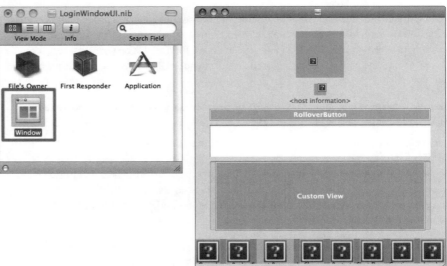

You can't tell easily by looking, but the window that opens is a representation of the login window. Once you see that, it is pretty easy to guess that *applelogo* is the big square in the middle. Single-click the square, and select Inspector from the Tools menu of Interface builder. If everything has gone properly, you should see windows on your desktop that resemble Figure 5-8.

Figure 5-8.
The Image View Attributes window

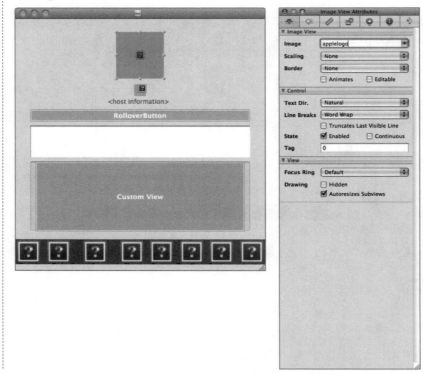

Note the text box next to the "Image" title was set to "applelogo." If you change "applelogo" to the name of some other TIFF file in the Resources folder (I've used one called *abide.tif*), the login window will display that image instead. For example, if you changed it to *contH.tiff*, you would see a continue button instead of the Apple logo.

Type in the name of the graphic you saved to the Resources Folder earlier. Go to File → Save to save the *.nib* file, and then quit Interface Builder with Command-Q. Now copy or drag your hacked copy of *LoginWindowUI.nib* back to the *English.lproj* folder, and replace the now outdated file. When you do, you're told you are not allowed to do that, but remember that this is your computer, so all you need to do is hit the Authenticate (or if you're using the command line, type `sudo` before the `cp` command) button, and type in your password. The system bows to your will and saves the file to the *English.lproj* folder, just as you wanted (er, demanded!). Here's how you'd copy it at the command line (do type a space after `LoginWindowUI.nib/`, but do not type a space between `loginwindow.bundle/` and `Contents`):

```
$ sudo cp -r ~/Desktop/LoginWindowUI.nib/ /System/Library/CoreServices/
SecurityAgentPlugins/loginwindow.bundle/ Contents/Resources/English.lproj/
LoginWindowUI.nib
```

It's payoff time. Log out of your account, and when you log back in, you'll see something that resembles Figure 5-9.

Figure 5-9.
That should freak the boy out

The dirtier way to do this is by simply replacing the *applelogo.tif* file with a TIFF of your own. Sure, that method works just fine, but something about it lacks the elegance and general usefulness of using Interface Builder.

 When you hack the Safari error icon in **[Hack #38]**, you'll probably think it will only be used when the Safari error page opens. This might not be the case with *applelogo*, and you don't want the Dude popping at odd times.

As you have guessed by now, you can use this methodology to completely revamp the login window. I think I'll leave mine with just the additional text and the child looking on, but you can use Interface Builder to change just about any visual element that is displayed when the login window is shown.

 Once you start modifying *.nib* files, you'll start giving into the temptation to mess with the *.nib* files of all kinds of applications. To look around inside an application in search of its *.nib* file, right-click on the application, and choose Show Package Contents. Not all applications have *.nib* files, but many do.

HACK 38: Change Safari's Error Page

Make Safari a little more informative when the Internet leaves you hanging.

If there is one page everyone hates to see, it is the page built-in to Safari telling you that you and the Internet have parted ways (Figure 5-10).

Figure 5-10.
Guess who's not connected to the Internet?

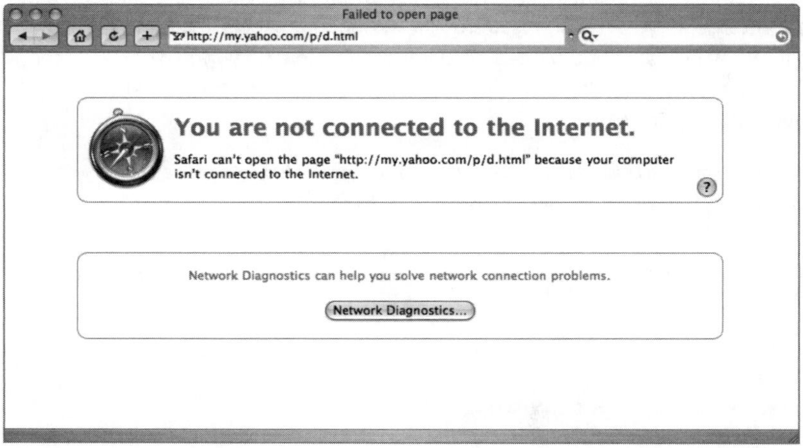

Everyone clicks the Network Diagnostics (a nice feature), but the problem is often with your ISP rather with your equipment, so there is likely nothing you can do but call your provider. Calling your Internet provider seems like something that you wouldn't need the Internet for, but if, like me, the Internet has replaced your phone book, finding the number of your ISP can be a real problem.

> You can't change the Safari error icon in Leopard because it doesn't exist. This hack will still work in Tiger with Safari 3. If you want to hack the Safari error page in Leopard, skip to the section "Hacking the Hack."

As careful programming would have it, the big Safari icon you see embedded in the page is just another image file. In this case, it's a TIFF named *error-page-icon.tif* (Tiger) or an icon file called *compass.icns* in Leopard. What you are going to do is change that image to something more useful, or at least less repetitive, than Safari's compass icon. Of course, in order to do this, you first need to find said bland image file. You might be tempted to use Spotlight at this point, but since the image is inside a package, Spotlight won't be able to find it. Don't worry. The hard work has been done for you:

1. Locate Safari in your Applications folder.

2. Right-click and choose Show Package Contents.

3. Open the folder called Resources, and most of your sleuthing is over.

4. At this point all that's left is to scroll down and find the file named *compass.icns*.

There is probably nothing more important than immediately copying the file to another location for safekeeping. I keep a folder on the Desktop called "Hacks in Progress," but any system that makes sense in your mind will do. Once the image is backed up safely, you can go about the business of replacing it with something spiffier.

Open up the image editor of your choice (ideally, something like Photoshop, because you'll need to work with transparencies), and set the stage to create a TIFF file. Create a new image sized 512 × 512 pixels. Feel free to fill the area with any artwork or text you wish. Save that as, predictably, *compass.icns* somewhere other than the location of the backup copy of *compass.icns*.

At this point you may think that by saving the image directly in the Resources folder of the Safari package. you'll save a little bit of everyone's favorite fleeting quantity: time. Unfortunately that method won't work, Applications can't navigate to packages to save files, so you'll have to do it the hard way. To make your new icon take the place of the generic, redundant Safari image, the steps are identical to the protocol we used to find the image. For the sake of clarity:

1. Quit Safari.

2. Open the Applications folder.

3. Ctrl- or right-click Safari's application icon and select "Show Package Contents."

4. Once you're bouncing around inside the package, open the Contents folder.

5. Finally, open the Resources folder. Inside, you'll see a ton of images, but the one you're interested in is—as you already know—is the image named *error-page-icon.tif*.

6. Open your Documents folder (or whatever folder you saved your replacement image in) and drag your replacement image to Safari's Resources folder (you may be prompted for your password).

7. Restart Safari.

The next time you find that your computer no longer has the close relationship it once did with the Internet, you'll see something like what's shown here in Figure 5-11.

Figure 5-11.
Safari's new error icon is now the Fictional 1-800 number of my ISP

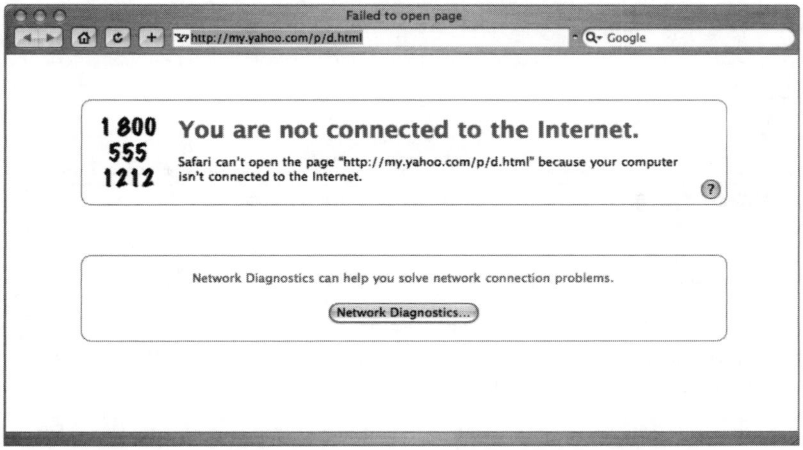

Hacking the Hack
That is plenty for Tiger people; you've got the image you need and replaced it with an image containing useful information. But what if you're using Leopard, or you want a little more? What if

you want your computer to really inspire you to harangue your ISP for not coming through when you needed the Internet? Why not change the error message?

Turns out that Mac OS X is full of localizable text. That is, OS X is full of strings that can be adapted for a particular place or language. Obviously, this is a good idea from Apple's standpoint; rather than having to recreate everything from scratch, programmers can simply change a few strings to adapt their program for Russia. Why not take advantage of this malleability?

The file needing attention in this case is in the *English.lproj* folder (if you're using English as the language for your Mac; if you're using another language, select the folder corresponding to the language you are using) and is called *Localizable.strings*. (Right-click Safari, choose Show Package Contents, then make your way to the *Contents/Resources* folder.) Before you get started, it is a good idea to back this file up so you can revert to the standard Safari strings if you tire of your customized messages.

Once you've located the required file, open it with XCode **[Hack #3]**, and you are well on your way to the land of personalized messages (see Figure 5-12).

Figure 5-12.
The extensive list of localizable strings

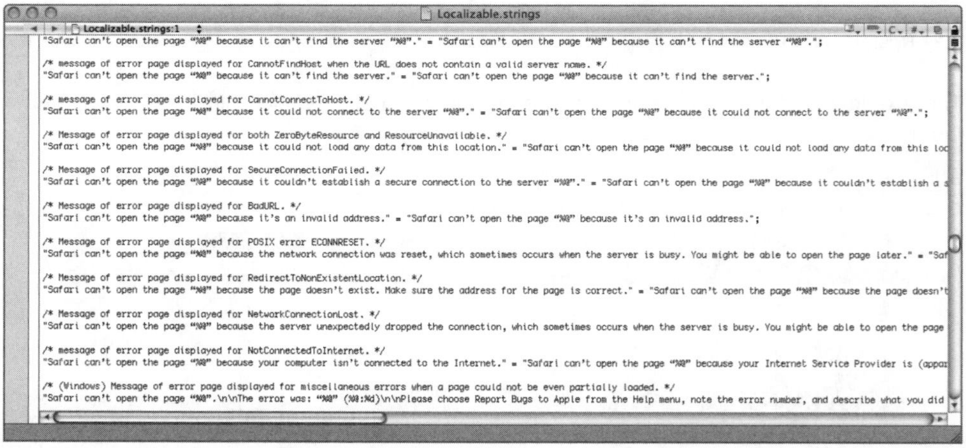

This is a long list of localizable strings but they all have this format:

```
/* Message of error page displayed for BadURL. */
"Safari can't open the page "%@" because it's an invalid address." = "Safari can't
open the page "%@" because it's an invalid address.";
```

If you want to change the message, you're interested in the bit of text that comes after the =. For this hack, I'm changing the message displayed when my computer isn't connected to the Internet. Searching for the line "NotConnectedToInternet" and replacing the message with "Safari can't open the page "%@" because your Internet Service Provider is (apparently) not bothering to provide." after the equal sign gives my error page a more honest look (Figure 5-13).

Figure 5-13.
Now I know who to blame

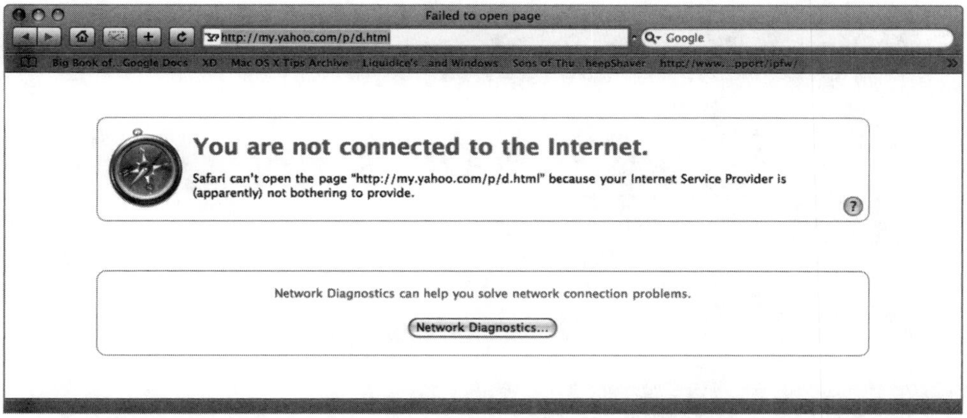

Armed with the knowledge of how to change the error icon and with the knowledge of how to change the text associated with the error, a little imagination is all you need to come up with some great error pages.

> **QUICK HACK**
>
> **CHANGE "%@"**
>
> While you're working away on this hack, you'll undoubtedly notice the "%@" symbols popping up incongruously in the middle of the error message. The symbols are there so the name of page (or some other replaceable text) will show up in the error message. If you want a static message, feel free to type over these; Safari will never know the difference.

HACK 39: Convert Audio Files with iTunes

There are a lot of options when it comes to converting audio with Mac OS X, but (if your needs are modest), iTunes will get the job done for free.

When it comes to audio manipulation, it is hard to beat the range of options available for Mac OS X. Everything from freeware to professional sound editing suites are available. This is great for people producing albums and podcasts but a little bit of overkill if you just want to convert a few sounds (which you might for the **[Hack #40]**).

iTunes isn't a full-featured sound converter, but it does support some of the more common formats. If your conversion needs (in and out) are limited to WAV, AAC, AIFF, Apple Lossless, or MP3, you're covered. If you have more robust conversion needs, consider third-party software such as Switch Sound Converter Plus (http://www.nch.com.au/switch) or Audacity (http://audacity.sourceforge.net).

Time to go about the business of converting file types with iTunes. Be warned that the process isn't intuitive, but also be assured that it is very easy. Launch iTunes and navigate to the Preferences (Command-,) and select Advanced, then choose Importing (see Figure 5-14).

Figure 5-14.
Getting iTunes to convert files

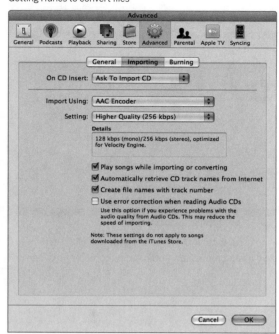

Choose the output format you want to use by making a selection from the Import Using pop up. If you want your converted file to end up as an AIFF, for example, you would use the AIFF encoder. For this Hack, we'll let AIFF be the preferred output, so adjust the pop-up menu to AIFF Encoder. iTunes will take care of the quality setting for you, but you can adjust the settings for other formats.

That finishes the setup; now the only thing left to do is convert a file. First, you must add the file to iTunes. Drag the file from the Finder into the iTunes library. Once the file is in iTunes, right-click or Ctrl-click to get the context menu where you'll see the option to "Convert Selection to AIFF" (Figure 5-15).

Figure 5-15.
Converting to AIFF

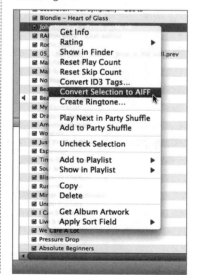

Drag the converted file out of iTunes, and you're done. Note that the changes you made affect how iTunes imports files from CD, so go back to the iTunes preferences, and change things back to the encoder you want to use for importing music.

If you're creating sounds for general OS X System hacking around, there is one thing to be aware of: you may have to change the file extension from *aif* to *aiff* (e.g., by renaming *filename.aif* to *filename. aiff*). iTunes defaults to adding *.aif* to the end of the filename; Mac OS X expects AIFF files used by the system and built-in applications such as Mail [Hack #40] to end in *.aiff*.

HACK 40: Replace Mail Sounds

Discover how to make Mail play custom sounds when checking mail.

Mail.app is a pretty nifty email client. Seamless integration with .Mac, the ability to generate high-quality colorful mail messages, and a clean, understandable interface all add up to make the time spent in Mail a pleasure. Of course, it would be more pleasurable if you had some more control over the sound, Mail teases you with the ability to change one of the four sounds (see Figure 5-16).

Figure 5-16.
Change only one sound? Are you kidding me?

Why stop at one? Sure, if you want to change the incoming mail sound, you are all set, but what if you're tired of the whoosh sound that mail plays when you send that missive off to the customer relations department of a big-box store that wronged you? What if the tink of no new messages grates upon your psyche every time you hear it? Changing one sound isn't sufficient; let's change all the sounds associated with Mail!

A little planning comes in handy at this point. Mail sound files are in *.aiff* format, so you create your sound using that format or convert an existing sound to it [Hack #39].

The choice of sounds can be critical. While it might be tempting to use something really long for your mail sound (and you could use an entire bootlegged Grateful Dead Concert if you wish), there are certain pragmatic things to consider:

- Unless you're a glutton for punishment, keep the sound short, the longest sound used by Mail is just under two seconds. The sounds are short for a reason. While it may seem like a great idea to use an eight-minute drum solo as your sent mail sound, if you do, you'll be undoing this hack in record time.

- The AOL "You've got mail" sound is way too clichéd to actually use.

Now that you have the hopefully short and appropriate sounds for Mail, it is time to get Mail to use your sounds instead of the Apple-supplied auditory masterpieces. For this, you'll be delving into the contents of the *Mail.app* package. You've got choices: you can use the command line (very fast) or use the GUI. This is a good opportunity to highlight the differences between the two approaches, so let's do it both ways.

Before you start, quit Mail.

The GUI Approach

Locate *Mail.app* in your Applications folder. Right-click or Ctrl-click on the application icon, and choose Show Package Contents. Navigate to the Resources folder, and sort through the mass of icons and other miscellanea to find the four files ending in *.aiff*. These are the sounds that you hear when you send a note, your accounts are checked, or when mail encounters an error (see Figure 5-17).

Figure 5-17.
The sounds of Mail

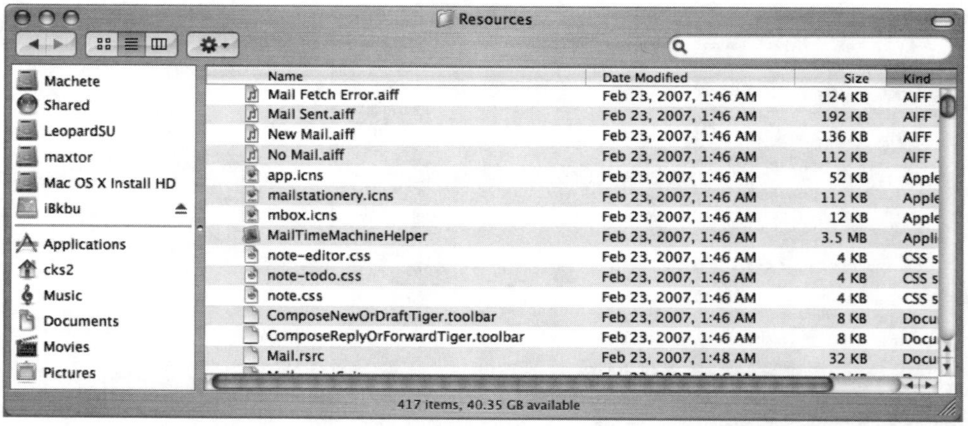

Once you've located the files, make backup copies of them and move the backups somewhere safe. With the backup files safely ensconced, rename the files you created earlier to names exactly matching the names of the *.aiff* files found in Mail:

- *Mail Fetch Error.aiff*
- *Mail Sent.aiff*
- *New Mail.aiff*
- *No Mail.aiff*

Once you've got the files named, drag them into the Resources folder where they will overwrite the existing sounds. If Mac OS X doesn't alert you that you're about to overwrite files, you've done something wrong (see Figure 5-18).

Figure 5-18.
You are on the right track!

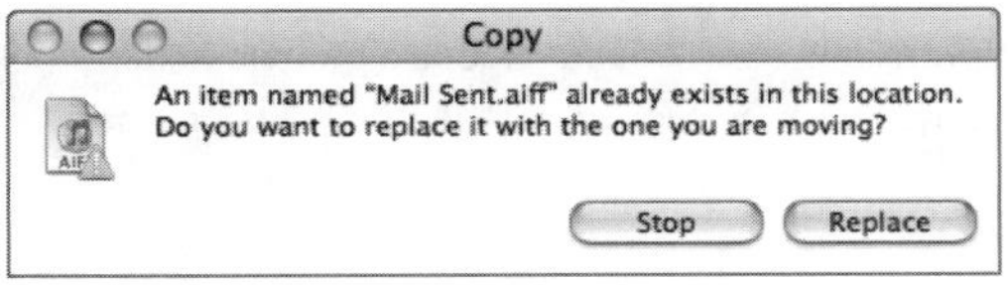

Replacing the files with other files of the same name is the brute force way of accomplishing the task, but in this case, also the easiest way. You could, however, use different filenames, fire up Xcode, and use the method described in [Hack #37] to tweak the Mail property list.

As I mentioned earlier, the same thing can be accomplished with the Terminal and can be completed much more quickly. First we'll change the directory we're working in to the *Mail.app* Resources folder, so at the Terminal prompt type:

```
$ cd /Applications/Mail.app/Contents/Resources
```

Next, create a directory (that is Unix-speak for "folder") to back up the sounds we are about to replace in the *Mail.app* Resources folder:

```
$ mkdir mailsndbu
```

Now move the files you are going to replace to the new directory. The backslashes (\) are there to indicate that the spaces within the filenames should be treated as part of the filename:

```
$ mv Mail\ Fetch\ Error.aiff Mail\ Sent.aiff No\ Mail.aiff Mail\Sent.aiff mailsndbu
```

All you need to do now is get the new sounds into the *Mail.app* Resources folder. Make sure the sounds you want to use are sitting on the Desktop; then use this command to change directory to the Desktop folder:

```
$ cd ~/Desktop
```

One more line:

```
$ mv Mail*.aiff /Applications/Mail.app/Contents/Resources
```

When you use this command, you're using a wildcard (*), so make sure that all the files on your Desktop that begin with Mail and end in *.aiff* are the ones that you want to move to the Resources folder of the *Mail.app*.

That puts all the sounds where they need to be, in Mail's Resources folder. The next time you use Mail, you'll hear your top four instead of Apple's!

Hacking the Hack

If you changed your Mail sounds, you have probably figured out that you can change a variety of sounds in this manner. Indeed, just about any sound resource file you find can be changed in this way. That method doesn't work if you want to add sounds where one doesn't already exist. Classic OS users likely remember SoundMaster and the fun that could be had setting sounds for a variety of system events. A worthy successor to SoundMaster hasn't shown up for Mac OS X yet, but you can add a bit of the fun back with SystemSound (http://systemsoundext.sourceforge.net/). SystemSound won't add all of the options SoundMaster offered, but the program will allow you to set a shutdown sound. At the price of free, it is worth the download. Once installed, SytemSound adds a preference pane to System Preferences where you can choose the shutdown sound.

Rename the Unrenameable

Some folders can't be renamed in OS X unless you know the special tricks. Uncover the hack to rename folders to fit your sensibilities.

Most of the folders on your Mac can be renamed with little effort. If you choose a generic folder buried in your Documents folder, you can rename the folder by clicking on the title, pausing, then clicking again (see Figure 5-19).

Figure 5-19.
Renaming a folder

Try that with your System Folder, and you'll be out of luck. No amount of clicking, swearing, and so forth will let you rename that particular folder. The reasons for the rigidity of Mac OS X when it comes to renaming particular folder are well founded. Applications and System services need to know where to look for the files they need to run properly. Were you to rename the "Library" folder to "Steaming Pile of Storage," programs that relied on support files inside that folder wouldn't be able to locate the resources they need to function properly. Even some of the folders you would generally consider only of use to you can't be modified through the regular methods. The Music folder, to cite one example among many (see Figure 5-20), is stuck being called Music.

Figure 5-20.
Where's the fun?

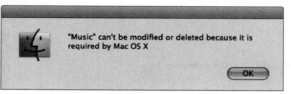

Hey, it's your computer and your folders; why not call them what you want? Begin the process of naming by departing on a voyage to the System Folder. The file you are looking for is called *SystemFolderLocalization.strings* and can be found in */System/Library/CoreServices/SystemFolderLocalizations/en.lproj*. Once you're there, make a backup copy of the file you're about to hack (as always).

If you've installed Xcode, double-clicking *SystemFolderLocalization.strings* will open the file up with Xcode. If not, you can open the file using TextEdit or your text editor of choice. TextEdit will open and edit the files without complaint; just right-click the file, choose Open with→Other, and pick TextEdit. The result of opening the file should be a shortish list of folders and their equivalent names (see Figure 5-21).

Figure 5-21.
See the pattern?

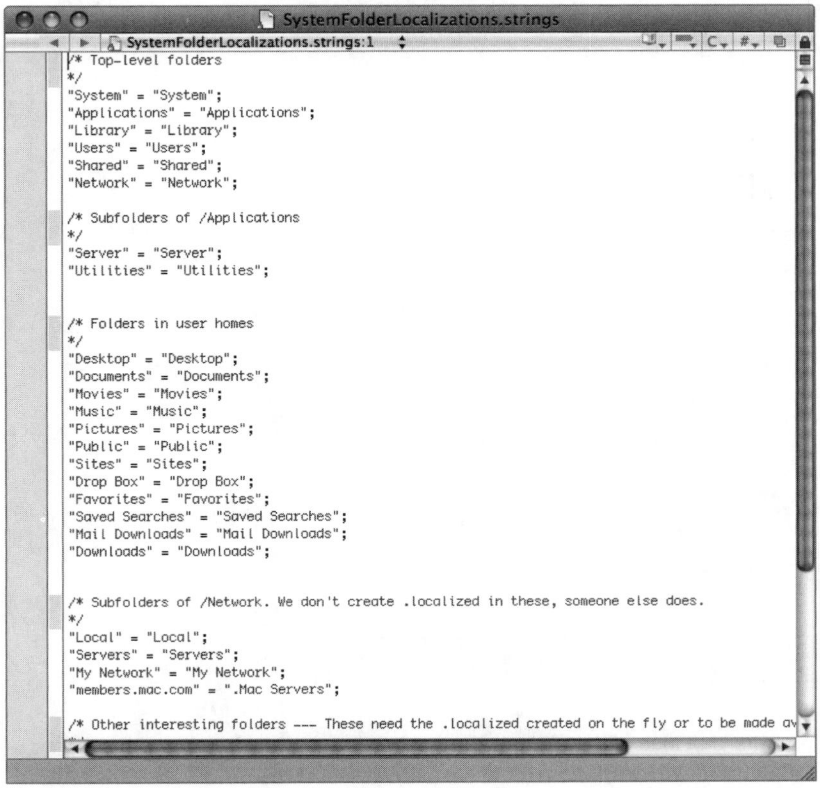

```
                    SystemFolderLocalizations.strings
◄  ►    SystemFolderLocalizations.strings:1    ◄►                    C   #      A
/* Top-level folders
*/
"System" = "System";
"Applications" = "Applications";
"Library" = "Library";
"Users" = "Users";
"Shared" = "Shared";
"Network" = "Network";

/* Subfolders of /Applications
*/
"Server" = "Server";
"Utilities" = "Utilities";


/* Folders in user homes
*/
"Desktop" = "Desktop";
"Documents" = "Documents";
"Movies" = "Movies";
"Music" = "Music";
"Pictures" = "Pictures";
"Public" = "Public";
"Sites" = "Sites";
"Drop Box" = "Drop Box";
"Favorites" = "Favorites";
"Saved Searches" = "Saved Searches";
"Mail Downloads" = "Mail Downloads";
"Downloads" = "Downloads";


/* Subfolders of /Network. We don't create .localized in these, someone else does.
*/
"Local" = "Local";
"Servers" = "Servers";
"My Network" = "My Network";
"members.mac.com" = ".Mac Servers";

/* Other interesting folders --- These need the .localized created on the fly or to be made av
```

When you see the result you'll pick up on the pattern quickly. You can probably guess that in a few moments, you'll be typing the new folder name in place of the deprecated (by you) folder name. The only question remaining is which side of the equation should you change? A good question: changing the left side of the equation would be very bad; changing the right side is fine. See Figure 5-22 for clarity.

Figure 5-22.
Only change the right side!

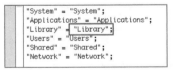

```
"System" = "System";
"Applications" = "Applications";
"Library" = "Library";
"Users" = "Users";
"Shared" = "Shared";
"Network" = "Network";
```

Make your changes within the quotation marks, and save the file (Figure 5-23).

Figure 5-23.
My changes; you'll come up with better ideas

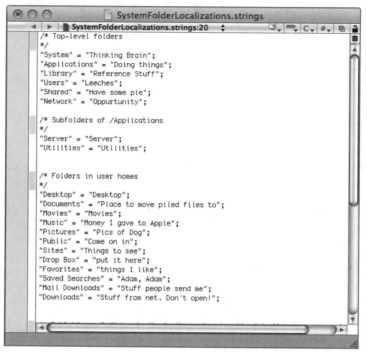

```
/* Top-level folders
*/
"System" = "Thinking Brain";
"Applications" = "Doing things";
"Library" = "Reference Stuff";
"Users" = "Leeches";
"Shared" = "Have some pie";
"Network" = "Oppurtunity";

/* Subfolders of /Applications
*/
"Server" = "Server";
"Utilities" = "Utilities";


/* Folders in user homes
*/
"Desktop" = "Desktop";
"Documents" = "Place to move piled files to";
"Movies" = "Movies";
"Music" = "Money I gave to Apple";
"Pictures" = "Pics of Dog";
"Public" = "Come on in";
"Sites" = "Things to see";
"Drop Box" = "put it here";
"Favorites" = "things I like";
"Saved Searches" = "Adam, Adam";
"Mail Downloads" = "Stuff people send me";
"Downloads" = "Stuff from net. Don't open!";
```

Now save the file, noting that Mac OS X won't let you overwrite the existing file. You can keep the same name by saving the file to the Desktop (or almost anywhere but the *en.lproj* folder).

The next step is to replace the *SystemFolderLocalizations.string* with the modified file. You can drag it from your desktop into the *en.lproj* folder. You'll be asked to authenticate (naturally), and Mac OS X will grudgingly accept your modifications.

Kill the Finder with your favorite technique (typing **killall Finder** in the Terminal works) and you'll see your changes (Figure 5-24 and Figure 5-25).

Figure 5-24.
New names in the Home folder and Sidebar

Figure 5-25.
New names at the root level of your hard drive

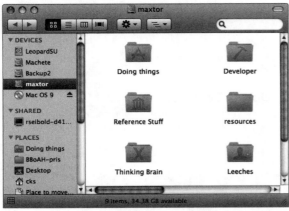

Unhacking the Hack

So you've decided you want to go back to the standard filenames? Well, if you've backed up before you started hacking, no problem. Just trade the backed up copy with your modified file. If you haven't backed up, then you've got some typing to do!

HACK 42: Create Custom Screensavers

Mac OS X brings a few screensavers along with the install but also offers the ability to create custom screensavers. Roll your own screensaver with this hack!

Before the desktop was overtaken by flat-panel monitors, screensavers were of (seemingly) critical importance. A static image would, given enough time, tire out the phosphors on the screen leaving a ghost image that would remain visible no matter what you were doing. Screensavers aren't the monitor-investment-saving programs they used to be, though. LCD screens are much less susceptible to burnt-in images, and people go through monitors much faster than they used to, but they are still fun to have around.

The list of screensavers that ship with Mac OS X is a list of the boring (no flying toasters?), but your choices don't have to stay on the meager side; you can create a custom screensaver of interest to you with a little work and the built-in abilities of Mac OS X.

The iPhoto Mosaic Screensaver

The iPhoto Mosaic screensaver is a no-work, big-payoff, semihidden feature of Leopard. It is difficult to describe in words but works as follows. A picture is chosen by OS X and zoomed away from, which reveals other pictures in your iPhoto library.

The zooming continues until the pictures become impossibly small to see, far beyond the limits of human visual acuity. At the same moment you think that Mosaic is a horrible method to glimpse large libraries, it hits you: The pictures have become part of a larger composition that is slowly morphing into another photo in your iPhoto library. Really, it is impossibly cool. Turning it on is no big trick:

1. Head to the Desktop and Screen Saver preference pane (System Utilities→Desktop & Screen Savers)

2. Select a Photo library

3. Click the Mosaic button, and you're done.

Build Your Own Screensaver with Quartz Composer

Now that the very interesting-to-look-at Mosaic screensaver is activated, you can turn your attention to making an even cooler, more personalized, screensaver with Quartz Composer.

Preparing for the hack

If you're wondering what Quartz Composer is, wonder no more. Quartz Composer is a part of the visual programming language that harnesses the technologies of Core Audio, Core Video, and Core Image—to name a few. The really good news is that Quartz Composer comes with the Apple Developer Tools, so it is free. This hack uses Quartz Composer 3.0, so if your version isn't on the cutting edge, head to Apple and download the latest version (you'll have to sign up for a Developer Account, but it is painless and free **[Hack #3]**).

Quartz Composer is seemingly infinitely flexible, but for this hack I'm going to use the powers of Quartz Composer to display a television show instead of a picture or generated effect. To smooth the process of creating the TV show screensaver, it is a good idea to pick a video test file and put it in an easily memorable place. The file should be something OS X can easily play: a plain old *.mov* file or an *.mp4* should be fine. For the purposes of this hack, I've placed a file called *Simpsons.mp4* on my Desktop.

With the test file in place, it is time to start using Quartz Composer. Quartz Composer is located in the Developer folder, which is located at the root of the hard drive by default (*/Developer/ Applications/Quartz Composer*). It might seem strange to see an application that's not in */ Applications*, but you can double-click this just like any other application.

Once Quartz Composer is up and running, the next step is choosing a starting point. In this case, it is wise to eschew any of the premade templates offered by Quartz and opt for "Blank Composition" (see Figure 5-26). You're not being a glutton for punishment by rejecting the templates; this particular project is actually easier if you avoid Apple's suggested starting points.

Figure 5-26.
Starting points for Quartz Composer

This is an opportune moment to become familiar with the Quartz Composer basics. The window layout seems like a decent place to start. Once you have chosen a starting point, you'll be left with three windows (as seen in Figure 5-27) and, unless you've used Quartz Composer before, very little idea of what is going on.

Figure 5-27.
The three windowed scheme of Quartz Composer

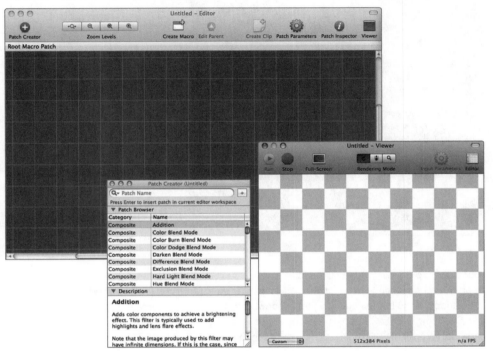

A quick look at what each window does will be helpful:

Editor window
Think of this window as a workspace. This is where you put *patches* (input sources and objects that act upon inputs) and hook patches together. As you work the results of your efforts will be displayed in the Viewer window.

Viewer window
This provides a preview of the final product will look like. Be forewarned that the Viewer window and the final product will often differ markedly.

Patch Creator window
This is where all the patches live. You add patches from this window to the Editor Window.

If you're still a little confused, don't worry. Quartz Composer is surprisingly easy to use but it is hard to get a handle on what is going until you actually start trying to build something. Which is what you're about to do.

Find your video file, and drag it onto the Editor Window. Quartz Composer will automatically add the appropriate path to the file. You can see the path by clicking the Patch Parameters button as revealed in Figure 5-28. Since you were able to get salient information by clicking Patch Parameters button, you should congratulate yourself; you've just made your first Source patch (in Quartz Composer speak). The patch in this Hack is called "simpsons".

Figure 5-28.
Your video clip has become an input patch!

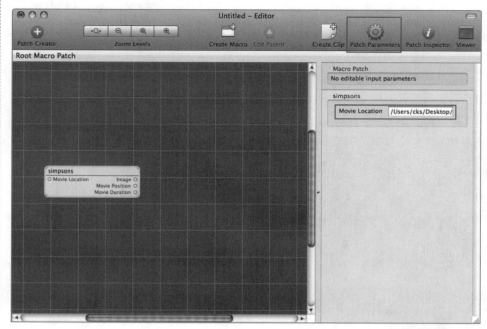

Your video clip is now in Quartz Composer, but you can't see it in the Viewer window because Quartz Composer needs to be told how to render the input. To achieve this, a Render patch needs to be added. Head to the Patch Creator window, and start typing "Billboard" into the search box. Like Spotlight, Quartz Composer searches as you type, so once you see Renderer and Billboard show up, you can drag Billboard to the Editor window as shown in Figure 5-29.

Figure 5-29.
Adding the Billboard renderer

The Billboard renderer works just as its name suggests. It creates a flat image of the input that can be moved in the x and y direction. But that's racing ahead. For now (believe it or not), you're one step away from a rudimentary screensaver that plays your video file. All that is left to do is connect the input to the renderer.

This is one of the places Quartz Composer really shines. Instead of some arcane text based link to connect the input to the renderer, you drag a line connecting the input to the renderer. In this case, click the image dot from the patch called simpsons to the image dot on Billboard patch. Once the connection is made, the video clip will start playing in the viewer window and, if you wish, you can save the file. Congratulate yourself, you've made a file that plays a video clip as a screensaver (see Figure 5-30).

Figure 5-30.
A rudimentary video playing screensaver

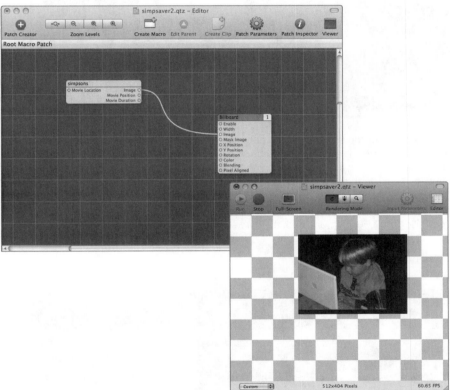

Well, the screensaver has been made, but it is honestly kind of lame. It just sits there in the middle of screen not doing much. You might as well just open a YouTube page and let video play. Why not crank up the interest level and add some movement to mimic the way screensavers have traditionally worked?

Since this screensaver uses the Billboard patch, it can be moved in the x and y direction. You will need another patch (or patches), however, to generate the coordinates you want the image to move to. You have a lot of choices at this point; Quartz Composer has a bevy of options to generate these values. To keep things on the simple side, try the LFO patch (type **LFO** into the search box in the Patch Creator window). This patch will generate values for x and y, plus you can adjust the numbers to suit our purposes. Drag the patch to the Editor Window twice (two separate copies, and connect one result to X Position and the other result to Y Position as shown in Figure 5-31.

Figure 5-31.
A moving image! Or rather a moving image that moves

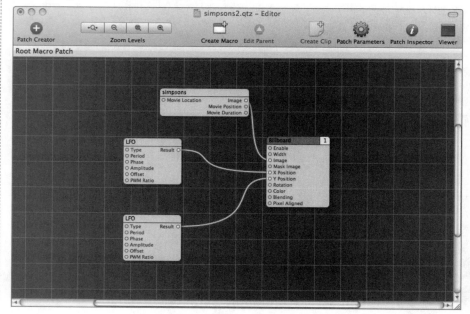

There isn't good way to convey what happens after you make those connections in a screenshot, but chances are your reaction will be "Well, that is simply horrible." And it is. The image is difficult to look at because it is moving too fast, and it oscillates repetitively to the corner of the screen and out of view and then back to the middle. This needs to be fixed.

To adjust the motion of the image, the patch parameters will need to be tweaked. Select the LFO patch controlling the X Position, and click the Patch Parameters button as shown in Figure 5-32.

Figure 5-32.
The defaults do not result in a pleasant screensaver

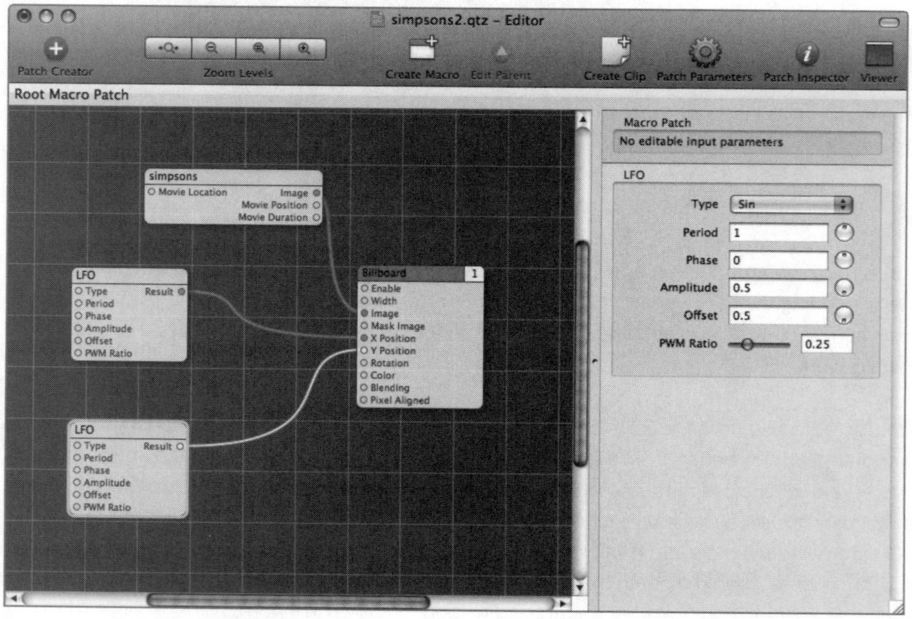

The question is, what should the defaults be changed to? It would better if the image didn't slide off the screen, if the movement was slower and if the image traveled in a gentle ellipse around the screen. To slow the image down, the Period will have to be changed to a larger value; trial and error reveals that a decent value for the Period is 10. To keep the image on the screen in the X axis, change Offset and Amplitude to .25. Finish tweaking the X Position LFO by changing Sin to Cos. Table 5-1 shows the settings in convenient table format.

Table 5-1.
X position LFO settings

Type	Cos
Period	10
Phase	0
Amplitude	.5
Offset	0
PWM Ratio	.25

With the movement in the X plane taken care of, it is time to adjust the movement in the Y plane. Those who are playing along at this point are being nauseated by the up and down jumping of the video clip, so it is better to head straight to Table 5-2.

Table 5-2.
Y position LFO settings

Type	Sin
Period	7
Phase	0
Amplitude	.3
Offset	0
PWM Ratio	.25

The lists don't tell you much about what is going on, so a quick explanation is in order. The Type indicates the function used to generate the position. In this hack, I wanted the image to travel in an ellipse, so setting one Type to Cos (cosine) and one to Sin (sine) results in the image traveling in a circular pattern.

Period sets the speed of the motion, the Period being the amount of time it takes for one complete cycle. A Period of 10 takes, well, 10 times as long as a Period set to 1. Matching Periods give a circularish motion; unmatched Periods (in this case) give a feeling of random movement.

Amplitude controls the amount of deviation from the center coordinate (0,0 for Quartz Composer). An amplitude of 1 sends the image off the edge of the display because the coordinate system of Quartz composer is bound by 1. Put differently, the edges of the Quartz Composer display are 1 and −1 in both the X and Y direction. Having slightly different values for Amplitude gives the image an elliptical path. Since most monitors are wider than they are tall, giving X the larger value ensures the ellipse will have a larger movement in the X plane than the Y plane.

Offset is the amount the image will be moved from the 0,0 coordinate. Setting both values to 0 ensures that the image will rotate about the middle of the screen.

Finally, PWM Ratio doesn't really seem to have an effect in this instance, so you can safely ignore that value.

That was one boring explanation. For real fun, start playing with the settings yourself.

At this point, the hack is seemingly done. The image is rotating slowly about the origin, is easy to look at, and you could fire up the screensaver and watch TV without anyone thinking you were spending time on YouTube. That is the obvious conclusion, but if you actually try the thing as a screensaver, something horrible happens as you can see in Figure 5-33.

QUICK TIP ✕

HACK IN SITU

With most hacks, it is a great idea to work on copies and change whatever you're going to be changing only at the very end. With this hack, you can work on your screensaver while it is sitting in its final destination. This can be a helpful step because there can be discrepancies between what the Quartz Composer Viewer window shows and what the screensaver actually does. If you want to test your screen as you're building it, save the file to the Screen Savers folder found in your Home folder's Library. Now you can test any tweaks you make to the project directly with the Screen Saver pane in System Preferences.

Figure 5-33.
The goggles, they do nothing!

What you'll see is that no images are erased, they are just written over. In and of itself, that can be pretty cool, but in this case, it looks like someone regurgitated pixels. Don't worry: it is an easy fix. To get rid of the trailing image, all you need to do is add one patch, and as a bonus, you don't have to connect any nodes. Search for the Clear patch and drag it in to the Editor Window. Your immediate thought will be that you killed the screensaver because the entire Viewer goes black, but the animation is still going: you just can't see it. Change the layer on the Clear patch from 2 to 1 by clicking on the yellow box in the upper right corner of the Clear patch.

✉ Be sure to quit and reopen System Preferences after you make changes to the screensaver, or you'll keep seeing the old one when you test it.

Everything looks perfect. The viewer looks just like you want it to, but if you try out your creation as an actual screensaver, it will seem like nothing has changed. It is still nine kinds of ugly (and not the nine good kinds). The last step is setting the opacity of the Clear patch. Yes, it seems oxymoronic, but you have to set the opacity to 100% (see Figure 5-34). This is also your chance to change the background color; in this example, I'll leave mine as black, but if chartreuse is more your style, go crazy.

Figure 5-34.
The last tweak

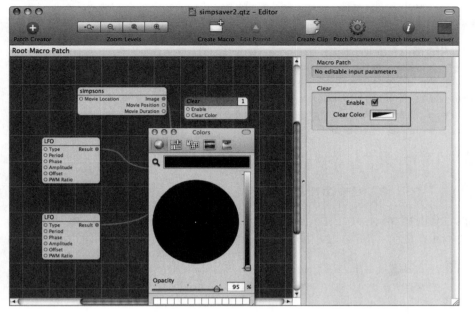

That's it, you're done with creating the screensaver. Give the thing a name and add the *.qtz* extension. Now all that is left to do is to put it somewhere that the Desktop & Screen Saver System Preferences pane can find it. A good place is in the Screen Saver folder of the System Library (/Users/username/Library/Screen Savers).

Figure 5-35 >>
Now you have sound

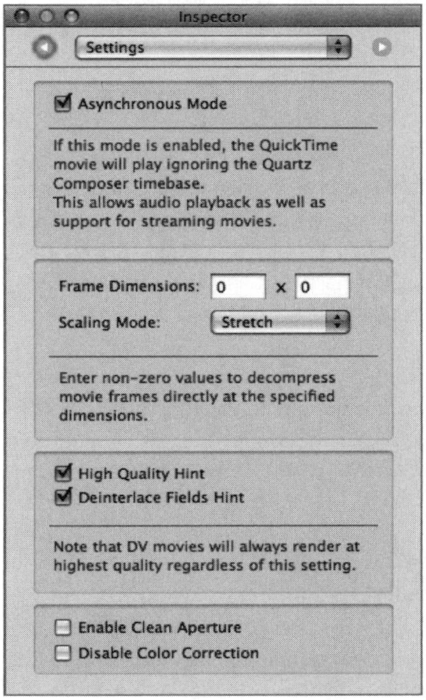

QUICK HACK ✕

ADD SOME SOUND TO YOUR SCREENSAVER

For this hack I left sound out. Usually you don't want sound with your screensaver, but it turns out that if you're using Leopard, adding sound to your screensaver is trivially simple to add. Select the Source patch (simpsons in this Hack) with a single click. Hit the blue Patch Inspector button found in the top of the Editor window, and choose Settings from the pop-up menu. Choose Asynchronous Mode, and the sound will play through (see Figure 5-35).

Sadly, this isn't available to Tiger users.

Once the file is safely ensconced in the appropriate place, head to System Preferences, open the Desktop & Screen Saver panel, and choose the Screen Saver option. Scroll all the way down, and the screensaver you created should be there. Choose test, sit back, and enjoy your creation.

Extending the Hack

Quartz Composer can do a lot more than just creating an interesting screensaver; the important thing about this hack isn't so much getting the video file to play in a pleasing way as your screensaver. The important thing is to create a tweakable working project. You can play with your new file as much as you like, and the worst thing that will ever happen is that you'll have either a nonfunctional or ugly screensaver. So have some fun with it!

HACK 43: Create Custom Icons

Bored with the standard icons found in Mac OS X? Disgusted by a particular icon? Change the icons to images that you find helpful.

Icons are a central part of the GUI experience: without pleasant pictures to click, how would you get things done? Apple has pages dedicated to helping you design the perfect icon for Mac OS X but the company's first piece of advice is:

> For great-looking icons, have a professional graphic designer create them.

Which is probably solid advice, but the hassle factor and the cost is too much for any true hacker to bear. You also have to wonder how seriously people take the rest of the advice, like these two paragraphs:

> Use universal imagery that people will easily recognize. Avoid focusing on a secondary aspect of an element. For example, for a mail icon, a rural mailbox would be less recognizable than a postage stamp.

> Strive for simplicity. Try to use a single object that captures the icon's action or represents the control. Start with a basic shape.

This advice is more useful, but is it actually adhered to? Take a look at two popular program icons. Obviously, the Safari icon adheres to Apple's guidelines; the shape is just a circle and the compass, and with just a small stretch of logic, the icon could be envisioned as a tool for navigating the Internet. The Photoshop icon is a basic shape, a square, but it is hard to imagine how someone firing up a Mac for the first time would guess that a square with Ps in the middle of it represented an image-editing program.

The lesson from all this is clear: forget the human interface guidelines unless you're trying to create a mass-market application. And if your mass-market application is very popular, forget the guidelines anyway. Since it's your computer and you're interacting with it, feel free to use or design the icons you want to see.

Changing Icons the Easy Way: Cut and Paste

The easiest, but least satisfying way, to change a problematic icon in Mac OS X is to simply find an icon that you like and paste it over the icon you want to change. For example, suppose you found the icon for your Time Machine backup disk annoying. Which you might: that odd blue hue with the inane backwards clock deal coupled with the fact that it looks more like a modded Apple remote than anything else make this a likely candidate for replacement. Once you've decided on the victim, er, replacement target, the next step is to find something to replace the icon with. If there is something on your computer, great; if not, there are several online sources for a vast number of icons that will be revealed with a quick Google search.

Once you find a suitable replacement, the process is straightforward. Click the file with the icon you want, and choose Get Info from the Finder's File menu (Command-I). Repeat the process with the file of the icon you want to use, as shown in Figure 5-36

Figure 5-36.
The target and the source

All that is left to do now is a quick copy and paste. Select the mini icon in the upper left corner with a click (it will surrounded with a soft blue hue), as shown in Figure 5-37, and select Copy (Command-C). If you've downloaded a picture, open it in Preview, then choose Edit→Select All (or press Command-A), and press Command-C to copy the image.

Figure 5-37.
Copying the source icon

Repeat the process with the target icon (click the file, choose File→Get Info), but change the copy command to Paste (Command-V). You're done; the new icon has replaced the old one (Figure 5-38)!

Figure 5-38.
Goodbye blue icon of annoyance

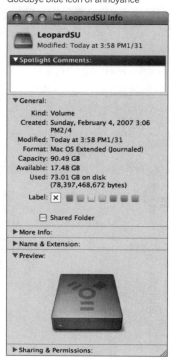

Designing Your Own Icons

As mentioned before, Apple has plenty of advice about icon design, and there are plenty of tutorials on the Web outlining how to design a great-looking icon. What the world is sorely lacking is a hack telling users how to make the ugliest icon possible. Don't fret: that void will soon be filled.

Generating the image

When creating or choosing an image to iconify, there are a few things to keep in mind. First is image size: Leopard features a maximum icon size of 512 × 512 pixels (that is a whopping .2 megapixels if you're scoring at home), so you'll want to start out with an image at least that big and preferably bigger. The second consideration is the file type. In this hack, we'll use Icon Composer (part of the Developer Tools, **[Hack #3]**), and Icon Composer is pretty accommodating when it comes to file types. Anything QuickTime can use, Icon Composer will accept. That means you are free to use GIF, PSD, TIFF, PNG, etc., but most icon designers stick with TIFF or PSD.

Now that the limits are specified, it is time to generate the image. In this case, I'm using Photoshop Elements, but (trust me), you could pull this off with any image editor you choose.

Begin by creating a new image with dimensions larger than 512 × 512. I want to see all the ugly, so I went for 1024 × 1024. If you have the option, set the background to Transparent (see Figure 5-39).

Figure 5-39.
The beginning point of the world's ugliest icon

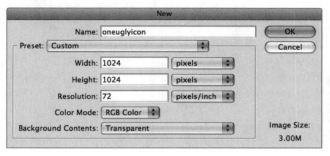

At this point, you're likely to be presented with a blank canvas to work with. Apple recommends simple shapes, and simple shapes are far easier to create than complex ones so create something simplistic. In this hack, I'm starting with just a solid circle generated with the Ellipse tool shown in Figure 5-40.

Figure 5-40.
Ah, a big circle

You could stop here. The icon is ugly and unrepresentative, and it could be the worst Mac OS X icon ever. But more fun than stopping is trying to make it look somewhat OS Xish. After all, if you're making the worst icon ever, this won't do; people will say you didn't even try. On the other hand, if you attempt to make it look OS Xish, people will think, "Man, that is sad, I can tell they put effort into it." The former scenario is utilitarian, and the latter scenario is endlessly hilarious. Hilarity is worth the extra effort.

To Xify the icon, we need a few more steps with Photoshop. To begin with, Mac OS X icons are supposed to look as though a light source is directly above them; a flat circle just isn't going to cut it. Time to light the top half of the circle. First, create a new layer (that is, Shift-Command-N for those looking to keep their hands on the keyboard). With the new layer created, you'll note that the moving dashed line is still present (this is called "marching ants" by Photoshop types). Since the light needs to come from the top and shine down, limiting the selection to half of the circle is useful. Choose the Rectangle Marquee tool and select the bottom ⅝ of the circle, while holding the option button (holding the Option key tells Photoshop to exclude the selected area from the overall selection). If everything went right, the top portion of the circle is selected. It would be better if the icon could display a hint of three dimensions, so refining the selection with the Elliptical Marquee Tool is a good next step. Again, hold the Option key to exclude the portion of the image you are selecting. Your result should look like Figure 5-41.

Figure 5-41.
The top portion is ready for enhancement

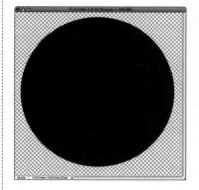

There are an infinite number of ways to proceed at this point, but invoking the power of the Gradient tool seems to be the favorite of Photoshop types. Set the foreground color to white and set the Gradient tool to Foreground to Transparent as shown in Figure 5-42. Then apply a Linear Gradient.

Figure 5-42.
The perfect gradient settings. Well, probably not

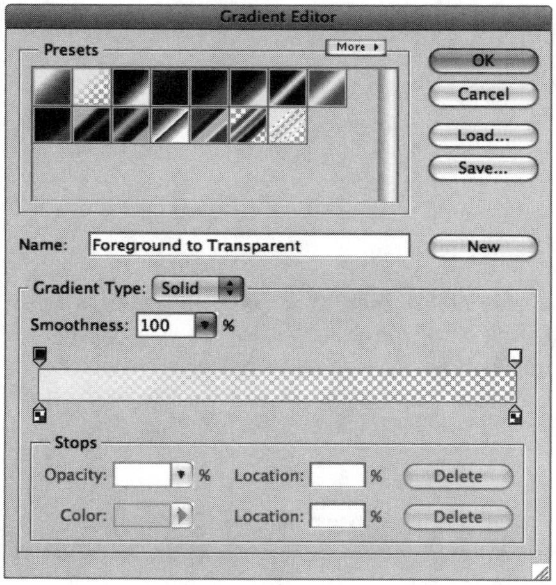

```
                    Gradient Editor
  ┌ Presets ──────────────── More ▸ ──    ( OK )
  │                                        ( Cancel )
  │                                        ( Load... )
  │                                        ( Save... )
  │
  Name:  Foreground to Transparent         ( New )
  ┌ Gradient Type: [ Solid  ◆ ]
  │ Smoothness: [ 100  ▾ ] %
  │
  ┌ Stops ──────────────────────────────
  │ Opacity: [    ▾ ] %  Location: [    ] %   ( Delete )
  │ Color:   [    ▸ ]    Location: [    ] %   ( Delete )
```

Apply the Gradient, ensuring that the white portion starts at the top, and the transparent portion ends at the end of the selection. This puts the gradient you just applied right at the top of the circle, and that isn't very OS Xish. Hit Command-T to invoke the free Transform tool. Move the gradient down from the top edge of the circle a comfortable distance. Continuing with the Free Transform Tool, you'll squish the bottom edges in a bit to follow the outline of the circle more closely. Hit return to make the changes stick. The result should look like Figure 5-43.

Figure 5-43.
Adjusting the gradient you added

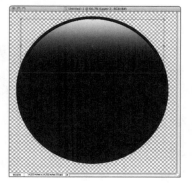

That's it for the top, but careful inspection of Mac OS X buttons reveals that the bottom of the button also shows a light source. One supposes there is really good lighting in the icon design offices of Apple, Incorporated.

To get the bottom looking lit up, though not as lit up as the top, a little more Photoshop work is required. At this point, a method of selecting most of the rest of the circle without selecting the part you already enhanced is required. I used the Elliptical Marquee tool followed by the Polygonal Lasso tool to refine the selection, but there are plenty of much more elegant ways to pull this selection off. Once the area is selected, create a new layer (Shift-Command-N) and head back to the Gradient tool. Again, use Foreground to Transparent, but this time, to give a more rounded appearance, change to the Radial Gradient option. Apply the gradient, and you should have something that looks something like Figure 5-44.

Figure 5-44.
Wow, this is really starting to become the ugly icon I had hoped for

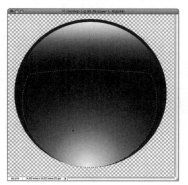

If you're happy with the shape and look of the gradient you just added, you can move to the next step. If you want to fine-tune it a bit, hit Command-T to bring up the free transform tool and tweak as necessary.

At this point, the icon is just a solid circle with some gradients on it. Not the most exciting blob in the world. Add to the unexciting nature that it isn't quite ugly enough. I'm going to fix that by adding a big red X in the middle. In this example, I've used the text tool with a 900 point Microsoft sans serif font. The results are approaching the ugly ideal I set out to capture in the beginning (see Figure 5-45).

Figure 5-45.
Full on ugly!

The good news is that the process of creating the image to use for an icon is almost complete. All that is left is a few small tweaks. First, reorder the layers so the layer with text is beneath the layers with the gradients as shown in Figure 5-46.

Figure 5-46.
Reordering the layers

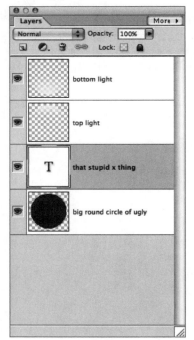

Some final adjustments to make: change the opacity on the gradient layers to 80% and hit all the layers with a Gaussian blur of 10. The last thing OS X icons usually feature is a drop shadow. In Photoshop Elements, there is a Drop Shadow table associated with the layer style option. Choose the background layer (the one with the big red circle) and add the "High" drop shadow. Good news: you've created the world's ugliest Mac OS X icon. Well, mine is probably much worse than yours, so compare your result to Figure 5-47.

Figure 5-47.
I win the ugly icon contest!

With the image complete and your eyes spurting blood from taking in that much ugly at once, it is time to turn this image into a proper icon. To get started, resize the image to 512 × 512 (the maximum size for a Mac OS X icon) and save the file in Photoshop's native PSD format.

Figure 5-48.
What, a solid-white bounding box? Unacceptable!

Composing the icon

All that is left to do is to turn the image you made into an icon. For that the easiest choice is Icon Composer, part of the Mac OS X Developer Tools. Launch Icon Composer (found at Developer→Applications→Utilities→Icon Composer) where you'll be greeted by a many-sectioned blank canvas (see Figure 5-49).

YOU'RE ALREADY DONE!

Once the image you want to use is saved, you're ready to use it as an icon replacement if you so desire. To pull this off, right-click (or use Command-click) the *.psd* file you just created and choose Copy from the contextual menu. Fire up Preview (found in the Applications folder) and choose "New From Clipboard" (Command-N) in Preview's File menu. Now hit Command-C to copy the image. Next, right-click the file whose icon you want to replace, and choose Get Info. Paste your new icon right over the old one as described earlier in this hack. If you're wondering why a trip to Preview is necessary—why you just couldn't cut and paste directly—the reason is that directly cutting and pasting between the image file and the icon you want to replace results in an icon without the transparency (see Figure 5-48). You worked hard to get the transparency right and a quick detour through Preview will ensure that the icon behaves as you expect.

Figure 5-49.
The starting point of Icon Composer

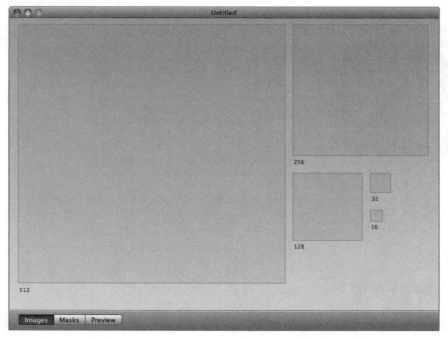

The rest of creating your icon is pure gravy; you can just drag your newly created image on to the square marked 512 and have Icon Composer generate the smaller sizes.

Once the process is complete, Icon Composer will create the appropriate masks (masks define if the click will activate the program associated with the icon or not: see Figure 5-50).

Figure 5-50.
Round masks everywhere

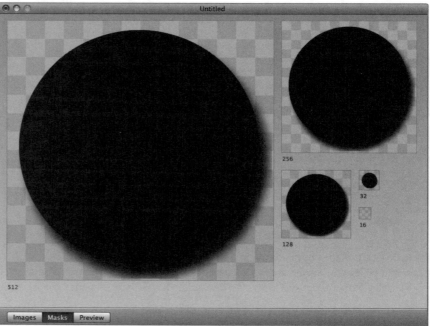

All that is left to do is save the file. That is a simple process—just visit the File menu and choose Save. Icon Composer will generate the necessary files and add the *.icns* extension. Now you can use the icons with any program you can come up with. I use it to identify the script from **[Hack #44]**. The easiest way to change a program's icon to the new *.icns* file is to open the program's resource folder and replace its *.icns* file with the the *.icns* file you created. (The resource folder is inside the *.app* folder. For example, Safari's resource folder is */Applications/Safari.app/Contents/Resources/*. Give it the same name as the existing *.icns* file and drop it in the folder. If you were to replace the *compass.icns* of Safari, the result would look like the icon shown in Figure 5-51.

Figure 5-51.
Wow, from beautiful to rueful in a few easy steps

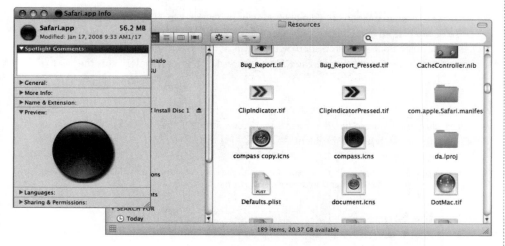

Just imagine how many Docks can be ruined with your new creation (see Figure 5-52), and it even has a reflection!

Figure 5-52.
One icon can ruin the whole Dock

HACK 44: Clean Up That Desktop with AppleScript

Everyone wants a clean Desktop, but no one wants to invest all the dragging and dropping required to achieve a tidy computing environment. Forget the drag and drop: let AppleScript do the work.

Everyone uses his Mac a little differently. Some people are conscientious and put all their documents in the Documents folder, all their pics in the Pictures folder, and all their movies in the Movies folder. Some people don't work that way: they use the Desktop just like you'd use a real Desktop—a temporary storage place for whatever you happen to be working on at the time. Still other users use the Desktop as a repository for every file they run across during a particular computing session. They don't bother putting anything away until the Desktop is cluttered beyond hope. Some people call these types slovenly; others refer to these people as some sort of stain on the computing community. You can call the desktop clutterer "that guy on the back of this Apple Hacks book."

Hi, I'm Chris, and I'm a Desktop clutterer. (Hi Chris.)

Desktop clutterers like me don't need pity or derision: we need help. As it turns out, the files on the Desktop are of predictable types, and since they are likely easily categorized ,that means the process of cleaning up the Desktop should be easily automated. You can't say "automation" without thinking of Automator when you're using a Mac, so guessing that Automator holds the key to a clean desktop is a good guess.

What would be ideal is an AppleScript that will put everything in the appropriate folder, a script that will put MP3s in the Music folder, documents in the Documents folder, movies in the Movies folder, etc. Turns out, this isn't much of problem.

> This script will fail if a file exists in the destination with the same name as the file being moved. Think of it as a safety precaution so that important data isn't overwritten.

Creating the Script

To get started on your AppleScript, launch the Script Editor, found at Applications→AppleScript→Script Editor. This is a straightforward script. What it will do is identify the files by their extension and then move the files to the appropriate folder. Here's the script I use:

```
tell application "Finder"
    set theDesktop to alias ":Users:cks:Desktop:"

    -- Where to put stuff
    set theMusic to alias ":Users:cks:Music:"
    set thePics to alias ":Users:cks:Pictures:"
    set theVideos to alias ":Users:cks:Movies:"
    set theDocs to alias ":Users:cks:Documents:"

    --filetype by extension
    set musicExt to {".mp3", ".aac"}
    set picsExt to {".jpg", ".gif", ".tif", ".tiff", ".png"}
    set videosExt to {".avi", ".mpg", ".mov", ".mp4"}
    set docsExt to {".rtf", ".txt", ".doc"}

    set allFiles to files of myDesktop
    repeat with theFile in allFiles
        copy name of theFile as string to FileName
```

```
        repeat with ext in musicExt
            if FileName ends with ext then
                move theFile to theMusic
            end if
        end repeat

        repeat with ext in picsExt
            if FileName ends with ext then
                move theFile to thePics
            end if
        end repeat

        repeat with ext in docsExt
            if FileName ends with ext then
                move theFile to theDocs
            end if
        end repeat

        repeat with ext in videosExt
            if FileName ends with ext then
                move theFile to theVideos
            end if
        end repeat

    end repeat
end tell
```

A closer look at what is going on is in order because you'll likely want to modify the script to suit your needs. The following bit of the script invokes the Finder and tells it to look at my Desktop. Here, the Desktop is being defined by the path *:Users:cks:Desktop*. You could change the folder you want the Finder to examine and clean it up by changing the path. If you wanted to run this script on your Downloads folder, change it to *:Users:username:Downloads:* Note the presence of the colons. In AppleScript, colons replace the more familiar slash used when working in the Terminal (/).

```
tell application "Finder"
    set theDesktop to alias ":Users:cks:Desktop:"
```

This next section of the script defines where the files are going to end up. You can adapt the script to folders of your choice by changing the paths to different folders. An example being if you wanted your music to end up in a folder called NewMusic within your Music folder. The change would be to have the script burrow one level deeper in the folder by adding one more level to the path: *:Users: username:Music:NewMusic:*.

```
-- Where to put stuff
    set theMusic to alias ":Users:cks:Music:"
    set thePics to alias ":Users:cks:Pictures:"
    set theVideos to alias ":Users:cks:Movies:"
    set theDocs to alias ":Users:cks:Documents:"
```

The next section of the script defines which extension belongs to which kind of file. If these extensions aren't sufficient, you can add your own. For example, if you want to include Photoshop files to files sorted as pictures you would simply add `,".psd"` inside the brackets of the `set picsExt` line.

```
--filetype by extension
    set musicExt to {".mp3", ".aac"}
```

```
        set picsExt to {".jpg", ".gif", ".tif", ".tiff", ".png"}
        set videosExt to {".avi", ".mpg", ".mov", ".mp4"}
        set docsExt to {".rtf", ".txt", ".doc"}
```

The rest of the script is all about moving the files, and there isn't much to change unless you want to add a new class of files. If you want this script to catch application files and move them to your Application folder, you will have to add the necessary code in this part.

If you type the script into Script Editor window, you'll end up with a rather bland-looking script as shown in Figure 5-53.

Figure 5-53.
That doesn't look right...

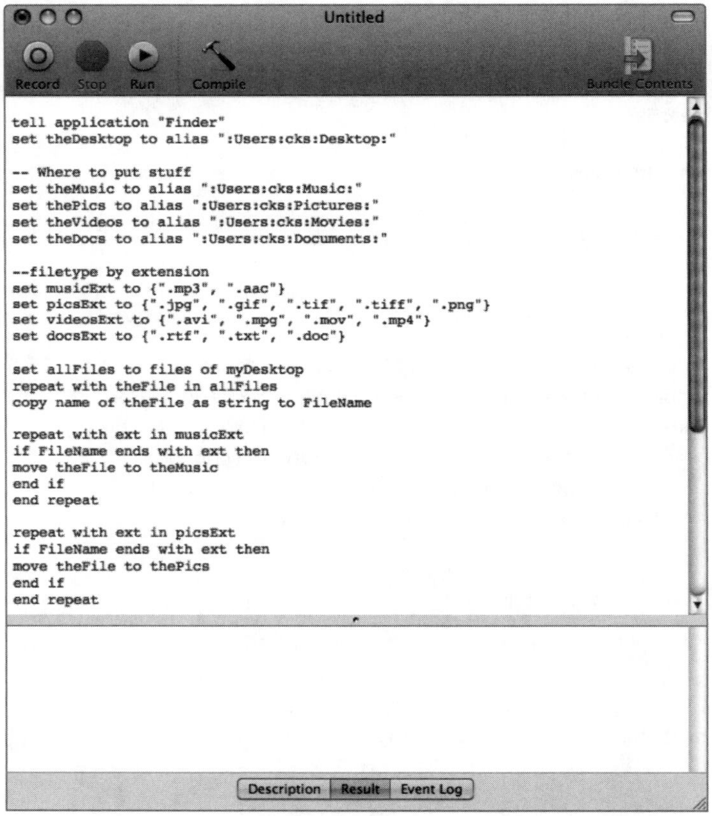

You know this isn't right: scripts are supposed to be color-coded and indented. Hit the Compile button (it looks like a hammer), the Script Editor will work a little magic, and everything will look as expected (see Figure 5-54). As a bonus, Script Editor will find any structural errors (unclosed quotation marks, for example) and alert you.

Figure 5-54.
That is more like it!

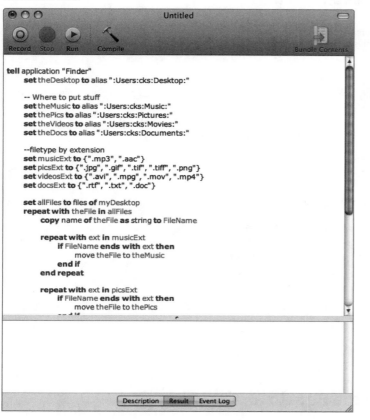

```
tell application "Finder"
    set theDesktop to alias ":Users:cks:Desktop:"

    -- Where to put stuff
    set theMusic to alias ":Users:cks:Music:"
    set thePics to alias ":Users:cks:Pictures:"
    set theVideos to alias ":Users:cks:Movies:"
    set theDocs to alias ":Users:cks:Documents:"

    --filetype by extension
    set musicExt to {".mp3", ".aac"}
    set picsExt to {".jpg", ".gif", ".tif", ".tiff", ".png"}
    set videosExt to {".avi", ".mpg", ".mov", ".mp4"}
    set docsExt to {".rtf", ".txt", ".doc"}

    set allFiles to files of myDesktop
    repeat with theFile in allFiles
        copy name of theFile as string to FileName

        repeat with ext in musicExt
            if FileName ends with ext then
                move theFile to theMusic
            end if
        end repeat

        repeat with ext in picsExt
            if FileName ends with ext then
                move theFile to thePics
```

If you're only going to need this script very occasionally, you could just save it as a script, fire up Script Editor, and hit the big green Run button whenever you want to clean up your Desktop. That is a great option for the occasionally untidy, but for Desktop abusers like me it isn't the best idea. What I would like is a way to run the script with a minimal amount of hassle. So I'll save it as an Application Bundle, using the pop-up menu next to File Format as shown in Figure 5-55.

Figure 5-55.
Creating a new application with AppleScript

All the necessary files will be generated and packaged with your script, and you'll be able to clean your Desktop any time you wish with a double-click.

 This script works recursively, meaning that any folders (not drives) on your Desktop will be sorted as well. It is a good idea to use this script only if your Desktop is cluttered with files, not folders.

Hacking the Hack

If you would like to modify the script to move another file type, such as applications, this is how to change it. Under "where to put stuff":

```
set theapplications to alias ":Users:cks:Applications:"
```

Under "filetype by extension":

```
set applicationsExt to {".app"}
```

And finally, within the main **repeat** loop:

```
        repeat with ext in applicationsExt
            if FileName ends with ext then
                move theFile to theApplications
            end if
        end repeat
```

HACK 45: Change the Boot Image

You've customized the login window, icons, and screensavers. Grab the gold, er gray, and customize the Boot Image Panel!

The Boot Panel is without a doubt the dullest visual in Mac OS X: it is gray on gray and just not that exciting. Worse yet, every Mac has the same boot image; where is the joy of customization? The good news is that you can change the boot image; in fact there is more than one method.

Change the Boot Image the Easy Way

If you don't feel like mucking about with hex editors and RAW files, the easy way to change the boot image on Intel and PowerPC-based Macs is to use a utility. One option is BootXChanger (http://namedfork.net/bootxchanger). It is a free download and using BootXChanger, you can change the boot image on PowerPCs to just about any image you want and change the boot image of Intel Macs to images within reason.

Using BootXChanger is simple, but there are some catches: You can't change the color of the background screen, images can't be bigger than 128 × 128, the number of colors available are limited and, on Intel Macs, simpler images are better (BootXChanger tells you if you can't use the image).

Those caveats out of the way, it is time to get started changing the boot image. After downloading BootXChanger, launch it and drag the image you want to use (BootXChanger comes with some useful sample images) to the BootXChange window (see Figure 5-56). Authenticate and you're done.

Figure 5-56.
Changing the boot image

Restart your computer and enjoy your new boot image (see Figure 5-57)!

Figure 5-57.
Your Mac is radioactive

Change the Boot Image Super Hack Style

I'd really like to use a Mac Mini for my MAME arcade cabinet [Hack #117]. I'm currently running Windows 98 on an old beige-box PC, and I really want to switch to more modern hardware and software. The Mac Mini is the smallest and quietest machine out there. The Wi-Fi, keyboard, and mouse make it a perfect fit. I could even run Windows XP on it because most emulators are designed primarily for Windows. But it would be nice to use Mac OS X, if for no other reason than to save the $200 XP license.

Since Mac OS X would be acting like an embedded operating system inside the arcade, I want to conceal the fact that it is a generic computer running a standard OS. This means, hiding as much of OS X as possible. Technote TN2602 (http://developer.apple.com/technotes/tn2002/tn2062. html) covers how to hide things like the menu bar and Dock, and even how to replace the Finder as the main application. However, I want to cover all the details, including images displayed at boot time. Res Excellence (http://www.resexcellence.com) has a wealth of information on how to customize your Mac, including replacing the boot image and boot panel. However, the boot images only work on PowerPC Macs. So I decided to figure out how to do the same for Intel Macs. It turns out that Intel Macs are far more restrictive of the image than PowerPC Macs, but I was able to replace it nonetheless. I'm going to walk through how I reverse-engineered the Intel boot loader and replaced the standard gray Apple with the Chalice from the Atari 2600 Adventure game.

Before diving into the Intel side, I felt it was important to understand how the PowerPC hacks worked. The Mac boot sequence is covered in detail by Amit Singh (http://www.kernelthread.com/mac/osx/arch_boot.html). The relevant part is that the boot loader, BootX, draws the Apple logo. Fortunately, BootX is Open Source, so you can see how it displays the image. The logo is a 128 × 128 image with a color palette. The pixel data is defined, pixel by pixel, in *appleboot.h*. The palette is defined in *clut.h* (which I assume stands for "color lookup table").

I wanted to make sure this was indeed the familiar boot image, so with a short C program, I dumped the pixel data to a file named *appleboot.raw* and the palette to a file named *clut.act*. Using some ImageMagick foo [Hack #36], I created a PNG from this raw data, and viewed it:

```
$ cat clut.act appleboot.raw > appleboot.map
$ convert -depth 8 -size 128x128 appleboot.map appleboot.png
$ open appleboot.png
```

Sure enough, *appleboot.png* is the image we all know and love. It is now pretty clear that you can replace the logo with any 128 × 128 image you want by changing the pixel data and palette, and recompiling BootX. But recompiling isn't very convenient to test out a new image, and you'd have to write a tool to convert raw image data into C arrays.

Fortunately, there are nice tutorials on how to patch the *BootX* binary that shipped with your system. Usually the process requires using a hex editor and Photoshop, and is not for the faint of heart. Even better, there are tools, such as Imagine BootX, that completely automate the process. However there are no tools for Intel users, so it's important to read and understand this tutorial. The Intel procedure is based on it. You'll notice the palette and pixel data extracted from the hex editor are exactly the same as the ones I extracted from the source code.

The boot sequence for an Intel Mac is similar to PPC Macs. However, instead of Open Firmware, the Extensible Firmware Interface (EFI) is used. Thus the *BootX* boot loader is replaced with an EFI boot loader called, aptly, *boot.efi*, and is still stored in */System/Library/CoreServices*. Unfortunately, *boot.efi* is not open source like *BootX*. Without the source, I wasn't even sure that *boot.efi* had the job of displaying the boot logo. So the first task was to verify that the standard Apple boot logo was somewhere inside *boot.efi*.

Time to break out a hex editor. With nowhere else to start, I assumed the Intel image was exactly the same as the PPC one. There are two main colors in the image: the light gray background, #BFBFBF. and the dark gray foreground, #737373. The palette indexes are 0x01 and 0 50, respectively. Using a hex editor, searching for the two three-byte color sequences turned up one match each. Looks like I hit the jackpot on the palette. The bytes from 0x010E40 to 0x01113F (in the 10.4.6 *boot.efi*) match the PPC palette exactly.

However, searching for a long string of 0x50 bytes (dark gray) turned up empty. So either the image is different, with the same palette, or the image was encoded somehow. After browsing the rest of the file, there didn't seem to by any long stretches of the same two values (like 0x01 and 0x50 in the original image), so I guessed that the image was encoded. Was it possible to figure out how it was encoded without having source code? I like a challenge, so I pressed on.

My next assumption was that the image data was near the palette data, probably directly after it. EFI has some built-in compression routines for just this kind of purpose. I figured this would be a good place to start. After reading the EFI documentation, though, I didn't see any data after the palette that matched the compression header. So I gave up on that. However, the data just after the palette (0x011140) had some interesting properties:

```
FF 01 FF 01 FF 01 50 01 01 02 01 17 01 34 01 47
03 50 01 13 76 01 01 03 01 20 01 40 06 50 01 13
75 01 01 1A 01 42 07 50 01 FA 01 0A 73 01 01 07
01 34 09 50 01 43 01 02 72 01 01 0E 01 43 0A 50
01 36 72 01 01 14 01 4A 0B 50 01 20 71 01 01 12
01 4B 0B 50 01 4D 01 0B 70 01 01 0B 01 48 0C 50
```

QUICK TIP ✕

HEX EDITING

A hex editor is a program you can use to look at and manipulate binary files. Usually when you're looking at files, you're looking at stuff that makes at least a little bit of sense. Binary data doesn't make any sense to you (though it isn't a problem for your Mac). Still, there are times when you want to manipulate binary files. To do that, you'll need a *hex editor*, which is so named because the binary numbers that make up a binary file are usually displayed in two-digit hexadecimal, or base 16, numbers, from 00 to ff. There are a lot of choices for hex editors around, the truly intrepid use Emacs (is there anything that program can't do?), but for mortals, a program such as Hex Fiend (http://ridiculousfish.com/hexfiend/) will get the job done.

While there are no long strings of 0x01 and 0x50, those two numbers do show up unusually often, but mostly on odd bytes. So what did the even byte mean? And then it clicked: run-length encoding! Those Apple guys are so clever! Run-length encoding (RLE) is a very simple compression algorithm in which long sequences of the same byte are replaced with a pair of bytes: (count, value). So the first two bytes, FF 01, are code for a sequence of 255 0x01 bytes. I first observed this technique when writing a DOS graphics program using the Allegro game-programming library years ago, and it's apparently used in fax machines, too.

Okay, so RLE was a good theory, but it's time to verify it. Using a Ruby script (there's an interesting discussion of Ruby and RLE, including some scripts at http://praisecurseandrecurse.blogspot.com/2007/03/haskell-for-short-attention-span-run.html.), I was able to decode the bytes from 0x011140 through 0x01169F as RLE. And sure enough, this data matched my *appleboot.raw* file I extracted from BootX. Full jackpot! I now had the palette and pixel data. Now could I replace the image?

Due to the RLE compression, you can't just stick any old 128 × 128 image in there, like *BootX*. No sir. Apple made it much more difficult to customize the image because it must compress down to 1,376 bytes or less. And this was no easy task. Nearly all of the boot images on ResExcellence are way too complicated to compress down that small. However, one stuck out: the Adventure chalice from Patrick Deuley's Atari collection (see Figure 5-58):

Figure 5-58.
If you had an Atari 2600, you remember this

First off, I love Adventure, so this would be perfect for my MAME machine. Plus, it had only two colors and large contiguous blocks of the same color, which should compress nicely. To keep things simple, I wanted to change the black and yellow to the same light gray and dark gray as the Apple logo. Using Photoshop, I was able to use the *clut.act* palette and change the colors. Also, the original image has some anti-aliasing on the edges. Since this blocky image really doesn't benefit from anti-aliasing, and the extra colors used for the smoothing would bloat the RLE compression, I removed the smoothing pixels.

Because Photoshop does not understand the RLE compression used, I saved it as a raw image, and I wrote a Ruby script to compress the raw image into an RLE image. Luckily, the image compressed down to 622 bytes, so it would easily fit within the alloted 1,376 bytes of the original image. Instead of modifying original *boot.efi*, I used a copy, called *chalice.efi*. Using a hex editor on *chalice.efi*, I overwrote the chalice's RLE bytes on top of the original Apple logo. Now, I needed to test out this modified boot loader.

The `bless(8)` command allows you to change the boot loader for a volume. This means I could use *chalice.efi* while keeping the original *boot.efi* completely intact. As it turns out, the Startup Disk pane of System Preferences also uses `bless` (or some equivalent API) to re-`bless` the original *boot.efi*. If I messed something up, I could boot to the original Mac OS X DVD and run the Startup Disk utility. I created a new directory, and copied my boot loader there:

```
$ sudo mkdir /efi
$ sudo cp chalice.efi /efi
```

One final detail needed to be covered before running `bless`. The startup boot menu invoked when holding down the Option key uses a special file to display the volume name below the icon, called the *volume label*. Since the `--label` option of `bless` is currently broken, I'll just use label file used by *boot.efi*:

```
$ sudo cp /System/Library/CoreServices/.disk_label /efi
$ cd /efi
$ sudo bless --folder . --file chalice.efi --labelfile .disk_label
```

Now, time to reboot to see if all this hex hacking actually worked (see Figure 5-59).

Figure 5-59.
Adventure on the Mac!

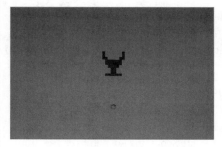

Holy crap, it did! This will make a nice detail on my MAME arcade cabinet experience. And it was fun to figure out, too.

— Dave Dirbin

HACK 46: **Empower the Finder Window**

The Finder window is one of the most often-seen Windows in Mac OS X—why not make it a little more useful?

The standard Finder window seems like a simple enough place. You get quick links to your drives, some standard folders, and canned searches (see Figure 5-60). For many users, that is probably enough. But the hackers among us demand a little more.

Figure 5-60.
A standard Finder Window

	Name	Date Modified ▼	Size	Kind
▶	Desktop	Today, 8:11 PM2/2	--	Folder
▶	Downloads	Today, 3:57 PM2/2	--	Folder
▶	Pictures1	Today, 2:22 PM2/2	--	Folder
▶	Movies1	Today, 2:22 PM2/2	--	Folder
▶	Documents1	Today, 2:22 PM2/2	--	Folder
▶	Music1	Today, 2:22 PM2/2	--	Folder
▶	Music	Today, 1:47 PM2/2	--	Folder
▶	Pictures	Today, 12:33 PM2/2	--	Folder
▶	Documents	1/30/08, 10:06 PM1/30	--	Folder
▶	Library	1/30/08, 11:01 AM1/30	--	Folder
▶	Movies	1/23/08, 8:49 PM1/23	--	Folder
▶	Sites	1/10/08, 10:57 PM1/10	--	Folder
▶	Public	1/8/08, 10:18 PM1/8	--	Folder
▶	Shared	11/11/07, 3:56 PM11/11	--	Folder

DEVICES: LeopardSU, Machete, Backup2, maxtor
PLACES: Applications, BBoAH-pris, Desktop, cks, Documents, Pictures, Movies, Music
SEARCH FOR: Today, Yesterday, Past Week, All Images, All Movies, All Documents

14 items, 31.74 GB available

See the Path

If you use the Terminal with any regularity, you're familiar with the concept of file paths. Finder can show you the paths if you take just a moment and add a path bar. This isn't much of a hack: just click View→Show Path Bar in the Finder's menu bar, and a convenient path bar will be added to the bottom of the Finder window (Leopard users only!) (see Figure 5-61).

Figure 5-61.
An ever useful path bar

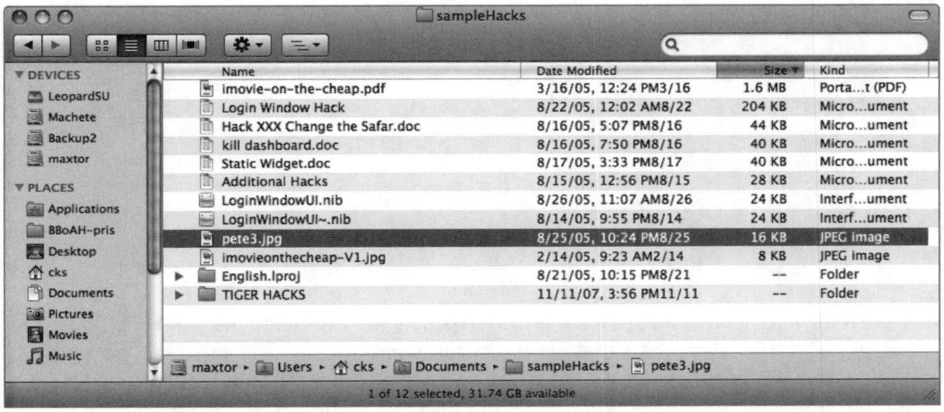

More Control Over the Sidebar

The Sidebar isn't new to Mac OS X 10.5, but it is improved. Some see it as a nod to the popularity of iTunes, and others see it as an annoyance. Whatever your feelings, the important thing to know is that you're not stuck with the Sidebar left by a standard install. The first thing to do is to decide what you want on the Sidebar. After all, if you never use the prebuilt searches or your Music folder, there isn't a compelling reason to have them cluttering up the Sidebar. To remove unneeded or unwanted items from the Sidebar, take a trip to the Sidebar Preferences (Finder→ Preferences→ Sidebar), as seen in Figure 5-62, and remove the check mark next to any items you don't want to be bothered with.

Figure 5-62.
Uncheck the items you don't want

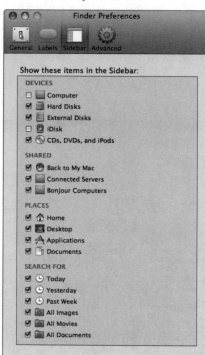

That is great for getting rid of things, but more often people want to add to the Sidebar instead. Fortunately, this is a simple process that works exactly as you would expect it to on a Mac: simply drag and drop any file or folder you want to be represented on the Sidebar, and your new addition will show up under the Places area. When you tire of the new addition, drag it off the Sidebar, and it disappears with a poof.

Adding folders and files to Places is useful, but it would be even better if you could add Smart Folders to the "Search For" area of the Sidebar. Turns out, this isn't a challenge, either. Create a new Smart Folder (in the Finder, choose File→New Smart Folder), and check the box to add it to the Sidebar when you save the folder (Figure 5-63).

Figure 5-63.
Adding a new search to the Finder Sidebar

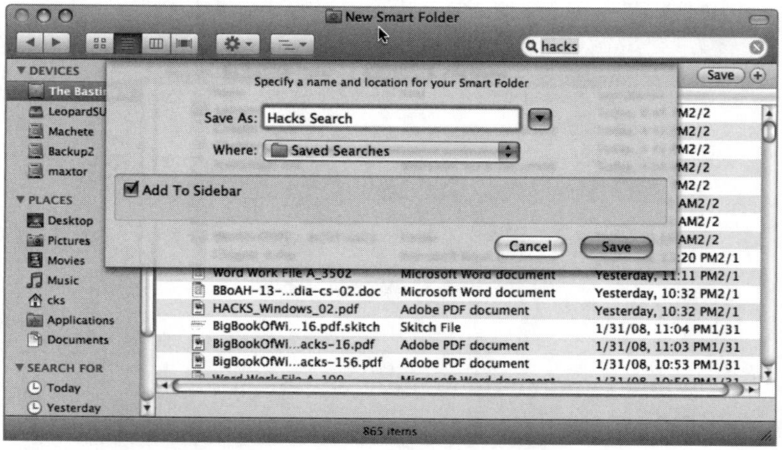

Add Apple-Built Searches

The default searches that show up in the Sidebar aren't the only ones Apple included in Leopard, they are just the searches Apple chose to enable by default. You can add the other searches Apple came up with by locating */System/Library/Core Services/Finder* in the Finder. Right-click Finder, select Show Package Contents, then follow the path: *Contents/Resources/CannedSearches*. You'll see all the searches Apple chose not to include (see Figure 5-64).

Figure 5-64.
Hey, extra searches, Apple is holding out on you!

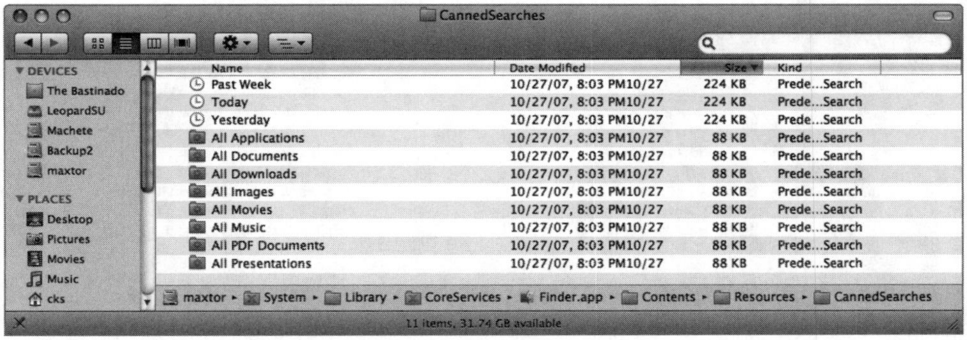

Getting these searches into the Sidebar can be a bit of a trick, you can't just drag the searches to the Sidebar, or they'll end up under Places. You can, however, right-click on the search you want to add and choose Show Package Contents. Inside this folder, you will find a folder called *search. savedSearch*. You can drag that file to the Sidebar and get all the functionality of the search, but the folder will show up with a very uninformative name, "search". To change the name to something meaningful, you could fire up the Terminal and use the mv command, but in this case it is easier to select and copy the searches you want to use (see Figure 5-65).

Figure 5-65.
Copying an Apple search

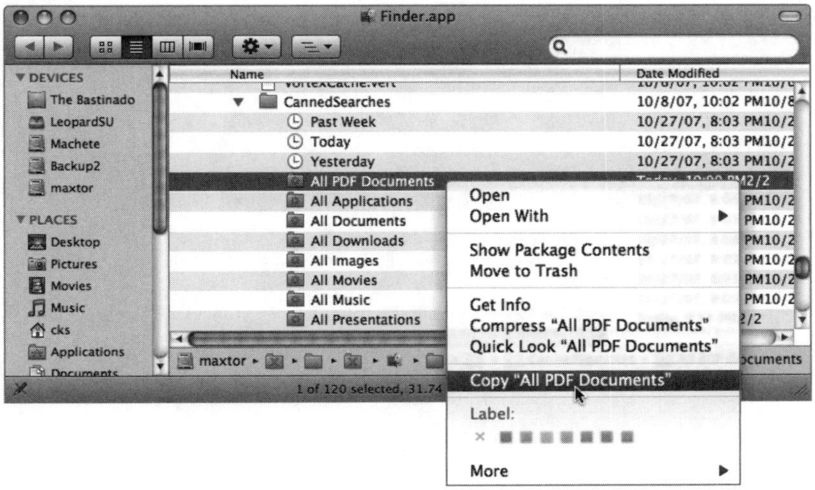

Once you have the file copied somewhere you can hack it, select the folder, right-click, and choose Show Package Contents. Rename the *search.savedSearch* to something more informative. Copy the renamed file and paste it into the Contents folder of the search you want to add to the sidebar and, voila, you've added an Apple defined search (see Figure 5-66)!

Figure 5-66.
Finally, the All PDFs search shows up

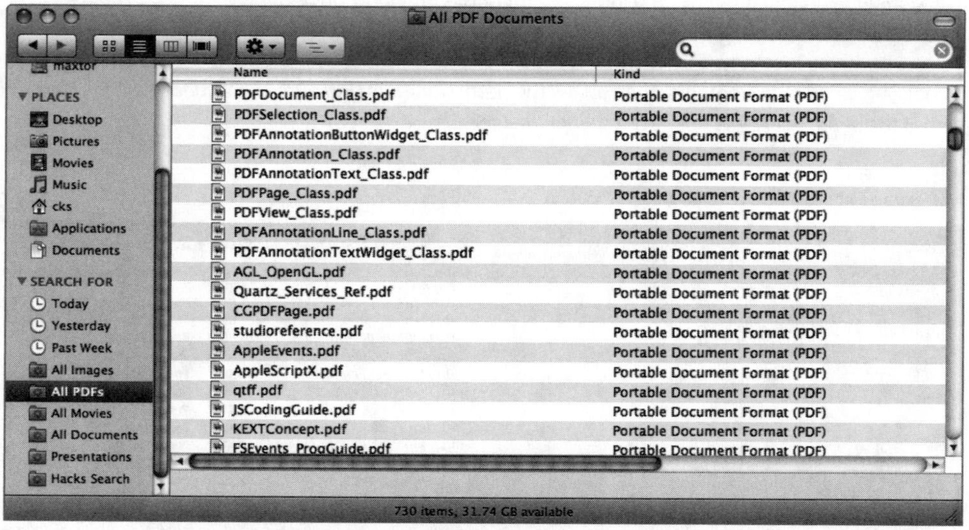

There are more things you can add or remove from a standard Finder window, but with these tips and hacks, the Finder window will be a much more useful window.

NETWORK AND SECURITY HACKS

Your Mac is a repository for all your digitized belongings and a gateway to a wider world. This chapter explores ways to protect your Mac's files while extending your ability to get at those files over the network. Discover how to make your Mac explorable over the Web, how to see just what data is leaving your Mac, browse anonymously, and tweak Mac OS X's firewall. From must-know security tips to safely sharing a Wi-Fi signal, this chapter will make your Mac's world a better place.

HACK 47: Automate Your Download Folder

You can combine AppleScript and Automator. Get a peek at the power with this time-saving hack.

Typically when I download a PDF, QuickTime, or document file, I have to open up my download folder to get the file. Sadly, you can't just click on the Downloads folder in the Dock and have it open in a Finder window. You have to Command-click the folder in order for it to open. I think that's a waste of time. So I figured out a way to have the folder open up when a file is downloaded into it. It's a neat little time saver that should be a folder action option built into the system.

Intrigued? Here's my method for automating this process. This how-to assumes that you're running OS X Leopard, but it will also work if you're using Tiger.

1. Open Script Editor (found in Applications→AppleScript→Script Editor) and Automator, which is found in your Application folder.

2. Open and close your Downloads folder a couple of times. This will ensure that your Downloads folder will be available from the Finder's Go menu.

3. Make sure all Finder windows are closed.

4. Now go back to Script Editor and create a new file. Click the Record button on the far right of the Editor menu bar.

5. Click on your Desktop, and then click on the Go menu in the Finder menu bar. Click down to Recent Folders→Downloads. It should be there because you just recently opened it. (If not, open a new Finder window and click on the icon for your home directory in the window's sidebar, then double-click on the Downloads folder displayed on the right side.)

6. Go back to the Script Editor and click the red stop button. After you click this button, you should get a script that looks similar to this one (see Figure 6-1):

```
tell application "Finder"

    activate

    make new Finder window to folder "Downloads" of folder "bakari" of folder
    "Users" of startup disk

    end tell
```

Figure 6-1.
Let Script Editor do the programming for you

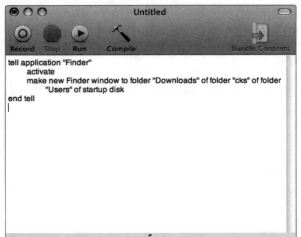

7. Now click the Compile button in the Editor menu bar. Next, click the Run button to see if the script indeed opens up your Downloads folder.

8. If everything is working okay, copy your script to the clipboard. If you didn't get the results you need, simply delete the script and try again.

9. Now open up Automator. When the Starting Points screen appears, click Custom in the Starting Points pane and follow that by clicking Choose at the bottom of the pane.

10. Click on the Files & Folders actions in the far left column of the Automator interface. Scroll down the list of actions and select Get Selected Finder Items. Drag that action over into the larger workflow window.

11. Go back to the first column and select the Utilities actions. Scroll down and select the Run AppleScript action. Drag and drop it into the workflow window.

12. Delete the script code in the Run AppleScript window and replace it with the Apple script that you copied in Step 8. Just press Command-V, and it should appear in the box.

    The completed workflow should look like Figure 6-2.

Figure 6-2.
Transforming your script into an Automator workflow

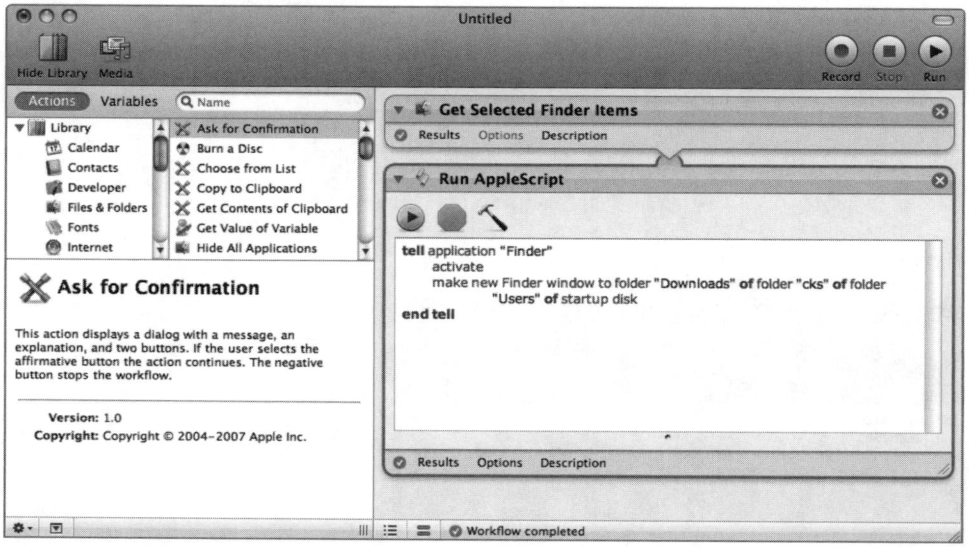

13. Click the Run button in the far right of the menu bar of Automator to check the workflow. It should again open up your Downloads folder.

14. If it works okay, click on File→Save As Plug-in. Select Folder Actions from the drop-down menu. Where it says "Attached to Folder," select Downloads from the drop-down menu. This is the folder for which the action will be applied and executed. Type in a title for the filename, such as "Open Downloads Folder."

15. Now test it out. Download something from the Internet that should go straight to your Downloads folder. Or simply drag a file from your Desktop into your Downloads folder in the Dock. When a file is added to the Downloads folder, the Automator workflow should run the AppleScript and open up your Downloads folder in about two to three seconds.

16. If something doesn't work right or if you decide you don't want to use the workflow after all, simply go to your home folder→Library→Workflows→Applications→Folder Actions. Delete the folder action that was saved there.

That's it. This workflow should be a nice time saver that will open your Downloads folder when something is added to it.

— Bakari Chavanu

HACK 48: Approximate a Static IP with NoIP for Mac

Most Internet service providers (ISPs) will provide a static IP address for a price, and often that price includes a forced upgrade to a commercial account. If you're one of the many who want static IP functionality without added expense, discover a free alternative with this hack.

If you want to run your own web server [Hack #11] or stream files from a home machine to a mobile machine over the Internet, it might have occurred to you that life would be much easier if only you had a static IP for your computer. If you always knew where your computer could be found via the Internet, copying files or serving up pages becomes much easier. A typical situation might be one in which you use a laptop while out and about, and want to access a drive on your desktop machine sitting at home. Guessing where the computer might be is an exercise in futility.

You can, of course, get a static IP address for your favorite Mac. Some ISPs will give you a static IP just for asking, but more often the ISPs see a static IP as something of value and want to charge a fee for giving you an unchanging IP address. The fees vary widely (I found rates anywhere from $5 to $35 a month), and if you use a laptop in multiple locations, a single static IP address will work at only one location.

What is required is a method to approximate the functionality of a static IP address without actually having a static IP address. One solution would be to give a name to your computer, store said name in a centralized location, and then have your computer relay its current IP address to the centralized location. When you or someone else goes looking for the computer, they can instead look for the name and then be forwarded the current IP address of your machine.

As luck has it, that is exactly the way that NoIP works on your Mac, and the best part is that it is a completely free service. Sounds cool: so cool that this process has a name—Dynamic DNS. The concept behind the process is simple: NoIP maps the current address of your computer to a specific name. This is the way DNS servers work; instead of having to remember a cryptic number, you can, for instance, type in www.Slashdot.org and end up at the site. The DNS servers translate the site name into an IP address. With a Dynamic DNS server (such as NoIP), the address is still mapped to an IP but the server updates the IP frequently.

The first step is, predictably, a quick trip to http://www.no-ip.com. Download the client for OS X. While you're at the site, you might as well sign up for an account; you won't be getting very far in this hack without one. The procedure is pretty standard, and a small price to pay for the increased functionality coming your way.

The install of NoIP is standard except that the NoIP installer installs a daemon during install. The daemon, which is required if you wish to run NoIP as a background process, is not activated just by installing (you'll have to turn it on manually), so don't worry that installing NoIP is adding another background process. It won't run in the background until you instruct the NoIP client to do so.

Once you've completed the registration and are waiting to do the activation dance (NoIP sends you a link to click on), you can go ahead and get started. Since you've downloaded the client, launch *NoIP.app* (by default NoIP installs in the Applications folder). You'll be asked for your user password. The process is safe, so go ahead and enter your magic string of authorization (see Figure 6-3).

QUICK TIP

WHAT'S THIS IP STUFF ANYWAY?

IP stands for Internet Protocol. An IP address identifies where your computer sits on the Internet. Most ISPs use dynamic IPs, which means that your computers address can change from time to time. This setup is fine when you're using your computer to browse the Internet but not very useful when you (or others) want to find your machine from somewhere on the Internet.

Figure 6-3.
NoIP is up and running, but it can't do much except tell you your IP address—for now

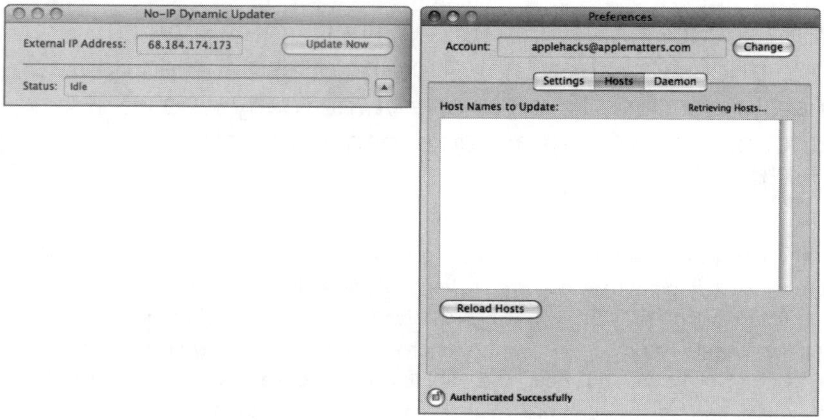

Hopefully, by the time you've installed NoIP, the NoIP web site has sent you an activation code. If you've got the activation code and activated your account, it is time for a trip back to *No-IP.com* to get NoIP to perform the dynamic IP redirecting you are after.

✉ We couldn't take care of this the first time we were at *No-IP.com* because until the client is launched, NoIP doesn't (excuse the unavoidable irony) know your IP address, and because we were waiting for activation.

Once your browser is at *No-IP.com*, log in to the account you created earlier and click Add under Hosts/Redirects. The first thing you'll have to decide is a name to identify your IP address. In this example, I opted for AppleHacks. You also get to choose an extension; pick whichever extension you like from along list of choices provided by NoIP (see Figure 6-4). I chose no-ip.biz for no particular reason.

Figure 6-4.
The basic NoIP setup

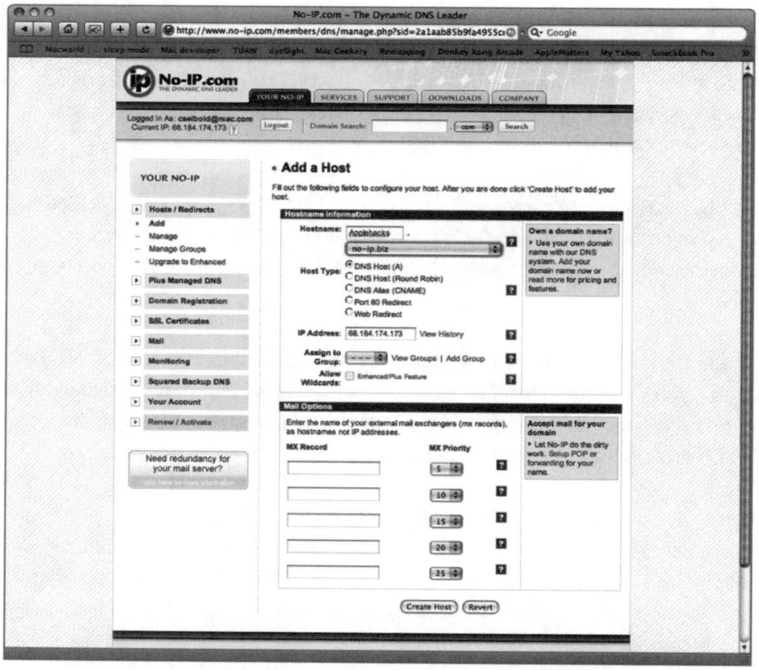

It seems as if you're suddenly inundated with cryptic choices. Port 80 redirect? MX Priority? Mail Options? For the purposes of this hack, just ignore most of those choices; we're trying to find one machine over the Internet, not run a mail server. The one choice that we might not be so lucky with is the Port 80 redirect. It turns out that Port 80 is the default port for serving files over the Internet, and to stop users from running their own servers, some ISPs will intentionally block port 80. If this happens to you, change the port to some other port and instruct NoIP to redirect the port 80 to your chosen port.

Almost done now: the server knows the name we want associated with our IP address. The only thing left to do is tell the computer to share that information. That is no problem. Fire up the *No-IP.com* client, enter the name you chose earlier, and let the *No-IP.com* client do its thing (see Figure 6-5).

Figure 6-5.
NoIP will find your hostname

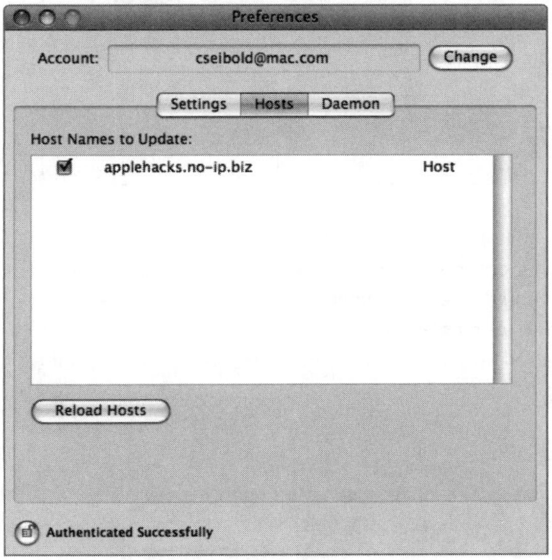

It can take a few minutes for everything to become active and working on NoIP's side of the equation so you might not be able to access your computer from a remote machine in seconds (see Figure 6-6).

Figure 6-6.
The No-IP.com client taking care of business

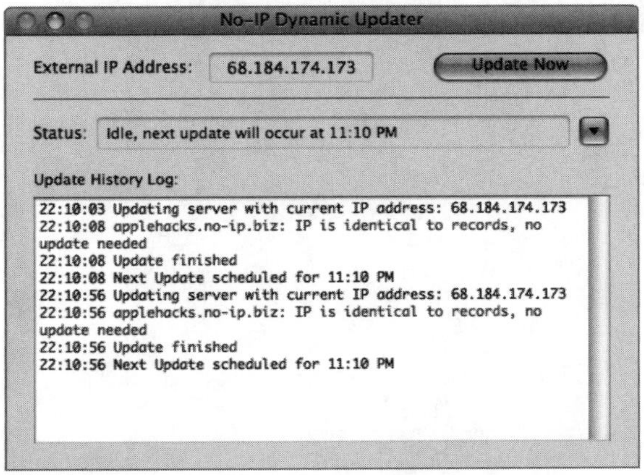

The process is complete; your IP address, and hence your computer, is now available to any device that can browse the Net. As you might expect, nothing is ever that easy. .Just typing in the name assigned to your computer will bring up an error page, which varies depending on how you've got your computer set up (see Figure 6-7).

Figure 6-7.
No joy with an Apache error page!

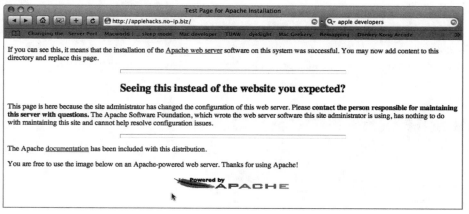

Getting the Hack to Pay Off

An Apache error page means you can find your computer, but there are a few things you need to do to make your Mac actually serve up the files you desire. You can go as crazy as you want **[Hack #11]**, but for the purposes of this hack, we'll keep everything as simple as possible. To make your Mac web-friendly, you'll have to head to your System Preferences and turn on the services you want to allow (see Figure 6-8).

Figure 6-8.
Firing up web sharing

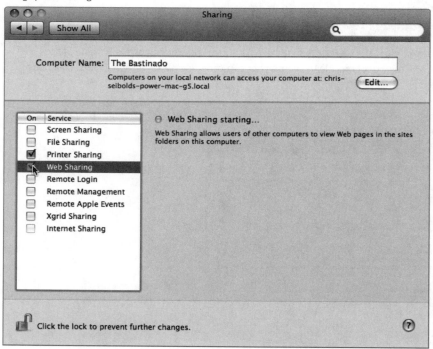

You can use Web Sharing to access files stored in one of your Mac's Sites folders, or you can share files via your Public folder. The choice should be based on your needs. I'm going to be using No-IP to access .*mp3* files and such, so I'm only sharing the Sites folder of my Home directory. After turning on Web Sharing and moving some files to my Sites folder, it is time to test out the dynamic domain name. You have to be a little careful here; when using No-IP, you type http://applehacks. no-ip.biz, omitting the www that some people insist on putting in the URL.

The second thing to be aware of is that it matters where you've stored your files. The domain name will take you straight to the Documents folder of the *WebServer* directory under */Library*. That folder contains various preinstalled web stuff but you can certainly use it. For the purposes of this hack, it is simpler to just throw files in the Sites folder of your Home directory. If you take the easy way out, remember to append the domain with the name of your home directory to get to the files you want to share. In my case, it looks like: http://applehacks.no-ip.biz/~cks. Typing that in results in an automatically generated index page, which is all I really wanted (see Figure 6-9).

Figure 6-9.
An automatically generated list of files stored in your sites folder

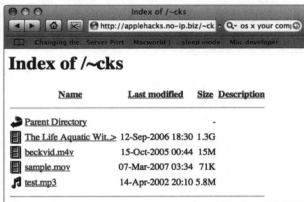

The only thing left to do to make sure everything is working is to try to stream a QuickTime test movie. You can do this right from a browser running on the machine serving the files, but where is the fun in that? Driving to a local Wi-Fi hotspot, I typed in the URL and selected the QuickTime test movie (see Figure 6-10). Success!

Figure 6-10.
Worldwide media access

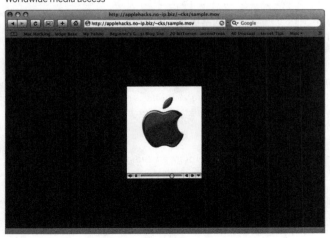

Hacking the Hack

Once the *No-IP.com* client is successfully installed, there is one tweak that will make the process better, and that is to make the application invisible. Select Preferences and then click on the Daemon button. *No-IP.com*'s update client can transform from the familiar program you've been configuring to an invisible Unix application.

Click Update Daemon Settings, Start and Launch Daemon at System Startup and you'll enjoy all the benefits of a seemingly static IP address without ever being bothered to do a thing (see Figure 6-11).

Figure 6-11.
Starting the background daemon to save a little Dock space

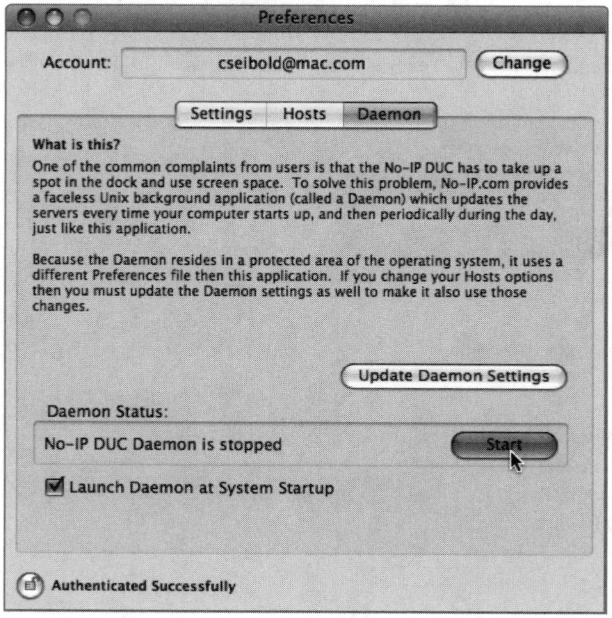

HACK 49: **Surf Anonymously**

While you're watching the Web, the Web is watching you. Discover how to jump around the Internet without giving away information about yourself or your computer using free tools and services.

Mac users as a group feel pretty smug about online security. There are good reasons for this attitude, since, as a rule, Macs are generally free of the spyware and adware that so bedevils the larger Windows-using world. On the other hand, just because your Mac is safe from malicious Windows programs doesn't mean you aren't spewing information about your machine and, by extension, yourself every time you click a link.

The simplest way to avoid passing out this information is through an *anonymizer*. These online sites route your traffic through their servers, leaving the impression that the associated IP address was the point of origin. There are a variety of sites providing this service but a favorite of mine is the Cloak (http://www.the-cloak.com/anonymous-surfing-home.html).

While using the Cloak or a similar web service seems like an ideal solution, there are some drawbacks. The first is that the majority of these sites provide you only a certain level of Internet fun. For example, if you try to leave a comment on some random blog through Cloak, you will be told that it isn't going to happen (see Figure 6-12).

Figure 6-12.
No flames from you

I'm not implying one of the reasons you'd want to surf anonymously is to sock-puppet comment boards or anything so mundane, but when you're surfing the Net you want all the functionality possible without thinking about worrying about running into a "no way" from the folks doing the anonymizing. (You can, of course pay for an upgrade.) In addition, there is a question of just how anonymous you really are. Sure, the sites on the other end won't know anything about you, but the anonymizers have logs as well. If they were forced to give up the logs... well, your browsing history would be exposed to prying eyes.

If the little inconveniences and the (unlikely) possibility of an eventual compromise of your information when using a web-based anonymous proxy are too much to bear, it is time to think about Tor. Unlike a web-based anonymizer, which makes it look as all your traffic is emanating from their server, Tor works by routing your traffic through numerous other computers.

Tor aims to keep you anonymous by making your path very hard to follow. Imagine the connection from your computer to a particular site as a piece of string. It is trivially easy to follow that string from the data-harvesting site back to your computer. With the way Tor works, the string doesn't point back to your computer, it points back to another computer, which points back to another, etc. Put differently, Tor transforms your connection from a single string to a ball of twine with 20 ends hanging in every direction.

There is a little bit of work involved in setting up Tor for the first time, and the starting point is (predictably) a download. Point your browser to http://tor.eff.org/download.html.en and download the appropriate installer. When you mount the disk image and open it, you're faced with something unfamiliar (see Figure 6-13).

Figure 6-13.
Where's the installer program?

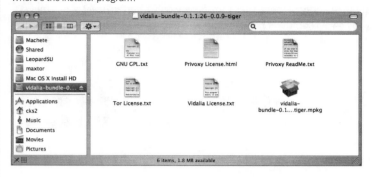

There doesn't seem to be an installer, but no worries: click the box icon, and the installation process will begin. You're asked for your password, and the *.mpkg* takes care of the rest. What you end up with is an application called Vidalia residing in your Applications folder. Firing up Vidalia doesn't seem to do much because first you have to configure your computer to take advantage of the application. That means a trip to some advanced settings in Network Preferences (System Preferences→Network→ Proxies).

This isn't a "configure once, and you're done" deal. If you use more than one way to connect to the Internet (perhaps Airport and an Ethernet connection), you need to configure the proxies for each interface you use.

> **QUICK TIP**
>
> **HOW MUCH CONFIGURATION DO YOU NEED?**
>
> Are you confused by all the proxies? You know a proxy is just an indirect connection to a server, but why so many? Each proxy you are configuring handles a different type of transfer. The File Transfer Protocol handles the transfer of files; Hyper Text Transfer Protocol (HTTP) handles the majority of your browsing, and so on. For maximum security, you should configure all the proxies, but if you are only interested anonymous file transfers, then configuring the FTP proxy will suffice.

Among these preferences, you are faced with a host of choices. Which proxies do you want to configure? The recommendation is to configure the following proxies:

- Web Proxy (http)
- Secure Web Proxy (https)
- FTP Proxy
- Gopher Proxy

You're configuring four proxies, but there are only two things to remember: the Web Proxy Server Box is always 127.0.0:8118, and be sure to hit the Apply Now button after each entry.

Believe it or not, within a few seconds of applying your last change, you'll be browsing anonymously, though you may not know it. The standard way to check is to visit a Tor Detector (e.g., http://www.anonymitytest.com), but the best way is to check the logs in Vidalia (http://lefkada.eecs.harvard.edu/cgi-bin/ipaddr.pl?tor=1). (See Figure 6-14).

Figure 6-14.
The truth is in here!

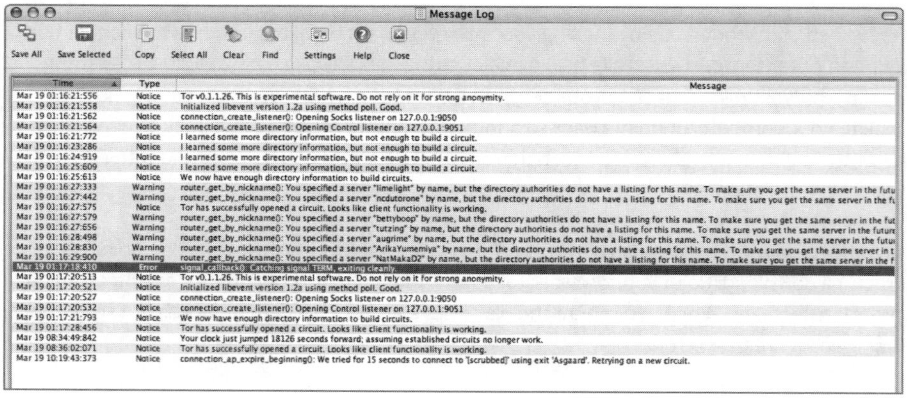

Finally, use the aforementioned Tor test page and compare the results the IP address found when you open the Network Pane in System Preferences to the result returned by Tor Detector. If the IP addresses given differ, you can be sure you are browsing anonymously.

 If you're behind a router, compare the address given for the DNS Server in the Network Preference Pane, not the computer's IP address.

When everything checks out, and you are certain you are browsing anonymously, realize that more people donating bandwidth make Tor more secure and consider heading back to *Tor.org* (http://tor. eff.org/). There you can set up your machine to be used as one of the trail-scrambling middlemen. The performance hit is not noticeable to most people, and you'll be making the Net a more anonymous place.

HACK 50: Monitor the Data Leaving Your Mac

Your computer is always connected to the Internet, and that means the Internet is always connected to your computer. Data transfer isn't a one-way street by default, and your Mac could be sending out information without your knowledge.

You don't have to be left in the dark about which programs are calling home and which applications are connecting to the Internet unbeknownst to you. Master your Mac's connectivity and control the transfer of data with Leopard's built in-firewall and, for even more control, Little Snitch.

Using Mac OS X's Firewall

When you load a program on your Mac, you usually do so for a specific reason. If you're after photo management, you install a piece of software to manage your photos. What most people don't knowingly do is load software on to their computer with the thought that the software is going to use your always-on Internet connection to phone home and report that status of the program to the company that produced the software.

Usually the check back to the corporation's servers is completely innocuous, the software is just checking for updates or getting help topics. Other times the call back to home isn't as benign. The software could be checking to see if the copy is valid, or the software might be relaying information you'd rather not be broadcasted. Of course, not all software does this. Some software is completely upfront about when and why the program checks in with home base. Other programs check with more stealth.

While it is easy to sympathize with a software company's desire not to have its titles pirated, it is a headache when legitimate use of a program is blocked by the company's antipiracy efforts. To put a face on this problem: I have multiple Macs and rarely bother quitting a program (preemptive multitasking, hooray!) but on more than one occasion I've been prevented from using a particular program on one machine because another instance of the program is running on another machine (Office displays this behavior). So even though I am only attempting to actively use one copy of the software, I am prevented from doing so by the program.

This is problematic. Denying users use of a legitimately obtained copy of software isn't just annoying, it means that the software is communicating to another computer somewhere without the user's knowledge. In some cases, it's just another computer on your network, as the running copies of a program compare license keys. But on some cases, this communication is with a server somewhere. That is a little disconcerting. If a program is calling home without your knowledge, you don't really have any idea what information the program is actually sending. This is something you'd probably like to put a stop to.

If you want more control of the data entering and leaving your Mac, what you're really after is a firewall. A firewall separates the Internet from your computer, and depending on which firewall you use, it can be highly customized to meet your needs. As you can probably imagine, customizing a firewall can either be so superficial as to be worthless or so arcane as to be indecipherable. What most users would like is just a little more control with a minimal amount of effort.

With the advent of Leopard, Mac OS X's firewall was significantly improved. Now users get three levels of security. The default "Allow all incoming connections," the fairly strict, "Allow only essential services" connection and the "Hey let the user decide" connection option—actually called "Set access for specific services and programs" (see Figure 6-15). You can access the Firewall via System Preferences→Security→Firewall.

Figure 6-15.
The default Firewall settings in OS X

QUICK HACK

ENABLE STEALTH MODE

This hack is about limiting the information leaving your Mac, but since you're adjusting the Firewall settings anyway, you might want to consider enabling Stealth Mode on your Mac. This won't stop your Mac from sending information out, but any other computer that tries to contact your machine will receive no response at all, essentially telling the other machine that nothing at all resides at your IP. To turn on Stealth Mode, click the Advanced button in the Firewall pane and select (unsurprisingly) Enable Stealth Mode.

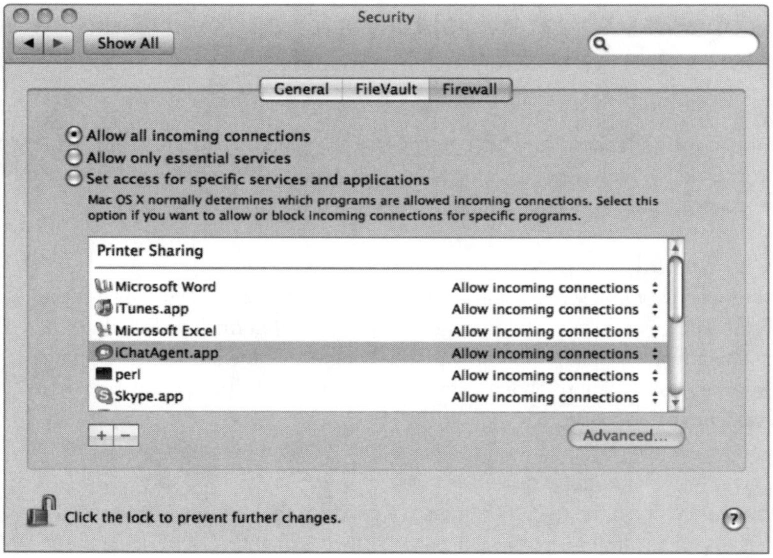

Since you want to limit what your Mac sends out without your knowledge, you've got two choices: you can choose either "Allow only essential services" or "Set access for specific for specific services and applications." If your pick is "Allow only essential services," everything is blocked but a few things OS X deems indispensable. So you'll still be able to use Safari because it relies on `configd` (`configd` is a Unix program that handles the Dynamic Host Configuration Protocol for OS X), but any file-sharing applications, VoIP applications, and most gaming applications will be unable to connect (see Figure 6-16).

Figure 6-16
You've killed No-IP!

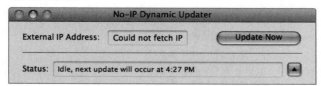

A better choice for most of us is to "Set access for specific services and applications." Selecting this option results in OS X asking you specifically if you want to allow a certain application to accept incoming connections. Since you probably know what applications you don't mind fielding calls, you'll build up a list of applications that can (or can't) accept traffic over time. It's a list you can modify at any time by visiting the Firewall pane and manually adjusting the permissions.

Little Snitch 2

The firewall included with Leopard is enough for most people, but if you want even more control, Little Snitch 2 is worth a try (http://www.obdev.at/products/littlesnitch/index.html, $24.95). With Little Snitch, you can monitor all the information entering and leaving your computer and set up specific rules to filter said information.

Installation is (as suspected) straightforward. Once the program is downloaded, click on the installer, and get prepared to type your password in twice. After you are fully authenticated, you can get down to the serious business of watching what data is leaving your computer. Little Snitch comes with a long list of preset rules as defaults, and these should be plenty to get you started (see Figure 6-17).

Figure 6-17.
Follow the rules!

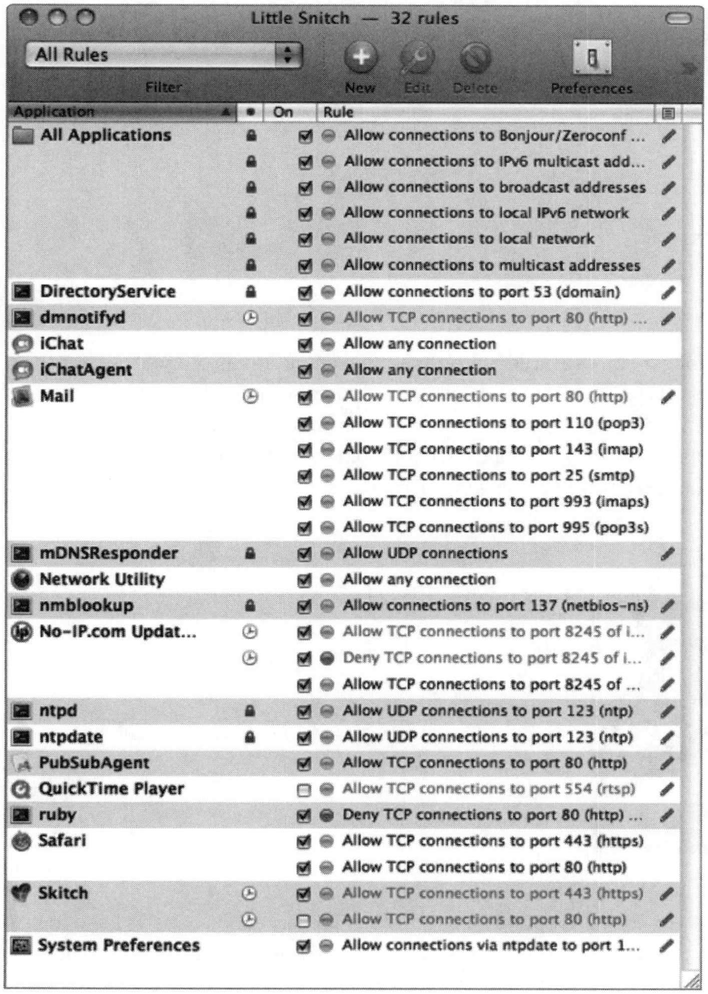

Of course just adding a long list of rules to your firewall only provides another hoop for some clever programmer to jump through. Where Little Snitch really shines is the program's ability to modify the rules as time passes. When Little Snitch finds some unexpected traffic, the program lets you know (see Figure 6-18).

Figure 6-18.
Little Snitch 2 is learning

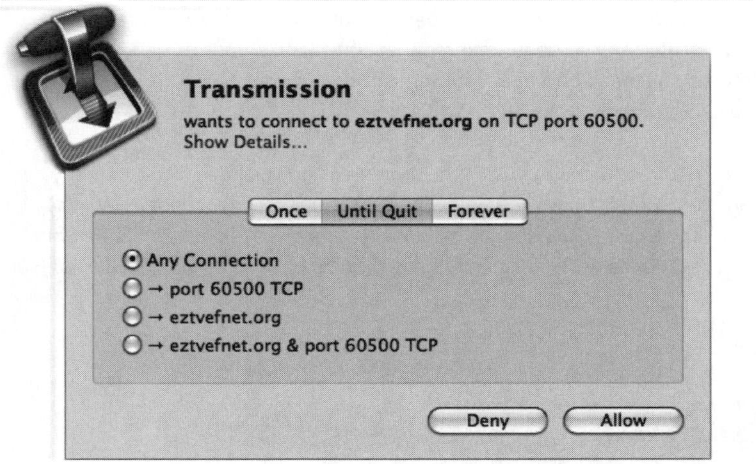

Take careful note of the choices:

- Once

- Until the application quits

- Forever

The choices mean that the longer you use Little Snitch, the more accurate the program becomes. In a few days, all the applications you want to send data will be doing so without intervention, and the programs that were sending stuff you didn't want leaving your computer will no longer be communicating with the larger world. As a bonus, Little Snitch throws in a graphical network monitor that fades in and out with network activity (see Figure 6-19).

Figure 6-19.
You'll see all your network activity

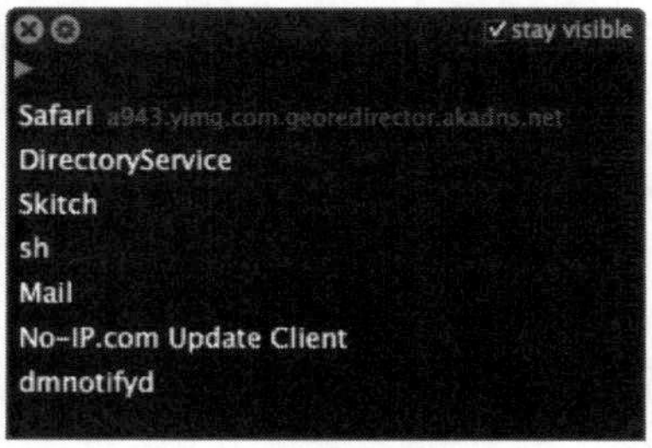

Both Little Snitch and Leopard's firewall displays are graphical representations of ports used to route network traffic on your computer. They have the advantage of being very easy to use and pleasant to gaze upon. Still, they aren't as easily customizable as IPFW (the command line firewall included in OS X). If you want scads of very specific control over everything going in and out of your Mac, investigating IPFW is worth your time [Hack #51].

HACK 51: Resurrecting the IPFW Firewall in Leopard

If Mac OS X's built-in GUI firewall or Little Snitch 2 isn't enough firewall control to satisfy your needs, you're not alone. Some people loathe OS X's new firewall, and some want more control than is offered by the standard firewall.

If you're willing to fire up your Terminal to achieve a little more control over your ports, you can be richly rewarded by configuring the kernel-level firewall that ships with Mac OS X: IPFW. The IPFW firewall that came with versions of OS X before Leopard came along with the Unix BSD *userland* that is now part of Mac OS X. IPFW is a kernel-level firewall as opposed to the new application firewall in Leopard. IPFW is a pretty serious firewall that has stood the test of time in the Unix/Linux world and should serve you well in protecting your Mac from certain types of attacks launched over a network or the Internet.

Having said all that, please understand that IPFW is only as good as the rules you set. Also, there really is no reason as to why you could not use the new application firewall in addition to the IPFW firewall. I really think Apple should have designed the new firewall in Leopard to work this way. Time will tell how effective the new Leopard firewall is. While the jury is still out to lunch on that one, let's focus on keeping our Macs as secure as possible by resurrecting the old IPFW firewall.

The rest of this hack is a step-by-step tutorial in setting up IPFW. We will do the following:

1. Configure the IPFW firewall for use in OS X 10.4 or 10.5

2. Install the IPFW firewall as a shell Script

3. Add the IPFW firewall script to your Startup items, so that it survives restarts

If you do exactly as this tutorial says, it should work as advertised without any problems. You can even visit my web site, and simply cut and paste the text from the blue boxes so you can avoid typing mistakes (http://macsecuritypro.com/2007/11/17/ressurecting-the-ipfw-firewall-in-leopard).

For those of you wondering if the IPFW firewall can be configured from the Aqua GUI, the answer is no. I have tried to make this tutorial as simple as possible so that you do not have to write any code or get too geeked out. If you can read, and cut and paste, you should be able to make it through this tutorial without getting too many battle scars.

Part I: Configure the Shell Script

The shell script below is nothing fancy but it's just right for the job. Again this IPFW firewall script works in both Tiger OS X 10.4 and Leopard 10.5. You will need to make adjustments based on what services you want to run on your Mac. The # sign you will see at the beginning at some of the lines tells the computer to ignore that particular line. It is great for letting people know what is going on with the script, and for turning on and off optional bits of the script.

I have configured the script to be pretty strict but reasonable for most people as is. However, you might want to also run a web server or email server, do file sharing, remote login, or who knows. So if you want to do remote login on the standard SSH port 22, just remove the # from the beginning of the line with dst-port 22 in it. This will open the port needed for remote login when the script is executed. Only edit the sections that have "Optional" in the line above them.

Here's the IPFW shell script you will need. Look it over to see if there are any ports you want to open. (The port numbers are after the "add" part of each command.)

```sh
#!/bin/sh
#
# ipfw script for Mac OS X 10.4 Tiger and 10.5 Leopard
# Created for MacSecurityPro.com
# Created by John E. 11.05.2007

# Enable Logging ***Do NOT Change This Section****
if [ `/usr/sbin/sysctl -n net.inet.ip.fw.verbose` == 0 ] ; then
/usr/sbin/sysctl -w net.inet.ip.fw.verbose=2
fi

# Use flush to remove any existing firewall rules
/sbin/ipfw -f flush

# Establish rules for localhost ***Do NOT Change This Section****
/sbin/ipfw -f add 00010 divert 8668 ip from any to any via en0
/sbin/ipfw -f add 02000 allow ip from any to any via lo*
/sbin/ipfw -f add 02010 deny log ip from 127.0.0.0/8 to any in
/sbin/ipfw -f add 02020 deny log ip from any to 127.0.0.0/8 in
/sbin/ipfw -f add 02030 deny log ip from 224.0.0.0/3 to any in
/sbin/ipfw -f add 02040 deny log tcp from any to 224.0.0.0/3 in
/sbin/ipfw -f add 02041 allow tcp from any to any dst-port 427 in

# Check states, ****Do NOT Change This Section*******
/sbin/ipfw -f add 02047 allow tcp from any to any out
/sbin/ipfw -f add 02050 allow tcp from any to any established
/sbin/ipfw -f add 02055 allow udp from any to any out
/sbin/ipfw -f add 02065 allow tcp from any to any frag

# Optional- Open port for "Remote Login" a.k.a SSH Connections
#/sbin/ipfw -f add 02075 allow tcp from any to any dst-port 22 in

# Optional- Open ports for Apple File Sharing (AFP)
#/sbin/ipfw -f add 02080 allow tcp from any to any dst-port 548 in

# Optional- Open port for Internet Sharing(Encrypt your signal)
#/sbin/ipfw -f add 02090 allow tcp from any to any in via en1

# Optional- Open ports for web server a.k.a web sharing
#/sbin/ipfw -f add 02100 allow tcp from any to any dst-port 80 in
#/sbin/ipfw -f add 02110 allow tcp from any to any dst-port 443 in

# Deny all other ***Do NOT Change This Section****
/sbin/ipfw -f add 12190 deny log tcp from any to any
/sbin/ipfw -f add 20000 deny log icmp from any to me in icmptypes 8
/sbin/ipfw -f add 65535 allow ip from any to any
```

Now we need to create and install this script. To do this, you will need administrator privileges. First, open the Terminal application (see Chapter 4).

At the $ command prompt, type the following command to get to the /Library/StartupItems directory where we will create and install the script. Be sure to hit enter after cutting and pasting (or typing) the commands. Also, you will be prompted for your Admin password whenever the sudo command is used, so have it handy.

```
$ cd /Library/StartupItems
```

Now make a new directory for the Firewall:

```
$ sudo mkdir /Library/StartupItems/Firewall
```

Lets, create the firewall script using the vi editor:

```
$ cd Firewall
$ sudo vi Firewall
```

After the editor opens, hit the "i" key on the keyboard to allow you to insert text (see Figure 6-20).

Figure 6-20.
Don't worry, that's how the Vi text editor is supposed to look!

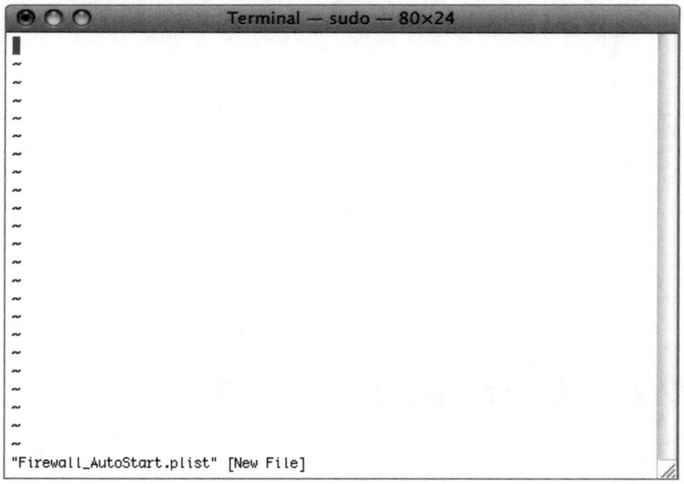

Now copy the entire script from the web page and paste it into the vi editor (right click paste). Make sure that all the lines are there. If so, hit your Esc key, and then the following text:

```
:wq
```

Finally, hit the Enter key.

Your script should now be created, but it is not executable yet. To make it executable, type the following command, which is the chmod with the +x option to make the file executable:

```
$ sudo chmod +x /Library/StartupItems/firewall/Firewall
```

Part II: Install the Firewall Shell Script
You are almost there. There are two more things we need to do in order to complete this tutorial. First, we need to make a .plist file in the StartupItems directory, so our script will automatically

launch at every boot of the system. If you fail to create a *.plist* file for your firewall script, then whenever you restart your computer, the firewall will be off, and you will have to manually start it. It's probably not the best idea from a security standpoint.

I have created the following *.plist* file, which you can copy and paste as is, without modification. Open the `vi` editor and name the .plist file *StartupParameters.plist*.

```
$ sudo vi StartupParameters.plist
```

Hit the "i" key once you are in the `vi` editor. Now copy and paste this code into the editor:

```
{ Description = "Firewall"; Provides = ("Firewall"); Requires = ("Network");
OrderPreference = "None"; Messages = { start = "Starting NAT/Firewall"; stop =
"Stopping NAT/Firewall"; }; }
```

Again, follow this with hitting the Esc key, and typing:

```
:wq
```

followed by the Enter key.

Now we are ready to start the firewall. Before you do though, I would recommend going ahead and turning the new Leopard Firewall off in the Security Preferences panel. Just set the Firewall to allow all. Once you've done that, return to the Terminal and type the command below to start your new IPFW firewall. Enter your admin password when the prompt asks for it.

```
$ sudo ./Firewall
```

Let's make sure the rules are up and running by entering the following command:

```
$ sudo ipfw list
```

You should see a list of all the rules that match what is uncommented in your firewall script (see Figure 6-21).

Figure 6-21.
Your new firewall rules

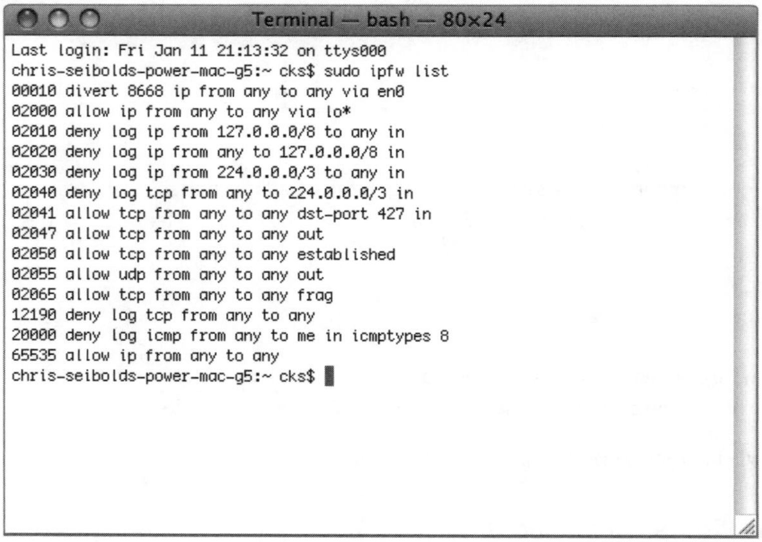

```
Terminal — bash — 80×24
Last login: Fri Jan 11 21:13:32 on ttys000
chris-seibolds-power-mac-g5:~ cks$ sudo ipfw list
00010 divert 8668 ip from any to any via en0
02000 allow ip from any to any via lo*
02010 deny log ip from 127.0.0.0/8 to any in
02020 deny log ip from any to 127.0.0.0/8 in
02030 deny log ip from 224.0.0.0/3 to any in
02040 deny log tcp from any to 224.0.0.0/3 in
02041 allow tcp from any to any dst-port 427 in
02047 allow tcp from any to any out
02050 allow tcp from any to any established
02055 allow udp from any to any out
02065 allow tcp from any to any frag
12190 deny log tcp from any to any
20000 deny log icmp from any to me in icmptypes 8
65535 allow ip from any to any
chris-seibolds-power-mac-g5:~ cks$
```

If so, it means the firewall is up and running, and you are almost done. The last thing to do is restart your computer to see if the firewall automatically starts. To do this, just restart your computer, then open the Terminal and type the previous command. It should give you the same result.

You can take a deep breath now... Take off the pocket protector and your geek hat; you are all done. Your secure firewall is now up and running.

> *For Mac OS X 10.4.x Tiger users*: If you install this script, you will no longer be able to configure the firewall through the Preferences panel as long as the script is running. If you want to go back to the Apple-provided firewall apparatus, delete the IPFW script and corresponding *.plist* file (*/Library/StartupItems/Firewall/ StartupParameters.plist*) and restart your computer. The firewall should be back to normal.

— John Edwards

HACK 52: Physical Security Measures for Your Mac

You've protected your Mac from the networks you use; now protect it from people who can touch it!

These days security seems to be a matter of firewall, antiviruses, and software updates. But that's only one side of the story: your Mac wouldn't be safe without physical protections. Physical access to your Mac means that someone could steal it or simply, if default settings are in place, turn it on (or wake it from sleep) and access files. Obviously stealing your Mac doesn't require a password, and until you set it, neither does waking your Mac. So how can you achieve maximum security for your precious files? The best option is never to lose physical control but that method can be unwieldy, especially in the shower. Let this hack show you the steps you can take to protect your Mac and files from someone with physical access.

You want your data to be safe from crashes, user error, and prying eyes. Apple (Time Machine) or solid backups have you covered for the user error and crash scenario, but you want more security than that. So just how do you protect your Mac from the nosey? There are three different solutions, shown in the next sections.

Kensington Cable

If you're afraid of thieves, this tough lock fits into the security port found on every Mac and Apple display. It is a physical tether that provides a huge impediment to would-be thieves. While these are extremely useful at home or work, they aren't as useful or convenient when you're hopping from Internet hotspot to Internet hotspot around town.

Screensaver/Sleep Password

Let's suppose you work in an office, and you're often away from your computer.

Probably you just leave your Mac on, but do you really want anyone to be able to access your files? The likely answer is no. Even if no one has malicious intent in your work environment, there is always one joker who is willing to mess with your computer just for kicks.

The simplest solution is to set a screensaver/wake-from-sleep password; just open System Preferences, click on the Security pane, and tick the box "Require password to wake this computer from sleep or screen saver"—in Leopard, it's in the General tab (see Figure 6-22 and Figure 6-23).

Figure 6-22.
Finding the Security pane on your Mac

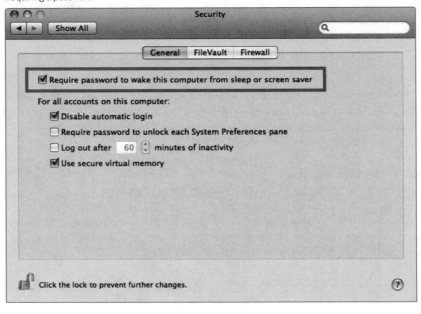

Figure 6-23.
Requiring a password

QUICK HACK ✕

PICK A GOOD PASSWORD...

The following passwords aren't any good: qwerty, 123, letmein. So now that you know three bad passwords, you might be wondering how to pick a better one. There are plenty of tips and techniques from misspelling (try substituting letters with symbols), your favorite book title (B|G_BOOK_0#_@pp[3_H@CKS) to using an online random number generator. These are good methods but don't provide any feedback about your password choice. Fortunately, OS X is here to help. When you're choosing a password for OS X, you'll note a key symbol (see Figure 6-24).

Once the password is assistant is running, OS X will helpfully volunteer passwords, or rate your manually entered password (see Figure 6-25).

So what's the difference between a good and bad password? Since the Password Assistant is running, it is an opportune moment for an experiment! Figure 6-26 shows a bad password.

Figure 6-24.
The key symbol will get you to OS X's password assistant

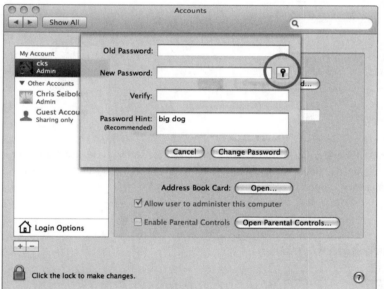

Figure 6-25.
That's a great password!

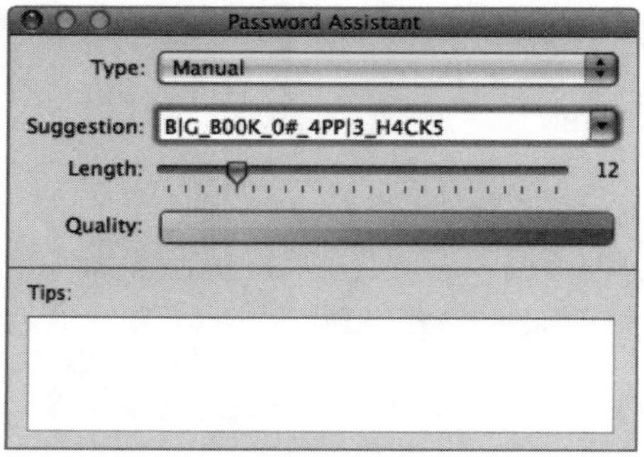

Figure 6-26.
Yes, "secret" is easily cracked

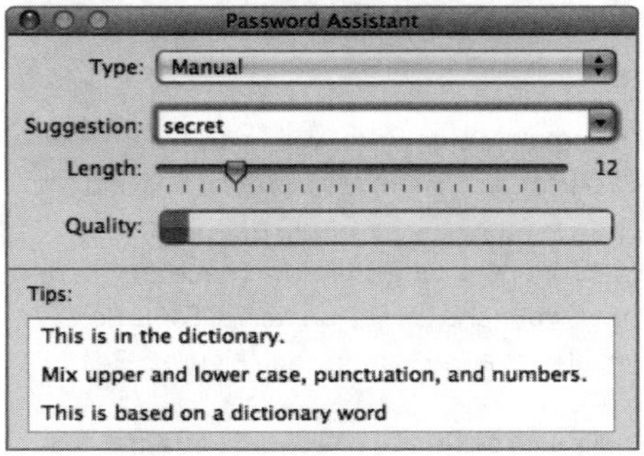

With passwords longer is better, but longer isn't enough (see Figure 6-27).

Figure 6-27.
A little better

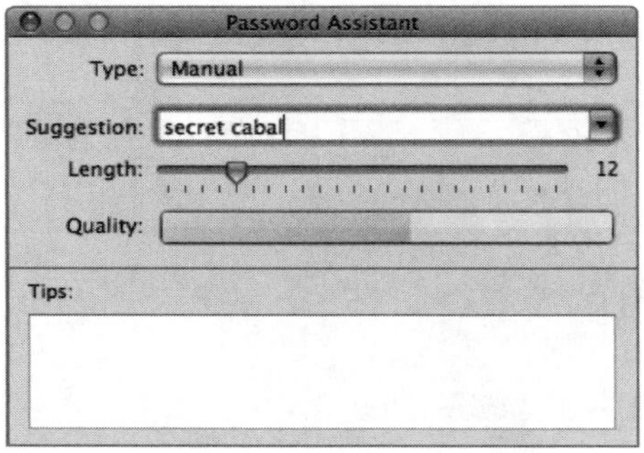

Password Assistant rates "secret cabal" as much better than "secret" not only because it is longer, but because a space has been added. That said, both words are in the dictionary, and you can do better and still have an easily memorable password (see Figure 6-28).

Figure 6-28.
3=e, @=a

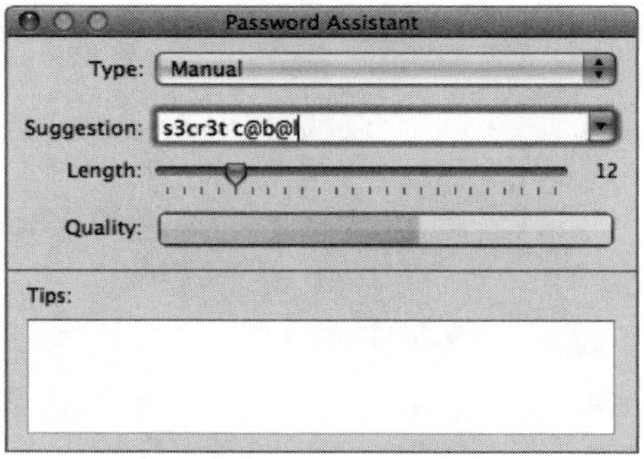

The reason s3cr3t c@b@l is seen as superior is because symbols have been mixed in. OS X will advise that it is a decent password but why not max out the password strength? (See Figure 6-29.)

Figure 6-29.
That is a tough password!

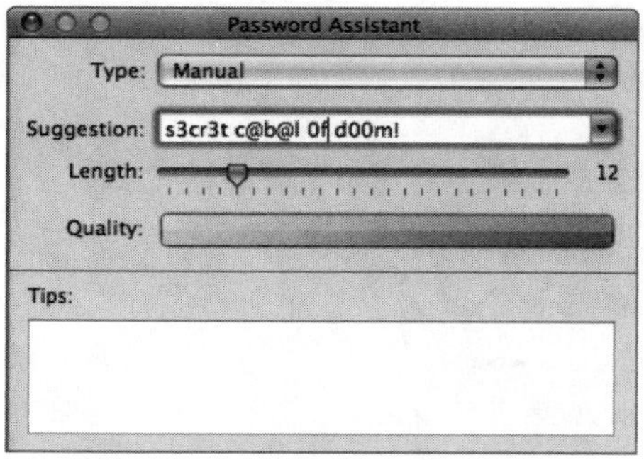

That is a great password! But don't use it, it has been published (here). Instead, come up with your own memorable phrase, substituting symbols and numbers for letters. If you're wondering why I didn't let OS X generate a memorable password for me, well to a get a password as strong as "s3cr3t c@b@l 0f d00m," OS X suggested "bunkoing4088#hostelry". The things that pass for memorable these days...

Use a Login Password

Does a screensaver password make your Mac any safer? Your Mac is safer from someone who casually wants to poke about on your machine, but your Mac isn't really any safer from someone even slightly determined to get access. The password can be avoided by restarting the Mac (holding down the power button for a few seconds is the simplest way to reach that end, and everyone knows about the power button). Once your Mac restarts, the malefactor will have wide-open access. Hence, you need to make your Mac also ask for a password at every login. Open System Preferences, click on the Accounts pane and choose, in the Login Options section: Automatic login: disabled (see Figure 6-30 and Figure 6-31).

Figure 6-30.
It's a security feature but you'll have to visit the Accounts pane

Figure 6-31.
Disabling auto login

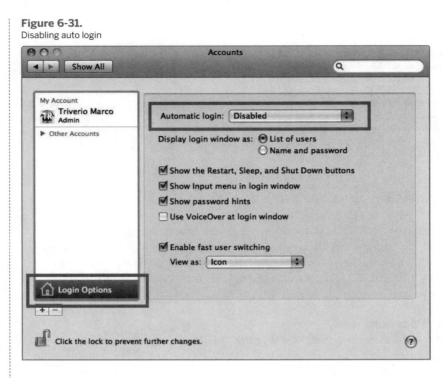

Use a Firmware Password

With a screensaver password and a login password required, is your computer and your data as safe as possible? No.

People can still access your files with one of the following methods:

Target-disk mode
1. Connect two Macs with a FireWire cable.
2. Restart the one whose data you want to access.
3. Press "T" just after the startup sound.
4. The target hard drive will appear on the Desktop of the other Mac.

Single-user mode
1. Reboot the Mac holding the data you wish to access.
2. Pres Command-S after the startup sound.
3. Enjoy root privileges (if you know how to use the command line).

Password-reset
1. Boot the Mac you want to reset the password(s) of from a CD/DVD (such as the Restore disks or any retail version of Mac OS X).
2. Open the Reset Password Utility.
3. Select the disk that contains the password(s) to reset (default is Macintosh HD).
4. Select the user whose password you want to reset.
5. Choose a new password.

As you can see, once someone has physical access, there are several workable options to get around your password machinations. Surely, there is some way to protect your Mac against intrusions of these sorts. There is: the best way to protect your Mac against these kinds of attack is to set a firmware password.

⚡ Unless you are very serious about security be very careful when applying an Open Firmware password. Maxing out the security and forgetting the password you chose turns your beautiful, functional Mac into a beautiful, nonfunctioning brick. Firmware is the first thing your Mac sees when booting; if the Mac sees something that doesn't (sorry) compute, your Mac won't boot.

It's quite easy and it works on both PowerPC and Intel Macs (there are differences, though). The firmware password option is a standard part of 10.4 and 10.5, and if you're using Mac OS X from 10.1 to 10.3.9 download it from:

http://www.apple.com/support/downloads/openfirmwarepassword.html

The other option is to get it from any Mac OS X installation CD: it's in *Applications/Utilities/*, and it's called Firmware Password Utility (see Figure 6-32).

Figure 6-32.
Grabbing the Firmware Password Utility from a disk

For all the protective power of the firmware password, using the Firmware Password Utility is straightforward:

1. Open the application.
2. Enable and choose a firmware password, avoiding the capital "U" character, which is not recognized on some Macs (see Figure 6-33).
3. Supply your administrator credentials (username and password) to save the new settings (see Figure 6-34).

Figure 6-33.
If Apple says it makes your computer more secure…

Firmware Password Utility

Version 1.3 (1)

The Firmware Password Utility application is used to prevent others from starting your computer with a different disk. This makes your computer more secure.

Copyright © 2000–2006 Apple Computer Inc. All Rights Reserved.

Figure 6-34.
Creating a new password

Setting a firmware password will:

- Block the ability to start up from an optical disc (using the "C" key)

- Block the ability to start up from a NetBoot server (using the "N" key)

- Block the ability to start up in target disk mode (using the "T" key).

- Block the ability to start up in verbose mode (pressing Command-V during startup)

- Block the ability to start up in single-user mode (pressing Command-S during startup).

- Block a reset of parameter RAM, also known as PRAM (pressing Command-Option-P-R during startup).

- Ask for a password to enter the Startup Manager (accessed by pressing Option during startup).

- Block the ability to start up in safe boot mode (pressing the Shift key during startup). (See Figure 6-35.)

Figure 6-35.
The Firmware password is protecting your Mac

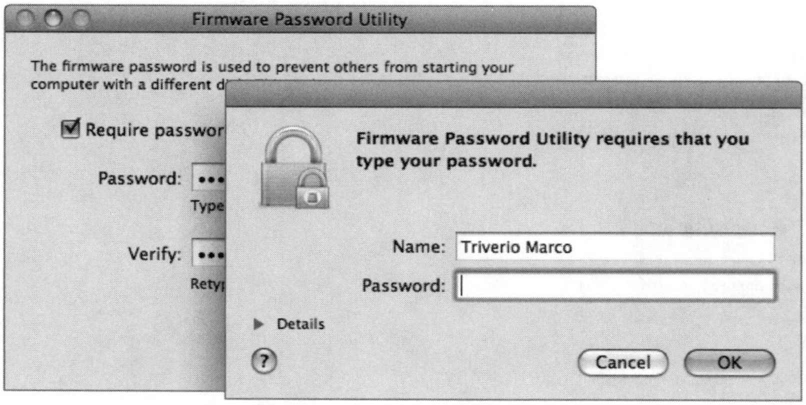

There are some differences between architectures when using a firmware password. On PowerPC-based Macs, it will also ask for a password to enter commands after starting up in Open Firmware (pressing the Command-Option-O-F key combination during startup). On Intel-based Macs, it will block the ability to use the D key to start up from the Diagnostic volume of the install DVD.

This is one of the safest ways to protect your Mac. When using a firmware password (excluding hardware operations and security breaches, see more below) *if your password is kept secret and is hard to guess*, you can feel reasonably safe.

Safer Still, Especially with a PowerPC

Firmware's options are called *variables*, and they are stored in a nonvolatile memory called NVRAM (which retains its values even in absence of power). On a PowerPC-based Mac, they control everything from the boot partition to several security settings, while on an Intel-based Mac, they control only a small number of the available options.

There are at least two ways to change the value of a variable:

- From the Mac OS X command line (works on PowerPCs and Intels)

- Simply open the Terminal (*/Applications/Utilities*) and play with these useful commands:

  — Show all firmware variables:
    ```
    $ sudo nvram -p
    ```

  — Show a particular variable:
    ```
    $ sudo nvram variable
    ```

  — Set a variable:
    ```
    $ sudo variable=value
    ```

Those with PowerPC Macs can use the Open Firmware command line accessed by pressing Command-Alt-O-F after the startup sound (see Figure 6-36).

Figure 6-36.
The Open Firmware console

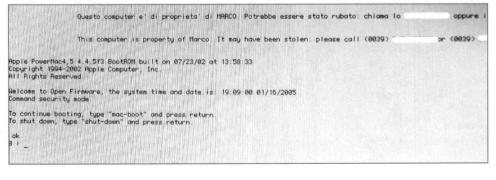

These are some useful commands:

- Show all firmware variables:
  ```
  printenv
  ```

- Show a particular variable
  ```
  printenv variable
  ```

- Set a variable
  ```
  setenv variable value
  ```

Working from the Open Firmware command line gives you more control, and that's why if you're using a PowerPC Mac, you should choose it over the Terminal.

Two really interesting variables are `oem-banner` and `oem-banner?`, which make OF show a welcome message at the top of the Open Firmware console screen. You might take advantage of this ability by forcing your Mac to print your contact information. Should an honest soul find your misplaced computer, she will have the information needed to return it to you.

To pull this off, you have to enable the banner by typing:

```
setenv oem-banner? true
```

Now enter the message you want to show:

```
setenv oem-banner text
```

For example:

```
setenv oem-banner This Mac is Steve Jobs' property. If found, please call 555-
123456 and you'll receive a dozen solid gold iPhones
```

When is the banner shown? By default, it is actually shown only when your Mac boots into the Open Firmware console. The chances of someone booting your Mac while pressing the Command-Option-O-F keys on accident are remarkably slim. And the odds that some random passerby is Mac-savvy enough to think about using the Open Firmware console are nearly as slim. Luckily, you don't have to hope against hope if you set certain variables.

There are two more variables worth knowing about. The first variable is `security-mode`. Security mode defines when Open Firmware should ask for a password. It can be set to four values:

`no password access`
Open Firmware is completely disabled, and the password will never be asked.

`none`
This is the default value: the password will never be asked (even if the password variable is set).

`command`
Password will be asked only in the cases listed below.

`full`
Your computer will enter the OF console every time it wakes from hibernation (but not from sleep) or when it starts up. It will ask for a password to perform any operation.

The second variable you should know about is **password**. This is the variable that actually stores the password you choose. A new password must *not* be set with the **setenv** command; it must be set with the **passwd** command.

Using those variables, you decide when the Open Firmware console is entered:

- If the **security-mode** variable is set to **none** or **command**, and you press Command-Option-O-F after the startup sound, the Open Firmware console will be launched.

- If the **security-mode** variable is set to **full**, the Open Firmware console will be launched each time you boot your Mac.

- If the variable **auto-boot?** (the question mark is part of the name of the variable) is set to **false**, the custom banner is displayed.

In the example that displays the custom banner, it would be useful if it were displayed every time your Mac is booted. The Firmware Password utility sets the **security-mode** to **command** by default but, for better security, you might prefer the **full** mode, which makes your computer enter the Open Firmware console at every boot and, thus, always show the banner you have previously set.

If you prefer the convenience of **command** but still want the banner to be shown at every boot, you have to set the **auto-boot?** variable value to **false** as mentioned earlier.

On an Intel-based Mac, you cannot set a firmware banner but you can make your Mac show a string at every login (this is possible on PowerPCs too). You just need to use the Property List Editor (installed along with Xcode tools) to edit the file */Library/Preferences/com.apple.loginwindow. plist* adding the child **LoginwindowText** and setting it to a **string** of value *Hello, I'm Phil Schiller* [Hack #6] (see Figure 6-37).

Figure 6-37.
You found Phil Schiller's Mac!

Circumventing Firmware Passwords

If you're wondering if the firmware password (on both PowerPC and Intel Macs) can be circumvented, the answer is (un)fortunately yes. This proves that 100% security doesn't exist.

How can the nefarious undo your hard work? Or how can you undo your work if you've forgotten your password? There are three methods; fortunately for people wanting to break into your computer, they are either obscure (OS 9) or a lot of work.

One way of getting around the firmware password involves using OS 9. Obviously, this is for PowerPC only. Boot into Mac OS 9 and obtain the password with FWsucker (http://www.securemac.com/openfirmwarepasswordprotection.php#fwsucker).

You can also obtain (without resetting) the password in Mac OS X with a little bit of work if you have administrator access.

If you have "played" a little bit with Terminal and the `nvram` command, you might have found that the following command:

```
$ sudo nvram -p
```

(which requires an administrator password) shows the `security-password` variable, which is in the form:

```
%c3%c4%c4%c3%df
```

It looks like unintelligible garbage, but the password is not ciphered; it has only been obfuscated! Every ASCII character has been XORed (exclusive OR) with 0xAA. Once you can see the password, you can decode it as you can see in Table 6-1.

Table 6-1.
A magic decoder table for XOR encrypted passwords

sp	%8a	3	%99	F	%ec	Y	%f3	L	%c6
!	%8b	4	%9e	G	%ed	Z	%f0	M	%c7
"	%88	5	%9f	H	%e2	[	%f1	N	%c4
#	%89	6	%9c	I	%e3	\	%f6	O	%c5
$	%8e	7	%9d	J	%e0	]	%f7	P	%da
%	%8f	8	%92	K	%e1	^	%f4	Q	%db
&	%8c	9	%93	L	%e6	_	%f5	R	%d8
'	%8d	:	%90	M	%e7	`	%ca	S	%d9
(	%82	;	%91	N	%e4	a	%cb	T	%de
)	%83	<	%96	O	%e5	b	%c8	U	%df
*	%80	=	%97	P	%fa	c	%c9	V	%dc
+	%81	>	%94	Q	%fb	d	%ce	W	%dd
,	%86	?	%95	R	%f8	e	%cf	x	%d2
-	%87	@	%ea	S	%f9	f	%cc	y	%d3
.	%84	A	%eb	T	%fe	g	%cd	z	%d0
/	%85	B	%e8	U	%ff	h	%c2	{	%d1
0	%9a	C	%e9	V	%fc	i	%c3	|	%d6
1	%9b	D	%ee	W	%fd	j	%c0	}	%d7
2	%98	E	%ef	X	%f2	k	%c1	~	%d4

Non-admin users can still remove an Open Firmware password following this procedure:

1.   Turn off your Mac and disconnect all the cables.

2.   Locate the RAM slots.

3. Remove or add a RAM bank.

4. Start up the Mac and press Command+Alt+P+R (which resets the PRAM).

5. Add or remove the RAM bank you have previously removed or added.

6. And voilà: no more Open Firmware password!

Safer Still

Is all hope lost; does physical access to your Mac mean that someone can get at your data no matter what? Not necessarily, if you correctly use cryptography.

Thanks to an easy-to-use feature of Mac OS X, called FileVault, your Home folder can be encrypted. Once encrypted with FileVault, it cannot be accessed, even when firmware password is removed, or your hard drive is stolen. In fact, the home directory is ciphered with AES-128 (Advanced Encryption Standard with 128-bit key), and files cannot be read if the correct password isn't provided.

To enable FileVault, open the Security panel in System Preferences and click on FireVault. Next, you have to set a Master Password (which can recover home directories of users who have forgotten their password) and then click "Turn on FileVault...". All the files in your home directory will be encrypted and will be automatically deciphered after login.

This feature is almost transparent to the user and, as you might have noticed, is most useful when the Master Password and the user password are kept secret and are hard to guess (see Figure 6-38).

Figure 6-38.
Filevault protects your data

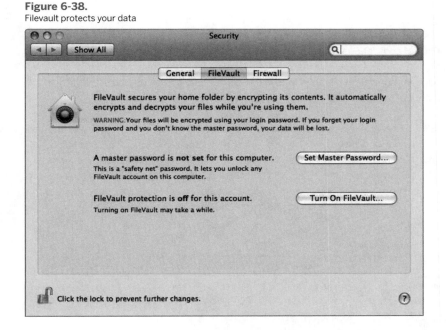

If you follow all of these procedures, your Mac won't just be reasonably safe from prying eyes; you'll have the safest Mac in the neighborhood.

Keep Your Traffic Private with Secure Shell

Like your data private? Find out how to keep your data safe from prying eyes using the SSH network protocol built in to every OS X install.

Secure Shell, or SSH, is a network protocol that provides secure communication between two computers. The data between the computers is encrypted, which allows for confidentiality and integrity. That is, if SSH is used correctly, no eavesdropping or tampering with your data is possible, unless you are under attack by an immortal miscreant with extraordinarily powerful computers.

SSH is available in many forms: proprietary, open source and free software from a variety of organizations. The most popular implementation is OpenSSH, which happens to be what is installed in OS X.

Typically, SSH is used to log in to remote machines securely in order to execute commands. You can also use this secure connection to transfer files, run GUI programs under X Windows, and forward ports. It is this last feature that will enable us to create secure tunnels between computers.

Tunnels: What and Why?

The purpose of an SSH tunnel is to secure the "last mile" of your connection. There are many reasons to want this, but the most common involve situations in which your connection is monitored, restricted, or not secure. For example, if you are at a coffee shop using your laptop over the provided unencrypted Wi-Fi connection, there is a chance that someone is eavesdropping on your communications. In such a situation, you could create a tunnel to a home machine to check your email securely.

Keeping prying eyes away from that email your sister-in-law just sent at the local Wi-Fi hotspot may seem like overkill, but SSH is useful for much more than protecting your inbox. Many people have certain kinds of applications or sites blocked or monitored by their place of work (or by their country). Setting up an SSH tunnel to a machine outside your work (or country) network will allow you to keep your communication private and to use applications that may otherwise be blocked; chat programs are one example.

Setting up an SSH tunnel requires two computers—one as the SSH client (machine C) and another as the SSH server (machine S). Machine C is insecure or restricted, while Machine S has full access to the Internet and is preferably under your control. In the example of an insecure wireless computer, Machine C is your wireless laptop, and Machine S is a desktop connected to the Internet. In the example of securing your work communication, Machine C would be your work computer, and Machine S could be a home computer connected to the Internet (see Figure 6-39).

Figure 6-39.
The typical SSH "last mile" configuration

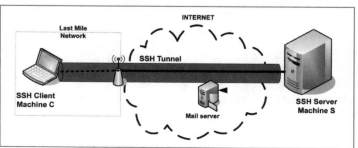

Configuring the Tunnel

SSH tunnels work by forwarding a port. For example, by default you access a web site on that server's port 80. For example, you normally access http://www.google.com at Google's port 80. (There are default port numbers for all the standard Internet services: mail on port 25, secure http on port 443, and so on.) If your network is insecure or port 80 is blocked, you could forward port 5580 on your local machine, through machine S, to port 80 on *google.com*. Locally, you imagine you're connecting to your own machine's port 5580, but SSH transforms this into a connection to a remote port 80 from machine S. For example, once this is set up, any connection in your browser to http://localhost:5580 connects you to http://www.google.com:80 through the SSH tunnel. Requests you send to localhost:5580 are transmitted to Machine S, via the SSH connection, and that machine sends the message to Google for you. Anyone monitoring your local network will see only an encrypted SSH connection to Machine S on port 22, securing your data and actual final destination.

In order to set up an SSH tunnel, you need the following:

* Two machines with SSH installed. Mac OS X comes with SSH, as do most variants of Unix and Linux.

* At least one of these machines (the one you'll use as the SSH server) has Remote Login enabled (or SSH server configured for non-Mac machines).

* An Internet-available IP address for the server machine. Most broadband connections provide a unique IP for your home, though it may change frequently [Hack #48]. You can find your global IP under the Network section of the System Preferences folder if you are directly connected to your cable/DSL modem. If you are connected through a wireless router, you can find your IP in the administration interface for that device. An IP is a unique address for a machine that is accessible from anywhere on the Internet and is of the form w.x.y.z (where w, x, y and z are numbers between 0 and 255—certain combinations, such as 255.255.255.255, are reserved for special purposes).

Before you enable SSH on your Macintosh computer, make sure your password is robust. If SSH is left in its default configuration, our password will be your only line of defense against an intruder. To enable SSH on your Mac, go to the Sharing preferences in your System Preferences and enable the Remote Login feature. Once you click Start, the SSH server will listen for incoming connections to your computer. You may configure SSH through the files located at *.ssh/config* in your home directory and */etc/ssh_config*, but this should not be necessary for most situations (type **man ssh_config** at the Terminal prompt for information about these files). If you use a wireless or wired router, you may need to forward SSH (port 22) to your server Machine S using the router administration interface.

In addition to the IP for your server Machine S, you need the following information:

* The site or IP that serves the service you wish to access (e.g., *pop.gmail.com*)

* The port on that server for the service (e.g., 80 for HTTP)

* An unused port on your client Machine C

The tunnel will be set up with a single command in *Terminal.app*:

```
$ ssh -L localport:remoteserver:remoteport -l serverUserName -N serverIPorHost
```

Here **serverUserName** is the your username on the server Machine S and **serverIPorHost** is the IP or hostname for Machine S.

For example, if you would like to secure all of your Google searches, you could run:

```
$ ssh -L 1300:google.com:80 -l serverUserName -N serverIPorHost
```

Forwarding ports with numbers less than 1024 requires root privileges. Any SSH port forwarding to these ports would be run with the `sudo` command, which prompts you for your administrator password:

```
$ sudo ssh -L 995:pop.gmail.com:995 -l serverUserName -N serverIPorHost
```

This command forwards `localhost:995` to the POP email service for Gmail. In order to get your Gmail in an application like Apple's Mail, you would have to set your POP mail server to be `localhost`. GMail uses port 995, which is the default for POP email over SSL. Normally (without SSL), POP email is accessed via port 110. So, in order to securely download your POP email from another service, you would forward a local port to port 110 on your mail server:

```
$ ssh -L 30110:pop.mailserver.com:110 -l serverUserName -N serverIPorHost
```

Here **pop.mailserver.com** is the name of your POP email server. Now, in order to get your email in Apple's Mail, similar to the GMail setting, set the POP server as `localhost` and under the Advanced settings, set the port to `30110`. Once this is configured, your email will be downloaded to your computer without being monitored on your local network.

You can similarly secure the email you send using SMTP by forwarding port 25:

```
ssh -L 3025:pop.mailserver.com:25 -l serverUserName -N serverIPOrHostName
```

Of course, the important thing to remember is that this secures your email onlybetween Machine C and Machine S, not between Machine S and the Internet.

Once you are comfortable with the theory behind setting up an SSH tunnel, you can try the GUI application, SSH Tunnel Manager (http://projects.tynsoe.org/en/stm/), to configure and set up multiple tunnels simultaneously. It makes it very easy to manage multiple tunnels.

A final word of caution: do not assume you have complete privacy or security until you have a deep understanding of what you are doing. For example, if you are tunneling web traffic through SSH, you may still be sending DNS requests unencrypted. This means that even though your web traffic is secure, someone can find out which web sites you have visited if the network is being monitored.

— Devanshu Mehta

HACK 54: Secure Your Wireless Network

Everyone (seemingly) has a wireless network but not everyone is willing to take the steps necessary to secure that network. If your network is completely open, people can intercept your packets and see exactly what you're doing over your network. Don't let this happen to you: secure that network!

Nothing is more convenient than the near ubiquitous wireless network: the 802.11x protocols fill the airwaves around us, put the "mobile" in mobile computing, and give everyone a reason to seriously consider a laptop. When out and about, an unsecured hotspot is a pathway to free Internet usage; at home, strangers mucking about on your network or leeching your bandwidth isn't as appealing (or is it? See **[Hack #55]**).

Before starting the process of locking down the network, taking the time to investigate who is using the network can be a revealing exercise. The process is simple; all it requires is a quick trip to the command line followed by:

```
$ ifconfig
```

This command returns this seemingly inscrutable output (see Figure 6-40).

Figure 6-40.
That's a lot of info

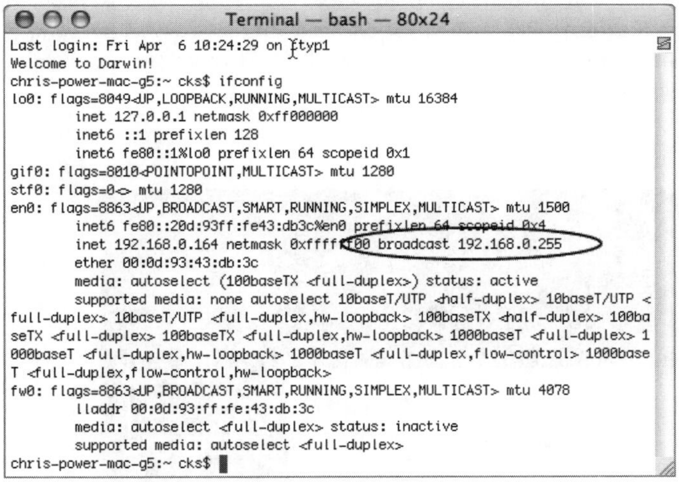

While the window is packed with useful information, the only part of interest for the current purpose follows the word "broadcast." That's the IP address of the wireless network and the small bit of information we need to perform the next test. Back to the command line and another simple line of code:

```
$ ping -c2 -i30 192.168.1.255
```

> **QUICK TIP**
>
> **YOU WON'T FIND EVERYONE ON YOUR NETWORK**
>
> This is not a perfect method to find network interlopers, not every computer will respond to a `ping` request (if you've enabled stealth mode on your Mac, this trick won't catch it). But using a `ping` command has the advantage of being quick and easy.

Most wireless security
happens inside your
wireless router. Typically,
users access their router
through their browser
of choice. Of course,
it doesn't do you any
good to know that you
can control your router
through your browser
if you don't know your
router's IP address.
You can derive this
data using the `ping`
command as described
earlier in this Hack and
analyzing the results
(one of the returned
IP addresses will be
your router, usually the
shortest). Let's make it
even easier with a short
list of the default IPs for
most common routers:

- Airport: 192.168.2.1

- Linksys: 192.168.1.1

- D-Link: 192.168.0.1

- Belkin: 192.168.2.1

That list obviously
doesn't cover every
router, but chances are
it will cover yours.

What the command accomplishes is straightforward: the computer sends out a data packet, and all the computers using the network send back a packet. It's the command-line version of "Can you hear me now?" Only not nearly as annoying. The `-c` specifies the number of packets to send, and `-i` indicates the amount of time to wait. In this example, two packets were sent, and 30 seconds was allowed for a response. The result is as follows:

```
PING 192.168.1.255 (192.168.1.255): 56 data bytes
64 bytes from 192.168.1.200: icmp_seq=0 ttl=64 time=0.325 ms
64 bytes from 192.168.1.200: icmp_seq=0 ttl=64 time=1.147 ms (DUP!)
64 bytes from 192.168.1.1: icmp_seq=0 ttl=150 time=1.860 ms (DUP!)
64 bytes from 192.168.1.203: icmp_seq=0 ttl=64 time=23.430 ms (DUP!)
64 bytes from 192.168.1.200: icmp_seq=1 ttl=64 time=0.311 ms
```

`DUP!` means duplicate and, ignoring those, the result is informative as to how many machines are using the network.

If `ping`ing the network reveals that others are using the network or if you just want to secure your network against future incursions, there some steps you can take. The method you choose to protect your network is up to you (of course). Some methods are less work and offer less protection; some methods are seemingly secure but still crackable, and at least one method is considered secure. The following sections take a look at your security options.

Basic Steps (Even if You Opt Not to Protect Your Wireless Network)

There are a few steps to consider taking even if you decide not to close your network to interlopers. First, you should give network a new name. Routers come factory-set with names like Linksys or D-Link. Names like that practically scream, "use me first." So changing the name of your network to something that means something to your is a good idea, and kind of fun to boot, like wearing a Homestarrunner T-shirt (see Figure 6-41).

Figure 6-41.
Give your network a custom name

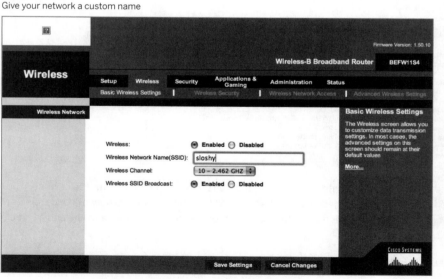

Secondly, and this is more important than giving your network a new name, is to change the password for your router. The default administration settings for wireless routers are easily accessible on the Internet, so there isn't any problem gaining access to your router if you don't change the values. It is also a good idea to turn off remote management so ne'er-do-wells won't be able to do incredibly nasty things to your router over your wireless network (see Figure 6-42).

Figure 6-42.
A few small tweaks makes your wireless network a better place

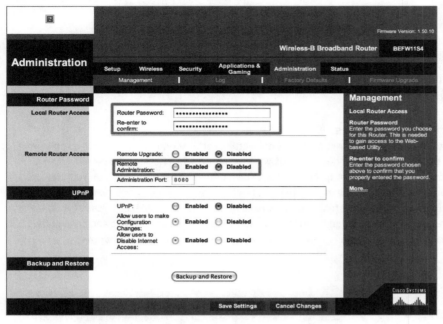

Disable SSID Broadcast

One of the easiest ways to add a modicum of security to your network is to tell your browser not to broadcast the service set identifier (SSID), which is the name you gave your network or the default name set at the factory. Most people when looking for an unsecured network to jump on, just pick a name associated with an unsecured access point. With no SSID being flung through the air, most people will overlook your network. If you're not broadcasting an SSID, your network won't show up in their list of choices. Turn off SSID by accessing your router configuration page (see Figure 6-43).

Figure 6-43.
Turning off the SSID with a Linksys router

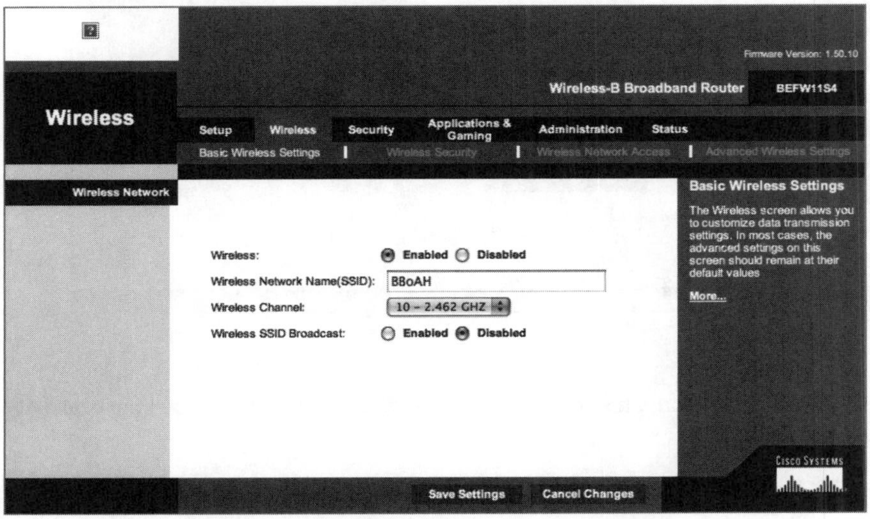

To rejoin the network, choose "Join Other Network..." in the Airport menu, and type the name in by hand.

How much security does not broadcasting the SSID offer? Not a great deal. There are a variety of programs that can detect the unbroadcasted network name (KisMAC is an OS X option), and once the name is known, the network is completely unprotected. That said, if you live in a sea of unprotected hotspots, turning off your SSID is probably enough to make the opportunistic leeches look elsewhere.

Restrict MAC addresses

Most routers allow you to restrict access by only letting certain computers and devices on to your network. Routers decide what devices to allow on the network by checking the device's media access control (MAC) address. If you're going to be filtering the people allowed on your network by MAC address, the first thing to acquire is the MAC addresses of the devices you want on the Internet. For Macs connecting to the router wirelessly, you'll need the MAC address of your AirPort card. To retrieve this information, head to the System Preferences of your Mac and consult the Airport pane—System Preferences→Network→Airport→Advanced (see Figure 6-44).

Figure 6-44.
Your AirPort card's MAC address

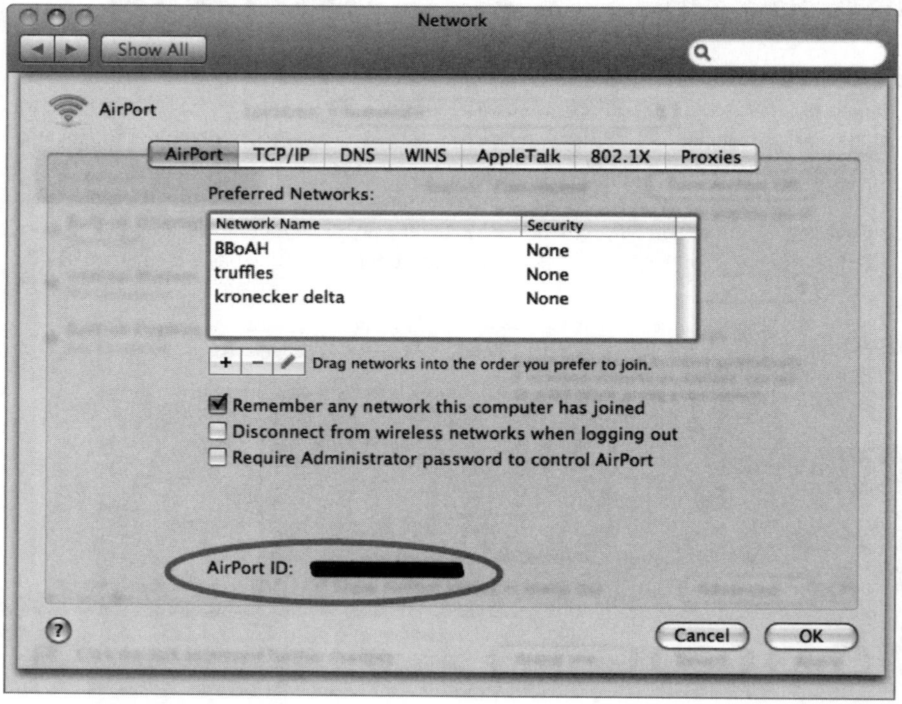

Once you've compiled the information, enter the MAC addresses of the devices you want to allow on your network.

QUICK HACK ✕

LET THE ROUTER DO THE WORK

Listing all the MAC addresses you want to allow can be tedious; typing them again can be even more tedious. Luckily, some routers will take care of the grunt work for you! Tom Sgouros explains how he pulled it off:

"I use a Linksys WRT54G wireless router. I logged onto the router control by using a browser to open up 192.168.1.1 and opened up the network by removing all the restrictions. Then I fired up the two laptops that needed access to the network. Under the Wireless tab of the router control page, I clicked Wireless MAC Filter, then the button that says Edit MAC Filter List. This opens another window with places for you to fill in the MACs. But at the top of that window, there's another button that says Wireless Client MAC List. Clicking there gets you a list of all the computers currently making a wireless connection.

"Click Enable MAC Filter for each computer you want to allow onto the network, and then click the Update Filter List button at the bottom of this window. The MAC addresses will be filled into the Filter List. Scroll down and click Save on that page, and all the computers will be saved. Now make sure that you've checked the button that says only to permit listed computers to access the network, then hit Save, and you're done" (see Figure 6-45).

Figure 6-45.
Adding allowed machines

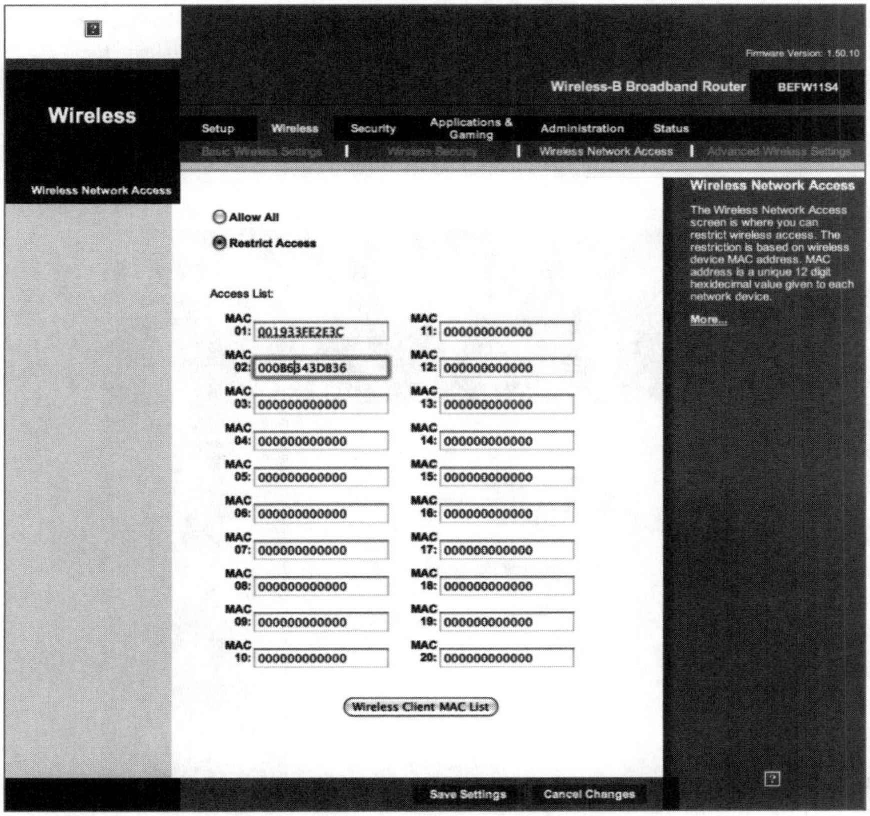

Filtering MAC addresses is tougher to crack than simply turning off the SSID broadcast but it isn't much tougher. Many programs capable of discovering a hidden wireless network can also sniff packets. Since your MAC address is sent with each packet and since the communication is unencrypted, if someone wants to get on your network, all they need to do is spoof their MAC address to match yours. On the other hand, adding MAC filtering to a nonbroadcasting SSID is increasing the hassle factor of using your network, and the hassle can easily chase away the slackers trying to get a free ride to the Web.

WEP and WPA-PSK

With the lightweight security out of the way, we can turn our attention to methods that don't simply obfuscate the network but actually encrypt the traffic. To put a finer point on the difference, if you use one of the previous methods, your network may be difficult to find, but all the traffic will be sent in plain text. Thus anyone who bothers to intercept our traffic can follow exactly what is going on with very little work.

Wired Equivalent Privacy (WEP) and Wi-Fi Protected Access (WPA) do not make the network harder to locate (though they can be used in conjunction with the earlier methods); these protocols encrypt the data being sent. Now it is time to make the critical choice: should you use WEP or WPA? This is one with an easy answer. Since both are equally easy (or difficult) to set up, the only sensible thing would be to go with the one that offers better security. In this case, the race isn't even close, WEP can be cracked in a few minutes (at most) with several freeware programs, while WPA is still considered secure.

Once you've decided to go with WPA, you might wonder just what version of WPA is right for you. Most routers come with two version of WPA: one called WPA-RADIUS or possibly WPA 802.1x and another protocol named WPA-PSK (Pre-Shared Key) or alternatively WPA-HOME. The difference is not trivial: WPA RADIUS relies on a server to authenticate clients and is generally used for businesses while WPA-PSK relies on a string entered into the clients you want to use the network (see Figure 6-46).

Figure 6-46
WPA-PSK is the one you want

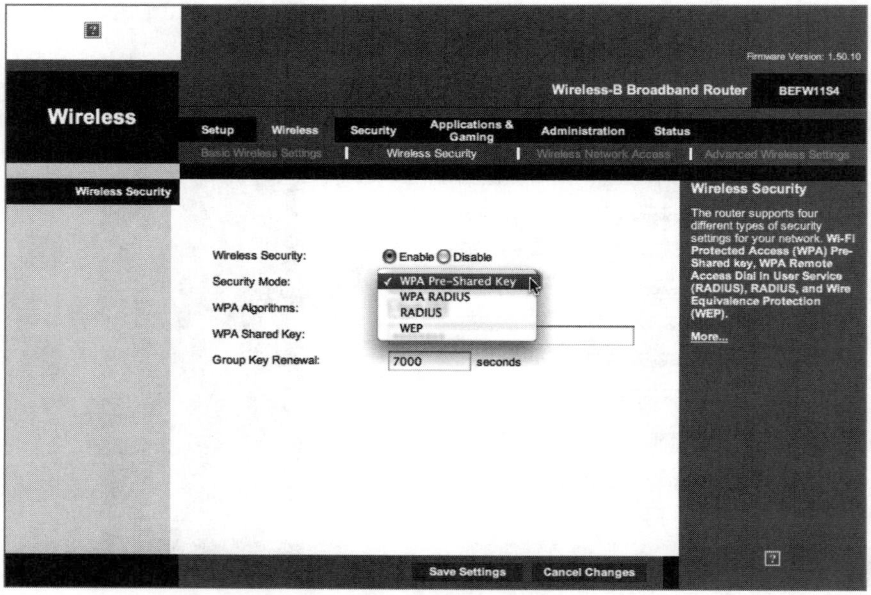

You've made your choice and decided for the protection of WPA-PSK. The good news is that the work is almost done. The bad news is that it isn't as straightforward as you would expect. With most routers, you can type any password you wish into the WPA shared key field. For example, if I set a password to "qwerty", the router will happily accept the key. Trying to enter that key to gain access to the router via Wi-Fi is a dead end. OS X won't let you enter any password less than eight characters. Here it turns out that OS X is smarter than your router. The WPA specification demands a key length of between 8 and 63 keys. Your router wasn't smart enough to tell you that, but OS X is. Now it is as simple as choosing a password and entering it in your router. If you're successful, a small lock should be displayed next to the network you just secured (see Figure 6-47).

Figure 6-47.
Locked tight... or is it?

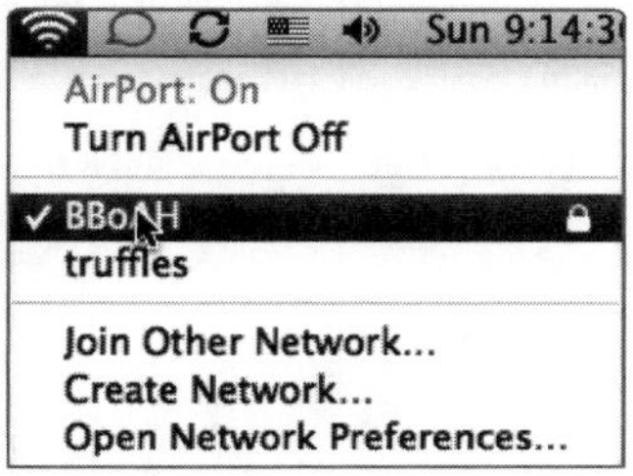

At this point you're feeling pretty good. You've locked your Wi-Fi down so those freeloading Wi-Fi crackers can't surf for free. But there is one more thing to consider—the security of your password. 123GOVOLS is memorable, but it is also very vulnerable. WPA networks aren't susceptible to the tricks that WEP networks are, but they can be compromised by dictionary attacks. How devoted are people to running through a WPA network with a list of possible passwords? Visit http://www.renderlab.net/projects/WPA-tables where you can find a rainbow of tables (useful for cracking) that range up to 33 GB in size. From the web site:

> The fact that we found a way to speed up WPA-PSK cracking does not mean that it is broken. Far from it. The exploit used by coWPAtty and other similar tools is one of dumb passphrases. The minimum number of characters for a WPA-PSK passphrase is 8. The maximum is 63. Very few users actually use more than about 20 characters. As well, they also choose known words and phrases, likely to be in a dictionary. This allows us to leverage a human element in obtaining the key.

So why not make a really good password? You won't be entering it often, your Mac will remember it for you and you'll be secure in the knowledge that it will take a really long time to crack your network. A quick trip to http://www.random.org/strings allows access to a tool that will generate random sequences of letters, numbers, or mixed results. Length is crucial: a randomly generated passphrase of 14 letters is thought to be very secure, so setting the page to output just such a string is advisable (see Figure 6-48).

Figure 6-48.
Hard-to-crack passwords live here

Here are the strings returned with my trial:

OVDQe1IOO4PWvz

qmSUMzsv0DOLzi

eVNc78lbXQixil

Kkfa8CrznNCIqz

MWyCiaYbo6W7wS

9hRRa7ZWSLI4hA

DzYNLmOYQLUI35

74kjKkbbUQMHO2

zxHnj8lnMgbV3A

SEJTL1ix4Zdyba

I couldn't find any obvious dictionary words or sequences of pi in any of the phrases; these will be hard to crack (though the fourth choice seems to indicate that Kafka ate craisins during an eye exam).

Once the string is generated and chosen, write it down. Store it in the Keychain or otherwise ensure that you will retain continued access to the passphrase because remembering a random 14-character string of letters and numbers is a challenge. Paste the newly birthed preshared key into the appropriate spot on your router configuration page and hit Save Settings (or whatever text your wireless router uses to indicate you want to make the change permanent). The router will restart, safe from prying eyes and bandwidth leeches.

To get your Mac back on the network, select the network you've secured and enter the key into the required field (see Figure 6-49).

Figure 6-49.
One long password

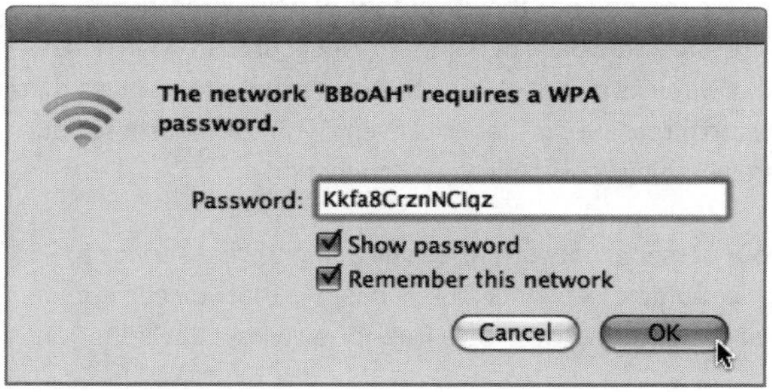

Unhacking the Hack

You've changed your router's admin name and password, hidden the SSID, crammed a completely random 14-letter phrase in as a password and forgotten or lost every scrap of information you used for the setting. If you try to unplug your router hoping the defaults will be restored, you are going to be stymied, so how can you get your router back when you've been blocked by your own security?

Don't worry: your router hasn't become a brick of plastic, circuitry, and electronics. On most routers, there is a recessed reset button that you can hit with a pencil tip or paperclip to return your router to factory defaults.

HACK 55: Share Your Wi-Fi

While some people want to lock down their Wi-Fi, others would like to share the bounty of high-speed access with the occasional passerby. Learn how to safely indulge your altruistic side with this friendly hack.

Brian Jepson once said that terms of service (TOS) contracts were akin to Neitzsche's void: stare at them long enough, and they stare back at you. It's a particularly apt description. Suffice it to say that this hack may violate the terms of service contract with your ISP. Or the hack may not, to be absolutely sure, consider employing a team of highly compensated legal professionals to provide sound legal advice.

Legal issues aside, there are good reasons to share your Wi-Fi. The most obvious being that your connection might make someone else's day a little better and not cost you anything. The more self-serving motive is one of momentum; if everyone felt obligated by custom to provide open access to their Wi-Fi network, you'd benefit when you were out and about and didn't have to hassle looking for a connection.

To every argument for sharing your Wi-Fi, there are a million objections to the notion. Someone could use your connection to download universally objectionable content, perhaps *Son in Law* featuring Pauly Shore, or something even worse. Again the legal ramifications of something like this and the defense of having an open access point are topics best left to courts, but you have to wonder how likely is the scenario that an inveterate file sharer will choose your network to use as the primary gateway for a P2P (peer-to-peer) connection.

QUICK TIP

DON'T GET IN THE TECHNICAL-SUPPORT BUSINESS

There is a temptation to share both the bandwidth and the cost associated with your connection amongst your neighbors. The reasoning is simple: if three neighbors chip in $25 a month, everyone will be getting cheap broadband. ISPs have known since the days of dial-up that providing access is easy; providing service is hard. And that is what happens more often than not when you decide to be a mini ISP. If the Internet goes out (at three in the morning during a tornado), you'll get the call. If your neighbor gets a new computer and can't figure out how to connect, you'll get the call. If the network seems slow, you'll get the call. If someone discovers a virus on their computer, you'll get the call and the blame. On top of that, you'll have to deal with collections. Maybe a few bucks a month is worth being the sole source of computer support for the tri-house area to you, but the decision isn't the no-brainer that it seems like on paper.

The simplest way to set up an open Wi-Fi access point is to simply disable (or never set up) the security features on your wireless router. This method has the advantage of being drop-dead simple—all it takes is inaction—but has the huge drawback of being very insecure. An open access point set up doesn't just give anyone with a wireless device access to the Internet, it also gives them access to all your network traffic. Not the most reassuring scenario. Even if you want to share your Internet, you probably don't want to share anything more than your connection.

The question becomes how to protect your personal network while still doing a great service to iPhone users and others. The answer lies in multiple networks. The concept is that you can set one network up in a secure fashion and let the other network be a free-for-all within the limits you choose to enforce.

The obvious solution to multiple networks is (wait for it): multiple routers. There are other ways to accomplish the same goal using firewalls and proxy servers, but then you're stuck managing the solution, and your once altruistic ideal of sharing the Internet becomes a burden. Using a second router minimizes the hassle of the process; it is a set-it-and-forget-it process (to steal a line from infomercial rotisserie cookery). Besides there is every chance you have an old 802.11b router laying around somewhere, why not put it to use?

Configuring the Open Access Router

The first step in the process of running an open unsecure network is configuring the router that is going to be handling the network operations. There are some very basic settings to modify to avoid conflicts and confusion. In this example, a D-Link router is being used, but almost all routers will accommodate these changes.

A good place to begin is with the IP address. If you're using the default setting, there is a good chance that it will conflict with the default setting of another device. Thanks to subnets and such, the conflict won't really matter, but it can get confusing if you want to access the router, so let's change the IP (see Figure 6-50).

Figure 6-50.
Changing 192.168.0.1 to 192.168.111.1

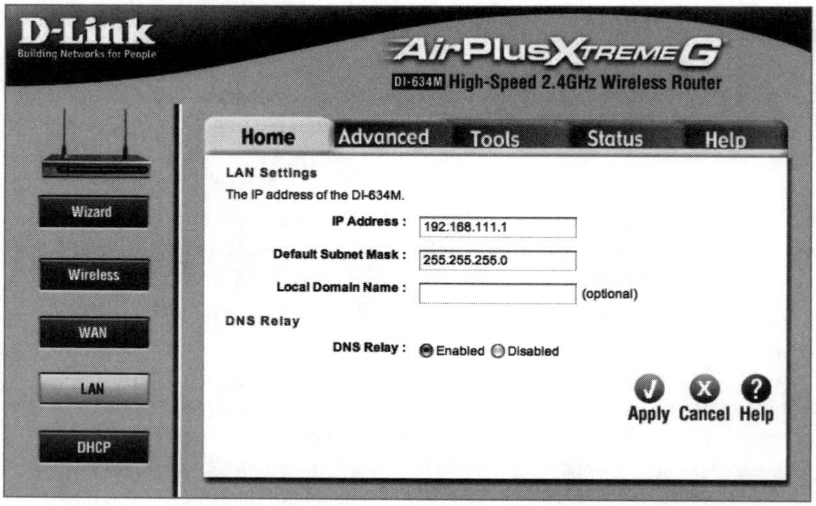

Since you're already logged in to your router, take the opportunity to make a few other configuration changes. Why not change the name so people know you don't mind them using your Wi-Fi? (See Figure 6-51.)

Figure 6-51.
A friendlier network name

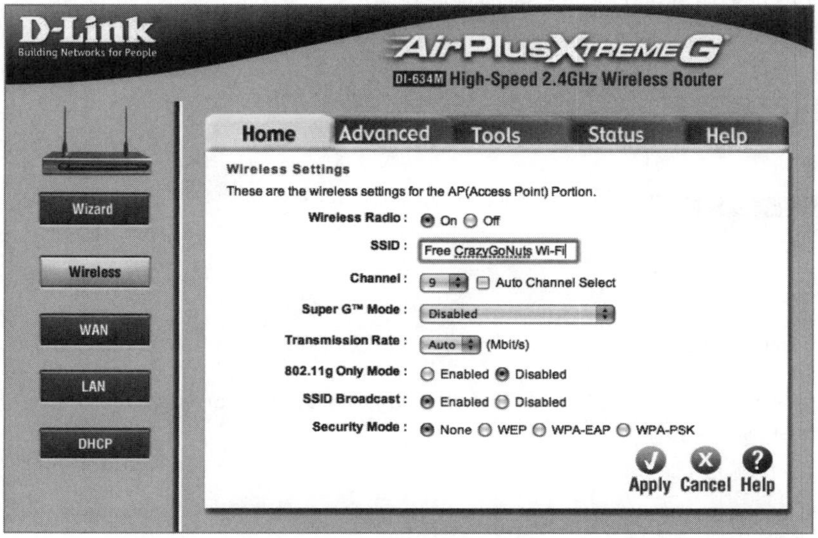

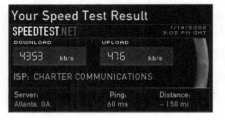

Depending on your router you can further adjust the settings. You can deny FTP connections, throttle the bandwidth both upstream and downstream, and even disallow access to LAN services. The implementation of these options varies widely from router to router, so if you're interested in applying these restrictions, read the manual that came with it. For the purposes of this example, I was interested in limiting the amount of bandwidth allocated to the free access point (see Figure 6-52 and Figure 6-53).

Figure 6-52.
The protected network runs at the maximum speed allowed by my ISP

Figure 6-53.
If you're using the free access provided, your speeds will be limited

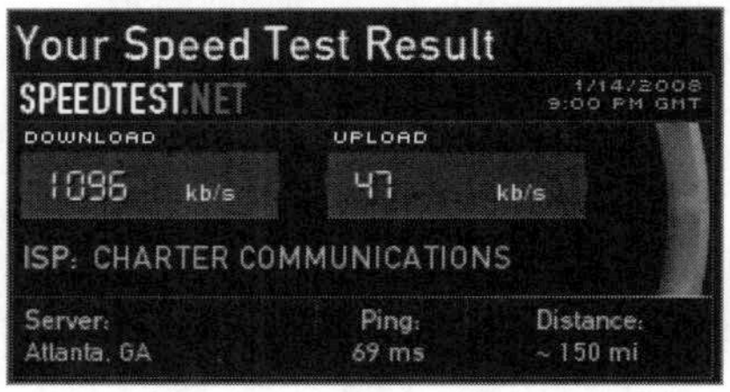

Physically Configuring the Routers

Finally, you'll need to physically configure the routers. The goal is to have the free router run in the subnet of your protected router. Fortunately, this is an easy trick to pull off. Simply plug the WAN port on the router you're going to use to provide free access to an open LAN port on the router you'll be using for your protected network. Once everything is set up, you can check the configuration by visiting the Airport menulet (see Figure 6-54).

Figure 6-54.
Everything as it should be

Success! You're now a provider of free Internet access: iPhone users and wardrivers within the range of your signal will love you.

HACK 56: Use Your Mac as an Access Point

Your Mac is a sharing machine! Plug in a printer, and it can share that; toss some files into your public folder, and users can get to them over the LAN. Want to run a site from your Mac? No problem. The sharing doesn't end there; you can even go so far as to share your Internet connection to those around you who can't connect, or with your wireless gaming console.

The situation where you might want to share your Internet connection without access to a router seems a bit suspect at first. Just where are you going to be that doesn't have an Internet connection? And if it has an Internet connection why would you want to share it; heck your laptop is already connected!

It seems like an unlikely scenario until it happens to you, then it seems like Apple really knew what it was doing when the company added the ability to share your Internet connection in the Network pane of System Preferences. Typically, the scenario goes something as follows: you're in a hotel room or some other not-home place where you can get Internet via the Ethernet but not wirelessly. Of course, you're sharing the room, and the other person also has a laptop. Naturally you both want to hit the Internet at the same time. Instead of the predictable knife fight over who gets to use the sole Ethernet hookup, hook your Mac up and use it to share the Internet connection.

Pulling Off the Hack

The good news is that this is a very easy trick to pull off. The bad news is that the process includes ominous warnings that may frighten the uninitiated. So let's get initiated.

Head to the Sharing Pane of System Preferences and check the box next to Internet Sharing.
Configure the right side of the pane as required for your particular situation. In the hotel example
would be: From Built-in Ethernet to Airport (see Figure 6-55).

Figure 6-55.
Configuring the sharing options

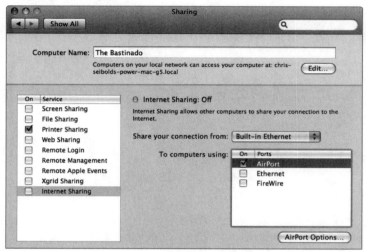

Time for a choice: the next step is to decide whether or not to rename your network (the default
name is the same name as your computer) and if your network should require a WEP password.
WEP is insecure. but a little security is probably better than none and requiring a password should
keep those looking far any usable network at bay. It should be noted that you'll only have to
make these decisions (as mundane as they may be) when going from wired Internet to wireless
Internet. If you're sharing your Internet over FireWire, for example, you won't be bothered with
authentication or network name options (see Figure 6-56).

Figure 6-56.
Options when sharing your Internet connection via Wi-Fi

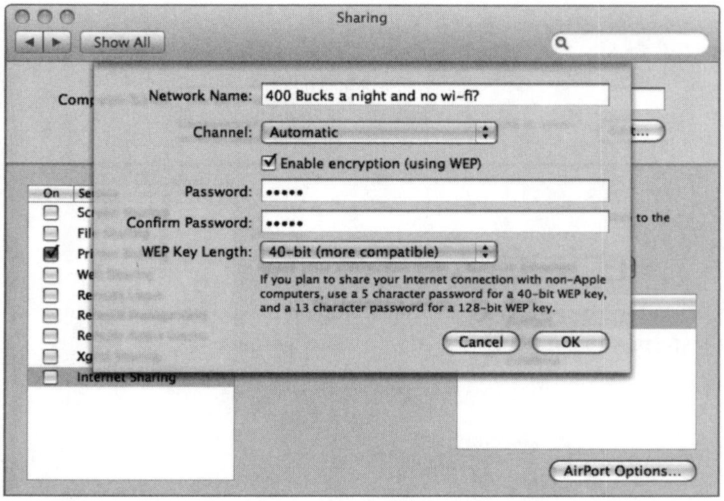

Once you've got everything set up according to your desires, it is time to start sharing that connection. This is where the ominous warning part comes in. Instead of simply checking the box and having the sharing begin, you get a stern warning that you're about to mess up everyone's Internet settings and instructions to contact the system administrator (see Figure 6-57).

Figure 6-57.
Don't worry, you won't break the Internet

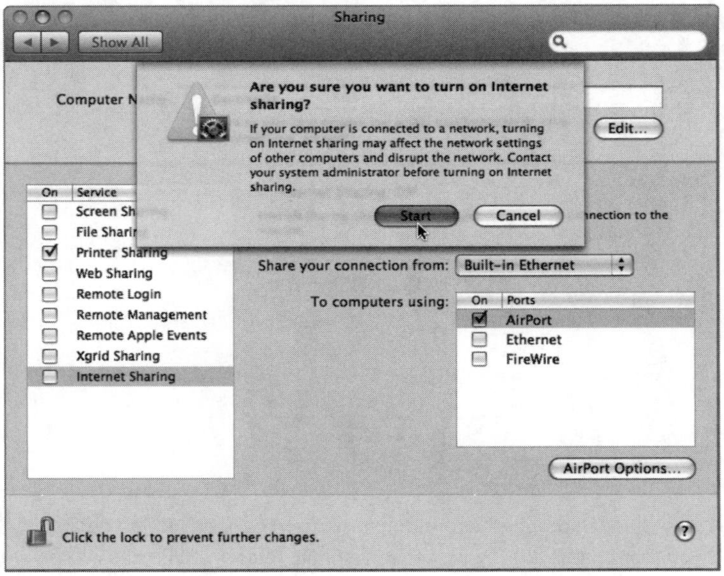

This hack is running your Mac as an access point, so the chances of you breaking the Internet are slim to none. Go ahead and start the sharing process. You'll know you're successful when the Airport menulet changes from the usual broadcast icon to a quarter pizza with an up arrow (see Figure 6-58).

Figure 6-58.
Now you're sharing the Net

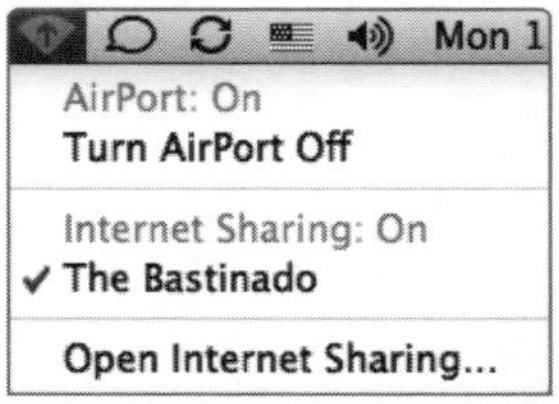

And that is all there is to it. If you have a desktop at home and a Nintendo Wii, Playstation 3, or an Xbox 360 you can use the same tip to share your Internet with these devices.

HACK 57: Hide Sensitive Files in OS X

There are plenty of ways to secure your files in OS X (see [Hack #52]), but good security takes planning, something you might not have done when you run across that must-save file. Even without planning and without being a system administrator, there are methods to hide the files you don't want others to see on OS X.

There are probably files on your computer you don't want people to see. It might be financial information, embarrassing poems, or the world's greatest invention. In fact, it really doesn't matter what it is; if it is something you don't want others to see, you need to know the tricks to keep other eyeballs off your work while keeping the data accessible to yourself (see Figure 6-59).

Figure 6-59.
Uh, avert your eyes!

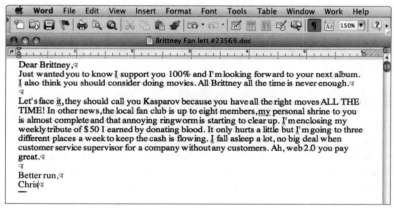

The most obvious solution to the problem is just proper security procedures. Use strong passwords, multiple accounts, encrypt everything with FileVault, etc. Taking those steps will provide a great deal of security for your files, but most people don't bother or can't take all those steps. If you work on a shared Mac in an office with lax security procedures, the system administrator might have everyone working off the same account. Or, if you use your computer around the house, you likely have it set to auto login and family members just come and use the Mac as they wish without separate, secured user accounts.

Many (probably most) users get by using their Mac in this fashion. It usually isn't that big a deal. If your computer mates aren't interested in delving into the Mac, and your family members are using the machine mainly for web surfing, everything will probably be okay. That isn't to say that one account for everyone can't lead to serious problems. It surely can, particularly if it is an administrator account. It's just that most people don't run into insurmountable problems.

A problem people do run into when using a shared Mac is one of keeping their really private stuff truly private. Say you've found a video you want to share with your friend, just to see their reaction. If you save it to your Desktop as a file called *hello.mpg*, there is a good chance someone else won't be able to resist the temptation to take a look. Some things just don't go over at work or at home. You need to hide that file.

The Quick and Easy Way: Bury It in Your Library

Probably the easiest way to hide files is simply to put them somewhere no one (even Spotlight) is likely to look. If you're logged in as an administrator, you can make this place just about anywhere you want: in the system library, deep in an application package or in a fake account you set up. These are all great places, but ones that require authentication to use. For non-admin users, their user library comes to the rescue. The user library is a pretty boring place and shoving a file somewhere inconspicuous inside it is likely to keep your plans secret (see Figure 6-60).

Figure 6-60.
Even Spotlight won't know

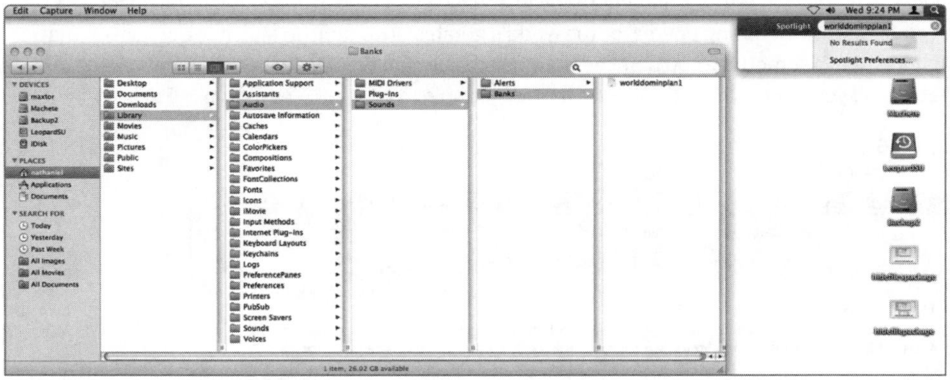

![Screenshot of Finder column view showing Library folders with Spotlight search showing No Results Found]

Hide It with a Dot

When OS X first came out, one of the common reactions among computer critics in the know was that OS X hid its Unix roots very well. The notion being that while OS X was based on a system that had been around forever (in computer years), not much of the text-based Unix came through. Thing is, all that Unixy stuff is still there; you just can't see it. OS X manages to hide the files from view, so the end user is presented with a clean GUI to play with. One of the ways OS X achieves this goal is by making a lot of files invisible. Visibility of a file or folder is controlled by a bit that is set either to visible or invisible. You can edit the bit by hand, rendering formerly invisible files visible or vice-versa, but there is a quicker way to get the job done. Any file beginning with a dot (.) is automatically invisible to OS X. Just as good: the file is also not indexed by Spotlight (see Figure 6-61).

Figure 6-61.
Creating an invisible file

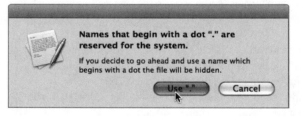

That is fantastic: no one but a Mac-savvy person will ever find the file, and Spotlight doesn't index invisible items. On the other hand, you might be wondering how you can access the file once it is invisible. Obviously you won't be able to double-click the file; it is invisible after all. To get access, you'll need to use the command line. Fire up the Terminal and type:

```
$ open /Users/cks/Desktop/.secretfile.docugly256.tif
```

And the file will open for your inspection. If you're worried that the file will open up with some weird Terminal-specific application, fret no more. The file will open with same program it would if you had used a double-click.

The dot fun doesn't have to stop with a single invisible file; creating invisible directories is only slightly more difficult. With a file, you were able to name the file directly from the Finder after reading a warning, but the Finder won't allow you to create a directory with a leading dot. The workaround is simple: use the Terminal to create a directory. Typing:

```
$ mkdir .worlddomplan1
```

Creates a hidden directory in your Home folder (see Figure 6-62).

Figure 6-62.
The hidden directory revealed by showing invisibles

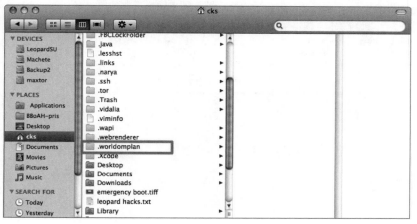

Since it is a directory, you can toss any files you want hidden in the folder without adding a leading dot to the filenames; the files will remain invisible. To access the files, use Shift-Command-G or choose "Go to Folder…" from the Go menu of the Finder. Type in the path to your folder (in the example the path is ~/.worlddomplan1), and you'll be able to browse the files in your favorite GUI manner.

How hard will these files be to find? Using either method will defeat a Spotlight or Google Desktop search (Google Desktop relies on Spotlight's database, so there is no surprise there), but things could get dicey if the folder or files get too large. No one is ever going to notice a few kilobytes being taken up by a small directory. but if you're slapping hi-definition rips of Pauly Shore movies into a hidden folder, that will likely be discovered if someone is trying to save some drive space.

Hiding Files in a Disk Image

Perhaps a more elegant way to hide files on the fly is with an encrypted disk image. This hack works on two levels. The first level is social engineering: we'll name the disk image something so boring that no one will to look at it. Second, we'll password-protect the data so even if they do try to take a peek, they'll still need a password.

Launch Disk Utility (Applications→Utilities→Disk Utility) and choose New Image. Now here's the crucial naming part. You'll want a name so impossibly boring that no one would ever want to look at the disk image. How about *Principia_Latin_Version*? That should keep the file unlooked at anywhere outside a university physics building. If you happen to be trying to pull this hack off in a physics building (like I once did), a better choice is probably *PORNO* or *interpretive_dance_reviews*. The important thing is to know the types of people likely to be using the computer and to adjust the name accordingly (see Figure 6-63).

Figure 6-63.
Creating an encrypted .dmg

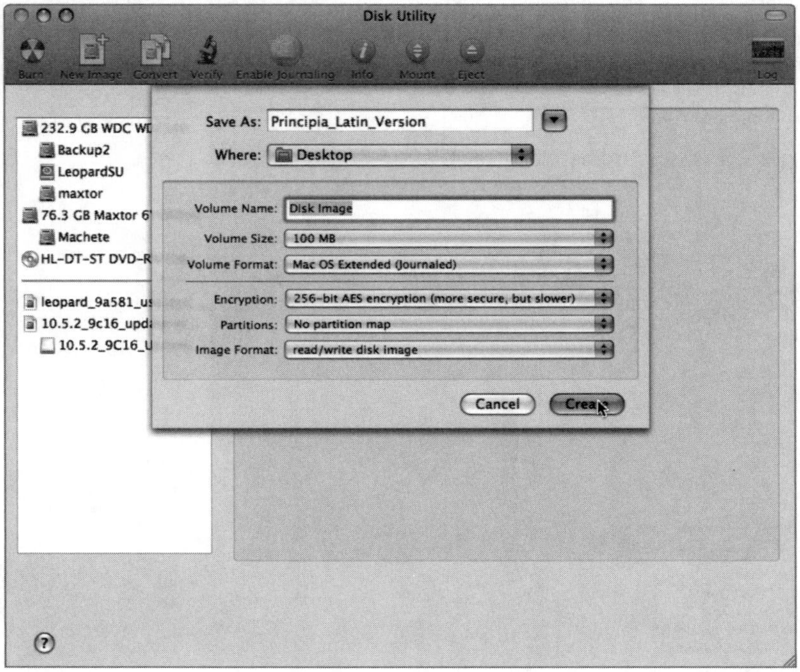

Once the name is chosen, pick an appropriate size. The default size is 100 MB, but obviously you'll want something big enough to hold all the files, so change the size as required. Finally, choose your encryption and pick a good password. Type the password twice and ensure the Add to Keychain box is unchecked because, unless you've changed the defaults, Keychain will automatically type the password in for you, which is obviously self-defeating in this case.

After the image is created, the disk will automount. Drag any files you wish to a disk and eject the disk (see Figure 6-64).

Figure 6-64.
Drag your files to the disk, not the .dmg

Principia_Latin_Versio
n.dmg

Interpretive dance

The *.dmg* you created will remain, but the files inside won't be visible with a Spotlight search, and anyone trying to open the *.dmg* will be required to enter the password you created.

It's Better to Be Better

Those are three quick and easy ways to hide your files from prying eyes. While they do provide a level of security for the files you'd rather hide, they are no replacement for proper security practices. You'll be much better off, and your data will be safer, if you use FileVault and individual accounts.

7

HACKING THE IPOD

Apple sells a lot of computers but the company sells even more iPods. How many iPods has Apple sold? Estimates put the number somewhere north of 125 million units since the introduction of the original FireWire-based 5 GB model that debuted in October 2001 as a Mac-only device.

When you've got as hit as big as the iPod on your hands, it is a good idea to keep the product fresh, and Apple has done just that. The latest iPods (iPod touch) run off a variant of Mac OS X (earlier iPods used an operating system developed by Pixo), and other features have been added over the years (the ability to play video is a notable example). For all the changes the iPod line has gone through, the iPod is still a storage device with a few specialized chips for replaying music and (shuffle and older models excepted) video.

A storage device with a screen? That sounds like an ideal device for hacking! And the iPod is a great thing for hackers to play with. With various tips and tricks, you can extend your iPod's abilities and turn the diminutive device into a Wikipedia reader to go, a take anywhere Home folder, or even boot disc for your Intel Mac.

QUICK TIP ✕

IT ISN'T ALWAYS IPOD-SPECIFIC

Many of the hacks in this chapter rely on your iPod's disk mode. When disk mode is enabled, your iPod can store data you can access any time you plug the iPod in. It's a great way to move files around without a carrying a separate drive or memory stick. The good news is that hacks that rely on this functionality work with any storage you can attach to your Mac. So, if you want a portable Home folder, you don't have to have an iPod to pull it off—just mobile storage with enough capacity (and flash drives are getting cheap).

HACK 58: Home Folder to Go

Most (but not all) of the information that makes your Mac uniquely yours resides in your Home folder. Discover how to take this folder with you everywhere you go so that any Mac is almost home.

Hard drive-based iPods, as of this writing, come in 80 GB and 160 GB versions. That is a mind-boggling amount of data. According to Apple's calculations, you can hold 20,000 songs, 25,000 photos, or 100 hours of video. Translated, that means an owner of the (lesser) 80 GB iPod could store enough photos to look at for 69 hours if they spent 10 seconds per photo, enough songs to last nearly eight weeks without hearing a replay, or a goodly chunk (272 episodes) of *The Simpsons* (that show has been on the air a *long* time).

That amount of storage on a device that, in terms of battery life, has at best 20 hours of music playback or 6.5 hours of video playback seems to be a bit of overkill. Thus, if you're a multi-Mac user, it makes sense to give up a little of that massive space to have the comfort of your Home folder no matter what Mac you find sitting in front of you.

The introduction of Leopard has made this hack both easier and trickier to pull off. The hack is very simple if all the computers you use are Leopard-based. If the computers you're using rely on different versions of OS X (or if you just want maximum flexibility out of your Home folder to go), knowing how to pull the hack off on both Leopard Macs and older Mac OS X-based Macs is a necessity. This hack gives the information you need to master the portable Home folder no matter what flavor of Mac OS X the target computer is running.

Burn Up Your iPod? The Debate Rages!

The criticism of using your iPod for anything but music, movies, and occasional file transfers has traditionally consisted of a claim that the iPod's hard drive was designed for short bursts of data transfer followed by longer periods of inactivity. That description accurately depicts the manner in which the iPod works but doesn't necessarily reflect the capabilities of the drive. The current drive found in the iPod is a 1.8-inch model manufactured by Toshiba and is rated for five years or 20,000 power-on hours. Compare and contrast this number with the supposedly more robust 2.5-inch hard drives found more commonly in computers. The computer drives made by Toshiba are rated for—five years or 20,000 hours.

At least from Toshiba's point of view, your iPod hard drive is made to last exactly as long as a regular hard drive whether it is used in short bursts or constantly accessed. Finally, if you're wondering if the temperatures generated by the drive spinning much more than when the iPod is being used as a music player will kill the drive, consider this: Toshiba gives the operating range of the iPod drive as topping out at 65 degrees C. For nonmetric-inclined folks, that is 149 degrees F. So, unless your iPod is hot enough to press laundry (light starch please), ruining the hard drive by using it for things other than playing music isn't going to happen.

What Your Home Folder Means to You

Your Home folder houses everything that you like about your Mac. Your music, your photos, and the veritable morass of preferences that tell your applications just how you like them to behave.

Of course, not everything travels with your Home folder. Your Applications folder houses the applications you use and they won't go for the ride unless you manually copy them to a folder on the iPod or are already on the Mac you'll be using away from home. You've got two choices: either make sure the applications you want to use are on the Macs you'll be using or take your unusual applications with you. In Figure 7-1, I've created a folder called *Applications to go* on my iPod. I can run those applications with my preferences by navigating to the folder and double-clicking the icon. While this method works with the majority of OS X applications, some won't yield to these machinations. Check out the sidebar, "Portable Applications," for a way to get stubborn applications fully portable.

QUICK TIP

PORTABLE APPLICATIONS

Not every application is a good traveler. While most OS X applications enjoy drag-and-drop functionality, some very important applications do not. Mail, to cite one example, stores preference files in your System Library so you won't be able to fire up Mail and use it as though you were on your main machine with this hack. All is not lost, however: a bevy of portable applications are available from Sourceforge. You've got choices, you can download the source and you can compile said code on your own or download the already built application for 99 cents. See http://www.freesmug.org/portableapps/ to get started.

Figure 7-1.
The recently created "Applications to go" folder

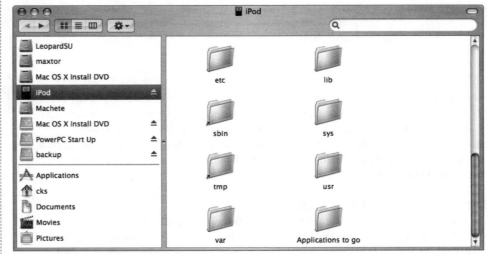

Enabling iPod Data Storage

The first obstacle to deal with is the fact that your iPod was delivered with music and video in mind. That means Apple doesn't send iPods out as preconfigured mass-storage devices, which is precisely what you need if you want to store your Home folder on your iPod. A logical place to begin would be to enable the iPod to store non-iTunes data. The process is painless: simply launch iTunes, select the iPod you want to use in the sidebar under Devices and check the box next to "Enable disk use." Click Apply to make your choice stick, and your iPod has gone from a music/movie/photo machine to a music/movie/photo/mass storage jack of all trades.

Figure 7-2.
The iPod shuffle's data storage slider

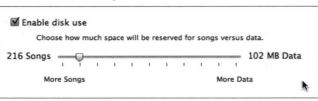

Figure 7-3.
Changing the factory settings

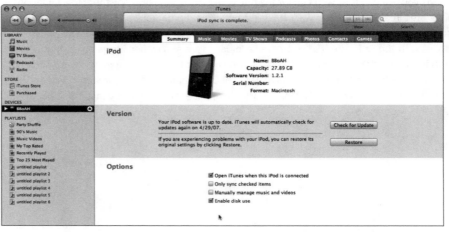

Transferring your account (pre-Leopard)

The Mac is easy right? So slapping your Home folder on your iPod is just as easy as a drag and drop right? Well it is, with one caveat. Turns out that a Mac needs to know where to look for your Home folder in order to use it and telling your Mac where to look for your Home folder is a nontrivial task. Here you have a decision to make: do you want the iPod to house your current Home folder and rely solely on your iPod for all your Home folder storage needs, or do you want your iPod to have a duplicate Home folder?

Whether you've decided to go with a new user or just go all-iPod all the time, the process is the same. First, locate the folder you want to use on the go and drag it to your iPod's icon. This copies the data from the chosen folder to your iPod, and you will be asked to authenticate during the process. While dragging you Home folder around may seem a bit scary, worry not: no data is destroyed.

Figure 7-4.
The Users folder is easily identified by the silhouette

Users

Once you've transferred the data, it is time to tell your Mac where to look. To pull off that trick, you'll need to invoke one of the Mac's less-used but more powerful programs: Netinfo Manager. You'll find the program hiding in the Utilities folder. Launch the Netinfo Manager, click on users, and then on your username. Click the lock found in the usual lower right corner, authenticate, and you're ready to make the necessary changes (see Figure 7-5).

Figure 7-5.
Netinfo Manager in action

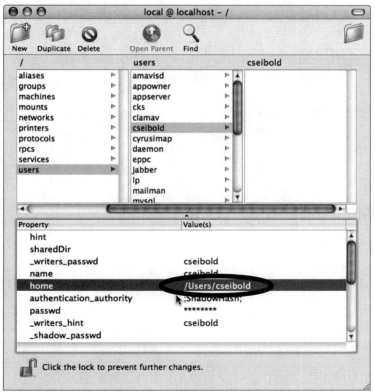

QUICK TIP ✕

WHERE IS THAT USERS FOLDER?

The Users folder is located at the root of your computer's directory. Which is a geeky way of saying that the Users folder can be found by double-clicking your hard-drive icon (the path is *Macintosh HD/Users/Yourusername*—replace *Macintosh HD* with whatever the name of your Mac hard drive is). Open the Users folder (see Figure 7-4) to find folders for each account (your active folder will look like a house; all the rest look like folders).

Notice the circled area in Figure 7-5. That is the information that needs to be changed for your Mac to find the folder. Here you've got options. You can change it the cool power-user way and type the path to your iPod (in this case, /Volumes/BBoAH/cseibold), or you can do it the Mac way and drag the desired User folder from the iPod to the input field. Once that task is accomplished, all changes to that user account will be saved to your iPod instead of your Mac's hard drive.

Transferring your account with Leopard

With Leopard, the venerable Netinfo Manager is no more. Replacing the functionality isn't another program but an extension of the Accounts preference pane. While some will miss Netinfo Manager, if you're hacking your iPod to hold your Home folder you won't be one of them.

Obviously you'll need the Home folder copied to the destination, so before you get started, use Leopard's copy-and-paste functions to copy your User folder's data to the destination iPod.

The deliciously easy procedure to get your Home folder on your iPod if you're using Leopard? Head over to the Accounts preference pane (System Preferences→Accounts) and authenticate. Once authenticated, you'll need to explore the Advanced options. Unfortunately, accessing Advanced Options isn't a simple click; Apple has cleverly hidden the functionality from view. To get to the Advanced Options, you'll be required to right-click or command-click on the account you want to change. Advanced Preferences will magically appear (see Figure 7-6).

Figure 7-6.
Accessing the Advanced Options of the Accounts pane

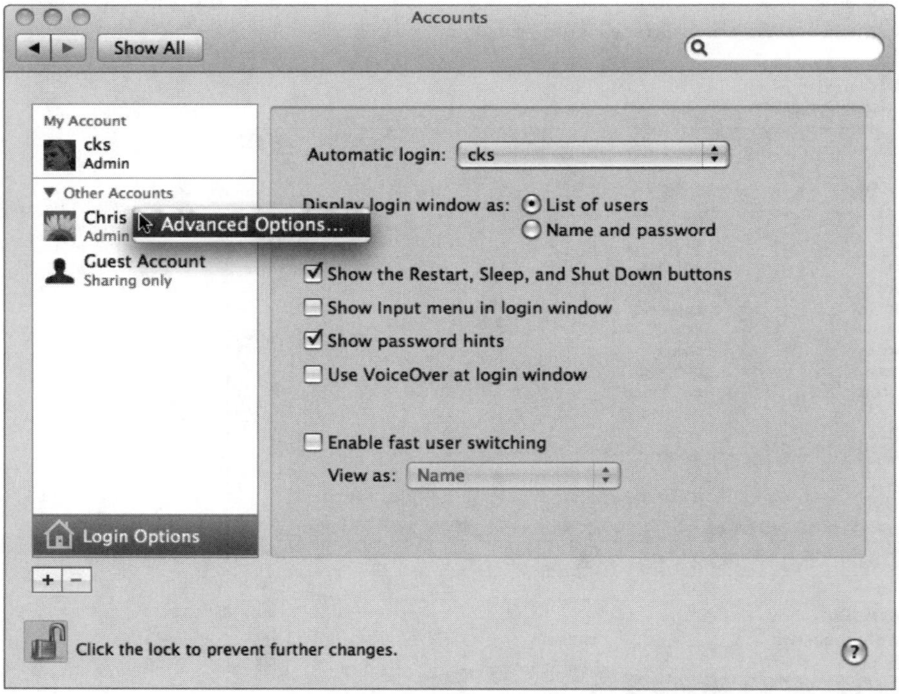

Once you've navigated to the Advanced Options, you can tell OS X to look for your Home folder data on your iPod (see Figure 7-7).

Figure 7-7.
Now OS X knows to look on your iPod for your Home folder

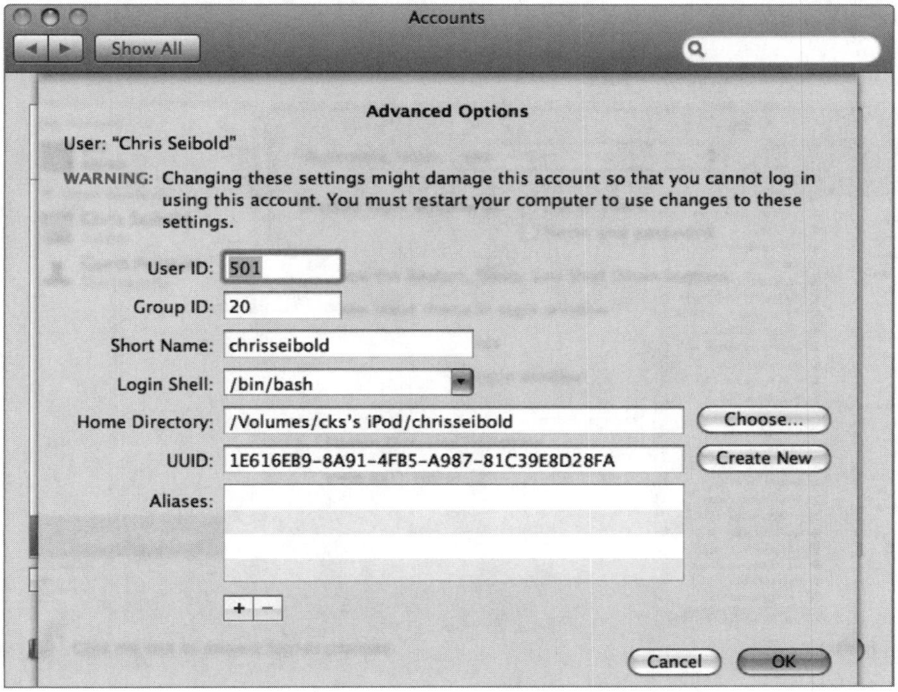

Be careful with this hack: for it to work properly, you'll need the iPod (or other drive) with you and attached to the computer whenever you want to log in. Trying to do so without your iPod connected isn't possible; all your stuff is on a different drive after all!

One account or an account to go?

So you want your Home folder to go, but you don't want to rely on your iPod for your Home folder all the time? For example, you want your Home folder on your iPod when you're away, but when you're in your dorm or apartment, you want your Mac to rely on the internal hard drive. That configuration makes a lot of sense; why not use the built-in hard drive when you're using your home computer?

Of course, if the latest files aren't at your fingertips, the purpose of a Home folder to go (convenience) is largely defeated. For example, if you modified a Keynote presentation while you were working on a Mac using your iPod as the Home folder, when you want to work on the same presentation at home, you won't want to dig through the iPod manually to find the latest revision.

What is needed is a way to keep the Home folder on the iPod synced up with the Home folder on your main Mac. There are many ways to get this done, using either the command line and something like rsync [Hack #1] or a third-party commercial application. There is no single "right" method for keeping the folders synced, but one of the easiest uses Automator.

You could start from scratch and create your very own Automator workflow [Hack #22], but why reinvent the wheel when someone else has done most of the legwork? Point your browser to http://www.apple.com/downloads/macosx/automator/syncfolders.html and download a copy of Sync Folders. Sync Folders is a very handy Automator action written by Ben Long that can take the contents of two folders and make sure the folders exactly mirror each other while ensuring the newest version of each file overwrites the older files. Install Sync Folders in Automator with a double-click (see Figure 7-8).

Figure 7-8.
An Automator workflow including Sync Folders

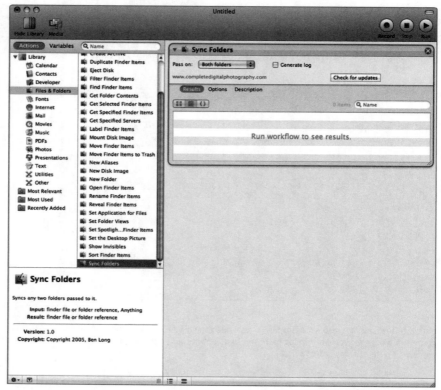

That's great, but it doesn't really get you anywhere. Sync Folders needs to know what you want synced. Since this hack is about syncing Home folders, that's what we want to sync. Furthermore, we want the folder synced both ways with the newest version of each file in both folders. The first thing to do is drag your Home folder to the workflow pane. Repeat the process with the Home folder you've created on your iPod. Make sure the pop-up menu is set to Both Folders, and you're ready to try it out. Click the Play button and witness the results of the Workflow.

Likely you don't want to fire up Automator every time you want to sync your iPod Home folder and the Home folder on your main machine. No problem: one of the great things about Automator is that it will let you save a workflow as an application so you can just launch the application instead of mucking about with Automator every time you want to sync the two folders. Choose File→Save As..., name the workflow something explanatory, and choose to save it as an application (see Figure 7-10).

Once the file is saved, you can sync the two folders anytime you want simply by launching your newly birthed application.

QUICK TIP ✕

BACK UP YOUR HOME FOLDER FIRST

Your Home folder is of crucial importance, and is one collection of files you really, really don't want to lose. Before you try this hack (or any potentially destructive hack), make sure your Home folder is safely backed up (see Figure 7-9).

Figure 7-9.
Automator will now sync your chosen folders

Figure 7-10.
A new application generated by Automator

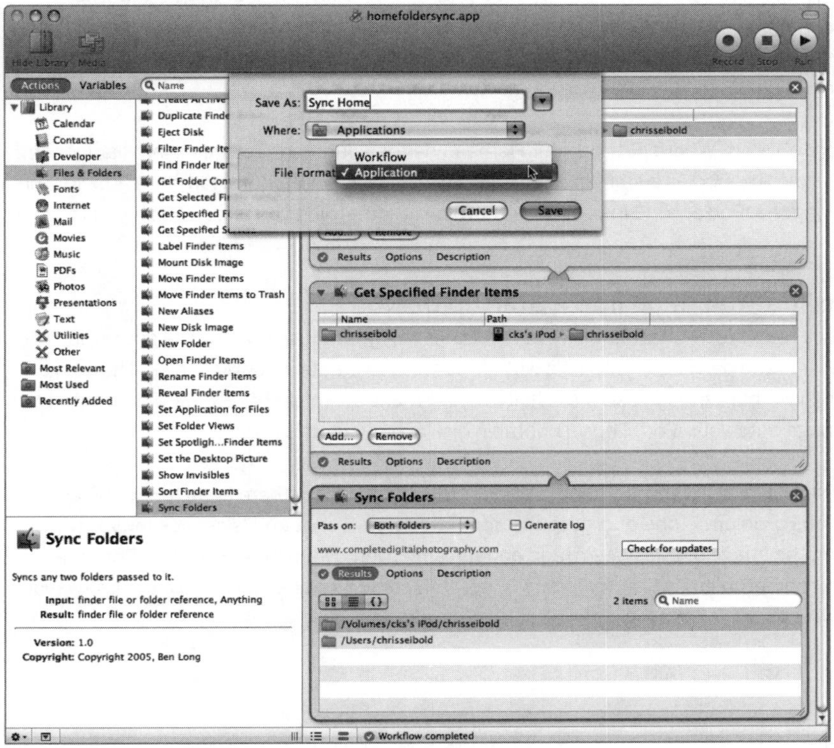

Using your Home folder on the go

Using your newly portable Home folder is simply a matter of reversing the steps outlined to create your new Home folder. Create a new account on the target machine with the same name as the account on your iPod, and you're ready to go. Once the account is created, either invoke Netinfo Manager for pre-Leopard installs or use the Advanced Options in the accounts preference pane to point OS X to the iPod-based Home folder.

HACK 59: Boot from Your iPod

iPods are becoming ever more spacious, and this increase in storage means that it is entirely possible to keep all your data not on your computer's hard drive, but on your iPod. Take your iPod with you, and any computer you boot from the device will seem exactly like the computer you use the majority of the time.

How would you like to put *everything* on your iPod? No more messing with syncing multiple Macs or updating software across multiple machines; the system and all your files will be right there on your iPod waiting for you.

> This hack won't work with the iPod touch or iPod shuffle. The flash memory-based iPod nano is probably a long shot.

Slap a screen, a few specialized chips, a scroll wheel, and a battery on a tiny hard drive, and you've got a homebrewed iPod. Once that realization is made, it is a short hop to fully embracing the idea that the difference between an iPod and a portable hard drive is that the portable hard drive is substantially cheaper and not nearly as impressive with white ear buds dangling from it. The coolness factor aside, the obvious use for an iPod, other than being an iPod, is using the conglomeration of chips, slick, and drive as a startup disk.

The benefits are obvious. Where putting your Home folder on your iPod provides a familiar working environment, using the iPod as a startup disk gives you access to your entire computer just for the hassle of carrying the iPod around in your pocket, which is something you already do if you're a big iPod fan.

Methods to Turn Your iPod into a Startup Disk

To the majority of people, the startup disk of OS X works in mysterious ways. You've got symbolic links, invisible files, and permissions to deal with if you want to create a bootable disk. The easy way around all these hurdles is to use Disk Utility to first make an image of your hard drive and then restore that image onto your iPod. Thus a bootable disk on your iPod is born.

While using Disk Utility to get the job done is straightforward [Hack #1], there are a few drawbacks. The most obvious problem is one of disk space. You have to have enough disk space for your original system, the image of the system, and enough space left over on the iPod to restore the system. The second problem is that the process is a little convoluted because you can't image your startup disk without unmounting it.

QUICK TIP ✕

NEW IPOD? THEN THIS IS AN INTEL-ONLY HACK

When the fifth-generation iPod appeared, it looked a lot like the fourth-generation iPod. There were some changes: the screen was a bit bigger, and black was suddenly an option, but the cosmetic changes weren't as big as an internal change. Gone was the FireWire controller chip. But what's a few chips between friends? The trouble is that with no FireWire controller chip, there is no FireWire data-transfer ability. Booting your PowerPC Mac from a newer iPod isn't impossible, but it's complicated and only possible with late-model PowerPC Macs. Mac OS X Hints has the steps if you want to try it out: http://www.macosxhints.com/article.php?story=2006 0301112336384.

Fortunately, you can avoid the hassle of booting your Mac with an install disc or a second drive, and then image and restore your startup drive to your iPod. Do this either by using Terminal or by downloading a donation-ware utility.

Making the iPod bootable with Carbon Copy Cloner

Mike Bombich's Carbon Copy Cloner utility, mentioned earlier, is available at http://www.bombich.com/software/ccc.html. Once Carbon Copy Cloner is downloaded and stowed safely in the Applications folder of your Mac, launch it.

Launching Carbon Copy Cloner yields a pleasant surprise; you get your choice of which items to copy and which items to skip (see Figure 7-11).

Figure 7-11.
Welcome options in Carbon Copy Cloner

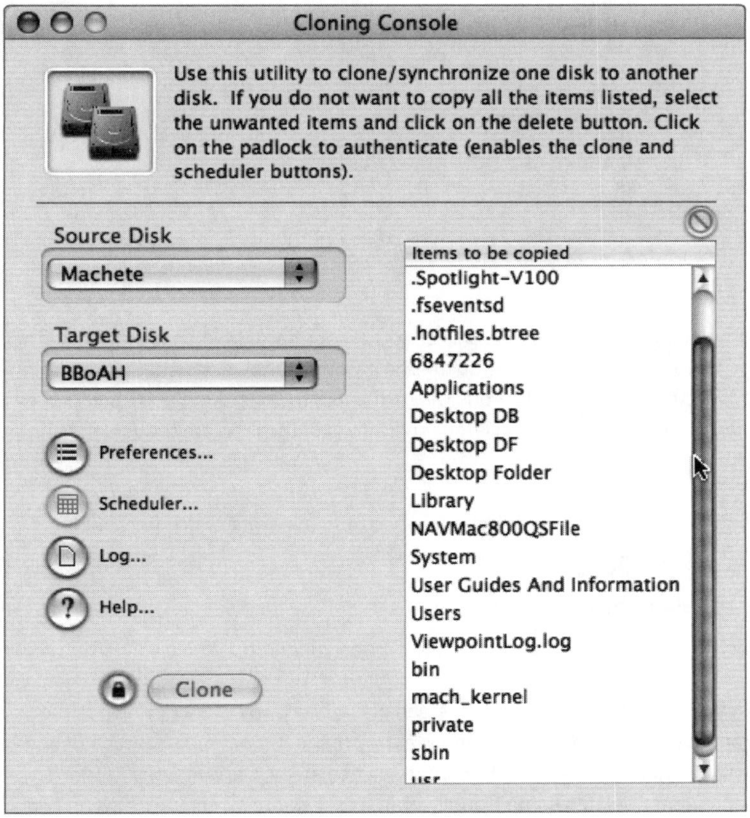

To create a bootable drive, certain items are must-have. You can't do without your */bin*, */mach_kernel*, */sbin*, */usr*, */System*, and */Library* files and folders. Leaving out */Users* would kill the point of making your iPod an everyday startup disk. In this example, and in most cases in which you want to use your iPod as the startup disk, accept the defaults. Click Clone, enter an administrator password, and Carbon Copy Cloner will get to work (see Figure 7-12).

QUICK TIP

MORE SPACE FOR SONGS!

Every file you transfer to your iPod is that much less room you'll have for music and video. Before you actually begin this process, it is a good time to get rid of the files you don't need. See **[Hack #24]** for a list of likely candidates.

Figure 7-12.
Authenticating so Carbon Copy Cloner can start working

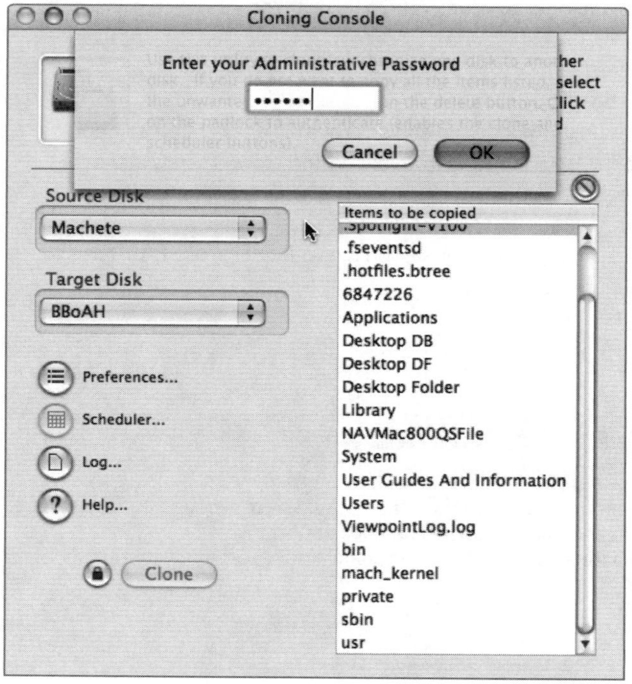

When the process is complete, you'll have a bootable version of your hard drive on your iPod. With iPod in hand, you can now use just about any Mac as though it were your own depending, naturally, on the iPod and the Mac. The most compatible iPods will be the fourth generation and earlier; they will boot any Mac. As mentioned earlier, fifth and later generations of the iPod are truly useful only with Intel-based machines.

You can do all this from the command line if you're so inclined, and the process is dead simple: you'll need only one command, which looks something like this:

```
$ sudo ditto -x / /Volumes/iPod
```

Where **/** is the root directory, and **/Volumes/iPod** is the path to your iPod.

Yes, it really is that easy. So why not just use `ditto` instead of Carbon Copy Cloner? Besides the fact that `ditto` runs from the command line—an intimidating prospect for some—`ditto` doesn't do a lot of what Carbon Copy Cloner does. Or rather, where `ditto` stops, Carbon Copy Cloner keeps going. Carbon Copy Cloner deletes some troublesome files if you're switching between two differently configured Macs (say a G4 and a G5-based machine). If the Macs you're using are the same, give `ditto` a shot!

You've discovered that making the iPod a bootable disk isn't a big trick, but it's likely that booting from your iPod all the time isn't the ideal situation. Most people find it preferable to boot from their iPod when away from their main computer, but boot from an internal drive when not.

If you're really after a "your computer to go" experience and want to use the built-in hard drive on your Mac the majority of the time, what you secretly desire is a way to use your Mac in a more or less standard manner while keeping the iPod updated so that any foreign Mac will seem like your machine at home.

QUICK TIP ✕

CAN I DO IT WITH WINDOWS?

iPod users aren't necessarily Mac users, so it is natural to wonder if you can pull off this hack with a Windows machine. It's possible, but the technique is very different from what's described in this hack. If you'd like to see what's involved, check out this Tom's Hardware article: http://www. tomshardware. com/2005/09/09/ windows_in_your_ pocket/.

Carbon Copy Cloner rides to the rescue. In the Advanced Preferences pane of Carbon Copy Cloner, you are presented with the option of scheduling regular backups. In this case, regular backups consist of comparing the disk on the iPod to your internal hard drive. That means the process is short, sweet, and schedulable.

To actually boot from your iPod, plug said iPod into the appropriate port on the computer you wish to use. Select System Preferences, choose Startup Disk, specify the iPod as your boot device of choice, and restart (see Figure 7-13).

Figure 7-13.
Ready to boot your Mac

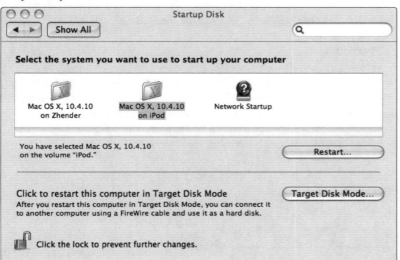

Here are a few things to remember. Booting a Mac off the iPod is a much slower process than booting the Mac off the internal hard drive or even an attached FireWire drive. Once booted, however, the performance is acceptable. Additionally (and obviously), you can use your iPod as an emergency boot device; think of it as an emergency toolkit in your pocket.

HACK 60: Manage Your Shuffle Sans iTunes

iTunes is a great program. It can manage tens of thousands of sings, hours of video, and enough podcasts to keep the longest commute interesting. For the iPod shuffle, iTunes is overkill. The shuffle holds a few hundred songs—a small enough number that the music can be managed (obviously) without a screen. Free your shuffle from being tied to a single computer and a single source of music with this nifty database replacement.

It is hard to fault the iPod shuffle. The device is small, light, and holds enough songs to outlast the battery. Really: what more do you need for a music player? Well, another nice feature would be the ability to manage the shuffle independently of iTunes. iTunes is great when dealing with very large libraries and iPods that hold multiple gigabytes of data, but for a device that holds

QUICK TIP

WHAT ABOUT PERFORMANCE?

If you're wondering about taking a performance hit by booting off your iPod, your concerns are well placed, especially if you are using a newer iPod. USB 2.0 has a higher theoretical speed than FireWire (480 Mbps versus 400 Mbps), but tests reveal that the overall winner in real-world usage is FireWire. Internally connected hard drives can easily surpass this speed; the drive in the Mac mini is capable of a comparably whopping 150 MBps. If the difference doesn't seem huge, remember that "b" stands for bits in the USB and FireWire specs, and "B" stands for bytes in the Serial ATA drive used by the mini. Performing the conversion, we find that the Serial ATA drive in the mini has sustained data transfer rates of 1200 Mbps—roughly three times as fast as FireWire or USB 2.0.

240 songs, iTunes is a bit like strapping a car battery to a Mac Pro, hauling the thing around and calling it a portable.

The other problem with using iTunes to manage the shuffle is that you're tied to a single computer. If you've got your shuffle tied to your Mac at home and find a file you want to listen to while you're at work, you're out of luck. You'll have to take the file home, import said tune into iTunes, and then get it on the shuffle; a bit of a hassle when you want to listen to that must-hear podcast on the long drive home.

Fortunately, things don't have to be this way. Thanks to a bit of nifty Python programming by Martin Feilder called iPod Shuffle Database Builder, you can use your iPod shuffle in the same fashion as any generic MP3 player, and for bonus points, you can still use iTunes as well.

Before You Get Started
It's been mentioned before in this chapter but, since it seems to be a key to every iPod hack, Disk Use must be enabled. On every other iPod, you can just enable disk use but with the shuffle, you're forced to choose how much of the shuffle's storage you want to allocate to disk use and how much you want to allocate to iTunes. For the purposes of this hack, let's choose a middle value though you could devote your entire shuffle to data storage if you wanted to eschew iTunes altogether and only use iPod shuffle database builder for your listening needs (see Figure 7-14).

Figure 7-14.
Using the slider to give the shuffle some limits

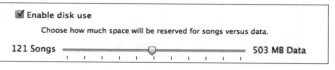

QUICK HACK ✕

WHERE DID THAT DOWNLOAD GO?

If you're using a pre-Leopard version of OS X and have a crowded desktop (or Downloads folder), small files that download rapidly can be hard to spot. Usually the result of a download is a visually uninspiring compressed file. Don't waste your time squinting and trying to find the file; let Safari do the hard work for you. Simply open the Downloads window (Window→Downloads in the Safari menu bar) and click on the magnifying glass to have the Finder reveal your file in a new Finder window (see Figure 7-15).

Installing iPod Shuffle Database Builder
While some Mac users cringe at the thought of using the terminal, iPod Shuffle Database Builder makes the point that just because a program invokes the Terminal and is written in Python doesn't mean that the entire process has to be messy and convoluted. Now that the shuffle is prepared, it is time to get the program. Point your browser to http://shuffle-db.sourceforge.net/ and download *rebuild_db-1.0-rc1.zip*. Note that the *1.0-rc1* will change as new versions are released.

Figure 7-15.
Ah, there it is

Once the download is complete, navigate to the *.zip* file and double-click to expand the file. Open the resulting folder, and you'll find a variety of files (see Figure 7-16).

Figure 7-16.
That's a bunch of files, but we need only one

rebuild_db-1.0-rc1
LeopardSU
maxtor
Mac OS X Install DVD
Machete
SHUFFLE IT
Applications
cks
Documents
Movies
Pictures
License.txt
Readme.txt
rebuild_db-win32.src.zip
rebuild_db.exe
rebuild_db.py
5 items, 38.44 GB available

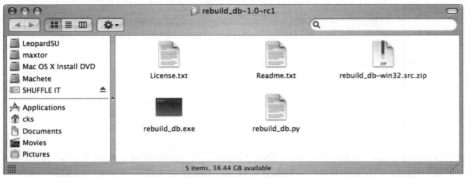

The file you're after is *rebuild_db.py*. Drag that file to the root directory of the shuffle you're hacking (which is a fancy way of saying drop it on the shuffle and check to make sure the file isn't in a folder). Once the program is safely ensconced, open *rebuild_db.py* with Terminal (see the sidebar "FORCE A PROGRAM TO OPEN A FILE"). Be careful: just double-clicking on this file defaults to opening with TextEdit, so make sure it's Terminal that opens the file. Once the *rebuild_db.py* program has done the job of rebuilding the database, you'll get a notice in the Terminal window (see Figure 7-17).

Figure 7-17.
It worked!

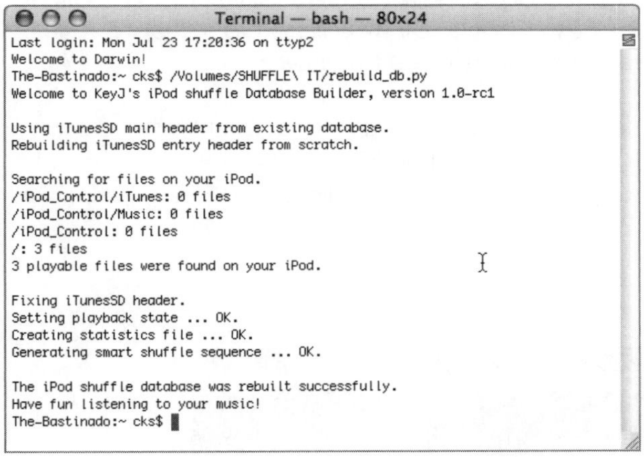

Terminal — bash — 80x24
Last login: Mon Jul 23 17:20:36 on ttyp2
Welcome to Darwin!
The-Bastinado:~ cks$ /Volumes/SHUFFLE\ IT/rebuild_db.py
Welcome to KeyJ's iPod shuffle Database Builder, version 1.0-rc1
Using iTunesSD main header from existing database.
Rebuilding iTunesSD entry header from scratch.
Searching for files on your iPod.
/iPod_Control/iTunes: 0 files
/iPod_Control/Music: 0 files
/iPod_Control: 0 files
/: 3 files
3 playable files were found on your iPod.
Fixing iTunesSD header.
Setting playback state ... OK.
Creating statistics file ... OK.
Generating smart shuffle sequence ... OK.
The iPod shuffle database was rebuilt successfully.
Have fun listening to your music!
The-Bastinado:~ cks$

In the example in Figure 7-17, I have used only three songs just to make sure everything performed as promised, but you can add as many songs or podcasts as space will allow. If you saved part of the shuffle for iTunes, *rebuild_db.py* will find any songs already on the iPod and add those to the mix.

Hacking the Hack

Now that all the hard work is done, you can use your shuffle in ways heretofore unthinkable. If you're away from your Mac and using another Mac, you can just add any MP3s you want to the shuffle, relaunch *rebuild_db.py* in the manner described earlier, and you'll be able to listen to the new sounds. The best part? When you're at home, you can still add songs via iTunes to your shuffle. Run *rebuild_db.py*, and those songs will be added to the database and available for your auditory pleasure.

QUICK HACK

FORCE A PROGRAM TO OPEN A FILE

In this iPod shuffle database hack, we are presented with a scenario in which the program we want to open a particular file with isn't the "recommended" program for that file type. You can always go through a menu and manually choose the program to open a file, but there is a faster way. Drag the icon of the file you want opened to the icon of the program you want to open it with (especially convenient when the destination program is in the dock), and OS X will force the destination program to open the file. For some combinations of files and programs, such as trying to open a Word document with TextEdit, this may make a mess, but others will work fine.

If you're going to be using a Windows machine away from home and want to add files via the Windows box, it is a great idea to drag the file *rebuild_db.exe* to your shuffle. After adding files from a Windows machine, double-click the .exe file, and the database will be rebuilt. (An .exe file is a program file executable by Windows; a .py file is a script in a language called Python that can run on a Macintosh.) This time a random playlist won't be created, and the songs will be played in alphabetical order. If there's a podcast you want to hear on the way home, slap it in a folder named "aa" and avoid a lot of clicking forward.

That's it: you've got a use-anywhere, add-music-from-any-machine iPod shuffle. Enjoy your music and podcasts without the restrictions of iTunes!

HACK 81: Uncap Your iPod's Volume

Do you need a louder iPod? Not scared of ear-damaging decibels? Remove Apple's volume limitation on your iPod, and crank the music to the hardware's maximum level.

Steve Jobs is a demanding taskmaster, and one of the things he demanded out of iPod designers was a louder iPod. Knowing who the boss was, the designers complied. The result was a music player that was substantially louder than most other players on the market. The downside was that the iPod's volume exceeded the standards set by some governments (France, to cite one example) and provided an invitation for lawsuits.

Once Apple realized that the arbitrarily high-volume limit of the iPod could result in lawsuits and governmental interference, the company added a volume limit to later versions of iPod software. It is a good idea: damaging your ears because you want to hear *We Built this City* by Starship at levels well above the threshold considered safe isn't the best idea. On the other hand, they are your ears.

To get around the cap, first visit http://gopod.free-go.net/ and download goPod. This can actually be a bit tricky because instead of the usual obvious download link, the goPod web page uses a bit of graphical interactivity. To actually download goPod, you have to click the GO button on the goPod page (see Figure 7-18).

Figure 7-18.
Click Go to get the required software

Once downloaded, you have to make sure disk use is enabled for your iPod. If you've read any of the other iPod hacks, you know that enabling disk use is a standard step in iPod hacking. If enabling disk use is new to you, simply make sure your iPod is plugged in and iTunes is running. Select your iPod's icon from the iTunes source list and click Enable Disk Use. The added functionality comes with a price, however: you must now manually eject your iPod each time it is plugged into your computer.

Once disk use is enabled, launch the very easy-to-use goPod with a double-click. GoPod will ascertain the status of your iPod's volume setting and report the result. As expected, the test iPod is capped (see Figure 7-19). (Every time you update the iPod's software, the volume is capped again; remember that when your music suddenly seems inexplicably faint).

Figure 7-19.
This iPod won't go to 11

The procedure is straightforward: simply click the GO button, and the volume is uncapped. Now you can listen to your iPod at highest, most ear-damaging volume possible. Once the process is complete, goPod will report the new volume status of your iPod (see Figure 7-20).

Figure 7-20.
That is better—well, louder

Undoing the Hack
It might occur to you that imposing a limit on the volume of the iPod might be a better idea than turning the volume up to eleven. To cap the volume with a shuffle, you have to invoke iTunes and adjust the slider in the application (see Figure 7-21).

Figure 7-21.
Recapping the shuffle to a comfortable level

To cap the volume on other versions of the iPod, you can use the functionality built into the iPod. Select Settings→Volume Limit, and use the scroll wheel to select the appropriate maximum volume. You can make the selection stick by depressing the center button. Now, you get a few more choices. Clicking Done ends the process, but if you're worried about someone else's hearing, by choosing Set Combination you can enter a password to prevent anyone other than you from adjusting the iPod's maximum volume limit.

HACK 62: The 2¢ iPod Case

Out-of-the-box iPods are beautiful to look at, but a few days stuck in a pocket with your keys or flopping around in the console of your car can leave your iPod with a depressing array of scratches and blemishes. Help your iPod avoid scratches by creating your own durable and amazingly inexpensive iPod case.

One thing people love about the iPod is the size; even the comparatively bloated iPod classic is a wonder of miniaturization. Oddly, the same people who love the small, compact nature of the iPod often purchase a case for their new iPod during the same transaction. The situation is a little confusing: after paying a premium for the ability to carry a huge music collection in their pocket, many users rapidly compromise one of the most compelling reasons to purchase an iPod by ensconcing the device in a bulky and unwieldy case.

Of course, it makes sense to protect your iPod. A scratched-up screen ruins the fun of looking at the stored photos, and a seriously marred iPod just doesn't project the aura of cool that a sweet-looking iPod does. Scratches are a sad fate for such a beautifully designed Apple product. What is needed is, obviously, a durable protective cover that can be replaced as necessary with a minimum of effort and expense. When faced with those requirements, most people turn to duct tape but everyone's favorite dull-gray panacea simply won't work in this instance. Blame the tape's inherent opacity and propensity to leave gummy residue on every surface it manages to contact. A better solution is required.

Why not packaging tape? The stuff is thick enough to prevent any but the deepest of scratches, has the required amount of adhesion but can be removed without leaving a sticky film. Sounds like a winner. Throw in the fact that packaging tape is both easy to work with and cheap (the tape used in the example was $1.98 for enough to make 130 cases), and you've got an ideal iPod protection material.

For this example, an original, super-scratchable iPod nano is being used in conjunction with a very sharp razor knife and a roll of 2-inch Scotch packaging tape (see Figure 7-22). If you're going to cover the full-size iPod, you'll want the harder-to-find, but available, 3-inch packaging tape.

Figure 7-22.
The required tools

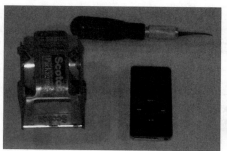

Once the tools are assembled, it is time to get to the business of protecting the iPod. The obvious way to go about this is to place a piece of tape sticky side up and slap the iPod on the thing face down. Unfortunately that method results in a protected iPod but also a plethora of unsightly bubbles (see Figure 7-23).

Figure 7-23.
Check out those unsightly bubbles!

There is a solution. Attach one end of the tape to the work surface (just stick it down) with the sticky side of the tape facing away from you. Now, slowly and gently stick the tape to the iPod with your free hand working from the bottom to the top. This allows you to smooth out any bubbles before they become a lifelong part of your awesome iPod case. Some patience and practice is required to get the hang of it, but because it is only packing tape, you've got plenty of raw material (see Figure 7-24).

Figure 7-24.
The bubble-minimizing method

Once you are satisfied with the result, it is time to get rid of the pesky extra tape (see Figure 7-25).

Figure 7-25.
Ready for some careful trimming

Trimming the excess tape varies according to the iPod model you're attempting to protect. The general idea is to remove any tape that would interfere with the Hold button or any ports. One of the easiest ways to locate the areas of tape that need to be removed is to simply fold the tape over and mark the areas to be removed with a fine-point Sharpie. Finally, you'll likely want to notch the tape at the corners of the iPod to prevent unsightly folds from forming. The cover will last longer if you terminate the tape on the back rather than the sides of the iPod, a few millimeters is enough to avoid premature peeling of the tape. You could, naturally, cover the back as well using the same process.

That's it, the project is complete, and you've not only got an iPod that is well protected from the hazards of being in your pocket (car keys and such), but you also likely have enough tape left over to send out that package you've been meaning to mail! Undoing the hack is as simple as pulling off the tape, so there isn't a reason not to give this hack a try (see Figure 7-26).

Figure 7-26.
A protected iPod

HACK 83: The Ultimate Zen Hack: iPod Video Cable

There are times you want to watch video on your iPod and times you want to watch that same video on a larger screen. Wanting to watch video from your iPod on your TV doesn't require a trip to the Apple and the purchase of a special cable. Chances are you can pull it off with a cable that's lying around the house.

Consider, if you will, the qualities of a truly great hack. Ideally, the hack is fun and provides a tangible benefit. Of course, the hack would be further enhanced if you could use something you already own, and the cherry that would top it all off would be if the hack denied a major corporation some small bit of profit.

Which brings us to the fifth-generation video-capable iPod. The machine is simply awesome—a spacious hard drive coupled with the diminutive size means that not only is there room for songs, there is plenty of room for videos. Naturally watching video on such a small screen isn't always an ideal solution. Two and a half inches is fine on a long plane ride, but if you're trying to watch that episode of *Heroes* you downloaded to your iPod with a few friends, the screen just isn't going to cut it.

Apple is in the business of selling things people actually want, and they've addressed the small screen size issue by letting you play video on your television (setting up your iPod to stream TV is simple: Videos→ Video Settings→ TV Out), but Apple says a special video cable is required to get the video from the iPod into your TV.

The proprietary video cable bears a strong resemblance to an ordinary video cable. Both cables sport a four-conductor 1/8-inch plug connected to standard RCA connections. The differences seemingly end there. Where standard A/V cable is black, chunky, and not attractive, the special iPod cable is sleek, white and looks about as good as a video cable can look. Still, the similarities are enough to make you wonder.

Here you could proceed in a variety of ways. Test each contact and RCA connector with a multimeter for continuity. Perhaps hook the RCA connectors to an oscilloscope and analyze the signals to identify which RCA connector transports the video and which two carry the audio signal. Or you could realize that the maximum number of combinations given by three. That means there are a total of six combinations and that is well within our ability to crack by brute force. Sparing you the rest of the trial, the result is as follows:

- Red (usually reserved for right channel sound) is video out.

- Yellow (usually reserved for Video out) is right channel sound.

- White remains the same—left channel audio.

Now you can use that A/V cable that you have laying in a desk drawer (they almost always ship with camcorders) to carry the video from your iPod to your TV (see Figure 7-27).

QUICK TIP

DON'T TRY THIS WITH THE NEWEST IPODS

If you're one of the lucky folks who have a video-capable nano, an iPod classic, or an iPod touch, this hack won't work. Whereas the fifth-generation iPods were able to push video out through the earphone jack, the newer iPods use the iPod-specific port found on the bottom of the iPod. It isn't a complete loss, however: the newer iPods offer better playback resolution than previous models.

Figure 7-27.
iPod video through a clunky black cable

HACK 64: Good as New: Clean Your iPod

Your iPod will get dirty. Restore that new iPod look with the tips and techniques revealed in this shining Hack.

Remember those first moments when you unwrapped your new iPod? So clean, so shiny...until you put it in your pocket. The iPod's metal back loves to be scratched, and its plastic front is not much better. Don't get out the bleach and silver polish, though. Your iPod needs the cleaning products and tools appropriate to its outstanding design.

Getting Clean

The best product for cleaning dirt, fingerprints, and small scratches off your iPod is a product called Plexus Plastic Cleaner. Originally designed to polish the windshields of F-16 fighter jets and other aircraft, Plexus does an amazing job of cleaning up any polymer surfaces, so you can use it on everything from CDs and DVDs to your car (which probably has a polymer-based clear coat on top of its paint). The company that makes Plexus sells it only by the case online (http://www. plexusplasticcleaner.com), but if you Google "Plexus Plastic Cleaner," you'll find a number of outfits selling it online at a price of about $10 for a big can that will last you years.

A cleaner is only half the battle; you also need something with which to apply it. For that, get a set of microfiber towels. Of course, microfiber everything (T-shirts, towels, mops) is all the rage these days, so you shouldn't have any trouble finding them. I use these towels for almost everything, from waxing my car to cleaning my laptop's LCD display to dusting around the house. The ones I like best come from an outfit in Tacoma, WA, called Griots Garage (http://www.griotsgarage.com/product/car+care/car+drying/pack+of+five+micro+fiber+wipe+down+towels.do). Their five-pack of microfiber towels goes for $9.99, which is expensive, but the ones they sell last forever and clean up like new if you put them in the washing machine (don't use fabric softener—it will ruin them!).

To clean your iPod, simply spray a small amount of the Plexus onto the towel (*not* directly onto the surface you're trying to clean). Use a toothpick to shove the towel down into the small crevices and lines to get dirt out.

Once your iPod is nice and clean, it's time to deal with all those scratches you've accumulated.

Getting Rid of Scratches

When we talk about getting rid of scratches, we typically use terms such as "polish them out" or "fill them in." These terms aren't quite accurate because the definition of polishing is that you are "removing material." When you make a surface nice and shiny with a polish, you're essentially sanding down the microscopic bumps that reflect light unevenly. When you polish out a scratch, you're removing the surrounding material so that it is even with bottom of that scratch. This might sound sort of frightening, but don't worry. Unless you have a gouge (i.e., a really deep scratch), we are only talking about removing a few microns of material here. I am telling you this because it's important to realize exactly what's going on when you're in the process of rubbing out that huge wedding ring scratch that goes right across the front of your iPod's LCD display.

There are a number of kits on the market that do a good job of removing scratches. The kits available from iCleaner (http://www.ipodcleaner.com) are good, but you probably already have the most effective iPod plastic polish in your garage or utility closet: Brasso. This old-school, $3-a-can metal polish does a pretty amazing job of safely removing iPod plastic scratches, because it contains a mild abrasive. Twist the microfiber towel so it forms a tight, smooth surface over the pad of your index finger, and put a small amount of Brasso on it. Press hard when you rub, and go back and forth, not in circles.

Back and forth and not in circles, you ask? But Mr. Miyagi told Daniel in *The Karate Kid* that one waxes and polishes in a circular motion! That's just how things are done!

Well, the problem with waxing or polishing in a circular motion is that it produces swirl marks that you can see from a mile away. When you polish anything, you leave tiny scratches, and if those scratches are circular, light will catch them from every angle, and they will be quite visible. If you polish in straight lines, though, those scratches will be visible only when light catches them in one of the 360 degrees of the viewing angle, so they will hardly be noticed. This also works on your car—wax/polish front to back for surfaces parallel to the ground, up and down for surfaces perpendicular to the ground.

Be patient: this job takes a good, long time to accomplish on your iPod, but the results are well worth it. Unlike the Plexus, I wouldn't use Brasso to polish out scratches in other plastics. I have heard about bad results from people who were so amazed that it worked on their iPods, that they went out and ruined their cell-phone screens, because the composition of the plastic was different.

The Ugly Truth About Pretty Chrome

The back panel on your iPod is made of an aluminum part that has been electroplated in chrome. When it's new out of the box, the surface is very pretty, but it scratches very, very easily. The ugly truth is that there's nothing you can do about those scratches once they are there, because you can't polish out scratches in chrome. Chrome is a plating process, and the shiny silver material you see is just a few microns thick, so any scratch you see probably goes all the way through the chrome layer and down to the bare aluminum. To polish out the scratch, you'd need to polish off the whole layer of chrome, and you probably don't want to do that.

Unless your iPod is subjected to the environment the same way the chrome bumper on a truck is, the best way to keep it shiny is just to use Plexus or another plastic cleaner along with the microfiber cloth; this removes any surface contamination that would dull the appearance of your iPod. Most of the chrome polishes you see on the market are intended for automotive applications where chrome is subjected to all sorts of crud (flying bugs, exhaust gasses, dirt, rain, etc.), and these products remove that fouling from the metal to make it shiny again.

With this hack, you now know how to keep your iPod in good aesthetic order. Don't overclean your iPod, though: once a month should keep its appearances up nicely.

— Greg Koenig

HACK 85: Read Wikipedia on an iPod

Who doesn't want Wikipedia with them all the time? Get a thousand pages of Wikipedia on your iPod with this hack.

I've commented now and again that I'd be willing to pay upwards of $100 for a handheld version of Wikipedia—one that I can sync via Wi-Fi, then take on the bus and read to my heart's content. Unfortunately, the market doesn't seem to be responding to my lone cry, so I wrote a Perl script that loads Wikipedia onto my iPod.

Wikipod starts from a Wikipedia page and traverses all the links it finds, downloading each page to the iPod. It then traverses each link on the new pages, continuing this process until it finds no new links or has reached the size limit you specify.

Here's the script in all its glorious Perl:

```
#!/usr/bin/perl
#
# wikipod 1.6
#
# Matthew M. Swann
# http://swannman.wordpress.com
#
# Usage
# -----
# wikipod <wikipedia URL> <path to iPod notes directory> <# MB to fill>
#
# About
# -----
# This perl script formats wikipedia articles for viewing on an iPod using
# the iPod's "Notes" feature.  Starting at the wikipedia URL specified on the
# command-line, all links are followed and the corresponding pages are saved
# to the iPod, continuing until the amount of space specified on the command-
# line has been filled.
#
# Note that the iPod may take some time to load the articles on first browse.
# Once it has completed this process (which seems to continue even if you leave
# and do other tasks on the iPod), notes load quickly.  I highly recommend
# plugging the iPod in while this process completes, as is it disk- (and thus
# battery-) intensive.
#
# Version History
# ---------------
# 1.0: 10/1/2006     Initial release
# 1.1: 10/14/2006    Fixed problem with / characters in URL,
#                    allowed users to leave off the trailing slash,
#                    and limited how many MB we'll fetch
# 1.2: 10/14/2006    Includes tag to properly display UTF-8 encoded chars
```

```
# 1.3: 10/14/2006    Stops after 1000 notes, since the iPod won't display
#                    more than that.  Also fixed missing slash in dupe check.
# 1.4: 10/14/2006    Script now sleeps for two seconds between page requests
#                    to comply with wikipedia's robots.txt file, which states
#                    that "friendly, low-speed bots are welcome viewing article
pages".
# 1.5: 10/14/2006    Sleep is set for four seconds now.
# 1.6: 11/22/2006    Now gives additional feedback to the user. (David Still)
#
###############################################################
use POSIX qw(ceil floor);

sub WritePage;
sub SanitizeHTML;

if (@ARGV != 3)
{
    print "usage: wikipod <wikipedia URL> <path to iPod notes directory> " .
          "<# MB to fill>\n\n";
    exit;
}

$numPages = 0;
$fullURL = $ARGV[0];
$notesDir = $ARGV[1];
$numMB = $ARGV[2];

# This should not be changed, lest ye feel the wrath of the Wikimedia folks
# TODO: allow pages to be read from a local db cache
if ($numMB > 50)
{
    $numMB = 50;
}

$numKBytes = $numMB * 1024;

# Get the locale-specific wikipedia hostname and initial page name
$fullURL =~ /http:\/\/(.*)\.wikipedia\.org\/wiki\/(.*)/;
$URLprefix = "http://" . $1 . ".wikipedia.org/wiki/";

# The pages to process
# (WritePage sticks links on to the end of this array)
@links = ($2);

# Loop until we've filled up all our allotted space (MB or 1000 notes),
# or until there are no more links to get
while ((($numPages * 4) < $numKBytes) && (@links > 0) && ($numPages < 1000))
{
    # Get the next page
    my $currentPage = shift(@links);

    # Process the next page
    WritePage($currentPage);

    # Keep the user informed
    print "\nTransferred " . $numPages . " pages...";
}
```

```perl
# We're done!
print "\nDone transferring " . $numPages . " pages!\n\n";

sub WritePage {

    my $name = shift(@_);

    # Replace slashes with underscore for the filename
    my $safeFilename = $name;
    $safeFilename =~ s/\///_/s;

    # Don't do anything if we've already processed this page!
    if (-e ($notesDir . "/" . $safeFilename))
    {
        return;
    }

    # Download the starting page ($ARGV[0] is the first param)
    my $CMD = "curl -s \"" . $URLprefix . $name ."\"";

    # Execute the command and store the results in $HTML
    my $HTML = `$CMD`;

    # Extract the content
    $HTML =~ /\<div id=\"content\"\>(.*)\<!-- end content --\>/s;
    my $content = SanitizeHTML($1);

    for ($count = 0; $count < ceil(length($content)/4000); $count++)
    {
        $section = substr($content, $count * 4000, 4000);

        $section = $section . "\n\n";

        # Hitting "menu" goes back, so an explicit "back" link isn't necessary.
#        if ($count > 0)
#        {
#            if ($count == 1) {
#                $section = $section . "<A HREF=\"" . $name . "\">Prev page</A>";
#            }
#            else {
#                $section = $section . "<A HREF=\"" . $name .
#                    ($count - 1) . "\">Prev page</A>";
#            }
#
#            if (($count + 1) < ceil(length($content)/4000)) {
#                $section = $section . " | ";
#            }
#        }

        if (($count + 1) < ceil(length($content)/4000))
        {
            $section = $section . "<A HREF=\"" . "z" .
                        $safeFilename . ($count + 1) . "\">Next page</A>";
        }
```

```perl
        # Prepend our content with a tag to let the iPod know we're doing UTF-8
        # More info: http://docs.info.apple.com/article.html?artnum=61894
        $section = "<?xml encoding=\"UTF8\"?>" . $section;

        # Calculate the filename and add a slash whether the user specified
        # one or not -- this is messy but it works.
        if ($count == 0)
        {
            $filename = ">" . $notesDir . "/" . $safeFilename;
        }
        else
        {
            $filename = ">" . $notesDir . "/z" . $safeFilename . $count;
        }

        # Open a new file
        open my $file, $filename or die "Can't write file: $!";

        # Write our data out to a file
        print $file $section;

        # Flush the buffer and close the file
        close $file;

        # Increment the number of pages we've done
        $numPages++;
    }

    # Sleep for four seconds to obey the wikipedia robots.txt file
    sleep(4);
}

sub SanitizeHTML {
    # Put the HTML to be sanitized in $raw
    my $raw = shift(@_);

    # Remove non-article content
    $raw =~ s/\<div id=\"siteNotice\"\>.*?\<\/div\>//s;
    $raw =~ s/\<div id=\"jump-to-nav\"\>.*?\<\/div\>//s;
    $raw =~ s/\<table class=\"messagebox protected\".*?\<\/table\>//s;
    $raw =~ s/\<div class=\"thumb tleft\"\>.*?\<\/div\>.*?\<\/div\>//s;
    $raw =~ s/\<div class=\"thumb tright\"\>.*?\<\/div\>.*?\<\/div\>//s;
    $raw =~ s/\<!-- end content --\>.*//s;

    # OPTIONAL
    # Remove disambiguation links... we generally don't want to follow those
    $raw =~ s/\<div class=\"dablink\"\>.*?\<\/div\>//s;

    # OPTIONAL
    # Remove tables
#    $raw =~ s/\<table .*?\<\/table\>//gs;

    # Remove category links
    $raw =~ s/\<div id=\"catlinks\"\>.*?\<\/div\>//s;
```

```perl
# Remove everything at and below the References section
$raw =~ s/\<ol class=\"references\".*//s;

# Convert the <h1> heading to a __TITLE__
$raw =~ s/\<h1 class=\"firstHeading\"\>(.*?)\<\/h1\>/__TITLE__$1__ENDTITLE__/s;

# Convert wiki links to __LINK__
$raw =~ s/\<a\ href=\"\/wiki\/(.*?)\".*?\>(.*?)\<\/a\>
    /__LINKURL__$1__LINKTEXT__$2__ENDLINK__/gsx;

# <p> and <br> become carriage returns
$raw =~ s/\<p\>/\n/ig;
$raw =~ s/\<br\>/\n/ig;

# <li> becomes -
$raw =~ s/\<li\>/- /ig;

# All other tags disappear
$raw =~ s/\<.+?\>//gs;

# Convert __TITLE__ back into an actual title
$raw =~ s/__TITLE__(.*?)__ENDTITLE__/\<TITLE\>$1\<\/TITLE\>/s;

# Get rid of __LINK__ tags that point to images or special wikipedia locations
$raw =~ s/__LINKURL__(\S+?):(\S+?)__LINKTEXT__.*?__ENDLINK__//gs;

# Convert all other __LINK__ tags back into valid links
$raw =~
  s/__LINKURL__(.*?)__LINKTEXT__(.*?)__ENDLINK__/\<A HREF=\"$1\"\>$2\<\/A\>/gs;

# Strip whitespace
$raw =~ s/\s*//;
$raw =~ s/\n/__W__/g;
$raw =~ s/\s\s+//g;
$raw =~ s/__W__(__W__)+/\n\n/g;
$raw =~ s/__W__/\n/g;

# Find all the links in the document
my @linkUrls = $raw =~ /\<A HREF=\"(.*?)\"/g;
push(@links, @linkUrls);

# Back where it came from
return $raw;
}
```

That would be a lot of typing, so why bother? Head to http://homepage.mac.com/swannman/wikipod.zip and download the script.

Once the download is complete, move it to your Desktop (it is likely in the Downloads folder).

Open *Terminal.app*, and type:

```
$ cd ~/Desktop
```

Once you've changed the directory to the Desktop, follow that command with:

```
$ chmod 755 wikipod
```

This command marks the script as executable, and the script is ready to be used.

Using the Script

This isn't a straightforward double-click and go deal, but it isn't difficult either.

Mount your iPod in disk mode (you can tell if your iPod is in disk mode by the presence of the iPod's icon on the Desktop).

Open *Terminal.app*, and type:

```
$ cd ~/Desktop
```

Pick a Wikipedia page to start from. We'll choose the iPod page for this hack.

Type the following:

```
$ ./wikipod http://en.wikipedia.org/wiki/IPod
```

(You can't see it, but there's a trailing space after the `IPod`.)

Double-click on your iPod icon and drag the Notes folder into the Terminal window to auto-complete the path. If you're comfortable with the Terminal, the path is:

```
/Volumes/youripod/Notes
```

Now type the number of megabytes of space for wikipod to fill:

The command should now look like this:

```
$ ./wikipod http://en.wikipedia.org/wiki/IPod /Volumes/youripod/Notes 10
```

Hit enter, and your iPod will start filling up with Wikipedia entries (see Figure 7-28).

Figure 7-28.
The Terminal is doing the hard work for you

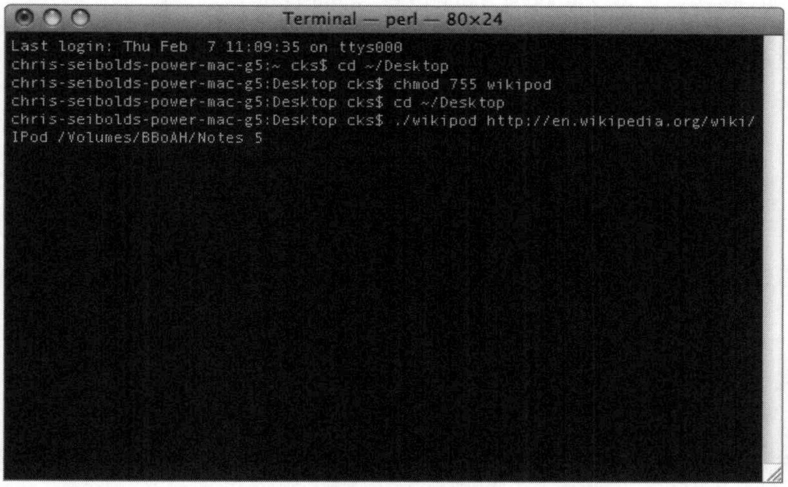

Go back to your iPod folder, double-click on the Notes folder, and watch the entries as they're downloaded, formatted for your iPod, and transferred over (see Figure 7-29).

Figure 7-29.
The Wikipedia pages are flying into your iPod!

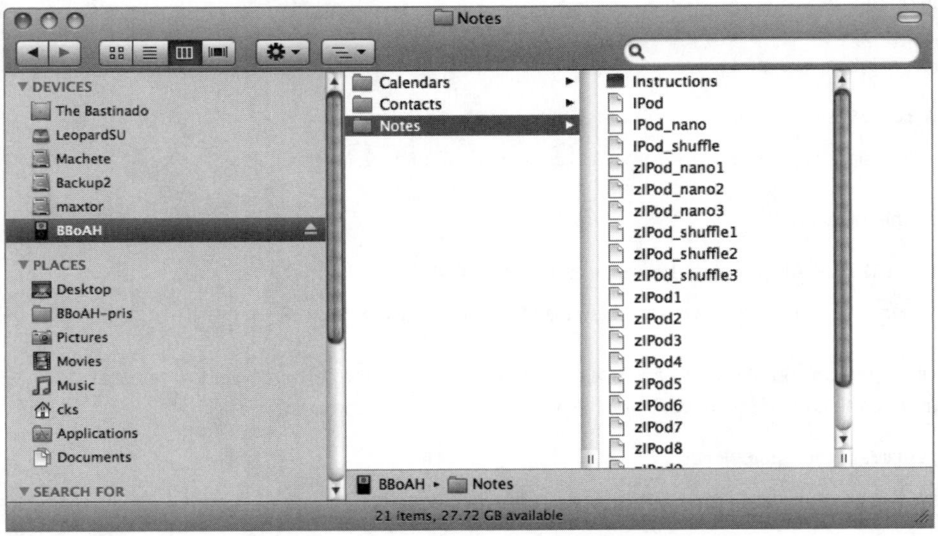

When the script exits and prints "Done transferring x pages!," you can unmount your iPod.

There's one caveat about using Notes on the iPod. The first time you navigate to the Notes menu after syncing with iTunes or downloading new Wikipedia articles, the iPod needs to inspect each page to see whether the links are valid. This can take a fair amount of time (and battery, because it's disk-intensive), so I recommend leaving the iPod plugged in until it finishes. (This is a real bummer; I'm looking into ways to work around it, but I'm not optimistic.)

Now, you might not want to use just Wikipedia as the source for Notes on your iPod. The good news is that you can modify the script to convert any web-based source to iPod Notes, but I'll leave that exercise to you.

— Matt Swann

MAXIMIZE YOUR MAC WITH MULTIPLE OPERATING SYSTEMS

Since the switch to Intel chips, Macs have become a viable option for those who want to run OS X but need to run Windows. However, your Mac can do more than just run Windows and OS X. Your Mac can run classic versions of the Mac OS, and you can swap drives from a Windows machine to the Mac and boot without installing OS X. You can even suck your information from your Mac to your newly installed Windows partition if you want your experience to be as seamless as possible.

HACK 86: Nondestructively Partition Your Hard Drive

Installing Leopard? Linux? Need partitions? Use the command line to partition your drives without losing that hard-earned data.

It has probably happened to you: you're sitting in front of your machine and find yourself wishing that you were running separate partitions on your Mac. The reasons vary, perhaps you want to install Linux on a second partition, maybe you want a second startup disk to repair the first hard drive, etc.

In the pre-Tiger days, partitioning your drive meant a willingness to lose all your data. You had to start up from a bootable CD, invoke Disk Utility (Disk Copy in the very olden days), and partition the drive. Of course, if you were willing to do that, it meant you had a rock solid backup of your data and likely another disk. Thing is, if you already had another disk, the reasoning behind resizing the drive was questionable. The long and short of it was that partitioning a drive before Tiger was something you usually either did the moment you bought your Mac or not at all.

That changed when Boot Camp came on the scene. Boot Camp partitioned your drive without compromising the your data, so clearly it was possible. What's more, using Boot Camp, you can partition your Intel Mac as much as you want. Trouble is, Boot Camp sets everything up for a Windows install, and you might not want to install Windows. You might want to install Leopard or the Apple TV OS on your new partition.

QUICK TIP

LEOPARD CAN DO THIS FOR YOU

OS X 10.5 has a lot of advantages over 10.4 and one of them is that you won't need to hit the command line to create partitions. The Disk Utility application that ships with Leopard can take care of adding and removing partitions without data loss. A true boon for Leopard users but useless if you want a new partition to upgrade to Leopard!

Figure 8-1.
The Partition Map Scheme line reveals the information you need to know

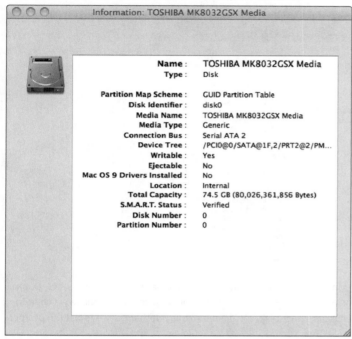

You should be able to run the commands that follow by shutting down every application except Terminal (which you need to run this hack). If you get an error running on of these commands, try booting your Mac in single user mode and running the commands from there (see the sidebar, "SINGLE-USER MODE: YOUR MAC IN COMMANDLINE-ESE").

Before you start, it is a good idea to plan out your partition strategy. Take into consideration the amount of data you have on your computer, the size of the hard drive, and your intended use. In this example, I am partitioning a 75 GB drive into three partitions: one 60 GB partition, one 10 GB partition, and one very small 4 GB partition. I chose this scheme because I want a simple partition with Mac OS X installed to troubleshoot the other partition, and I want to use the very small partition to store photos while swapping them betwixt computers.

> **Remember [Hack #1]?** This is one of the hacks where a good backup is critical, and a backup on the drive you're about to partition doesn't qualify as a good backup for this hack. A flicker in the power or some other unforeseen event could lead to massive data loss.

QUICK HACK

SINGLE-USER MODE: YOUR MAC IN COMMAND LINE-ESE

You enter single user mode by starting your Mac while holding down the Command–S keys. You'll boot into a command line instead of the familiar Mac OS X GUI. You can see why you'd want to do that if you are partitioning disks, but there is more, well actually less, happening behind the scenes. Single user mode avoids firing up a lot of the services your Mac usually runs and not just the things you associate with the GUI. While single user mode is useful for this hack, it is an old Unix standard, designed to allow maintenance on a multiuser machine without interference from the dreaded (by the admin anyway) users.

Time for some prepartitioning fun. One thing you'll probably want to do is make sure your mental plan for the partition matches the reality of the disk you're about to partition. Open up Terminal **[Hack #30]** and type this command:

```
$ diskutil list
```

This command lists the properties of your currently mounted hard drives. In my case the output looks like what's in Figure 8-2.

Figure 8-2.
The information about all mounted disks

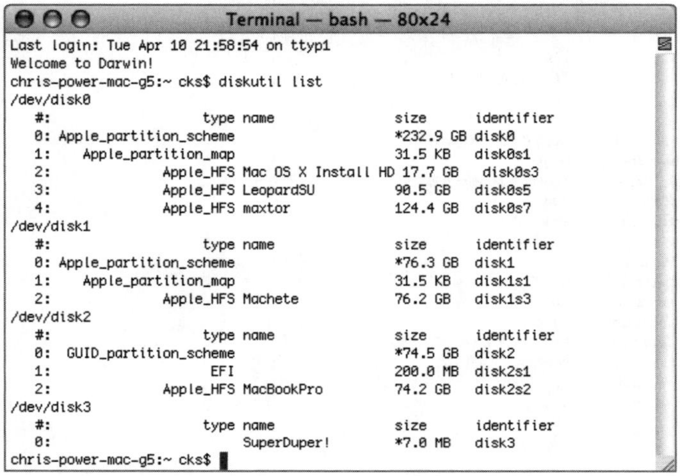

The disk I want to modify is "MacBook Pro" (oooh, such an original name for a drive in a MacBook Pro), and the identifier (important) is "disk2s2". This is important information because we want to know a little bit more about that particular disk. You'll need to use another command at the prompt:

```
$ diskutil resizeVolume disk2s2 limits
```

This returns the current size of the partition, the maximum size of the partition (a number bounded by the size of the disk), and the minimum size (a number dictated by the amount of data already on the disk).

```
Current size:   79682387968 bytes
Minimum size:   45766385664 bytes
Maximum size:   79682387968 bytes
```

Thus far, all that has been done is harmless probing but the realm of "break out the restore disks, I just lost all my data" is about to be entered. In other words, time to get down with a little partitioning.

Before you partition your own disk, you'll need to calculate your minimum size in gigabytes (GB). Divide the number (45,766,385,664 in the preceding example) by 1,073,741,824. In this example, you'd get 42 GB, the smallest size you can shrink your boot disk to. You should also perform the same math on the current size, because that lets you know how much total space you have for the other partitions (74 GB in this example).

And yes, the total number you get is smaller than what the drive size is advertised as. That's because drive makers calculate a GB as $1{,}000^3$, but the operating system calculates it as 1024^3. That's why a drive advertised as 250 GB ends up being 232 GB when you get it home!

The command is deceptively short for the result (be sure to replace the numbers and partition names with whatever is appropriate for your configuration):

```
$ sudo diskutil resizeVolume disk2s2 60G JHFS+ NewPartition 10G JHFS+ Smalldisk 4G
```

You can create as many partitions as space will allow, and the partitions don't have to use the Journaled Hierarchical File System (JHFS+). You can use a variety of schemes (HFS+, MS-DOS, etc.) To generalize from the previous example:

- **diskutil resizeVolume** is the command to get things started.

- *disk2s2 60G* gives the size of the partition you want to shrink. After the command is finished, this will be the size of your Mac OS X boot disk. You don't name it because it is already named (in this case, MacBook Pro).

- *JHFS+* indicates the types of scheme you want to use on the new partition. As mentioned earlier, a variety of formats are supported. This can be an important consideration depending on your intended use for the partition. In the example, I'm just using the new partitions for convenience, so I'm sticking with JHFS+, but if you're installing Linux or Windows on the new partition, it is worth your time to make a conscious decision on which filesystem to use.

- *10G* is the size of the new partition. I've used G for gigabytes throughout the example, but you can use M for megabytes or T for terabytes.

- *JHFS+ Smalldisk 4G* is another little partition.

The question is, did it work? Terminal is happy to report the success or failure of the attempt (see Figure 8-3).

Figure 8-3.
Success!

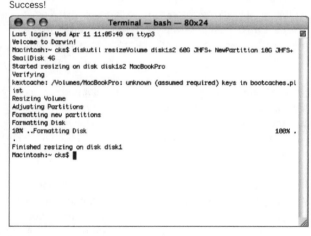

Once **diskutil** is done performing whatever partitioning magic it does, you can use the disks as though they were separate entities as shown in Figure 8-4.

Figure 8-4.
All one disk, three partitions!

MacBookPro   NewPartition   SmallDisk

HACK 87: Run Windows on Your Mac

You've got a wealth of choices for running Windows—and even a few other operating systems—on an Intel Mac.

With the release of the Intel Macs came the speculation that they might run Windows applications right out of the box. Some people speculated that Windows might be the new Classic, with Mac OS X and Windows applications running side by side. They weren't exactly right, but they were prophetic. Not long after the Intel Macs came out, two of the leading virtualization packages, VMware Fusion and Parallels Desktop, supported a seamless mode in which Windows programs and Mac OS X programs coexisted happily on the same desktop. But there's another way to run Windows on your Mac, and no doubt you've heard a lot about it. Boot Camp configures your Mac's hard drive so you can install Windows on some spare space, and choose between booting Windows or Mac OS X. Peaceful yes; coexistence—not really.

> Virtualization software takes your computer's resources (such as hardware devices, CPU time, chunks of memory, and disk space) and hides them really well. It hides them so well in fact, that it can trick an otherwise clever operating system into thinking this ragtag assortment of resources is a complete computer. So when that copy of Windows boots up in a VMware or Parallels "virtual machine," it sees what it thinks is a standard PC BIOS, CPU, memory, hard disk, and more. And it starts running and does its job just fine, mostly unaware that VMware or Parallels is brokering all its interactions with this virtual hardware.

Boot Camp or Virtualization?

When you go to install Windows on your Mac, you've got two choices. If you want to run Mac and Windows programs at the same time, you need to use virtualization software, either Parallels or VMware. Both cost $79 (shop around for rebates and such), and both are excellent. You'll still need a licensed copy of Windows to run under this virtualization environment, so figure on spending at least another $200 to get Windows. If you have a PC that came with Windows install disks, they are most likely locked to that computer, so you won't be able to use that copy of Windows with VMware or Parallels.

If you're planning on using Linux, I suggest VMware because it has slightly better support for Linux. For example, at the time of this writing, Parallels did not allow you to copy and paste between Linux applications and Mac OS X applications, although VMware does. Both VMware and Parallels allow seamless copy and paste between Windows and Mac OS X applications, so if you're only going to be running Windows, either one is a fine choice.

If you don't need to run Windows applications side-by-side with Mac OS X, and you don't mind interrupting your flow to reboot your Mac every time you want to switch between Windows and Mac applications, you can use Boot Camp (included with Leopard) to run Windows. What's more, you can choose to use Boot Camp with one of these virtualization packages. Both VMware and Parallels can boot off of your Windows partition. So if you need to get at your Windows applications while you're in Mac OS X, they will be there for you; if you need to run Windows at maximum speed, you can reboot into Windows and give it direct access to the full power of your Mac.

> Boot Camp is a good choice if you're a gamer or you need to run 3D-intensive applications. Because Parallels and VMware support 3D acceleration for some popular games and applications, they might also work for you. However, if you have a Mac with integrated graphics, you're going to get the most speed using Boot Camp. MacBooks and Mac minis have the slower Intel-integrated graphics; iMacs, Mac Pros, and MacBook Pros have more powerful discrete graphics cards from NVIDIA and AMD. Systems with integrated graphics run most modern games slowly or not at all, and using Boot Camp will let you squeeze every last bit of power out of them.

Installing Windows with Boot Camp

To install Windows on Boot Camp, you usually open up the Finder, make your way to /Applications/ Utilities, and run the Boot Camp Assistant. When you've done that, you're prompted to insert your Windows (XP or Vista only) CD or DVD, and then the computer reboots into the Windows installer.

I suggest that you take a slightly more difficult route that will, in the end, make your life easier.

Windows prefers to run on a disk partition that's been formatted with the Windows NT File System (NTFS). Windows XP is content to run on the older FAT32 format, but this format is unreliable and prone to errors. And Windows Vista will flat out refuse to install on a FAT32 partition. So for best results under Windows, you really should have the Windows installer format your Boot Camp partition as NTFS. Unfortunately, this causes a problem: Mac OS X cannot write to NTFS partitions (it sees them as read-only). And Windows can't see Mac OS X partitions at all, without the use of third-party software. So if you use NTFS for Windows, you won't be able drag files between your Windows and Mac OS X partitions. So what I suggest you do is create three partitions:

- Your original Mac OS X partition (you'll be taking away some of its free space to give some space to Windows)

- A FAT32 partition with a few gigabytes of space for transferring files

- Another FAT32 partition with lots of space for Windows (you'll instruct the Windows installer to format this as NTFS)

The only problem is that if you do this, you won't be able to use the Boot Camp Assistant, because it works only on a disk that's been formatted with a single Mac OS X partition. But the truth is, you don't need the Boot Camp Assistant. All you need is an Intel Mac, your Leopard Installation DVD, and a Windows installation CD or DVD. Oh, and a little trip to the Terminal [Hack #30] to prepare your disk.

You're going to be taking some space away from your Mac and giving it to Windows. So after you've opened the Terminal, you need to figure out just how much space is left and repartition your disk. This is an inherently risky operation, so don't do it unless you have made a reliable backup. The diskutil command can do everything you need; you'll first use its list option to see how your disk is set up. Here you can see that partition 2 of disk 0 is full of Mac OS X:

```
$ diskutil list
/dev/disk0
   #:                      TYPE NAME              SIZE       IDENTIFIER
   0:     GUID_partition_scheme                  *298.1 Gi   disk0
   1:                        EFI                  200.0 Mi   disk0s1
   2:        Apple_HFS Macintosh HD               297.8 Gi   disk0s2
```

Next, use the resizeVolume option to resize the disk. You need to choose how much disk space to give to Mac OS X, how much for the shared data partition (let's call it "Data"), and how much for Windows. This command gives 220 GB to Mac OS X, 12 GB to the shared data partition, and whatever's left over for Windows:

```
$ sudo diskutil resizeVolume disk0s2 220g "MS-DOS FAT32" Data 12g \
  "MS-DOS FAT32" Windows 0b
```

If you get an error, use the `resizeVolume diskname limits` option to see how much space you can take away from Mac OS X. You may have to free up some space or be content with less space for Windows if you don't have enough:

```
$ diskutil resizeVolume disk0s2 limits
For device disk0s2 Macintosh HD:
    Current size:   319723962263 bytes
    Minimum size:   139510571008 bytes
    Maximum size:   319723962263 bytes
```

When it's done, run `diskutil list` again to see what you did:

```
$ diskutil list
/dev/disk0
   #:                       TYPE NAME                 SIZE       IDENTIFIER
   0:      GUID_partition_scheme                     *298.1 Gi   disk0
   1:                        EFI                       200.0 Mi   disk0s1
   2:           Apple_HFS Macintosh HD                 219.9 Gi   disk0s2
   3:    Microsoft Basic Data DATA                     12.0 Gi    disk0s3
   4:    Microsoft Basic Data                          65.9 Gi    disk0s4
```

Now you've got three partitions: your old Mac OS X partition (now with less space), and two partitions formatted with FAT32. Now you can put your Windows disk in, shut down your Mac, and then power back up while you hold down the Option/Alt key. The Option key will cause a list of bootable drives (internal disks and optical disks) to appear, and you should select the Windows installation disk and proceed through the installation. Install Windows on the partition that you created (you'll be able to recognize it by looking at its size), and choose the NTFS filesystem when asked how to format it. In Vista, you'll be notified that Vista can't install to that disk, so you'll have to click "Drive Options (Advanced)" to format the target drive.

Be super-careful here. If you pick the wrong target disk, you could wipe out your Mac OS X installation!

Here's one thing that Boot Camp does that this manual procedure won't do: it sets up your Mac so that it boots into Windows by default (you can change this later). So if you walk away from your Mac while you are installing Windows, you will probably come back to find that it has booted back into Mac OS X. This is because Windows reboots at the end of the installation. So, shut down your Mac, start it up with the Option/Alt key held down, and select the Windows drive (not the installation disk this time).

You can use the Startup Disk pane in System Preferences under Mac OS X to make Windows the default, and you can do the same from the Boot Camp utility in Windows. You can also force your Mac to offer you a choice by holding down the Option/Alt key while it boots. You might want to do that at this point, because you'll need to reboot Windows a couple more times: at least once after installing the Boot Camp drivers and probably a couple of times for the various Windows updates that are needed. When you're done, you can use the Boot Camp utility (it's in the Window system tray/notification area) to reconfigure your Mac to always boot Mac OS X.

After Windows has finished installing and you've logged in to your pristine Windows desktop, insert the Leopard install DVD (if the Mac eject key doesn't work, click Start→My Computer or Start→ Computer to open up Explorer, find your DVD/CD drive, right-click it and select eject). The Boot Camp driver and utility installation will start up. This is essential if you want Windows to run properly on your Mac.

Installing Windows on a Virtual Machine

Although I've mentioned that VMware Fusion and Parallels Desktop are both excellent, you will have to make a choice because I don't recommend installing both of them on the same machine at the same time. I did that once, and even tried running both of them at the same time, and my Mac punched me in the face (well, it was a kernel panic, but it felt like a punch in the face). So pick one: if you plan to run Linux in a virtual machine, I suggest VMware. If not, flip a coin or take an informal poll of your most geeky friends.

Both VMware and Parallels offer trial versions of their software, so you could try them both (just not at the same time!). Head on over to http://www.vmware.com/mac or http://www.parallels.com/en/products/desktop, and download a trial version. Install it on your Mac, and you're ready to roll.

Using VMware or Parallels with Boot Camp

If you've already used Boot Camp, you can instruct VMware or Parallels to use your Boot Camp partition to run Windows. This requires a little background tweaking on the part of VMware and Parallels, because as far as Windows is concerned, the virtual machine and your Macintosh are two different computers, with slightly different sets of hardware, and as a result, a different identification as far as Windows XP and Vista's product activation is concerned.

Fortunately, both Parallels and VMware include software that rearranges things behind the scenes and smooths everything over, for the most part. If you use VMware or Parallels to boot an activated copy of Windows, it will probably trigger the Windows Activation procedure again. But once you've gotten through the initial setup and that activation procedure, you can use Parallels or VMware to access your Boot Camp partition and run the exact same copy of Windows under Mac OS X. When you need to flip over to running Windows directly on your Mac's hardware, you can shut down the virtual machine that's hosting Boot Camp, and reboot your Mac with the Option/Alt key held down to choose Windows.

To boot your Boot Camp partition from VMware, simply run VMware and look for the Boot Camp entry in the list of virtual machines, as shown in Figure 8-5.

Figure 8-5.
VMWare goes to Boot Camp

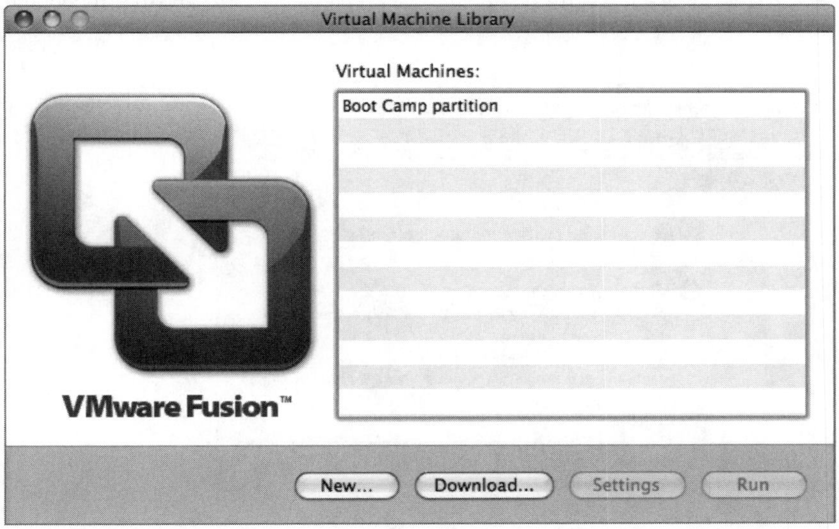

VMware should detect your Boot Camp partition automatically. (If it doesn't, check the VMware support web site for tips, tricks, and answers.) To run it, select "Boot Camp partition" and click Run. VMware will make some changes to your Boot Camp partition, you'll be asked for your password, and after a few minutes, it will start up your Boot Camp partition in a virtual machine (see Figure 8-6). In order for it to function properly, you'll need to install VMware Tools (this takes care of all the behind-the-scenes wrangling needed to keep Windows happy), and you're ready to enjoy your Windows any way you want: in a virtual machine, or running right on the "bare iron."

Figure 8-6.
VMware locating the Boot Camp partition

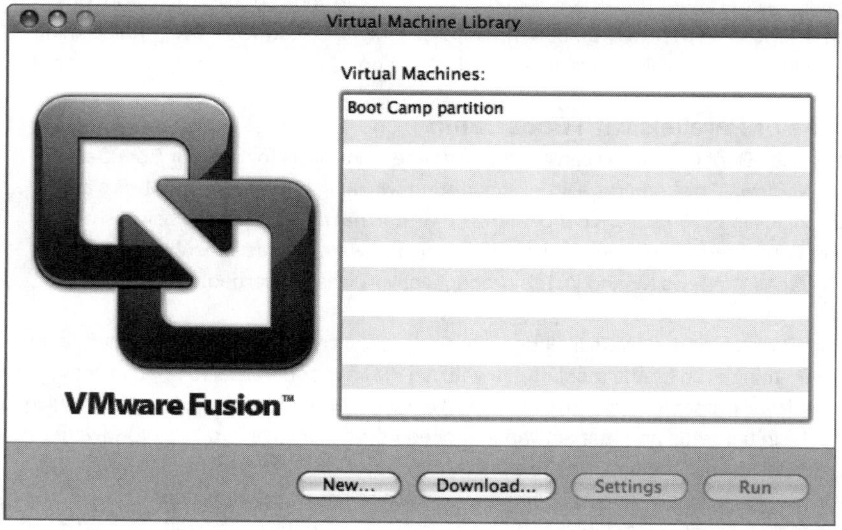

Parallels is similar, except it doesn't automatically detect and configure the Boot Camp partition. Instead, you need to create a new virtual machine and select the Custom option (see Figure 8-7). Specify the version of Windows you have installed under Boot Camp, choose the amount of memory to give it, and when you come to the virtual hard disk option screen, choose Use Boot Camp. You'll take a few more steps through the configuration, and when it's done, Parallels will boot up Windows, explain to you that it has some one-time configuration to perform, and then reboot the virtual machine.

Figure 8-7.
Configuring a custom virtual machine for booting your Boot Camp partition

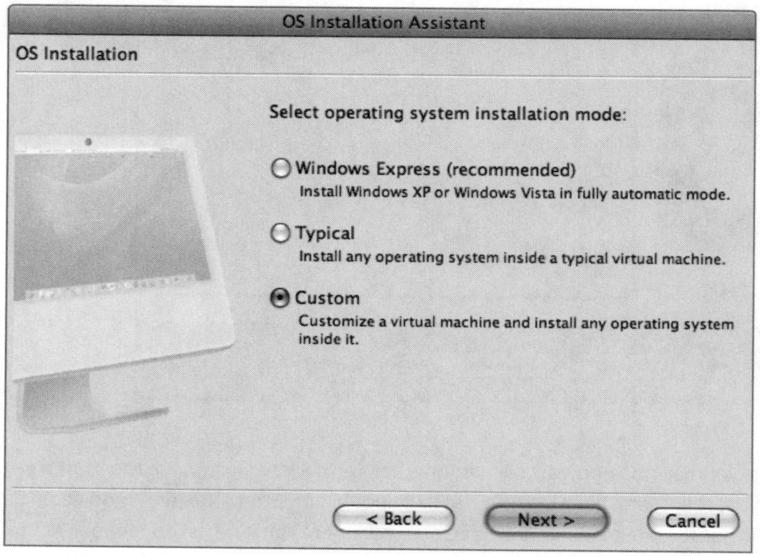

Creating a Virtual Machine from Scratch

You can also set up a virtual machine that doesn't use your boot camp partition, or any real disk partition for that matter. In Parallels and VMware, when you create a new virtual machine, you are asked to choose a location for the virtual disk image (the default is fine; you can always move it around later). This is a multigigabyte file that contains the entire operating system. The great thing about this is that you can easily back up the virtual machine. The bad thing about this is that these virtual disk images are huge, and if you are using Time Machine, it will make many backups of it (hourly, daily, weekly) and quickly fill up your Time Machine drive. If you don't have a lot of free space on your Time Machine drive, consider opening System Preferences and configuring Time Machine to exclude (Options→Do Not Back Up) the directory that holds your virtual machines.

To create a new virtual machine, launch Parallels Workstation or VMware Fusion, select File→ New, and follow the instructions for creating a virtual machine. You'll need your Windows DVD or CD handy, as well as your product key. Both Parallels and VMware Fusion can make life extremely easy for you by giving you the option to specify your username, password, and Windows product key before you start the installation. This lets the installation run largely unattended, so you can go for a walk or climb a mountain while you are waiting.

When you've got Windows up and running, be sure to give VMware's Unity (shown in Figure 8-8) or Parallels' Coherence mode a try. These modes integrate your Mac and Windows desktop for a seamless virtualization experience.

Figure 8-8.
VMware's Unity mode

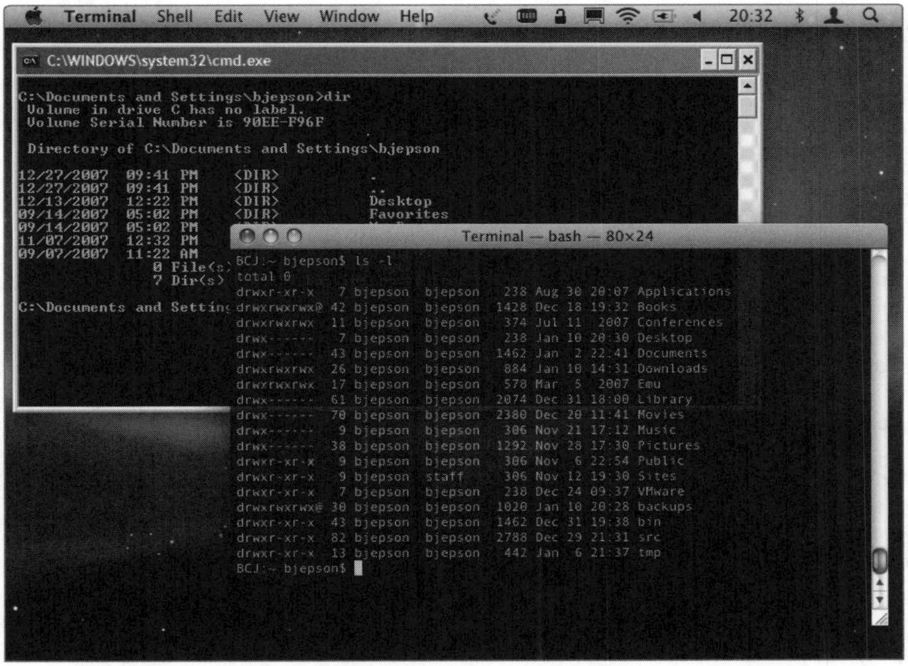

If you are installing Windows Vista, I suggest that you do not use the option to supply your product key. Here's why: the Vista installer will let you install without a product key (leave it blank), but it still enforces the activation after the grace period. The nice thing about not providing the product key is that it makes it harder for you to absentmindedly activate Windows before you are ready. If you're planning to install Windows for a quick test or evaluation, why use up your precious activations? And if you plan to use Windows only for evaluation, you should look into Microsoft's TechNet Plus, which costs $349 a year and gives you a number of benefits including complete versions of Microsoft operating systems licensed for evaluation purposes.

Crossover Mac

There's one other option open to you, and it doesn't even require a copy of Windows. Crossover Mac (http://www.codeweavers.com/products/cxmac) is a software package that builds upon the open source WINE (http://www.winehq.com) project. WINE stands for "WINE Is Not an Emulator," a clever recursive acronym that hints at what WINE actually is. Unlike VMware and Parallels, which use a combination of virtualization (abstracting the physical devices on your Mac) and emulation (using software components to duplicate the function of physical devices), WINE does neither. Instead, WINE is best described as a clone of the software components that make up Windows. Windows is made up of a collection of executable programs (EXEs), dynamic link libraries (DLLs), and other software components. WINE duplicates the functions of most of the components that come with Windows.

Because it's not a complete reimplementation of Windows, Crossover is not compatible with as much software as Windows running under VMware, Boot Camp, or Parallels. But, it can run software extremely fast; pretty much as fast as the software would run on a Boot Camp installation. This is because there's not much in the way between the Windows application and your Mac's hardware. If a 3D game tells Windows to draw a polygon on the screen, it takes certain steps to make that happen. Crossover does nearly the same thing Windows does in performing the same task, without the overhead of any virtualized or emulated hardware. It's as if someone "ported" Windows (albeit incompletely) to Mac OS X!

— Brian Jepson

HACK 88: Suck Windows Onto Your Mac

You know you can install Windows onto your Mac but what if you already have Windows installed on another machine? It turns out you don't have to reinstall, you can suck the installed Windows right onto your Mac!

When most Mac users here the words, "Windows" and "sucks" in the same sentence they think of the phrase, "Windows sucks!" Well, the veracity of that statement aside (there are certain applications that are only available on Windows, after all), there are a couple of products that make it very easy for your Mac to suck Windows in. By having a Windows virtual machine on your Mac, you can avoid having to go get a Dell. In this hack, we are going to cover how to get a Windows machine on your Mac without ever installing Windows. How? By the power of suck.

As noted in [Hack #68], there are a couple of products battling it out for Virtual Machine supremacy on the Mac—Parallels and VMware, to name two. For the purposes of this hack we are going to use Parallels. You can either purchase Parallels, or download a trial and try this out without the pesky financial commitment. To get this hack to work, you'll also need an Intel Mac and a Windows machine running XP or Vista.

Prepping the Windows Box

First go to your Windows machine, and download and install Parallels Transporter (see Figure 8-9, Figure 8-10, and Figure 8-11). Transporter will let you create an image of your Windows hard drive in a format that Parallels on your Mac will be able to understand and use. You do need to make sure you have at least the size of your hard drive available as free space on your Windows machine. So, if you have a 60 GB hard drive on your Windows machine, your drive should have at least 30 MB free. Don't worry, once you are done transporting the image, you can delete it from your Windows box; you'll have all that free space back.

Figure 8-9.
This is the welcoming screen to Transporter on your PC

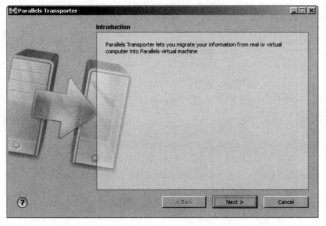

Figure 8-10.
For most cases, just select Express

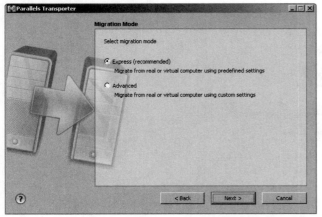

Figure 8-11.
Since you want to create an image of your Windows machine, select "Migrate from this computer into Parallels virtual machine"

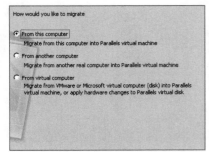

QUICK HACK

WHAT HAPPENS IF TRANSPORTER DOESN'T WORK?

Sometimes Transporter will kick back an error. Usually it has to do with the amount of free hard drive space (what did I say above?), but sometimes something else is going on. Here are some troubleshooting tips:

- Switch off any virus software you have running on your Windows machine.
- Defragment the hard drive.
- Turn off any third-party firewall software you have running on your Windows machine.

Once Transporter is running, sit back and relax. Or better yet, go back to your Mac and do some work. Because Transporter is making a mirror image of your Windows hard drive (much like Carbon Copy Cloner can do with your Mac OS X boot disk), this is going to take some time.

Eventually Transporter will be done creating an image of your Windows hard drive. Now it's time to suck it over to your Mac. The simplest way to do this is to connect your Mac and PC together, Ethernet to Ethernet. If you are all wireless, all the time, head on down to your local computer store and buy a regular old Ethernet cable. Attach one end to your Mac and the other end to your Windows machine with the machines powered on.

If you are lucky enough to have a PC with a FireWire cable, you can also connect your Mac and PC this way.

On your Mac, open up System Preferences→Network and double-click the Built-in Ethernet option making sure DHCP is selected.

Now that your machines are hooked up, go to Applications→Parallels Transporter on your Mac. After you open it up, it should look exactly the same as the Windows version, albeit with luscious OS X chrome (see Figure 8-12, Figure 8-13, and Figure 8-14).

Figure 8-12.
On your Mac selection, "From another computer"

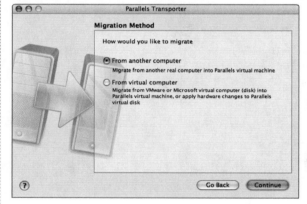

Figure 8-13.
Select your connection type

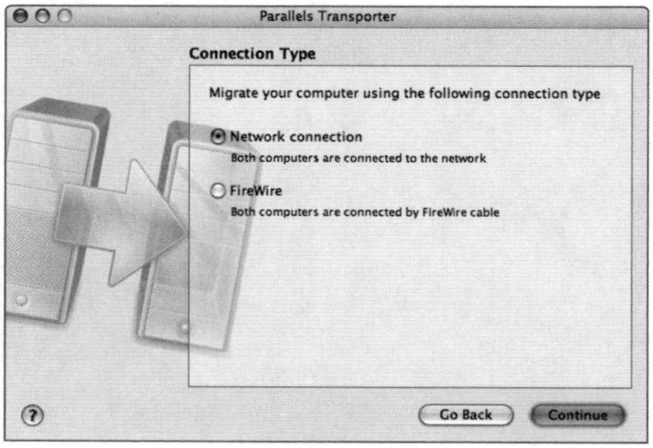

Figure 8-14.
Confirm that your Windows machine is on, connected to your Mac, and has the Parallels Transporter agent running

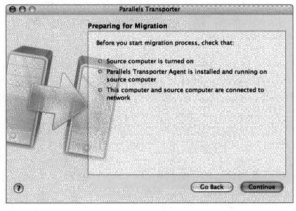

Once your machines are seeing each other, you can start the transfer process. It's time for another break now, but it will likely last even longer than last time because now the disk image Parallels created on your Windows machine needs to be transferred via Ethernet to your Mac. This also means that you must have enough free space on your Mac to accommodate the disk image. (Don't worry, Parallels will inform you if you don't.)

After sucking over the entire image, you're almost done! The new virtual machine will show up in Parallels. The final step to get everything working smoothly is to install the Parallels Windows tools on your virtual machine. These tools will make working with Windows on your Mac much smoother.

HACK 89: Move from Windows to Mac OS X Painlessly

The differences between Macs and Windows-based machines aren't negligible, but the differences don't have to be insurmountable. Learn the answer to all those pesky Mac versus Windows questions with this guide.

Maybe you've switched to the Mac; maybe you're supporting a switcher. In either case: welcome! If you still feel like you're stumbling around in the dark wondering what the switcher is saying or what your Mac is wanting, hopefully the following article will turn a few lights on. Maybe you're thinking about switching but still a little worried about how compatible you will be with Mac OS X. Again, this article should hold your hand as you cross over.

Although switching to Mac from Windows is a relatively simple process, you still need to reeducate yourself a little on the Mac's way of doing things and its terminology. If you're supporting a switcher, learning the keystrokes of Windows will help immensely because you'll be able to tell him (for instance) that Command-C on the Mac is the same as Ctrl-C on Windows.

Recently, having undertaken study at a college where the computers are all Macs, I've encountered many students with no Mac experience who are struggling with the differences. It's been interesting to hear their frustration at not knowing how to do the simplest little things on the Mac—and what they've said hasn't been flattering to the Mac.

So for them, and every other switcher and the people who support them, this article provides a list of the equivalences: terminology, applications, and general way of doing things on a Mac. It is by no means complete or comprehensive. It also assumes Windows up to XP because at the moment, that is the version the majority of switchers are familiar with.

Modifier Key Definitions

On a standard QWERTY keyboard with a U.S. layout, the modifier keys on a Mac are the Command, Control, and Option keys. The Command key is the one at either end of the Space bar. In shorthand form, the Command key is represented by a cloverleaf symbol. It is often also called the Apple key because older versions of Apple keyboards had the Apple logo on it. The Option key is the next key out from the Command key. The Control (Ctrl) key is the third key out from the Space bar.

On other keyboard layouts and laptop keyboards, these keys may be laid out differently.

Table 7-1 shows the differences in Windows/Mac desktop terminology.

Table 7-1.
Mac vs. Windows terminology

On Windows	On OS X
Windows Update	Software Update
Command Prompt	Terminal
Control Panel	System Preferences
Directory	folder
Explorer	Finder
My Computer	Finder
Options	Preferences
Program	Application
Recycle Bin	Trash
Context menu	Context menu
Taskbar	Dock
Blue Screen of Death (less common on Windows since XP)	Kernel panic (very rare on Macs)

Table 7-2 shows the equivalent methods of doing things on Mac and Windows. Not all methods are shown, only those where the method differs. For instance, just like Windows, you can close a window via the File menu; or copy, cut, and paste via the Edit menu.

Table 7-2.
Mac and Windows equivalents

Function	On Windows	On OS X
Abort an application	Ctrl-Alt-Del, select application, and click End Task	Option-Command-Esc, then select and click Force Quit
Applets	Bottom right of Taskbar	Top right of menu bar
Applications: accessing running applications	Alt-tab Click on program's name in the Taskbar	Alt-tab F9 Click on the application's icon in the Dock. Running applications are indicated by a black triangle or dot below the application's Dock icon.
Applications: finding and launching	Start Menu	Dock Applications folder

Table 7-2.
Mac and Windows equivalents *(continued)*

Function	On Windows	On OS X
Basic troubleshooting of application crashes (after performing each of these, test if the problem is solved)	Restart application Reboot Scandisk Defrag Reinstall troublesome program	Restart application Reboot Delete troublesome application's Preference file (found in *Library/Preferences* folder of your User folder and often named something like *com.vendorname. applicationnme.plist*) Repair disk permissions using the Disk Utility in the Applications→Utilities folder (requires administrator access)
Close a window	Close button (top right of window)	Close button (top left of window). Note: If the Close button displays a grey dot in the middle of it, the document in the window is unsaved
Context menus	Right mouse click	Ctrl-left mouse click on single button mice, otherwise, also right mouse click
Copy	Ctrl-C	Command-C
Cut	Ctrl-X	Command-X
Drive names	C:, D:, E: etc	OS X uses the name given to the disk (the label in Windows) to reference disks (e.g., "iMac Hard Disk")
Ejecting CDs and DVDs	Push eject button on disk drive Right-click on disk and select Eject	In a Finder window, click eject symbol to right of disk Drag and drop the disk's icon on to the Trash icon (it will turn into an Eject icon) Push the Eject key on the keyboard Note: a disk in use can't be ejected
File navigation and management	Windows Explorer My Computer	Finder
Files: Location of personal files	My Documents	Documents
Help	F1	Command-?
Installing programs	Run install program (if not automatically run)	Some applications have an installer (usually indicated by a *.pkg* or *.mpkg* suffix). Double-click to install. Others you simply drag and drop to the Applications folder.

Table 7-2.
Mac and Windows equivalents. *(continued)*

Function	On Windows	On OS X
Maximize a window	Maximize button (top right of window)	Zoom button (green button in top left of window). Note: Zoom is not functionally equivalent of Maximize, but is the closest thing to it on Macs. Zoom only enlarges the window enough to display the full width of the document within it
Menu bar: accessing by keystroke	Alt key	Ctrl-F2
Menu bar: location of an application's menu bar	Top of its window	Top of screen
Minimize a window	Minimize button (top right of window)	Minimize button (orange button in top left of window)
Monitoring system performance	Task Manager	Activity Monitor (found in the Applications/Utilities folder)
Move cursor one word right	Ctrl-Right arrow (cursor) key	Option-Right arrow (cursor) key
Move cursor one word left	Ctrl-Left arrow (cursor) key	Option-Left arrow (cursor) key
Move cursor to beginning of the line	Home key	Ctrl-Left arrow (cursor) key
Move cursor to end of the line	End key	Ctrl-Right arrow (cursor) key
Paste	Ctrl-V	Command-V
Properties: getting information about an item	Properties menu item. Usually in context menu (also Alt-Enter)	Get Info. Usually in either context menu or File menu (also Command-I)
Options and settings: location in menus	Usually under the Tools menu item	Usually under the application's named menu item
Removing media	Right-click on device and select Eject Open "Safely Remove Hardware" from Taskbar and choose the device to remove	In a Finder window, click eject symbol to right of the device Drag and drop the device's icon onto the Trash icon (it will turn into an Eject icon) Note: a device in use can't be ejected
Resize a window	Click and drag any edge	Click and drag bottom right corner
Run an application	Locate via the Start menu	If not already in the Dock, applications are stored in the Applications folder and its subfolders, and can be run directly from there. They can be kept permanently in the Dock by right-clicking on their Dock icon and selecting "Keep in Dock".
Screen brightness	Usually on the monitor	F14 to decrease F15 to increase

Table 7-2.
Mac and Windows equivalents. *(continued)*

Function	On Windows	On OS X
Screen capture	PrtScn to capture full screen to clipboard	Command-Shift-3 to capture full screen to a file
	Alt-PrtScrn to capture current window to clipboard	Ctrl-Command-Shift-3 to copy the full screen to the Clipboard
		Command-Shift-4 to capture selected area of the screen to a file. Press Space bar to automatically select the window under the cursor
		Ctrl-Command-Shift-4 to copy the selected area to the Clipboard
Select All	Ctrl-A	Command-A
Separator used in pathnames	Backslash (\)	Forward slash (/) (occasionally a colon (:) for old-style pathnames
Show desktop	Click Show Desktop shortcut in Taskbar	F11
System information	System in Control Panel (also right-click on My Computer and select Properties)	"About this Mac" in the Apple menu (top left corner of the screen)
Tabbed browsing	Available in Internet Explorer 7 and Firefox	In Safari, is off by default. Enable in Safari's preferences
Undo	Ctrl-Z	Command-Z

Table 7-3's list of applications is merely based on commonly used ones and is no recommendation for those listed, nor against any not mentioned. Those that are preinstalled on new Macs are shown in italic.

Table 7-3.
Common applications on OS X vs. Windows

Purpose	On Windows	On OS X
Browser	Internet Explorer	*Safari*
	Firefox	Firefox
Calendaring (home)	Outlook	*iCal*
Calendaring (professional)	Outlook	Microsoft Entourage
	Lotus Notes	Lotus Notes
Database	Access	Filemaker
Desktop publishing (home)	Microsoft Publisher	Apple Pages
	The Print Shop	The Print Shop
Desktop publishing (professional)	Adobe InDesign	Adobe InDesign
	QuarkXPress	QuarkXPress
Email client (personal)	Outlook Express	*Mail*
	Thunderbird	Microsoft Entourage
		Thunderbird
Email client (professional)	Outlook	Microsoft Entourage
Flash content creation	Flash	Flash
Illustration	Adobe Illustrator	Adobe Illustrator
	Inkscape	Inkscape

Table 7-3.
Common applications on OS X vs. Windows. *(continued)*

Purpose	On Windows	On OS X
Image editing (home)	Adobe Photoshop Elements	*iPhoto*
		Adobe Photoshop Elements
Image editing (professional)	Adobe Photoshop	Aperture
		Adobe Photoshop
Instant messaging	Microsoft Messenger	*iChat*
	ICQ	Microsoft Messenger
	Yahoo Messenger	ICQ
		Yahoo Messenger
Internet telephone calls	Skype	Skype
Movie editing (home)	Movie Maker	*iMovie*
	Adobe Premiere Elements	Final Cut Express
Movie editing (professional)	Adobe Premiere Professional	Final Cut Pro
Music player	Windows Media Player	*iTunes*
	iTunes	
Music recording	Adobe Audition	*GarageBand*
	Cakewalk	Logic Studio
	Cubase	
PDF viewer	Adobe Reader	*Preview*
PDF creation/editing	Adobe Acrobat	*Built-in print-to-PDF facility*
		Preview
		Adobe Acrobat
Photo management (home)	Google's Picasa	*iPhoto*
Photo management (professional)	Adobe Lightroom	Apple Aperture
		Adobe Lightroom
Presentation	Powerpoint (Microsoft Office)	Keynote (Apple iWork)
		Powerpoint (Microsoft Office)
Spreadsheet	Excel (Microsoft Office)	Numbers (Apple iWork)
		Excel (Microsoft Office)
Text editor	Notepad	*TextEdit*
	Wordpad	
Web page authoring (professional)	Dreamweaver	Dreamweaver
Widgets	Yahoo Widget Engine	*Dashboard*
		Yahoo Widget Engine
Word processing	Word (Microsoft Office)	Pages (Apple iWork)
		Word (Microsoft Office)

Clearly this information isn't useful for only the recent switcher; those who support switchers or are jumping headlong into Parallels will find the lists of inestimable value.

— Chris Howard

HACK 70: Panic Swap

Planning on using a Mac as a Windows-only machine? This hack reveals the method to boot your Mac into Windows using a drive swap!

I had been working for the same company for over 18 years and decided it was time to move on. Yeah, it took me a while. This company was giving us laptops for the last 15 years, and even though I'd used about four or five different laptops, my IT people always transferred my mail to the next computer. Once I decided to leave, I was thinking about what I wanted to take with me.

The big thing for me was my mail. I had accumulated thousands of messages and attachments through the years and stored them in folders within the Lotus Notes mail program. I asked the company if they would just sell me the laptop. They said "no." Bummer. So I started emailing myself some of the messages. It became abundantly clear pretty quickly that this process just wasn't going work; there were just too many messages. Knowing there is a Mac client for Lotus Notes, I thought maybe I could just buy the client and copy over the database? A little research told me that the Notes for the Mac client cost thousands of dollars—so that option was out.

Starting to run out of time, I figured I would just copy the drive contents to another drive and hope I could figure out some way to access my emails. I was very disappointed. Then, working on my MacBook, one day a light bulb went off—if I could not take the laptop, why not take the drive? At this point in my story, let me point out that it helps tremendously to have an excellent relationship with your IT manager. I called him and asked if it would be OK for me to replace the drive with another. He said "yes," which turned out to be easier said than done. Time was running out for me at the company, so I ran to every computer store I could find in New Hampshire.

No one had a 120 GB, 2.5-inch SATA drive. Checking online that evening, I found a few places, but I know that many that claim to ship the same day actually don't guarantee overnight delivery. Time being of the essence, I found a place that did promise next-day (or over the weekend in this case) delivery. I ordered up the drive I needed, made sure the next-day delivery option was checked. It was a Friday, so I knew the drive would come on Monday morning—which meant that I would get the drive on my last day at the company—not much time to get things right. The drive arrived at 9 a.m. I swapped it with the drive in the Dell and went off to my final day at the company. Whew!

Required Items
Here's what you need to swap drives:

- Valid Windows activation number

- Windows USB keyboard

- Boot Camp Driver set

- A quarter

- Torx T8 screwdriver

- Phillips P0 screwdriver

- Patience

Swapping the Disks

I needed to swap out the internal hard drive on my MacBook, and even though I had upgraded the memory, I had not pulled the HD. However, to learn how to install the memory upgrade, I discovered a MacBook hard-drive installation video from Other World Computing (http://eshop.macsales.com/tech_center/index.cfm?page=Video/macbook/macbook/med.html).

Using this as a reference, I pulled the hard drive out of my MacBook. It is a fairly simple process if you have the correct tools:

1. Turn your MacBook over, remove the battery (Figure 8-15), and there are instructions printed inside the compartment (Figure 8-16).

Figure 8-15.
In this step you use the high-tech tool known as a quarter (state designation unimportant)

Figure 8-16.
Apple includes instructions for installing RAM, unfortunately I want to take the drive out!

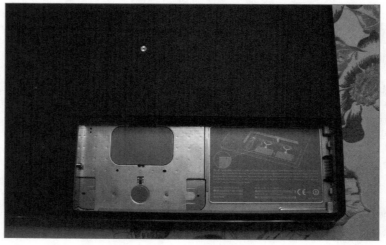

2. Remove the L-shaped shield using the Phillips screwdriver (Figure 8-17).

Figure 8-17.
Shield removal

3. Lift the plastic flap on the left side and pull on it, and the hard drive will slide right out (Figure 8-18 and Figure 8-19).

Figure 8-18.
Pull the tab!

Figure 8-19.
The hard drive makes an appearance

4. Remove the carrier bracket by unscrewing the four screws on the sides. Note the orientation. Place this bracket on your Windows hard drive and reverse the entire process (Figure 8-20).

Figure 8-20.
The replacement drive

Booting the Mac

I start up the MacBook and hear the familiar Mac start-up chime. At first, a large folder icon appears on the screen with a flashing question mark. I'm starting to think this isn't going to work, but after a long minute or so, the folder disappears, and I hear the Windows chime (Figure 8-21).

Figure 8-21.
Booting from a Windows drive

A Windows login screen appears telling me to invoke the Ctrl-Alt-Delete key combination to get to the login screen. Try as I might, I cannot get past the screen shown in Figure 8-22.

Figure 8-22.
You can't give the Windows salute with a Mac keyboard

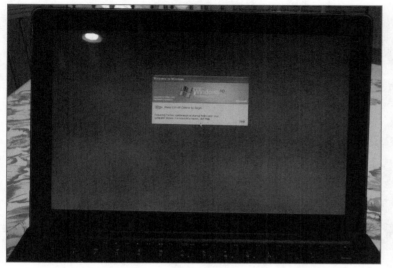

I send an email out asking a few friends what they think, and the "driver" word pops up. Sure, I probably don't have the right keyboard drivers that map the Mac keyboard to Windows. I call a friend of mine down the road and ask if I can borrow a Windows USB keyboard. Once I get that, I plug it into the MacBook, invoke the Ctrl-Alt-Delete key combo. and voilà, I get to the Windows login screen. All through this process the screen resolution is blocky and fuzzy.

After login, I get a Windows verification screen. This screen asks you to type in your Windows registration number. I dig out my documentation, and find the number. I type that into the screen, and it sends me to a new screen with a 1-800 number and a new set of numbers. This screen tells me to dial the 1-800 number and give this sequence to the tech support guy. I call the 1-800 number, and the fellow on the other end asks me why I need a new registration number? I tell him I'm doing a drive swap, and he tells me to read him the sequence of numbers on the screen. After that, he reads a new sequence back that I am supposed to type into the new set of boxes on the screen. Interesting to note that all through this process, the technician never asks for my name or any other personal information. I input the new key into the screen, and I am sent directly into Windows XP.

Getting Everything Working
Almost at once the "Installed New Hardware" window pops up and stays up. I click the damn thing more than a dozen times, but it refuses to die. I finally drag it off the side of the screen to get it out of the way.

QUICK HACK ✕

GET BOOT CAMP DRIVERS WITHOUT INSTALLING BOOT CAMP

Launch the Boot Camp application but instead of installing, choose Utilities→Save Mac Windows Drivers to Folder. Once the process is finished put the folder on the media of your choice (CD, thumb drive, etc.).

With great anticipation, I launch Lotus Notes, and with little fanfare I get to the login screen. I log in, and Lo and Behold, there are all of my emails (see Figure 8-23).

Figure 8-23.
Great, my email is there!

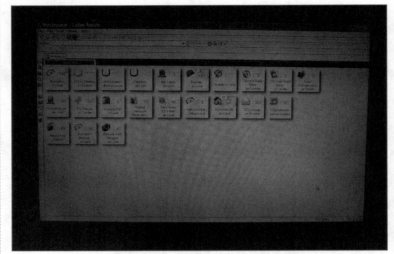

I click on a few, and everything seems to work fine. For fun, I launch MS Office, and it fires right up. However, I cannot make an Internet connection, I still need the Windows keyboard I borrowed, and the screen resolution is still lousy. I am not able to adjust anything, so the driver problem continues.

So, I shut down and reinstall the old Mac OS X drive so I can access the Boot Camp application. I learned that Boot Camp has a menu option to extract the drivers, so I save myself the hassle of burning a CD-ROM. I copy the folder to a USB pocket drive, plug that into the MacBook, and drag the folder to the Windows desktop.

Inside this folder there is an *.exe* file. I launch this file and sit back. For the next 10 minutes or so, my MacBook is on autopilot. The "Installed new hardware window" starts popping up in rapid-fire progression. Chimes sound, things flash across the screen; it's very entertaining. After it's all done, a screen pops up suggesting I restart.

After the restart, it's amazing. The screen resolution is perfect and crystal clear. The MacBook airport card is recognized, and an Internet connection screen pops right up. The Alt key on the MacBook now functions properly, so I can give back the Windows keyboard I borrowed. Just like a Mac, everything just works.

What I like best is I did not "pollute" my Apple HD with Windows. I like the fact that it's on another drive in a drawer, just where it should be, when I need it (see Figure 8-24).

— Rich Lefko

Figure 8-24.
Well, it is kind of Macish...

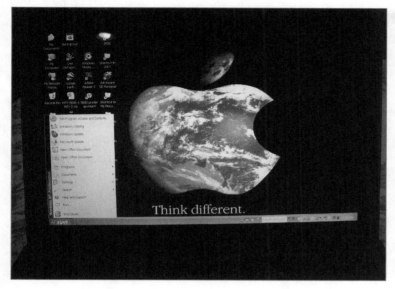

<u>HACK 71:</u> **Using Windows Keyboards with OS X**

If you're an Apple fan, you can choose from four different keyboards to suit your tastes. Of course, choosing three of them will also require that you buy the laptop they are built into, so they are an expensive way to get a keyboard you like. If you're buying an Apple-designed standalone keyboard, you get one choice, and it is a choice that may or may not suit your tastes.

If Apple's version of a keyboard doesn't suit your taste—perhaps you need more key travel or a stiffer feel—all is not lost. There are plenty of third-party keyboards manufactured with Mac OS X compatibility in mind. On the other hand, the number of keyboards manufactured for Mac OS X pales in comparison to the number of keyboards designed to work with Windows, and it can be a frustrating experience to see the perfect Windows keyboard sitting on the shelves and then discovering that there is no true Mac analog.

What would be ideal is the ability to use any old USB keyboard with OS X without losing the functionality.

Out of the Box

If you just plug in a random Windows-compatible keyboard to your Mac's USB port, chances are it will work. That is to say that you'll be able to type, but there will be plenty of weirdness. A quick trip to System Preferences is required to get Mac OS X to recognize the keyboard. Open the Keyboard and Mouse Pane (System Preferences→**Keyboard & Mouse**) and choose the Keyboard option. Then click the Change Keyboard Type button as shown in Figure 8-25.

Figure 8-25.
Opting out of Apple-crafted keyboards

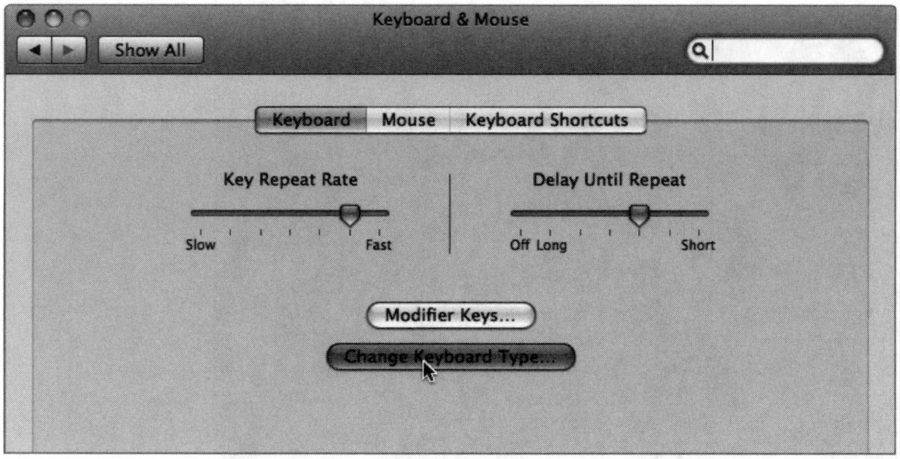

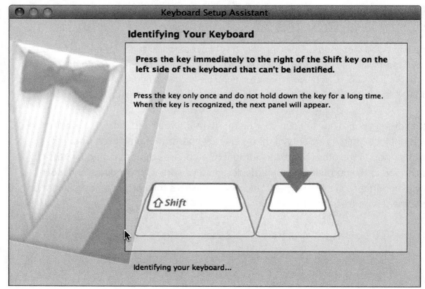

The assistant will ask you to push a few keys, and OS X will identify the new keyboard (see Figure 8-26).

Figure 8-26.
OS X is playing detective and identifying a Windows keyboard

A this point, you can go keyboard-remapping crazy and try to get the Windows keyboard behaving as much as possible like your old Mac keyboard by modifying the keyboard shortcut to your heart's content. The process is simple but a bit time consuming. In the Keyboard and Mouse pane, click the Keyboard Shortcuts button, and you'll be presented with a longish list of keyboard shortcuts. You can modify the list by double-clicking the shortcut you want to change and assigning new keys. To get a Windows keyboard behaving like a Mac keyboard means going through all the combinations and swapping the Alt key with the Command key. Once the process is complete, you'll be able to use your Windows keyboard in the Mac fashion you're accustomed to (see Figure 8-27).

Figure 8-27.
Wow, this is going to be a lot of work

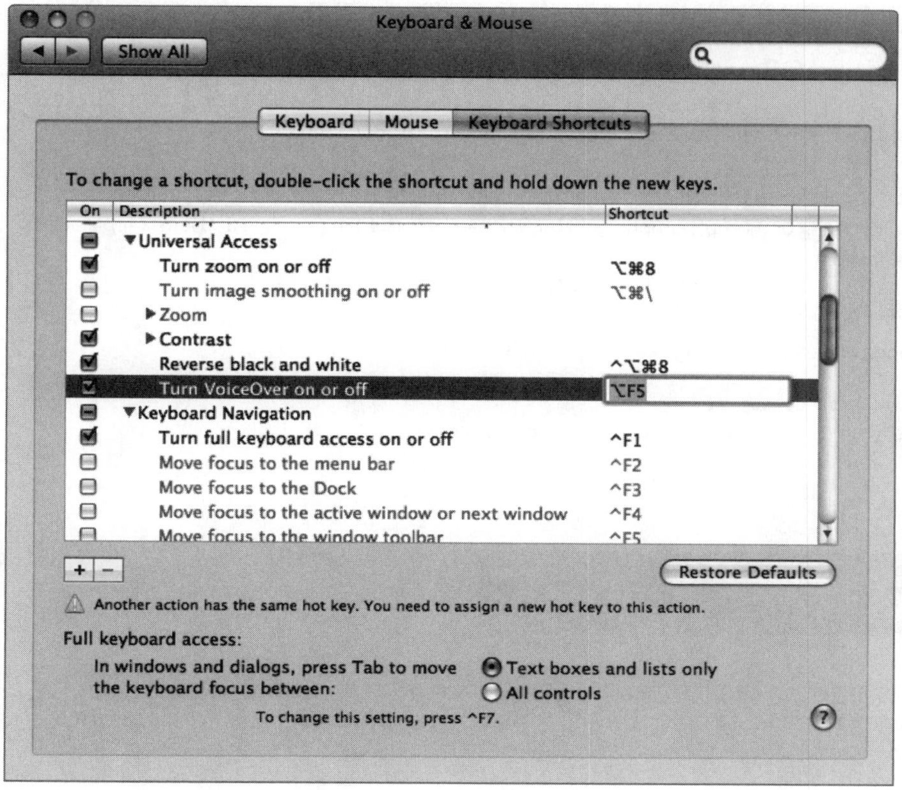

![Keyboard & Mouse preferences window screenshot showing Keyboard Shortcuts tab]

Keyboard & Mouse

Show All

Keyboard | Mouse | **Keyboard Shortcuts**

To change a shortcut, double-click the shortcut and hold down the new keys.

On	Description	Shortcut
▣	▼ Universal Access	
☑	Turn zoom on or off	⌥⌘8
☐	Turn image smoothing on or off	⌥⌘\
☐	▶ Zoom	
☑	▶ Contrast	
☑	Reverse black and white	^⌥⌘8
☑	Turn VoiceOver on or off	⌥F5
▣	▼ Keyboard Navigation	
☑	Turn full keyboard access on or off	^F1
☐	Move focus to the menu bar	^F2
☐	Move focus to the Dock	^F3
☐	Move focus to the active window or next window	^F4
☐	Move focus to the window toolbar	^F5

+ −   Restore Defaults

⚠ Another action has the same hot key. You need to assign a new hot key to this action.

Full keyboard access:

In windows and dialogs, press Tab to move the keyboard focus between:
- ⦿ Text boxes and lists only
- ○ All controls

To change this setting, press ^F7.

Some Windows keyboards are more OS X-accessible than others. Logitech keyboards (just to cite one brand) have keybindings for the volume keys that control the volume on your Mac. If the volume keys work, the only thing you're really missing is the eject key. Macs have one; Windows keyboards don't. There is probably some arcane way to add a key to eject removable media to a Windows keyboard, but if you're stumped, it might be time to try the next best thing: add an eject option to the menu bar. This is a really easy hack. Dig through your System folder according to the following path: System→Library→Core Services→Menu Extras. Once you're in the proper directory, double-click Eject.menu, and an Eject menulet will be added to your menu bar as seen in Figure 8-28.

Figure 8-28.
You can eject from the menu bar

Open SuperDrive ⏏

If you were hoping the cornucopia of dedicated keys found on most Windows keyboard could be assigned to do something useful on your Mac using the Keyboard Shortcuts pane, you're out of luck. OS X won't recognize that superfluous email key; trying to use it as a function button (or something) only results in the Mac beeping at you to say, more or less, "I know you've pressed something but I'm not listening."

HACK 72: Boot Another OS Without Losing Uptime in Mac OS X

Cherish your Mac uptime? Discover the tricks to booting into an alternative OS without losing that all-important uptime!

Have you ever wondered how long can your Mac persist without a reboot?

If so, you should know that there's a command-line utility that tells you how long your Mac has been on (working or asleep); simply open the Terminal application (you can find it in */Applications/ Utilities/*) and type:

```
$ uptime
```

The ouput will read something like (see Figure 8-29):

```
Doddy:~ marco$ uptime
14:22  up 1 day, 15:52, 2 users, load averages: 1,78 2,30 1,70
```

Figure 8-29.
That's a lot of uptime!

```
Doddy:~ marco$ date; uptime
Fri Feb 23 20:51:28 CET 2007
20:51  up 35 days,  6:45, 4 users, load averages: 5.09 5.76 5.80
Doddy:~ marco$
```

I personally love to show off to my geek friends by saying that my Mac has been up weeks or months; it shows how stable Mac OS X is and makes people understand how well the sleep mode works on Macs.

There are two reasons why you sometimes have to reboot:

Mac OS X updates
You should always install Apple-provided updates; they usually fix bugs and patch security holes, so rebooting your Mac after an Apple update is unavoidable.

Other operating system(s)
Maybe, along with Mac OS X, you also use Linux, and if you have an Intel-based Mac, chances are that you have installed Windows.

If you want to retain your uptime while booting into Linux or Windows, you can do so by exploiting the so-called Safe Sleep (also known as "hibernation," "suspend to disk," or "deep sleep"). But how does Safe Sleep work? The idea is very simple: when your Mac is sleeping and a power failure happens, it usually forgets everything stored in the RAM (usually opened applications and documents), and you will lose all changes to documents that have not been saved to disk.

However, with Safe Sleep, this problem has been solved. Whenever your Mac goes to sleep, it saves to disk enough information to completely restore your session (open applications, unsaved documents, etc.) even in the event of a power failure. Technically, when in deep sleep, your Mac is actually off, and thus another OS can be started.

If you're not sure about what sleep and deep sleep are please, give the following table a look:

	Normal Sleep	Deep Sleep
Also known as:	Sleep Suspend to RAM	Hibernation Suspend to Disk Safe Sleep
Invoked by:	Apple Menu→Sleep Closing laptop lid Quick press of power button	Power failure in normal sleep
Remains on:	RAM Select ports	Nothing
Information stored in:	RAM	File: */var/vm/sleepimage*
Wake method:	Press any key Mouse activity Connecting a peripheral Opening laptop lid	Power button

Is Your Mac Safe Sleep–Enabled?

Most recent Macs (desktops and laptops) support Safe Sleep including:

- All Intel-based Macs

- PowerPC-based Macs sold after October 2005

If you have bought a Mac before October 2005, it might be Safe Sleep–capable, but you might need to turn on the feature.

To check whether Deep Sleep is enabled, simply put your Mac to sleep, wake it after a few seconds and open the Console application (*/Applications/Utilities*) selecting *system.log* (*/var/log/system.log*). If you can read:

```
Sep 19 19:01:43 computername kernel[0]: System SafeSleep
```

You can rest assured Deep Sleep is enabled.

If it is not and if:

- You have at least Mac OS X 10.4.3 (Apple menu→About this Mac)

- You have at least as much free disk space as physical memory plus 750 MB

You can try to enable Deep Sleep (users report it working even on 2003 PowerBooks). Open a new Terminal window and type:

```
$ sudo nvram nvramrc='" /" select-dev " msh" \
  encode-string " has-safe-sleep" property unselect'
$ sudo nvram "use-nvramrc?"=true
```

Restart your Mac and type in Terminal:

```
$ sudo pmset -a hibernatemode N
```

Where **N** is:

- 3: (most cases)

- 7: if you have secure virtual memory enabled (System Preferences →Security)

- 1: if you want to disable Normal Sleep and always enter Deep Sleep

- 5: if you want to disable Normal Sleep always entering Deep Sleep, and you have secure virtual memory enabled

- 0: to disable Safe Sleep

For a full undo, you should type:

```
$ sudo nvram "use-nvramrc?"=false
```

And restart your Mac.

How do you get into Deep Sleep? There are at least two ways. Before trying either, please make sure that hibernation is enabled on your Mac (using the Console application as explained above). These are the options:

- Download and use an application such as Suspend now! or the Deep Sleep widget.

- Put your Mac to Sleep (Apple menu→Sleep) and unplug the power or remove the laptop battery until the white LED goes off.

Now your Mac is off, which means that you can make it boot into another OS. Of course, don't change anything in the Mac OS X partition (especially the sleep image) because that might make it impossible to restore the session saved on disk.

The Easy Way (PowerPC and Intel)
There are a few ways to do this, although the specifics of your firmware security settings and the architecture of your Mac (PowerPC or Intel) might mean that only one will work for you.

On a PowerPC-based Mac
1. Put your Mac into Deep Sleep.

2. Turn it on by pressing the power button.

3. Press the Alt (also known as Option) key right after the startup sound.

4. Choose the partition from which you wish to boot; for example, the Windows partition if you're after a session playing your favorite Windows-only game (if you choose the Mac OS X partition, the previous session will be restored).

When you're done with the other OS, you can simply reboot, Mac OS X will be the startup OS by default, and the previous session will be restored.

On an Intel-based Mac

On an Intel Mac, you can also use the Option key method shown earlier, or you can go one step farther and use rEFIt. You can grab a copy of rEFIt from Sourceforge (http://refit.sourceforge.net). The install nets you a very nice boot menu that lets you choose the partition you wish to boot from. You can also permanently install the rEFIt files, and the menu will be shown automatically every time your Mac turns on. If you've installed rEFIt, you can switch to another operating system like this:

1. Put your Mac into Deep Sleep.

2. Turn it on and choose the operating system you wish to boot again; if you choose Mac OS X, the previous session will be restored.

The Open Firmware method (PowerPC only)

If you have customized Open Firmware security [Hack #52], you might find that the first solution doesn't work.

This is because access to the Startup Manager (the screen that appears when pressing Alt during boot and that lets you choose the partition from which to boot) is disabled. This behavior is displayed when you have set the Open Firmware variable `security-mode` to `full`. This special security mode makes your Mac start up in Open Firmware every time it is turned on and asks for the Open Firmware password to perform any kind of action (boot, shut-down, variable modification, etc.).

This second solution can also be used when Open Firmware security has not been customized: simply press Command-Alt-O-F right after the startup sound to start the OF console.

Now all you have to do is to give the correct commands:

```
$ boot
```

This makes your Mac boot from the default partition (usually Mac OS X); if Mac OS X is in hibernation, the session will be restored. This command turns your Mac off:

```
$ shut-down
```

This command boots from the second partition of your hard drive, which is where the Linux bootloader usually is (check your setup for the actual location):

```
$ boot hd:02,\\:tbxi
```

To discover the number of the Mac OS X partition, you can use Disk Utility (*/Applications/Utilities*).

You can even get inside a graphical menu and boot from there; type:

```
$ dev /multiboot
multi-boot-menu
```

Now, type the number of the boot device:

```
$ setenv boot-device hd:N,\\:tbxi
```

N is the number of the partition from which you have to boot; you can find the correct number in Disk Utility or in the multiboot menu.

> Using `setenv` permanently changes the selected partition from which your machine will boot.

To boot, issue the `mac-boot` command.

If you know the number of the partition from which you wish to boot, you can use the `boot` command (or change it permanently with `setenv`). If you are not sure, you might prefer to get into the multiboot menu. If your Mac freezes while restoring a Mac OS X session, you might feel stuck, but don't worry: simply enter Open Firmware (pressing Command-Alt-O-F after the startup sound) and type:

```
$ setenv boot-image
boot
```

This will make your Mac boot from cold start. Enjoy your uptime!

— Marco Triverio

HACK 73: Run Classic Mac Applications with SheepShaver and Basilisk II

Relive the glory (or gory) days of the Classic Mac operating systems on your Leopard or Intel-based Mac.

The transition from Classic Mac OS to OS X was tumultuous for many users. Apple fans had become truly attached to the familiar operating system, and many were loath to give up the comfort level they enjoyed with the OS that had powered Macs since the beginning. Apple tried to ease the transition for end users with various measures, ranging from dual-boot Macs to Classic mode, which let users run Classic applications using emulation on OS X-based Macs.

The attempts at Apple-sponsored Classic Mac compatibility began to end when the Intel Macs were released (Intel Macs could not run the necessary Classic environment) and were truly dead when Leopard was released without any Classic support. You might expect some gnashing of teeth at the omission of Classic with Leopard. However, six years had gone by since the Classic OS was the primary option for Mac users, and OS X had proven to be far superior, so very little outcry was heard as the Classic Mac OS was left for dead.

But just because few complained about the loss of Classic functionality, doesn't mean it isn't missed. There are some great old games that run only under Classic Mac as well as programs that are extremely useful but lack a Mac OS X analog. Also, nostalgia is a non-negligible factor in all of this; those who have been using Macs since the beginning might pine for the old days of the smiley Mac on occasion.

Running Classic Operating Systems with SheepShaver

Whatever the reason, it turns out you can still run OS 9 on your Mac with an emulator and a little hacking on your part. To pull this hack off, you'll need a few things:

- System 9.0.4 or earlier

- Mac ROM

- Copy of SheepShaver

Perhaps the hardest part of this hack is collecting the software you need to pull it off. SheepShaver is no problem; just head to http://gwenole.beauchesne.info/en/projects/sheepshaver and download the Mac OS X universal binary. Since this hack is focused on installing 9.0 I'm not going to cover installs of other versions of the Classic Mac OS (other installs won't change much). Apple is also happy to provide the ROM. Get a working ROM by visiting http://tinyurl.com/2hkjea (which is a reduced length URL pointing to Apple's download page for a Mac ROM update). Once you have the ROM, you'll have to extract it using a Classic OS program called Tome Viewer (http://www.versiontracker.com/dyn/moreinfo/macos/4561).

Getting a copy of the OS 9 install disk is the tricky part. Your usual resources might not come through. If you have an old version lying around, that's ideal. If not, you'll need some serious search skills or a trip to eBay where you can get a copy of OS 9 for less than $5. Be picky about which disk you buy; the ideal will be a full retail version of OS 9 for maximum compatibility.

Once everything is collected, you can get started on actually installing an environment in which OS 9 can run and bring back memories of the olden days. At this point, it is probably wise to create a central repository for all your OS 9 needs. For the purposes of this hack, I'm creating a folder called *baldsheep* on my Desktop (it doesn't really matter where you do this) and putting all the required files in the newly generated folder. So, into *baldsheep* I'll toss the ROM and the folder generated when I expand the SheepShaver download.

It is time to go about the business of installing OS 9. Open up the SheepShaver folder and you'll see two applications: SheepShaverGUI and SheepShaver. If you're thinking SheepShaver GUI is an easy-to-use graphical version of SheepShaver, you're wrong on both counts, SheepShaverGUI is neither easy to use nor a different version of SheepShaver. SheepShaverGUI is merely a separate program to set the preferences for SheepShaver (see Figure 8-30).

Figure 8-30.
Don't be confused by dual applications

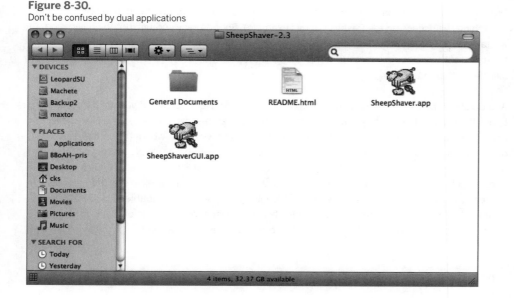

You can use SheepShaver to generate a disk (called a "hard file") for the OS 9 installation. To do that, you'll get to work with one of the most maddening implementations of a windowed interface ever seen on a Mac. Launch SheepShaverGUI and click Create. Change the disk size from 40 MB to something more appropriate (500 MB is sufficient) as illustrated by Figure 8-31.

Figure 8-31.
Creating the "hard file"

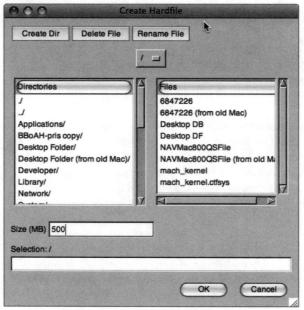

Once you've allocated space for OS 9, navigate to the folder where you've decided to keep everything (*baldsheep* on the Desktop, in this example). Sounds easy enough, but the navigation will take some getting used to, so you might want to consider just typing the path and appending the name of the file you're creating. In this example the path would be */Users/cks/Desktop/ baldsheep/OS 9 HardDisk*.

And *OS 9 HardDisk* is the name of the file you want SheepShaver to create. If you are determined to use the GUI method, be aware that SheepShaverGUI operates in a manner you've likely never encountered. The left window is for directories, and the right window is where the contents of directories are displayed. And, for some unknown reason, SheepShaver always starts you off at the root of your hard drive. To create the hard file using the GUI of SheepShaverGUI, click Create and navigate by double-clicking the directory you want to move to. In this example, the exercise proceeds as follows: double-click Users→double-click your username→double-click Desktop→ double-click baldsheep. Once the maddening clicking is over, type the name of the hard file you want created and hit OK (see Figure 8-32). The process takes a few seconds.

Figure 8-32.
Creating a disk for OS 9

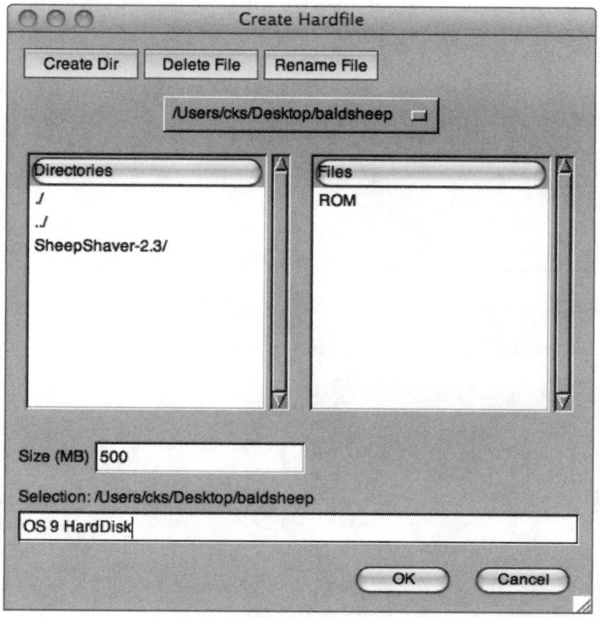

With the area to store Mac OS 9 created, it is time to tell SheepShaver where the ROM you secured earlier resides. Click the Memory/Misc tab in SheepShaverGUI and click the "Browse..." button in the pane that appears. Repeat the clicking process until you've reached the ROM. This is also a good time to allocate RAM to OS 9; the minimum amount of RAM to run OS 9 was 32 MB with 8 MB of virtual memory. RAM capacity has increased since OS 9 was released, so set the value to a comfortable amount. I use 128 MB (see Figure 8-33). Be aware that the amount of memory you allocate to OS 9 will not be available to OS X while SheepShaver is running.

Figure 8-33.
Setting the ROM and RAM

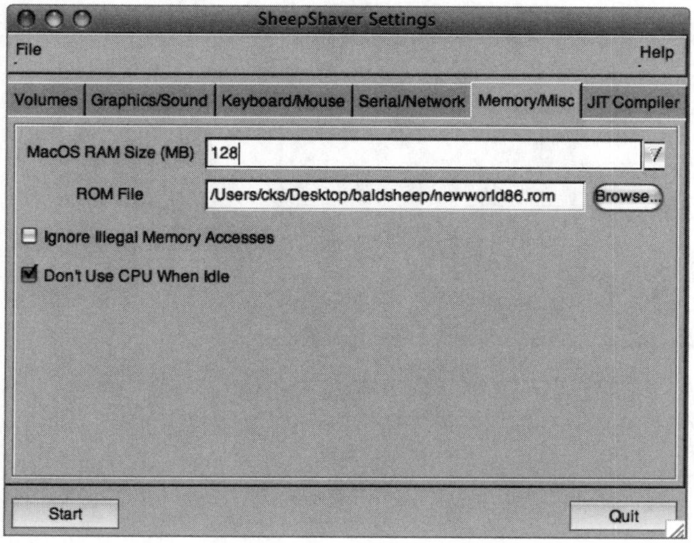

With the hard disk file created, memory allocated, and the ROM out of the way, there are a few other tweaks you'll want to make. In the Serial/Network tab, change the Ethernet interface to *slirp* as shown in Figure 8-34.

Figure 8-34.
Letting OS 9 share your OS X Internet connection

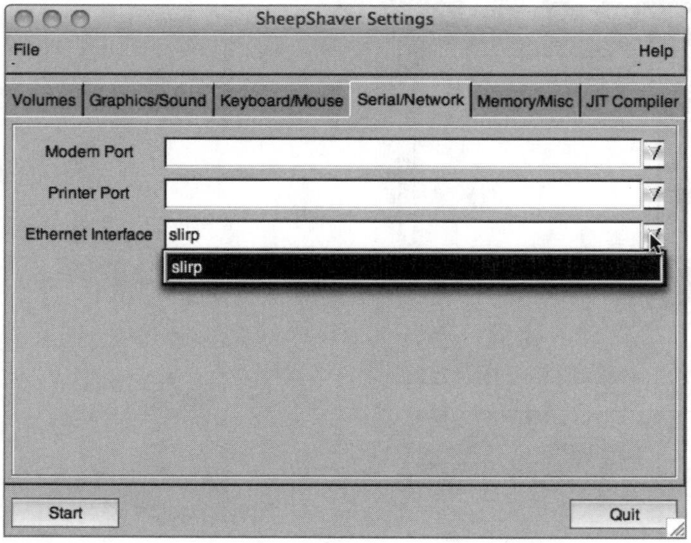

Finally, you might be interested in changing the Window size to something a bit larger (I couldn't get full screen to work). For best results, choose a resolution with the same aspect ratio as the defaults (see Figure 8-35).

Figure 8-35.
Bumping up the screen size

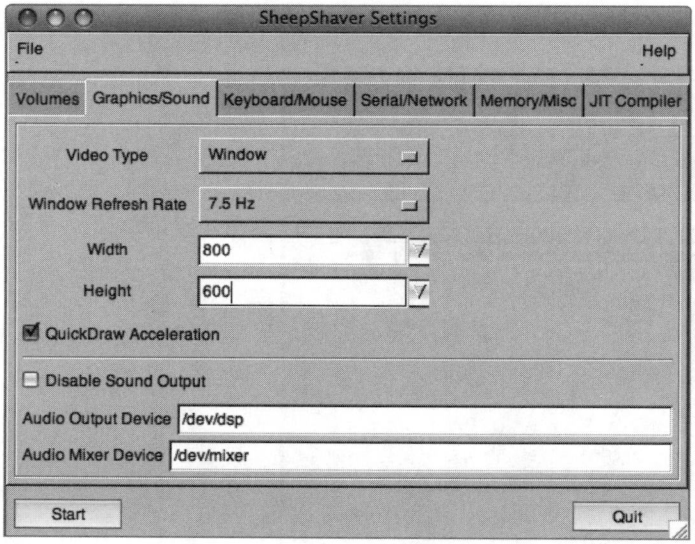

The good news is that the install is almost over. Insert your OS 9 disk in the CD drive of your Mac and visit the Volumes pane of SheepShaver. Choose Boot from CD ROM, and the install will get underway (see Figure 8-36).

Figure 8-36.
Leopard and OS 9 together!

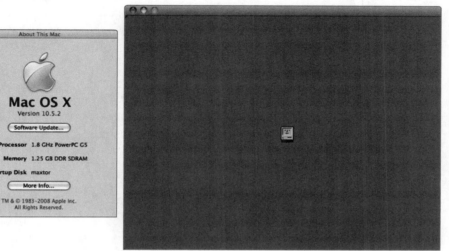

You can't quit SheepShaver in the expected manner when OS 9 is running. Instead you have to shut down OS 9. If it has been some time since your last foray into OS 9, choose Special from the Finder's menu bar and select Shut Down.

Extending the hack
If you want to use a disk accessible to both OS 9 and OS X, it isn't much of a challenge. All you really need to do is create an image and add it to the volumes recognized by SheepShaver. If you're comfortable with the Terminal, you can issue the appropriate commands, but if you're more of a GUI-oriented person, Disk Utility (Applications→Utilities) will do the trick without any fuss.

Once Disk Utility is up and running, the goal is to create a disk image to house OS 9. The first decision you need to make is the size of the image. Hard drive space is cheap these days, and OS 9 is a relatively small operating system, so a 500 MB image is more than enough and has the added bonus of being a preset option in Disk Utility. You'll want the disk to behave like a hard drive, so set the Partitions menu to "Hard disk" (see Figure 8-37).

Figure 8-37.
A new home for OS 9

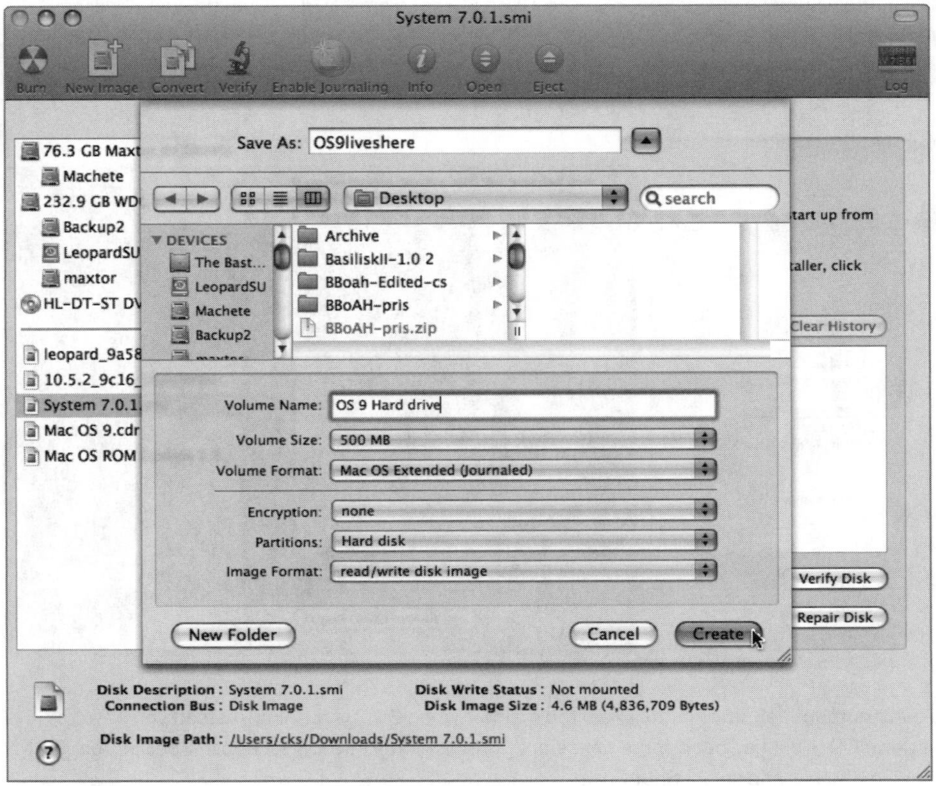

QUICK TIP ✕

SHEEPSHAVER MIGHT NOT BE THE ANSWER

SheepShaver is great if the programs you want to run are 9.0.4-compatible; not so great if the programs you want to run require 9.1. You're probably wondering what a fractional difference of a release could make. Programs that require 9.1 require virtual memory or a MMU emulator, neither of which SheepShaver supports. Want to run MDK from your first iMac? No problem. You want to run a program that requires 9.2? Forget it buddy: you need features SheepShaver doesn't offer. Is there recourse available? Not really: if you've got a new Mac with Leopard installed and/or a Mac with an Intel processor, you're simply out of luck. If you can't live without OS 9.2 support, the only options seem to be acquiring an OS 9-capable Mac if your machine is Intel-based (cheap on eBay) or running 10.4.x if your Machine is PowerPC-based.

After your drive is created by Disk Utility, eject the drive using the Eject button. This step is crucial because SheepShaver won't use a mounted disk well (if it uses it at all).

Once the installation is complete, you can get back to your OS 9 roots by firing up SheepShaver whenever a yearning for the old days hits you. If you're wondering about performance, SheepShaver supposedly runs at about 1/8 of native processor speed. So if you're using a 2.0 GHz Mac, you'd expect SheepShaver to feel like you're a 250 MHz iMac. Honestly, it doesn't feel that peppy. A 250 MHz Mac was sufficient to almost comfortably run OS 9, but the experience isn't the best with SheepShaver. Still, in a Leopard and Intel world, SheepShaver is your best bet for firing up 8.6-9.0.

Running Older Versions of Mac OS with Basilisk II

SheepShaver is great for 8.6-9.0, but for versions of Mac OS released before 8.6, most users prefer Basilisk II. The obstacles for installing Basilisk are the same as the obstacles you'd face if you tried to install SheepShaver, and the obstacle was getting the files. Fortunately you don't need an OS 9 retail disk to pull this hack off; Apple will give you System 7.0.1. A quick list of the things you'll need:

· Mac ROM

· Basilisk II

· Version of Mac OS earlier than 8.6

If you think you already have a ROM from the SheepShaver section of this hack, it turns out that ROM won't work. If you attempt to use the ROM you downloaded from Apple earlier, you'll get an unfortunate error message (see Figure 8-38).

Figure 8-38.
You need an old-world ROM

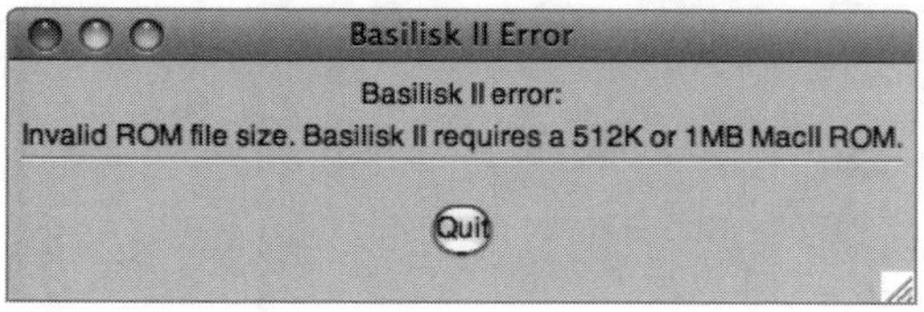

One way or another, you'll need to get an old-world ROM. One method is detailed at "Capturing a Mac ROM image" (http://mes.emuunlim.com/tips/capturing_a_mac_rom_image.htm) but careful searching with Google will likely reveal easier methods of acquiring a old world Mac ROM.

Once you have the ROM, the hard work is over. You can download Basilisk II at http://gwenole. beauchesne.info/projects/basilisk2, and you can download an older version of Mac OS from Apple (http://www.info.apple.com/support/oldersoftwarelist.html).

The Mac Classic was the first Macintosh I ever owned; it shipped with System 6.0.8 but was much better with System 7. Since I'd like to have that Classic Mac feeling again, I'm going to install System 7.0.1 with Basilisk II. Using Basilisk is almost exactly like using SheepShaver.

The basic procedure is summarized as follows:

1. Create a hard file for the OS (or use a image created with Disk Utility)

2. Allocate Memory and locate ROM

3. Add the install disks in the volumes pane

4. Tweak preferences

5. Start Basilisk II

Again, you are presented with two applications after expanding the Basilisk II download—Basilisk II and Basilisk IIGUI. You set up Basilisk II using Basilisk IIGUI, and navigating in Basilisk IIGUI is exactly like navigating in SheepShaverGUI. If you're wondering why the programs seem so similar, it is because they are products of the same project. If confusing navigation is good enough for 9.1 emulation, obviously it is good enough for 8.6 and lower. Double-click to open the directory you want to move to in the left pane; select files you want to use in the right pane.

Get started by creating a volume (100 MB should be more than enough) or using an image file created with Disk Utility. Add the install images (see Figure 8-39) you downloaded from Apple. In the case of System 7.0.1, there are six images; if you decide to install 7.5, there are 19 separate files. That is a lot of clicking when you're using Basilisk IIGUI.

Figure 8-39.
Adding the install images to Basilisk II

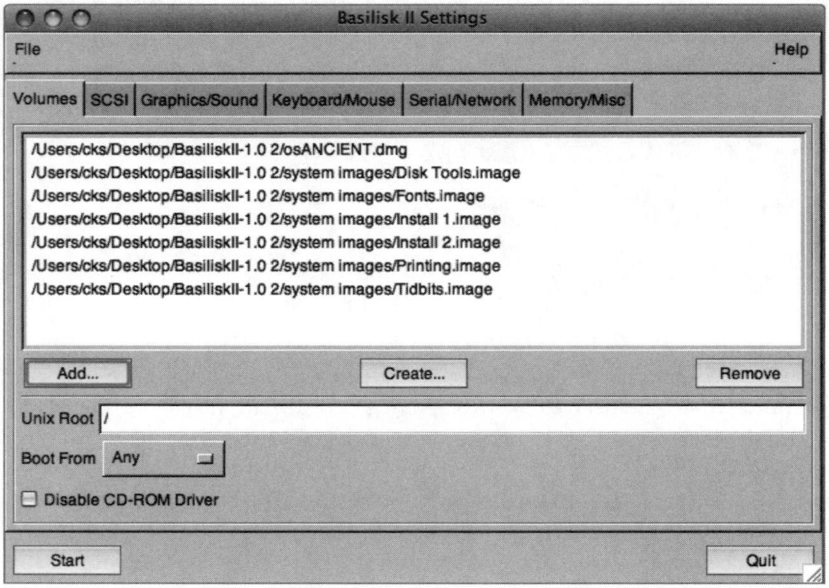

Figure 8-39. screenshot shows Basilisk II Settings window with the Volumes tab selected:

```
/Users/cks/Desktop/BasiliskII-1.0 2/osANCIENT.dmg
/Users/cks/Desktop/BasiliskII-1.0 2/system images/Disk Tools.image
/Users/cks/Desktop/BasiliskII-1.0 2/system images/Fonts.image
/Users/cks/Desktop/BasiliskII-1.0 2/system images/Install 1.image
/Users/cks/Desktop/BasiliskII-1.0 2/system images/Install 2.image
/Users/cks/Desktop/BasiliskII-1.0 2/system images/Printing.image
/Users/cks/Desktop/BasiliskII-1.0 2/system images/Tidbits.image
```

The next step is to allocate memory. System 7 shipped on the Quadra 700, which featured 4 MB of RAM. RAM prices have dropped considerably, so bump the RAM up to the Quadra's maximum of a whopping 68 MB (see Figure 8-40).

Figure 8-40.
This configuration costs tens of thousands of dollars in 1991

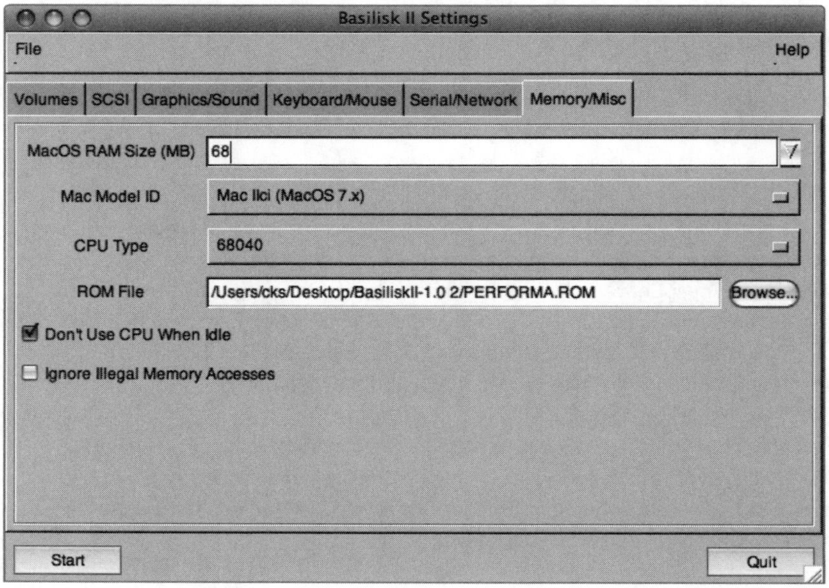

Screenshot shows Basilisk II Settings window with the Memory/Misc tab selected:
- MacOS RAM Size (MB): 68
- Mac Model ID: Mac IIci (MacOS 7.x)
- CPU Type: 68040
- ROM File: /Users/cks/Desktop/BasiliskII-1.0 2/PERFORMA.ROM
- ☑ Don't Use CPU When Idle
- ☐ Ignore Illegal Memory Accesses

Finally, you may want to tweak the video settings. I like the default in this case, so I'll stick with that. Click Start and the magic begins (see Figure 8-41 and Figure 8-42).

Figure 8-41.
You can initialize the disk without worry

Figure 8-42.
Ah, the good old days, and snappy too!

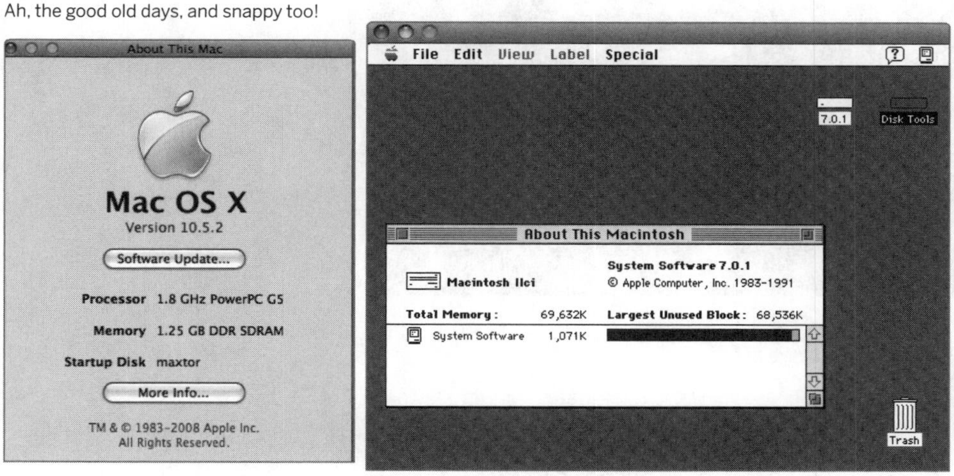

It is a lot of fun to play around with System 7, and there is a ton of software available for the price of a Google search. But who needs any of that? You've got the puzzle desk accessory back and that is minutes of fun!

Build a Screaming Fast Darwin Machine for $935 (or Less)!

You don't need a Mac to run Darwin; build your own Darwin Machine for a fraction of the cost of a Mac.

At the time of this writing, there was no officially Apple-sanctioned method for installing Mac OS X on a non-Apple PC. Although there are many techniques for this available on the Internet, I wasn't able to find one that didn't involve using untrusted binary code from file-sharing sites. So, in the hopes that the future brings us an official method for running Mac OS X on an ordinary PC, here's

QUICK TIP

WHAT IS DARWIN

Darwin is an open source OS developed by Apple computer based on the NeXT's NeXTSTEP operating system along with other free projects including FreeBSD and NetBSD. Darwin can run most of the command line applications you've been using on your Mac and comes with the X11 window Manager so you can even get some GUI goodness rolling.

almost everything you need to know to do this. Although Darwin, the Open Source foundation of Mac OS X, will happily load on commodity PCs, I'm using it in this hack as a placeholder for the Mac OS X version I hope to see in the bright shiny future.

The Parts

There is no definitive hardware selection to build a perfect "Hackintosh" box, but the following gear worked very well for me and for others (see Figure 8-43). To be more accurate, the wrong hardware can cause serious issues, and drivers can be a problem, too, so be sure to check that your stuff is going to work. You can also expand on what I have selected here, such as adding more drives for RAID because the motherboard I chose supports this. That's one of the nice things about building your own system: you can configure it to your needs.

Figure 8-43.
The internal parts I'm using for my Hackintosh

Here's the hardware list:

- Motherboard: Asus P5W DH Deluxe

- Processor: Intel Core 2 Quad Q6600 LGA775 (retail package).

- RAM: 4 GB DDR2 5300 @ 667 MHz

- Video card: eVGA eGeForce 8600GTS w/256 MB RAM

- Hard drive: Seagate 320 GB SATA II, 7200 rpm, 16 MB buffer

- DVD drive: Creative 8x (ancient, from old computer, Model DVD8401E, May 2000!)

- Case: Ultra Wizard ATX Mini-Tower with 350 watt power supply

Let's now take a look at some of the costs involved.

> I am a real bargain hunter as you will see here, but your price shouldn't be too far off mine if you search around. Feel free to gloss over this section if you want to get straight to the machine building.

Motherboard: Asus P5W DH Deluxe

The motherboard was bought from a seller on eBay who lived in my city, so I picked it up for $140 with no shipping cost. Cost online new today is around $180. Check around for the best prices.

Processor: Intel Core 2 Quad Q6600 LGA775 (retail package)

The processor was bought from Fry's as part of a processor + motherboard package. The combo cost $274 plus tax, or $298. I then sold the motherboard on Craigslist (http://www.craigslist.org) for $60. So the net cost of the processor was $238 for me. I see them selling online for around $280 or even less.

RAM: 4GB DDR2 5300 @ 667 MHz

My RAM was bought from another Craigslister who seemed a bit desperate for money. I bought a 2-GB Kingston kit from him for $30. Also bought from him two 1-GB sticks (matching) for $12 each. All of it was DDR2 @ 667 MHz. Total for 4 GB was $54. I'll admit this was a great deal, but I see 4 GB of Kingston Value RAM going for around $100, so shop around; 2GB will work fine too.

Video card: eVGA eGeForce 8600GTS with 256 MB RAM

The video card was bought from some gaming fanboy on Craigslist who must have needed to get the latest video card. I bought a matching pair from him for $135. Cost for one was therefore $62.50. Buying one off the shelf will set you back around $160. Check prices.

Hard Drive: Seagate 320 GB SATA II, 7200RPM, 16 MB buffer

The hard drive was purchased new from Fry's for just $64.99 plus tax, or $71. Online I see them for around $90.

DVD Drive: Creative 8x (ancient, from old computer. Model DVD8401E. May 2000)

My DVD drive is some relic from an old computer. It's an 8x CD burner and DVD reader. I'll be generous and value it at $5. Obviously you can buy a better drive, and it should work fine in OS X. A decent new one will set you back around $40.

Case: Ultra Wizard ATX Mini-Tower with 350 watt power supply

The case was purchased from the same guy I bought the RAM from. It was brand-new in the box with a 350 watt power supply and a complete set of nice shielded cables. Got it for $30. They go for around $85 new.

With the processor, make sure you get the one that has G0 stepping (not B3 stepping). The G0 version runs cooler, and thus can be overclocked with a stock cooler more safely than its B3 counterpart.

The following table shows the total cost:

Part	My Cost	Retail
Motherboard	$140	$180
Processor	$238	$280
Memory	$54	$100
Video card	$62.50	$160
Hard drive	$71	$90
Optical drive	$5	$40
Case	$30	$85
Total	$600.50	$935

Building a PC has become much easier over the years, and your methods will vary according to the components you pick. I've included some pictures, but for more detailed instructions specific to the components you choose, a Google search or a visit to the manufacturer's web site is in order (see Figure 8-44 through Figure 8-49).

Figure 8-44.
The open case. Mmm new! The nice pin headers from Asus are already on the panel wires. These are nice because they slip right onto the board with no fuss

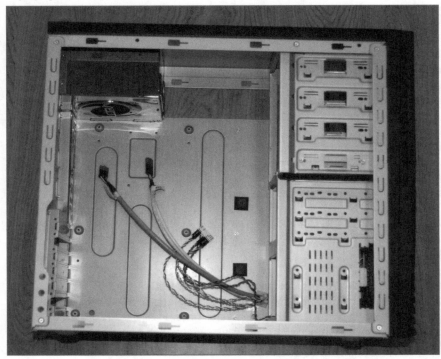

Figure 8-45.
The I/O panel of the motherboard. Lots of stuff including eSATA, plenty of USB ports, and firewire. Notice the WiFi antenna jack!

Figure 8-46.
Most of the SATA connectors. Plug the hard drive into the RED one

Figure 8-47.
All of the components mounted in the case. Not much to it!

Figure 8-48.
Another view with everything in the case

Figure 8-49.
And the finished tower from the front

Tweaking the BIOS

Next we'll need to tweak the BIOS a bit for this to work properly. Again your motherboard may be different than mine, but the settings are usually the same. Most BIOSs can be accessed by pressing DEL or F1 right after system boot.

My BIOS version 2301 comes built in with the motherboard. Some people say to use version 2206, but so far I haven't seen any problems with the version I'm using. If you experience problems with a BIOS later than 2206, or have an earlier one, then certainly change yours to 2206.

The following is a list of BIOS changes I made. There are a lot more options in the BIOS, but I changed only the ones shown here. I have laid them out in the same hierarchy as found on your BIOS screen(s).

Begin by restoring your BIOS to default values (this option is under the EXIT menu in your BIOS). Then edit the options in the list that follows. When you are finished, the values should look like this:

```
[Main]

    Legacy Diskette : [Disabled]

    [IDE Configuration]
        Configure SATA As        [AHCI]
        ALPE ans ASP             [Disabled]
        IDE Detect Timeout (Sec) [0]

[Advanced]

    [Jumper Free Configuration]
        AI Overclocking    [Manual]
        CPU Frequency      [333]
        DRAM Frequency     [DDR2-667MHz]

    [CPU Configuration]
        Note: the top part of this section is grayed out.
        Modify Ratio Support        [Disabled]
        Microcode Updation          [Enabled]
        Max CPUID Value Limit       [Disabled]
        Execute Disable Function    [Enabled]
        Enhance C1 Control          [Auto]
        CPU Internal Thermal Control [Auto]
        Virtualization Technology   [Disabled]
        Intel(R) SpeedStep(tm) tech. [Disabled]

    [Chipset]
        Configure DRAM Timing by SPD   [Enabled]
        DRAM ECC Mode                  [Disabled]
        Hyper Path 3                   [Auto]
        DRAM Throttling Threshold      [Auto]
        Memory Remap Feature           [Enabled]

    [Onboard Devices Configuration]
        HD Audio Controller       [Enabled]
        HD Audio Mode             [Non-Vista]
            Front Panel Support Type [AC97]
        Onboard 1394 Controller   [Enabled]
```

```
                    Onboard PCIE GbE LAN_1        [Enabled]
                    Onboard PCIE GbE LAN_2        [Disabled]
                        LAN Option ROM            [Disabled]
                JMicron SATA/PATA Controller      [Enabled]
                     JMicron Controller Mode      [AHCI]
                     JMicron SATA/RAID BOOTROM     [Disabled]

        [PCI/PnP]
              Plug And Play O/S        [Yes]

    [Power]
          Suspend Mode                 [S3 Only]
          Repost Video on S3 Resume    [No]
          ACPI 2.0 Support             [Yes]
          ACPI APIC support            [Enabled]

          [Hardware Monitor]
                AI Quiet [Disabled]

    [Boot]
          [Boot Device Priority]
                1st Boot Device  [CDROM/DVD ROM]
                2nd Boot Debice  [HDD]
                3rd Boot Device  [Disabled]
```

Finally, save your BIOS changes and reboot.

Installing Darwin

This is the best part of the hack; you're about to turn your carefully constructed amalgamation into an exceedingly peppy Darwin machine. How fast will the machine be? Noting that there is plenty of commonality between the Darwin machine you just built and an Apple-manufactured Mac Pro, you can expect this machine to keep up easily with the Mac Pro for any task that both machines can do.

Time to get Darwin running. This is a relatively painless install and if you've gone through all the work of building the machine, well within your level of skill. To get started, find another computer and point your browser to http://www.opensource.apple.com/projects/darwin/6.0/release.html. You'll see a link to *x86 ISO image*; that is the file you're after and it weighs in at 315 MB. Download the file, expand the file, and burn it to a CD (Disk Utility works great if you're using a Mac).

Once the CD creation process is finished, insert the CD into the drive of your lovingly built computer and restart.

Darwin will boot from the CD in the drive (you changed the BIOS earlier so the computer will be looking for the drive) and start asking questions. Since this is a brand-new PC there are no wrong answers though if you're installing Darwin on to a previously used machine be careful: choosing the wrong partition can lead to data loss. The install takes some time, so don't get antsy. Once the install is complete, you'll be prompted to create a root password: do it. You've probably heard that not having a root user on OS X is a good idea. Not so with Darwin; no root user means no functional computer. So use your favorite password; eject the CD and reboot. When Darwin comes up, your username will be root, and the password will be the one you just created.

Hacking the Hack

Okay, you've got a machine running Darwin, but it is also a fully capable Windows box, Linux box, and just about any other OS that comes in an Intel-compatible flavor. Should some clever person devise a way to install Mac OS X that doesn't infringe on Apple's intellectual property, this box will run that too. Until then you've got a speedy, do-almost-anything-machine.

— Martin Smit and Chris Seibold

9

HACKING THE ILIFE

What's the best thing about a Mac? Is it the industrial design? Mac OS X? Or is it the iLife Suite? The answer is different for everyone, but one thing most Mac users seem to agree on is that iLife is a pretty nice part of the Mac experience. Out of the box (or when you boot up your new Mac), the iLife applications are useful, fun, and intuitive. But there is more power in the iLife applications than is revealed by a cursory inspection. Here are ways to get the most out of your new electronic life.

HACK 75: Get More Out of iTunes

There is a lot of power (and media manipulation) hiding under the hood of iTunes. Discover some lesser-known, but very useful, iTunes features with this handy guide.

Apple missed the start of the peer-to-peer music-swapping revolution. When music swapping was bringing university servers to a crawl, Apple was hawking Macs with DVDs so users could watch movies on their computers. What users really wanted was the ability to rip and burn CDs. A product cycle or two later, Apple realized its mistake and decided to jump into the music game as quickly as possible. Thus iTunes was born. Well, maybe not so much "born" as purchased from Cassady and Greene. Once the sale went through, Apple slapped a new interface on the program and released it to the adulation of users at the 2001 MacWorld.

iTunes morphed into more than just a digital media player application and become a store, a web browser married to a single site, an iPhone update interface, and a bevy of other useful things. All that utility in one program practically ensures that a lot of features—features users may love—will go overlooked, lost in the cacophony of everything that encompasses iTunes.

Get Out of Sorts with Your Music

At the heart of iTunes is a database. Databases are really good at being sorted, but you wouldn't know it from the standard iTunes install. Sure, you've got a few headers that you can sort, but iTunes is capable of much more. To see all the options for sorting your media, all you need is a right-click on the Mighty Mouse or Option-click on the old no-button mouse (see Figure 9-1).

Depending on how you use iTunes, other sorts may be much more useful to you than the standard columns. Download a ton of TV shows? Airdate will get the shows you haven't seen in front of you faster. In fact, if you use iTunes to watch a lot of TV, a Smart Playlist might be in order. Figure 9-2 shows an example that sorts through your iTunes files and grabs any TV shows you've added but haven't watched within the last week.

Figure 9-1.
That's a lot of options

Figure 9-2.
No reruns here

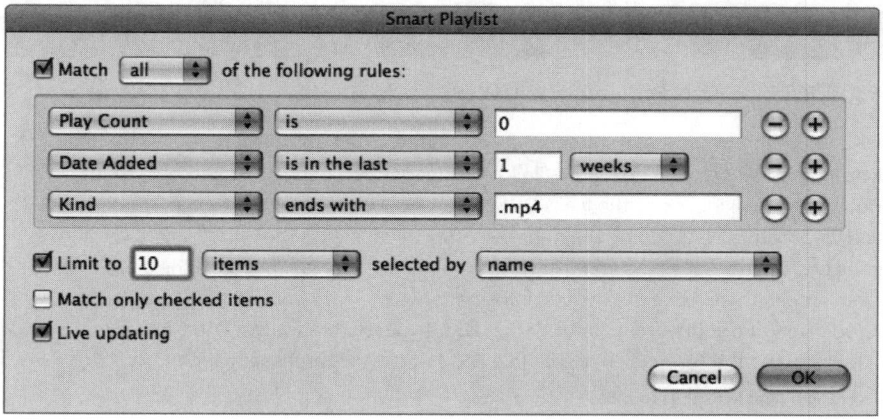

With so much going on with iTunes, the best place to start hacking is getting around the limitations of iTunes. In this instance, the limitations aren't overlooked parts of the program but things Apple positively discourages.

In this hack, I recommend that you lose the DRM by burning the files to a disc as MP3s. The choice makes sense; a standard audio CD can hold (surprise) about 75 minutes of music, while a CD full of MP3 files can hold much, much more, somewhere around 12 hours worth of music. Thus if you're trying to minimize burning and ripping, the MP3 route makes sense. On the other hand if you actually plan to listen to the discs you burn, the Audio CD option is a better choice. Many CD players are not capable of playing MP3 CDs.

Lose the DRM on iTunes Tracks

Digital rights management is a way to protect files from unauthorized sharing. The methods vary; Apple's implementation is called Fairplay and, in day-to-day use, probably won't bother most users. Even though FairPlay is transparent to most users, Apple is slowly transitioning to DRM-free tracks. Currently these tracks are limited to music from EMI and some independent labels, but as time passes, hopefully more and more of the media will arrive free of pesky DRM restrictions.

Truth is that many of the tracks bought from iTunes are laden with DRM. (As mentioned earlier, Apple calls its DRM version FairPlay—never say that the company doesn't know a good name when it sees one.) You don't want DRM on your music; you want to use your purchases how you see fit! Why not get rid of the DRM? You've got a lot of choices.

The long, tedious DRM workaround

The most obvious way to get rid of DRM on the tracks you buy is to burn your files to an audio CD as MP3 files. Once the burn is complete, reimport (rip) the songs into iTunes. There are downsides to this methodology. First, there will be some quality loss in the processing of the files. Tracks purchased from iTunes are encoded with advanced audio codec (AAC), but the format changes when they are written to the audio CD. The change from AAC to MP3 necessarily results in some data loss, and the tracks will sound a bit worse to sensitive listeners. (I can't tell the difference, but my ears are made of solid, lab-grade tin.)

Once the MP3 CD is burned, simply reimport the tunes back into iTunes and you now have slightly worse, but DRM-free, copies of your music.

The downside of all this is that if you have a large library of purchased music, the process positively eats time and requires enough disk swaps to cause repetitive strain injury. To top it all off, a big reason a lot of us buy music from the iTunes store is because of convenience. Going to all this trouble for your entire library defeats the purpose of buying songs from the store in the first place.

iTunes Plus is free from DRM restrictions meaning that you can do anything you wish with a track as long as it is legal. Sending the file to a jillion friends, posting it online, etc., is not legal. But, you're thinking, since the file is DRM-free, how would anyone ever know? This isn't the place for a lecture about doing the right thing just because it is the right thing to do, and respecting copyrights is the right thing to do. Still, be aware that just because the file is DRM-free doesn't mean the file doesn't contain information about who bought it, as Erica Sadun discovered. To assure yourself that information about you is stored with a DRM-free purchased iTunes track, fire up the Terminal, navigate to a DRM track you purchased, and type:

```
$ strings /pathtosong/foo.m4a | grep name
```

If you're wondering what is going on here, `strings` runs through the file specified for ASCII strings (that is, letters and numbers to 0you and me). The result is then sent to `grep` via a pipe (`|`). `grep` searches through the results of the `strings` command and pulls out the text that appears with the word `name`. My result looked precisely like this:

```
$ cd ~/Music/iTunes/iTunes\ Music
$ cd Danger/09\_14\ 2007\ -\ EP/
$ strings 01\ 11h30.m4a | grep name
nameChris Seibold
```

On the other hand, if you're burning your music to listen to while driving, then why not lose a little DRM cruft in the process?

If you're using Windows, you can use a utility such as myfairtunes (http://hymn-project.org) to strip the DRM from your iTunes DRM music, automatically. The trouble is that each new version of iTunes brings in a new form of DRM, and there tends to be a lag between the release of iTunes and the ability of myfairtunes to free the music.

If you're determined to get rid of iTunes DRM using your Mac without burning disks, you can use iMovie HD to strip off the DRM. The process is cumbersome, but the drill is as follows:

1. Fire up iMovie.

2. Import the song you want to strip of DRM into iMovie HD. This is easier than you might imagine because iMovie HD provides a convenient listing of all the music you've purchased. So just grab the track, and drag it to the timeline (see Figure 9-3).

Figure 9-3.
iMovie is a DRM stripper's best friend

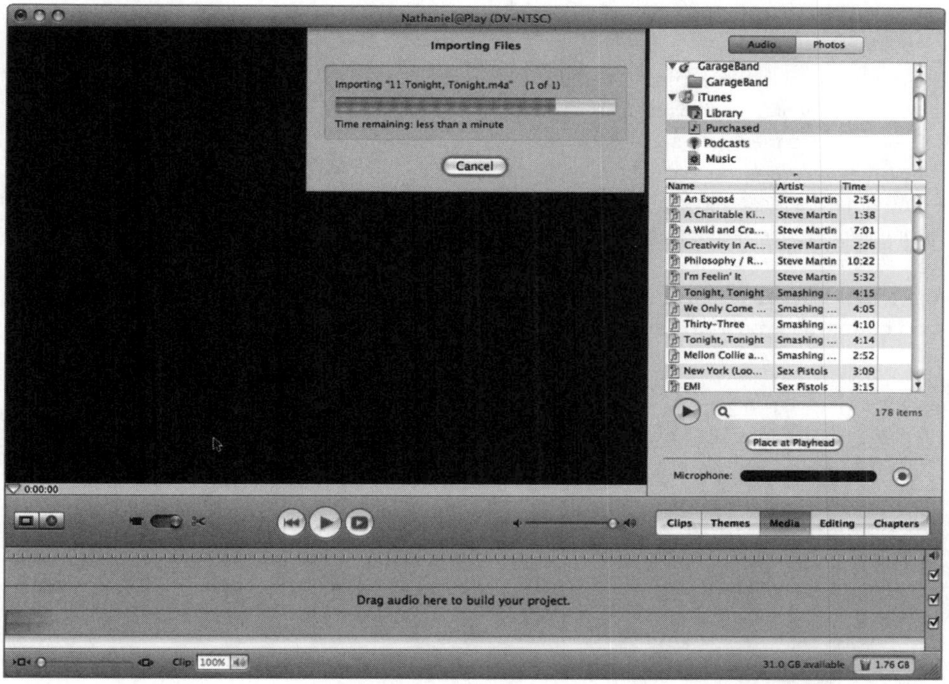

3. At this point you'd imagine that you could just export and be done. No luck: iMovie HD requires an image to be associated with the file. That isn't much of an obstacle; just drag an image (any image will do) to the main window of iMovie HD. Now it is time to turn this "movie" back into just music.

4. Choose "Share..." from iMovie's Share menu and choose QuickTime as the method you wish to use.

5. Once that choice has been made, refine the selection by opting for Expert Settings. Finally hit the Share button, and you'll be prompted to save the file as something. This is where the

QUICK TIP ✕

BURN, RIP, ERASE, REPEAT...

If your plan is to do this for a large number of tracks, why waste blank CDs? Burn to a CD-RW disk, and as soon as you're done burning, rip the MP3 files onto your hard drive, then erase the CD-RW disk and start again.

picture-losing trick comes in. You're going to export the Movie without the image. Name the file something meaningful and choose "Sound to AIFF" from the pop-up menu (see Figure 9-4).

Figure 9-4.
Exporting to AIFF

Give iTunes Better Ears

Earlier in this hack, I mentioned exporting and ripping MP3s. What I didn't mention (because of file types) were options for ripping music. iTunes is set up for ease: when you insert a music CD, the standard behavior is to ask if you want to import the tracks into iTunes. There is even a checkbox to make the behavior standard practice.

If you use the default iTunes import method, you'll end up with a MP3 file sampled at 160 Kbps. The acceptability of the audio quality is completely dependent on the listener but in the age of 160 GB iPods, perhaps the space-saving, audio-quality sacrificing, 160 Kbps isn't the optimal choice. After all, there is every chance that a rip of a physical CD will outlive the physical CD. So why not maximize the quality of the rip? iTunes is happy to let you do just that after a quick trip to the Advanced Preference settings of iTunes.

Simply choose iTunes→Preferences, click on the Advanced button, followed by a click on the Import button, and you'll have all the choices you could ever desire (see Figure 9-5).

Figure 9-5.
Adjust away, it is your music!

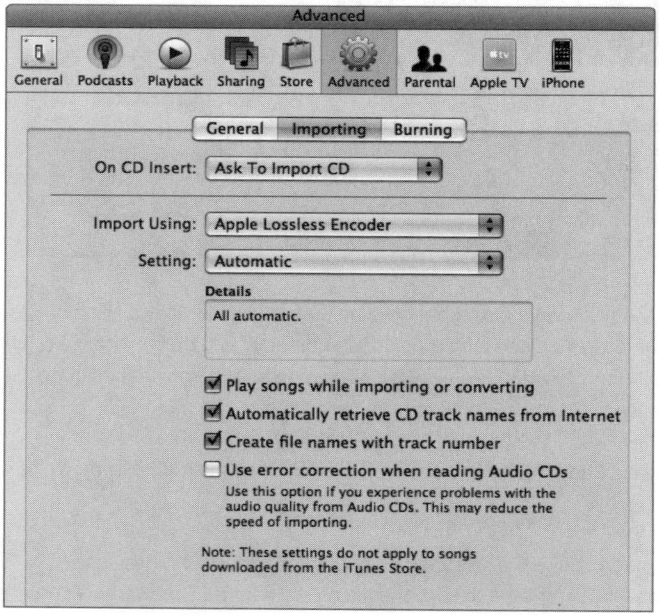

Here you have to balance file size with quality—or you would if today's devices were limiting. If you are all Apple, all the time, the best choice is Apple lossless. If you desire enhanced compatibility, a high bit rate MP3 rip is in order. The tradeoff, as alluded to earlier, is one of file size. A standard MP3 rip of a CD results in file sizes of a few megabytes per song. An Apple lossless rip of an audio CD results in files that are about half of the original size, so a rip of an entire CD can be expected to require somewhere between 300 to 400 megabytes.

If your ears don't crave lossless quality, or if you want your music to be more compatible, consider bumping up the sampling rate of the MP3 rips. MP3 is a *lossy* algorithm meaning that there is a lot of information lost in the encoding process. That doesn't mean you can hear the information that is lost. Encoders are clever programs and are able to exclude the data you wouldn't have heard anyway. How good the MP3 turns out to be has a lot to do with the quality of the encoder, so you can be satisfied with a sampling rate less than iTunes' default setting. The general consensus among audio fans (as far as there can be a general consensus on a topic so inherently subjective) is that a sampling rate of 192 Kbps results in a file nearly indistinguishable from the source. iTunes comes with three presets: 128, 160, and 192 Kbps. You can go higher than 192 Kbps using the custom option, but you can't go crazy: the MP3 format tops out at 320 Kbps. Of course, there is only one way to know what is right for you and that is to experiment and then choose the bit rate you find satisfactory.

You've considered the lossless option that veritably eats disk space, and you've considered the MP3 option that uses far less disk space and is more compatible but maybe doesn't sound quite as good as you would like. If only there was an option for better sound at lower sampling rates. Apple to the rescue: the AAC format results in rips that sound much better than the equivalent rip in MP3 format or, put differently, better sound per bit of data. In Preferences→Advanced→Importing, iTunes gives you two options for your music-importing needs: 128 Kbps and 256 Kbps. Obviously if you're not satisfied with a 128 Kbps rip, don't be afraid to bump up the quality to 256 Kbps.

Overlooked iTunes Features

With the annoying restrictions out of the way, it is time to get to what iTunes can do for you instead of avoiding what iTunes wants to do to you. This is a lot more fun because iTunes wants to do a lot for you, so much it is hard to remember it all.

See the music

You've probably run across the trippy, oddly entrancing iTunes visualizer during your forays into iTunes. While most of us just hit Command-T and let the visualizer do its thing, you have much more control over the visualizer than you realize. The first bit of fun is full-screen mode: hit Command-F, and iTunes will flip back and forth between running in a resizable window and filling the entire screen. Think how much fun you'll have with iTunes visualizer dancing along on your plasma screen at the next soirée you throw.

Once you've got the visualizer running on a big screen, or even if it is running on your computer monitor, you might want a little more control over just what the crazy, flashback-inducing visualizer is doing. In a triumph of intuitiveness that is so intuitive you'd never think of trying it, the first thing to do is to type **?**. That's right, hitting on the universal symbol for "Huh?" results in a useful menu outlining your visualizer options (**H** also activates the menu).

And iTunes gives you a bevy of options when it comes to the visualizer. You can view the song information, change the volume, skip ahead or back on your playlist, and even display the frame rate the visualizer is running at (you can also cap the frame rate). Those are interesting options and all self-explanatory with the built-in help viewer.

QUICK TIP

GAH! I'VE ALREADY IMPORTED ALL MY CDS!

So you've imported a lot of audio CDs, and you're worried about song duplicates if you reimport your CDs at a higher quality. Worry not: you won't be reduced to using the iTunes "find duplicates" feature. iTunes will ask you if you want to replace your existing songs with the higher quality rips; the answer in this case is "yes."

Things get more interesting when you discover the options not covered by the help viewer. By tapping the Q and W key, you can choose from various built-in themes. These are basically the lines that react to your musical selection. The iTunes visualizer applies effects to these lines, and you can scroll through the various effects using the A and S keys. iTunes isn't done with your visualizer options yet; you can also control the color palette used to color the form and effect using the Z and X keys.

The iTunes visualizer gives you a lot of choices with each effect, form, or color. Counting haphazardly and applying simple math, you'll find that there are over 80,000 possible unique combinations. Double that if you use the optional high-contrast colors. As you can imagine, if you have a favorite configuration, it can take quite some time to cycle through all the options to get back to combination you want to see. That is where the Shift and the number keys come in to play. You can save your favorite option at any time by hitting Shift and the number (1 through 9) you want to associate with your beloved configuration. Here's one final iTunes visualizer secret: when you've got a waveform as the form, hit the plus and minus keys to adjust the amplitude.

At this point you might want to check out Table 9-1. Is there anything in the table you want to save in perpetuity? Is it something you might want to refer to at a later date? If so, get the scissors ready, and cut out this handy guide to the iTunes visualizer controls (you might want to make a photocopy first).

Table 9-1.
iTunes visualizer controls

Keys	Action
Q, W	Cycle back and forth through forms
A, S	Cycle back and forth through effects
Z, X	Cycle back and forth through colors
T	Toggle frame rate capping
I	Display song information
? / H	Toggle Help
D	Reset visuals to default
Arrows up, down	Volume
Arrows left, right	Previous/next track
C	Display current configuration
M	Select configuration mode
0–9	Display saved configuration
Shift 0–9	Save configuration
N	Toggle normal or high contrast color
R	Random Configuration
B	Display the Apple logo

Control your library with Smart Playlists
Smart Playlists were mentioned in passing earlier in this hack, but they are just so useful—particularly with large libraries of varying media types—that a little closer scrutiny is warranted.

Smart Playlists work like any database query; you define a set of criteria, and the results that match the criteria are returned. Apple is happy to get you started with Smart Playlists, and five are included with the standard iTunes install. Just because they are already there doesn't mean you can't mess with them. Let's get one of Apple's Smart Playlists running in a fashion that differs from the manner envisioned by Apple. Pick your least-favorite Playlist, right-click, and select Edit (see Figure 9-6).

Figure 9-6.
Editing a preconfigured Smart Playlist

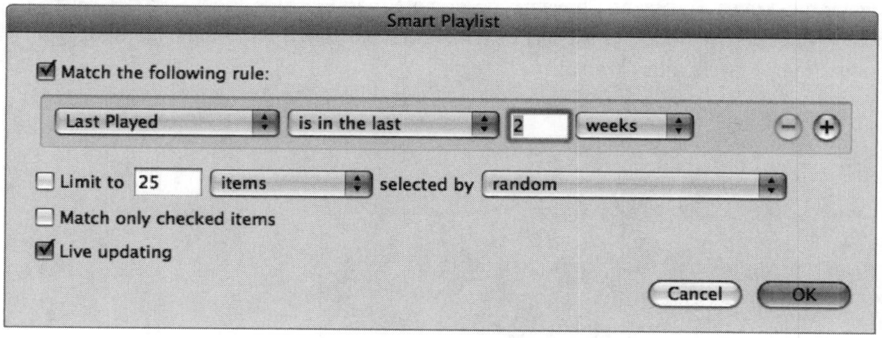

Smart Playlist

☑ Match the following rule:

| Last Played ⬍ | is in the last ⬍ | 2 | weeks ⬍ | ⊖ ⊕ |

☐ Limit to 25 | items ⬍ | selected by | random ⬍ |

☐ Match only checked items

☑ Live updating

(Cancel) (OK)

For this example, the Smart Playlist Recently Played has been selected. The default configuration includes 25 songs that have played during the last two weeks in the Playlist. But suppose this Playlist doesn't really fit the needs of this iTunes user. What if I played "We Built this City" by Starship to torture someone in the last two weeks? If that dreck comes out the computer speakers, and I'm not fully prepared, bad things could befall my hardware. Plus, I'm either listening to iTunes all the time or never, limiting the Playlist to the last few weeks could severely limit my choices.

So a little tweaking is in order. Using the + button results in a new line for a new rule being added. With the menus that come up, it is easy to exclude anything by Starship. It is similarly easy to change the time frame of the Playlist to a more encompassing six months. Finally, leaving checkboxes unchecked means that the number of songs is unlimited and that the Smart Playlist is updated as more songs are played (see Figure 9-7).

Figure 9-7.
The revised, much more livable, Smart Playlist

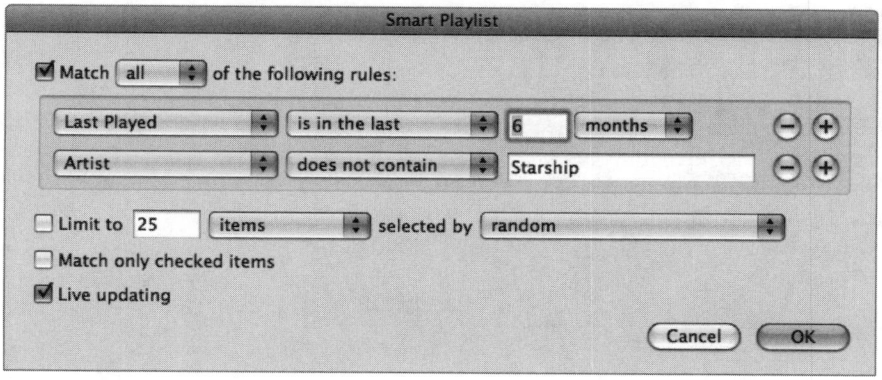

Smart Playlist

☑ Match all ⬍ of the following rules:

| Last Played ⬍ | is in the last ⬍ | 6 | months ⬍ | ⊖ ⊕ |
| Artist ⬍ | does not contain ⬍ | Starship | | ⊖ ⊕ |

☐ Limit to 25 | items ⬍ | selected by | random ⬍ |

☐ Match only checked items

☑ Live updating

(Cancel) (OK)

As you'd expect, you aren't limited to tweaking Apple-supplied Smart Playlists. You can create your own Smart Playlist (and you undoubtedly should). To get a new Smart Playlist going, the process is simple. Use the iTunes File menu (or Option-Command-N) to create a new Smart Playlist. Once the new Smart Playlist shows up on your screen, edit away to your heart's content.

While a Smart Playlist is easy to set up, coming up with a good or useful Smart Playlist can be challenging for most of us. For Bakari Chavanu, the king of Smart Playlists, great Smart Playlists are child's play. Why not peruse five of his excellent examples (see Figure 9-8 through Figure 9-12) to get your inner Smart Playlist muse fired up?

Figure 9-8.
Back in the Day: Captures your old school cuts

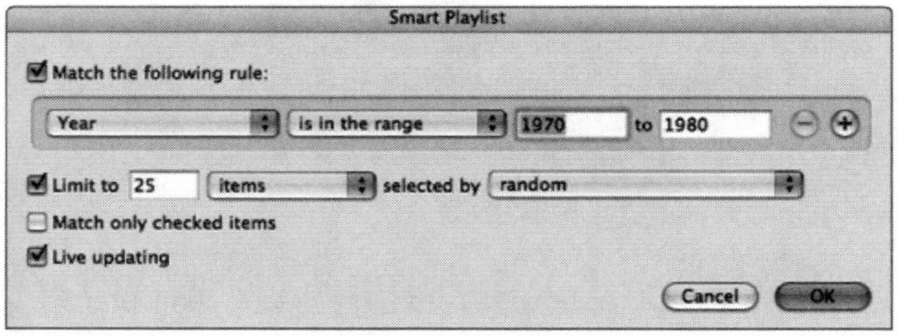

Figure 9-9.
Forgotten Gems: Favorite songs you haven't played in a while

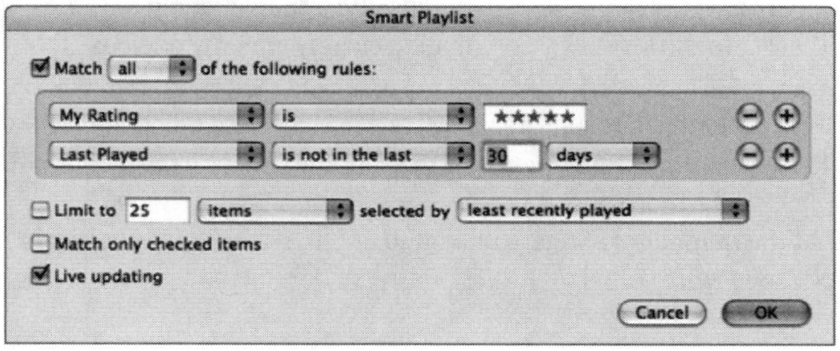

Figure 9-10.
iTunes Free Songs captures all the free iTunes songs you've downloaded from iTunes

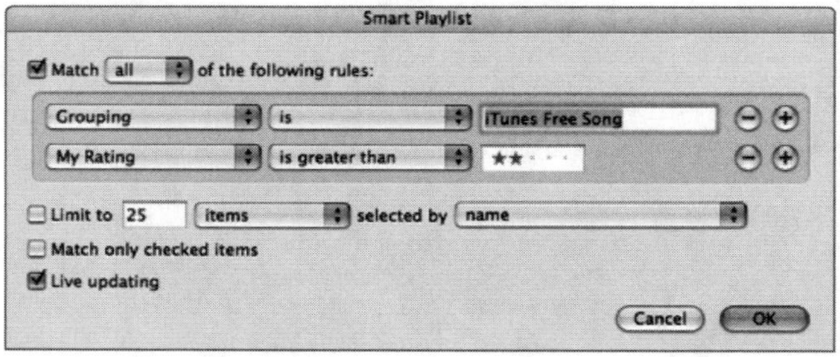

Figure 9-11.
Quickie: Short songs about two minutes long

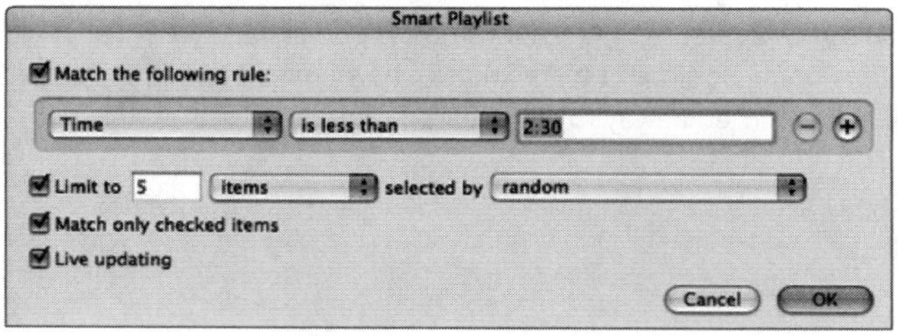

Figure 9-12.
Rising Stars: Songs that are becoming my favorites because they're being played more often

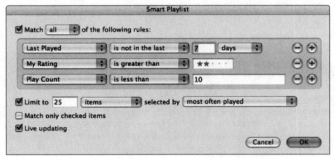

Add album art to iTunes

Album art has been a part of iTunes for some time, but with the release of the iPhone and Cover flow, album art has become more critical for easily browsing your music. Besides looking fairly lame, the question mark on black displayed by songs missing album art conveys no useful information unless you consider "Hey, you don't have album art for this song!" useful knowledge.

You can, of course, search for album artwork within iTunes by invoking Advanced→Get Album Artwork from the iTunes menu bar. If a song's ID3 tags are correct, and if the iTunes store has the artwork, iTunes will take care of adding the artwork. If the album doesn't exist in the iTunes music store, predictably, nothing happens. A sad, sad state of affairs.

The solution is relatively simple. You can manually locate the image (Amazon seems to be the favorite for most people) and move it to the Drag Album Artwork Here area. No need to drop the artwork on the Desktop first; a straight trip to the Album Artwork area works just fine.

The drag-and-drop method is fine if you're missing the occasional album cover, but looking for and adding hundreds (or perhaps) thousands of album covers in that fashion would be an invitation for unmowed lawns, neglected children, and repetitive stress injury. And you shouldn't have to do it by hand anyway; you're using a computer, and these things are supposed to be taken care of automatically.

Good news: you don't have to do it all by hand. Amazon has a larger database of album art than iTunes so intrepid programmer Aric Friesen has married Amazon's album cover library with ID3 tags and produced the super-useful Fetchart (http://www.aric.org/fetchart/index.html). Simply download, install (you'll have to authenticate), and you'll notice a new script in the iTunes menu bar (see Figure 9-13).

Figure 9-13.
A new script in iTunes

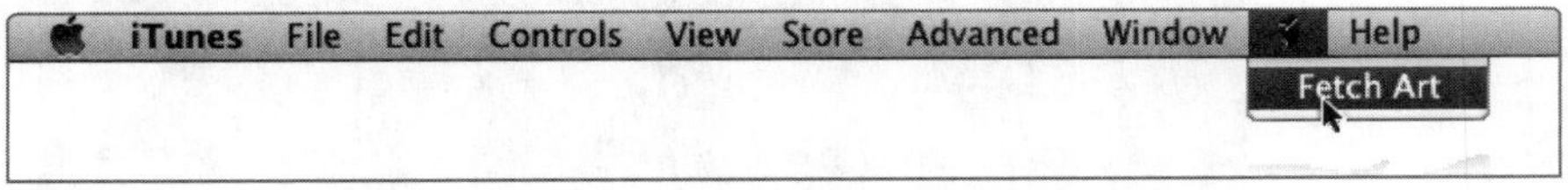

|  | **iTunes** | File | Edit | Controls | View | Store | Advanced | Window | ✂ | Help |

Fetch Art

When you find one of those pesky question marks, just hit Fetchart via the drop-down menu, and you'll be asked if you want to import the album art into iTunes (see Figure 9-14).

Figure 9-14.
Art found!

Fixing bad track information and tags

Fetchart is great if each track is properly identified and the album is listed, but when I had a friend try out this hack, Fetchart didn't work for him. As it turned out, his library was full of badly labeled tracks with no album listed. For example, he had imported "Under Pressure" by David Bowie with Queen playing backup as a single file and called it (for no apparent reason) Under_Pressure_Queen. His imports from the days before spacious hard drives (and iTunes) played fine, but their tags were hopelessly messed up.

Well maybe things aren't as dark as they would seem. Perhaps there is a way to get those tags corrected automatically and thus find the missing album artwork. This is where MusicBrainz enters the picture. MusicBrainz is a user-maintained system that attempts to identify music by acoustic fingerprints. If only they had a handy client to run your music through to repair tags! The good news is that just such a utility exists (http://musicbrainz.org), and the Mac OS X version is called iEatBrainz. Download and install the client, then select any songs that have questionable tags in the iEatBrainz browser (see Figure 9-15).

Figure 9-15.
Choosing the songs with iffy tags

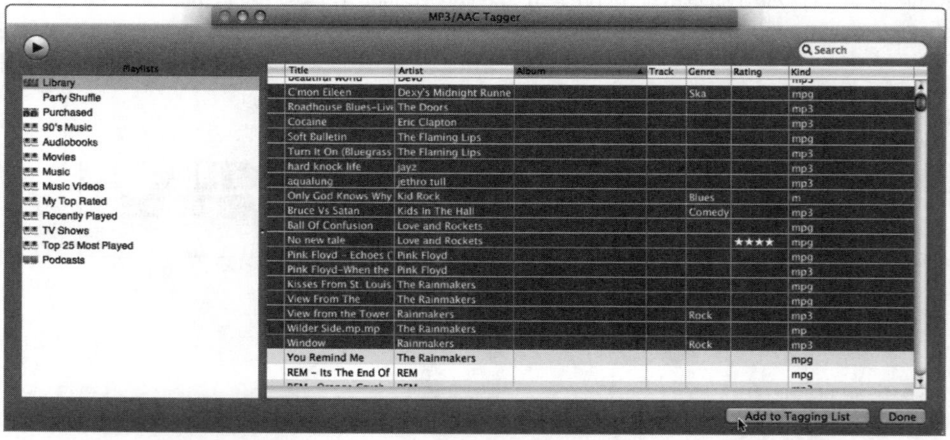

Once the songs have been selected, iEatBrainz compares the selected songs to the MusicBrainz database and generates the proper tags. The method isn't perfect, but if you have more than a dozen songs in need of tag help, using the iEatBrainz client beats typing the information in by hand (see Figure 9-16).

Figure 9-16.
Typical results for iEatBrainz.

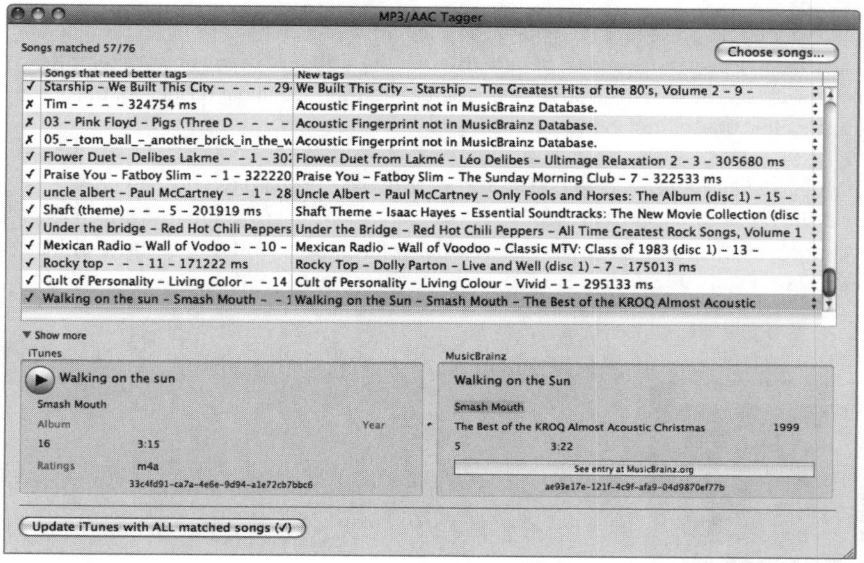

The client (of course) works over the Internet so it can take some time to check all your songs. Once iEatBrainz finishes its attempt at identifying your tracks, you can review the results. If you are comfortable with the identifications, click the "Update iTunes with All matched songs" radio button. (You'll be warned that you can't undo this action.) Once iEatBrainz is finished, you can go back and fetch album art for your now properly tagged music with any of the methods discussed previously (see Figure 9-17).

Figure 9-17.
All your hard works pays off with a completed library of album art

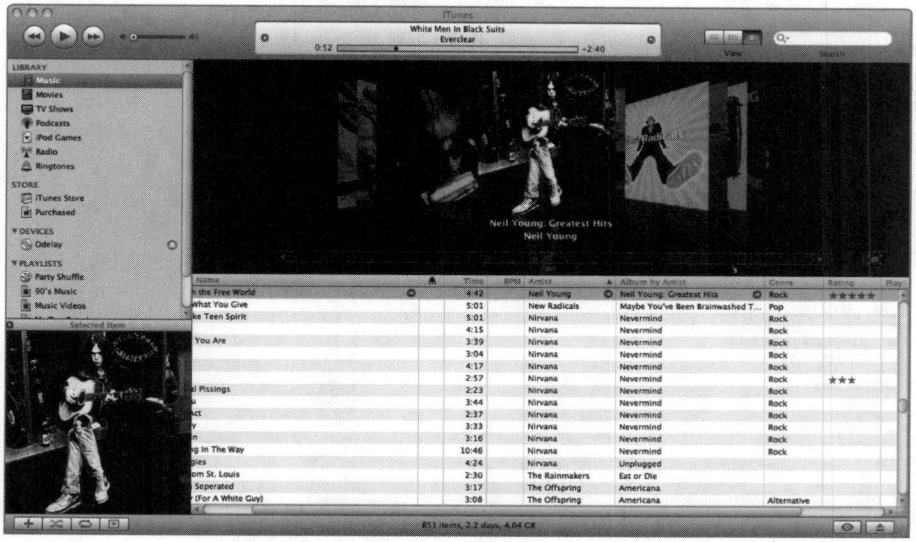

QUICK HACK

OF COURSE YOU CAN UNDO IT!

When iEatBrainz says you can't undo the action, what the program really means is that any mistakes will be a chore to edit. You can always edit the data associated with your tracks by hand with the "Get Info" option. You can change the artist, delete the art, rename the album, give props to the artists that inspired Elvis. The options are all yours as long as you're willing to spend time editing the data.

Add lyrics for music

"My head smelled just like tuba lube" is not an actual lyric from Pink Floyd's song "Comfortably Numb." The actual lyric is "My hands felt just like two balloons," and while there is an argument to be made that the misheard lyric is actually better than the one penned by Roger Waters, there is only one correct answer. Why argue with someone when you can whip out your iPod and have them read the lyric?

To add lyrics to your tracks automatically, you're going to have to do a little hacking. In the olden days, you could just use pearLyrics and be done with it, but the author of pearLyrics, Walter Ritter, was threatened with legal action, so he pulled the program. You can still find it online, but the standalone application doesn't run in Leopard.

Luckily pearLyrics also came as a widget that continues to work in Leopard (you won't find at Apple's widget site but you can find it at http://mac.softpedia.com/get/Dashboard-Widgets/Music/pearLyrics-Widget.shtml). The widget automatically finds lyrics for the song currently being played in iTunes (see Figure 9-18).

Figure 9-18.
pearLyrics in action

Flip the widget over by clicking the small "i", make sure Copy Lyrics to iTunes is checked, and as your music plays, the lyrics the pearLyrics widget finds will automatically be added to iTunes (see Figure 9-19).

Figure 9-19.
Lyrics are automatically added to iTunes

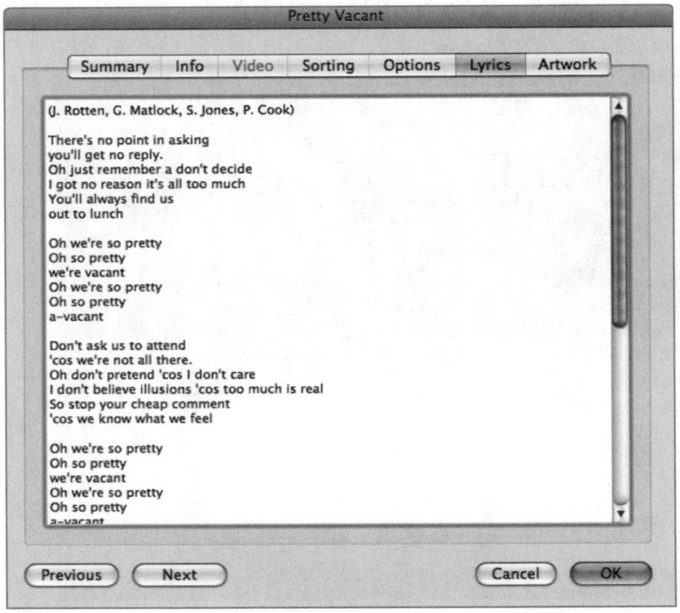

As you can imagine, if you have a big library this process can take quite some time, but it does have the advantage of downloading only lyrics to the songs you listen to.

HACK 78: Build a Custom Visualizer with Quartz Composer

If you want to see your music in different ways, Quartz Composer is the answer. Learn how to build a custom visualizer for your music.

Starting with OS X 10.4 (Tiger), Apple included a very powerful tool for creating beautiful realtime graphics with every system. It's called Quartz Composer, and it's easy to use, though it looks daunting. Quartz Composer is great at visualizing information. For this hack, we'll build a real-time animation that responds to the music you're playing in iTunes (for more on Quartz Composer, see **[Hack #42]**.

First, you need to install Quartz Composer if you haven't already **[Hack #3]**.

For those of you who may have dabbled with Quartz Composer and are hoping to build upon your knowledge, we're going to explore the Audio Input, Iterator and "Replicate in Space" patches, how and why to make macro patches, and all about publishing your inputs. Now it's time to open Quartz Composer and get patching.

First, let's create something on the screen and get it moving to Audio Input:

1. Launch Quartz Composer and choose File→New Composition from Blank (see Figure 9-20).

Figure 9-20.
Your visualizer begins life as a blank slate

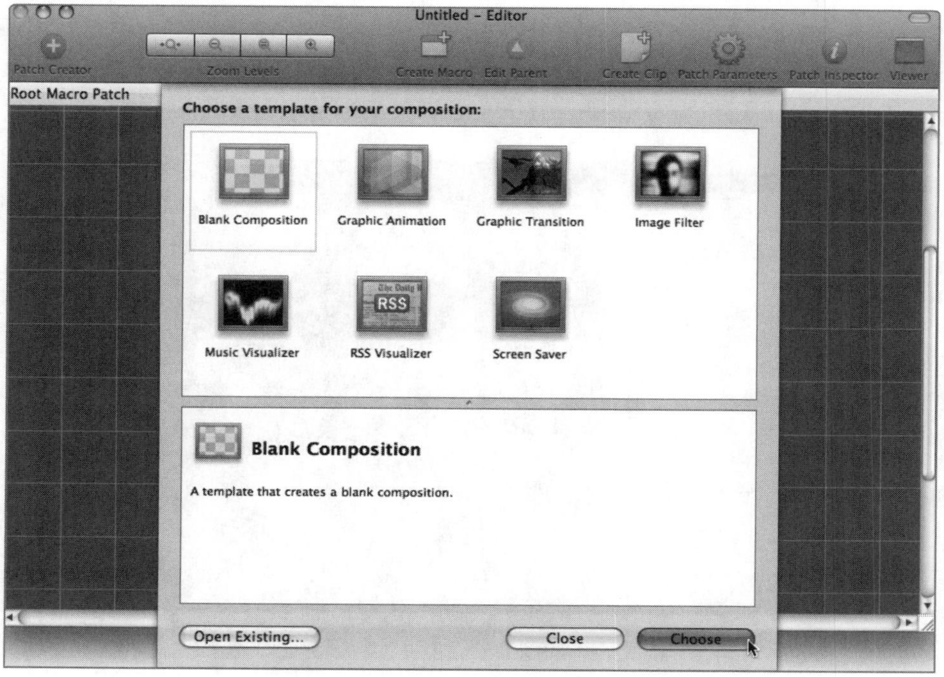

> **QUICK TIP**
>
> **SEE THE LYRICS ON YOUR IPOD**
>
> You've gone to the trouble of adding lyrics to your iTunes library, so you probably want to see the lyrics on your iPod. Doing so is easy. Select any song that you (or pearLyrics) have retrieved the lyrics for and depress the select button four times. Please don't use this tip for portable karaoke; the world has too much of that already.

2. In the Patch Creator (called the Patch Viewer in Tiger), type Clear to find the Clear patch, and drag it to your editing window. You've now cleared away the background and are ready to draw.

3. Type **Cube** into the patch creator and drag the "Renderer - Cube" patch into your editor (see Figure 9-21).

Figure 9-21.
Wow, that is one big cube!

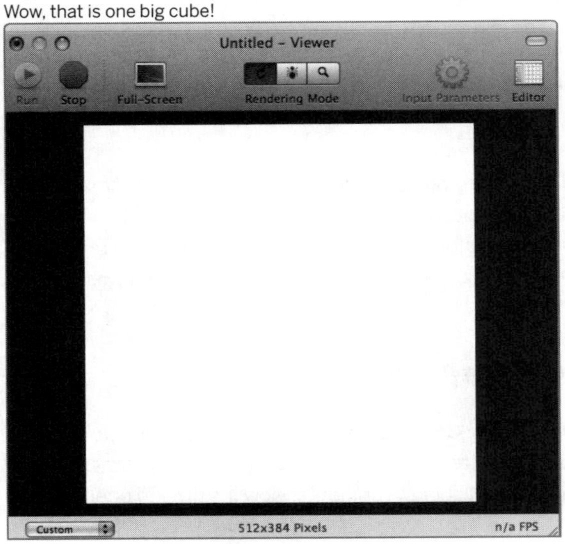

It's huge! Let's size it down a little bit:

4. Click on your Cube patch to select it; then press Command-I on your keyboard to open the Inspector.

5. Change the width, height, and depth of the cube each to 0.1 by typing the new number into the corresponding text field.

As soon as you input each number, you'll see the cube shrink accordingly (see Figure 9-22).

Figure 9-22.
That is better.

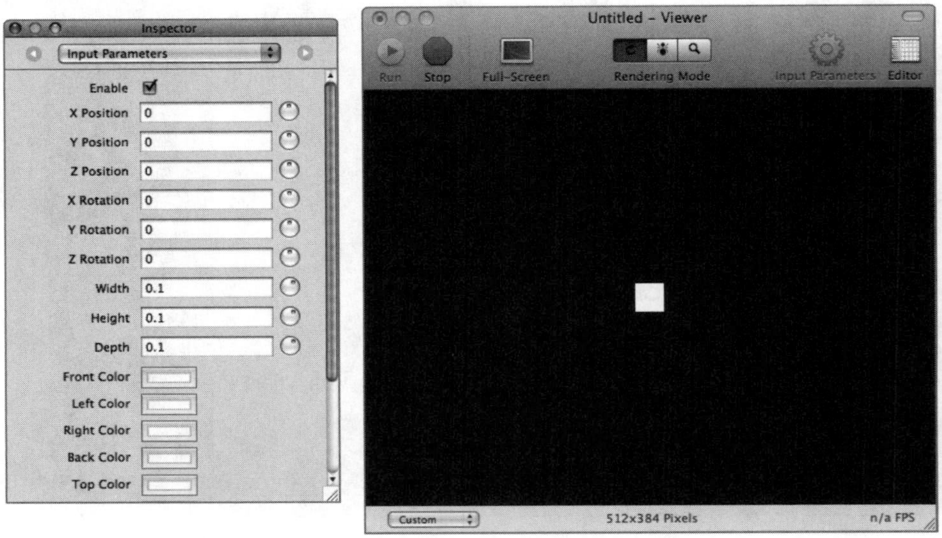

Now let's get an audio patch:

1. Type `audio` into the patch field and drag the Audio Input patch into your editing window.
2. To connect these two pieces, click on the little circle just to the right of Volume Peak, and drag a connection to the little circle just to the left of Y Position on the cube (see Figure 9-23).

Figure 9-23.
Your first connection in Quartz Composer

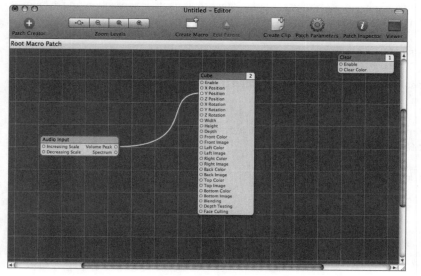

Now you should see the cube bounce in your viewer whenever you make noise!

Let me guess, it's not working. If it's not moving at all, click on the Audio Input and then bring up its Inspector with Command-I. You may need to change pages using the arrows at the top of the Inspector. You're looking for the page with drop-down menus for the Audio Device and Input Source. To use an internal microphone on a MacBook, choose Built-In Audio for your device and Built-in Microphone for your input source. See what choices you have, and try any that look promising. For example, if you have a Logitech microphone attached to a G5 PowerMac, your setting might look like Figure 9-24.

Figure 9-24.
Settings for a basement configuration

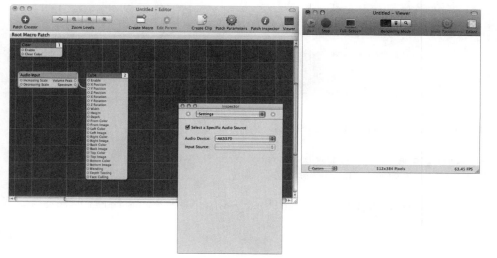

Once you see the cube bounce, you know you've got it nailed.

Connect to iTunes

Now it's time to route iTunes to Quartz Composer, so your animation can respond to some phat beats instead of your yapping.

To pull this off, you need to install Soundflower—a freeware utility lets you route audio from iTunes to other applications. This is great because Quartz Composer is another application! You're four steps away from Quartz Composer jamming to your iTunes library.

1. Download Soundflower from http://www.cycling74.com/downloads/soundflower.

2. Run the installer and then copy Soundflowerbed to your Applications folder. Be forewarned: installation requires a restart.

3. Now, in your System Preferences, click on Sound and take a look at what has been chosen under the Output option.

4. Write this down, and then choose "Soundflower (2ch)" for your output as shown in Figure 9-25.

Figure 9-25.
Built-in Audio has been changed to Soundflower (2ch)

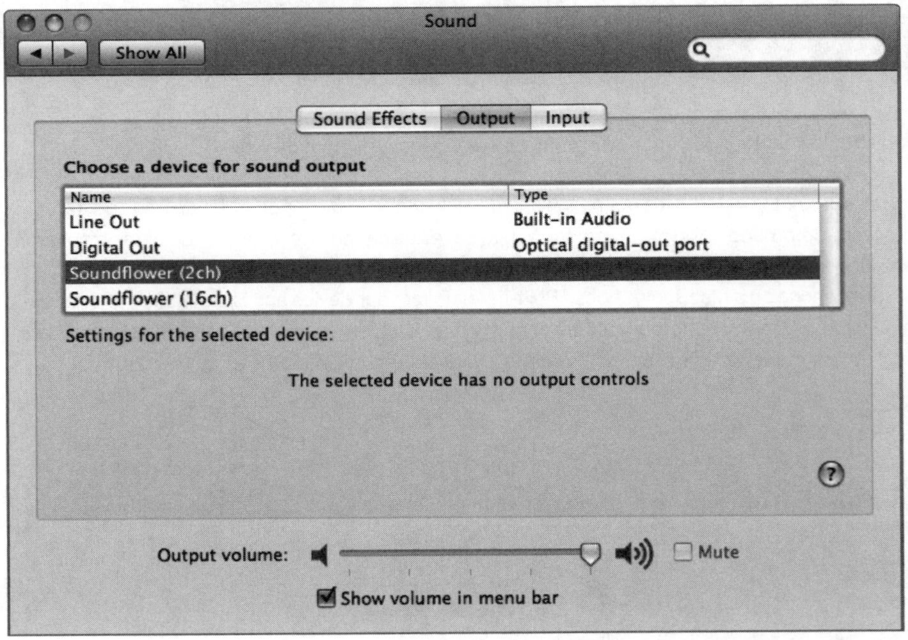

Now iTunes will play its audio through Soundflower!

The sound is being routed internally, but we're not hearing it. And what good is an iTunes visualizer if you can't hear the music the visualizer is visualizing?

1. Open your Applications folder and run Soundflowerbed, which creates a cute little flower icon in the Mac menu bar.

2. Click on this flower icon, and underneath "Soundflower (2ch)," choose the output you wrote down earlier (probably Headphones or Built-in Audio). That should do it. Now iTunes is sending audio to Soundflower, which sends it on to your regular output while making it available to every audio application on your Mac (see Figure 9-26).

Figure 9-26.
You want to hear your iTunes music don't you?

Now that SoundFlower's up and running, let's switch our Audio Input patch to use it instead of a microphone.

1. Select the Audio Input Patch, bring up the Inspector (Command-I), and use the arrow icons at the top of the Inspector to switch it to the settings page (if it's not there already).

2. Select "Soundflower (2ch)" as the audio device and play some tunes. You should now see the cube on the screen bopping to the beat (see Figure 9-27).

Figure 9-27.
This boring change will get your cube moving!

Elaborating the Hack

Quartz Composer can do much more than simple volume detection. We'll now expand our patch to use the Spectrum output of the Audio patch, drawing boxes that represent 12 distinct bands of the audio spectrum. First, we'll build one box that reacts to the spectrum instead of the volume, and then we'll use the powerful replication and iteration features of Quartz Composer to automatically generate the rest.

1. Disconnect the Audio and Cube patches by grabbing the connection where Audio plugs into the y position of the cube, pulling it out and letting it drop onto an empty section of your editor.

2. Drag and drop a Replicate in Space patch into your editor (see Figure 9-28).

Figure 9-28.
Four patches, but not for long

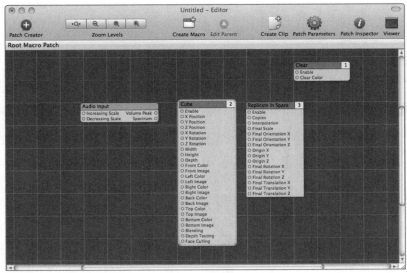

Notice the corners of the Replicate patch. They are squared instead of rounded like our Clear and Cube patches. This signifies that it can hold other patches inside it. In this case, we want to put the Cube patch inside. We'll cut and paste just as you do in a word processor.

3. Select the cube.

4. Press Command-X to cut it to the clipboard.

5. Double-click on the Replicate in Space patch to go inside.

6. Press Command-V to paste the Cube patch back to the editor.

Now you see a cool pattern of cubes in your viewer, created by the Replicate in Space patch (see Figure 9-29).

Figure 9-29.
You're inside a patch, and creating cubes

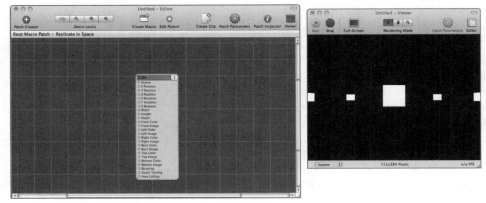

There is more tweaking to do:

7. Press the Edit Parent button above the Editor to go back up a level.

8. Choose the Replicate in Space patch and open up the Inspector (see Figure 9-30).

Figure 9-30.
Hmm, settings to play with

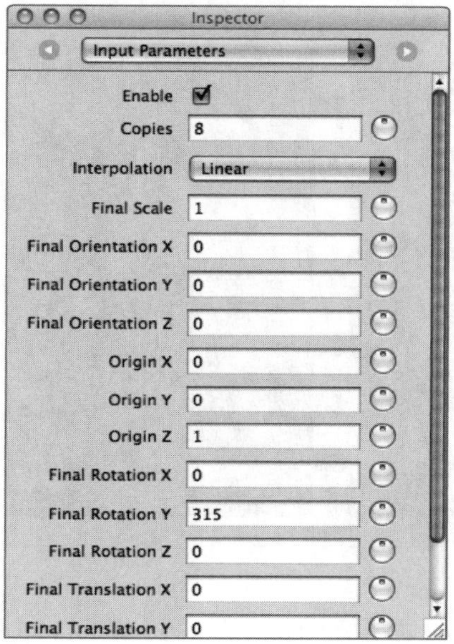

Pumping Things Up with the Inspector

One of the things you'll be using a ton is the Inspector window. The Inspector will often have multiple pages. You can flip through them using the arrows at its top; or by pressing Command-1 for page one, Command-2 for page two, and so on. Whenever you open up the Inspector during this tutorial, try switching pages and seeing what sorts of properties you can access.

You'll see that Quartz Composer has made eight copies of your cube, and that "Final Rotation Y" is set to 315 by default. All this creates the cool pattern. But not so cool you can't make it better.

Reset this by typing **0** (zero) in the text fields next to "Final Rotation Y" and "Origin Z," which makes our viewer appear to contain only the one cube again.

We'll move the cube to the bottom of the screen by hand:

1. Spin the dial next to Origin Y counter-clockwise until the cube sits right along the bottom of the screen.

2. Now twirl the dial next to "Final Translation Y" clockwise. You may have to spin it all the way around many times. This way you can see the cubes slowly separate as they spread out to reach for the top of the screen.

QUICK TIP

SKIP THE SPINNING

Quartz Composer uses tiny hard-to-control dials for many adjustments. You can (of course) just type a value in the box, but that is time consuming and doesn't offer the serendipity enjoyed when spinning the dials. It turns out there is a third way to spin that dial. Use the Tab key to move through the input boxes, and you'll notice that the dial is suddenly highlighted with a soft blue glow. Once you see that glow, you can use the arrow keys to twiddle the dial!

It isn't clear from the steps but what is happening is that the Replicate In Space patch is creating eight cubes, starting at the Origin Y point and ending at the Final Translation Y point, with equal spacing in-between. Your final product will resemble Figure 9-31.

Figure 9-31.
Evenly spaced cubes

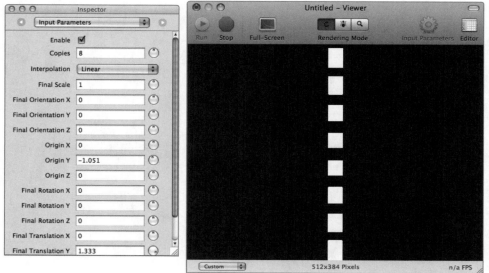

Drag-and-drop a new connection between Volume Peak and Final Translation Y, and check out your result (see Figure 9-32).

Figure 9-32.
Final settings: your cubes have become a pulsing line

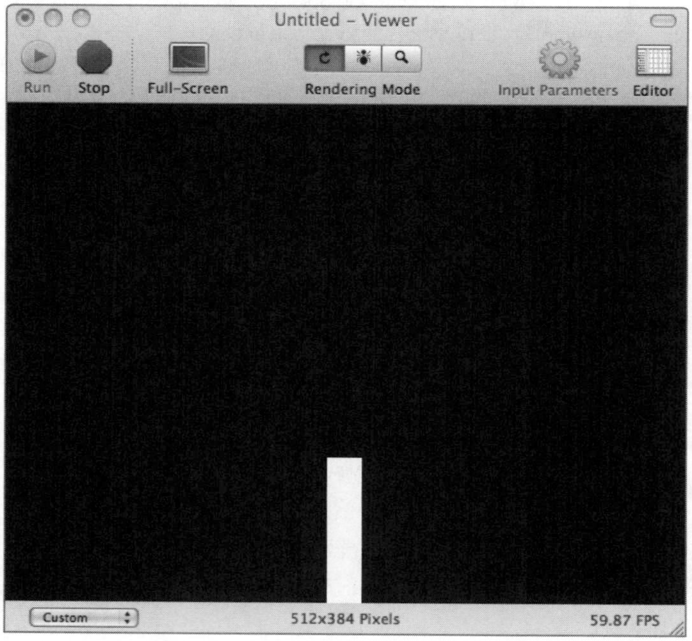

✉ You've got iTunes running but your cubes aren't jumping? Recall that the visualizer is relying on Volume Peak for instructions on how to move the cubes. The louder you set the volume in iTunes (not on your speakers), the bigger the movement will be.

You've now got the basic animation for your visualizer. But there is a lot more going on behind the scenes. Hover your mouse over the Spectrum output from the Audio Input patch, and you'll see the constantly changing spectrum information (see Figure 9-33). Notice how the information is stored as a Structure with 12 members, labeled with numbers zero through 11 (16 if you're a Leopard user).

Figure 9-33.
Quartz Composer generates a lot of data

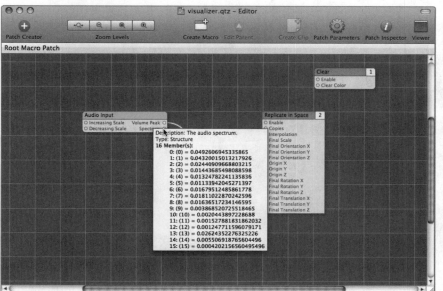

Tighten up the Design

Next, we're going to create a Macro patch, which will be a custom container for our Cube patch, combining all the properties we want to change in an easy-to-modify package. The name may sound forbidding, but the process is simple:

1. Double-click on the Replicate in Space patch to jump back inside.

2. Bring in an Input Splitter (type **Splitter** into the Patch Creator), and use the Inspector to set its type to Color (see Figure 9-34).

Figure 9-34.
Adding color with an input splitter

3. Connect its output to all the color inputs on the cube: Front Color, Left Color, Right Color, Back Color, Top Color, and Bottom Color.

4. Now, drag an HSL Color patch into the Editor, and connect its color output to the input on the Input Splitter. Your final product should resemble Figure 9-35.

Figure 9-35.
Hooking up the inputs

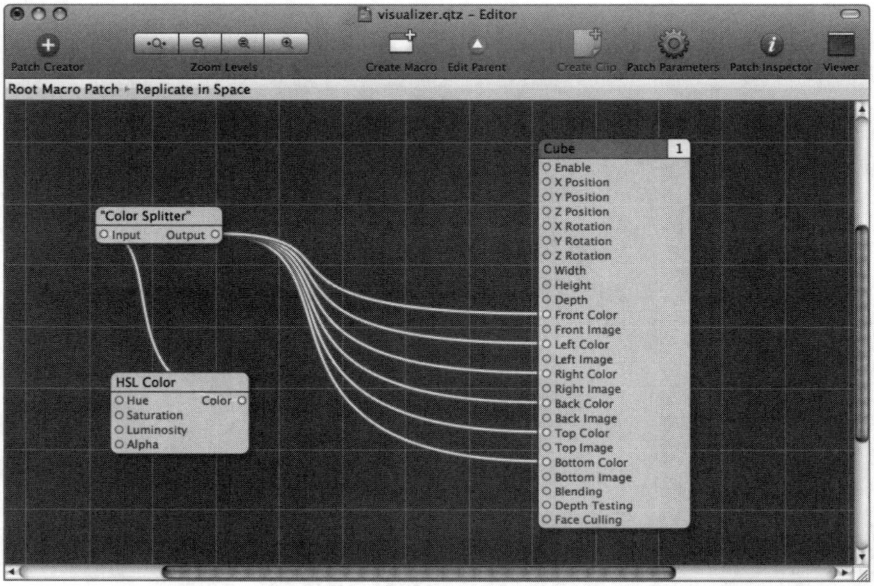

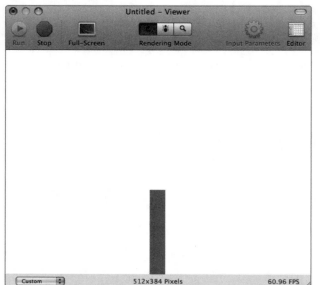

Now you can change the color on every side of the cube with just one patch. Time to try it out!

Use the Inspector to change the Luminosity to 0.5, and then slide the Hue back and forth to see a change (see Figure 9-36).

Figure 9-36. A pulsing purple bar!

QUICK TIP

BEST CODING PRACTICES COUNT EVEN WITH QUARTZ COMPOSER

Why bother running the Color through an Input Splitter instead of connecting it directly to the six Color Inputs on the cube? We do this as a "best coding practice." Let's say that down the line we decide to use something beside the HSL Color patch to make a color. To do this, we'll need to connect our new patch up to all six inputs again. If we've abstracted the input by one layer like this, then we only need to plug it into the Input Splitter, which doesn't require any more processing power than connecting it directly.

Publish the Hue Inputs

In our final visualizer exercise, we'll change the hue of each band separately. To get to this buried property, we "Publish" the Hue input:

1. Right-click on the Hue Input (Ctrl-click if you've only got a one-button mouse), then choose "Published Inputs - Hue," and hit Enter on your keyboard. You'll note that Hue changes to "Hue" (the quotation marks are added by Quartz Composer in Leopard) and that the circle next to Hue is darkened.

2. Press Edit Parent, and you'll see the Replicate in Space has a new Hue input at its bottom.

3. Publish the Hue, Origin X and Origin Y from your Replicate in Space patch as shown in Figure 9-37.

Figure 9-37.
Publishing an input with Quartz Composer

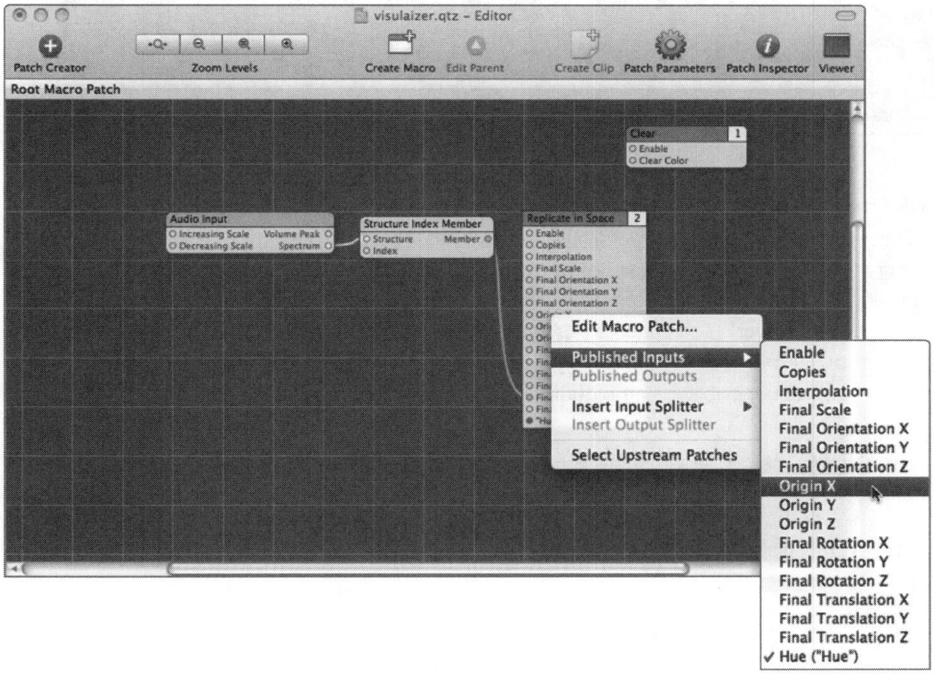

The Hue is published, which means that you'll be able to control it with another patch on a different layer of the visualizer. Once you're done with that, bring a Structure Index Member patch into the editor, and connect the Member output to Final Translation Y (see Figure 9-38).

Figure 9-38.
Connect the Member output

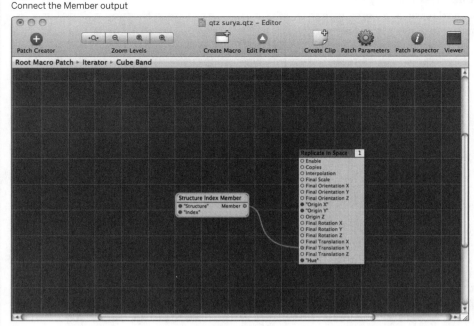

Hook the Hues Up to Various Frequencies

A real project will often include several layers of patches. This can make your project window look like a big mess. Fortunately, you can define macros to contain the complexity; they allow you to hide complexity (keeping your work from looking like a bowl of spaghetti), and also allow you to reuse complicated bits of work. This patch picks one of the 12 bands in the Spectrum, calling it up using its index (those zero through 11 numbers you spied earlier), and spits out a number representing that particular frequency band's amplitude to our handy-dandy cube replicator.

1. Publish the Structure and Index inputs.

2. Drag-select the Replicate in Space and Structure Index Member patches, and press the Create Macro button above the editing space.

This creates a Macro patch that simplifies a number of items into one compact patch. You'll also notice that the cube has jumped to the middle of the viewer. Its Origin Y was reset when we created the Macro. Let's fix that, change our title, and add another variable that will be useful later on.

3. Use the Macro patch's Inspector to change its Origin Y so that it sits on the bottom of the screen again.

4. On the first page of the Inspector, find the text field next to Title: and type in **Cube Band**. Leopard users won't have that option, but you can double-click the title of the patch (Macro Patch) and change it to Cube Band.

5. Connect Audio Input's Spectrum to the Structure in the Cube Band, and you'll see the cube jumping like it did when you had it hooked up to Volume.

What has all this effort earned you? You can now change the Index to cycle through the different bands. You'll appreciate this shortly.

We're in the last stretch now. It's time to use an iterator to have Quartz Composer automatically cycle through all the bands and create our dancing bars. You've dealt with iterators before; Replicate in Space is a specialized version of an iterator.

6. Bring an Iterator patch into your composition.

7. Cut and paste to put your Cube Band inside.

8. Double-click on the Iterator to dive in.

9. Bring in an Iterator Variables patch.

Once you place your items inside the iterator, Quartz Composer cycles through these inner bits 10 times (the default Iteration value), and the Iterator Variables patch will change each time, with the Index output corresponding to the number of times we've cycled. Here's how to do that:

10. Connect the Current Index of the Iterator Variables patch to the Index on the Cube Band. This way each cycle through the patch will affect a different band of the audio.

11. Drag an iterator into the editor.

12. Cut and paste the Cube Band and Iterator Variables inside.

13. While inside, publish the Structure and Origin Y inputs of the Cube Band so you can still access them from the root level. We did something similar with Hue in an earlier step.

14. Click on Edit Parent to return up a level.

15. Connect the Spectrum output to the Structure on the Iterator.

Our bar begins bouncing. We could use the Inspector to move the Origin Y of the iterator back to the bottom of the screen, but that's getting a bit tiresome, isn't it? Let's take a minute to have Quartz Composer do this for us automatically. Start by bringing in a Rendering Destination Dimensions patch and a Math patch. We're going to calculate how big our viewer is, and move the Origin Y property so that it always sits on the bottom of the screen.

16. Run a connection from Height in the Dimensions patch to Initial Value in the Math patch.

17. Run another connection from Resulting Value in the Math patch to Origin Y in the iterator.

Our box disappears. That's all right: we need to use the Inspector to adjust the math we're doing. In Tiger, the patch will automatically have two operations; in Leopard, it will have only one, so add another (Patch Inspector→Settings→Number of Operations).

18. Set Operation #1 to Divide, and Operand #1 to "1".

19. Set Operation #2 to Subtract.

20. Connect the Height Output of the Dimensions patch to Operand #2.

21. Twirl the dial next to Operand #1 clockwise until the box sits on the bottom of the screen; for me, this happens around 1.78.

Now we can resize the viewer into any aspect ratio without losing our Y Positioning.

22. Double-click on the Iterations input of the iterator. Take care to click on the little circle and not the patch itself. You'll see a small text box appear, which will allow you to set the iterations directly, without opening the Inspector (see Figure 9-39).

Figure 9-39.
Changing the numbers of iterations

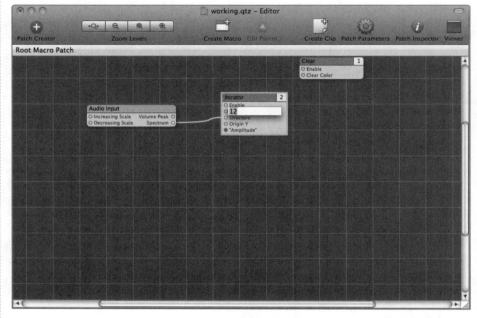

23. Change this number to **12**, and then double-click on the Iterations patch to jump inside.

All 12 boxes are actually on the screen right now, but they are overlapping. They are all there but if you can't see them (this is a visualizer, after all) the functionality is wasted. Let's compress the spread a little so they're all visible.

24. Bring in a Math patch and run Current Index from Iterator Variables to Initial Value on Math.

25. Connect the Resulting Value to Origin X.

We can see a few of the boxes now, but we'll need to adjust the math to have them spread out evenly. No problem, set the Math patch to first Subtract 5.5 from the Initial Value, and then Multiply by 0.16.

Now our boxes are all spread out nicely (see Figure 9-40).

Figure 9-40.
The Math patch spaces the cubes out nicely

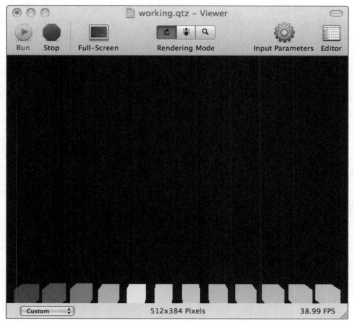

Let's put on a couple of finishing touches: the first one will make the bands easier to differentiate; the second will give a certain level of control over the final animation.

26. Add another Math patch.

27. Connect Index from the Variables patch through the Math patch (via Initial Value) and into the Hue input on the Cube Band.

28. Set the Math patch to Divide the value by 24.

That's a much nicer look, and it's now much easier to distinguish the bands. The last item on our agenda is to publish a control for adjusting the overall amplitude of our animation:

29. Go inside your Cube Band patch.

30. Bring in a Math patch, and place it in the stream between Member and Final Translation Y.

31. Set it to multiply our Initial Value coming from the Member output by 1.

32. Bring in an Input Splitter, set its type to Number, and connect its output to Operand #1.

33. Publish the Input from the Splitter as "Amplitude" by right-clicking, choosing Published Inputs →Input, and then typing over Input with Amplitude.

34. Go up a level in the hierarchy and publish Amplitude again.

35. Go up one more level (back at root now) and publish Amplitude one last time.

Now click on your viewer and press Command-T. You get a drop-down menu with a text field and dial for Amplitude. Spin the dial and watch how it changes. Once you find a nice range you like for Amplitude, perhaps between 0 and 10, dive all the way back down to that Input Splitter to peg the value at the level you found pleasing.

36. Double-click on Iterator, then on Cube Band.

37. Use the Inspector to change its Min and Max values from "NaN" to **0** and **10**, respectively.

38. Press Command-T to hide the Heads Up Display (HUD), and then press it again to show.

Now there's a handy slider next to Amplitude, which you may find much easier to use than the dial.

You've done it! You've built a fully operational graphic visualizer. Save a copy and start messing around with it. Try adding Math patches, changing the colors, perhaps throw the whole visualizer into another Replicate in Space patch! Experimentation is the key to learning Quartz Composer. Twiddle every dial and try using every patch. You're bound to stumble upon beautiful combinations in no time.

— Surya Buchwald

HACK 77: Get More Out of iChat

iChat is fun, useful, and a great way to keep in touch (among many other things). Maximize your iChat experience (or find an alternative) with this interesting guide.

As the Internet has grown in popularity, it has both redefined how people do things and been used to do things people want to do. One of the things people want to do is talk to each other. This is no surprise: we're social animals. It was inevitable that real-time communication would come to the Internet.

iChat is Apple's method of real-time interaction. With iChat, you can carry on a conversation via text, voice, or even engage in a video chat. You can do a lot more than just chat; the moniker is increasingly misleading as capabilities are added to the program. Swapping files, troubleshooting a remote computer, and even administering a Mac over an iChat connection are all possible. With everything you can do over an iChat connection, you'll find yourself using the program frequently. And of course, you'll want to customize such an often-used application with time-saving tips and tricks. This hack will help you customize iChat and get it to do what you want it to do.

Buddy Control

It's your Mac, but when you fire up iChat, all your buddies get to pick their pictures and screen names. Generally this is no problem but if one of your buddies is using an annoying picture or an uninformative handle, you might want to change their picture or handle to something more informative.

iChat lets you do just that. Right-click or command-click on the name of the iChat offender and select Show Info (see Figure 9-41).

Figure 9-41.
Sorry Tanner, I'm making some changes

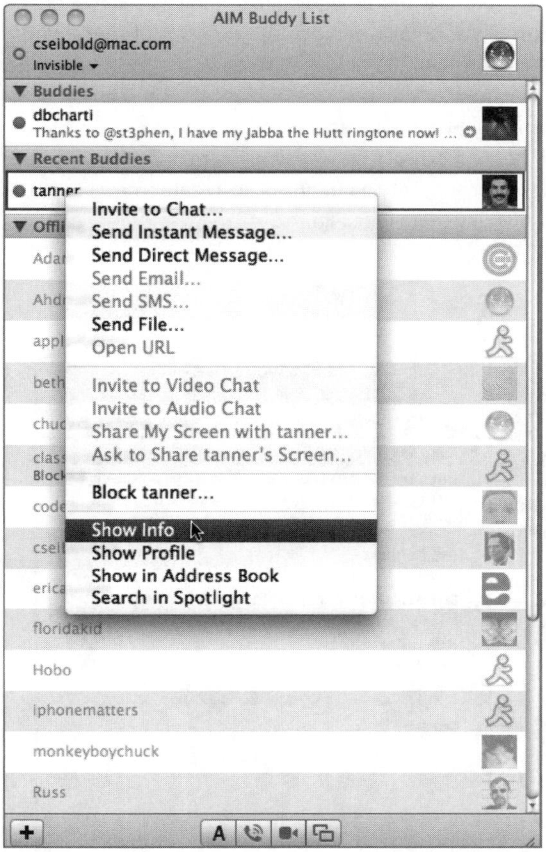

This opens your buddy's address card in which you can change just about everything about them. Annoying nickname? Come up with one of your own. Tired of the picture? Drop in the photo you want to use and check the "Always use this picture" checkbox (see Figure 9-42).

Figure 9-42.
Make your buddies conform to your wishes

You can also control the sounds made when your friend logs in, becomes available, and a variety of other things by clicking the Alerts button. Be careful with this, adding too many noises that are associated with your buddy's moves can result in a decidedly distracting experience if your friends are very active on iChat.

If your buddy's biggest problem is that he won't shut up, the most obvious thing to do is to invoke iChat's almighty Block option. This prevents the blocked user from seeing you're online at all. The method isn't fool-proof; the intrepid iChatter might suspect something is up, create a new screen name, add you to it, and discover that you're ducking them (see Figure 9-43).

Figure 9-43.
Chris Howard has blocked me!

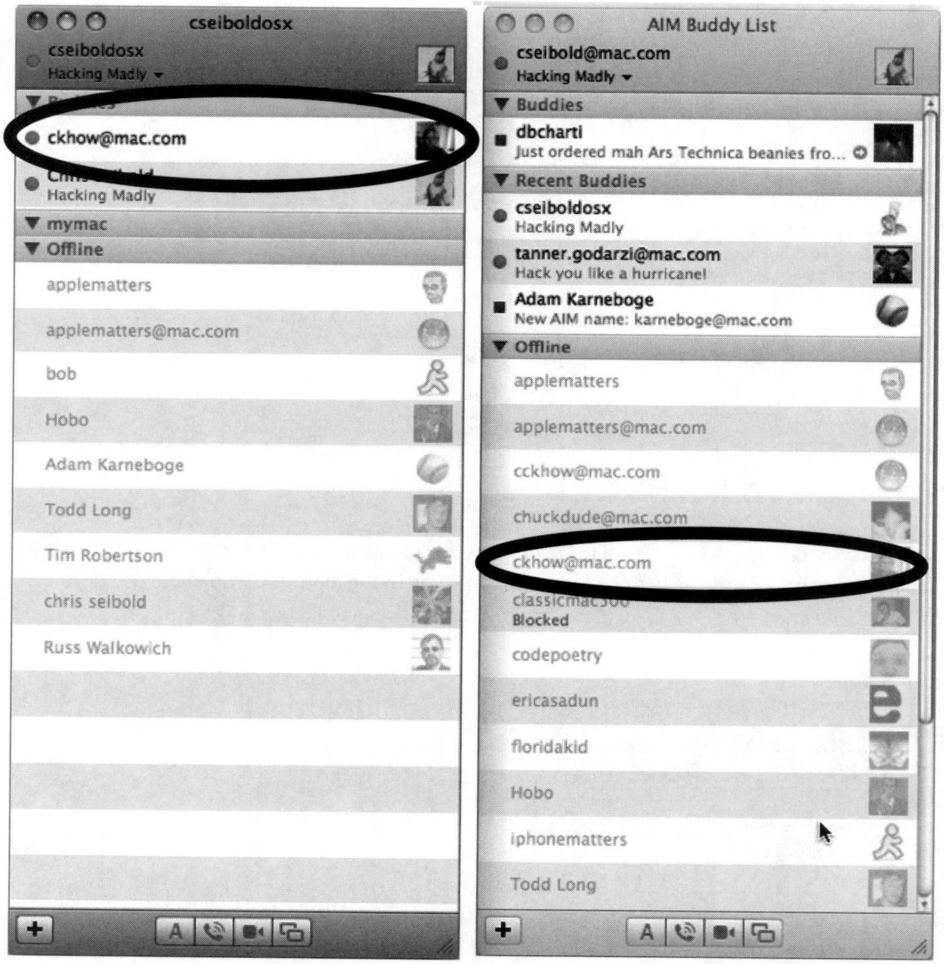

Simply blocking someone is (usually) effective, but it lacks elegance and you never get to waste the time of the overly annoying iChatter. If you want to have a little more fun out of annoying iChatters instead of blocking them, try having them chat to a bot [Hack #78].

Go Invisible or "Don't Call Us, We'll Call You"

One of the niftier features available in iChat 4 is the Invisible feature (see Figure 9-44). Setting your status to Invisible does exactly what you expect: you can see others, but they can't see you. It's a nice feature when you're looking for someone and don't want to be bothered, but the etiquette of going Invisible is questionable. What are you really saying: it's okay for you to ring people up but not vice versa?

Figure 9-44.
Go Invisible and iChat is an outgoing calls-only concern!

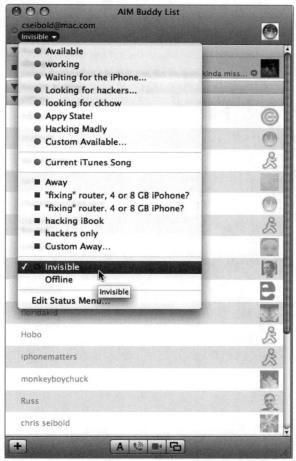

Free .Mac Screen Names for iChat Accounts

All the cool people have iChat accounts that end in mac.com. Actually, that probably isn't true, but if you want a screen name that ends in mac.com, you can get one without shelling out the $99 usually required to get a mac.com screen name. To pull it off, you'll have to sign up for a .Mac trial account. Choose your .Mac email address, and it doubles as your iChat screen name. Sixty days later you'll lose .Mac functionality, but you'll get to keep the .Mac screen name.

Changing Your Own iChat Buddy Picture

iChat pictures are fun to play with, so much so that for many people getting on iChat is just an excuse to show off their latest iChat picture. For those who aren't aware of what kind of fun can be had with iChat pictures, well, you're missing a great part of iChat.

Changing your own picture is easy; just find the picture you want to use and drag said picture on top of whatever picture you're currently using. Once the image is there, iChat will automatically open up a window (assuming the picture is large enough) that will allow you to scale and place the picture in whatever manner you see fit (see Figure 9-45).

Figure 9-45.
Tweaking a buddy picture for iChat

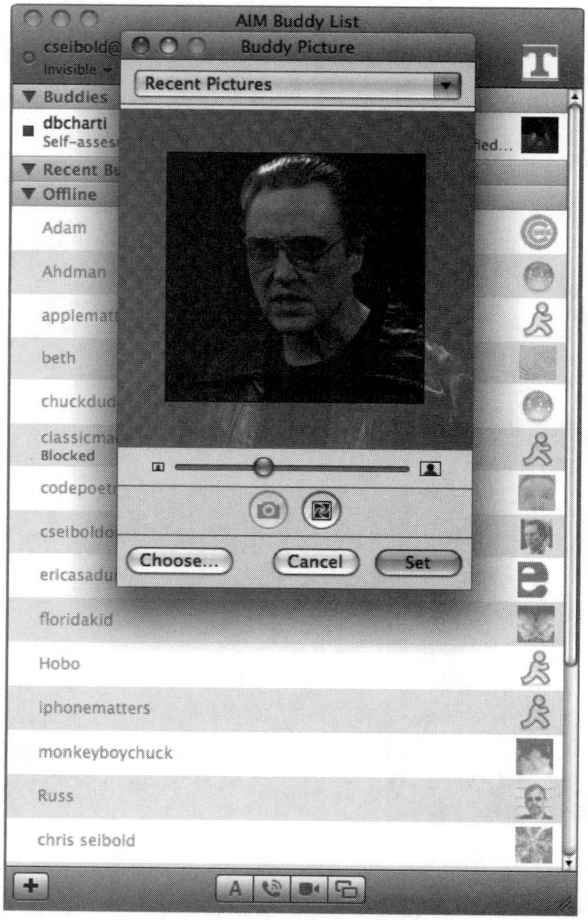

QUICK TIP ✕

IT WORKS IN ADDRESS BOOK TOO!

The OS X Address Book and iChat feature a goodly amount of integration. Any changes you make to your iChat buddies are reflected in your Address Book.

It wouldn't be iChat AV 4 if you couldn't use effects from PhotoBooth on your pictures. Clicking the Pinwheel button brings up a bevy of different effects you can apply to your iChat picture (see Figure 9-46). It must be noted that the usefulness of some of the effects are suspect. iChat buddy pictures are limited to 64 × 64 pixels, so people aren't going to see the effects you apply in any great amount of detail.

Figure 9-46.
Doctoring an iChat buddy picture

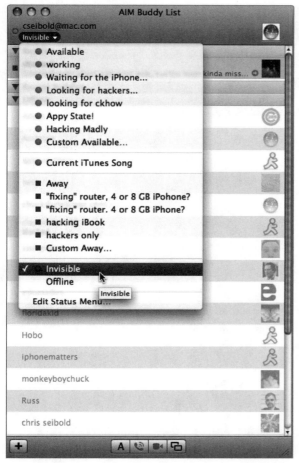

Secure Your Chats

By default, iChat relays all of your chats over a centralized server. The server is an AOL system
if you're using the default configuration of iChat, or a GoogleTalk server if you're using `jabber`.
Because the chats are unencrypted by default, there is a small possibility that someone could read
the chats betwixt you and your friends. If that worries you—if your chats include plans on derailing
Google and/or AOL, for example—you can skip the server part altogether. To avoid the servers, you
want to have the chats go directly from your computer to the person you're talking to. This is an
easy trick to pull off: right-click or Command-click on the person you want to chat with, and select
"Send Direct Message..." (see Figure 9-47).

Figure 9-47.
Skip the mega servers

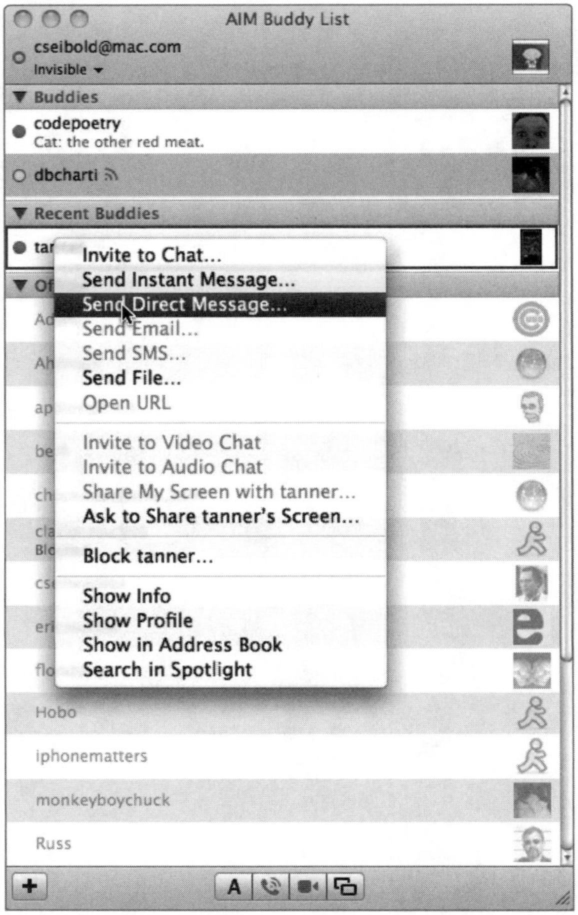

Once a direct message is started, and you force a direct message session by attaching a file to one of your chats (to start a direct session, pick any short file and drop it in the area where you type outgoing IMs), the data won't populate AOL's or Google's servers. Of course, the chat still goes over servers, just not Google's or AOL's servers. Conceivably someone with access to the servers that are used to transmit your data could still read the notes being passed back and forth. Alternatively, if you're IMing folks at a local hotspot, the messages are sent in HTML-formatted text. That guy behind you can intercept your chats electronically if he is determined to discover what you're chatting about. It should also be noted that a truly determined person can read over your shoulder. Threats are everywhere!

What you want is an encrypted chat. When your chats are encrypted, the stream of text, video, audio, and files leaving your computer are unintelligible junk to those who intercept said stream. iChat provides you with just such a tool, accessible by going to iChat→Preferences→Security. Select Enable next to the iChat security status indicator, and your once-clear-as-day chats are encrypted with 128 bit security (see Figure 9-48).

Figure 9-48.
No one will be reading this

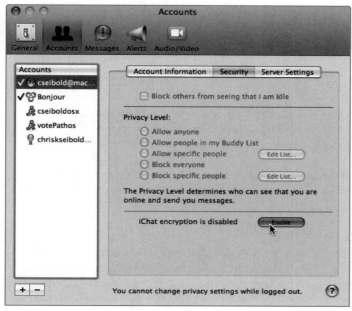

The drawback to enabling iChat encryption is that it only works between two users who have
.Mac accounts. You can tell that a chat is encrypted in two ways: first, you won't get that scrolling
"unencrypted chat" warning across the top of the message window when you start a new chat.
Second, a small lock icon will appear in the upper right corner of the message window. (Incidentally,
encrypted chatting won't work with the trial .Mac account you got earlier in the section "Free
.Mac Screen Names for iChat Accounts"; Apple restricts the encryption feature to paid-up .Mac
accounts.)

Not surprisingly, people who don't have .Mac accounts want private chatting as well. The father
of the year, for example, doesn't want the world listening in as he lovingly describes his brand-
new minivan and how cool it makes him look. What's a non .Mac account holder to do? It isn't
widely advertised but by tweaking the preferences in iChat ever so slightly, all your chats can be
encrypted. Under iChat Preferences (iChat→Preferences...→Accounts), click the Server Settings
button and put a check mark next to Use SSL. The server changes, for example, from login.oscar.
aol.com to slogin.oscar.aol.com, and you're chatting with SSL.

Improve That Video

In the early days of iChat video conferencing a FireWire camera was required. For most people, that
meant an iSight. Sadly, Apple has discontinued the external iSight, but happily iChat now supports
a wide array of USB cameras. The Xbox 360 camera works flawlessly with iChat, for example. So
how can you tell if your USB camera is compatible with iChat? All you have to do is check that your
camera is UVC-compliant (USB Video Class).

QUICK TIP

HOW DO PEOPLE
LISTEN?

You hear a lot about
how insecure chats and
other forms of Internet
communication are
if you don't take the
proper precautions, and
you're likely wondering
just how much trouble
it is to listen on your
iChat. It turns out it is
surprisingly simple.
All that is needed on
the part of a would-be
cracker is a packet-
sniffing program and
a little interest. Packet
sniffers and packet
analyzers (such as
WireShark, available
from http://www.
wireshark.org) have
many legitimate uses,
such as network
diagnostics and
application testing, but
can also be used to
snoop on your network
activity. Such tools
are available for just
about any platform you
can think of, and the
chats are sent in easily
readable text, so using
a Mac is no protection
at all. If you're worried
about people listening
in, secure your chats. On
the other hand, if you're
like me, your chats are
boring enough that you
can tell the crackers by
the way they suddenly
nod off.

The rest of this hack
is about sharing more
than text with iChat.
Unfortunately when
it comes to iChatting,
not all Macs or Internet
service providers are
created equal. To get
the most out of iChat,
you'll need either a Core
Duo 1.83 GHz processor
on Intel-based Macs
or a dual 2 GHz G5 for
Power PC-based Macs.
You'll also need some
pretty heavy bandwidth:
1500 Kbps upstream
and downstream.
Those are requirements
for initiating certain
processor-intensive
chats; requirements
to merely participate
are much lower. You
could commit all
the requirements to
memory so you can plan
who can participate
in the chats, but iChat
gives you an easier
way to know if your
friends can join. Right-
or Command-click on
the buddy in question,
select Buddies→Show
Info, and click Profile.
The capabilities of your
buddy will be revealed
(see Figure 9-49).

Compliance to the USV standard is one thing; a good image is something completely different. Most webcams are cheaply made, and the image quality shows it. The good news is that there is every chance you own an iChat-compatible camera that is leaps and bounds ahead of webcams or even built-in iSights. Examine your shelves and locate your old, never used, dusty digital camcorder. Hook it up to your Mac via a FireWire cable, turn the digital video camera to VCR mode, and presto, you've got an iChat cam that will yield superior video and audio.

The drawback of the video-camera solution is that the digital camcorders tend to be unwieldy. You can stick a webcam just about anywhere, but the bulky camcorder makes getting the thing pointed at your face a bit of a trick. The solution will vary from camcorder to camcorder, but one good option is that super cheap, very-small tripod found in digital camera starter kits or in the digital camera section of the big box stores. While mini tripods are usually just a worthless gizmo to make you realize you need a much bigger tripod for your camcorder, with iChat the situation is a bit different. You're only after a stable base and the ability to point the cam where you want, perfect for using your digital camera as a webcam.

Fix a Remote Computer with iChat

Screen-sharing is a new feature in iChat 4. The feature sounds innocuous; one imagines that it would be a great collaborative tool because both users can see each other's screen at the same time. However, that is not what screen sharing is; rather, it's a one-way deal. The person doing the sharing is more or less turning the other person loose on their Mac. You can see what they're doing; the mouse moves around and such, but if they aren't active, you'll forget they are even there. A momentary lapse is enough for damage to be done, so only try this with people you can trust. What's the quickest way out of screen sharing if something unexpected happens? Quit iChat with the Command-Q key combo. Sure, you'll have to restart iChat, but the possible damage prevented will be worth the small inconvenience.

Figure 9-49.
Can they participate? Now you know

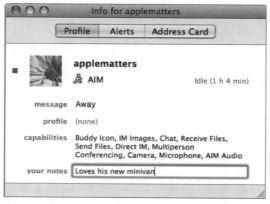

What, exactly, can someone sharing your screen pull off? Anything that doesn't require a password. iChat allows someone to empty your Trash, delete documents, change your bookmarks, and burrow through files. In other words, keep a careful eye on the screen when you allow someone else to share your screen. On the other hand, the access is great when you are trying to fix some else's computer.

HACK 78: Use a Chatbot with iChat

There are a variety of ways to get rid of annoying people on iChat, but they're no fun. Discover a method to keep that chatty friend occupied with this automated response system.

You likely know that you can set up iChat to respond to messages automatically when you are away. People will then know you're away because they get the canned message. With iChat AV 4, you can come up with a far more entertaining alternative.

Why would you want to do such a thing? Obviously, seeing iChat interact with your buddies sans input from you has entertainment value, but the reasons go deeper. If you have someone who constantly wants to chat about nothing of import, you can give him the "I'm chatting with you" feeling he is craving. Or if you're a telecommuter, and your boss is pinging you every so often just to make sure you're online, this hack will make him believe you never leave the computer, even when you're outside playing with your dog.

To pull this hack off, you need to do some minor iChat tweaking, and download a sample AppleScript from Apple and a copy of the Virtual Psychotherapist Eliza. You already have iChat, so the next steps pertain to the other files you'll be using.

Apple is happy to provide sample iChat scripts at http://developer.apple.com/samplecode/ iChatAppleScriptSamples/iChatAppleScriptSamples.zip. So you've got the files for the AppleScript part, but you need the files for the Eliza bit.

No problem, instead of yet another browser trip to yet another URL, you can let the Terminal take care of all the work. Type:

```
$ sudo cpan
```

You'll be prompted to type your password [Hack #5]. You might get some error or configuration messages; just ignore them (type **no** if **cpan** asks you if you want to do a manual configuration, and it will configure itself automatically). Once the initial negotiations are dismissed, you should be left with a prompt that reads **cpan>**. This is normal. At this new prompt, type:

```
cpan> install Chatbot::Eliza
```

Lo and behold, the Terminal will take care of the rest. It will grab the required files off the Internet and install them in the proper destinations on your computer. It is very nifty. The result looks like Figure 9-50.

QUICK TIP ✕

THEY'RE LISTENING

One completely nonobvious thing about screen sharing in OS X is that an audio conversation automatically starts. Presumably, this functionality is there so you can tell the person whose computer you are trying to control to keep their damn hands off the mouse.

The interesting stuff happens when one machine has a microphone and the other doesn't. The conversation is completely one way, and the person sharing audio generally doesn't realize it. If you can imagine a situation in which you are troubleshooting a friend's Mac, and your microphone is turned off. Extend your mind a bit further, and realize that you can hear every word they say and they have no idea.

Figure 9-50.
cpan took care of all the drudgery

With Eliza installed, you can turn your attention to the AppleScript part of the equation. As it turns out, just using the script provided by Apple generates errors, but this is easily remedied. Begin by expanding the Zip file you downloaded earlier, then copy *Chatbot-Eliza.applescript* and *Chatbot-Eliza.pl* to *~/Library/Scripts/iChat*. (If the folder doesn't exist, create it with Command-N.)

Open *Chatbot-Eliza.applescript* with Script Editor (*/Applications/AppleScript/Script Editor.app*). Once you've got the script opened and editable, three parts need to be changed.

First change:

```
set elizaScriptDir to POSIX path of (((path to desktop) as string) & "Chatbot-
Eliza-1.04")
```

To:

```
set elizaScriptDir to null
```

That was easy; now just a few more changes. Cut the block that reads:

```
on received text invitation theMessage from buddy theBuddy for service theService
for chat theChat
        tell theChat
            accept invitation
            post message "Hello! What can I help you with today?"
        end tell
    end received text invitation
```

Replace the lost text with:

```
on received text invitation theMessage from theBuddy for theChat
    tell theChat
        accept
        send "Hello! What can I help you with today?" to theChat
    end tell
end received text invitation
```

One more change to make: cut the block that says:

```
    on message received theMessage from buddy theBuddy for service theService for ¬
chat theChat
        set theResponse to runChatbotEliza(theMessage)
        tell theChat
            post message theResponse
        end tell
    end message received
```

Replace it with:

```
  on message received theMessage from theBuddy for theChat
      set theResponse to runChatbotEliza(theMessage)
      tell theChat
          send theResponse to theChat
      end tell
  end message received
```

Compile, save the script, and you can move on.

Youve tweaked Apple's script and installed Eliza. The only thing left to do is to let iChat in on your nefarious plans. The process is simple:

1. Launch iChat.

2. In the menu bar, choose iChat→Preferences... and click the Alerts tab.

3. Drop down the Event list and choose Message Received.

4. Check the "Run AppleScript" box and choose "Chatbot-Eliza.applescript" from the list.

5. Drop down the Event list and choose Text Invitation.

6. Check the "Run AppleScript" box and choose "Chatbot-Eliza.applescript" from the list.

7. Close the Preferences window.

You've done all the hard work; now when people try to chat with you on iChat, they'll get Eliza's "helpful" responses.

Target a Chatter

If you follow the earlier instructions, a chatbot will start up whenever anyone rings in. It is loads of fun, and you'd be surprised just how long the unsuspecting will talk to Eliza before realizing that they aren't talking to you (personal record: 27 minutes). The setup is somewhat limiting though; either everyone who chats with you talks to the chatbot, or no one does. It would be better if just selected folks ended up talking to Eliza. For example, your boss would get the Eliza bot, while you carry on a chat with the people you want to talk with. You can pull off just such a hack. Head to Buddies→Alerts, change Event to Text Invitation, and check the Run AppleScript box. Choose the Eliza script, and the selected buddies get the Eliza treatment.

Hacking the Hack: Get Chatbots Chatting

Well, you've got the chatbot chatting to real people, but you might be wondering what if two chatbots talked to each other? It is easy to set up if you have more than one iChat account. Just adjust the settings for each to launch the AppleScript you modified earlier. Send a message from one chatbot-enabled account to another and, well, they don't make a lot of sense, but those chatbots don't give up (see Figure 9-51)!

Figure 9-51.
These bots aren't solving any problems but at least they are talking

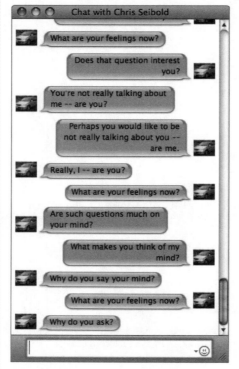

— Matt Swann and Chris Seibold

HACK 79: Quick iPhoto Tips and Tricks

iPhoto 08 is fantastic, but you can make your experience even better with these tips and hints.

iPhoto is Apple's iLife answer to all your photo needs and likely one of the most popular of the iLife programs. Who doesn't love the drop-dead simplicity of plugging your camera in and getting all its photos sucked right onto your Mac?

Sure, iPhoto is great right out of the box, but that doesn't mean you can't make it even better.

Print N-Up Pages

iPhoto 08 gained some excellent functionality, but it also shed one of the printing options people really enjoyed: the ability to print N-up pages. In previous versions of iPhoto, you would select some number of images, and iPhoto automatically sized them to fit on a single page. It was easy, it was convenient, and now it is gone.

The good news is that you can still print your photos in an N-up fashion with just a little extra work. Here's how to pull it off:

1. First select the photos you want to print.
2. Go to File→Print...
3. A new window will open; hit Print.

Don't worry, iPhoto doesn't start printing your photos right away; instead the Print window will appear, presenting scads of printing options. Once you see the Print window, choose Layout from the pop-up menu as shown in Figure 9-52.

Figure 9-52.
Adjusting the printing options

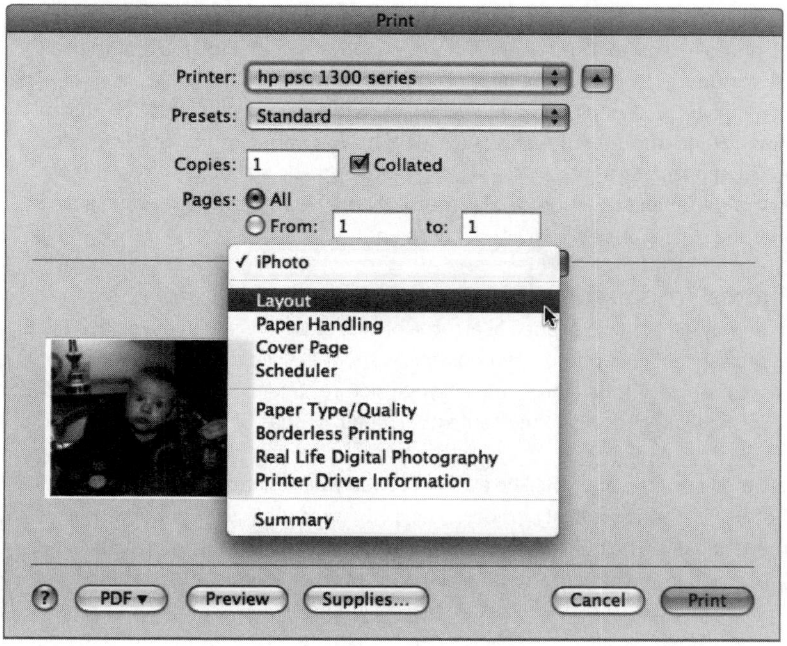

Once you choose layout, the Print window will change substantially. Good news: it is time for the return of N-up printing. Change "Pages Per Sheet" to the number of images you want to print (you are limited in your choices), and choose Single Hairline for the Border option as shown in Figure 9-53, and you're ready to print away.

> **QUICK TIP**
>
> **N-UP AND CONTACT SHEETS AREN'T THE SAME**
>
> If you've never used N-up printing, you're likely wondering what the difference is between N-up printing and iPhoto's built-in contact sheet format. When you're using contact sheets, you specify the number of columns, and iPhoto takes care of the rest. That means your options are limited: choose too many columns, and your photos will be shrunk smaller than you want; not enough columns and you're wasting paper. When you use N-up printing, you specify the number of photos per page. You get more control and less white space than with the contact sheet option. The most popular use of N-up printing is setting four photos per page and using 4 x 6 photo paper. The result is four wallet-sized photos—perfect for those cute snaps of your kid dog or lolcat.

Figure 9-53.
Your iPhoto printing options are back

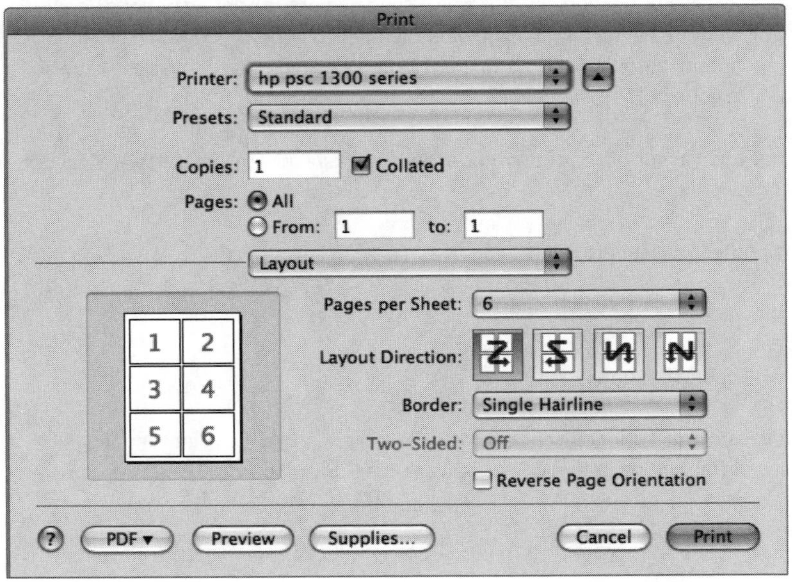

Print to a Given Size

If you want to print a photo to a certain size paper, iPhoto is happy to do that for you, but the program takes the unfortunate step of automatically cropping the image. What you're really looking for is a print-to-file option, and you won't find that in any of iPhoto's myriad of menus. It turns out the option is hidden in a contextual menu. Just select the photo you want to print, hit the Print button, and choose "Customize..." from the resulting page. Once you do so, the photo pops up in iPhoto. Right-click the photo, choose Fit Photo to Frame Size, and you'll get the largest possible print of your photo for the page size selected without cropping.

Get at Those Photos Without iPhoto

iPhoto 08 changed the way iPhoto works. Specifically, the old file structure has been replaced with a package, so direct browsing of your photos isn't possible without a quick hack. To browse your photos directly, navigate to your iPhoto Library (it is in your Pictures folder if you haven't moved it), and right-click (or Control-click) to bring up the contextual menu; choose Show Package Contents.

A new Finder window then appears, and you'll be able to browse your iPhoto library without being encumbered by iPhoto. This method is a bit cumbersome if you want to access your photos in this manner on a frequent basis. The quick workaround is to create an alias of the Originals folder (right-click the Originals folder and choose Create Alias) and put it somewhere easy to get at, such as your Desktop or Pictures folder. Once the alias is in place, any time you want to access your original photos, they are just a few clicks away. Be warned though, this is a one-way street; do not attempt to add photos to your library through the folder alias.

HACK 80: Tips for Pics

As great as iPhoto is, it won't help you take decent pictures. Turns out that getting great-looking shots isn't that difficult; learn the basic tips of taking great snaps and how much camera you need from professional underwater photographer Eric Cheng.

Although the art of photography has infinite layers of complexity, there are a few tricks that can almost guarantee great-looking images. Aside from instinct and artistic talent, there are really only a few things to keep in mind. Here are a few:

Focus

Learn how to use your camera's focus lock function. For most cameras, this is accomplished by holding the shutter button down half way, which forces your camera to choose a focus point and stay there. By using this technique, you will be able acquire a focus on your chosen subject while reframing for a more pleasing composition.

Composition

Perhaps the most important trait of a good image is an aesthetically pleasing composition. Try not to just place the center of your frame on your subject's head and click away. The Rule of Thirds is a good guideline (see Figure 9-54). This says that if you divide up your frame into thirds both vertically and horizontally, you should place the most interesting elements in your photo at the intersection points of the dividing lines. Try to place eyes, heads, and horizon lines along dividing lines and their intersection points.

Figure 9-54.
The author and a friend. Eyes and mouths are arranged along dividing lines according to the Rule of Thirds.

Exposure

Modern cameras are pretty good at choosing good exposures but still tend to fail in extreme situations. Remember that your camera chooses its exposure by averaging the brightness of the entire scene and setting the shutter speed and aperture so that the resulting image is gray (a middle brightness).

When shooting something very white that fills the frame (such as snow or a bride's wedding dress), set your camera to overexpose. Otherwise, the camera will expose so the subject becomes gray, and everything will be too dark.

Conversely, if you're shooting a very dark scene (like a groom's tuxedo), you have to underexpose so the camera won't make everything too bright.

How Much Camera Do You Need?

There's no question that there's a digital camera arms race going on out there. Unfortunately, we, as consumers, are caught right in the middle; with so many camera models out there, it can be difficult to choose a camera.

At the moment, low-end digital cameras are using 4-megapixel sensors, while high-end point-and-shoot cameras are capturing upwards of 12 megapixels. On the SLR front, the newest cameras have sensors that record a staggering 21 megapixels. But how many pixels is enough for a decent print?

As a general rule, making a print from an image that contains 200 pixels per inch (PPI) will yield excellent results. At 200 PPI, an 8 × 10 inch print requires 1600 × 2000 pixels, or exactly 3 megapixels. However, you don't need to print at 200 PPI to get a print that looks pretty good. Even a well-exposed, sharp, 2-megapixel image can yield a decent 8 × 10 inch print (see Figure 9-55).

Figure 9-55.
Choose the resolution of your camera wisely.

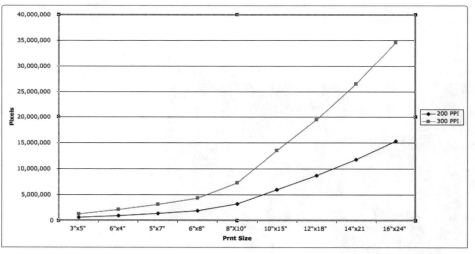

So why buy a 12-megapixel camera when 2 megapixels is enough? There are quite a few reasons, but here are my three favorites:

- Having more pixels gives you insurance. If you didn't quite get close enough to your subject, you can crop the image and still have enough pixels for a large print. Also, having more pixels gives you room to print that image you didn't quite nail. When reducing a 12-megapixel image down to 4 megapixels, the slight blur at full resolution might come out looking sharp after all.

- A 12-megapixel camera produces an image that can be printed natively at 20 inches at 200 PPI. A well-exposed, sharp image should be able to produce a good-looking 30-inch poster!

- Storage is cheap these days, so it doesn't hurt to capture the best image possible. And if you happen to capture a spectacular image instead of the snapshot you were planning on getting, you'll be glad you had the extra pixels so you can blow up that image as a full-sized poster.

Now that you have the knowledge to get great-looking pictures and know what equipment you need to get the job done, get out there and start snapping!

— Eric Cheng

HACK 81: Get More Out of iWeb

You want a beautiful web site, and you want an easy web site—the answer is iWeb. It isn't as easy as Steve Jobs promised, but it is as beautiful. Maximize your iWeb experience with this hack.

The latest version of iLife (as of September 2007) is iLife 08. If you have created sites using iWeb from iLife 06, be very careful. While Apple has updated iWeb 2, it still doesn't always play nice with sites created by its predecessor. If you're going to open a previous iWeb project in iWeb 2, make a backup copy of the Domain file first. See the section "Starting Off with iWeb," which tells you where the file is and an easy way to copy it.

iWeb is Apple's easy-to-use web site-creation software and as such, it's remarkably simple to use—as long as it's done Apple's way. Apple's way entails the use of nothing but their web-page templates with your content uploaded to your .Mac account. Using it this way ensures that all the incredibly uncomplicated features work exactly like Apple told you they would, but nothing screams "I'm an iWeb template, and the person who made me can't do much of anything else for site creation" more than, well, using it in this way. You can make some pretty interesting sites with it, but it takes more work than just dragging and dropping pictures from your iPhoto library.

Apple's iWeb isn't alone among easy-to-use Macintosh web site-creation software packages. Others include Goldfish from Fishbeam Software, RapidWeaver from Realmac Software, Freeway Express and Pro from Softpress Software, and SandVox from Karelia Software.

What these programs have in common are ease of use, WYSIWYG editing, and power. They each take a different approach to creating web pages and sites. This doesn't make one or the other better or worse, just different. In almost every case, each publisher offers a free trial version with either limited features, saving options, or a time limitation that will allow you to evaluate their software. Just because Apple includes iWeb with the purchase of a new Macintosh computer does not mean that it would be the best fit for the way you work. Take the time to visit the home pages of each program and take it for a spin.

So, assuming you've read this far, you want to make a web site, and you want it to be easy. You also don't want it to look like everyone else's web site, so you want the ability to make some basic changes in the program's templates to make yours unique. Either iWeb or one of the others will fit the bill, but which one you choose depends entirely on how you want your web site to function.

An Aerial View of iWeb

You know what iWeb is: web site-creation software. But knowing what a program is designed to do is different than knowing how the program will do it. When you're using iWeb, you're engaging a program that allows you to do a lot of things visually that would be difficult to code by hand, and it

---

allows you to do this without resorting to some high-end editor. In short, with iWeb, you can create visually stunning sites without knowing a lick of HyperText Markup Language (HTML) or a smidgen about Cascading Style Sheets (CSS)—to name a few acronyms you'll never need to understand.

You will want to know a few things about publishing your sites. You can create all the pages you want, but iWeb won't generate the necessary files until the page is published. That is great, nothing taking up extra space on your Mac; but that won't do you any good if you want other people to see your stuff. To get the files needed (iWeb generates XML files, JavaScript files, HTML files, and appropriate media files), you have to publish the site. Until that happens, your pages exist only in iWeb.

The easiest way to publish a page or complete site created with iWeb is to use .Mac. The integration provided by .Mac means that setting up hit counters, comments, and such, are easy. In fact, all it takes is a click on the Publish button found on the lower left corner of the iWeb window. That doesn't mean you can't use iWeb without .Mac. You can let your Mac serve up your web page **[Hack #11]**, or you can go with a third-party host. To publish your site on your Mac or with another host, choose File→Publish to Folder. This results in a folder with all the needed files including the media you included (if you've got a big image gallery, the process can take some time) in a host-friendly hierarchy (see Figure 9-56).

Figure 9-56.
Publishing to a folder

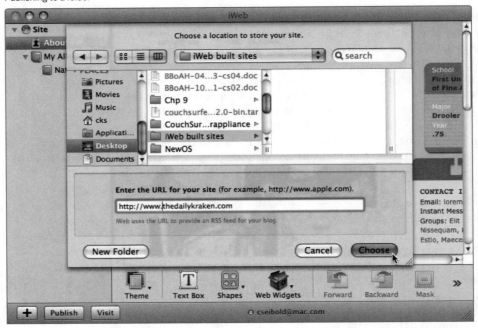

Once the your site is published to a folder, uploading the folder and all the files in it to your web host results in an iWeb generated page on a non-Mac host that works as you would expect.

Starting Off with iWeb
Creating a new site in iWeb is simplicity itself. Start the program. If you haven't played with it before, you'll be presented with a screen that will ask you to select a template (see Figure 9-57).

Figure 9-57.
The default templates page

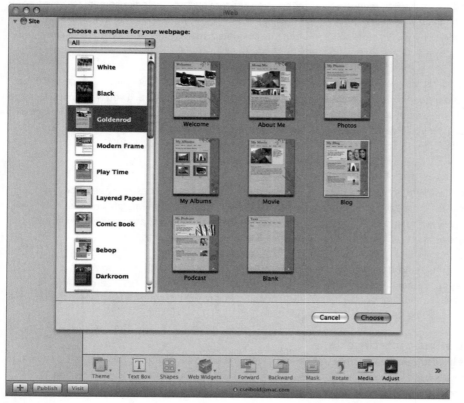

If you have played around with iWeb before, the site you started in your last session will show up. As long as you don't care if your previous work will be blown away, you can select the name of the site in the sidebar on the left and hit your Delete key. Poof! It's gone, and the iWeb templates will show up in a separate window.

You may however want to keep your previous site. This gets a little trickier. You can, of course, always just go to the File menu and select New Site. This allows you to create a new site, but your previous site will also be uploaded to .Mac when you publish it.

Backing Up an Existing Site

If you don't want to discard the work you've done on the previous site, but you also don't want to publish it automatically, you can back up your existing site and move it out of the way. You'll need to move the Domain file in your user library. This file is where iWeb keeps all the information about a site you're about to create.

To get to your Domain file, here is what you do. First, quit the iWeb application and then follow this path in the Finder: */Users/user name/Library/Application Support/iWeb*. Inside this folder is your Domain file for your previous site. Make a new folder within this folder. Call it whatever you want (preferably something descriptive like the site name) and drop the Domain file into it. If you wish, make another folder at the same time with the new site name. It's not a bad idea to make duplicates of your Domain files and keep them in these folders as a backup.

To make a copy, select the Domain file, right-click it, and select the Duplicate command (or do the same through the Edit menu). Store it either in the folder you just created or someplace safe from harm. Nothing will make you sound more like a pirate (argh!) than discovering that your Domain file with everything you've done so far has become corrupted, making it impossible to recover all your hard work.

After either saving your existing Domain file to another folder or trashing it, when you restart iWeb, the template window will appear as if you never had created a site before. If you want to work on the site you moved out of the way, follow the same instructions as above, move the current Domain file to the folder you created just for this purpose, and move the Domain file you now want to work on out of its folder. Restarting iWeb will now choose the file you moved.

Templates and Themes

When you are first creating a web page, or an entire site, you get to choose between a bevy of templates. Under each theme in the sidebar there are some standard template choices. The templates are designed with a particular kind of page in mind, a movie, an image gallery, etc. If none of those templates fit your style, go with blank and customize away.

On the other hand, if the look of a particular iWeb theme is good for you, then go with it and just create your content. Keep in mind that many other people are using the exact same theme, so you'll get no points for originality, but if you're just trying to post images for friends and family, are they really going to care how original the site looks?

iWeb's Basic Interface

Apple likes to create software with as many onscreen buttons as possible. This makes it easy to find commonly used functions and speeds up the workflow. The iWeb interface is no exception. While there are certainly many things you'll need to do via the menu bar commands (or through keyboard shortcuts), you'll find that most of the time you'll be using the various icons or onscreen windows to accomplish your tasks.

The one you'll use most often will be the Inspector (see the section "Inspecting the Inspector (Expect the Unexpected)"), but a systematic approach is more useful. I start with the icon at the lower left of the iWeb window and move right. Each icon is useful; they either add some functionality or allow for easy insertion for common elements on to your web page.

Themes

You've seen them from when you first start up iWeb, but just in case you didn't read the first part of this hack, here it is again. The first button all the way over to the right at the bottom is Themes (see Figure 9-58).

Figure 9-58.
Your gateway to Apple-supplied themes

You can select a different theme (from iWeb's 26 or so choices) for the page that is currently displayed. How it will look depends on the type of page in question, but keep in mind that this doesn't change any of your other pages. If you've created more than a single page, you'll need to go to each page in turn and select the new theme to make them consistent. You could naturally choose a different theme for every page on your site, but please don't! If you go this route, don't send me a link because my eyesight is bad enough already. Your best bet is to choose a theme before you start or accept that changing your mind later will have consequences.

Text Box

This button puts a text box on your currently viewed page. Once it's there, move it to where you want your soon-to-be-created beautiful prose/insightful commentary to go. What? You expected some long-winded explanation?

Shapes

Another easy one: want a shape like an arrow or square amongst others? Here's where they are. Select one and move it where it's needed. Once there, resize the shape with the handles. It doesn't get any easier than that.

Web Widgets

Web Widgets are all new for iWeb 2. Prior to adding Web Widgets, the only way to add things like Google Ads or YouTube videos was to do it through third-party software that you had to run every time you updated the page. Major pain now removed.

At first glance your choices might seem somewhat limited, but the add-ins are very powerful and will accept just about anything you can throw at it. Some are prebuilt for you such as Google Ad-Sense advertisements (that can actually make you some money for every time you con ...uh, trick ... err *convince* a visitor to click-through your links). You do have to set it up through Google, but it's not very difficult.

Speaking of Google, you can also add Google Maps to your site. Adding a Google Map is as easy as specifying the map (you know, like where in the world you want to show) in the address field of the Google Map widget (see Figure 9-59). iWeb will even give you a live preview so you know just what it's going to look like before posting.

Figure 9-59.
Adding a Google Map

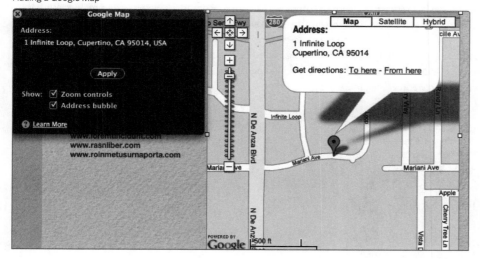

Getting away from the Google lovefest for a moment, iWeb also lets you add embedded HTML code into a box Apple calls a Web Snippet. Ever see those little weather widgets that some people have on their pages? Now you can tell the world just how crappy the weather is on your page too! Doesn't thrill you? No problem, there's code available from many of the currently popular sites such as digg, FaceBook, MySpace, and Twitter (see Figure 9-60); the list goes on and on. You can also add your own HTML code here, if you know how.

Figure 9-60.
Let the world see your Twitter feed.

The last bit you can do from Web Widgets is the .Mac Web Gallery. If you've published iPhoto events or smart folders to your .Mac account, you can easily add them to an iWeb page. Because iWeb is tied to your .Mac account, it already knows about any photo galleries you've created. If you go to the Web Widgets icon, check the .Mac Web Gallery part of the drop-down menu, and any galleries you've published will show up in the submenu. Don't have a .Mac account and/or any galleries? Then that part of the Web Widgets will be grayed out.

One step forward, two steps back

Since every element in an iWeb page is essentially text and graphic boxes, it's easy to cover one with another. Many times you may have different layers of graphics or text purposely on top of each other. In order to change the order or just bring out a layer hidden behind another, select the one that needs to move forward or backwards and use the (what else?) Forward or Backward button.

Unmask

The Unmask button is another one those "Gee, what can we call this?" Apple moments.

In my opinion, it doesn't actually unmask anything. Instead it brings up the Edit Mask function that works for almost every type of image other than those presented via galleries and movies. With the mask window selected, you can crop out certain sections of an image that aren't needed, or expand an image or part of an image to fill a given dimension area to the size you wish. Keep in mind that this function can do only square or rectangular edits. If you have an oddly shaped image you want to resize or edit, you're better off using a real image editor to do so. Unmask works well for easy, or quick and dirty edits (see Figure 9-61).

Figure 9-61.
Quickly editing a picture, zoom or crop

Sit on it and...

The Rotate button allows to you to quickly rotate almost any object 90 degrees at a time—clockwise, naturally. Holding down the Alt/Option key rotates the same objects counter-clockwise. Movies and .Mac galleries will not rotate.

Media

The Media button brings up audio, movies, and pictures from the default locations of iTunes and iPhoto (or wherever you have designated them to be in each program's Preferences). Keep in mind that both iPhoto and iTunes can store and display movies from their default folders, and that iTunes and GarageBand have default folders for audio. One weakness of iWeb is that you can't designate different folders to pull content from outside those pesky default folders of the other iLife applications (together the entire suite is often referred to as the *iApps*). Fortunately, from the Finder, you can just drag and drop from almost any graphic or audio element, and iWeb will do something with it. Maybe not what you intended for it to do, but chances are it will be available for you to use.

Adjust

Ever play with the some of the possible adjustments to your pictures within the iPhoto edit window? If you have, then you know exactly what iWeb's Adjust window looks like.

This only works for individual pictures, not movies or frames with multiple images in them. How to access this magic window of photo editing? Just hit the Adjust button.

The Inspector

By an amazing coincidence (or maybe not so amazing since I knew I would write this), the Inspector is going to play a huge part in the next part of this hack. I'm not going to say too much about it now except to say that iWeb would be almost impossible to use without the Inspector (see the section "Inspecting the Inspector (Expect the Unexpected)").

And the rest...

The last two buttons you can kind of put in the "Sure is nice to have, but I probably wouldn't miss them if they weren't there" category: Colors and Fonts. The Colors button brings up the Apple color-selection window that we've all seen before in various other programs, and the Font menu does much the same. These are convenient ways to select the pertinent function, but you can just as easily do so through the View menu. Various parts of the Inspector will also bring up these windows automatically.

I've described in detail most of the onscreen icons and separate windows that are available in iWeb 08 with one major exception: the Inspector window. There's so much functionality packed into that one box that it deserves its own section!

Inspecting the Inspector (Expect the Unexpected)

One part of iWeb that you'll get to know very well is the Inspector window; it is responsible for all behind-the-scene changes. iWeb relies on this window and its subwindows for almost everything you need to do beyond dragging and dropping graphics and text boxes. A bit about the Inspector: please note that the Inspector I'm talking about is the one for iWeb 2 (part of the aforementioned iLife 08), which added a few tricks not available in iWeb 1.

The Inspector window has several tabs on it, each of which performs various tasks. You can bring it up (if it isn't already there) using a menu command (View→Show Inspector) or by hitting the Inspector icon at the bottom of your site window.

Site tab: Site and Password

The first tab is the Site tab (see Figure 9-62). It has two buttons on it; Site and Password. Under the Site button, you can name (or rename) your site, publish your site to a group, enter your email address, and see how much room is left in your .Mac iDisk account.

Figure 9-62.
Name your site!

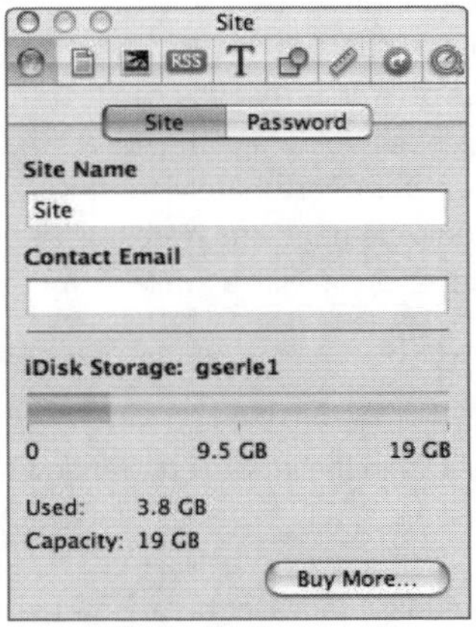

The Password button allows you to make your site private by adding one (and only one) name and password for access. iWeb will suggest that you don't use your .Mac password, and this a *good* idea. Once you create a password, you'll be giving it to people so they can access your site. If you use your .Mac password, well, clever people who can guess your .Mac name (not that hard) will be able to access a whole lot more than your web site. The two most important parts here are your site name and your email address. Your site name is what is listed when you upload it to your .Mac account or publish the site to a folder. Your email address is used if you employ the Send Email icon anywhere on your site. You can naturally use whatever icon or text that you wish and have it link to the email address (or addresses) of your choice, but using the iWeb email icon makes it very simple, and it's one less thing to think about.

Page tab

The second tab is the Page tab. Like the Site tab, it has two buttons: they are labeled Page and Layout. The Page button has a field to name each page in your site and whether or not you want it show up in iWeb's default navigation bar. If you're making your own navigation window (see the "Site navigation" section), uncheck it for each page.

Under the Layout button, you can determine the width and height of the page along with the height for your header and footer. Using Layout, you can also select a background color for the page (including gradients which can look pretty cool) or choose an image (see Figure 9-63). Choosing a color will bring up a different window with several different options for choosing colors. While you can choose between millions of different shades, the best bet is to select the simple crayons or web-safe color icon at the top. Choosing an image gives you several other options, including tiling (if the graphic doesn't fill the page, it will be repeated until it does) or stretching (it distorts the image, which can have its own pluses or minuses). Remember that iWeb does not make any changes to the image itself, so you may want to open it in a graphics program to reduce its opacity and more easily allow the rest of your content to show up without distractions. The last option here is the

Browser background color; it adds whatever color you choose to any overlap in size between the pages you've created and the actual browser window as selected by whoever is viewing your site.

Figure 9-63.
Size your page, set your background

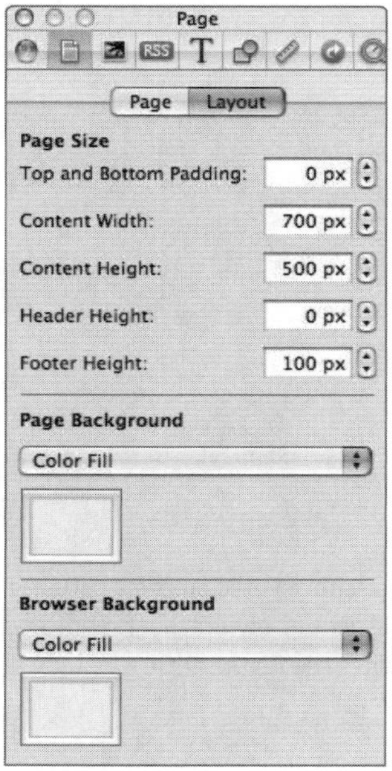

Photos tab

The Photos tab also has two buttons: Photos and Sideshow. The Photos button allows you to select your photo file size...kinda. The only real choice you have is a range of a few, Apple-chosen sizes, from "small" (allowing for faster downloads with some degradation of picture quality) up to and including full size.

The Photos tab is also the first place where you run into Apple's way of allowing others to be notified when you've made changes on your photo pages. This facility allows people to subscribe to your site with Real Simple Syndication (RSS). If you enable the syndication (iWeb will ask), a small icon is put on your photo pages that a subscriber can click. When new stuff appears on the site, the subscriber will be notified in her browser bookmarks. Maybe. If the person who wants to subscribe uses a Mac, then it's no real problem. The two most popular browsers for the Mac (Firefox and Safari) both support RSS and will drop a notice to you the next time you use them. Windows users who prefer Firefox should also have little to no problems either. Internet Explorer users might have problems using the stock version of IE before Version 7; they will need a dedicated RSS reader to keep up with your site. So when you're harangued at the next family reunion, tell the complainers to switch browsers!

Back on topic, this tab is also where you allow or disallow comments from others on your pictures of, say, your Aunt Betty at the last family reunion (or whatever). The comments do not show up on Photo or Album pages, but they will appear to the user when individual pictures are selected. This feature seems a little weak to me and not particularly well thought out. You can also allow attachments (perhaps other people posting pictures of their own on your site), but this makes me nervous, and I'm not going to allow it until I get it a bit more figured out on the security end of it. Both the Photos and Albums iWeb pages use these settings (see Figure 9-64).

Figure 9-64.
Spice your page up with pics

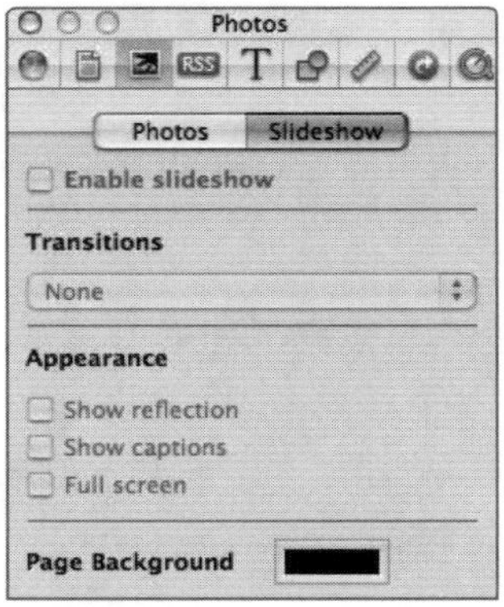

With the Slideshow button, if you hit the checkbox labeled Enable Slideshow, you'll create a slide show of selected photos. You can then determine what transitions will occur between each photo when visitors to your site hit the Play Slideshow icon on any photo page (see Figure 9-64).

Figure 9-65.
Choose your transition

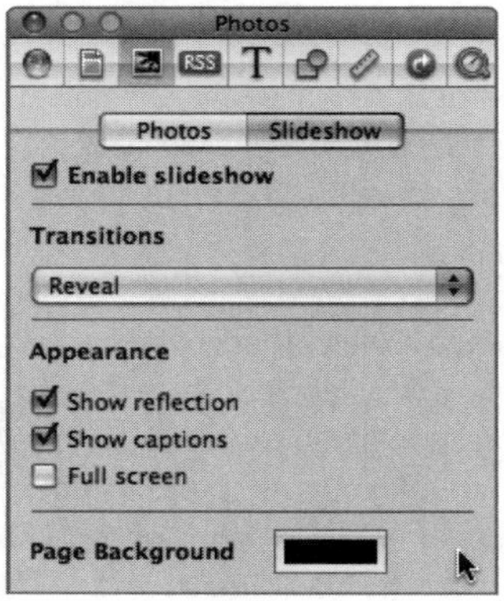

If you have played around with iMovie, you've seen these transitions before. Which one you choose is a matter of taste. Unfortunately, you can't determine how long each image will be onscreen before the next picture blasts its way into the foreground; you're basically stuck with what iWeb deems a sensible choice. Other selections here include Show Reflection (a slightly faded mirror image of the photo), Show Captions (your titles for each image), and Full Screen (whether or not you want your images to show in...um...full screen).

Blog and Podcast tab
The fourth tab controls some of your RSS settings. (As mentioned earlier, RSS is a scheme for getting changes to your web site delivered to subscribing users as they happen.)

If you look at the default Blog and Podcast pages (these pages are accessed by choosing New under the file menu), they are remarkably similar. Each has a Main page, an Excerpts (or posts) page, and an Archive page. I'll go into more detail later, but here is a brief description of these three pages. The Main page is where you can give a description of what the viewer will typically find in your blogs or podcasts; it's also where iWeb puts the RSS badge for your content (see Figure 9-66). The Excerpts page is where you'll actually create your content, and the Archives page is where someone can go to look at all your past submissions.

Figure 9-66.
Set your RSS preferences

You're still in the Inspector and you have two buttons to choose from yet again. Here, the Blog button (which also works the same for podcasts) has settings for how many excerpts you want to show and how long they will be on the opening or main page for your blogs or podcasts (the default being 5). Also here, you can decide whether or not to allow comments or attachments, and whether or not to display a Search field. The Search field isn't a connection back to the Web for Google; it only searches your site. The Podcast button allows you to enter the name (typically your own) of the podcast series creator, a contact email, and whether or not you want to set an overall parental advisory for your podcasts. This dialog also asks you if you want to be able to post your podcasts in the iTunes store (.Mac only). Each podcast created can be attributed to an "Artist" and have a parental advisory of its own.

Text tab

Next on the Inspector hit parade is the Text icon. It should probably come as no surprise that this tab is mostly for dealing with the written word as created for your site, though it does do a few other things as well. All text created for an iWeb site must be within a text box. How that text in those boxes looks is determined here. You can change some other things about the box itself elsewhere. Don't worry, we'll get to it later. (Tired of me saying that yet?) Breaking all the rules so far, this part of the Inspector has not two, but three buttons.

The first button is simply labeled Text. From here you can change the color of the text itself; if you want it aligned on the left, center or right; and what color (if any) you want the background to be. The controls for spacing your text are also here along with what kind of margins you want to choose (see Figure 9-67). These are a matter of taste, so when you start to actually create your site, play with them to your heart's content.

Figure 9-67.
Control your text fields

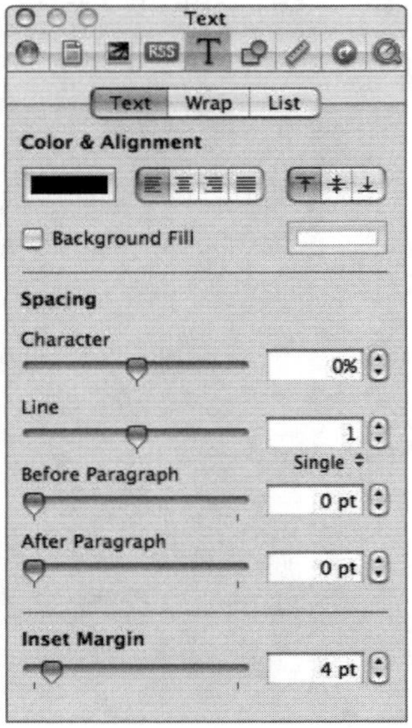

The Wrap button lets you insert a graphic into a text box. It also lets you decide if you want the text within the box to flow to the left or the right of this graphic, and how many spaces there will be between the graphic and your text (see Figure 9-68).

Figure 9-68.
Wrap text around images!

If you're a big fan of creating lists, you will love this last button: List. Here you can choose what kind of bullets or numbering you want, or even select a different graphic of your own. Align the bullets and resize them however you desire and even scale it. The bullet and text indent controls are here as well.

Graphic tab

The Graphic tab is a personal favorite (see Figure 9-69). It's a bit misleading as far as the title goes because the functions here work with more than just graphics, but text as well. So, as I'm explaining these, don't just see them in relation to pictures, but individual words and text boxes as well. This increases the number of effects you can easily do in iWeb. OK, no more cheerleading; let's talk about what it does.

Figure 9-69.
The Graphic tab offers a lot of control

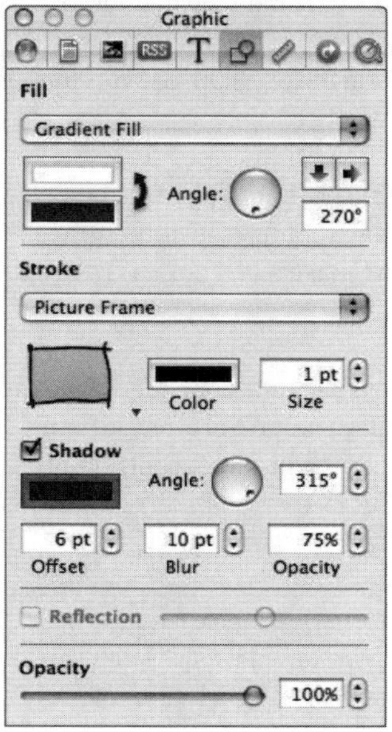

The top uppermost section has your Fill functions. Solid colors, gradients, and a few other tricks live here. Change their orientation by 90 degrees with a push in either direction or use the Angle spin wheel for a little more control. Keep in mind that the spin wheel doesn't change the orientation of the box, just the direction in which the colors fade into one another.

The next section for unknown reason is called "Stroke." I guess calling it Frame wasn't sexy enough for Apple. No matter: adding a frame to a text, picture, or graphic box is what Stroke is designed for. Choose from a few different types; change the color of the frame and even its pixel size from right here.

The Shadow section does what you might expect; it adds a drop shadow behind whatever type of box you might have on your page. Change the color, the angle of the shadow, its offset, blur, and opacity all with a few clicks. For images, you can also add a cool, slick looking reflection by checking the box next to the Reflection slider.

The last slider is a control for the overall opacity of the selected object which explains why it is named Opacity. Maybe you want the image or text dimmed to allow for something else to shine on top of it: dim it here. Maybe you want something transparent to sit on top of another work of art: fade it here.

Metrics tab
At first glance, the Metrics tab might not seem all that big a deal. It doesn't have multiple buttons and has very few options when compared to the other selections in the Inspector. But Metrics is where you can fine-tune almost every section of each page in iWeb. If some text or graphics object gets lost behind some other object, this is where you can start moving things around to find those items and put everything back to where it started. Don't worry, we'll get more on that bit when we get into making pages.

The first part of this section is a text box called File Info that tells you the filename of the object you're manipulating. It looks as though you could change the file name to something memorable, but you can't actually change the name of the file (which makes little sense because iWeb saves every graphic in the Domain file kept in its Library so you're not altering the original), but you can view it.

In the next part down (labeled appropriately "Size"), you can adjust the physical size of the graphic or text box and, in the case of pictures or graphics, decide whether you want to keep both the width and height in the same proportion. Keep in mind as well that you can't make a text box smaller than the size required to display the text within it.

The third part of this box is the Position section. Use this to position an item on your page. It's not a bad idea if you start moving stuff around with the intent to move it back later to note the file name and position as labeled here; it's a snap to revert back simply by reentering these numbers. Apple labeled these position markers as X and Y. Changing the X number moves them left and right, and Y moves them up and down.

The last part of the Metrics tab is called Rotate. Almost any object in iWeb with the exception of some of the template's default graphics (this can change in almost every template so I won't list them here) can be made to flip through a full 360 degrees (embedded text in a graphic will flip as well, so be careful) or angled using the spin-wheel or with exacting degree in the angle box (see Figure 9-70).

Figure 9-70.
Fine tuning for your web page

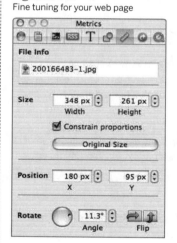

Link tab

OK, take a deep breath; we're almost through with talking about the Inspector. Just two more icons to go, but they are very important when creating an iWeb site. The first one, Link, is where, as you might imagine, you create hyperlinks not only to other pages in your site, but to the whole Web itself. If there is some content you need that isn't on your site, Link allows you to select a word or graphic to create a link to that other page. The original version of iWeb in iLife 06 allowed you to do this as well, but iWeb 2 takes it to a whole new level of customization. You'll spend a lot of time here if you create your own navigation links instead of using iWeb template's default navigation bar.

This icon has two buttons: Hyperlink and (new to iWeb 2) Format.

Hyperlink

Creating a link couldn't be simpler. Select a graphic, text box, word, or line of text you want to use for a link. Begin the process of making the link by clicking on the "Enable as a hyperlink" checkbox. There's a drop-down menu labeled "Link to" that is enabled when you select the checkbox. Use it to select whether you want the link to go to one of your pages, a page somewhere on the Internet, an email link, or a file. Once you make the selection, stuff happens; what kind of stuff depends on the kind of link you make, or where you want the link to go to. Let's go over them quickly one by one. More details will be in future sections as we get more into the meat and potatoes of making an iWeb site.

If you want the link to go to one of your other iWeb pages (when you choose the "One of my pages" from the "Link to" drop-down menu), the second drop-down menu labeled Page will have a listing of all the pages you've created so far for this site. Select the appropriate one, and the hyperlink is automatically created.

If you want a link to go to another page somewhere on the Internet (and have selected "An External Page" from the "Link to" drop-down menu), a text box will appear in which you will enter the Internet address. It is important that you have the exact address of the page or site that you want to go to. Some browsers handle links differently than others, so neatness counts. The easiest way to do this is to open a browser window and go to the site or page you want to link to. Usually (unfortunately not always though) you can copy the address by selecting the entire thing via the URL window near the top of the browser. Go to the edit menu (or right-click/Ctrl-click) and copy the address. When you go back to iWeb and select "An External Page" from the drop down menu, iWeb will put the copied address right into the window for you. How freaking cool is that?

Next is an email link: this is usually your own email address, though you can choose whatever (or whoever's) email address you wish. Just select from the "Link to" drop-down menu "email," and a text window opens. Type just the email address (example: youraddress@mac.com), and you're done. iWeb does everything else including whatever call-ups are required to open the viewer's primary email application.

Finally, you can link to a file. This can be just about anything, a picture, a movie, a PDF or other office document, a presentation, whatever you need it to be. When this option is selected via the "Link to" drop-down menu, a Finder window opens, and you can scroll to the actual file you want to link to. When the user selects this via your link, the browser window will display the contents of the file (see Figure 9-71).

Figure 9-71.
Master of the links

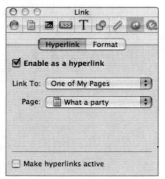

Format

The second button under the Link tab is called Format. This is new to iWeb 2 and was sorely missed in the first version. Under the original version of iWeb, the normal, rollover, visited, and disabled font link colors were defined for you and, unless you knew how to get into the guts of the page, they could not be changed. Even if you knew how to get to the guts of the page, iWeb would change it back the next time you updated the site. (And quite frankly if you knew that much about web technology and its languages, you were never going to use a program like iWeb anyway.) Once again there were some third-party software gurus who figured out how to change this, but it was software you had to run every time you updated your site (see Figure 9-72).

Figure 9-72.
One link style to rule them all

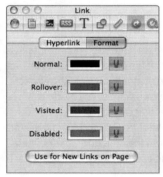

So what can you do when you're in this area? Obviously change the colors of the normal, rollover, visited, and disabled font link colors. Just select the condition you want to define, choose a color, and you're done. Unless you are extremely picky about color, just use the crayon color picker. All of them are web-safe. Couldn't be easier. You can also select whether you want the text underlined in any of these four conditions.

The button on the bottom of the page ("Use for New Links on Page") is for making all links on the current page work identically. Unless you have a need for links to appear differently (and hey, it's your site), this can save you a lot of time by taking the decision out of your hands and just selecting whatever default settings you've made.

QuickTime Tab

The QuickTime tab is for adjusting all those iMovie 08 files you will undoubtedly be dropping into iWeb. Nothing says love like 10 to 50 MB downloads of some family function for all your relatives. I'm kidding of course. By reducing the size and using default compression schemes in either iWeb or iMovie, your file sizes can be much less than this, and we will certainly discuss some of these options when we start making pages with iWeb (see Figure 9-73).

Figure 9-73.
No need to handcode QuickTime files

Some of the options here include setting start and stop points within the movie. In other words, moving the first flag (on the left) changes the point in which your movie will begin to play for viewers of your web site. Why would you do this? Several reasons come to mind. Perhaps you don't want people to have to bother viewing the opening credits, or you just hate the beginning of your movie. The other flag allows to you pick what point the movie will end. If web space is an issue, this is where you can make some cuts to reduce the file size being uploaded or downloaded.

The flag just below is called "Poster Frame." As you move the slider, you'll notice that the movie is also moving along. This setting allows you to select the still frame seen by visitors to your site for the movie you're presenting. If your actual first frame is a black screen just before the opening credits roll, or is a "Fade from Black" sequence, this is where you can pick a different frame to give your audience a view of what the movie may be about.

There's a couple of checkboxes to check out before we end this part.

The first checkbox on the bottom is called Autoplay. Much as it sounds, it begins to play the movie content (or audio or video) as soon as enough has loaded in your Mac's opinion to allow it to play without interruption. How well this works depends on your Internet connection, so it's by no means an exact science.

The Loop checkbox plays your content over...and over again until your target audience hates you. Don't use Loop unless this is the effect you were looking for. It has other uses as well: maybe there's an audio snippet you want to have play while the page is open. Use sparingly.

The last checkbox is called "Show movie controller." It puts the start, stop, and movie slider controls onto the movie, giving control of it to the viewer. Naturally this all requires QuickTime to operate, and if your viewer is not on a Mac, this isn't always a given. Most modern browsers will show some kind of pop up saying what software is required to view the content, so you may be forcing otherwise kind and patient people to download software they may or may not want. Good luck with that.

You've Got the Theory, Time to Practice

With the discussion of iWeb and its interface out of the way, it is time to start talking about making web pages! What you want your web site to communicate to your audience is entirely up to you, but remember that if they can't figure out how to navigate your site and read your content, you've failed to make a good web site. You're welcome, of course, to have obscure pictures that fade in and out for your navigation (and yes that is technically possible in iWeb), but unless having the audience hate you is the look and feel you're going for, standard internal and external links will probably do nicely.

Because most of the functionality I'll be talking about in this part of the hack is done through the Inspector window, when I talk about which part of the Inspector to go to, you'll see something like this: Inspector→Page→Layout. The first part (in this case the Inspector) is the window, the second (Page) is the icon to choose within the window, and the third (Layout) is whatever other button within the icon choice is required. I'll be doing much the same once we start talking about other floating menus (like the Color and Media windows).

Before you put a single pixel on screen, think about what you're doing. What do you want the page to look like? With iWeb 08 (or 06), changing your mind later on some design element can create some serious reworking and, on occasion, may be impossible for a few of the page templates. So give it some serious thought. One great place to find design ideas is the rest of the Internet. Think about your visits to pages that you enjoy and consider what it is about the site (beyond the content) that makes you return there. Ask friends for ideas and look for elements from unlikely places. Make your site look different and interesting without sacrificing those bits that will make it easy to move around in.

Faking Master Pages

One feature that iWeb does not have in either the 06 or 08 version is the "Master Page." What exactly is a Master Page? It's a selection of common graphic and text elements that you want to appear on every page in your site. Done properly, it is a huge time saver in putting your site together. It is not done properly in iWeb. Oh sure, you can have the common elements that Apple has created for each of their templates, and they look good, but having your own Master Page is not supported. You can fake it with iWeb, though, and while it takes a little more work that it should, you can get some pretty nice results. How is it done?

Start by hitting the plus symbol (+) on the bottom left of the main iWeb screen or by going to the File menu and selecting New Page. I found that the white blank template (as opposed to the black blank template) made it easier to place my custom elements and not have to delete a bunch of stuff I didn't want. If the page isn't as wide as you want it to be, here's how to change it before you add content (and do some other stuff too).

Size matters

iWeb's default page size is 700 pixels wide. Using the Inspector, you can easily adjust this to any size you wish. Keep in mind that any pages you add will have to be changed (if you want them to be the same size) as well because all new pages default to this size. To make your page a different size than the default, go to the Inspector and select Inspector→Page→Layout. This will have lots of information about the current page you are viewing, some of which is covered later, but for now let's just change the width. You'll see a Page Width box with the number "700px" in it. Select or highlight this number and put in whatever number you would like. Don't fret about the "px" part; iWeb is smart enough to know you mean pixels and not inches or feet (that's a good thing). There is also a Page Height box, but don't worry about it unless you absolutely have to. iWeb will resize your page length automatically beyond the default 480 pixels if the content requires it. If you don't have enough to fill the provided 480 pixels, feel free to shorten it if you wish.

To change the Page's name, go to Inspector→Page→Page. There will be a generic name there, associated with whatever type of page you selected. Select or highlight the name, and replace it with one of your choosing. Don't worry about any spaces between words either; both versions of iWeb will fill in the data required by an Internet browser. In this case, the page won't actually be viewed on your site. This is your Master Page, and while it will be sent when you upload your site to either .Mac or some other domain, unless you actually link directly to it with your iWeb's or your own custom navigation menu, most people will never see it.

You've changed the page width and given your page a name. Next, let's make a menu for navigating your site.

Site navigation

Your first decision is what you want your navigation links to look like. Navigation links are what get you from page to page on your site and for the sake of people trying to view your content beyond the first page, please make it as identical as possible on every page. iWeb's default navigation system puts links to all page categories (blogs, podcasts, photo pages, and the like) across the top of your site in most templates on every page. This works great, and you can choose whether or not you want a page to be linked there in each page's Inspection box. Actually, calling it a default is a bit misleading. This is the only way iWeb displays your links to other pages on your site automatically. Want a vertical navigation bar in the white template? You are out of luck unless you make it yourself, and again, you'll have to insert a link manually for each and every page.

To include a page in iWeb's standard menus, go to the page you wish to add and then go to Inspector→Page→Page. At the bottom of the window, there are two selections, "Include page in navigation menu" and "Display navigation menu." Hitting the checkbox for "Include page in navigation menu" puts the page into iWeb's navigation menu. No real surprise there, but you won't see the menu until you also select the checkbox labeled, "Display navigation menu." Ah! There it is. Looks the same in almost every template, and it's about as exciting as unbuttered toast. So, uncheck both boxes and make them go away. Let's make our own.

In iWeb 2, the process is easy. Just make a text box and arrange your text however you want it. Go ahead and make your hyperlinks in the first box you've made. In iWeb 2, you can now cut and paste your links box into multiple pages, and all your formatting will remain intact. Using the Inspector→Link→Format dialog, you can also specify what color the links should be before clicking, when your mouse hovers over it, and after clicking. So get it just the way you want it, put it exactly where you want it to be, and then cut and paste it to every page on your site. Voilà! You now have a custom-made navigation bar that will make your iWeb pages stand out from the others. If there are other elements that you want to have on each page, don't do the copy-and-paste thing just yet. First, you have to finish your Master Page. By a remarkable coincidence, instructions for that process are in the next section.

Not doing it the Apple Way

You've sized the page the way you want it and created a custom navigation section. Now it's time to start arranging things to your liking. First, make sure there are no other elements of iWeb where you plan on putting these graphics and text boxes. Most likely, your bits and pieces will cover them up, and trying to get at them after can be a pain. So on your blank page, either delete them or move them out of the way. As I said before, if you're going to make your own navigation bar (see the previous section), go to Inspector→Page→Page and deselect both "Include page in navigation menu" and "Display navigation menu."

Next, place whatever graphic and text elements you want on the page in the exact location you want them to be. Remember if you want to change it later, you'll have to revisit every page created and redo it. So, once the graphic and text elements you've created are in place, visit your good friends Copy and Paste in the Edit menu. To select the elements you want repeated, you have three options. You can go to the Edit menu and choose Select all. You can also drag your mouse across the screen until all the elements are captured, or you can hold down the Shift key on your keyboard and manually select each element.

The good news is that once you have made a page for each iWeb page type (podcast, gallery, and so on) of your web site, you most likely won't have to repeat the procedure. Most often, you can simply Duplicate (also in the Edit menu) a page when you need a new one with similar content, and all the graphic elements will be duplicated as well. Simply delete the repeated content (or select all the text in each text box), and put the new stuff in. If you accidentally cover one graphic with another, or you need one graphic to be in front of another graphic and they're backwards in order, don't fret. The Forward and Backward buttons at the bottom of your iWeb window will move a graphic element or text box forwards or backwards in order on your page. If you want elements to be all the way up front or all the way to the back, go to the Arrange selection in iWeb's menu bar and select either Bring to Front or Send to Back. If you make a mistake, and the graphic is covered with no way to select it, you can still get to it, but you'll have to move the other elements covering it out of the way. Before you do this, go to the Inspector→Metrics window and in the Position section, note the graphic's exact position in pixels, horizontally and vertically. Write those numbers down, move the graphic to get what's behind it, and when you've made the changes necessary, reenter those numbers with the moved graphic selected. iWeb will then place the element at that spot.

The upside to this is that you can make similar themes on each page, maybe just slightly changed in color or size to make them stand out. The downside is that when your guests browse your site, they'll have to redownload every element of that page even if it's repeated on a previous one. This is one reason why iWeb sites have a tendency to balloon in size as compared to other web-site creators, and why it takes longer to download iWeb sites.

Congratulations! You now have the skills required to create as many Master Pages in iWeb that you'll ever need. In the next section, we'll create your Welcome Page and go over using some of iWeb's built-in page creation templates (but tweaked to your own style).

What else do I need?

In all honesty, you don't really need any other tools beyond what iWeb and the other programs that make up the iLife suite provide. Apple has been kind enough to include very powerful text- and graphic-manipulation software to get you started. However, no man is an island, and no web site worth its weight in pixels is typically made alone. As I said, iWeb includes some very good tools, but they are far from complete. For some other really cool and creative text and graphic manipulation, you may need to go outside the Apple-enclosed world.

You may already have some great text tools and not realize it. Do you have Microsoft Word for the Mac? Within Word, there's a text-manipulation program called WordArt. It's nothing fancy, but it might suit your needs without having to spend another dime. More good gear for making text dance is BeLight software's ArtText (http://www.belightsoft.com/products/arttext/overview.php). It's a bit of a one-trick pony as compared to, say, PhotoShop Elements, but the learning curve isn't nearly as steep.

For manipulating graphics and pictures, there are few tools more complete than Adobe's suite of ground-breaking software known currently as CS3. However, most people who use iWeb don't have $600 to $1,200 just sitting around for the full suite, nor the time and patience to learn the complete interface. So get Photoshop Elements instead for $80 to $100 (or whatever your currency of choice is). Most of what you'll actually use is right there. If you want to go cheaper than that, there is the venerable and most excellent GraphicConverter, DrawIt, Painter, and many more.

iWeb's Welcome Page

Your Welcome Page is the first thing someone will see when they visit your site initially unless they have a direct link to some other posted content. You want it to be representative of what they will find on your other pages, so if it's boring or looks like everyone else's site, they might not linger for long. So make it symbolize the way you think or write. Apple's iWeb allows the use of templates, which is the easiest way to start, but remember you want it to reflect you and not someone else's idea of a web page.

If you want your page to look different, your best bet, as said before, is to choose either the white or black blank template and work from there. What? You mean you don't have to use iWeb's Welcome template for your first page? Of course not: use whatever page or template you want. Choice is good. Just remember that the more complicated the iWeb template, the more work you'll have to do on every Master Page you create to tweak and make it your own.

Hold on a second? *More* Master Pages? What in the seven hellish trials of the Woz am I talking about? Remember the previous section I wrote about creating Master Pages? I talked about creating the basic structure of your pages so that you don't have to reinvent it every time. Well, I won't go into great detail here, but some templates and pages are easier to manipulate than others and may require some gentle modification to work within the parameters of your Master Page. Deal with that later, getting the Welcome page right is the first step.

Choose your template and page and get it on the screen. At this point, you can effortlessly change the background color or the browser color of the page in the Inspector→Page→Layout box. Depending on the template you choose, there may be lots of default text boxes with "Loren Ipsum" text written inside. You can either edit the text to say what you want (most times), get rid of the text box altogether by highlighting it and hitting Delete, or you can make the box as small as possible and then change its opacity in the Inspector box to zero. It will still be physically present; you just won't see it anymore.

Add text, photos, graphics or whatever other elements you wish to make it look the way you want it to. One of the best parts of iWeb is that all the graphics created in other programs are pretty much a drag-and-drop affair from a Finder window. iWeb accepts most common graphic file types including JPEG, GIF, and PNG. There are others as well, but those three are the biggies. Of course you can import all the graphic files you might use into iPhoto and just drag and drop them directly within iWeb's Media window as well. Reshape and resize them using the Inspector→Graphic and Inspector→Metric windows.

Now think about how you want your text to look. Do you want to go with a single or double column? For one of my sites (http://www.macparrot.com), I went with three columns, and because I chose a wide layout (915 pixels wide to be exact), I had plenty of room not only for the three columns, but also my homemade Navigation menu, some graphic site links, Google ads, search bar, and also a favorite links section. You can make your web site as wide as you want to, but keep in mind that many people will be looking at your site with browsers somewhere in the 800 to 1024 pixel width range. Going beyond that will force people to scroll left or right, which can be irritating to your viewers.

Besides your layout, something else to consider is how you want people to find your most recent content. The Navigation menu you created should be used for going to the main sections of your site, not for letting people know about new blogs, photographs, or podcasts. Consider using the remaining space to talk about and link to new things you've added to your site.

How to do this is very easy. Assuming you have room for a column or two, you have a few options. For the three columns at MacParrot.com, I have each listed according to the kind of content I would typically add. The first column has Mac news stories I found interesting and would add my own comments to. The second column I use for reviews. and tech articles I've written. The third column is for my blogs and whatever podcasts I might create. Each column consists of one large text box that you can make either by selecting it in the Insert menu or by hitting the Text box icon at the bottom of your main iWeb screen. I use one long column for each section and update it by copying and pasting similar text to the top and then changing the date and title. My old stuff goes down in the column, and my new stuff is at top.

All of your text is fully editable within iWeb. Make it bigger or smaller using the keyboard shortcuts (Command- + and Command- -), hitting the Fonts key at the bottom to open the separate fonts window, or by using the menu commands. The Fonts window is also the easiest way to change the font within the text box or just the highlighted text you have chosen. You can change the color of the text and spacing and a few other neat tricks in the Inspector→Text→Text window. Make bulleted lists; go hog wild! Explore your options and have fun.

One thing I've haven't really talked about yet is just what you're going to use your web site to convey to the world at large. There is an excellent reason why I haven't; what you want to say and how you want to say it is entirely up to you. You may have a fascination with the mating habits of an aboriginal plaid spider from lower Albania (if this is something you find interesting, I really don't want to meet you) or how many thumbtacks it takes to recreate the Eiffel Tower in full size. It doesn't really matter. Your passions and what you find interesting are reasons enough to make a web site. The first step is to make it look interesting enough for visitors to stick around.

What's Next?

You've now created your Master Page and used it to make up your Welcome page. Maybe one page is all you need. Most people can't resist the lure of adding more pages especially when it's so easy to do so. So get started: you have all the tools now. Share your thoughts and media with the billions of Internet users out there!

— Guy Serle

HACK 82: Fun with Photo Booth

At first glance, Photo Booth seems like a goofy, unremarkable program. Use this hack to transform Photo Booth into a tool you'll want to use!

Photo Booth is Apple's answer to a question no one asked. The question? I've got an iSight; can I do something goofy? That noted, it is a fun answer. Kids love it, and the application is a surprisingly powerful tool for creating quick movies, GIFs for your iChat icons and snaps of whatever your iSight camera happens to be trained on at the time.

Better Movies

If you're an owner of an Intel-based Mac running Leopard, you can do something no G5 owner can do: use background images with iChat. The process is simple: fire up Photo Booth, and you can record a movie in front of the Eiffel Tower without ever leaving the basement. Or you should be able to anyway. The problem that most people complain about is that Photo Booth isn't quite good enough at distinguishing you from the background. Hence, when you put yourself in front of an aquarium full of fishes, the fish often bleed through. This isn't good: after all, a fish swimming in one eyeball kind of ruins the illusion.

So how can you get rid of the annoying and all too common bleed-throughs and make yourself stand out against the background? It helps to understand what Photo Booth is trying to do. First Photo Booth analyzes the actual background (after asking you to step out of the frame) and when the program has acquired the necessary information, you're invited to step back in. The difference detected by the program is what separates you from the background. When Photo Booth isn't sure if some pixel is part of you or the background, you get that annoying bleed.

The key to minimizing this is to understand that this is a problem that was solved before computers made the (forgive the pun) scene. The technique is called *bluescreening* (among other names), and the idea is to create a background that is easily differentiated from the subject. Any screen color that is sufficiently different from the foreground image will work, but the traditional choices are blue and green because these supposedly vary the most from human skin.

It shouldn't come as much of a surprise that what works for Hollywood will work for you as well. The trick is to choose a plain background (a green sheet works great or even the blue sky) and have Photo Booth sample that. It makes the final product much better, and if you're doing this a lot, well worth the time.

The remaining gotcha is one of shadows. Even with a strong, easily differentiated background, shadows can get in the way. A shadow on your blue background may appear as black or purple, and confuse the program. Usually it isn't too big of a deal but if you're going for that perfect image you want to adjust the lighting to avoid shadows that might confuse Photo Booth. So if you're still having problems with Photo Booth after finding an appropriate backdrop, turn up the lights to turn down the shadows. The movie studios that use this technique put the blue background well behind the talent, and light it as flat as they can. You can try that, too, by stepping well forward of the blue wall or whatever you're using. If you're far enough forward, your shadow won't fall on the wall. You can also try dedicating one or more lights exclusively to the background to erase any shadows that fall on it.

Add Backdrops and Effects to Photo Booth

If you went to all the effort of making sure there is no bleed in Photo Booth, you're probably also interested in expanding the number of backdrops and effects available. The good news is that the process is very easy. Just navigate to the effects page of Photo Booth and drag the image of the *.mov* file you want to use to one of the empty spaces.

Although Apple demonstrated, but never officially released, a *Star Wars* hologram effect, someone has taken the time to recraete it. If you don't remember, the effect was one Apple used to hype Photo Booth, but to the annoyance of *Star Wars* fans everywhere, the effect wasn't included in the final release. MacRumors has the effect available, along with instructions, at http://www. macrumors.com/2007/10/27/star-wars-hologram-effect-for-ichat/

Create an Animated GIF with Photo Booth

Creating smallish moving images with a computer is something that people have been doing for years. But you can make it easy on yourself and let Photo Booth take care of the labor. Hit the "Take four quick pictures" button and get the pictures snapped (Figure 9-74). Select the resulting image in the drawer of Photo Booth and choose Export. You'll be presented with a dialog box to name your creation, and once you do that, bam, you're done. You've now got a nifty animated GIF to use on web pages or in iChat.

Figure 9-74.
Pics for a GIF

QUICK TIP

CONSIDER COMPRESSION WHEN YOU'RE FILMING

When you're filming your work of art, it is wise to consider how the final product will be displayed. In the case of YouTube, the first step is transforming your movie into QuickTime. This darkens your footage a noticeable amount, so if your final goal is YouTube (or even QuickTime), use extra lighting. Also, be aware that the compression algorithm used by YouTube favors static shots over sequences with a great deal of motion so if you are determined to have lots of close-up action, expect the end result to not be all you had hoped. All that said, if you read the rest of this hack, even the jumpiest videos will stay watchable.

HACK 83: Optimize iMovie HD for YouTube

iMovie 08 makes it easy to get your videos "YouTubed," but what about those iMovie HD projects? Discover the methods to make your movies all they can be once they are on YouTube.

If you're using iMovie 08, getting your movie onto YouTube is a trivial process; the functionality is built right in. Unfortunately that convenience comes with a price. While iMovie 08 is much easier to use when uploading videos to YouTube, as a movie-making solution, it isn't in the same class as iMovie HD.

What makes iMovie HD superior to iMovie 08? That depends on what kind of movies you're making, but to sum it up and avoid editorializing: if you're just looking into your iSight and gabbing (leave Britney alone!), then iMovie 08 is the clear winner. On the other hand, if you're telling a story with multiple scenes and special effects, then most people prefer iMovie HD.

Which leads directly to the best iMovie 08 trick: it comes with a free download of iMovie HD (http://www.apple.com/support/downloads/imovieHD6.html). Once you've downloaded iMovie HD, you'll discover that there is a world of third-party effects available to you that iMovie 08 doesn't support (check out http://www.geethree.com/slick/free.html for some free effects).

Once you've got a copy of iMovie HD and made a great movie, it is time to get that movie onto YouTube and share your masterpiece with the world. But, if you are used to iMovie 08, you're going to have to do a little work to make the final product all it can be.

There isn't anything difficult about exporting your movie for YouTube. The trouble arises because there are so many options. Wading through them all and discovering the tweaks that make a difference and the ones that don't would take you longer than making the movie to begin with.

Get started by opening up the project you want to post to YouTube and hitting Share→Share… from iMovie's menu bar. This brings up a new pane with a bunch of options, even one (Web) that seems like it would be perfectly suited for the job.

What will happen if you use the web compression setting is that iMovie will run through your final film, compressing everything down to make a decent compromise between file size and image quality. That is great if you're putting the movie on your site but if you're uploading said flick to YouTube, you'll be in a bit of trouble because YouTube will run through the movie and compress it yet again. The result is far from optimal.

So the mission is clear: you want to export the movie in a format that maximizes the quality after YouTube gets done compressing the movie! With that in mind, you'd think the rest would be easy: just pick the right format and export your movie in the highest quality possible. Sure, it will make YouTube's computers work a little harder when compressing the movie, but YouTube is a faceless corporation, so what do you care?

It turns out YouTube has limits both on the length of posted movies and the original file size. The maximum length of the movie is 10 minutes; the maximum file size is 100 MB. The goals are now clearly defined; you want the best possible movie that will fit in a 100 MB file. iMovie can help.

Again head to Share→Share… and get ready to do some tweaking. Choose Expert for the export settings. It will appear as though iMovie is going to export your movie without further interference, but a half second later, a new window pops up. Click Options, and you are ready to set up iMovie to create video that will result in maximum YouTube quality.

Time to maximize the export. Once you've clicked options, you are presented with a brand-new window called Movie Settings with an abundance of tweakable settings. .A logical place to start is with the Settings… options. Choose H.264 for the Compression Type, change Frame Rate to 30 fps (to match iMovie's settings) and, naturally, move the Quality slider to Best.

Next you'll want to turn your attention to the Size… options. The temptation is to create a larger size than the standard YouTube format and let YouTube scale the video down. But you want YouTube mucking with your video as little as possible, so choose 320 × 240 QVGA (YouTube's native size). If your video isn't in the same aspect ratio as 320 × 240, check the box next to Preserve Aspect Ratio so that the video isn't distorted by being forced into the new dimensions. Finally, check Deinterlace Source Video, because if you don't do it, YouTube will. The final settings should look like Figure 9-75.

Figure 9-75.
Size settings

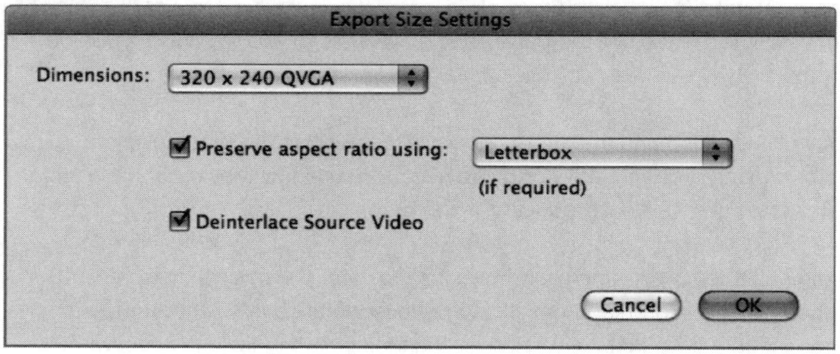

Finally, turn your attention to the Audio portion of the Movie Settings window. If you've recorded in stereo (or if you are using a stereo track for background music), select the Stereo (L, R); choose AAC for the Format option; and 128 Kbps for the target bit rate. If you're going with mono sound, 64 Kbps is more than adequate.

That's it; you're done! Export that movie. If you run up against the file-size limitation hop back to Settings... and add a limit for the Data Rate. Your goal is a file under 100 MB, so for a 10-minute movie, the maximum data rate you would allow would be about 165 Kbps.

One final warning: all of these settings are processor-intensive, and the resulting file size is (necessarily) large. Expect to spend some time both compressing and uploading the movie. Once you've seen how good your movie can look on YouTube, you'll be sure the effort was worth it!

HACK 84: Tips for Making Great Movies

If you're moving beyond your Mac's built-in iSight and filming with a camcorder, these simple tips will take your movies to the next level.

Making movies is fun; there is just no doubt about it. That said, the process can also be very frustrating. Typically, you're the person in charge of lighting, sound, cinematography, and direction. With that much responsibility foisted on one person, it isn't surprising that when you sit down to edit your movie, you find that something has gone horribly wrong. The lighting might be terrible, the sound might be uneven or unintelligible, the movie might look nothing like you thought it did when you were filming, or the camera might shake all over the place. These problems are all too common, and more than one would-be movie has been relegated to the digital scrap heap because the footage someone thought would be great turned out to be utterly unwatchable. Worse than the projects that were scrapped are the ones that someone decided to forge ahead with even though the source material left much to be desired.

With a few quick tips, you can avoid the soul-crushing moment that occurs when you open up your footage and discover it is unusable.

Get Some Headphones

You've got to get a pair of headphones, no doubt about it. It doesn't matter if they are cheap headphones from the closeout end cap at Target or high-end Sennheiser products. Just make sure they are compatible with your camera (which almost always use a mini-jack connector). Why? Your camera's microphone doesn't "hear" the same way you do. To hear what the microphone is picking up, put some headphones on and take a listen. For an example of how important headphones can be, envision this scenario. You're off camera filming someone 10 feet away. The scene calls for you to talk to the person. To you, it sounds like a normal conversation (because it is), but to your camera it sounds like you're shouting, and your subject is whispering. A cheap pair of headphones can alert you to this discrepancy and save time and reshoots. The kind that cover your ears are especially desirable for this kind of work.

Buy them, but more importantly use them. Why not buy really high-quality headphones? That's a good question. After all, today's digital camcorders can record really nice audio (44 kHz, roughly CD quality), so you'd expect top of the line headphones to make a huge difference. The truth is, they will make a difference but not enough to justify the cost. You won't have the equipment to design a top-notch sound stage, so you don't need the very best stuff to monitor your less than top- quality recording environment.

Spring for a Microphone

I know you're thinking "why would I need to buy a microphone; the camcorder has one built in?" You're right: all low-end camcorders have a built-in microphone. However, the built-in microphone on camcorders is often worthless (this is often true of moderately priced camcorders as well). It is not the case that the microphones are of low quality (most camcorders feature an electret condenser microphone); rather they invariably pick up the hum of the camcorder motor making for a very unpleasant audio experience. They also don't work well if your subject is more than a few yards away. So the question now becomes: What kind of microphone should you get? You've got a ton of choices: everything from a shotgun microphone, handheld microphones, wired and wireless lavalier microphones, stereo and mono—the list goes on and on.

There are lots of kinds of microphones. The most important variable is the pickup pattern. An omnidirectional microphone picks up sound from all directions; a *cardioid* microphone favors one direction over the others; and a shotgun microphone, also called a hyper-cardioid microphone, favors one direction even more. Perhaps a look at the popular choices is in order:

Shotgun microphone
These attach directly to your camera and look fairly silly on a small camcorder, but they generally perform adequately. Expect to spend around $100 for a decent model. These are probably the best all-around choice, because the sound they pick up best is the sound coming from the location where your camera is pointed. Still, they may not be the best choice if you're filming something tens of yards away.

Lavalier microphones
These are sometimes referred to as "tie-clip" microphones. The wired ones are cheap ($10 to $15) and easy to find; the wireless ones are a bit trickier to find and cost more (still as low as $50). These are the best choice for interviews (you'll need one for each person) and similar situations. A cardioid lavalier will pick up little more than the person who's wearing it, but an omni will get a decent (though fainter) signal from people nearby as well. You may want to avoid lavaliers if you're determined to record your project in stereo (you can get stereo lavalier microphones but be prepared to pay a lot more).

Handheld condenser microphones
These are your basic roving-reporter microphones. What you have is basically a ball on top of a stick, useful if you're interviewing random people. You can get omni-directional or cardioid models, and it will make a difference. Prices vary widely depending on quality and whether you're interested in a wired or wireless model. This type of microphone has a few drawbacks. They look positively

silly if not used in the right kind of setting, and their plug is likely incompatible with the jack on your camcorder (you can buy adapters). Still they can be your best bet for some certain kinds of projects (think Michael Moore movies and similar documentaries).

The right one for you will depend on your filming habits, but for general using a shotgun microphone is a good bet.

Get a Tripod

Tripods, like camcorders, start out very cheap and get very expensive. If you've got upwards of $8,000 dollars to spend on a Cartoni fluid head tripod, skip the rest of this section. If you're doing this on the cheap, you still need a tripod. It will do a much better job than any image-stabilization feature your camera may have, and you won't get that shaky hand-held look. So plan to drop thirty bucks on a tripod and consider it money well spent. If you ask any camera-using professional about a thirty-dollar tripod, they will swear to you that the thing is positively useless, and for the pros it is. You can't do a smooth pan with a cheap tripod (though if you really lube the thing and make sure your image stabilization is on, you can almost get there), and every tiny adjustment made while taping will be noticed on the final product. Fortunately you don't have to be an overly retentive pro to use iMovie, and all you want out of the tripod is a really steady base (if you need to move the camcorder during shots there are other solutions), so the really cheap tripod from Wal-Mart (or other oppressive mega center; they keep them next to the asparagus usually) is fine.

Light Up the Subject

The importance of adequate lighting cannot be overstated. Poor lighting is the hallmark of sub-amateur videos; everything looks unintentionally murky and renders your entire movie unpleasant to watch. That doesn't mean you want harsh lights illuminating every single scene; sometimes a brightly lit shot just isn't appropriate, either. Remember that you're not trying just to capture a scene; you're trying to get the appropriate feel as well. The only thing separating erotica and pornography is a few hundred watts of illumination. With the importance of lighting firmly in mind, we can turn our attention to decent lighting at rock-bottom prices.

Purchase three work lights that use incandescent bulbs. These will provide maximum flexibility and ease of use. Avoid the halogen and neon options because these generally don't look as nice on tape. (It's worth spending some time at this point familiarizing yourself with the "white balance" feature of your camera.) Also stock up on various wattages of bulbs to further the flexibility of your new lighting system. As a general rule of thumb, three 100-watt lamps placed carefully, yields a pretty nice picture. Your mileage may vary; be prepared to experiment.

The final question is "How can you tell when you have enough light?" Pros use expensive meters, but that's not something most of us have lying about. Most camcorders list recommended light levels (usually above 100 lux). You are going to have to rely on your eyes and the camcorder's viewfinder (it is especially important to use the viewfinder and not the LCD screen when doing this) and see how the shot looks. Are the light areas bright, or are they muddled? Is the contrast at an acceptable level, or does everything seem muted? Once you're happy, add some more lights because chances are you've got the scene too dimly lit. (Particularly important if you're going to export to QuickTime: use extra light because the QuickTime codec results in darker footage).

What if you want a steady short while you're moving the camera? You can pull this off with a homebrewed steadicam. A *steadicam* is a piece of filmmaking equipment that allows shots made with a handheld camera to appear incredibly smooth. Steadicams were used with great effect in key scenes of Stanley Kubrick's *The Shining*, grabbing smooth and low shots of Danny Torrance riding his Big Wheel through the deserted resort, for example. The drawback of real steadicams is the cost. Even the cheapest steadicam will set you back several thousand dollars. On the other hand, the homebrew device costs roughly $14 to build and provides excellent results. To discover how to build your own very useful steadicam, visit http://www.cs.cmu.edu/~johnny/steadycam.

10 HACK THE APPLE TV

Steve Jobs once said that the Mac was one leg of the Apple chair, the iPod was the second, and he hoped the Apple TV would someday be the third. This tells us two things: First, Steve took a long-term view when it came to the Apple TV, and second, he isn't much of a carpenter: the minimum number of legs for a stable chair is three after all, so until the Apple TV really takes off, that is going to be one hard-to-use chair.

The Apple TV didn't take off as hoped. Sales were lackluster, so Apple made adjustments. First the company released a software update that added YouTube videos to the mix. That didn't result in much of a bump, so at MacWorld 2008, Apple unveiled Apple TV Take 2. It was a consumer-friendly revision. You could rent movies directly from iTunes without the need for an intervening computer. The resolution was bumped up to HD, and, best of all: Apple dropped the price.

Hackers already thought the Apple TV was pretty sweet. It is easy to see why: at a fundamental level, the Apple TV is a low-powered Mac. It has a single-core Intel processor, wireless and Ethernet connectivity, a USB port, a hard drive, and a video out. All that packaged in a small, unobtrusive package is a hacker's dream. Well, if the hacker can get into the thing....

HACK 85: Use Your Apple TV with Standard Definition Sets

The Apple TV is made for a high-definition world, but you might want to hook to a standard-definition TV set. It isn't much work; find out how to use your Apple TV with any TV that has composite video input.

When you look at the back of an Apple TV, you see a lot going on. The predictable power port is there, a USB port, a HD port followed by component video, RCA audio jacks and an optical audio port. That's great if you have a TV with component video in or optical audio speakers, but if you want all the benefits (sans the resolution) of an Apple TV on a regular TV, you're out of luck; the ports just aren't there.

Most standard televisions feature composite video input and two inputs for sound. You might be more familiar with this as the yellow-red-white RCA inputs you see almost everywhere (it is how the Nintendo Wii connects). You can get the sound out of the Apple TV using red and white audio, but if you want to see the video, you've got to rely on either the HD port (not a viable option in this case) or the component video. Unfortunately, component video has three RCA plugs (red, blue, and green), while composite video has one plug (yellow).

QUICK TIP ✕

COMPONENT VIDEO VERSUS THE HDMI PORT

The Apple TV offers two ways to connect to your HDTV. You can pick from component video and audio (the five multicolored RCA jacks on the back of your Apple TV), or you can opt to use the high-definition multimedia interface (HDMI) port. Some HDTVs offer only one type of connection, so the choice is easily made, but if you're staring at a HDTV that offers both, you might be wondering which is better. From a cabling perspective, the answer is obvious: HDMI takes care of audio and video through one small cable, while component jacks require five different connections.

From a quality standpoint, the answer isn't as clear. The HDMI port outputs a pure digital signal, while component video is analog. The easy conclusion is that the HDMI signal will be substantially better; thing is, it isn't always. Testing the Apple TV on a few different sets produced different results depending on which cabling system was used, with the standard result being no noticeable difference. The answer for maximum video quality is to try both and pick the one you like better.

QUICK TIP ✕

APPLE TV REMEMBERS YOUR SETTINGS

If you've had your Apple TV plugged in the standard manner to a HDTV, and try and pull this off on a standard TV, you won't be able to see the black-and-white screens. You'll see the Apple logo, but after that, you'll just see slanting dots. The simple solution: hook up your Apple TV to the HD set you were using earlier, and change the settings. However, this isn't a good option if it is tough to get to the ports on your HD set. You need a way to cycle through the available resolutions. To do so, grab your Apple TV remote, and depress the menu and + buttons. Keep holding them down; when you can see the selection menu, choose the resolution you require.

Everyone knows yellow plus blue makes green right? That may work when mixing colors with crayons, but will it work when mixing signals from different colored cables? Try plugging the green cable of component video into the composite video input. (Actually, I just tried each plug.) If you run through the exercise, you are in for a good news/bad news scenario. The good news? When you try the green cable, you'll get a picture! The bad news? The picture is in black and white.

Buster Keaton made some great movies, and who doesn't enjoy the purposeful maiming of dear friends as displayed by the Three Stooges? Still, black and white isn't going to cut it as a solution. If you're plugging your Apple TV into the video composite jack, you're already sacrificing some video quality, so sacrificing color is too much to ask. Besides, movies just aren't as good without color: *Traffic* without the nuance of color is just a boring movie. With the color added, it's an Oscar winner.

Getting Color to the Composite Video Plug the Easy Way

While others were looking for a more complicated solution, Mauricio Pastrana devised an easy hardware hack to get your Apple TV to feed color video to the composite video port on a standard TV. The hack is both a hardware hack and a software hack in the strictest sense, but in the work-versus-result category, it is one of the niftiest Apple TV hacks ever. The hack isn't hard, but you'll need two items:

- HDMI to DVI adapter cable

- DVI to VGA adapter

Screw the HDMI to DVI adapter to the DVI to VGA adapter (see Figure 10-1).

Figure 10-1.
The completed assembly with DVI to VGA adapter plugged into HDMI to DVI cable

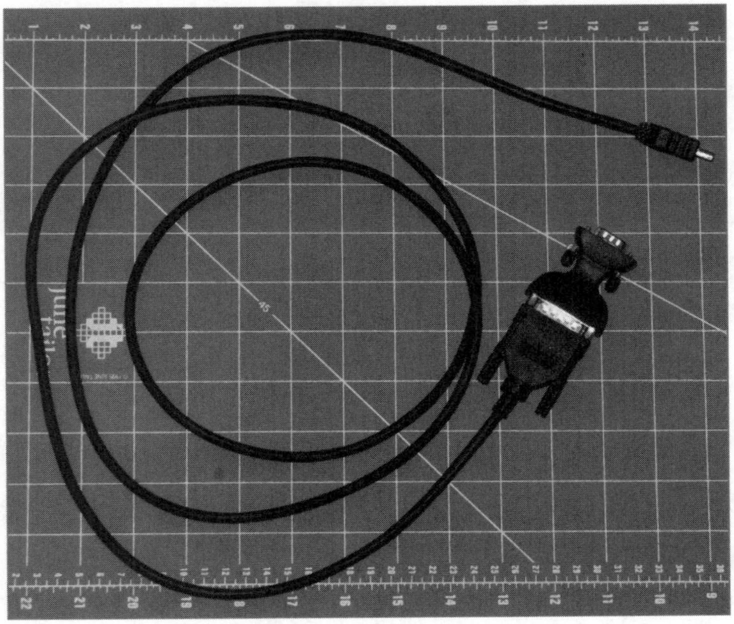

Once your materials are ready, the procedure is deliciously simple.

1. Connect the green output of the Apple TV to the yellow input (video) of your TV. The image will be in black and white.

2. Press the menu button, and navigate to the video settings page.

3. Change the video settings (if necessary) to 480i.

4. Unplug the video cable from your TV. Plug in the HDMI/VGA combo adapter to the HDMI output of the Apple TV. Wait a few seconds.

5. Unplug the HDMI/VGA combo from the Apple TV, and plug the video cable back in.

6. Press the play/pause button on the Apple TV remote for five seconds.

7. Plug the green composite cable back in, and wait a few seconds (my TV show scrambled red lines for a few beats).

Bingo: color on your standard definition set (see Figure 10-2)!

Figure 10-2.
Color on your old TV

HACK 86: Upgrade Your Apple TV Hard Drive

Whether you just want more disk space for your media, or you want to have a backup of your Apple TV to protect you from yourself, your very first Apple TV hack should be this: replace the hard drive and put the original in a safe place.

The original Apple TV included a mere 40 GB of disk space, which isn't enough to store all the music, photos, and videos that people tend to accumulate. What's more, that 40 GB leaves you with hardly enough space to put any cool applications that can run on the Apple TV. So before you do anything else with it, it's time to put a new hard drive in it. If you've got the 160 GB hard drive, you can probably avoid this hack for awhile, but not forever.

This procedure has been tested (and retested several times) on the 1.0 release of the Apple TV operating system. If you have the 1.1 or later operating system, it may not work. However, because you're removing, backing up, and safely storing the original hard drive, you can always go back to where you started. I've found the AwkwardTV Wiki (http://wiki.awkwardtv.org) to be a great source of up-to-date information on tips, tricks, hacks, and cool software, so be sure to check it out if you want to do some serious background reading before attempting this project.

Before you upgrade the hard drive, you need to choose which one to get. I generally go to Newegg. com first, partly because they have great prices, but mostly because they have two things I can't shop without: a search engine that works and an excellent user review system. The first (and as of this writing, only) generation of Apple TV uses parallel ATA notebook computer disk drives. These are older-style disk drives with 44 pins that you connect with a ribbon cable (most modern desktop and notebook computers use serial ATA, which uses a smaller connector with far fewer pins).

To find a new drive, search for laptop or notebook hard drives, and narrow it down to ATA, ATA-6, IDE, or parallel drives (these four terms are used interchangeably to refer to the same thing). Then make sure you're looking at 2.5-inch drives, and not 3.5- or 1.8-inch. Once you've done that, you've eliminated a lot of incompatible drives, so you can now search on the next most important thing: capacity. When you've found the capacity you want, you should be looking at a much smaller list of drives. Now, click through on each one, and read the reviews that users have submitted. For the Apple TV, you want to look for people complaining about noise or heat. Either one of those would be a problem (you certainly don't want your Apple TV to be louder than the television, and you definitely don't want to melt your home theater system). If you find some reviewers with specific comments about how well it worked with the Apple TV, that's a happy bonus. Order the disk drive you want, and you'll be one step closer to an upgrade.

You're going to need something to connect the old and new disk drive to your Mac so you can back up the old drive and restore it to the new one. An external enclosure that's designed for 2.5-inch parallel ATA drives will do the trick. Although you can find cheap USB 2.0 enclosures, I strongly suggest you get a FireWire enclosure for two reasons: they are much faster than USB, and they don't need a separate power supply because they can draw power from your Mac. Plus, when you're done with this project, you can buy a big disk drive, install it in the enclosure, and use it as a Time Machine disk that you can take on the road [Hack #92].

Other World Computing's (http://www.macsales.com) Mercury On-The-Go FireWire Portable Kit ($65) is a good enclosure, but there are many less expensive ones, such as the Coolmax (http://coolmaxusa.com) HD-211-Combo ($25).

Once you've gotten your new drive and an enclosure, it's time to take your Apple TV apart and back up the old disk drive. To do this, you need some tools, some time, and some patience. First, make sure you have the following:

- Clean work surface

- Torx-10 screwdriver for the Apple TV case screws

- Torx-8 screwdriver for the Apple TV hard disk screws

- Small Phillips head screwdriver (or whatever your external enclosure requires)

Now it's time to disassemble the Apple TV and remove the hard drive. The first step is to gently remove the soft material on the bottom of the Apple TV, as shown in Figure 10-3. Be careful: this material rips easily. You will want to replace it when you're done.

Figure 10-3.
Removing the bottom of the Apple TV

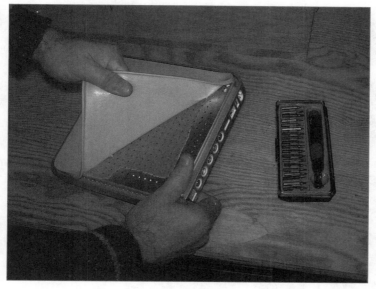

Next, use the Torx-8 screwdriver to remove the four screws in each corner, and the Torx-10 screwdriver to remove the smaller group of four screws (this holds the hard drive in place), as shown in Figure 10-4.

Figure 10-4.
Removing the screws

Now you need to gently lift the case up, as shown in Figure 10-5. Even though you removed the hard-drive screw, it is still held on by a small sticky surface. Be sure not to tug or strain the cables. Once you have it opened, remove the hard drive cable gently. The pins are extremely weak, and you don't want to bend them.

Figure 10-5.
Gently opening the case

Next, you need to work the hard drive off the case. This can take some effort, but you need to do it gently and with a steady pull. Avoid the temptation to pry it off with anything heavy duty. If you need more muscle, stick with something that won't pierce you or the hard drive. Figure 10-6 shows the drive still affixed to the pad that holds it on. Gently remove the green material, set it aside, and keep it clean. Even though it's not as sticky as it was before you yanked the drive off of it, it will still hold the drive in place when you need to drive the screws back in.

Figure 10-6.
Removing the disk drive

After you've removed the Apple TV hard drive, install it in the external enclosure you secured, and plug it into your Mac. Figure out which disk is the Apple TV disk (it's the disk with the partition named OSBoot). One way to do this is to open up a Terminal window [Hack #29] and use the `diskutil` command:

```
$ diskutil list
...
/dev/disk1
   #:                       TYPE NAME              SIZE        IDENTIFIER
   0:      GUID_partition_scheme               *128.0 Gi   disk1
   1:                        EFI                34.0 Mi     disk1s1
   2:             Apple_Recovery               400.0 Mi    disk1s2
   3:             Apple_HFS OSBoot             900.0 Mi    disk1s3
```

On my computer, it came up as `disk1`. It might be different on yours, so in the examples that follow, replace `disk1` with the name of your Apple TV disk.

> Disk numbers are handed out by Mac OS X on a first come, first serve basis, so if you are using FileVault or have some disk images mounted, your Apple TV disk may have a different number. Because it's so easy for this numbering to be changed, you should check the drive numbering each time you go to modify your Apple TV disk. You can use `diskutil list` to do this whenever you need to.

Now, unmount the disk, and use the Unix `dd` command to back up the Extensible Firmware Interface (EFI), Recovery, and OSBoot partitions:

```
$ diskutil unmountDisk /dev/disk1
Unmount of all volumes on disk1 was successful

$ dd if=/dev/disk1s1 of=EFI.img bs=1m
34+0 records in
34+0 records out
35651584 bytes transferred in 5.244276 secs (6798190 bytes/sec)

$ dd if=/dev/disk1s2 of=Apple_Recovery.img bs=1m
399+1 records in
399+1 records out
419405824 bytes transferred in 52.719368 secs (7955441 bytes/sec)

$ dd if=/dev/disk1s3 of=OSBoot.img bs=1m
899+1 records in
899+1 records out
943714304 bytes transferred in 126.457199 secs (7462717 bytes/sec)
```

You've now got three files: *EFI.img*, *Apple_Recovery.img*, and *OSBoot.img*. Keep them safe: back them up.

Next, remove the old Apple TV drive from the enclosure, and store it somewhere safe. This is your only working version of the disk right now, so take good care of it! Install your new disk drive in the enclosure, and recreate the partitions. First, run `diskutil list` again to figure out which disk number to use, then unmount that disk:

```
$ diskutil unmountDisk /dev/disk1
Unmount of all volumes on disk1 was successful
```

Now, blow away the partitions on the disk. Make sure you have verified which disk number you should use (may not be `disk1`), because this step will delete all the data on the disk:

```
$ gpt destroy /dev/disk1
```

You will probably get a warning that the disk you inserted was unreadable. You need to click Ignore. Next, create the partition table with this command:

```
$ gpt create -f /dev/disk1
```

Now you need to create the EFI, OSBoot, and Recovery partitions. This information is drawn from the AwkwardTV Wiki page http://wiki.awkwardtv.org/wiki/Prepare_a_Hard_Drive. You should visit that site for more details and for any new developments in the Apple TV hacking world. Next, create the EFI partition:

```
$ gpt add -b 40 -i 1 -s 69632 -t efi /dev/disk1
```

Ignore the disk insertion warning if you get one; then create the OSBoot partition:

```
$ gpt add -b 888872 -i 3 -s 1843200 -t hfs /dev/disk1
```

Ignore the disk insertion warning if you get one. If you've partitioned this disk for Apple TV earlier, there might be a partition still living in the space, so unmount the disk just to be sure:

```
$ diskutil unmountDisk /dev/disk1
```

Next, create the Recovery partition (ignore the insertion warning if you get one):

```
$ gpt add -b 69672 -i 2 -s 819200 \
  -t 5265636F-7665-11AA-AA11-00306543ECAC /dev/disk1
```

Finally, restore the Recovery partition using the image file you created earlier. You can skip the EFI and OSBoot partitions. The EFI partition seems to take care of itself, and you'll be performing a factory restore, which restores the OSBoot partition.

```
$ diskutil unmountDisk /dev/disk1

$ dd if=Apple_Recovery.img of=/dev/disk1s2 bs=1m
399+1 records in
399+1 records out
419405824 bytes transferred in 44.511941 secs (9422322 bytes/sec)
```

Next, create a filesystem for OSBoot and unmount the disk:

```
$ newfs_hfs -v OSBoot -J /dev/disk1s3
Initialized /dev/rdisk1s3 as a 900 MB HFS Plus volume with a 8192k journal

$ diskutil unmountDisk /dev/disk1
Unmount of all volumes on disk1 was successful
```

Now, check the output of `diskutil`. It should look like it did when you started:

```
$ diskutil list disk1
/dev/disk1
   #:                       TYPE NAME              SIZE       IDENTIFIER
   0:      GUID_partition_scheme                  *93.2 Gi    disk1
   1:                        EFI                   34.0 Mi    disk1s1
   2:              Apple_Recovery                 400.0 Mi    disk1s2
   3:              Apple_HFS OSBoot               900.0 Mi    disk1s3
```

Next, add a media partition using what remaining space you have. Use `gpt show` to find where the current partitions end and use the first number that appeared after the last partition, which is 2732072 in this case:

```
$ gpt show /dev/disk1
    start       size  index  contents
        0          1         PMBR
        1          1         Pri GPT header
        2         32         Pri GPT table
       34          6
       40      69632      1  GPT part - C12A7328-F81F-11D2-BA4B-00A0C93EC93B
    69672     819200      2  GPT part - 5265636F-7665-11AA-AA11-00306543ECAC
   888872    1843200      3  GPT part - 48465300-0000-11AA-AA11-00306543ECAC
  2732072  192639463
195371535         32         Sec GPT table
195371567          1         Sec GPT header
```

Unmount the drive, add the new partition, and format it:

```
$ diskutil unmountDisk /dev/disk1
Unmount of all volumes on disk1 was successful
$ gpt add -b 2732072 -i 4 -t hfs disk1
disk1s4 added
$ diskutil unmountDisk /dev/disk1
Unmount of all volumes on disk1 was successful
$ newfs_hfs -v Media -J /dev/disk1s4
Initialized /dev/rdisk1s4 as a 92 GB HFS Plus volume with a 8192k journal
```

Now, eject the disk from the Mac, and reinstall it in the AppleTV by reversing the procedure given earlier. When you turn on the Apple TV, you'll be asked to choose the language and screen resolution, and then you'll be greeted with the screen shown in Figure 10-7.

Figure 10-7.
Upgraded Apple TV is ready to be restored

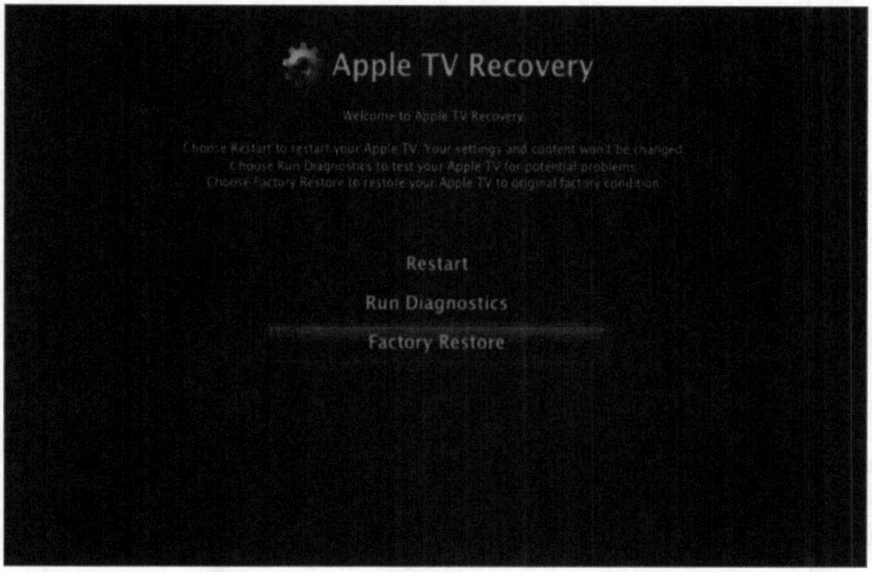

Choose Factory Restore, and follow the steps. This will install the Apple TV operating system software on the OSBoot partition, and you'll be set up with a blank media partition, which you can fill (or refill) with music by firing up iTunes and connecting it to your Apple TV as usual.

Configure the Apple TV for Remote Shell Access

You don't want to have to crack open your Apple TV every time you want to install software or tweak something. If you install the secure shell (SSH) server, you can connect to it remotely, install various mods and hacks, and muck around with your Apple TV without having to open it up again.

SSH is a service that lets you connect securely to a remote machine [Hack #53]. The `ssh` command when entered from the Unix shell opens a command-line interface similar to what you get when you open the Terminal application on a Mac. Essentially you are running a command-line shell on the remote machine, but you can't directly interact with any graphical applications running on it. However, you can do an awful lot with SSH, including modifying files, copying files over, and changing the way the remote machine behaves.

Unfortunately, Apple TV does not include the SSH server software, so you'll need to obtain it either from a compatible Mac OS X system (at the time of this writing, Apple TV was compatible with Mac OS X 10.4 Tiger). If you don't have a copy of a compatible Mac OS X system, you can probably find the SSH software in one of the combo updaters (these are the jumbo update packages that contain cumulative patches). For example, if you're using an Apple TV that is compatible with 10.4, you need to download the latest Mac OS X 10.4 (Intel) combo updater disk image from http://www. apple.com/support/downloads/, and double-click to mount the image. Next, you need to right-click on the combo updater *.pkg* file, and choose Show Package Contents. Open the Contents folder, and drag the file *Archive.pax.gz* to your desktop. You can now unmount the image and even delete it to save space.

Next, you need to extract SSH from the archive onto your Apple TV hard drive. You'll need to remove the hard drive from your Apple TV and install it in an external enclosure, as directed in Hack # Upgrade Your Apple TV Hard Drive". Next, make sure the OSBoot volume is mounted.

> The OSBoot volume should mount automatically; if it doesn't, make sure you are using a hard drive from a working Apple TV. If you upgraded your hard drive, make sure you went through the restore procedure and got your Apple TV working before trying this.

Next, open up a Terminal (located in */Applications/Utilities*), and change the directory to the OSBoot volume:

```
$ cd /Volumes/OSBoot
```

Now, use the `pax` command to extract the `sshd` (SSH daemon) program:

```
$ pax -rvz -f ~/Desktop/Archive.pax.gz ./usr/sbin/sshd
```

The next thing you need to do is create a property list in the directory that controls the programs that run at startup. Use your favorite text editor (if you don't have a favorite text editor, consider the free Smultron: http://smultron.sourceforge.net/) to create the */Volumes/OSBoot/System/Library/LaunchDaemons/ssh.plist* containing the following:

```
<?xml version="1.0" encoding="UTF-8"?>
<!DOCTYPE plist PUBLIC "-//Apple Computer//DTD PLIST 1.0//EN" "http://www.apple.
com/DTDs/PropertyList-1.0.dtd">
<plist version="1.0">
<dict>
```

```
            <key>Label</key>
            <string>com.openssh.sshd</string>
            <key>Program</key>
            <string>/usr/libexec/sshd-keygen-wrapper</string>
            <key>ProgramArguments</key>
            <array>
                    <string>/usr/sbin/sshd</string>
                    <string>-i</string>
            </array>
            <key>SessionCreate</key>
            <true/>
            <key>Sockets</key>
            <dict>
                    <key>Listeners</key>
                      <dict>
                            <key>Bonjour</key>
                            <array>
                                    <string>ssh</string>
                                    <string>sftp-ssh</string>
                            </array>
                            <key>SockServiceName</key>
                            <string>ssh</string>
                      </dict>
            </dict>
            <key>StandardErrorPath</key>
            <string>/dev/null</string>
            <key>inetdCompatibility</key>
            <dict>
                    <key>Wait</key>
                    <false/>
            </dict>
    </dict>
</dict>
</plist>
```

Double-check to make sure that you've opened and closed your angle brackets; one mistake, and this won't work. Next, unmount the drive, unplug it, and remove it from the external enclosure. Reinstall the drive in the Apple TV, and turn it on (make sure it's connected to the network). After it boots up, use `ssh` on your Mac to connect (hostname `appletv.local`, username `frontrow`, password `frontrow`). It will take a very long time (up to a minute) for the password prompt to appear the first time (the `-1` specifies the SSH 1 protocol because the Apple TV will not support SSH 2 without additional modification):

```
$ ssh -1 frontrow@appletv.local
Password:
Response: frontrow
```

Before you can make any changes to your Apple TV, you need to mount the filesystem in read/write mode. Use this command, typing `frontrow` when prompted for your password:

```
$ sudo mount -uw /
```

When you are done, you should mount it as read-only again:

```
$ sudo mount -ur /
```

The following code is a transcript of an **ssh** session with an Apple TV:

```
$ ssh -1 frontrow@appletv.local
The authenticity of host 'appletv.local (192.168.1.206)' can't be established.
RSA1 key fingerprint is 1c:c3:3e:06:42:58:ce:ea:bb:be:7a:b6:d6:d6:d8:db.
Are you sure you want to continue connecting (yes/no)? yes
Warning: Permanently added 'appletv.local,192.168.1.206' (RSA1) to the list of
known hosts.
Password:
Response: frontrow
Last login: Sun Nov 18 21:36:33 2007 from computer.local
-bash-2.05b$ uname -a
Darwin AppleTV.local 8.8.2 Darwin Kernel Version 8.8.2:
Mon Jan 29 18:57:29 PST 2007; root:xnu-792.94.18~1/RELEASE_I386
 i386 i386
-bash-2.05b$ ls
Desktop         Documents       Library         Movies          Music
Pictures        Public          Sites
-bash-2.05b$ df -k
Filesystem      1K-blocks       Used     Avail Capacity Mounted on
/dev/disk0s3      921600      467568    444816    51%    /
devfs                 95          95         0   100%    /dev
fdesc                  1           1         0   100%    /dev
<volfs>              512         512         0   100%    /.vol
/dev/disk0s4    96319728     1089240  95230488     1%    /mnt
```

There's a lot more you can do once you've enabled **ssh** on your Apple TV. Check out the Awkward TV Wiki at http://wiki.awkwardtv.org/ for all sorts of cool tips and tricks.

**Gain Remote Shell Access to the Apple TV
(Running Take 2) Without Opening the Case**

Not interested in expanding the internal storage of your Apple TV,
but you still want SSH access so you can perform all those nifty
hacks? Create your own *patchstick* to enable SSH on your Apple
TV without ever cracking the case.

Apple TV hacks have been floating around the Net since shortly after the first Apple TV got into the
hands of the first hacker. To be honest, as a platform, the Apple TV wasn't very compelling, so the
hacks made a lot of sense. Hackers were taking something that no one seemed to want and making
it do interesting (and useful) things.

The situation changed when Apple TV Take 2 came out. The box that was formerly derided became
desirable. HD movies, Airtunes Express functionality, and usability without a second computer all
added up to a much more compelling product. Of course, a better product doesn't mean people don't
want to hack the Apple TV; it just means that recreating the effort put into opening the case (again) to
reenable SSH might not be as appealing as it was when the Apple TV was a boring product.

The good news is you can get SSH running on an Apple TV Take 2 without cracking the box; the bad
news is that it might take some effort depending on your setup. Of course, getting SSH running on
an Apple TV by cracking the box takes a fair amount of effort as well. If extra storage is paramount
to you, by all means crack the box. If you envision the Apple TV as a movie-renting machine, this is
probably the more convenient method.

Once the decision has been made to go the noncracking route, it is time to collect the necessary
resources. This is trickier under Leopard but still doable; in fact with the right files, you can even pull
it off on your PowerPC Mac.

Here's how the hack works: the Apple TV won't, generally, boot off an external drive, but the
machine will boot off an external drive under specific circumstances. The circumstance you're
going to exploit is the diagnostic mode, Presumably Apple techs use this mode to troubleshoot a
problematic Apple TV. You're going to use the same mode to install a mess of files. The trouble is
that the Apple TV is fickle about which files it requires to run. You can't just slap any old kernel on it
and expect everything to go okay; you'll need specific files from OS X 10.4.9. Once all the required
files are collected, you cram them onto a USB flash drive, work a little command-line magic and
you'll have a stick that will install SSH.

Required Items

This hack covers multiple ways to pull off enabling SSH on an Apple TV, but there are a few things
you'll need no matter which method you choose. Better to get them together before you start
hacking than to flail about to find them midway through the hack. Here are the items you'll need no
matter which method you employ:

Flash memory greater than 512 MB
You've probably got this laying around already. It could be a compact flash card if you have a USB
card reader or a Flash drive that plugs directly into the USB port.

Apple TV 1.1 update
This is available from http://mesu.apple.com/data/OS/061-2988.20070620.bHy75/2Z694-
5248-45.dmg.

A patchstick creator

You can do the entire process by hand, but patchstick creators make the process much faster. There are a million flavors of patchstick creators, but the one I had success with was the one for installing Jaman TV. Get your copy at http://appletvhacks.net/downloads/jaman-patchstick-2.0.zip

Before You Get Started

After you've downloaded the *Patchstick* file from AppleTVHacks, it's wise to familiarize yourself with the conglomeration of files. If you open the folder and poke around, you'll see a few binaries, some *.plists*, and a couple of PDF files. Of particular interest is the *createPatchstick* executable; it's actually a script, and it's always a good idea to inspect scripts before you execute them. The majority of this hack will be taken care of by a script that came with the downloaded **Patchstick** folder. It is probably a good idea to take a look at the script before you run it. Open the **Patchstick** folder, right-click the *createPatchstick* binary, and choose Open With Other (see Figure 10-8).

Figure 10-8.
Inspect the script before you run it

For other, choose your favorite text editor or, if you don't have a favorite text editor, use TextEdit. You'll be able to read through the surprisingly understandable script (see Figure 10-9).

Figure 10-9.
Reading through this will let you know what is going to happen

Basically, the script formats and partitions the flash drive (make sure there isn't any valuable data on it) and copies a plethora of files from your **System** folder. The process, as far as your Mac is concerned, is completely nondestructive; all the script does is copy files. Once you are satisfied the script is safe, you can create a stick to enable SSH on your Apple TV.

The easiest way to pull this hack off is to find an Intel-based Mac running 10.4.9+. Once you have access to a 10.4.9+ machine, mount the Apple TV 1.1 update you downloaded earlier and insert the flash memory in an open USB slot on your Mac. Head to the Terminal and relocate to the the *Patchstick* directory:

```
$ cd ~/Desktop/Patchstick
```

From the *Patchstick* directory, type:

```
$ sudo ./createpatchstick
```

The *./* tells the Terminal a script is coming. In the case of this particular script, the first thing that happens is that you'll be prompted to pick which disk you want the patchstick created on as shown in Figure 10-10.

Figure 10-10.
Pick your disk

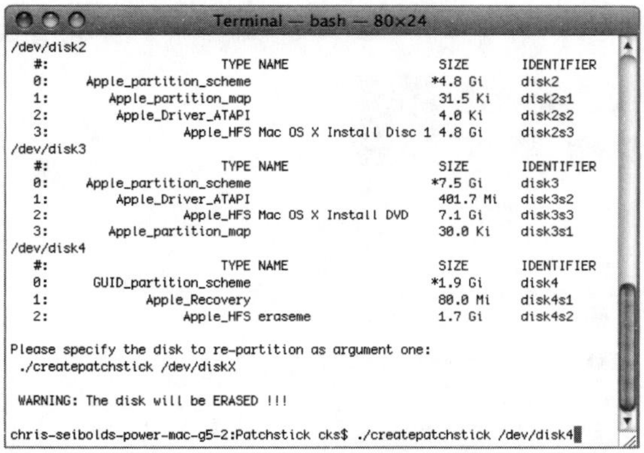

> Be careful when choosing the disk; you're running this script as *sudo* so if you pick the wrong disk, you could end up losing a great deal of data because *createpatchstick* doesn't check to see what disk you picked. When it comes to *createpatchstick*, you are the authority.

Once you've given your final answer, type:

```
$ sudo ./createpatchstick dev/disk2/
```

Where the disk identifier matches the disk you want to use as the patchstick. *createpatchstick* will run through the script doing all the heavy lifting (see Figure 10-19).

Figure 10-11.
createpatchstick gets to work

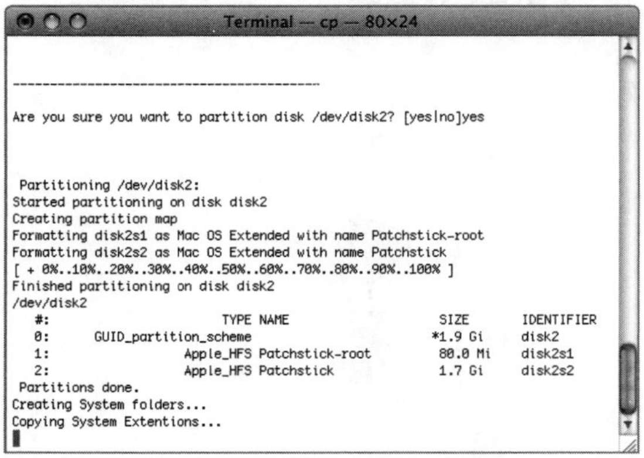

When the process is complete, *createpatchstick* will unmount the disk. Pull the stick out of your Mac's USB slot (you don't have to eject, in fact you can't: it is unmounted), and get ready to patch your Apple TV with it.

The Hard Work, No 10.4.9 Machine Handy Method

To pull this off, you need all the items listed earlier and Mac OS 10.4.6+ install discs.

To start, create a new folder on your desktop (or wherever), and give it a meaningful name. I'll use *patchfiles* but use whatever convention works for you.

Next, download and install Pacifist. Pacifist is a package inspector that allows you to get at files that are normally inaccessible. Now, insert the Mac OS X install disc (Disc 1). Launch Pacifist, click Open Package, and select *Essentials.pkg*. Pacifist then loads the *Essentials.pkg*, and you'll be faced with a semiconfusing but semifamiliar array of folders (see Figure 10-12).

Figure 10-12.
Hey, it looks like a basic system install

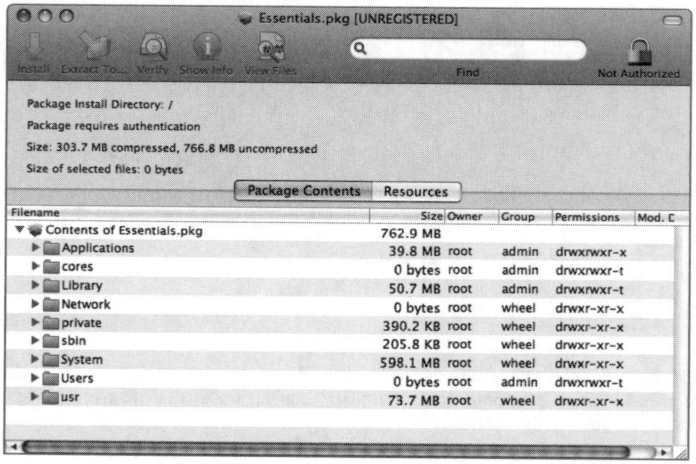

Now, instruct Pacifist to extract the files to the folder you created earlier by clicking the Extract To button and choosing the appropriate folder (see Figure 10-13).

Figure 10-13.
This step saves a headache

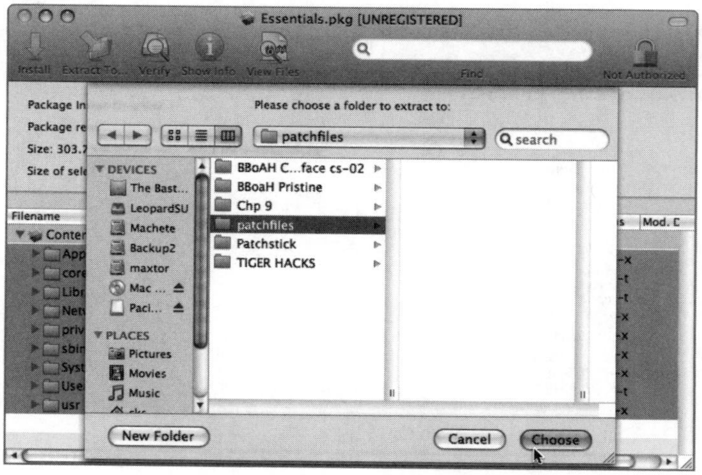

You'll be prompted for an administrator password, and Pacifist will take care of the rest, Be warned though, the process does take some time.

This next step is pure drudgery but necessary to create a working patchstick. The folder that was targeted as the destination of the extraction is now chock full of files and folders. Patchstick (the name of the conglomeration of files, binaries and folders you downloaded earlier) needs a good number of those files to work. You can find the files at *patchfiles/Essentials Folder/System/Library/ Extensions*. There are hundreds of files in there, but you're only interested in 32 of them; they are listed here:

AppleACPIPlatform.kext	*IOATAFamily.kext*
AppleAPIC.kext	*IOAudioFamily.kext*
AppleEFIRuntime.kext	*IOGraphicsFamily.kext*
AppleFileSystemDriver.kext	*IOHIDFamily.kext*
AppleFlashNVRAM.kext	*IONDRVSupport.kext*
AppleHDA.kext	*IONetworkingFamily.kext*
AppleHPET.kext	*IOPCIFamily.kext*
AppleIRController.kext	*IOPlatformPluginFamily.kext*
AppleRTC.kext	*IOSCSIArchitectureModelFamily.kext*
AppleSMBIOS.kext	*IOStorageFamily.kext*
AppleSMC.kext	*IOUSBFamily.kext*
AudioIPCDriver.kext	*IOUSBMassStorageClass.kext*
BootCache.kext	*NVDANV40Hal.kext*
GeForce.kext	*NVDAResman.kext*
IO80211Family.kext	*OSvKernDSPLib.kext*
IOACPIFamily.kext	*System.kext*

The mission is to get those files into the Extensions folder of the Patchstick folder created when you downloaded *Patchstick* at the very beginning of this hack. If you put it on your Desktop, you'll find it under *~/Desktop/Patchstick/Files/System/Library/Extensions*. It is a tedious drag-and-drop process but not much of challenge if you sort the folder's contents by name. When you're done, the Extensions folder of the Patchstick folder should have 32 items.

After you're done moving those files, there is another folder you need to move. The Kerberos. Framework folder is located in **Frameworks** folder of the **System** folder of the package you extracted. In my case, the file is located at *patchfiles/Essential Folders/System/Library/ Frameworks*. Move this file to *Patchstick/Files/ System/Library/Frameworks*.

If you enjoyed that exercise, you are in luck: there is plenty more where that came from. Head back to Pacifist, choose Open Package, and navigate back to the Mac OS X install disc. From there, follow the same path as earlier (*System/Installation/Packages*), but choose *BaseSytem.pkg* as the package to extract. Instead of extracting the entire package as in the previous step, you'll look for a few files. Once Pacifist is done extracting the files, you are presented with a window showing a list of everything Pacifist has found. Type **corefoundation** in the search box in the upper right corner of Pacifist, and Pacifist will find matching files and display the results in a side drawer (see Figure 10-14).

Figure 10-14.
Let Pacifist do the work

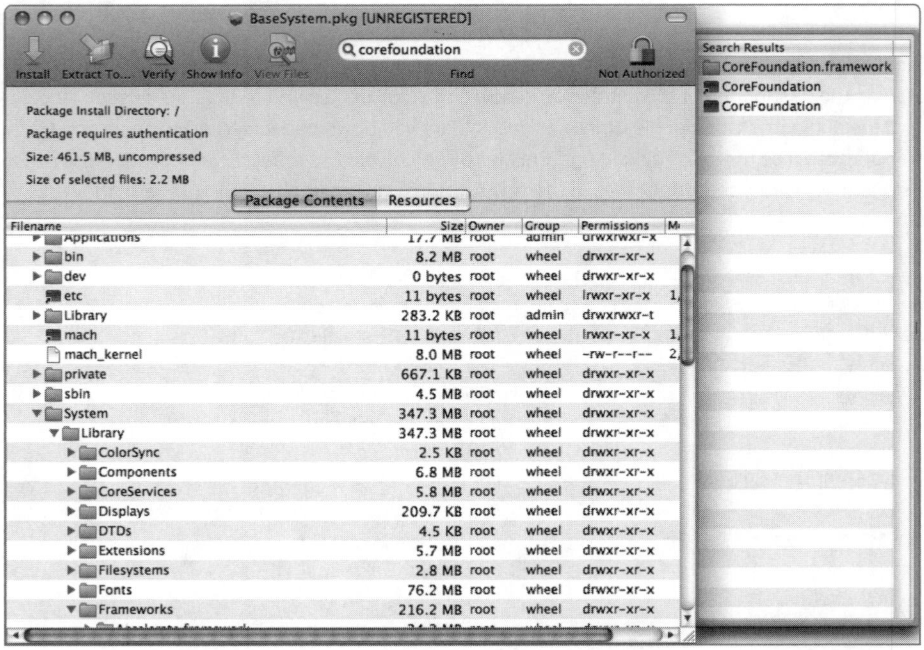

Once you've found the file you need, *CoreFoundation.Framework*, you need to get it in the right place in the *Patchstick* folder. Click the "Extract to" button in Pacifist, and point the program to the **Frameworks** folder of the *Patchstick* folder on your Desktop (*Patchstick/Files/System/Library/Frameworks*) as shown in Figure 10-15.

Figure 10-15.
Skip the middleman: extract straight to the right folder

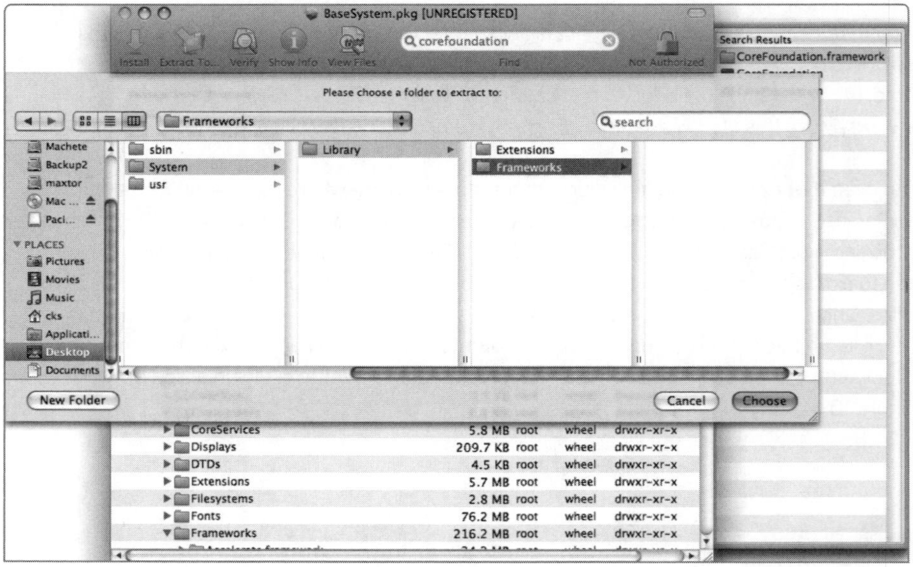

Repeat the process with *IOKit.Framework*. If you look at the **Frameworks** folder, it should now have three subfolders (see Figure 10-16).

Figure 10-16.
Patchstick's Frameworks folder should look like this

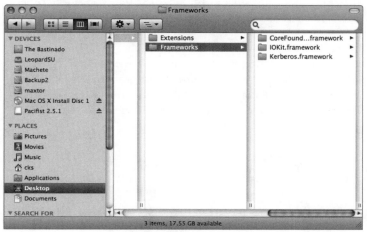

A few more moments with Pacifist: using the same method (search and expand directly to the required folder of the *Patchstick* directory) search for *dyld, ibgcc_s.1.dylib, libncurses.5.4.dylib,* and *libSystem.B.dylib.* Then, move these files to the *lib* directory of the **Patchstick** folder (**Patchstick/Files/usr/lib**). The end result should look like Figure 10-17.

Figure 10-17.
The final look of the lib folder

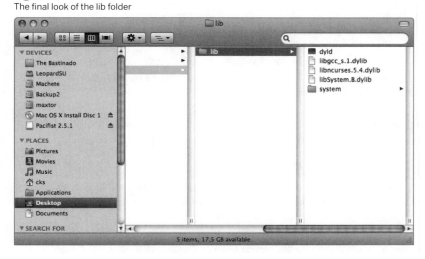

One more bit of copying from the install disk. Search for *libmathCommon.A.dylib* using Pacifist, and have Pacifist extract the file to *Patchstick/Files/usr/lib/system.*

That is a lot of work, but you're not done yet. Mount the Apple TV updater you downloaded earlier. You'll discover that the expanded disk image is called OSBoot. No need to rely on Pacifist this time because for a single file, the Terminal is much faster. Type:

```
$ mv /Volumes/OSBoot/usr/standalone/i386/boot.efi ~/Desktop/Patchstick/Files
```

That command copies *boot.efi* from the invisible *usr* folder on the Apple TV update disk to the Files folder of the Patchstick folder you downloaded much earlier in the hack.

There is one file left to add, but you'll have to get it from the 10.4.9 updater. You can get the updater from Apple at http://www.apple.com/support/downloads/macosx1049comboupdateintel.html. It's a big download—around 310 MB—so be prepared to kill some time unless you have a speedy connection.

Once the update is downloaded, your Mac will automatically mount it and report (unless your Mac is running something below 10.4.9) that the updater can't be used. No big deal: you just want a single file, not a system update! Head back to Pacifist, and point the program to the *Mac OS X 10.4.9 Combined Update (Intel) Disc*. Pacifist will find one package: tell Pacifist to open it (see Figure 10-18).

Figure 10-18.
There's only one choice

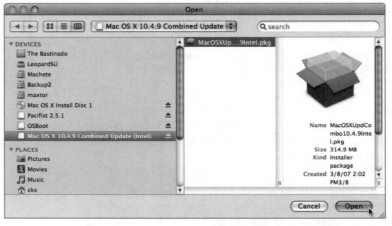

Once Pacifist is finished extracting the files, use the built-in search functionality to find *AppleIntelCPUPowerManagement.kext*. Next, it is more of the same: set Pacifist to extract the file to *Patchstick/Files/System/Library/Extensions*.

The good news is you're done transferring files! The bad news is that there is still some work to do. The permissions on the file *boot.efi* need to be changed, so visit the Terminal and type:

```
$ chmod 775 ~Desktop/Patchstick/Files/boot.efi
```

This step changes the permissions for *boot.efi* to readable by everyone, executable by everyone, and writable only by the file's owner. A minor change, it would seem, but the Apple TV needs to be able to read and execute the file, so it is a step you can't skip.

The rest is taken care of by the script you downloaded earlier. The drill is the same as the one you used if you tried the 10.4.9 method:

```
$ cd ~/Desktop/Patchstick
```

From the *Patchstick* directory type:

```
$ sudo ./createpatchstick
```

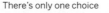 Be careful when choosing the disk, you're running this script as *sudo* so if you pick the wrong disk, you could end up losing a great deal of data because *createpatchstick* doesn't check to see what disk you picked. When it comes to *createpatchstick*, you are the authority.

Once you've given your final answer, type:

```
$ sudo ./createpatchstick dev/disk2/
```

Where the disk identifier matches the disk you want to use as the patchstick. *createpatchstick* will run through the script doing all the heavy lifting (see Figure 10-19).

Figure 10-19.
creatpatchstick gets to work

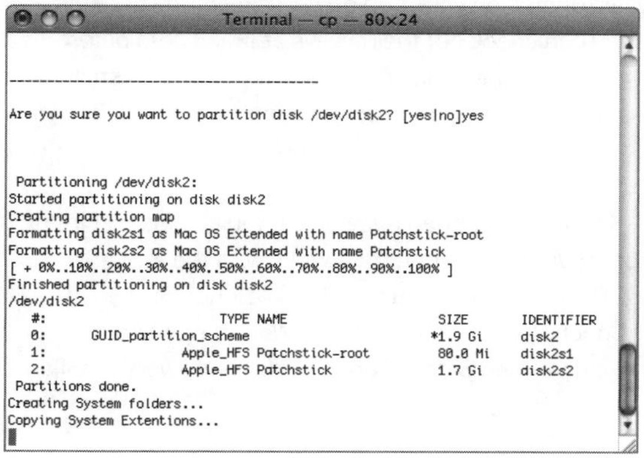

When the process is complete, *createpatchstick* unmounts the disk. Pull the stick out of your Mac's USB slot (you don't have to eject; in fact you can't, it is unmounted) and get ready to patch your Apple TV with it.

Patching the Apple TV Box

Once your patchstick is ready, patching the Apple TV is remarkably easy. Plug the patchstick into the Apple TV's sole USB port, and press Menu and – on the Apple TV remote for a few seconds. The Apple TV will automatically reboot, and the patchstick will get to work. White text will scroll on the screen, and some errors will be reported, but when you get back to your Mac, you'll be able to create an SSH connection to the Apple TV.

To create the connection, head to the Terminal and type:

```
$ ssh -1 frontrow@appletv.local
```

You'll get an interesting response:

```
The authenticity of host 'appletv.local (192.168.1.206)' can't be established.
RSA1 key fingerprint is 1c:c3:3e:06:42:58:ce:ea:bb:be:7a:b6:d6:d6:d8:db.
Are you sure you want to continue connecting (yes/no)? yes
Warning: Permanently added 'appletv.local,192.168.1.206' (RSA1) to the list of
known hosts.
Password:
Response:
Last login: Tue Mar  4 03:50:44 2008
-bash-2.05b$
```

The password is the same as the username: `frontrow`. There you have it—an SSH connection to your Apple TV without cracking the box. What good is an SSH connection? Check out "Hack # Browse from the Couch" for one fun hack!

Browse from the Couch

If you've got SSH installed on your Apple TV, why not take advantage of the increased functionality and use your Apple TV to browse the Internet?

If you've gone to the trouble of getting SSH running on your Apple TV, you might be wondering just what to do next. Why not get a custom browser running on your Apple TV? Think of the benefits: when you're thinking about renting a movie, you can check out the reviews at IMDB.com before laying down your hard-earned cash. You can check out the TV listings to see if you should stick to Apple TV content or go for traditional TV. Plus, web browsing on your flat-panel 52-inch HD TV while reclining on the couch just looks cool.

When it comes to browsing on your Apple TV, there is more than one choice. You can install Firefox and other browsers, but a custom browser for the Apple TV—one that works with the Apple TV remote—is the way to go for casual browsing. The choice for casual surfing is Couch Surfer (http://www.brandon-holland.com/software.html). Couch Surfer is based on the WebKit open source project (http://webkit.org/) as Safari is, so if you've used Safari, Couch Surfer has a very familiar feel.

Installing Couch Surfer

Installing Couch Surfer is easy; the process consists of three basic steps:

1. Download Couch Surfer.

2. Transfer Couch Surfer to the target Apple TV.

3. Run the installer script.

When you visit the Couch Surfer home page, you're presented with nine choices. You can opt for a plug-in version, which comes with an installer for either Apple TV 1.1 or Apple TV Take 2. What you need depends on how your Apple TV is set up. The important thing to remember is to get the proper version for your Apple TV software revision.

The Apple TV used in this hack runs Take 2, and I opted for the standalone version. Once you've made your choice and downloaded the software, it is time to get it over to the Apple TV. You could do this with the command line, but there are few files to put in different places, so it might be easier to use something with a GUI frontend.

Fugu is a graphical frontend for the built-in Secure File Transfer Protocol (SFTP) client that comes standard as a part of Mac OS X. It makes transferring files to your Apple TV a graphically friendly process. To download a copy of Fugu, point your browser to http://rsug.itd.umich.edu/software/fugu/download.html, and let the process take care of its self.

Once Fugu is downloaded, a double-click fires up the program. Once Fugu is running, instruct the program to connect to your Apple TV by typing **AppleTV.local** in the "Connect to" box and setting the username as **Frontrow**. Click the Advanced Options arrow, and check the box next to "Force SSH1 connection to server" (see Figure 10-20).

Figure 10-20.
Configuring Fugu

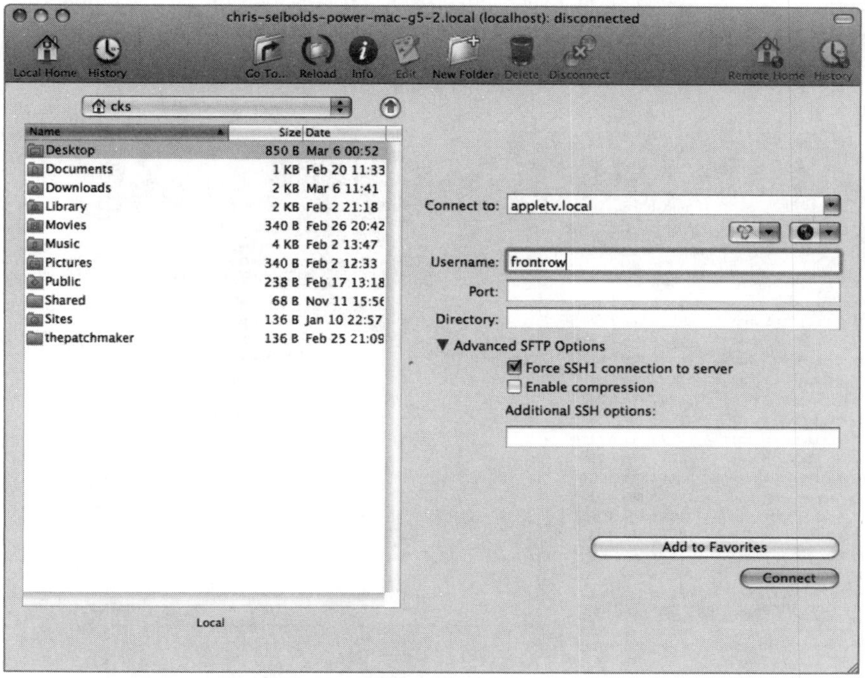

Now, click connect, and you'll be asked for your password (**frontrow**); once it's entered, you'll get the Apple TV file structure on the right side (see Figure 10-21).

Figure 10-21.
Hey, that layout is familiar!

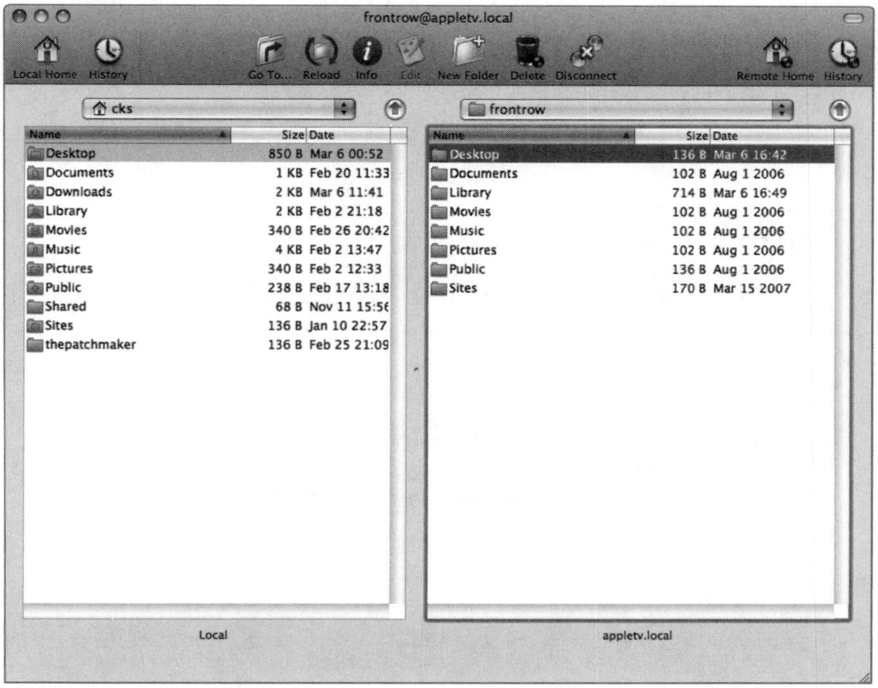

Moving files to and from the Apple TV is now a simple matter of drag and drop. In the specific case of Couch Surfer, locate the **Couch Surfer** folder you downloaded earlier and drag it to the **Home** folder (or wherever you want the program to live) of the Apple TV (see Figure 10-22).

Figure 10-22.
Adding Couch Surfer

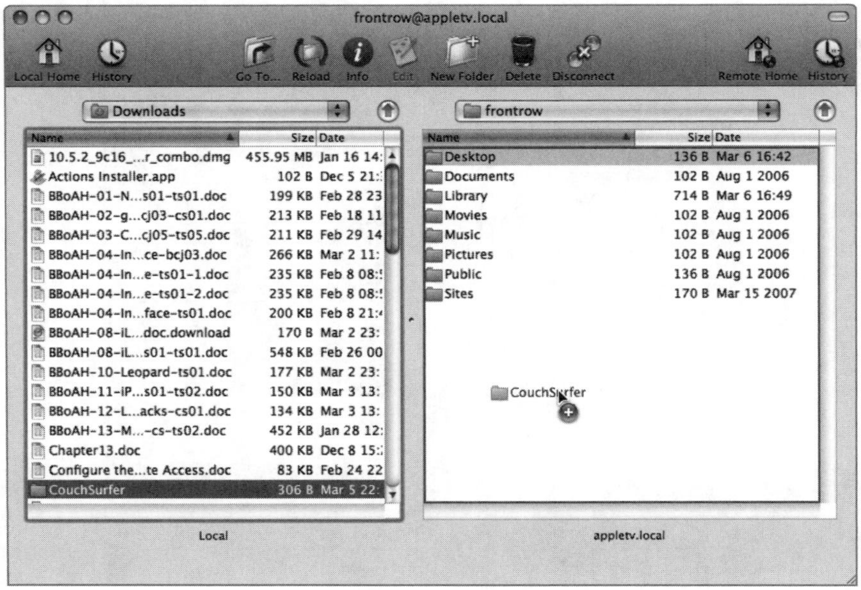

This is a good moment to add some bookmarks. Couch Surfer is completely controlled by the Apple remote so typing is cumbersome. Back on your Mac, grab the *Bookmarks.plist* file from the Couch Surfer folder you downloaded earlier, open it in a text editor, and add your favorite links to the list.

```
<?xml version="1.0" encoding="UTF-8"?>
<!DOCTYPE plist PUBLIC "-//Apple Computer//DTD PLIST 1.0//EN" "http://www.apple.
com/DTDs/PropertyList-1.0.dtd">
<plist version="1.0">
<array>
        <dict>
                <key>title</key>
                <string>brandon-holland.com</string>
                <key>url</key>
                <string>http://www.brandon-holland.com</string>
        </dict>
                ...
        <dict>
                <key>title</key>
                <string>your title for this bookmark</string>
                <key>url</key>
                <string>http://www.whatever.who/where.html</string>
        </dict>
</array>
</plist>
```

Put the resulting file in the Documents folder of your Apple TV. With everything in place, it is time to install Couch Surfer.

Back at the Terminal, launch the Terminal and connect to the Apple TV:

```
$ ssh -1 frontrow@appletv.local
```

Now, navigate to the directory where you put the Couch Surfer folder. In this hack, I put Couch Surfer in the Home folder so getting to the folder is easy:

```
$ cd couchsurfer/
```

A quick check with the `ls` command to make sure everything is where I (and the installer) expect it:

```
$ ls
About.txt        CouchSurfer.pkg       WebKit.pkg
Bookmarks.plist      Install.txt       installcouchsurfer
```

Everything is there; time to install Couch Surfer:

```
$ sudo ./installcouchsurfer
```

And the installer takes care of the rest:

```
Installing Couch Surfer...
installer: Package name is Couch Surfer
installer: Installing onto volume mounted at /.
installer: The install was successful.
Installing WebKit...
installer: Package name is WebKit
installer: Installing onto volume mounted at /.
installer: The install was successful.
Restarting Finder...
```

A few seconds later, you're browsing (see Figure 10-23)!

Figure 10-23.
Surfing from the couch

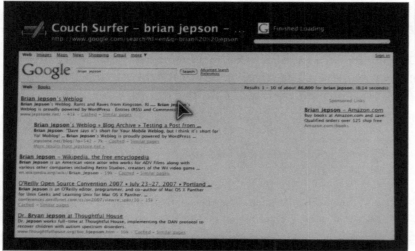

Couch Surfer might take a little adjustment if you are used to browsing with a mouse and keyboard (or if your fingers are iPhone-enabled), but it is a relatively simple system. You scroll around the page using the +, -, and the fast forward and rewind buttons. To follow a link, press Play/Pause to bring up a pointer for selecting links to follow. Now you never have to leave your couch!

11

HACK THE LATEST AND GREATEST: LEOPARD

Mac OS X 10.5 Leopard was originally scheduled for a late 2006 or early 2007 release. That date slipped, and the release wasn't available until October 26, 2007. Apple blamed the iPhone for the delay. The truth is that once the new release was in the hands of users they didn't care about the delay, they were just happy to have it.

Leopard features (according to Apple) over 300 enhancements and features. That's a nice round number and good for marketing purposes, and although some of the 300 were minor, many of these were significant changes. Leopard changed much more than previous iterations of Mac OS X. The big changes included Time Machine for very easy backups, Back to My Mac for GUI Mac remote management, and an iTunesish Finder with a Cover Flow-like method of browsing files just to name a few of the bigger changes.

The good thing about the changes: more hacking opportunities! Learn how to customize Mail stationery, bend Time Machine to your will, and get Back to My Mac functionality without a .Mac subscription, among other tricks in this chapter.

HACK 90: Make Mail Templates Yours

The version of Mail (3.0) that ships with Leopard includes a new feature—stationery. Discover a way to generate your own stationery or modify existing Mail stationery.

A new version of Mail ships with Leopard and with the latest version of Mail, Apple offers a special treat for users looking to spice up the usually boring mail message. Apple calls the new addition *stationery*, and it can give the messages you send a much more visually stimulating look (see Figure 11-1).

Mail offers up templates for all the usual suspects: stationery to make your letters look more like they just came out of an envelope, designs to show off your photos, and templates to convey those sentimental thoughts each of us experiences on occasion. The templates look uniformly great, and it is easy to tell that a lot of thoughtful design went into to each template. All the more remarkable is that the stationery is composed of plain old HTML and just a few images.

Figure 11-1.
You can replace the text, but not the images

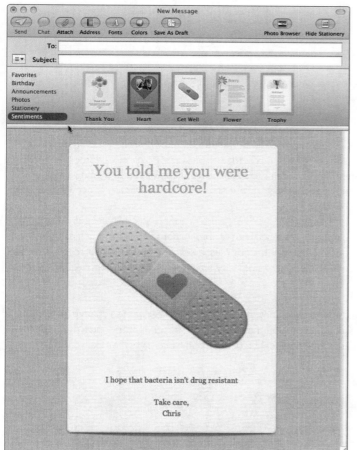

QUICK TIP ✕

BEFORE USING STATIONERY, CONSIDER RECIPIENT

While this hack covers customizing the HTML in Mail's stationery option, a lot of people hate getting HTML-formatted mail. The objection is valid: HTML doesn't render well in text-only email programs such as Mutt, takes up more space, and can be hard on the eyes. In fact many people despise formatting altogether in any email. To send all your messages as plain text (and make the HTML haters you know happy), go to Mail's Preferences→ Composing menu option and change the value next to Message Format: from Rich Text to Plain Text. Sure, your mail is a little more boring, but those picky about their mail will thank you. Well they won't really thank you, but they won't get angry at you either.

Wait! Plain HTML? Just a few images? Nothing very complicated? Sounds like a perfect thing to hack! And it is. There is a ton of fun to be had hacking away at the new stationery found in Mail. A two-tiered approach is best for this hack. First, we'll modify the existing templates, and then we'll create a custom template for any purpose you desire.

Modifying Existing Templates

Mail comes with 28 fun, good looking, and easy to modify templates. For this part of the hack, we'll use the Trophy template found filed under Sentiments. The first step is locating where Mail hides the HTML and images the program uses to generate the templates. Time to use the standard hacking trick of just poking around in the Library folder. Since Mail is available to all users, the more likely place for the files to reside is the main Library folder found down one level on the hard drive.

The hacking instinct is correct; no drill through the Library folder deep enough, and you'll find the files that hold the key to customizing the built-in templates. The precise path is: */Library/ Application Support/Apple/Mail/Stationery/Apple/Contents/Resources* (see Figure 11-2).

Figure 11-2.
A portion of the path, it's a long walk!

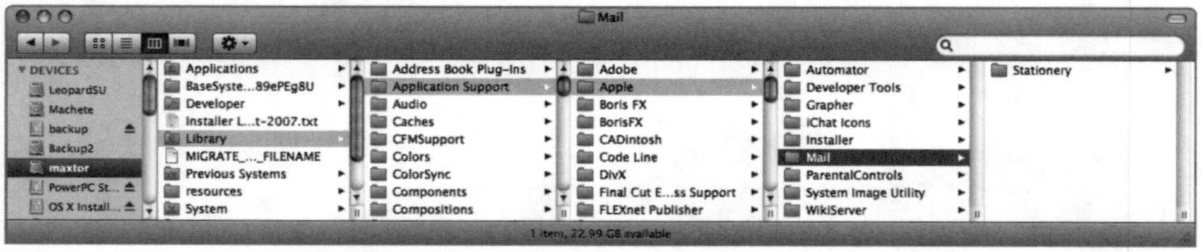

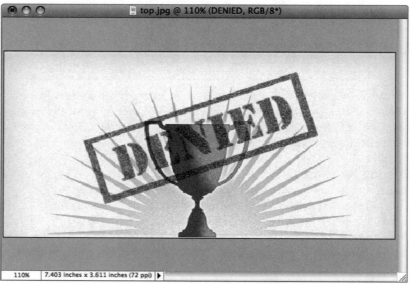

Once you've located the resources folder, copy the folder to someplace different while you hack away on it.

Time to get to the good stuff. Open up the Resources folder and navigate to the package *Trophy. mailstationery*; go to *Resources/Sentiments/Contents/Resources/Trophy.mailstationery*. While *Trophy.mailstationery* looks like a single file, it is actually a package. Right- or option-click, and choose Show Package Contents. Time for a little more navigation (yes, you're digging a total of 15 levels deep), but there isn't much further to go. *Contents/Resources* will finally get you to the files you want to modify.

When you are in the correct directory, you'll see a lot of *.lproj* folders and a few *.jpg* files laying around. For the moment we are interested in the *.jpg* files; modifying these files will result in unique stationery for Mail to use. For the purposes of simplicity, we'll keep everything simple and just do a dirty hack on the *.jpg* files.

This is the time for your creativity to shine through. Open the files you want to change in your favorite image editor and modify them to your heart's content. If you want to send a message to your favorite sports team, perhaps a modification of the trophy *.jpg* might look like Figure 11-3.

Figure 11-3.
Man, those guys only gave 108%

Edit the rest of the images in any manner you see fit, and drop them all back in the *Trophy.
mailstationery* package. Drop your modified package back into the folder where you first got it, and
the next time your team lets you down, you can send the coach an email that looks like Figure 11-4.

Figure 11-4
Let the team know how you really feel

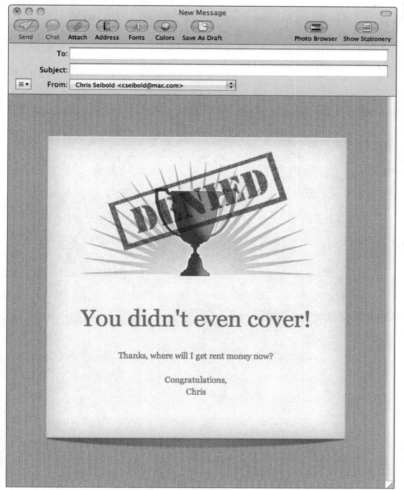

Undoing the Hack
Undoing this hack is straightforward. Simply drop the backup package in the folder, and your
Trophy sentiment stationery will return to the previous innocuous version.

Heavily Modifying or Creating Your Own Stationery
There is a lot of fun to be had simply editing the images, but you might want to do more. You might
want to generate stationery from a web page you already have or really modify one of Apple's
templates without replacing it.

The first step is to get the HTML code you want to use for your stationery, I'm using the Psst
stationery as a starting point, but standard HTML code will do (no ASP or PHP stuff). Create a new
folder and name the HTML file you want to use *Content.html*.

The next step is deciding where you want the editable text to go in your new stationery. Once that decision has been made, you'll have to add a section to your code to let Mail know you want it to be editable. The tags are simple:

```
<span contenteditable="true" apple-content-name="body" style="display:block; ">
```

This lets Mail know that that part of the page is editable. It is a good idea to add some display text so you'll know where to type. Get as fancy or as plain as you want. I'm going very plain:

```
Chris, you stooge type text here
```

Close the tags and your editable block of text is all set.

```
</span>
```

This takes care of adding text to the message. The rest of the steps are about turning your creation into stationery. Open up a Plist Editor (I'm using the Property List Editor that comes with Apple's Developer tools) and create a new *.plist* file. Click New Root followed by a click on the New Child button that appears. Name the Child "HTML File" and set the class to String with a value of *content. html* (see Figure 11-5).

Figure 11-5.
Creating the Description.plist file

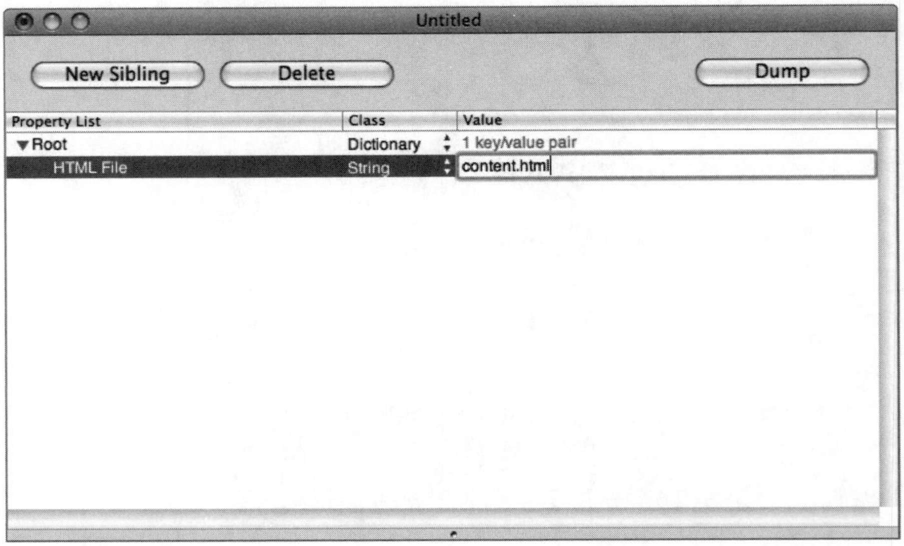

Generating the rest of the *.plist* file creations follow the same general process: click Create Sibling and set the values as follows:

Thumbnail Image
A thumbnail of the stationery; you'll have to create this; it's PNG format, 90 pixels high, 60 wide.

Folder Name
Whatever you want to call the folder; e.g., *newstationery.mailstationery*.

Stationery ID

Also in the *Description.plist*, you'll need a Stationery ID. Adding a new sibling for Stationery ID is as easy as clicking the New Sibling button, but you need a value to go along with the entry. Fire up the Terminal and type:

```
$ uuidgen
```

The Terminal will create a Universally Unique Identifier; copy and paste this number for the value of Stationery ID.

The images in your stationery have to be identified in the *Description.plist* as well. So add a New Sibling called Images. Set the class to Array and click New Child. Each image you use will need an entry, but since the numbering starts at 0, you'll end up with one less image than you might think you need (e.g., three images will be numbers 0,1 and 2). Repeat the image exercise for the background images you're using (if any). When you're done the *.plist* should look like Figure 11-6.

Figure 11-6.
The completed.plist file

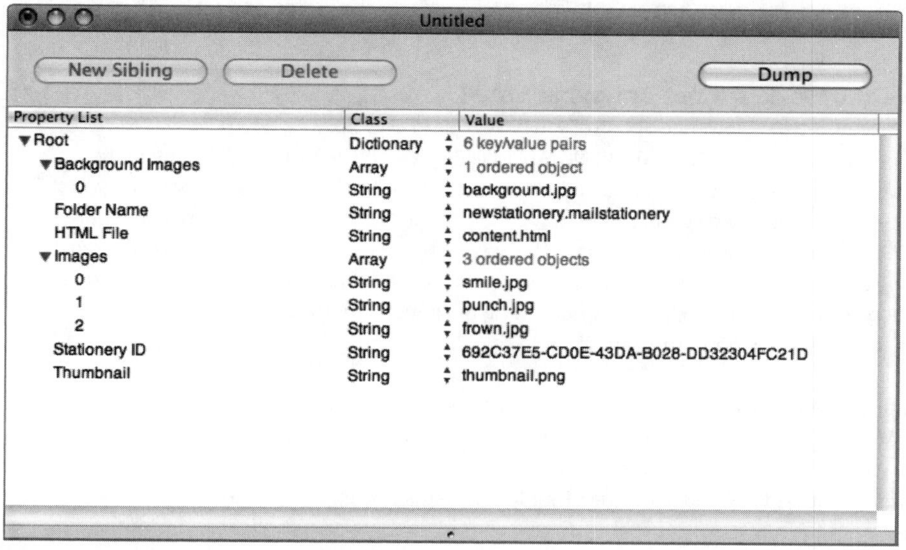

Finally save the file as *Description.plist* in the same folder as *content.html*.

The hard work is out of the way; now all that is left to do is to add all the files you want to use to the same folder where you saved *Description.plist and content.html*. Rename the folder *Resources* and place it in a folder with the same name you specified in the Folder sibling you created earlier (in this case *newstationery.mailstationery*). Double-click the result and Mail will ask you if you want to add the stationery. You've come this far, so click Yes.

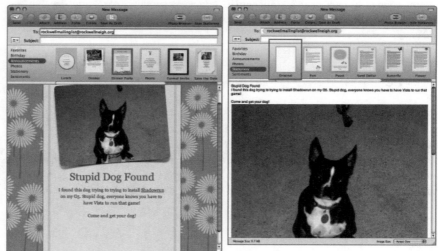

If you find yourself
typing up an email
using stationery and
decide you would prefer
to send a more vanilla
note, you don't have
to paste your text into
a new email. To revert
to the standard email
format you have chosen
(plain text or RTF mail),
simply click the Original
template found with the
Stationery options (see
Figure 11-7).

Create the World's Most Annoying Email

You've discovered just how much control you have over mail templates; now it's time to live dangerously. The sidebar "BEFORE USING STATIONERY, CONSIDER RECIPIENT" mentioned how many people detest HTML-formatted mail. Examining that statement for a moment, you realize that since only some people hate HTML mail, there must be others who are neutral or even like HTML-formatted mail. Why not change the world one mail at a time by generating the most annoying email possible? Email enough people and not only will you save time since you won't be getting any email in return, you may help swing the pendulum from general apathy to outright hostility towards HTML-formatted email.

To decide how annoying we can make an email, first we have to ascertain what to include in the email. We want stuff that is patently irksome, but we also want stuff that will render in most email clients. What is more annoying than the Internet of the 90s? Nothing springs to mind. Perhaps we can leverage the bad web design of the 90s into the loathsome email of tomorrow.

You could, naturally, go through and discover by trial and error which tags worked and which do not. I've saved you that trouble. Embedding a *midi* file is out straight away; that won't work on Yahoo, OS X or Gmail (pity really). So the old `embed autoplay=true` coupled with a *midi* of "Livin La Vida Loca" just isn't going to happen. Thankfully (or perhaps ruefully), there are few very annoying HTML elements that will work and plenty of generally benign HTML you can use. So how can you create the most annoying email template ever?

First, think colors: bright, vivid colors. Colors that never occur in nature; colors that would make a peacock vomit. Second, think animated gifs. Finally, consider the marquee element and an unclosed tag. Put them all together, and you've got one supremely annoying email.

HACK 91: A Brighter Spotlight

You can't miss Spotlight in Leopard, it is always on the screen. But the little magnifying glass in the upper right corner is far more than just a quick way to find files. Enhance your Spotlight experience with this hack.

As hard drives grew ever larger, the need for a systemwide search facility became obvious. Apple stepped up to the plate by adding Spotlight to Tiger. The reception was mixed: some found Spotlight invaluable, but others found the addition maddening in real-world use.

Leopard features an enhanced version of Spotlight, a version that addresses much of the complaints about the application's original incarnation. If you've been avoiding Spotlight, it is time to give it another look.

Spotlight as a Calculator or a Dictionary

Don't want to open up the Calculator application just to do a quick calculation? No problem: Spotlight has access to all the functions of the Mac OS X's built in calculator. Typing **sin (45)** in Spotlights search field yields the expected result (see Figure 11-8).

Figure 11-8.
Quick access to the calculator

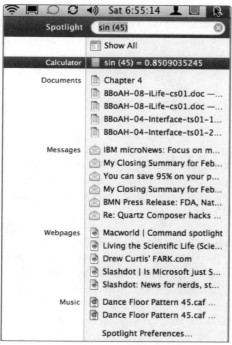

If numbers aren't your thing, Spotlight can help out with definitions as well; just type the troublesome word into Spotlight, and the definition will be revealed (see Figure 11-9).

Figure 11-9.
Ah, now I remember

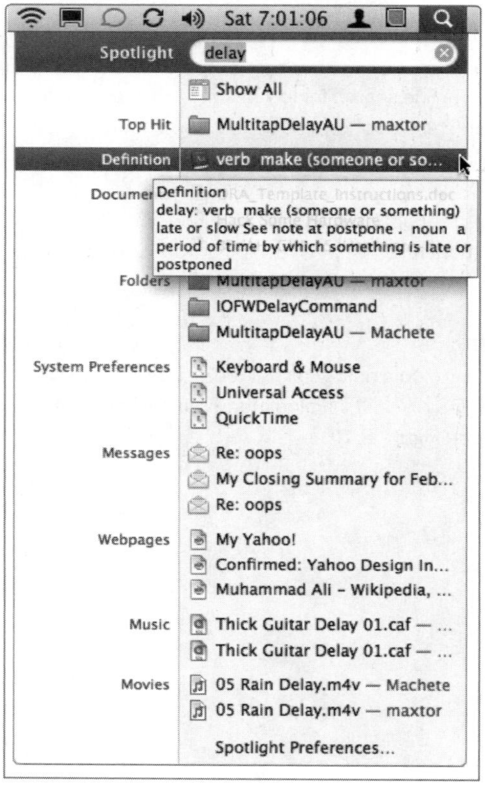

Use Boolean Searches with Spotlight

In Tiger you could use Boolean searches, but the methods were a little cryptic. For example "chris seibold(- jerk)" would find all the files in which the words "chris" and "seibold" appeared, but the word "jerk" did not. Conversely, "(chris|seibold) jerk" would return all the documents that had the words "chris" or "seibold" and the word "jerk"—useful, but not memorable.

Leopard addresses this shortcoming by allowing you to perform a Boolean search in a more obvious manner, with the more widely used terms "NOT," "AND," and "OR". If you're not familiar with Boolean terminology, the searches work just like you'd imagine. "Macintosh NOT OS X" returns all files fitting the criteria of containing "Macintosh" but not containing "OS X". The Spotlight search "Macintosh OR OS X" would return all files containing either the term Macintosh or the term OS X. Finally, the Spotlight search "Macintosh AND OS X" limits the result to files containing the terms "Macintosh" and "OS X".

A More Refined Spotlight Search

Boolean operators are great, and with clever usage, you can quickly zero in on the data you are looking for. In Leopard, OS X offers a method for even more refined searching. Hitting Command-F brings up a new Finder search window (see Figure 11-10).

Figure 11-10.
The standard Finder search interface

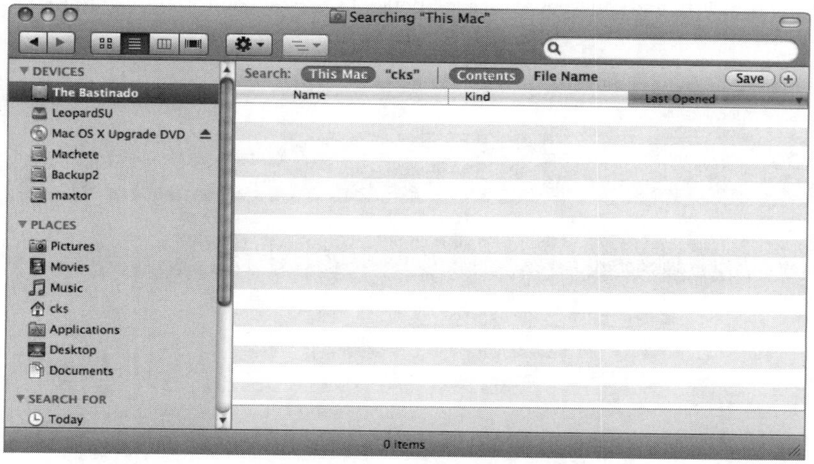

In Figure 11-10 you'll note you have some readily apparent options. You can restrict your search to your home folder (in this case "cks") or expand the search to include the entire computer. Any computers connected via Bonjour can be searched as well. Useful stuff, but not as great as the hidden functionality. Clicking on the "+" button reveals a brand-new search bar. You can set additional criteria for Spotlight to use when searching for files. In fact you can keep hitting the + button to add even more criteria. That method gets a little repetitive and confusing. Things are cleared up, and searching made easier when you hold the Option key. The + sign turns to ... and you get to the ability to filter the results of the earlier search using Boolean operators (see Figure 11-11).

Figure 11-11.
Refine your searches

Set Limits for Spotlight

Spotlight is great at finding things. That file you misplaced 18 months ago by accidentally burying it in the Legal folder that comes along with programs such as Acrobat, won't stay hidden from the indexing powers of Spotlight. The power of Spotlight's index cuts both ways. Sure, you can find any file, but you'll also find files you don't want to find. Why needlessly complicate your search? If there are locations you want to hide from Spotlight, Mac OS X has you covered. Head to System Preferences→Spotlight (or start a Spotlight search and choose "Spotlight Preferences..." from the very bottom of the results list), and you'll get access to Spotlight's master control (see Figure 11-12).

Figure 11-12.
Spotlight Preferences: reorder your results

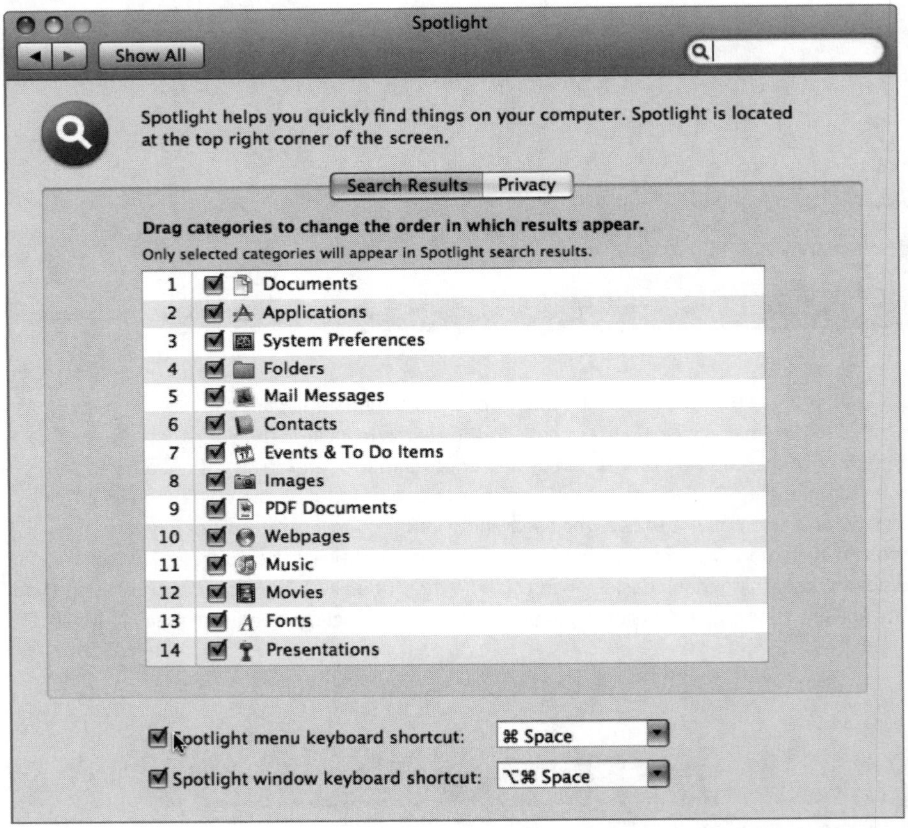

The first pane that you'll see lets you control the order and what results show up. To change the order, just click and drag the items around. If you don't want to be bothered with certain results—you don't care about Fonts, for example—just uncheck the checkbox.

Not seeing the results isn't the same as not indexing the results. If you uncheck Fonts, the files are still indexed; you just won't see the results. You might be wondering what the difference is between not being indexed and not being seen. In either case, you won't see the results. From a practical perspective, removing something from the results menu of Spotlight would seem to be the same as not indexing the file.

There are two nontrivial differences: the first is that your control over which files to return and which files to omit is limited. The less obvious, but just as critical, factor is that other applications rely on Spotlight's index. So if you've decided not return PDF documents in your Spotlight searches, those files will still be returned if you use another program that relies on Spotlight's index (one example would be Google Desktop).

What would be preferable is a method to have Spotlight skip indexing the files instead of indexing them and not returning the results. This turns out this is a simple step. Again in System Preferences→Spotlight, click the Privacy button, and a new pane will open to which you can drag Folders and drives you want Spotlight to skip, as shown in Figure 11-13. Note that you can't drag individual files.

Figure 11-13.
Adding a disk for Spotlight exclusion

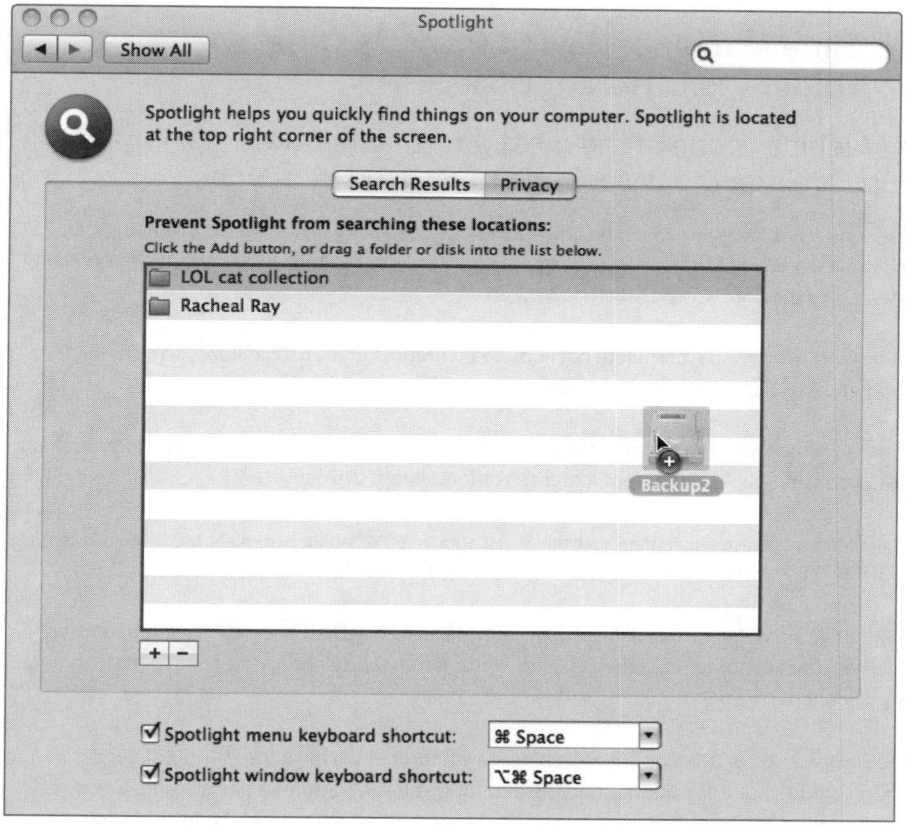

Use the Spotlight Index from the Command Line
If you want even more Spotlight searching ability, eschew Spotlight itself, and head for the Terminal. The Unix executable of most interest is `mdfind`. Typing:

```
$ mdfind Bavaria
```

Returns (just for the sake of example):

```
/Users/cks/Library/Caches/Metadata/Safari/History/http:%2F%2Fbadgas.
co.uk%2Flynndie%2F.webhistory
/Users/cks/Library/Caches/Metadata/Safari/History/http:%2F%2Fwww.cartalk.com%2Fcont
ent%2Fpuzzler%2Ftranscripts%2F200804%2Findex.html.webhistory
/Users/cks/Library/Caches/Metadata/Safari/History/http:%2F%2Fen.wikipedia.
org%2Fwiki%2FAnneliese_Michel.webhistory
```

A moment's inspection reveals that `mdfind` has returned the paths of all the items on my Mac that contain "Bavaria" in the file, the metadata, or title. This is great, but obviously of limited use. Were I to type in "hacks," I would be in for a lot of scrolling and too many results to be useful. Luckily, you can restrict searches to specific places:

```
$ mdfind hacks -onlyin /Users/cks/Backup
```

This returns all relevant files in the Backup directory of my Home folder. There are many more tools for limiting or broadening searches (including a method to constantly update the results) that you can discover and try out by typing:

```
$ man mdfind
```

HACK 92: ## Time Machine: How to Back Up Different Folders to Different Disks

Time Machine is one of the most amazing features of Leopard: backups are finally easy enough to be used by anyone.

Many users may not find Time Machine powerful enough. Backing up lots of data requires a big hard drive that isn't easy to carry in your bag, which means that all the work you do on the road is not protected by the hourly Time Machine backup.

The solution seems obvious: complete backups when home and partial backups, on a smaller (both in size and capacity) drive, while on the road.

Unfortunately Time Machine doesn't offer such an option: it is possible to back up to different hard drives, but you can't back up different folders to different hard drives.

 Before reading, please understand that this is not supported by Apple and might be dangerous for your data: please perform an extra backup on a different disk before proceeding.

Suppose that you own two external hard drives: one is called BigDisk, which you want to use for complete backups; the other is LittleDisk, which you want to use while on the road to back up only some significant folders.

Connect BigDisk and set it up for TimeMachine. I went for manual backups (the big slider on the "OFF" position), but this option is not relevant for this hack. Perform a backup and, when completed, unplug BigDisk (if you chose manual backups, you'll have to start a backup by right-clicking on the Time Machine icon and selecting "Backup now").

First, navigate to */Library/Preferences/* (the Library folder found at the root of your hard drive). Now, copy the file called *com.apple.TimeMachine.plist* in a safe place and rename it *com.apple.TimeMachine.BigDisk*.

For those Terminal lovers out there, simply type:

```
$ cd /Library/Preferences/
$ sudo cp com.apple.TimeMachine.plist com.apple.TimeMachine.BigDisk
```

Now plug LittleDisk into your Mac and set up Time Machine, excluding all the folders you think are of no vital importance. This might take a little more time than you'd expect: in fact, you have to set all the folders you do not want to back up.

As an example I backed up only:

~/Library/Mail
All my *Mail.app* emails

~/Library/Application Support
Among the other things here is the Address Book database

~/Library/Calendars
iCal calendars

~/Documents/Polimi
My university files

~/Desktop
My desktop folder

~/Downloads
Default folder for Safari, Mail, etc., downloads

Once again, I selected manual backups and started a backup.

When finished, save the file */Library/Preferences/com.apple.TimeMachine.plist* (it has changed now!) to a safe place and rename it *com.apple.TimeMachine.LittleDisk*.

Terminal fans will type:

```
$ cd /Library/Preferences
$ sudo cp com.apple.TimeMachine.plist com.apple.TimeMachine.LittleDisk
```

Whenever you want to perform a complete backup to BigDisk, you have to follow these steps:

1. Close the Time Machine Preferences pane!

2. Unplug LittleDisk and plug BigDisk.

3. Copy (do not move) *com.apple.TimeMachine.BigDisk* and rename the copy *com.apple.TimeMachine.plist*.

4. Replace */Library/Preferences/com.apple.TimeMachine.plist* with the one you have just created.

5. Open the Time Machine Preferences pane, select "Choose another disk," and select BigDisk

Again I selected to do manual backups.

Those of you using the Terminal can replace Steps 3 and 4 by typing (administrator password is needed):

```
$ cd /Library/Preferences
$ sudo cp com.apple.TimeMachine.BigDisk com.apple.TimeMachine.plist
```

You can now back up!

If you want to back up to LittleDisk again, the same procedure applies.

1. Close the Time Machine preferences pane!

2. Unplug BigDisk and plug LittleDisk.

3. Copy (do not move) *com.apple.TimeMachine.LittleDisk* and rename the copy *com.apple.TimeMachine.plist*.

4. Replace */Library/Preferences/com.apple.TimeMachine.plist* with the one you have just created.

5. Open the Time Machine Preferences pane.

6. Select "Choose another disk" and select LittleDisk.

Again I selected manual backups.

Those of you using the Terminal can replace Steps 3 and 4 by typing (administrator password is needed):

```
$ cd /Library/Preferences
$ sudo cp com.apple.TimeMachine.LittleDisk com.apple.TimeMachine.plist
```

You're done!

This hack is flexible and can be used to make a redundant backup of some vital folders to a smaller hard drive but also to an iDisk or an AFP disk.

— Marco Triverio

HACK 93: Two Ways to Make a Widget

Like widgets? Like Customization? Discover ways to create widgets to satisfy all your Dashboard needs.

If you're a CSS and HTML expert, you can whip out widgets for OS X without much trouble because at the heart of every widget is just plain old HTML and CSS. That doesn't mean widgets can only be composed of HTML and CSS. Far from it: widgets can use all the Unix commands you're familiar with, as well as Java instructions and Quartz Composer, just to name a few. But all the flexibility aside, all you really need to get going is HTML and CSS.

On the other hand, if you just want to create one widget, learning HTML and CSS is a bit much to ask. That is why when Leopard arrived, Safari supported the brand-new Web Clip functionality. Web Clip is a method to generate almost instantaneous widgets from any page on the Internet you find of interest.

To create your own widget with Web Clip, navigate to a page with information you want displayed using a widget, and choose File→Open in Dashboard (or click the Web Clip button in Safari's menu). For this part of the hack, I'm going to log in to my cable modem so I can check and make a widget of the Status page, in order to troubleshoot connectivity issues quickly (see Figure 11-14).

Figure 11-14.
With this widget, I can keep an eye on my modem

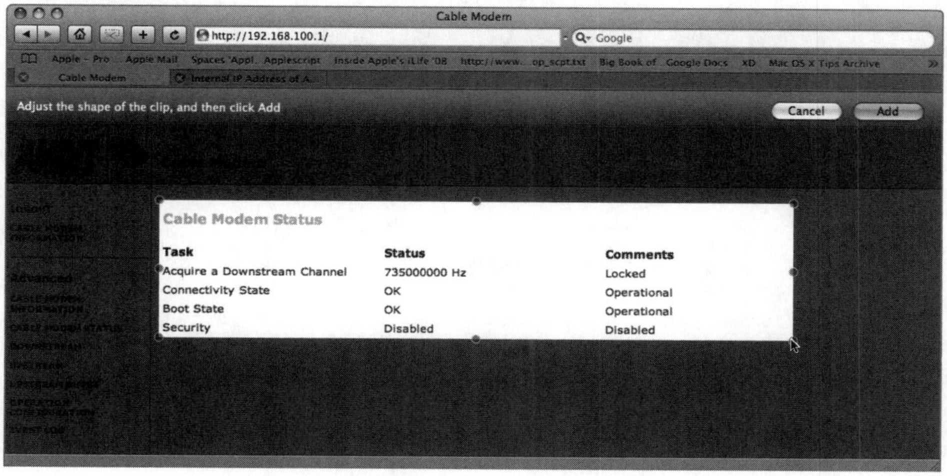

The circles on the edges of the highlighted area let you drag the area, so you can select only the salient parts of the web page you want to widgetify. Once you're happy with your choice, hit Add, and OS X will automatically take your choice, add some widget magic so it looks good on the Dashboard, and add it to widgets (see Figure 11-15).

Figure 11-15.
Your choice with has been transformed into a widget

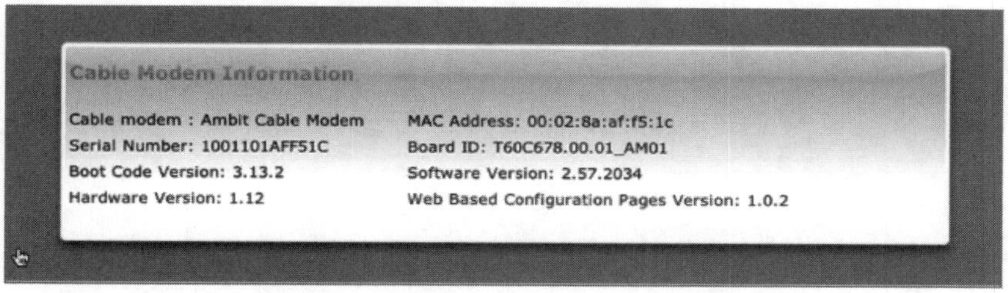

Web Clips are a great way to create widgets for stuff on the Internet, but not so great if you want a non-Internet-associated widget. Again, you could go through the rigmarole of hand-coding the widget, or you could grab a copy of Dashcode (http://developer.apple.com/tools/dashcode) and get some Apple-supplied help creating your widget.

Create a Widget with Dashcode

Widgets are supposed to be easy. That was the pitch when they first came out: just some CSS, a few links, and you'd be done. Designing a widget didn't turn out to be as easy as advertised. Anyone who heard the pitch was expecting a widget to be as easy to make as a web page. Trouble was, there are a lot of tools available to make web-page creation easy, but no applications to make widget creation easy. Apple got the message and released Dashcode, a tool specifically designed to make widget creation much less challenging.

How easy is it to make a widget with Dashcode? Play along and create an RSS reader!

Fire up Dashcode and choose the RSS reader template (see Figure 11-16).

Figure 11-16.
A Dashcode starting point

Dashcode generates a mostly blank, but mostly built widget. Drag the feed you want to use to the widget (see Figure 11-17).

Figure 11-17.
Hey your widget is done!

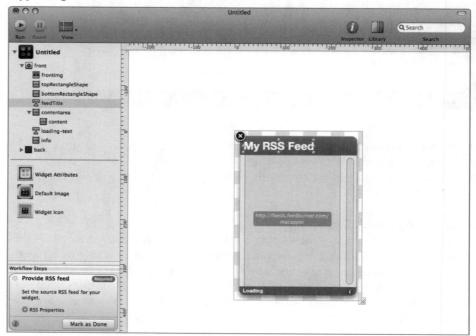

At this point, you could consider yourself done, but that widget doesn't look very MacApperish. If you take a look at MacApper.com, you'll note that the top is a darker blue than our widget's top, and the bottom is white. I don't want to mirror the exact look of MacApper, but I do want to keep a bit of the MacApper feel. Select the element you want to adjust from the source pane (e.g., top rectangle for changing the top) and click the blue Inspector button. Click the Fill and Stroke button in the Inspector and adjust away (see Figure 11-18).

Figure 11-18.
Customizing your widget

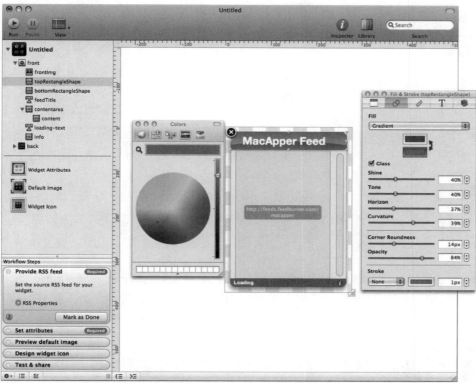

Repeat the process with all the elements you want to adjust.

Once your widget looks like you want it to—and feel free to go crazy—it is time to add an icon for your widget icon. Just find an image you want to use. (I'm using a PNG of Apple's generic Applications icon to fit in with MacAppers theme.) Click on widget Icon in the sidebar and drag your image on to the widget Icon in the center of the window (see Figure 11-19).

Figure 11-19.
A new widget icon

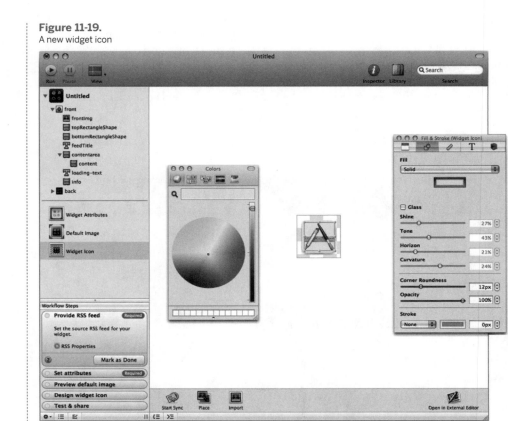

You're almost done. Click Run in the upper left corner, and the widget will start going about its widgety business right in Dashcode (see Figure 11-20).

Figure 11-20.
The widget is running

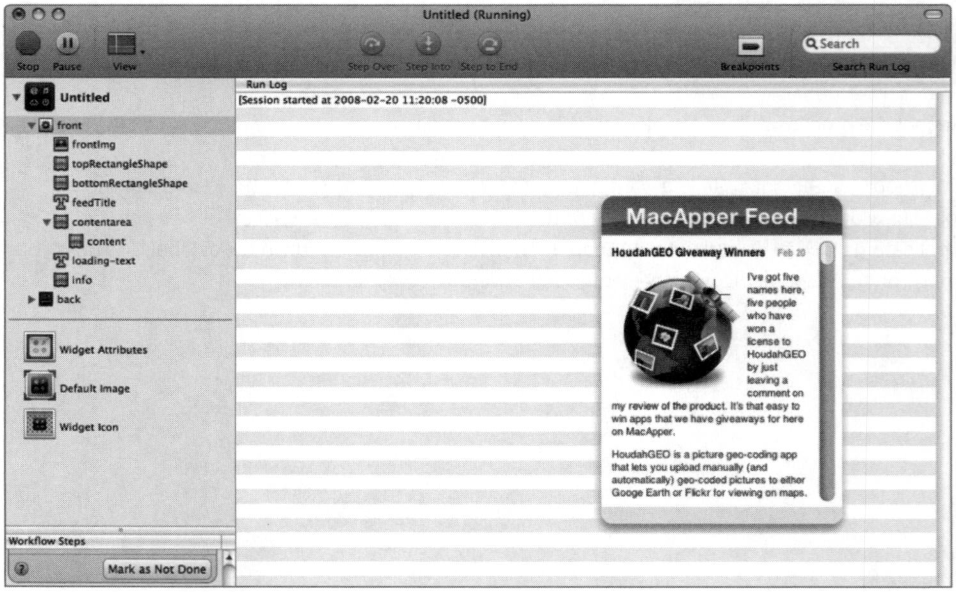

The feed is what I expected, but the size is a little constraining. I'll go back and adjust it by clicking on Front and resizing the entire thing. One more test run, and I'm satisfied. Time to put some polish on the thing. I'll change the widget title so it isn't so generic (see Figure 11-21) and save the file to my Documents folder so I can play with it later.

Figure 11-21.
Give your widget a name

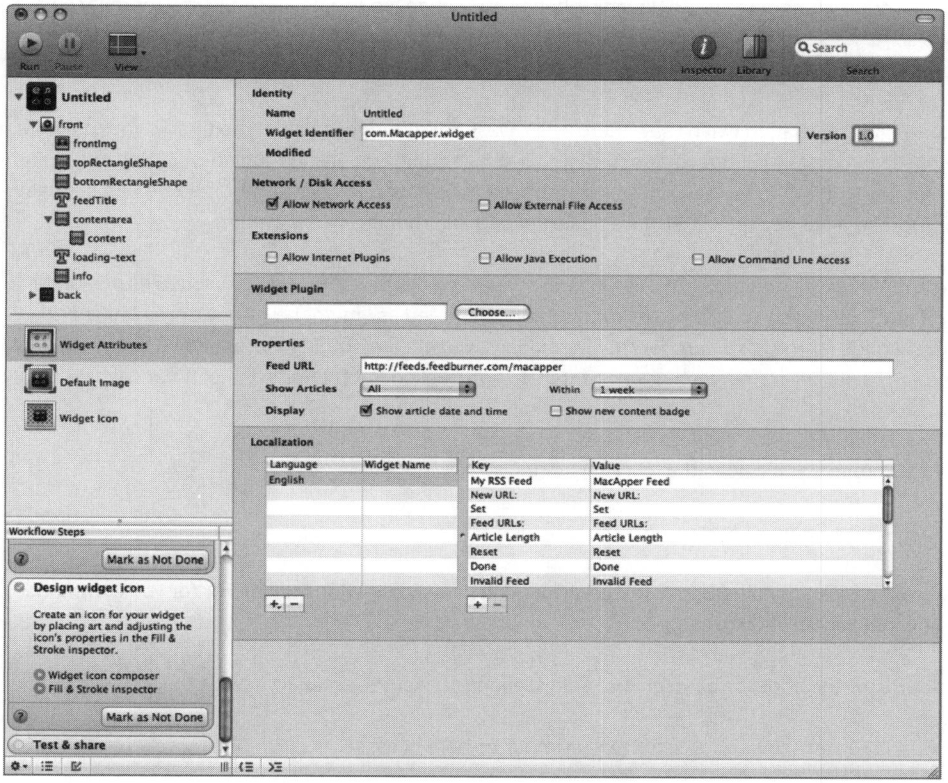

For the final step, send the widget to the Dashboard by clicking "Deploy Widget to Dashboard" under Dashcode's file menu. Your new widget is waiting (see Figure 11-22)!

Figure 11-22.
All done, enjoy your new widget

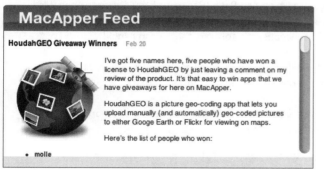

HACK 94: Tweak an Existing Widget

Building your own widget is great, but why make a widget when you can tweak one?

I love listening to NPR. When I commuted to and from work at O'Reilly, I'd have my car radio tuned to the local NPR station so I could get traffic information, hear the latest news, and more. But now that I work from home, my NPR listening habits have changed to when I'd make my morning coffee run (some habits die hard) or while running errands on the weekend (which I'd time appropriately so I could listen to *Car Talk*).

So, imagine my elation when I saw there was a Dashboard widget called Rabbit Radio (http://www.apple.com/downloads/dashboard/radio_podcasts/rabbitradio.html) that lets you tune into a select few NPR stations. I think it took me about a millisecond to decide Rabbit Radio was a widget for me, and a few seconds later, it was downloaded and running on my system.

Except, there was one problem: I live in Portland, Oregon, and KOPB wasn't included as one of the NPR stations you could listen to in Rabbit Radio. Bummed as I might be, it took only a few more milliseconds for me to remember that Dashboard widgets are nothing more than HTML, JavaScript, and CSS. I put my former web developer hat on and hacked Rabbit Radio to get it to do what I wanted.

For this project, you'll need the following items:

- The Rabbit Radio widget

- A text editor, such as BBEdit, TextEdit (found in your Applications folder), or for you command-line junkies, `vi` or Emacs

- A URL for the audio stream for the radio station you want to listen to

This isn't rocket science, folks: it's really simple, so here goes...

In the Finder, select your Home folder and go to Library→Widgets. This is the folder where all the widgets you've downloaded are installed on your Mac.

Select the Rabbit Radio widget (it's named *RabbitRadio.wdgt*). Right-click on it to get the context menu, and select the "Show Package Contents" option.

In the window that appears, you'll see a file named *RabbitRadio.html*. You'll want to open this file in your text editor of choice. You can do this by Ctrl-clicking on the file and selecting Open With → your text editor. For me, I use BBEdit (because it's software that doesn't suck!).

Scroll down in the document until you find a block of code that looks like Figure 11-23. Specifically, you're looking for commands such as `stationList.push`.

You'll find a line like the following in there somewhere. KQED is also a radio station, so let's copy their line, and paste another copy of it into the file:

```
stationList.push(new Station('KQED', 'West', 'QT', 'http://www.kqed.org/w/
streamingfiles/kqed_qt.mov'));
```

Figure 11-23.
Find this code

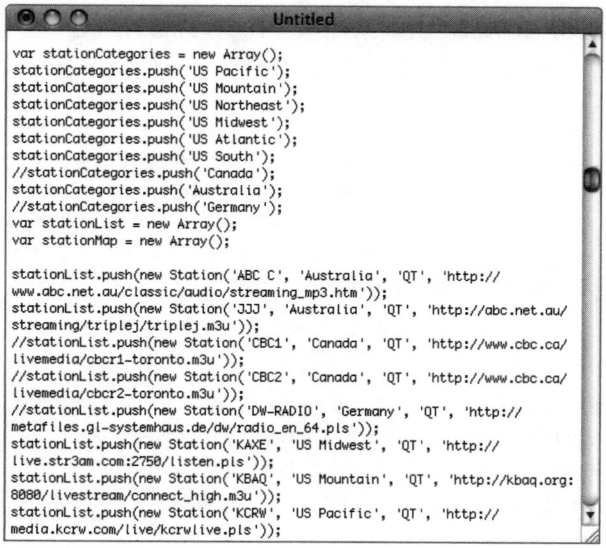

```
var stationCategories = new Array();
stationCategories.push('US Pacific');
stationCategories.push('US Mountain');
stationCategories.push('US Northeast');
stationCategories.push('US Midwest');
stationCategories.push('US Atlantic');
stationCategories.push('US South');
//stationCategories.push('Canada');
stationCategories.push('Australia');
//stationCategories.push('Germany');
var stationList = new Array();
var stationMap = new Array();

stationList.push(new Station('ABC C', 'Australia', 'QT', 'http://
www.abc.net.au/classic/audio/streaming_mp3.htm'));
stationList.push(new Station('JJJ', 'Australia', 'QT', 'http://abc.net.au/
streaming/triplej/triplej.m3u'));
//stationList.push(new Station('CBC1', 'Canada', 'QT', 'http://www.cbc.ca/
livemedia/cbcr1-toronto.m3u'));
//stationList.push(new Station('CBC2', 'Canada', 'QT', 'http://www.cbc.ca/
livemedia/cbcr2-toronto.m3u'));
//stationList.push(new Station('DW-RADIO', 'Germany', 'QT', 'http://
metafiles.gl-systemhaus.de/dw/radio_en_64.pls'));
stationList.push(new Station('KAXE', 'US Midwest', 'QT', 'http://
live.str3am.com:2750/listen.pls'));
stationList.push(new Station('KBAQ', 'US Mountain', 'QT', 'http://kbaq.org:
8080/livestream/connect_high.m3u'));
stationList.push(new Station('KCRW', 'US Pacific', 'QT', 'http://
media.kcrw.com/live/kcrwlive.pls'));
```

As you can see, this identifies the station name (KQED) and provides a link to the live streaming feed from that station. We'll edit this line to make a line for KOPB.

Before I can insert the link into the HTML file, I need to get the URL for KOPB's live feed, so I went to Oregon Public Broadcasting's web page, clicked on their "Listen Live" graphic, and right at the top of the next page was a set of links for "Live Radio Stream (MP3)". It's perfect: just what I'm looking for.

Ctrl-click on the link that says "Stream for iTunes, Quicktime, Winamp or Real Audio Player", and then select Copy Link from the context menu that appears. This copies the URL for KOPB's live feed to the pasteboard (which, of course, means you can paste it into something else...hmmm...I wonder what that could be...)

Now go back to your text editor to the line you copied and pasted earlier. Select the text for KQED and replace it with KOPB.

Next, select the URL for KQED's feed, and then hit Command-V to paste in the URL for KOPB's feed. That line should now look like this:

```
stationList.push(new Station('KOPB', 'West', 'QT', 'http://www.opb.org/programs/
streams/stream-radio.pls'));
```

Hit Command-S to save the changes you've made to the file, and then quit your text editor.

Now when you open the Dashboard, check the back of Rabbit Radio's interface, and you'll see KOPB listed in the pop-up that lists all the stations.

What's great about this is that you don't just have to add NPR stations to the list. If your favorite local radio station offers a live feed over the Internet, you can add that feed to Rabbit Radio as well. So, go on, mix it up. Hack on those widgets; it's just code.

— Chuck Toporek

Leopard introduces a host of new visual tweaks, If you're not a fan of the new look of OS X, discover hacks to make the looks of Leopard bearable.

Each new OS X iteration introduces a spate of new visuals. While the changes aren't as great as the optic shock Mac fans experienced when OS X was introduced, there are enough differences between Leopard and Tiger to leave some people pining for the olden days. There is no reason to forgo Leopard and miss out on such highly beneficial features as Time Machine just because you can't stand the graphics. The rods and cones of your eyes screaming in agony can be calmed with a few hacks.

A Different Dock

One of the big complaints about Leopard is the Dock (also a big complaint about OS X in general). First, there is the problem of continuity. If the dock is placed at the bottom of the screen, you get a distracting 3D reflective dock with blue globs telling you what applications are up and running. Put the dock on the right or left sides, and the 3-Dness is gone, replaced by a less distracting gray box with rounded corners (see Figure 11-24).

Figure 11-24.
Standard Dock choices in Leopard

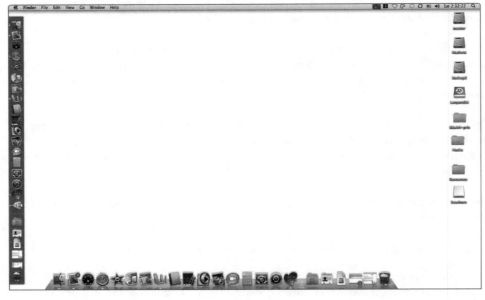

It would be nice to replace the glass dock at the bottom with the fully functional but less visually intrusive look used when the Dock resides on the side of the screen. Luckily you can do just that. There is more than one way to get the rounded grey rectangle of goodness to show up at the bottom of the screen, but the quickest was discovered by Jackilyn Hoxworth (see Figure 11-25). Fire up the terminal and issue the following command:

```
$ defaults write com.apple.dock no-glass -boolean YES
```

Hit return and follow the earlier command with:

```
$ killall Dock
```

Figure 11-25.
A Dock that is easier on your eyes

If you want to see all Dock's options, dig through the Library folder in your user space until you find *com.apple.dock.plist* file (the path is *~/Library/Preferences/com.apple.dock.plist*). Open said file with the Property List Editor and marvel at all the options (see Figure 11-26).

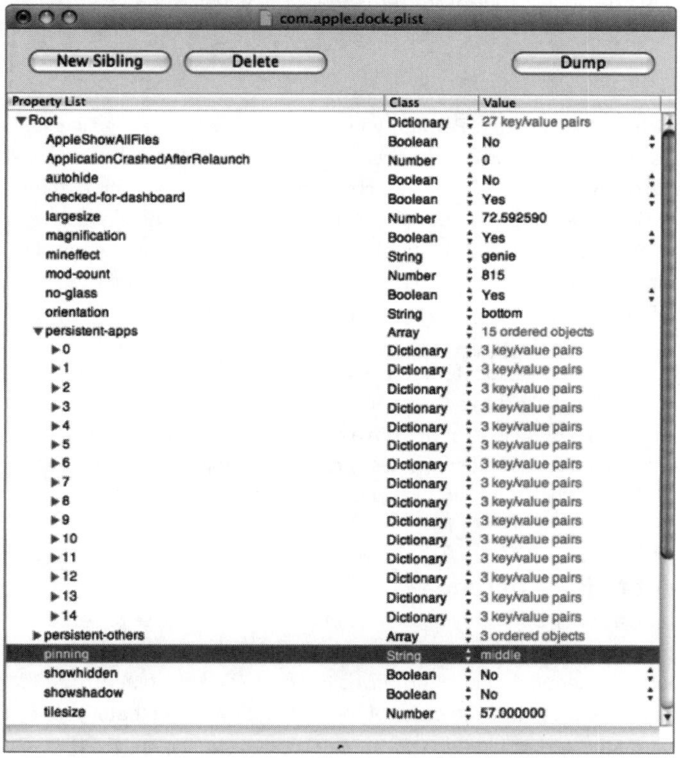

Figure 11-26.
You can change a lot with by editing the .plist file

One thing you can't change with the *.plist* settings or a quick trip to the terminal are the blue globules indicating which apps are currently running on your Mac. The blobs of neon blue have been the source of much derision for Leopard, and some users positively loathe the things. If you're one of those glowing dot haters why not get rid of the things?

As with most hacks, there is more than one way to accomplish this mission. You could dig through the system folder, find the glowing dots whose very existence is an affront to your vision, and replace them. You'll have to replace three different files (*indicator_large.png*, *indicator_medium. png*, and *indicator_small.png*) if you're using the glass dock; two files (*indicator_medium_simple. png* and *indicator_small.png*) if you're using the simple Dock. This is useful information if you want to replace the blobs with an indicator of your own devising, but overkill if you're just yearning for the little black triangles that were standard until Leopard.

Why is navigating to the *Dock.app* and opening the package overkill if you want the triangles back? Because you're not alone: a lot of people want the triangles back, enough people that Chris Owen put together an AppleScript to take care of the heavy lifting for you: it's called Change_ Dock_Indicators (come on, not Triangle Buddy or something?). Find it at http://home.hubris.

net/owenc/misc/Change_Dock_Indicators.zip. Run the Applescript application. Authenticate with an administrator's password and, as Emeril might say, BAM! You've got black triangles (see Figure 11-27).

Figure 11-27.
Oh triangles, how I've missed you

If you want to go back to the Leopard-supplied indicators, rerun the script and you can switch back with no work at all.

Get the Tiger Dock Back

Get the Tiger Dock Back

Maybe triangles or a simple Dock isn't good enough. Perhaps you truly crave the Dock from Tiger. Why not? The Dock in Tiger looks clean; clicking on a folder there generates a simple text list instead of the grid or fan view of Leopard (though with 10.5.2, Leopard now supports list view). In short, there are a lot of reasons to love the dock in Tiger. Well, the Dock is just an application, and there isn't any reason you can't have the Tiger Dock in Leopard. The first thing you'll have to do is secure a copy of Tiger's Dock. Depending on the method you used to install Leopard, you might have one on your Mac already (look in the folder called Previous Systems at the root of your hard drive).

Once the version of the Dock you want to use is located, you've got a little more work to do. You can't directly replace the Dock because the Dock is always running, and OS X won't let you replace an application that is running. The workaround is to boot from a different drive. Once your Mac has been booted from a different startup disk, replace the Leopard Dock (Version 1.6.2 or above) found at *System/Library/CoreServices/Dock.app* with the version you scavenged from Tiger (likely Version 1.3.9).

Sometimes You Just Want to Be Different

If none of the previous options satisfy your Dock cravings, all is not lost. You don't have to settle for the simple Dock, the glass Dock, or even the Tiger Dock. You don't even have to settle for a custom mixing of the three. There are plenty of Dock alternatives for you to download at http://leoparddocks.com. Some of the Docks are great, and some of them are ugly enough that if you printed them out and hung them on the wall, you'd ruin your property value (see Figure 11-28).

Figure 11-28.
Some dock options from LeopardDocks.com

QUICK HACK

USE THE SCRIPT TO EXPERIMENT

The tried and true method of changing the visuals of OS X by finding the icons and replacing them manually doesn't work as well as it used to, but it does work for the Dock indicators. Still, it can be a bit laborious. Use the script supplied by Chris Owen mentioned in the main body of the hack (http://home.hubris.net/owenc/misc/Change_Dock_Indicators.zip) to speed up your Dock experiments. Use the Show Package Contents option on the script and put whatever crazy indicators you want to use in place of the supplied versions (remember to keep the filenames constant) and let Chris' script do the rest of the work. You'll be able to skip killing the Dock with the Terminal, and your experiments can be instantly undone!

More Discernable Folders

Another common complaint about Leopard concerns the folder icons. In the days before Tiger, the Music folder was easily distinguishable from the System folder. In Leopard the folders have lost their color, and the understated symbols on the front aren't as eye catching as they used to be.

If the lack of differentiation bothers you, the news is good: you can change it. The usual method is to find the source image and swap it out with an image of your choice. That is the general methodology here as well, but there is a wrinkle. Folders displayed in the Finder don't display a standard image type; they use icons (file extension *.icns*). Why not just a *.png* file? Folders (in this case) need to scale; what looks great in CoverFlow might not look so great to someone who views the files as 16 x 16 icons. To avoid this conflict, Apple includes different size images in the *.icns* file. Unfortunately, none of the more popular image editors support editing *.icns* files directly, so there will be a little bit of work to do to get the Folder icons just the way you want them.

Figure 11-29.
Adjust the look of the Calculator.app icon

The first step is finding the file. This involves another foray into the System folder and invoking the Show Package Contents option. The path to the required files is */System/Library/CoreServices/CoreTypes. bundle*. Use Show Package Contents (right-click for a context menu displaying this option) to open the bundle and dig around until you find the folder with the *.icns* file you want to change. Fortunately, the names of the files aren't cryptic. In this hack, the Applications folder is going to be modified, and the file is named *ApplicationFolderIcon.icns*, so there isn't any confusion (see Figure 11-30).

Figure 11-30.
The folder icons are easily identified

AppleScriptBadgeIcon.icns

AppleTalkIcon.icns

AppleTalkZoneIcon.icns

ApplicationsFolderIcon.icns

Once the files you want to change have been located, copy them, and move them to a place where you feel comfortable working on them. After making a backup copy (in case you want to change back), you'll need a way to edit the files. You can't just open the files with, for example Photoshop, because the .icns file has variety of images inside. A little trickery is needed. Open the .icns file with Preview and then use the Save As... command to save the file as something you can work with. I used the largest icon for this step because with a bigger image, you'll have more control over the finished product, but other sizes would work, too (see Figure 11-31).

Figure 11-31.
Grabbing the file

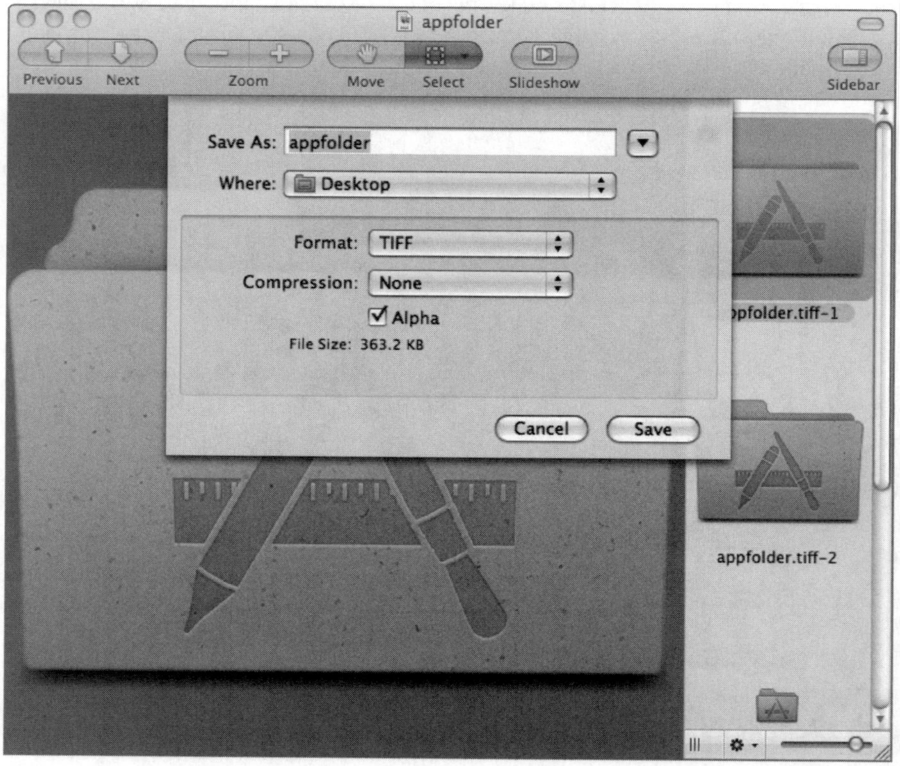

Once the file is saved, you can start with the fun stuff: editing the image. Choose an image editor that supports transparencies and open the image with the editor. Do whatever you wish to the folder or create your own from scratch. Once you're done with the creative process, save the file in just about any format you wish (including the native Photoshop format, .psd) and get ready to turn your efforts into something usable (see Figure 11-32).

Figure 11-32.
Designing a very bad replacement folder with Photoshop

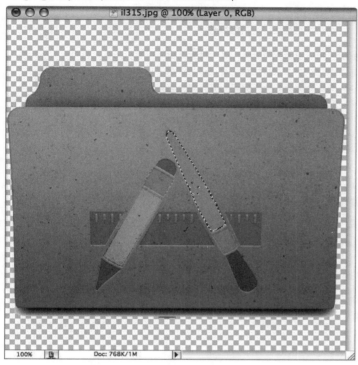

When you're done editing, open the file you want to iconize with Icon Composer, part of the Developer Tools install [Hack #3]. Export the file from Icon Composer, and your new folder icons are ready to go (see Figure 11-33).

Figure 11-33.
Icon Composer will create all the necessary resources for a new icon set

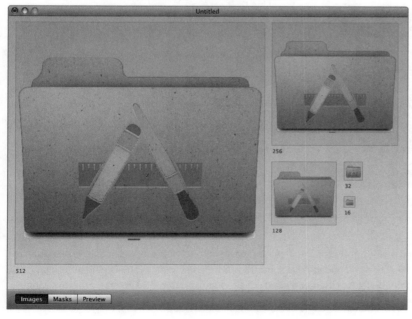

The rest of the hack is the usual drill: go back to the bundle where you first found the folder you wanted to customize and replace the standard *.icns* file with the file of your creation.

Unhacking the Hack

So say you've made your great folder icon and decided that you don't like it. Do you have to go through all that work to get the original folder icon back in place? Turns out that undoing the hack is a simple process of cut and paste. Find the spot where you backed up the original *ApplicationFolderIcon.icns* file, select said file, and use the Get Info command (Command-I). Highlight the small icon in the upper left corner and copy said icon. Highlight the icon you want to change and use the Paste function to drop it onto a Get Info window for the folder whose icon you want to replace. It is just that easy (see Figure 11-34).

Figure 11-34.
Copy and paste to get the old folder icon back

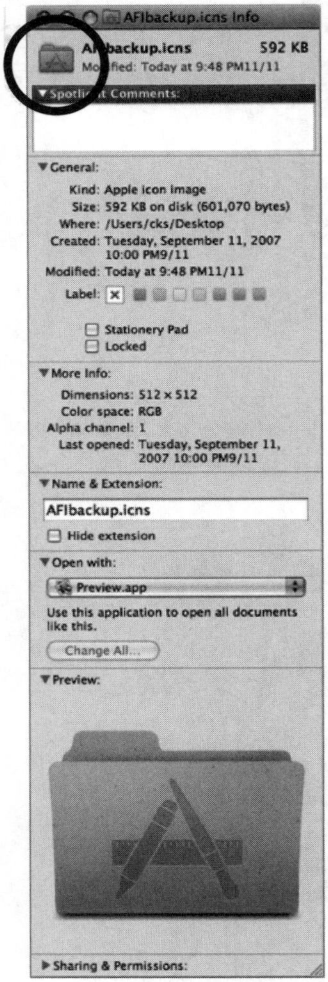

If you're wondering why you couldn't just cut and paste in the first place, well it only works when the folders already exist, and you had to have something brand new, didn't you? On the other hand, if you can find a premade folder (there are plenty of sites with custom OS X icons), you can change the look of Leopard's dull folder using the old copy-and-paste trick.

HACK 88: Install Leopard on Unsupported Hardware

If you've got a Mac officially unsupported by Leopard, it doesn't mean you can't trick Leopard into installing on your machine.

With every 10.X version of Mac OS X some older hardware is left by the wayside. The exclusions make sense; the capabilities of Macs change over time and what the latest and greatest machine will run zippily, a G3-based Mac would choke on. That disparity in capabilities noted, the cutoff for which Mac will run Leopard seem a bit arbitrary. The official requirements for Leopard are as follows: Intel, G5, or an 867 MHz or faster G4 Mac.

Those seems like reasonable numbers but you really have to wonder if the performance will be that much different on a 800 MHz dual processor machine when compared to a single 867 MHz-based PowerMac.

Of course, the level of acceptable performance varies widely from person to person, but if you have a Mac that doesn't quite meet the Leopard specs (or if you own a Mac with an upgraded processor), you might want to install Leopard on the machine to find out if Leopard's benefits are worth the performance tradeoffs.

In this hack, we'll be examining two separate methods. The first uses FireWire target disk mode and has the advantage of being remarkably simple but has the downside of requiring PowerPC-based Macs. The second is a more universal method that requires a trip to the command line.

The Fairly Obvious FireWire Target Disk Mode Method

If your $1,000 Mac has a FireWire port, one of the benefits of the machine is that it can be turned into a $100 hard drive for some other Mac. The good news is that the process is both easy to implement and completely undoable. All that is required is a restart of the Mac you want to use as a hard disk while holding Command-T. Once the machine is started this way, and the FireWire symbol is floating across the drive of the target Mac, connect it to your other Mac with a FireWire cable, and it will show up on your other Mac just as any other FireWire- or USB-based portable hard drive would.

If you've got your older Mac started in FireWire disk mode, your hard work is over; you can slide the OS X install DVD into the newer Mac it's connected to and launch Leopard's installer from the DVD. All the normal install options will be available, and once the install is complete, you'll have Leopard on your older Mac.

If that sounds too easy and obvious, there are a few catches. The first is that you'll need two Macs and one of them has to be of a recent enough vintage that Leopard will install on that machine. (That is where the trickery is; the Leopard installer looks at specs of the machine it is running on, not the specs of the machine in FireWire disk mode.) While the trick works, it doesn't work if you're going from an Intel-based Mac to a PowerPC-based Mac. Sure, the installer is universal, but what gets installed depends on what kind of processor you have powering the machine. Hence, if you booted an 800 MHz PowerMac into FireWire Target Disk Mode and hooked it to a brand new MacBook, when the process was over, you would find your efforts had gone for naught.

The Less Intuitive but Universal Method to Get Leopard to Install on Older Machines

If the FireWire method won't work in your setup because you lack redundant Macs or because you have an environment with both Intel and PowerPC machines, you're not stuck. Every time you attempt to install Leopard on a machine, the installer compares the specs of the machine to a file contained on the install disk. Change that file to fit the specs of the machine you want to install Leopard on, and the installer will happily chug away, installing Leopard on whatever Mac it is crammed into.

The obvious stumbling block in this process is changing the appropriate file. You might think that you can just copy the DVD to your hard drive and edit away but, sadly, it isn't so easy. Before bothering to copy the DVD, you need to make some preparations for hacking the necessary files.

For one thing, you'll need the right tools. In the past, Apple relied on *pax* files (*pax* files are generated by the **pax** utility, which was created to resolve issues between the **tar** and **cpio** format) but with Leopard, they switched to eXtensible ARchive (**xar**) format. The change isn't a big deal most of the time, but this is one case in which the old tools for decoding the files won't work. The first step is, predictably, downloading **xar**. Navigate to http://code.google.com/p/xar/downloads/list and pick your favorite version for downloading. Chances are you'll want the latest version that is in *.tar.gz* format. As of this writing, the most recent version is **xar** 1.5.1 (see Figure 11-35).

Figure 11-35.
Be sure to grab a .tar.gz version!

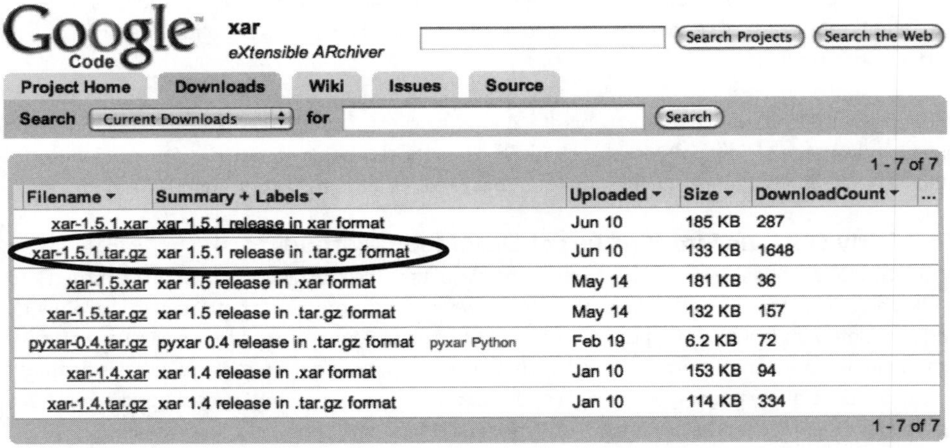

Double-click the download to expand the compressed files, and you'll be treated to a folder full of Unix executables, documents, and subfolders without an intuitive step in sight (see Figure 11-36).

Figure 11-36.
Unless you're familiar with Unix, this doesn't do much for you

At this point, you know a trip to the command line is order, so go ahead and launch the Terminal application (Applications→Utilities→Terminal). Navigate to the folder containing the `xar` files with the `cd` command.

```
$ cd /Users/cks/Downloads/xar-1.5.1
```

Once you're in the correct folder, use Terminal to issue the following command:

```
$ ./configure
```

While `configure` does its thing you'll be treated to a list of just what it is accomplishing:

```
config.status: creating cfgoutputs.stamp
config.status: creating Makefile
config.status: creating include/xar.h
config.status: creating lib/Makefile.inc
config.status: creating src/Makefile.inc
config.status: creating cfghdrs.stamp
config.status: creating include/config.h
```

(There will be much more.)

The `configure` command generates a Makefile, so now all the instructions are in place to use the `make` command. This will recompile everything necessary to get `xar` running on your Mac. The necessary command:

```
$ make
```

Hit return and again you'll get a long list of actions the command is performing. Once everything is settled down, you'll see the $ prompt again, and it's time to install `xar` in your machine. Type:

```
$ sudo make install
```

You'll be asked for your password, and once that crucial bit of personal information has been entered, the command should install `xar` into your *bin* folder. You can assure yourself that the install ended up in the right place by examining the feedback issued as the command was run.

```
/usr/bin/install -c -d /usr/local/bin
/usr/bin/install -c -m 0755 src/ixar /usr/local/bin/xar
```

If you see output that matches the above, you'll know everything is where it needs to be.

With `xar` installed, let's turn our attention to the file that requires modification. Since Leopard ships on a DVD, you'll first have to convert the Leopard install DVD into something a bit more malleable. Time for a trip to Disk Utility and some data duplication.

Disk Utility [Hack #1] can do many different things, but in this case, you're after only one of its many features, the ability to turn a data-packed DVD into something you can edit. To achieve this goal, launch Disk Utility (found in Applications→Utilities). Once running, instruct Disk Utility to restore the DVD to another partition (see Figure 11-37). Disk Utility will refuse to restore the disk to the partition used to start up your Mac.

QUICK TIP ✄

TIP FOR TIGER USERS

Disk Utility has been improved in Leopard, and you can drag the source and target disk from anyplace. In Tiger, for some maddening reason, you have to drag the source and target destination from the Disk Utility sidebar.

Figure 11-37.
Copying, err, restoring an install DVD

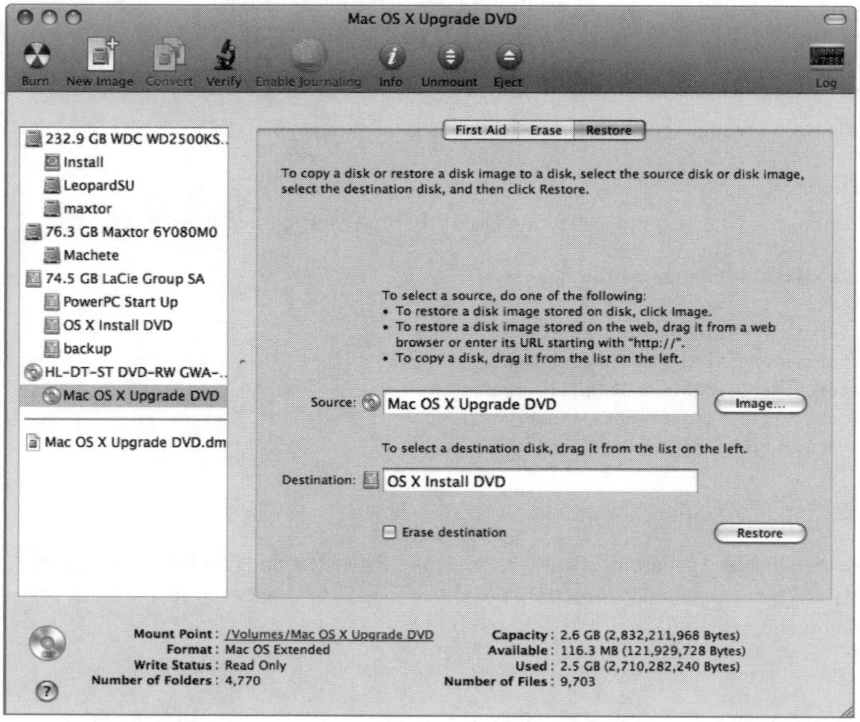

Restoring the install DVD takes some time, depending on the speed of your DVD drive, so be prepared to wait. Once the waiting is done, you'll have an exact copy of the Leopard install disc, but one that can be manipulated (see Figure 11-38).

Figure 11-38.
It looks like the Leopard install disk, but it's editable!

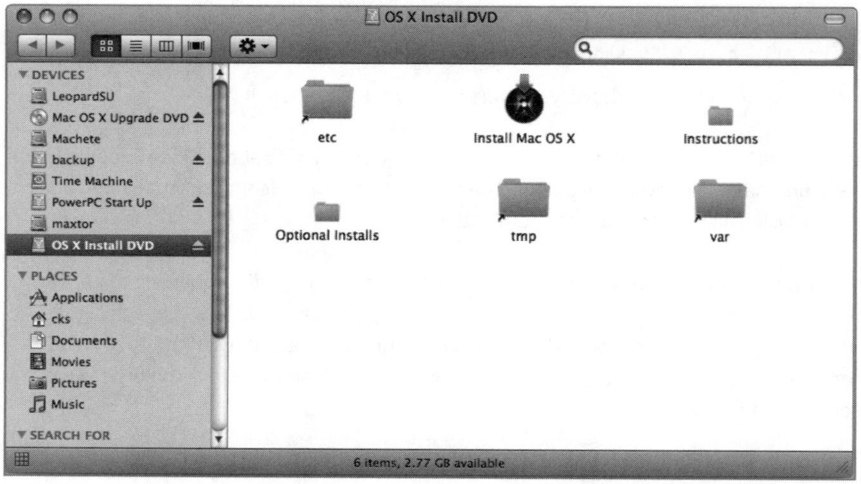

Once the copy of the Leopard install disk is available, it is time to get about the business of changing the requirements the installer looks for when giving you a yea or nay during the install process. You might be tempted just to open up the copy of the DVD and start rooting around for the required file, but you won't be able to find it. It turns out that the file resides in an invisible folder. You can either use a hack to reveal the invisible items or use the Terminal to move the file somewhere where you feel comfortable mucking about with it. Either way the path to the file is the same:

/OS X Install DVD/System/Installation/Packages/OSInstall.mpkg

Where "OS X Install DVD" is the name of the drive you copied the Leopard install disk to. To move the file to the Desktop (as good as place as any for a temporary home):

```
$ cp /Volumes/Mac\ OS\ X\ Install\ DVD/System/Installation/Packages/OSInstall.mpkg
~/Desktop
```

Hey, what do you know, suddenly you're working with a file you can actually see! Create a new folder to house the file temporarily (Finder→File→New Folder) and toss *OSInstall.mpkg* into the newly birthed folder (in this example, the folder holding the temporary copy of *OSInstall.mpkg* is named *Aged*). Now it's time to start messing with the file. Earlier in the hack, you installed `xar`, and this is where the work pays off. Issue the following command:

```
$ xar -x -f ~/Desktop/Aged/OSInstall.mpkg
```

In this command, the `-x` option tells `xar` to extract the files and the `-f` option tells `xar` which archive to open.

Once `xar` has finished extracting the files, open the enclosing folder and look for a file called *Distribution*. You can't tell by looking, but this is an XML file, which means it is raw text inside. Open the file with a text editor—in this example I'm using TextEdit (see Figure 11-39).

Figure 11-39.
Open the Distribution file

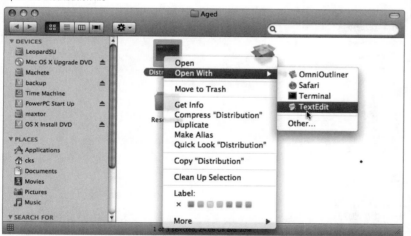

Once you have the file open, you are presented with a document that would be 26 pages if printed out. There is no reason to be concerned with the entire document; the information you want to change occurs early into the text. What we want to do is change the file as little as possible—just enough that it will install on your target Mac.

With that in mind you'll notice that one line specifically lists Macs to exclude:

```
var badMachines = ['MacBook3,1','iMac','PowerBook1,1','PowerBook2,1',
'AAPL,Gossamer', 'AAPL,PowerMac G3', 'AAPL,PowerBook1998', 'AAPL,PowerBook1999']
```

If your Mac is on the exclude list, you'll want to delete that entry.

The other line to look at it is:

```
// require 867Mhz+
if (system.sysctl("hw.cpufrequency") &lt; 866000000) {
    return false;
}

return true;
```

You can tell what is going on here. The comments (`// require 867Mhz+`) indicate that the installation will be checking the clock speed of the machine. The clock speed it looks for is a value greater than 86600000. If your Mac runs at less than 8.6 MHz, change the value to something that will suit your configuration.

You could also change the RAM requirements, but the value is set to 512 MB, and running Leopard with any less memory than that is likely inviting a very unpleasant computing experience. Once you've changed the necessary text, save the file, and check that it has been updated (see Figure 11-40).

Figure 11-40.
You can tell by the modification date that the file has been hacked

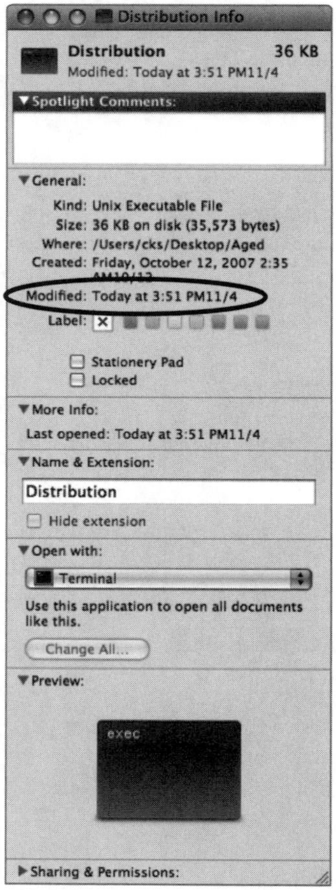

With the hacked file saved, it is time to get everything back into place and format the Leopard installer expects. First we'll use `xar` to compress the files:

```
$ xar -c ./ -v -f /Users/cks/Desktop/Aged/OSInstall.mpkg
```

The last thing to do is to move the *.mpkg* back to the install disc. One final command in the Terminal:

```
$ cp ~/Desktop/Aged/OSInstall.mpkg \
    /Volumes/OS\ X\ Install\ DVD/System/Installation/Packages/
```

Now you should be ready to install Leopard on almost any Mac you so desire using the hacked install partition as the start up drive [Hack #97]. Note that this install disc is not limited to just older Macs, it should also work fine on newer Macs. Enjoy the new school operating system on an old school Mac.

HACK 97: Burn Leopard to a Single Disk; Install Leopard from an Image

If you've got a disk image of Leopard, installing from that image can be a challenge. Learn the tricks to installing Leopard from an image or discover a method to bun Leopard to a single-sided DVD.

The recommended way to install Leopard from a disc image (DMG) is to restore the image to a dual layer DVD. That is great if you have a dual-layer burner, but if you don't, you are not hopelessly stuck. You can pull the install off with a blank partition or a single-layer DVD.

To install Leopard from a DMG file, you'll need at least one blank partition (two if you don't want to install over your current installation of Mac OS X). For more on partitions, check out [Hack #66].

Once the partitions are ready, you 're ready to dive into installing Leopard. Fire up Disk Utility (*/Applications/Utilities/Disk Utility*). The DMG will show up in the source list on the left side of the Disk Utility interface (see Figure 11-41).

Figure 11-41.
Locate the installation file

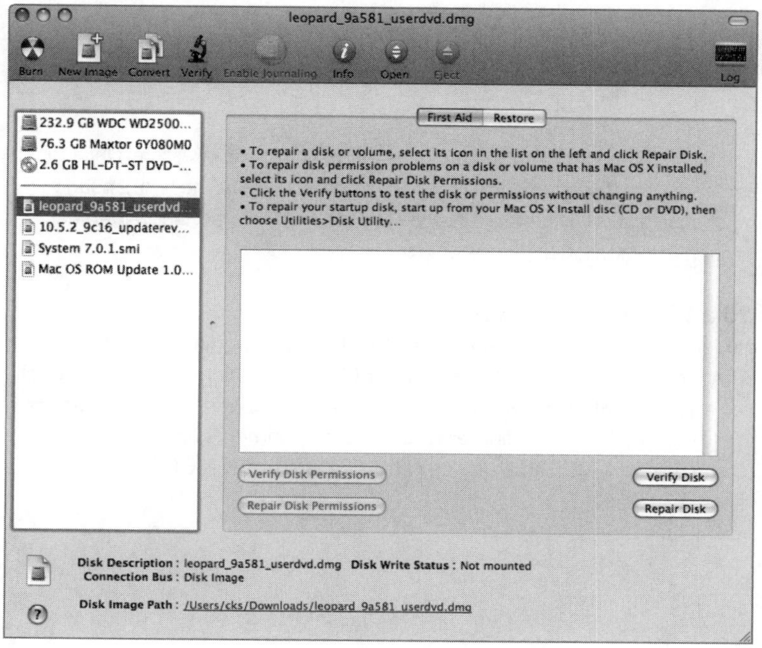

Now for the tricky part: restoring the disk. Click the Restore button and drag the disk you want to restore from to the Source: line. If you're tempted to drag the disk from a folder or your Desktop, don't: it won't work. You have to drag the disk from the source list in the right side of the Disk Utility window (see Figure 11-42).

Figure 11-42.
Drag the disk from the source list

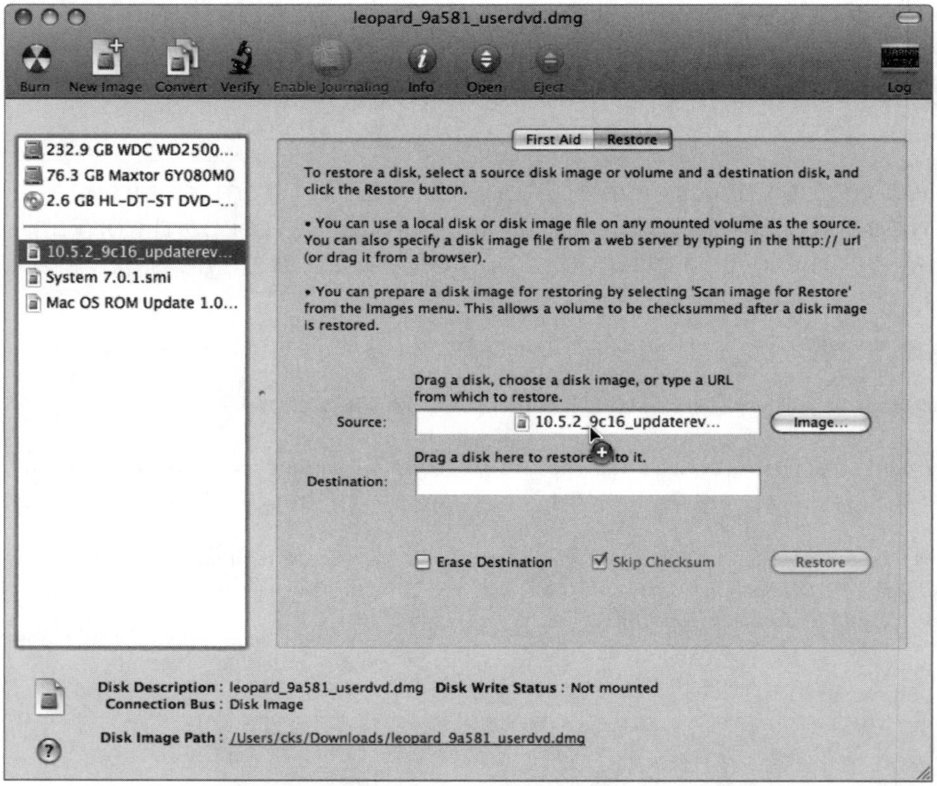

Repeat the process with the destination for your Leopard install DMG and click Restore. Once Disk Utility has finished the process of restoring the disk (be forewarned, it takes some time), head to System Preferences and choose the newly restored disk as your startup volume. Once your Mac restarts, you'll be led through the installation process.

Burning Leopard to a Single-Layer DVD

If you can't create a partition, installing Leopard from a DMG isn't going to work for you. The obvious solution is to burn the Leopard installer to a dual-layer DVD. No problem if you have a dual-layer DVD burner, but not every Mac of recent vintage is equipped with a dual-layer burner (original MacBook Pros, for example). Single-layer DVD burners are far more common, but the maximum amount of data the DVD can hold is 4.7 GB, and the size of the Leopard install is 6.6 GB.

The problem is obvious: there is too much data for a single-layer DVD. The most obvious solution: get rid of some unneeded information, specifically, about 2 GB worth. You could mount the Leopard DMG, poke around, and try to figure out if there is 2G worth of stuff you don't want, but that would be an extra step because the research has been done. Jettisoning Xcode Tools and some optional installs will shrink the Leopard DVD to workable size.

Time to get started. Fire up Disk Utility (Applications→Utilities→Disk Utility) and click New Image. Time to choose some settings. The ideal options for this hack are 4.7 GB (DVD+R DL) for Size, none for Encryption, and sparse disk image for Format (see Figure 11-43).

Figure 11-43.
Work-saving settings

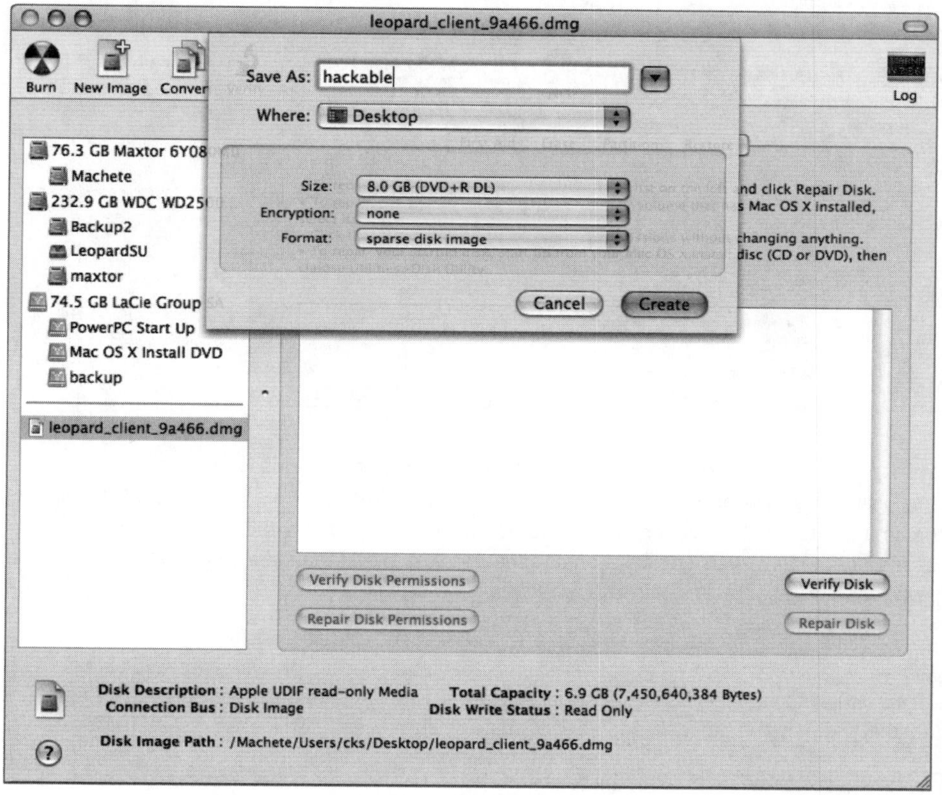

WHAT'S SO SPECIAL ABOUT A SPARSE IMAGE?

With a disk image (DMG), once you set the size you are done. The disk image will always take up the amount of drive you specified. For example, if you create an 8 GB DMG, it will take up 8 GB of room on your hard drive even if it completely empty. Sparse images work differently; instead of taking up the entire amount of drive space assigned, sparse images use only the storage needed for the files it contains. A 200 GB sparse image with 50 MB worth of files on it takes up 50 MB of hard drive space (plus a little overhead). Sparse images grow as the data in them grows but they can't exceed the original limit you provided when setting up the sparse image.

The sparse disk-image format may seem confusing, but it will save a step or two down the road. Once the image is created, mount it with a double-click if it doesn't auto-mount, and you'll find a generic drive icon on your Desktop. Restore the Leopard DMG file to the newly created sparse image by clicking the Restore button and dragging (from the left source pane) the Leopard DMG file to the source box and the mounted sparse image drive to the Destination box as shown in Figure 11-44.

Figure 11-44.
Restore to the sparse image

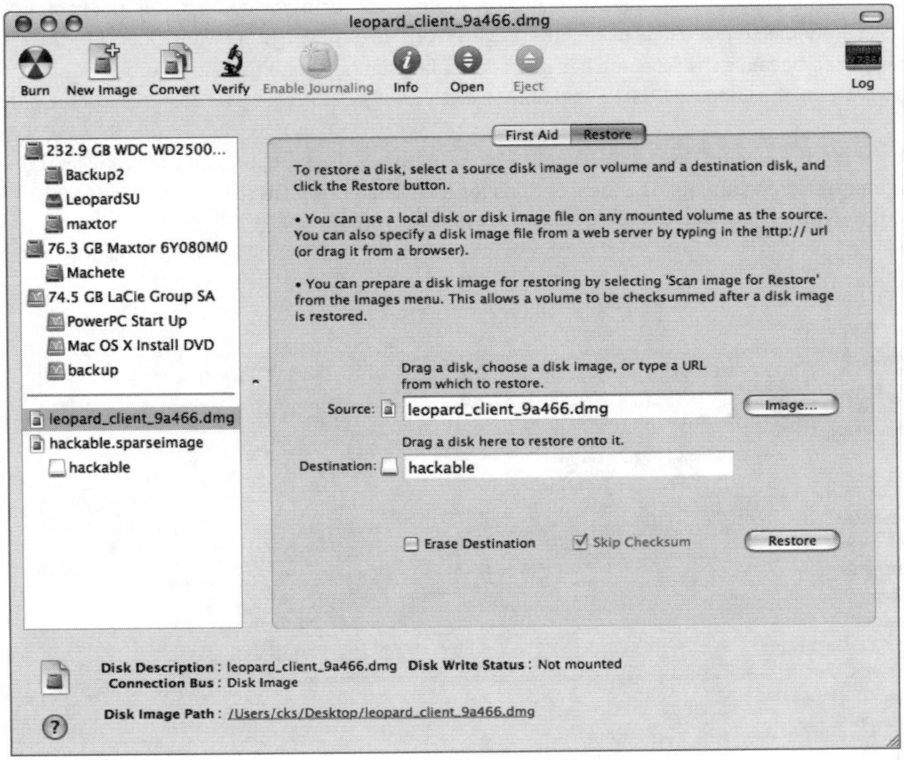

The process takes some time, but once Disk Utility has completed the job, opening up your new sparse disk image will yield something that look remarkably like a Leopard installation disk. This is the time to ditch that unneeded data. If you take a moment to look at the respective sizes of the files (see Figure 11-45), you'll quickly come to the conclusion that there are only two things worth messing with: the System Folder and Xcode Tools.

Figure 11-45.
Ignore the small stuff!

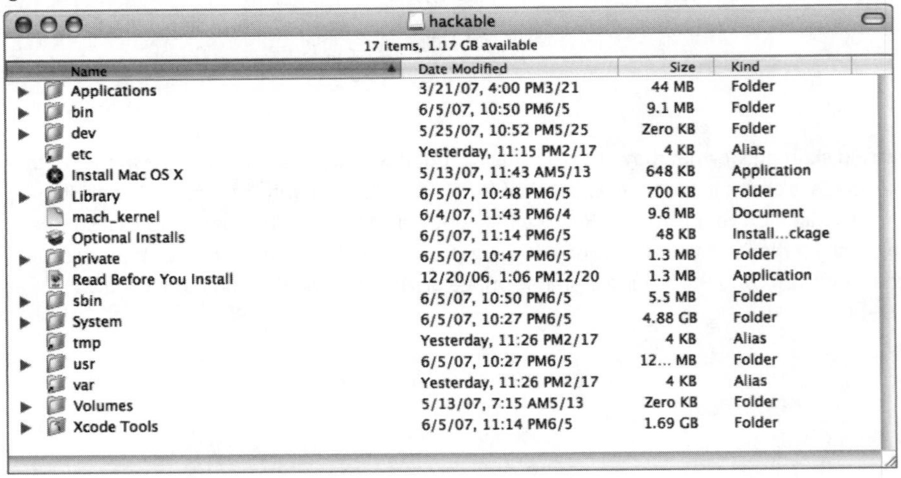

At this point the question becomes "What can I get rid of?" Obviously, you can trash Xcode. You don't need Xcode to get your Mac to run, and you can always download Xcode from Apple. The remaining files still take up too much room to fit on a DVD so create a little more free space by getting rid of *HewlettPackardPrinterDrivers.pkg*, *EpsonPrinterDrivers.pkg*, *CanonPrinterDrivers.pkg*, and *XeroxPrinterDrivers.pkg*. You'll find these in *System/Installation/Packages* of the sparse image.

You've deleted Xcode (1.69 GB), and four packages of printer drivers (about 1 GB), so the files left in the sparse image should total somewhere around 4.1 GB. That amount of data will fit on a single layer DVD! However, if you try to cram that much on a DVD, you'll be out of luck. The math tells you you're within the limits, but if you check the sparse image 's size, you'll see that it is still several gigabytes too large (see Figure 11-46).

Figure 11-46.
That can't be right!

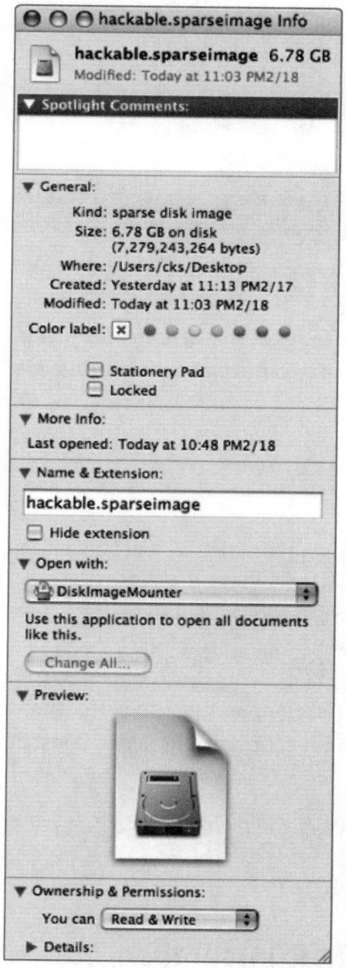

Logic will tell that the reported size can't be right. You deleted 2.69 GB of data, and the sparse image is still larger than the original Leopard DMG? The good news is that you're right: the actual data is around 4.1 GB. The vagaries of disk imaging are responsible for the disconnect between what you think the size should be and what is being reported. This discrepancy can be fixed with a trip to the Terminal (Applications→Utilities→Terminal). Since you're working with a sparse image, you can resize the disk after the files have been removed:

```
$ hdiutil compact filename
```

Where **filename** is replaced by the path to the sparse image you wish to compress. The entire command in this example is:

```
$ hdiutil compact ~/Desktop/hackable.sparseimage
```

Once you hit the return key, `hdiutil` will go about the business of reclaiming the free space as shown in Figure 11-47.

Figure 11-47.
The Terminal will give you a reasonably sized image

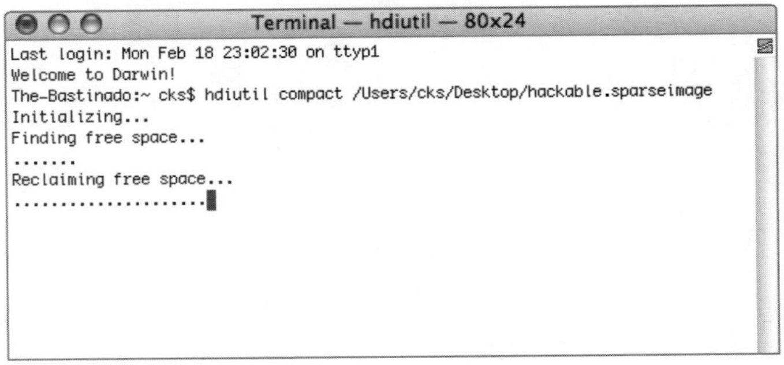

When the Terminal is done reclaiming space, you're left with an image of burnable proportions. But Disk Utility won't let you burn the image even though it's well within the size requirements. Create a new image by clicking the New Image button and use the settings:

- Size: 4.7 GB (DVD-R/DVD RAM)
- Encryption: none
- Format: read/write disk image

Restore the sparse image file you had been working with to your new DMG. This is exactly the same data that was on the sparse image disk, but now Disk Utility will willingly burn the data. Just select the DMG and hit the awesome Burn button in the upper right corner of Disk Utility. Once the data writing process is complete, head to System Preferences, choose the newly minted disk as your startup disk, and you're ready for a Leopard install from a single-layer DVD. Since this is a hacked DVD, you'll have to be careful when using it to install and remember to customize the install, omitting printer drivers and developer tools.

HACK 98: Approximate .Mac with Free Tools

Everywhere you turn on your Mac there is .Mac integration, but you can get most of the functionality using free tools.

There is more to .Mac than most people realize. You don't only get a .Mac email address, you get web space for files (up to 10 GB), you get a spot to host your web site, a method to synchronize data between your Macs, and you get Back to My Mac, just to name a few of the more popular features of .Mac.

If you use all .Mac's services, the package is a good value. You can cobble together the functionality but if your time is worth anything, $99 per year is actually a good deal. It isn't such a great deal if you only use one or two if its features. You'll be spending $99 every year for just a little convenience. If you're just using a few services, that is cash you can save by picking and choosing from following hacks.

Mail

One of the benefits of .Mac is a .Mac mail address. Not only do users get the cred of having a .Mac address, they also get up to 10 GB of mail storage. That storage comes with a price, however: every megabyte you devote to .Mac Mail is one less megabyte you can devote to the web storage part of .Mac.

Ideally we would like to be able to replace the mail functionality of .Mac with something equivalent. The usual choice is Gmail. Gmail has the advantage of being free, well supported with various widgets and Google Desktop, and an ever-increasing amount of storage. The big drawback to Gmail as a .Mac mail replacement used to be that Gmail was POP only, but that has changed. Gmail now supports IMAP, the same protocol that .Mac mail uses, so there isn't a reason not to switch.

The first thing to do to get Gmail functioning as close to .Mac Mail as possible is to enable IMAP access. By default, Gmail is web-based, but IMAP access is no big trick (though it seems people are always asking how to pull it off). Click the Forwarding and POP/IMAP tab (see Figure 11-48).

Figure 11-48.
Almost there

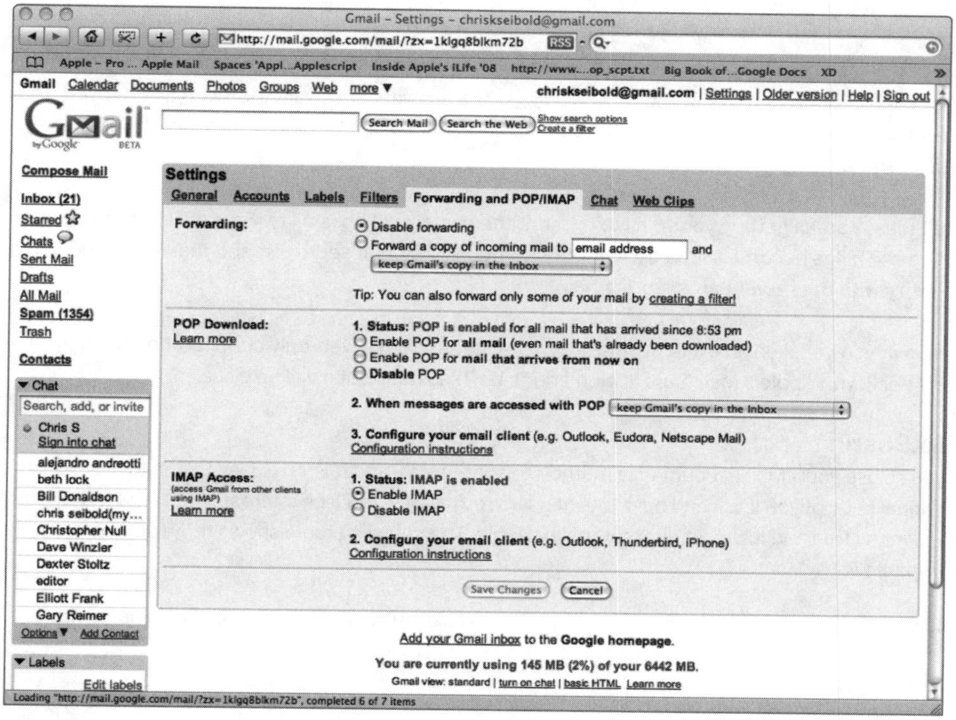

Select Enable IMAP (this is where most people seem to go wrong), and, of course, save changes.

That takes care of configuring Google, but for the system to come close to replication .Mac mail, OS X Mail will need to be configured. This process isn't difficult. (OS X Mail 3.0 is used throughout in this example, but the process is very similar with earlier versions of OS X mail.)

Select Mail→Preferences→Accounts and click the + sign in the lower left corner of the accounts pane. You're presented with something akin to Figure 11-49.

Figure 11-49.
Setting up your new account

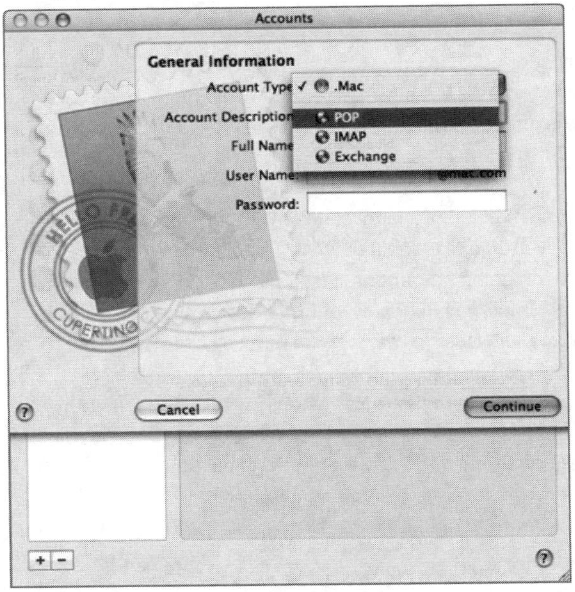

There really isn't much to say about the settings. The answers are straightforward and derived from the information given when you set up your Gmail account. Even the server name is obvious: *imap. gmail.com*.

That takes care of getting your mail to you, but there is a good possibility that you'll want to send mail out. Things become a little trickier but not much. Click Edit server list and the + sign, and add an entry with the server name *smtp.gmail.com*.

That's it: you've taken an existing or new Gmail account from a web-only configuration to one you can check with Apple's Mail. Sure, it won't quite be .Mac mail, but it will be close.

File Sharing

If you're use your .Mac account as a method to share files—and it is very easy to just toss a file into the local copy of you iDisk and have lots of users retrieve it—you'll be interested to know that there are a many free and low-cost alternatives available. The following table shows three alternatives compared with .Mac:

Name	Storage	Maximum file size	Data transfer limit
.Mac	10 GB	10 GB	100 GB
Media Max	25 GB	25 GB	1 GB
Omni Drive	1 GB	1 GB	5 GB
Openomy	1 GB	1 GB	Not stated

All the choices are easy to use, offer a way to share files with others, and feature the same rock bottom price of free—though you can pay for upgraded features.

Syncing

People love the syncing feature of .Mac. Bookmark a site on one Mac, and it shows up on your other Macs. Add a rule for Mail, and it will be deployed on all the associated Macs. Mail and bookmarks aren't the only things that get synchronized: also included are contacts, calendars, widgets and even System Preferences. The allure is obvious, and it turns out that replicating .Mac syncing is also one of the more difficult tricks to pull off. To get something approaching .Mac syncing, consider SyncTogether (http://www.markspace.com/synctogether.php) . This program will set you back $49.95 and limit you to using the product on three Macs. Additionally, syncing Keychains (one of the most delicious features of .Mac syncing) is not supported.

Back to My Mac

Back to My Mac is a feature that requires both a .Mac account and Leopard. Using Back to My Mac, you can access other Macs you own from anywhere you're using a Mac running Leopard. Using Back to My Mac is as simple as visiting the .Mac Preference pane, enabling the service, and clicking on the Mac you want to visit in the Sidebar of a Finder window (see Figure 11-50).

Figure 11-50.
Share the screen, transfer files

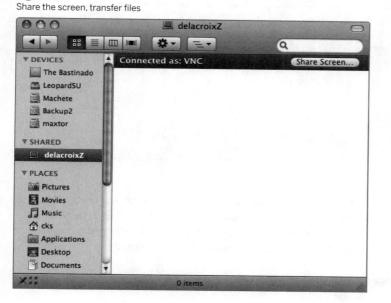

If you're on the road and left a file at home, you can imagine how useful this functionality could be. On the other hand, if you could get the same functionality for free that would be even better. Well, you can share screens and transfer files in iChat, and iChat can automatically launch a script. It seems conceivable that you could use iChat as a gateway for your very own Back to My Mac solution. The idea is easily conceivable, but Melvin Riveria was most likely the first guy to pull it off.

It is probably a good idea to create a new iChat account for this hack, one that you will use only to access your Mac. Sure, the step isn't required to pull the hack off, but you'll want this to be as secure as possible. Lots of people probably know your iChat handle, and since it was just iChat, you probably picked a simple password. Creating a new iChat account with a tough password will rectify these vulnerabilities.

Once you have a new, safe account it is time to do the legwork of configuring your Mac. The firsts thing you'll have to do is turn off sleeping. This probably seems like a huge energy sink but it is something you have to do to use Back to My Mac as well. Head to System Preferences, and click on Energy Saver. Move the Sleep slider to Never (see Figure 11-51).

Figure 11-51.
Caffeine for your Mac

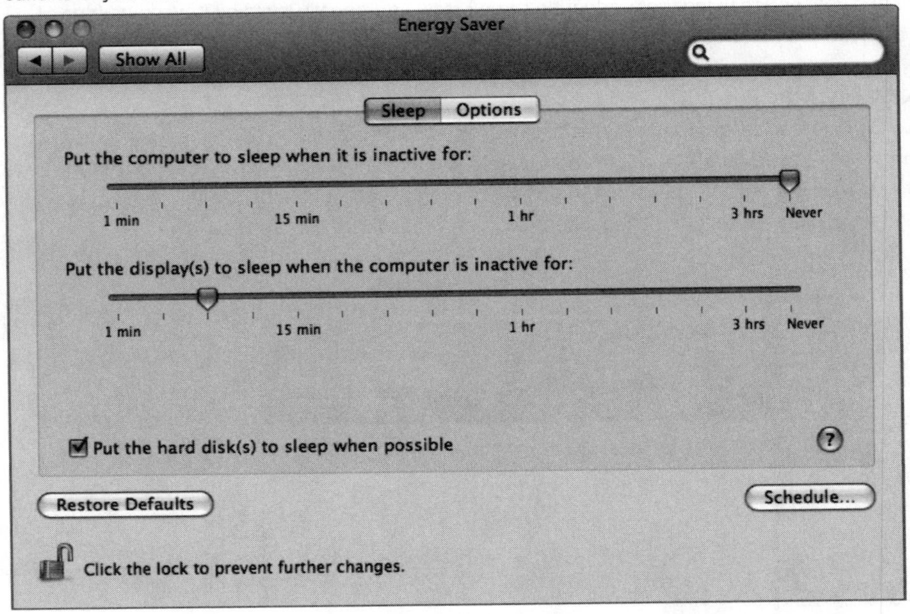

To pull this hack off, you'll need a script to automatically answer when you call out to your Mac. The good news is Apple supplies one with your Mac. The path to the required script is */Library/Scripts/iChat*, and the file you're after is *AutoAccept.applescript*. You're going to have to modify this script just a little, so open it up with Script Editor (*Applications/AppleScript/ScriptEditor*).

There is only one change to make, but it is crucial because if you don't change it, iChat will refuse to let you share the screen. Change:

```
on received audio invitation theText from theBuddy for theChat
        if (screen sharing of theChat is none) then
            accept theChat
        end if
end received audio invitation
```

to:

```
on received audio invitation theText from theBuddy for theChat
        accept theChat
end received audio invitation
```

Save the script and toss it into */Library/Scripts/iChat*.

The groundwork is complete. All that is left to do is to configure iChat. Unless you're very lax about security, you'll want to limit the people who can get into your computer via iChat. Select the account you wish to use for this task (in Leopard you can have multiple accounts open so this won't result in any loss of iChatting fun) and click the Security button. Choose Allow Specific People and add the iChat address you want to use for logging in to your Mac (see Figure 11-52).

Figure 11-52.
Only you can get in!

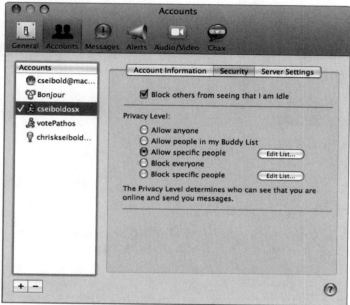

You're almost there. Click the Alerts button in iChat's preferences, change Event to Audio Invitation, check the box next to Run AppleScript and use the pop-up menu to choose the AppleScript you modified earlier (see Figure 11-53).

Figure 11-53.
Everything is in place

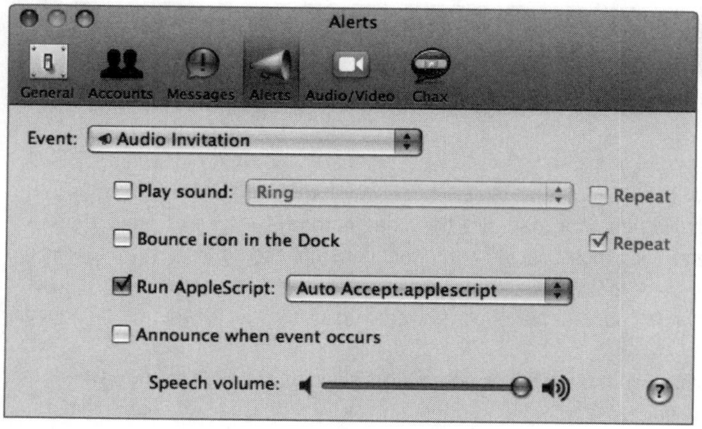

All that is left to do is to try it out! Fire up iChat on two separate Macs and ask to share the target Mac's screen (see Figure 11-54).

Figure 11-54.
Hey, that's my computer now let me in!

Thanks to the changes you made, iChat will accept your invitation to share the screen, and you'll have the Back to My Mac functionality of .Mac without the $99 entry fee (see Figure 11-55).

Figure 11-55.
Access to your files

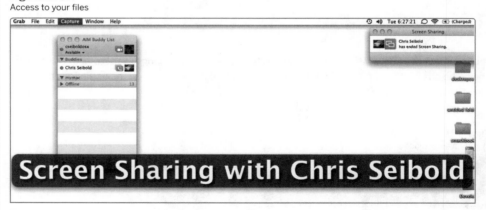

Hacking the Hack
iChat will get the job done, but the iChat method isn't the only way. If the Macs share a common network (they use the same Wi Fi signal, for example), the iChat method is a little excessive. There are simpler methods. Before tackling those, decide if you want constant access to the remote Mac or access only when the Mac happens to be awake. Of course, you want constant access, but if you get an electric bill, you might not want your Mac to be fully powered up just to wait for your remote needs.

To get constant remote access even though the remote Mac is sleeping, it needs to know when to wake up. You can configure your Mac to wake up when it receives a message. To enable this energy-saving option, head to the Energy Saver panels in System Preferences, select Options and put a check in the box next to "Wake for Ethernet network administrator access" (see Figure 11-56).

Sadly, waking your Mac only works when the Mac is wired via Ethernet to a network, so if you use Wi-Fi to connect, you can't pull this part of the hack off.

Figure 11-56.
Wake your Mac from afar

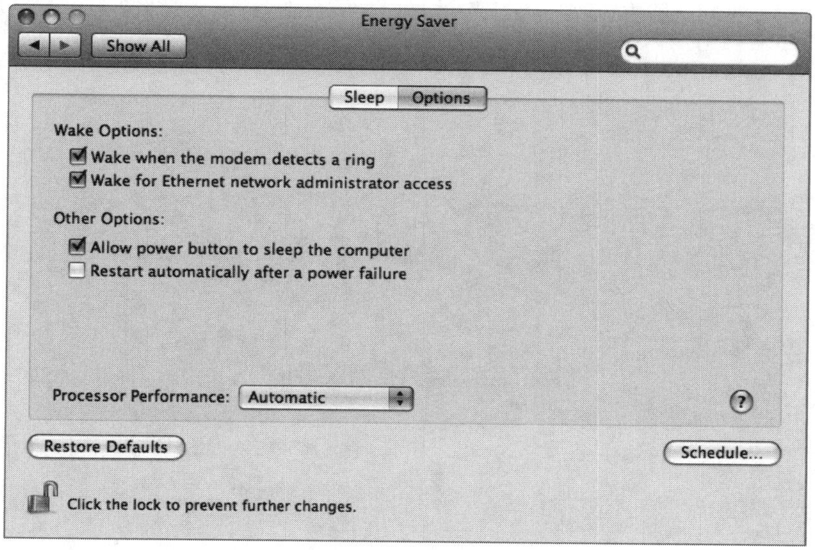

Time to enable screen-sharing access. Again, point your mouse to System Preferences and choose Sharing. Click the box next to Screen Sharing (see Figure 11-57).

Figure 11-57.
Turning on Screen Sharing

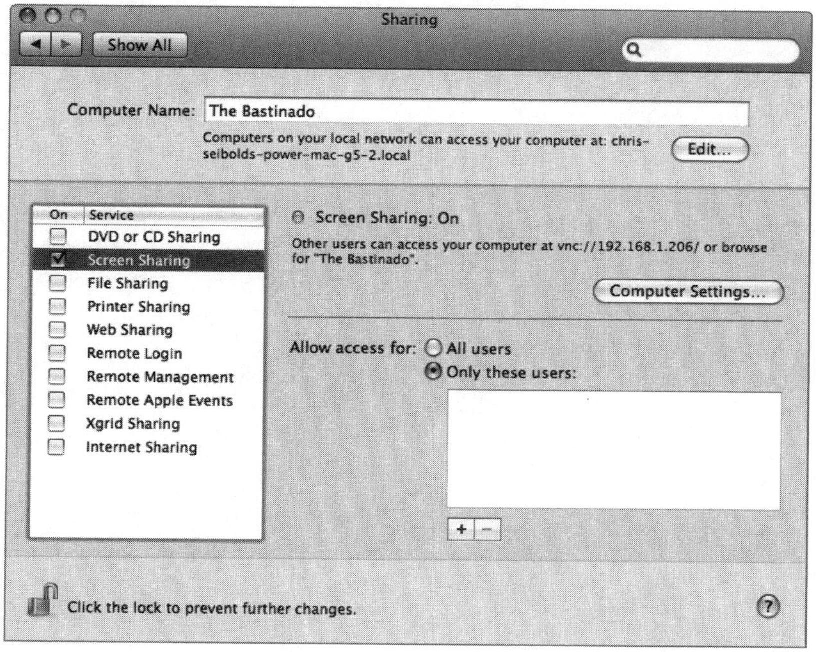

That is really enough; you can now share the screen by following the onscreen instructions. But it isn't the best set up. You can control the remote computer but transferring files, for example, will be tedious, and the configuration isn't very safe. Typically, you'll want you—and just you—to be able to hop on to your computer. To control who can and can't get on your machine, click the "Only these users" button and hit the +. Choose who you want to be able to log in and control your Mac (see Figure 11-58). In this example, I'm adding my main account so the login name and password will be the same one I use to log in to this computer.

Figure 11-58.
Only you can play!

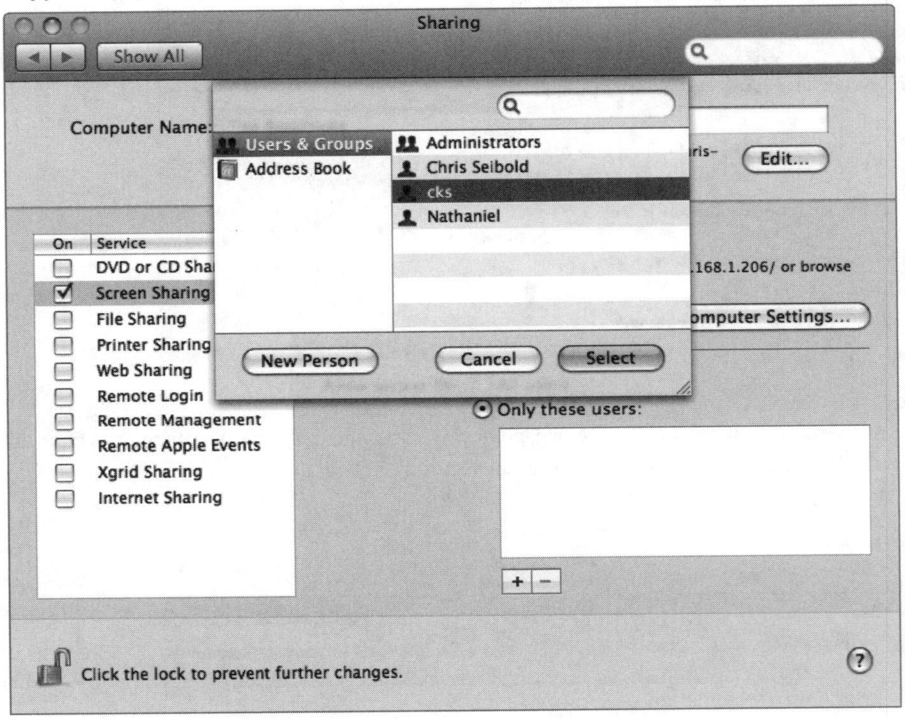

You're done. Or you would be if you didn't want to transfer files easily. Chances are you do want to transfer files. A little more work in System Preferences is required. Start by checking the box next to File Sharing and adjusting what you want shared using the + and - minus buttons located under Shared Folders area. (I want to share an entire drive but you can fine-tune which folders to share easily.) Once the choices are configured to your taste, you can decide who can share the folders and what kind of access they have with the + and - buttons found under the Users area (see Figure 11-59).

Figure 11-59.
Selecting folders and users

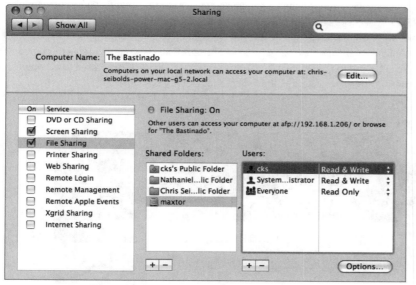

One final step: how do want the files transferred? If you're going to be swapping files between two computers on the same LAN, Apple Filing Protocol (AFP) is all you need. If you'll be transferring files from somewhere far away, say a hotel room, File Transfer Protocol is the answer. To tell your Mac which one to use, hit the Options button at the lower right side of the Sharing pane. I'm enabling both, when I'm at home and on the same network, AFP is easier but I want FTP when traveling (see Figure 11-60).

Figure 11-60.
The best of both worlds

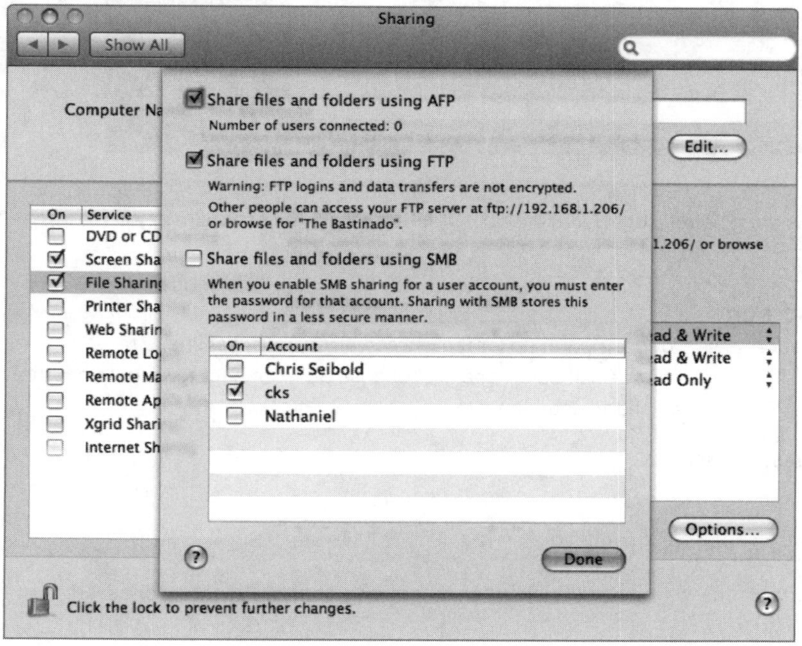

If your Mac is behind a router, chances are that your router will need to be tweaked a little for this hack to really work when you're on the road. Specifically, you'll have to configure your router to forward port 21 for FTP transfers and port 5900 to carry the screen-sharing data. Each router varies on how exactly to do this but generally you'll find an option page to forward ports somewhere in your router's configuration page (usually accessible at 192.168.*x.x* and configurable through a web browser). Two entries in the table are all you'll need so your router will know what to do when the requests come in. With a linksys router, the final product looks like Figure 11-61.

Figure 11-61.
The ports are ready

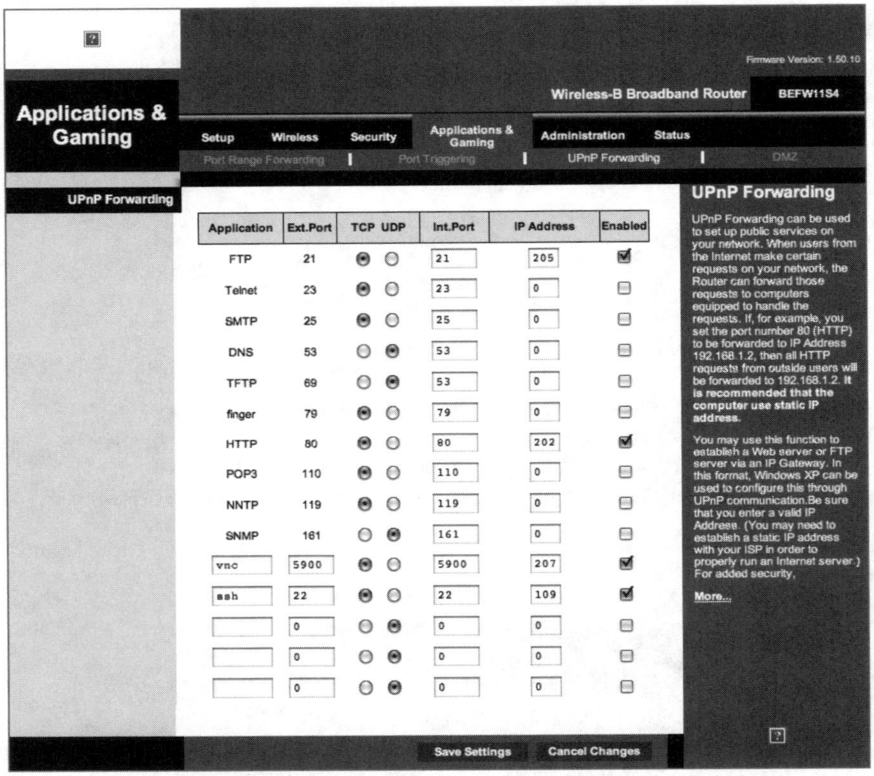

To make the whole thing better, consider using a dynamic domain name service [Hack #48] to learn how to set one up.

Sharing the screen

You've taken the effort to set your computer up for remote screen sharing; it's time to take advantage of the all your hard work. Click Command-K or choose Go→Connect to server from the Finder's menu bar. For a screen-sharing session, type:

```
$ vnc://192.168.0.0:5900
```

For an FTP session:

```
$ ftp://192.168.0.0:21
```

Once the connection is made, you can transfer files or remotely control your Mac for as long as you wish.

12

HACK THE IPHONE

As this book was being completed, the iPhone Software Development Kit (SDK) was released. In the future, the iPhone will have applications by third-party developers, so owners will have plenty of choices of games, business applications, blogging tools, and more. The existence of third-party applications won't mean that jailbreaking your phone will be useless, Apple is planning on exerting a fair amount of control over just what applications will be available. So there will very likely be good reasons to hack your iPhone in the future.

HACK 99: Jailbreak Your iPhone

Your iPhone is capable of much more than Apple intended you to know about. For those who dare unlock it, some very interesting things are possible.

There is a lot of buzz out there about hacking the iPhone to make it do things Apple didn't anticipate.

> Hacking an iPhone is a daunting task and one that, for many, should probably be avoided. Apple, at this writing, has released an iPhone Software Development Kit that allows third-party applications to run on the Mac OS X-based handset. This will open up the platform, for sure, but not as far as hacking it can. It is important to proceed with caution when using these hacks. If you don't understand what you are doing, it might be best to skip this hack. Although some of these hacks can be wiped out with a mere software restore, problems can arise that may "brick" your handset if you are not careful.

Warnings aside, if you are ready to have the coolest iPhone on the block, read on and don't look back. If not, then flip to somewhere else in this book; you might find something cuddlier and more n00b friendly.

iPhone Hacking Terms

Understanding these common hacking terms will help you follow the instructions to come, as well as help you exchange information with other iPhone hackers.

Jailbreak

Except for Apple applications such as iTunes, read/write access is not available for iPhones without jailbreaking it. The *jailbreaking* process enables read/write access on the iPhone's filesystem so that third-party applications can be installed. A jailed iPhone refers to the opposite: an iPhone that does not have read/write access enabled.

Unlock

Global System for Mobile Communications (GSM) cell phones like the iPhone can function on any GSM cellular network using Subscriber Identity Module (SIM) cards. Unfortunately, iPhones in the United States are tied to AT&T (not at the time of purchase but when it's activated through iTunes), which may not be your preferred cellular carrier The only other major U.S. carrier that supports GSM-based handsets is T-Mobile. There are many more, though, in Europe and other foreign countries.

In order to use the iPhone on a different cellular network than the one it's tied to, it is necessary to unlock the handset. An unlocked iPhone can be used on any network that supports GSM.

Firmware

Firmware is the underlying software that powers the iPhone. This core is where everything happens and without it, your handset would be a very shiny and pretty brick. Apple provides occasional firmware updates via iTunes to enhance the iPhone and offer additional functionality. You can get more use out of the iPhone by adding third-party stuff to the firmware. Be wary though: Apple hasn't officially endorsed third-party applications (yet) or officially allowed similar modifications. Installing third-party software risks damaging your iPhone due to incompatibility with the next revision of Apple-supplied iPhone firmware. Before applying new firmware updates, it's always best to check major news sites and Apple blogs for the progress of unlocking and jailbreaking future firmware upgrades.

Bricked

Bricked, in normal computer terms refers to a piece of hardware that no longer functions; its usefulness is equivalent to an actual brick. This term has been used to describe an iPhone's state after being modified in some way, whether it was upgraded with new firmware or rendered inoperable because it was unlocked and then upgraded. While bricking generally means unrecoverable, in the case of the iPhone, there are instances in which a "bricked" iPhone can be resuscitated.

Activated

If an iPhone has been restored or was newly purchased, it must be *activated*. If you performed a firmware restore, chances are you have a backup file containing activation data archived by iTunes. If it was newly purchased, you must sign up to a predetermined cellular carrier before it can be used. An unactivated iPhone can be used to make emergency calls, but it will otherwise not function.

Baseband

The *baseband* is what makes the iPhone's communications tick. It's one of the key components in keeping the handset locked to a specific carrier yet it's the first thing modified to allow its unlocking. Specifically, baseband is the part of the iPhone's firmware used by the radio chip. Since cell phones are, in a basic sense, glorified two-way radios, you can imagine that this bit of code is crucial. Having a permanently modified baseband could pose some problems if Apple decides to upgrade the baseband's firmware.

Restore

For some reason or another, you might have to erase everything on your iPhone and perform a *restore*. A restore in a sense resets the iPhone but not to factory conditions because it does not interact with the baseband. If your iPhone was unlocked and upgraded (from 1.0.2 to 1.1.1) or downgraded improperly (only if reverting from 1.1.1), the baseband will lose its original functionality resulting in the need for a patch.

DFU mode

Device firmware upgrade (DFU) mode allows direct access to the iPhone's firmware. Applications such as iNdependence use this mode to downgrade or upgrade your iPhone's firmware. An iPhone in DFU mode appears to be turned off. iTunes can detect if your iPhone is in DFU mode (iTunes calls it "Restore mode") so before you give up on an iPhone, plug it in to your Mac and see what is reported by iTunes.

Springboard/home screen

When you first wake your iPhone from the lock screen, you will see all of your applications above the Dock. This is called the *home screen* but is loosely referred to as *Springboard*. Usually the area above the Dock is only referenced, but the home screen can encompass the Dock as well.

Installer.app (aka AppTapp)

A repository for developers to distribute applications, *Installer.app* has become the easiest way to install third-party software. While applications can be installed over SSH to the iPhone's application directory, *Installer.app* manages updates and distribution, streamlining the process for the end user.

Using Different Firmware Versions

One of the biggest hurdles when hacking an iPhone is maintaining compatibility when upgrading to new firmware updates. As each update rolls out, it will take time for people you might call "unofficial developers" to gain access. The amount of time depends on how intricate the security is. We've seen with firmware version 1.1.1 that it took quite a while to push out a working jailbreak method while firmware version 1.1.2 took mere hours before it was cracked (even before Apple could initiate its widespread release).

So that brings up the ever-burning question: "How do I maintain compatibility with Apple's updates alongside third-party developers?" The simple answer: You don't, and you never will. This is part of a cat-and-mouse game between the hacking community and Apple. (You can decide which is the cat.) Apple pushes out an update, hackers catch up, and then Apple issues revisions to better lock it down. Probably, this will continue right up to the day Apple decides to open up the iPhone and unlock it.

One way to avoid becoming a victim of the cross-fire in this battle is to settle on older firmware. The one sure thing in this changing landscape is that earlier firmware versions are going to be well exercised and stable. As of now, no third-party applications require updated firmware to maintain stability. An iPhone running 1.0.2 will function the same way an iPhone running 1.1.1 does in terms of third-party software.

But Apple has released a few firmware updates since the iPhone's launch from 1.0.0 to (as of now) 1.1.3. Here's a little guide to which firmware is right for you.

Initial release: firmware version 1.0.0

The first public release (on an iPhone at least) is firmware version 1.0.0 and, while it doesn't contain many bugs, developers were already hard at work trying to crack the handset wide open for third-party software to take root.

A significant flaw exists in 1.0.0's Mobile Safari that allows attackers access to the iPhone's innards using a malformed TIFF file. This same method is used to jailbreak an iPhone running firmware version 1.1.1.

Firmware version 1.0.1

The first update to arrive to iPhone users via iTunes, firmware version 1.0.1 patched a few minor bugs and brought iPod hi-fi compatibility but the previously mentioned TIFF exploit still exists and is unpatched in this version.

Firmware version 1.0.2

This plain ol' update brought bug fixes and the like. It was reported that the OS was more responsive. Although firmware version 1.0.2 brought nothing significant, by this time the hacking community was flourishing alongside third-party developers. *Installer.app* (now known as AppTapp) provided an easy-to-use interface for downloading third-party software with ease while maintaining compatibility with all previous firmware versions.

The big one: firmware version 1.1.1

Announced at Apple's "The Beat Goes On Event" almost a month before its release, firmware version 1.1.1 caused widespread problems for users who had hacked and/or unlocked their iPhones. AppTapp users were left in the dark, literally, when a patch to Springboard hid non-Apple applications, making it impossible to install third-party software. The iPhone's security was enhanced, making a jailbreak attempt that much harder, but the most significant effect was for already unlocked iPhones. Depending on which method you had used, you could end up with a bricked handset.

Firmware version 1.1.2

Firmware 1.1.2 brought relatively minor updates such as the inclusion of more languages and was relatively unchanged. This allowed it to be cracked within hours of release, including a fully functional jailbreak method.

Firmware version 1.1.3

Just as 1.1.1 made a big splash for the hacking community, 1.1.3 had the same effect but in different ways. Before its debut at Macworld 2007, it was leaked to Nate True and Andru Edwards who posted the major details on their blogs. This gave them enough time to work out a single jailbreaking method, but a rift in the development community led to several being posted. Some worked with minor setbacks while others caused unintentional damage, all of which could be fixed with a software restore in iTunes.

Jailbreaking firmware 1.1.3 is a very different beast than the previous revisions covered here. Downgrading, which is a key part of this guide, is very difficult to do and if not done correctly will force you to start over again. The process requires restoring your iPhone to its original state. This is because 1.1.3 upgrades the baseband to use cellular triangulation, and that causes conflicts with 1.1.2 and earlier, such as having EDGE and calling capabilities terminated until either you revert or patch things up.

It should be noted that although Nate True had good intentions, his posted jailbreak broke some essential components such as Google Maps' pseudo GPS and Nikita, which powers third-party application installation.

HOWTO Jailbreak Each Firmware Version

Now that we've prepped you on the nitty gritty, and you've selected which firmware you want to call home, you, soldier, are ready to conquer foreign data sectors and liberate the 1s and 0s of the iPhone's core OS.

The goal here is to wind up with a firmware version that runs the applications you want to run on it, which probably means jailbreaking it, if you're still reading here. For some firmware revisions, this means installing a previous version and upgrading. Other revisions can be jailbroken straight off. This section discusses jailbreaking each version, and the next section discusses how to find these firmware versions.

1.0.0-1.0.2

For the initial firmware release, as well as the first couple of updates Apple pushed out for the iPhone, jailbreaking isn't nearly the daunting task it is for later versions. It's the exact opposite: so simple a seven year old could do it (always great to start them young) without destroying important user data or having to play tech support to bring back a bricked iPhone.

The fine developers of Nullriver Software compiled a one-click application (AppTapp Installer) that does it all in a matter of minutes without any fuss. Navigate your browser to http://iphone.nullriver. com/beta/, and download the appropriate installer for your operating system. From there, the rest is automated, and you'll be enjoying third-party applications in no time.

1.1.1

The process is just as easy as the previous one. The only real twist was the amount of time and energy put into finding the needed exploit to jailbreak the iPhone. Until 1.1.2, Apple had yet to patch a security problem with Safari that would allow a malformed TIFF file to gain access to the root filesystem of the iPhone and wreak whatever havoc it so desired. A malicious exploit of this problem hasn't been observed yet, but the hacking community seized the opportunity and tried to jailbreak the iPhone once more. The final result was a web-based version of the standalone installer that once again, managed a one-click no-fuss jailbreak.

Navigate on your iPhone using an open Wi-Fi connection (EDGE is usable but not bearable) to http://www.jailbreakme.com/, and consult the brief guide on this exploit's inner workings and what comes with Jailbreak. One upside to this hack is that after it's installed, the Safari TIFF exploit that made it possible will be fixed. Just to note, you'll probably be returning to 1.1.1 on several occasions, so it's best to have an extra copy of this firmware package on hand.

1.1.2

To jailbreak under 1.1.2, you'll need to jailbreak an iPhone that's running 1.1.1 and install OktoPrep. Essentially, what you'll be doing is upgrading your iPhone to 1.1.2 after jailbreaking a 1.1.1 iPhone. If you went the way of the web-based Jailbreak installer for 1.1.1, you're in luck; OktoPrep is preinstalled, but before JailBreakMe's update in early February, this package was not included and had to be installed separately through AppTapp.

The beauty behind OktoPrep is that it allows a seamless upgrade from 1.1.1 to 1.1.2 that does not involve nuking your personal information or post-upgrade regret. You can continue using 1.1.1 unjailbroken with OktoPrep present, and normal functions will not be affected. But to keep with the "I'm gonna hack it whether Apple likes it or not" attitude, we'll continue our jailbreak by downloading the needed tools from Conceited Software (http://conceitedsoftware.com/iphone/112jb.html), longtime developers for unofficial third-party iPhone applications.

The tools include a small Java application that once again, automates the jailbreaking process, but it takes a while to finish—10 minutes or so. In the mean time you can grab a cup of coffee and contemplate tackling 1.1.3.

1.1.3 and 1.1.4

Before you begin and take on the untamed beast that is firmware 1.1.3, you must not upgrade to 1.1.3 using Apple's updater yet. While you can revert back to 1.1.1 and then upgrade to 1.1.2, you'll lose all the cellular functions you had previously. In order to use cellular triangulation for the pseudo GPS in Google Maps, the baseband was upgraded and does not play nice with anything earlier than 1.1.3 (boot loader 3.9). While you can downgrade to earlier firmware or do a full restore, it gets tricky when you try to stay under 1.1.3 with the latest baseband revision. You'll have to restore your iPhone's baseband to its original state, but the process is not impossible, just time consuming. We'll cover that in a bit.

There are multiple ways to jailbreak an iPhone running 1.1.3 (iJailbreak and Soft upgrades), but an unintended side effect is losing YouTube functionality. Searching for content and playing most videos will result in an error, due to an authentication problem between the iPhone and YouTube. Users have reported various fixes, but from what I've found, they don't work for everyone. To avoid all of this, there is only one method I recommend using: the official jailbreak posted by the iPhone Dev Team (a group of top notch hackers obsessed with the iPhone). Not only is it simple, but it can be run directly from the iPhone and does not cause any problems.

You must be running a jailbroken 1.1.2 iPhone to prepare for the next step. It is very important to disable Auto Lock in Settings→General→Auto Lock. From Installer, update to the latest version if you haven't done so already; then proceed to install the BSD subsystem. Once complete, navigate to Sources in Installer then tap Edit→Add. Type in the URL installer.iClarified.com (make sure to include the `http://` if it's not present in the text field) and then tap Done.

After the source refreshes, select iClarified from the main category list. The official application is called "Soft 1.1.3 Jailbreak"; it was created by the Dev Team and is distributed by iClarified. The process will take 15 to 20 minutes; you can set your iPhone down, grab some more coffee, proclaim to your coworkers that you have gained super-powered hacking abilities, or ponder how long it will take for SkyNet to overtake your iPhone and subsequently the human race. Once done, you'll have an iPhone running 1.1.3, fully jailbroken.

How to Jailbreak Each Firmware Version

Once you know what firmware version you're planning to jailbreak, you have to figure out how to get your phone to that version. Here's how to get from where your phone is to where you want it to be.

Any model iPhone can be downgraded, but how far you can roll back depends on your boot loader revision. But wait, how do I find what my boot loader is? Elementary, my dear Watson: just flip over your iPhone, and turn to the serial number. The fourth and fifth digits determine what week the iPhone was manufactured while the third digit determines the year. For example, mine is 740, which shows it was manufactured week 40 (October) of 2007. Weeks 42 and earlier contain boot loader 3.9; weeks 45 and up contain boot loader 4.6. For weeks 43 and 44, you'll have to find it using the HWinfo application, available from the Installer source: http://www.trejan.com/irepo. (It will also work on the other weeks, too, if you want to double-check the serial number.)

iPhones running boot loader 4.6 can roll back only to firmware 1.1.1 while iPhones running boot loader 3.9 can roll back to firmware 1.0.0—the original version that first shipped with handsets back in June 2007.

Now that you know how far back you can downgrade, choose which firmware revision you want to stay on, and download the file from the following links that lead directly to firmware downloads from Apple:

- **1.1.3 (4A93):** http://appldnld.apple.com.edgesuite.net/content.info.apple.com/iPhone/061-4061.20080115.4Fvn7/iPhone1,1_1.1.3_4A93_Restore.ipsw

- **1.1.2 (3B48B):** http://appldnld.apple.com.edgesuite.net/content.info.apple.com/iPhone/061-4037.20071107.5Bghn/iPhone1,1_1.1.2_3B48b_Restore.ipsw

- **1.1.1 (3A109a):** http://appldnld.apple.com.edgesuite.net/content.info.apple.com/iPhone/061-3883.20070927.ln76t/iPhone1,1_1.1.1_3A109a_Restore.ipsw

- **1.0.2 (1C28):** http://appldnld.apple.com.edgesuite.net/content.info.apple.com/iPhone/061-3823.20070821.vormd/iPhone1,1_1.0.2_1C28_Restore.ipsw

- **1.0.1 (1C25):** http://appldnld.apple.com.edgesuite.net/content.info.apple.com/iPhone/061-3614.20070731.Nt6Y7/iPhone1,1_1.0.1_1C25_Restore.ipsw

- **1.0.0 (1A543a):** http://appldnld.apple.com.edgesuite.net/content.info.apple.com/iPhone/061-3538.20070629.B7vXa/iPhone1,1_1.0_1A543a_Restore.ip

From iTunes, connect your iPhone, hold down the Option key, and click the Restore button. A Finder window will pop up asking you for a file that ends with the extension *.ipsw*, (remove the .ZIP, but do not decompress the file). This is the iPhone firmware restore in its entirety. If you have a folder containing what appears to be a bunch of cryptic files, make sure that you're not decompressing the files after they are downloaded.

However, if you're running 1.1.3, you have your work cut out for you. To prepare for the downgrade process, you must be running iTunes 7.5 and the latest version of iNdependence (http://code.google.com/p/independence/) for Mac plus a copy of the iPhone 1.1.1 and 1.1.2 firmware.

1. Put your iPhone into DFU mode by holding the Power/Sleep button and Home button until the screen goes black.

2. Release the Power/Sleep button once the screen goes black, but continue to hold the Home button for another 10 seconds. If you are unsure about properly putting your iPhone into DFU mode (since there is no distinction with a powered-down device), connect your phone to iTunes. If you've done it right, iTunes will display a pop up letting you know your iPhone is in recovery mode.

3. From here you must hold down the Option key, then click restore. Navigate from the Finder window until you select the 1.1.1 firmware file (with the extension *.ipsw*) and let iTunes attempt to restore it.

4. The restore process will fail, spitting out "Error 1015, your iPhone could not be updated." Go ahead and launch iNdependence to break your iPhone out of recovery mode.

5. You'll be prompted to activate your iPhone and restore your personal data; when done, you'll have a downgraded iPhone and, depending on your boot loader, fully functioning calling capabilities.

6. If you're running boot loader 3.9, download *Installer.app* from http://repository.apptapp.com/ packages/System/Installer.zip, unzip the file, and add *Installer.app* to iNdependence under the Customize tab. Then add this source to *Installer.app*: *i.unlock.no* (it's just a web page), and wait for it to refresh. Navigate to the category titled Category Tools, install Baseband Downgrader, then restart when it's complete.

7. If you're running boot loader 4.6, you cannot downgrade any further but you can jailbreak and upgrade to your heart's content. If you are running boot loader 3.9, you can downgrade back to 1.0.2 and then 1.0.0. First, download a copy of AppTapp from http://iphone.nullriver.com/ beta/.

8. Now, put your iPhone into DFU mode by holding the Power/Sleep button and Home button until the screen goes black.

9. Release the Power/Sleep button once the screen goes black, but continue to hold the Home button for another 10 seconds. If you are unsure about properly putting your iPhone into DFU mode, (since there is no distinction with a powered-down device), connect your phone to iTunes. If you've done it right, iTunes will display a pop up letting you know your iPhone is in recovery mode.

10. From here, hold down the Option key, and then click restore. Navigate from the Finder window until you select the 1.0.2 firmware file (with the extension *.ipsw*), and let iTunes attempt to restore it (see Figure 12-1).

Figure 12-1.
The firmware you're looking for

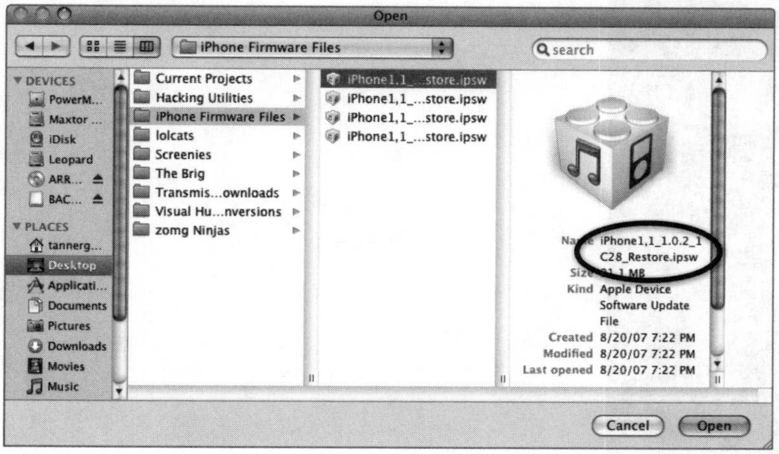

iTunes will spit out an error message and put your iPhone into recovery mode. Run AppTapp (from the Desktop) to save your iPhone from purgatory, and disregard any error messages.

Open up iTunes to ensure it recognizes your iPhone; then perform a jailbreak with AppTapp.

Bypassing Activation

Should you need to jailbreak 1.1.1 without activating, there is a method you can use to bypass activating your iPhone through iTunes. If a restore has been performed or it's been torn open from the box like it's Christmas morning, your iPhone should display the "Activate iPhone/Connect To iTunes" screen. Directly underneath you can unlock the screen to make emergency calls. We'll be leveraging this to gain access to the Home screen and jailbreak an iPhone running 1.1.1.

First, access the emergency calling menu, dial in *#307#, then click call (see Figure 12-2).

Figure 12-2.
Well, it is kind of an emergency

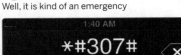

The iPhone will proceed to call itself but fret not, you're not being saved from the Matrix. Delete all the numbers in the text field, enter the number 0, then tap the call button and wait for the call (see Figure 12-3).

Figure 12-3.
You're calling yourself, go ahead and answer it, it is you after all

You will be called again; go ahead and accept the incoming call, then very rudely hit hold. You will be called yet again, but this time decline the call (see Figure 12-4). Your local law enforcement does not need to be notified of these mysterious calls; no one is hiding in the upstairs bedroom in your house.

Figure 12-4.
More calls

You should now see the keypad screen; go ahead and tap Contacts. After that tap, you'll be navigated to an empty contact list. Tap the plus button to add someone; then fill in the following information (Figure 12-5).

· URL 1: prefs:

· URL 2: http://www.jailbreakme.com

· Name: Mr. Smiths (This is optional but it makes the process that much cooler.)

Figure 12-5.
iPhone trickery

Save the contact information, and then tap the URL that contains prefs:, This will take you to the Settings menu, allowing you to turn Wi-Fi on and disable Auto Lock.

Go back to the Home screen, and repeat the steps until you get to the point where you tap contacts. You'll now be able to see the contact you made earlier (either that or he'll be able to see you, but that's not important right now) allowing you to go to the second URL, jailbreakme.com.

Once you're done, the iPhone returns to the activation screen, and you will have a jailbroken iPhone ready to run all that third-party goodness.

I personally would like to thank the various third-party developers and hackers who made jailbreaking possible, along with George Hotz, who first led the collaboration to unlock the iPhone.

— Tanner Godarzi

HACK 100: After You Jailbreak

You've jailbroken your iPhone: now what? Discover how to get more out of your freed iPhone.

So you've jailbroken your phone, and nothing seems to have changed. Wait, check that out: there's a new application added to your screen (Figure 12-6).

Figure 12-6.
Hey, that installer application is new...

This new application—Installer—is where the magic of a jailbroken phone starts. Give Installer a quick tap, and you are treated to a welcome screen. Still not very exciting. but at the bottom of the screen, you'll see something different from the familiar Springboard (see Figure 12-7).

Figure 12-7.
Installation starts here

Figure 12-8.
Don't install blindly, get more info

Now, tap Install, and get ready to be transported to a world of iPhone applications heretofore unimagined. If you're worried that you've just downloaded a million applications to your phone that are sitting around waiting be installed, fret not. The applications you see aren't on your phone; the list is comprised of links to the files, and until you choose to install something, the applications aren't taking up space.

Tapping All Packages will list everything available for your jailbroken iPhone, but the list is very long, long enough to result in some kind of repetitive stress injury on your pointer finger. You're better off relying on the screens that group applications by their intended purpose.

At this point you will probably tempted to go install-crazy and revel in your iPhone's newly increased utility. Resist the urge. Before installing any application on your iPhone, exercise care. Some applications might be malicious, some might be not be compatible with the firmware you chose, and some might be plain dogs. So, as with your Mac, research any program before you actually install it. A good starting place for your research is the More Info link at the bottom of the Package page (see Figure 12-8).

After you've found a program that is safe and possibly fun or useful, tap it. You'll be taken to the Package page. In the upper-right corner, there is an install button.

Hitting the Install button doesn't actually install anything; it just lets the installer know that you're feeling very serious about the process. A pane will slide up, and you get your choice: Install, Add to Queue, and Cancel. Install, as you expect, installs right away. Add to Queue adds the application to a list of applications to be installed (useful for those days when you feel like installing lots of software) but won't install anything until the next time you tap Install, when it will install all the programs you've chosen.

Once you actually tap Install, your iPhone will go about the business of downloading the application from the Web and installing it on your phone. Your phone will lock, and when you slide the lock open, your new application will be sitting on your home screen. Have fun: there's a world of iPhone applications out there.

To uninstall any or all the apps you've installed, tap the Installer, then tap Uninstall at the bottom of the screen, and you'll get a list of all the apps you've installed. Select the app you want to uninstall, and tap Uninstall (see Figure 12-9).

Figure 12-9.
Undoing the install

HACK 101:   Add a Hard Drive to Your iPhone (Kind of)

Is 16 GB not enough to hold your vast media collection? Forget about trying to decide which movies and songs to load on your iPhone (or iPod Touch), and discover a method to get to all the files on your Mac from your iPhone.

For some, the space afforded by an iPhone and iPod touch easily accommodates all of their media. For others, even the 32 GB of storage afforded by the top-end iPod touch isn't enough to hold all their media. At this point the arguing begins. Some opine that 8 GB is plenty to hold all the media a user could possibly want between charges, while the media-collecting-frenzied among us retort that while the capacity is enough to get them through the next charge, what is really lacking is choice. Why should they be forced to omit items from their iPhone's library when Apple could sell an iPhone or an iPod touch that includes the hard drive found in the 160 GB iPod classic?

One can argue that anyone with 160 GB of media doesn't have the most discerning palette, but hacking is all about getting your stuff to do the things you want the way you want them to. If you want to have access to 160 full-length features via your iPhone or iPod Touch, why not?

Turns out you can tweak your Mac so that your iPhone can access any file on your hard drive, and if you have access to any file, you have access to all your movies and music. No more hand wringing is needed now to decide what to add to your iPhone playlist and what to leave behind.

Pulling Off the Hack

This hack relies on a piece of open source software for your Mac. It's called iPhoneRemote and is available at http://code.google.com/p/telekinesis/. Download the program and drag it to the desired folder on your Mac (Applications is a good choice). That's it for installation—no ZIP or DMG here—the application you download simply shows up as an application.

Once iPhoneRemote is ensconced in your folder of choice, fire it up with a double-click. The application's icon will bounce like mad in the Dock, and you'll be presented with a window demanding you enter a username and password (see Figure 12-10).

Figure 12-10.
Create a name and a password to get started

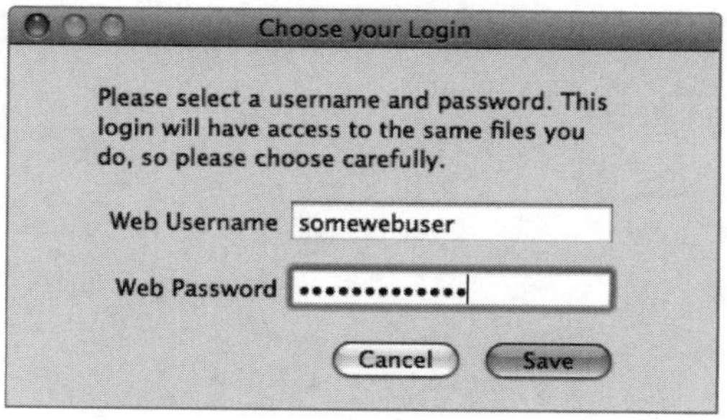

This isn't a password to access the program; it's a password to access the files on your Mac from the outside world. So create both a good username and a strong password **[Hack #25]**. Safari (if it is running) then attempts to load *https://localhost:5010/*, and you'll be greeted by a scary-looking warning (see Figure 12-11).

Figure 12-11.
Don't worry, you're only headed to your Mac

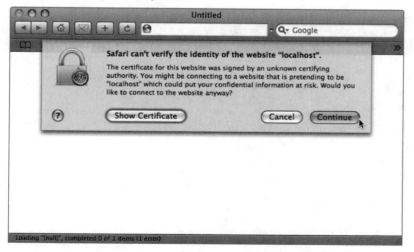

You are then hit up for your password, and once that information is accepted, you are whisked to a page that would look good on an iPhone (see Figure 12-12).

Figure 12-12.
This looks like it should be on an iPhone

What has happened is that iPhoneRemote has opened a port (5010) on your machine to allow access to your files. Pretty spiffy: you can browse your own Mac via Safari. But where is the iPhone-browsing goodness?

What you need now is an IP address of your Mac that will make sense to your iPhone. If you're at home using a wireless network for both the Mac and the iPhone, you can find it from System Preferences→Network→Airport (see Figure 12-13).

Figure 12-13.
Your local IP address

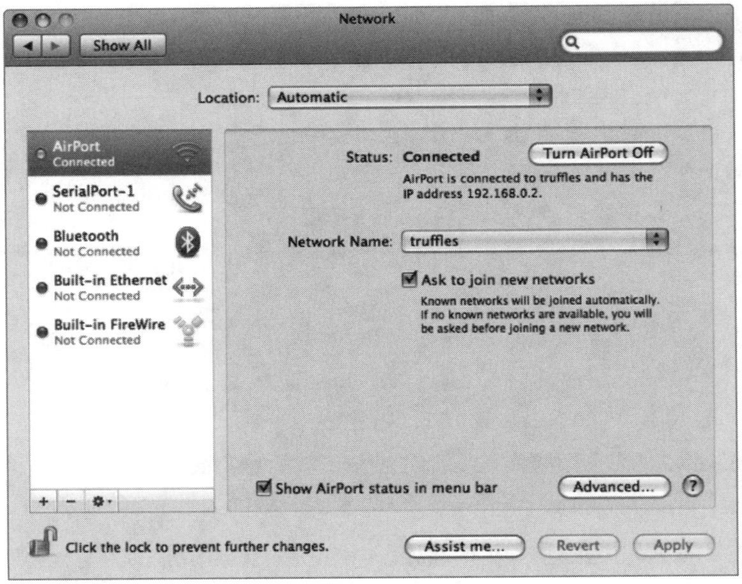

Once you have the IP address, you can enter **https://youripaddress:5010** to get access to your Mac. But where is the fun in that? If you're on the local network, you can probably walk over to your machine and get the file you're after! What you're really after is a way to get at your stuff when you are far far away. In that case, you need to know your Mac's external IP—the IP address the world uses to find your machine. To determine the magic number, head to a site such as whatismyip.com, and the information will be revealed (see Figure 12-14).

Figure 12-14.
Your external IP address

WhatIsMyIP.com
The fastest and easiest way to determine your IP address.

| IP Address | IP Command Lines | IP Addresses Explained | Speed Test | What's New |

Your IP Address Is 75.130.67.195

Automators, DynDNS users, MAC automators, coders, script writers, Click Here

It's likely that your home network uses a dynamically allocated IP number, or sits behind a firewall or router. **[Hack #48]** can help you.

Once you know the external IP address, the drill is the same: type in **https://youripaddress:5010** to get access to your Mac. See **[Hack #11]** for instructions on setting your router to maximize the experience. Make sure that port 5010 is among the open ports.

Accessing Your Media

You've got access to your Mac but not to your media. Trying to stream a song or a movie results in another window popping open asking for a name and password. Typing the name and password you generated earlier doesn't do any good. Time to head back to the Mac and iPhoneRemote and enable media sharing. Select "Preferences…" under the file menu, and check "Share media insecurely" (see Figure 12-15). Then click Restart Server.

Figure 12-15.
Share that media!

Now it's time for the fun to begin. Back to the iPhone, reconnect to your Mac, tap the Files icon, and navigate to the media you want to play. Tap once, and you'll be hearing or watching your media! The reason that the process is labeled insecure is because once you enable media access, any media sent will be streamed insecurely. The iPhone won't, according to the authors of Telekensis, accept self-signed security certificates so the media must be streamed in a less-than-secure manner. Anyone who knows your IP address, knows what port you're using, and knows the precise path to your media could copy all your media files. That's a lot of specific information, so there's a limited amount of security via obscurity.

I think the risks are worth it; somehow there is nothing cooler than streaming a movie from my home machine at the local Wi-Fi hotspot!

HACK 102: The iPhone as a Mobile Educational Tool

Sure the iPhone is cool, but it can also be very useful—useful in ways you might not expect. Discover how the iPhone can make you smarter.

Many colleges and some schools allow students to bring electronic devices to class for note taking or to record lectures, but this isn't the most convenient of solutions. High-school students face a somewhat strict ban on gadgets in the classrooms, but you want to learn all the time, even when you're not learning anything in class.

This is where the iPhone excels. Its small footprint allows it to be hidden and can be used when needed quickly without much hassle. These tips will help you use your iPhone in a learning environment for legitimate purposes.

Web Resources

This could change in the future, since no one knows what great applications will be made using the iPhone SDK. For now, the best bet to extend your knowledge with an iPhone is to rely on the Web.

Facebook

Perhaps the most important link I can put in here is Facebook (www.facebook.com). Yes, I mean the social network all the cool kids use to communicate with one another. True it won't teach you anything, but it will let you socialize with students who go to your school. I've found this to be an invaluable tool; it's great to talk with other students about upcoming projects and collaborate about it because face it, as much as you would rather your friends make an iCal entry, publish it to .Mac, and send you the subscription link, it'll never happen. They'll find it more convenient to publish it on a social network and leave it up to you to manipulate it.

In addition, an iPhone/iPod touch-optimized version of Facebook is available and really quite slick. Visiting the site through your iPhone via the normal link will auto-format the page for your iPhone.

PogoNotes

Now say you need an online text editor. You could rock it with Stickies, which is a good option. It works for my blogging, but if you just yearn for an online editor, you don't have many options.

As of this writing, Zoho apps and Google docs are read-only when accessed from the iPhone (that could change as time goes on). This isn't so useful when you actually want to type something, unless of course you don't mind Stickies. But a very useful alternative exists. PogoNotes (http://www.pogonotes.com) was designed specifically for the iPhone. It's a very basic editor and limited by what the iPhone's keyboard can do, so don't expect it to be a full-blown replacement for the more powerful online office suites. That said, PogoNotes is custom-built for Mobile Safari; it scales well and is plenty fast when on EDGE, which more than makes up for its shortcomings (see the sidebar "Edge Isn't Just a Guitar Player").

Vitalist

Organization is key for students, and the getting things done (GTD) methodology is a great way to accomplish it. Vitalist (http://iphone.vitalist.com) is your one online resource center that incorporates organization and task tracking into one clean iPhone application.

The real advantages of Vitalist is that it is web-based and beats iCal for jotting down new tasks and prioritizing them. iCal can do most of this, but the lack of customizing To Do's really hinders that application.

Miscellaneous Resources

Even though the Web is a powerful tool, there are better resources to use with a computer and iPhone that allow a lot of flexibility in how a student can archive and receive aggregated content.

Voice Notes

This application is not officially sanctioned by Apple, but is available through the premier iPhone third-party *Installer.app* [Hack #99] and is a great help for recording lectures. Voice Notes does exactly as its name implies: creates voice notes from your iPhone's microphone. However, instead of actually having your iPhone out during class, the application can record audio from the microphone embedded in the ear buds that came with your iPhone. This allows you to have your iPhone on and running, yet be tucked away, but that had probably already occurred to you.

iTunesU

Most people think of iTunes as the place to get singles, but iTunes offers access to more than just hit albums, award-winning movies, and highly acclaimed television shows: it also offers content from major universities from such schools as MIT, UC Berkeley, and Stanford. You can't attend UC Berkeley and MIT at the same time, but you can subscribe to hundreds of podcasts, and download videos and audio recordings of many lectures. Any topic you're interested in can be found somewhere with iTunesU. Visit http://www.apple.com/education/itunesu/index.html for the full details.

Keynote and iPhone AV Cables

Just because an iPhone comes in handy for students, doesn't mean a teacher can't use it. Just as it can be a tool to gather and facilitate information, it can be an exceptional teaching tool. Case in point: Keynote's export options. Keynote, part of iWork '08, allows you to create and edit presentations, but instead of playing them back on any Mac or PC, you can export them as a QuickTime file that's playable on the iPhone. Coupled with Apple's AV cables, Keynote is an easy and quick portable projector replacement.

— Tanner Godarzi

HACK 103: The iPhone as a Mobile Blog Machine

Forget carrying around a laptop or waiting until you get home to blog your thoughts. Blog in the moment from where the action is, using your iPhone.

When he introduced the iPhone, Steve Jobs opined that it was an excellent Internet device. He's correct but an excellent Internet device doesn't equal an excellent blogging device. Occasionally you'll need to make some adjustments in your workflow and adapt your tools to a mobile interface. Luckily for you this isn't too difficult, and once completed, it will unlock the true potential of the iPhone.

Get the Right Tools

Even though the iPhone boasts a spacious 3.5-inch screen and delivers a healthy portion of the Internet, it hasn't stopped developers from creating web pages optimized specifically for the device. Checking to see if sites you frequently visit have an iPhone-optimized page cuts down on loading time and displays only important content or, at the very least, make everything easier to use and faster to load. A few blogger favorites are Digg's optimized site, (http://www.digg.com/iphone) and Meebo's optimized IM client (http://www.meebo.com).

Gathering Content

A blogger's best friend and often times inspiration is content that can be gathered quickly and easily. Maintaining a workflow that does not compromise organization is essential.

Chances are you'll be obtaining content through RSS feeds and will probably be rocking a desktop or web-based reader. If your preference is online, your choices are easy: Newsgator (http://m.newsgator.com) offers an iPhone-optimized reader as does Google (reader.google.com) and Netvibes (http://iphone.netvibes.com/). If you prefer a desktop-based reader, you can always use one that supports Newsgator and, if you're desperate, bookmark your links on del.icio.us (http://www.del.icio.us).

Manipulating Content

Finding news and actually blogging it with an iPhone likely brings up thoughts of why it won't work. After all, the differences between an iPhone and even the smallest laptop are monumental. Add to those differences the fact that there are plenty of popular blogging tools that just won't work on an iPhone, and you have reasons to be skeptical.

It is important to understand what you can and can't do when it comes to blogging, In the end, you'll be surprised just how much blogging power lies in the iPhone's diminutive shape.

Creating a Blog Post

A blog post at the core is nothing more than someone's thoughts in text form that can be digitally manipulated. Getting this text from your iPhone to the front page of your blog isn't hard because you have two options: using your preferred content management system (CMS) or an alternative.

Besides using something like Wordpress to type your post, you might want to consider something local, for example, Stickies. As archaic and basic as this might seem, it'll serve the purpose quite well.

Now you must be wondering how you'll get that Stickie Note into a blog post without some sort of hackery or going near your computer. It's actually simple: email it to your blog. Blogging by email or *moblogging* isn't new; its' been around for quite awhile and has taken off now that most cell phones can access the Internet.

Fortunately for you, most of the major CMSs support moblogging. The following list is a compilation, along with links for instructions on getting everything set up:

- **Wordpress:** (http://codex.wordpress.org/Blog_by_Email)

- **Expression Engine:** (http://expressionengine.com/docs/modules/moblog/index.html)

- **Drupal:** (http://drupal.org/node/39172)

- **TypePad:** (http://preview.tinyurl.com/2s3p6y)

- **Vox:** (http://preview.tinyurl.com/3dtqce)

I recommend that you create a unique email address only you have access to when using the moblogging function of your CMS. So you won't forget that special email address, add it as a contact with the name of either your blog or the name of your CMS. If you name it Drupal, just start typing it out in the email address field, and the contact will pop up.

Time for an iPhone blogging limitation: even though many CMSs support posting images via email, the process does pose a significant problem with the iPhone: you cannot email your post along with an image. This isn't a limitation of your CMS but rather a limitation with the iPhone. Your only alternative if you want to combine an image with a post is to create it as a draft (with Mail) and type out your thoughts before sending it.

Organizing Additional Media

We've got the basics down already, but blogging has evolved beyond text; it encompasses a wide sphere of content ranging from text to video. As vibrant as you want to make your posts, it's just not as easy on the iPhone. Online content sharing platforms support only a limited range of blogging platforms for posting media. YouTube allows easy posting to some of the well-known platforms, and Flickr supports most of the major and lesser-known platforms.

But when you start getting into adding multiple types of media such as a Flickr images and Google videos, your only recourse is to use a plug-in that lets you link directly to the content and then display it properly.

A good example would be the plug-in for Wordpress, which allows you to insert a YouTube link wherever you please in your blog (http://www.ejump.co.uk/wordpress/easytube-plugin-for-wordpress). This is a tough trick to pull off with an iPhone because the process requires copying a convoluted link and pasting it. You can't copy and paste with an iPhone, so you'll be forced to transcribe the link. A major hassle: that video had better be really compelling.

Promoting Content with Bookmarklets

Besides creating content, bloggers often like to promote it across social networks. The most popular are Digg, del.icio.us, Reddit, Propeller (formerly Netscape), and Newsvine.

Submitting content from your blog and others' web sites isn't too much of a hassle on the iPhone if you use bookmarklets. Del.icio.us, Newsvine, Reddit and Propeller offer a bookmarklet you can grab from the story submissions page to fill in important information that speeds up the process. Digg, on the other hand, does not have a native bookmarklet but others have stepped in to offer their own. (http://skattertech.com/2006/06/digg-this-bookmarklet/).

Besides using bookmarklets to submit content to social networks, they serve a greater purpose especially when blogging. Take for instance a situation in which you need to find a word amongst a sea of text to edit out. Thankfully, Lifeclever (http://www.lifeclever.com/17-powerful-bookmarklets-for-your-iphone/) has compiled a list of 17 essential bookmarklets for the iPhone including find text, English translation, and shortcuts to many popular online tools, just to name a few.

As a blogger myself, I found the iPhone a bit of a challenge to get used to initially. I knew it would be a big help because I could type up a blog post anywhere, but I needed to learn how to adapt my workflow to a mobile device. Hopefully this helps but it's important to know that no matter how much you slim your needs down, the iPhone, in its current form, will not offer the same functionality as a UMPC, laptop, or desktop.

— Tanner Godarzi

Going Mobile with PasswordWallet

Frustrated by iPhone password woes? Let this hack blow away your password-entering troubles.

Let's face it: the number of passwords we all have to keep track of is growing rapidly. Not only is it harder to keep track of them because of their sheer number, but, as good security practices become more common, we are forced to change passwords more frequently and can't keep using the same, poorly formed password, over and over.

I frequently find that I need to know a password when I'm away from my computer. For example, I might be traveling and want to change the outgoing message on my voice mail at home. I need a password to do that, and it's one that frequently seems to leak out of my brain.

Truth be told, I've been forgetting passwords for a long time. That's why I've been using Selznick Scientific Software's PasswordWallet (http://www.selznick.com/products/passwordwallet/) application since before Mac OS X existed. Not only was it was one of the first password-keeping applications, it has long offered the ability to sync a secure copy of your password list to Palm devices. And back in the day, I didn't go anywhere without my trusty Palm V.

But these days, it's an iPhone I carry everywhere, so that's where I need my password list. In fact, even more so now, thanks to the utility of Safari. Thankfully, the latest version of PasswordWallet now includes the ability, at extra cost, to export an encrypted copy of my password list to iPhone. It's a handy solution that's cleverly implemented. It works by wrapping the entire password list inside of a Blowfish-encrypted HTML document that is then encoded as a `data://` URL. This URL is added to the desktop Safari bookmarks, so it can be synced to iPhone. You can even set it up so that every time you change your password list, the bookmark is automatically updated.

> A data:// URL is a self-contained resource so that no web connectivity is necessary. I have over 200 items in my password list, and while the resulting, encoded URL is incredibly long and complex, it renders and syncs just fine.

In other words, you don't need to install any special software or hack your iPhone. When you want to view a password, you select the bookmark in Safari, enter your password to open the list, and then find the password you need. In my opinion, it works well, and I'm happy with it. The following tips can make it work a bit more smoothly:

Categorize your passwords
Despite the alphabetical navigation afforded in the exported HTML, a long list is too cumbersome to navigate. To help with this, use PasswordWallet's categorization ability. In all my years using the desktop version, I never felt compelled to do this, but with the iPhone export, I think it's a must; it helps you find a particular entry more easily. At the very least, create just one category for those passwords you're most likely to use when mobile.

Customize the export
The template used to create the HTML for the iPhone is located in the *PasswordWallet.app* bundle. Right-click or command-click, and look in *Resources/[language].lproj* for a file named *iPhoneTemplate.html*. You can edit this file to your heart's content, but the only change I make is to change the password-entry field to a standard text field.

Use a password
On the desktop, PasswordWallet is locked with, well, a password. I use a strong one, which means it's long and includes some nonletter characters. This same password is necessary to open the

password list on iPhone. But typing a long, complicated password with the onscreen keyboard is tedious and prone to error because, in the password field, every letter is replaced with a bullet character. You can easily make a typo and not even know it.

So that you can see your password when you enter it, find this portion of the HTML template file:

```
<input style="font-size: 18px;" type="password" id="password"
  size="12" maxlength="255" />
```

Change the type definition from **password** to **text**. The result will look like this:

```
<input style="font-size: 18px;" type="text" id="password" size="12"
  maxlength="255" />
```

Re-export your password list to iPhone, and you'll find that now you can see your password as you enter it. Of course, you'll want to make sure that no one is peering over your shoulder while you do this, but I consider the moderately increased risk of this approach better than the alternatives of being frustrated by mistyping my password, or selecting a less secure and easier to type password.

Keep a copy
Sanford Selznick, author of PasswordWallet, further suggests that you might want to keep a copy of your modified template outside the application bundle and make a symbolic link to it in the same location as the original. This will preserve your changed template during application upgrades (note that you'll have to redo the symbolic link when you upgrade).

There are other password-keeping applications for Mac OS X, but I think the ability to create a secure, mobile version of my password list is a killer feature.

— Gordon Meyer

QUICK TIP

MAKE A SYMBOLIC LINK

A symbolic link is a way to have multiple copies of a file that point to some original file. For example, a symbolic link on your desktop to *Volumes/foo.file* allows you to manipulate *foo. file* from the desktop without actually going to *foo.file*. This is great, but you need to know how to make one. Fire up the Terminal, and type:

```
$ ln -s filename
linkname
```

Where **filename** and **linkname** are the original file you want to link to, and the name of the new link to that file. Hit return, and your new symbolic link will show up in your home directory.

13   HACKS FOR LAPS

Steve Jobs declared 2003 to be the "year of the laptop." He was probably right: 2003 was a big year for laptops but small machines have kept growing in market share every year since Steve's pronouncement. So 'Books (that's iBooks, PowerBooks, and MacBooks) seem like a natural target for hacking. In this chapter, you will learn how to repurpose a broken laptop, max out onboard storage, and even teach your 'Book to respond to slaps.

HACK 105: Three Ways to Disable a Built-in iSight

All currently shipping MacBooks feature a built-in iSight; learn how to disable this component if you don't want or can't use this functionality.

If you've got an Apple-designed laptop made after 2005, you're got an iSight camera built in. The camera is a nice piece of hardware; it's unobtrusive, fun to use for video iChats and playing with PhotoBooth, but, like everything, it isn't for everyone.

Some would-be Mac users are prohibited from carrying anything with a camera into their workplace because of security concerns. This may seem draconian because, on the surface, the prohibition seems to stem from a deep-seated distrust of users. Still, it is easy to imagine certain circumstances in which outlawing cameras of any sort is a good idea. For example, anywhere Carrot Top is appearing is a great place to ban cameras.

Besides the obvious corporate security objections (no one would want early pictures of the next iPhone to leak out), some people are plainly unnerved by having a built-in camera in their computer. It is one of those things: you rationally know that there aren't a million people watching you when you walk in front of your MacBook, but the fact that some super clever hacker could figure out a way to slurp the images from the built-in iSight and spew them all over the Web can be disconcerting.

What is needed is a way to allay the fears of all MacBook users and those who deal with them.

If iSight Bugs You...
If you're bugged by iSight's ever-staring square, the fix is simple though it requires a trip to the Terminal. Once you have the Terminal fired up, type:

```
$ sudo mv /System/Library/QuickTime/QuickTimeUSBVDCDigitizer.component \
  /Users/cks/Desktop
```

This command moves the *QuickTimeUSBVDCDigitizer.component* file to your desktop, but it won't kill iSight if you're using Leopard. Whereas Tiger relied solely on that component to access the camera, Leopard has a redundant driver. If you're a Leopard person, you need to move another file:

```
$ sudo mv /System/Library/PrivateFrameworks/CoreMediaIOServicesPrivate.framework/
Versions/A/Resources/VDC.plugin /Users/cks/Desktop
```

There ya go: no more iSight for you. Any effort to invoke iSight will result in failure (see Figure 13-1). The camera is still physically there, but it has become the computing equivalent of a vestigial organ. Until the files are restored, iSight won't be doing anything. If you are certain you never want to use iSight again, drag the two new files now residing on your Desktop to the Trash, and delete them forever.

Figure 13-1.
iSight is no longer functional

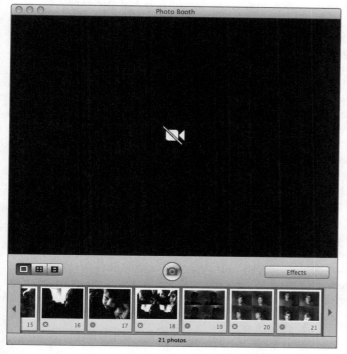

If You're Surrounded by the Paranoid...

Maybe you like the idea of having iSight, but you employer doesn't. The obvious solution is a physical barrier; after all, merely stating that iSight is disabled through a software hack is right up there with saying you're not interested in the money. Even if it is true, no one is likely to believe you.

The solution at this point is obvious: a sticker or a piece of opaque tape. The tape has easy availability going for it, but the sticker can add a level of personalization not offered by the tape. Figure 13-2 shows how cool this makes a machine look.

Figure 13-2.
A goofy "O" sticker

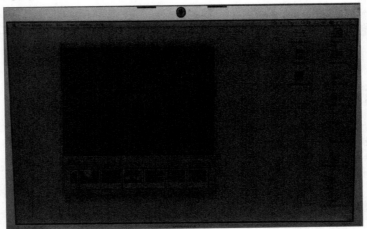

Somehow it is hard to imagine even a professional-looking piece of tape or sticker inspiring confidence. There is only one option left.

Pretend You Have an iBook or a PowerBook

The difference between the Powerbook and a MacBook Pro is all about the internal components. A few changes and passing off a MacBook Pro as its earlier non-iSight-owning sibling is easy. It is a bit harder to do the same thing with a MacBook; the keyboard is quite different, but it is still doable. That said, what this part of the hack is about isn't convincing people you don't have a MacBook, but rather convincing them that your machine doesn't have a camera.

You could take this part of the hack to any extreme you want. You can create a custom bezel that replaces the Apple-made bezel, but that involves disassembly. The easier way, which you can undo any time, involves Scotch Magic Tape (the matte finish helps) and paint—specifically (for my MacBook Pro) Testor's Model Master Aluminum (nonbuff) B-1418.

Lay the tape out on flat surface and paint the tape carefully to avoid buildup and brush strokes. Once the paint has dried, cut a section slightly larger than the iSight out with a razor knife, and place it over the iSight lens. You'll be able to spot it but, from actual experience (yes, as dumb as it sounds, I had to do exactly this once, in order to bring my computer into a work site), most people will pass right over iSight when performing a cursory inspection.

HACK 106: Two Hacks for the iBook

In the age of Intel everything and scrolling trackpads, it can be easy to forget that the iBook is still a viable machine for a lot of people. Upgrade your iBook in a MacBook world.

Leopard requires an 867 MHz G4 processor or better. Sure this leaves a lot of the older PowerBooks and iBooks stuck squarely in the Tiger era, but any PowerBook introduced after November 2002 can run the latest and the greatest as can any iBook introduced after April 2004. Couple the ability to run Leopard with the low prices, these models generally fetch less than half the price of a new MacBook, and it is easy to see how a used 'Book can be an attractive proposition.

Generally, when buying used, you're trying to save some money (obvious exceptions to this rule include, for example, art and antique autos), and if saving money is the goal, the obvious choice is the iBook. The unfortunate thing about choosing an iBook is that it lacks in two key areas. First, the iBook doesn't support **two-finger gestures** on the trackpad—the greatest addition to cursor control since Apple replaced the trackball with the trackpad in 1994. The second thing the iBook lacks, which can be a deal killer, is **dual-monitor support**. Instead of doing the sensible thing and increasing the amount of monitor real estate users had when plugging into an external monitor, Apple sought to differentiate the PowerBook and iBook by forcing the iBook to mirror the video displayed on the iBook's screen. If only there was a way to get around those limitations, a Leopard-capable iBook would be a nice choice as a laptop, particularly if you already have a desktop to do the heavy lifting.

Two Finger Scrolling

Fortunately (and predictably), you can get around the limitations imposed by Apple. As it turns out, the trackpad in the iBook G4 can perform *two-finger scrolling*; the machine simply lacks the required driver. You can overcome this limitation by installing iScroll2, an open source driver written by Daniel Becker (http://iscroll2.sourceforge.net/).

Installing iScroll2 is straightforward: there is a GUI installer, and once the process is complete, you get a brand-new preference pane in System Preferences (see Figure 13-3).

Figure 13-3.
The preference pane of iScroll2

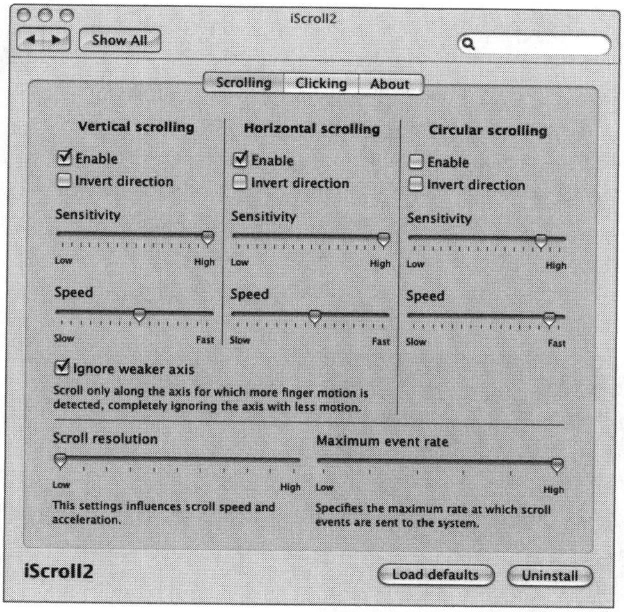

There is a good chance that iScroll won't be optimized for your personal track preferences right out of the ZIP file. Don't get discouraged: playing with the adjustments for just a short time will leave you wishing you could get iScroll2 to run on your MacPro. (One available option allows you to map a two-finger tap to a right mouse click.)

QUICK TIP

WHAT ABOUT MY SINGLE-FINGER POWERBOOK?

A few PowerBooks use a trackpad that can perform two-finger scrolling but, maddeningly, the feature isn't present on standard OS X installs. The same recipe to add two-finger scrolling to the iBook G4 can be used to add the same feature to the PowerBook. If you've got an aluminum PowerBook that lacks multitouch capability, iScroll2 is the answer to your single-finger woes.

QUICK TIP ✕

RECYCLE THAT MAC

Apple will gladly recycle any iPod or cell phone you drag into the store but it isn't so easy with a Mac. If you buy a new Mac from either the Apple Online Store or an Apple retail store you can get Apple to recycle your old computer (one machine, one monitor, brand unimportant) by jumping through the additional hoops of either selecting the "Apple Recycling Program" option while checking out online, or asking one of the Apple employees about the program when making your purchase at a retail outlet. Apple will send you an email with instructions on how to proceed but be aware that you're going to have to pack the thing up and haul it to the nearest FedEx location. Too much work? Your local Apple store will be able to tell you where to recycle your computer locally.

Monitor Spanning

With two-finger scrolling out of the way, it is time to tackle the less universally desired but still often deal-killing *monitor spanning*. iBooks are limited to monitor mirroring, but what people really want is monitor spanning: that way you get to use each of the pixels built into the screen of your iBook and the pixels of the added monitor.

There are two basic ways to go about this. You can opt to fiddle with your iBook's firmware (the method I first used), or you can let some free utility muck with the firmware for you. Both methods have their advantages and disadvantages. Meddling with the firmware yourself is exhilarating (for some folks anyway), and you know exactly what was changed. Letting a program fiddle with your firmware takes a lot of the fear and time out of the process. Either way, mucking about with your Mac's firmware is a good method to take your Mac from functional computer to pretty doorstop very quickly. Be careful. I'll stick with the script for this part of the hack.

Point your browser to http://www.rutemoeller.com/mp/ibook/ScreenSpanningDoctor.dmg, and download the file. Before you mount the installer, recall that you are about to authorize a program to toy with your firmware, and the results could be troublesome. I used this installer before I demobilized my iBook without problems, but that doesn't mean you won't have issues. This is one time it's worthwhile to read the *README* file and to visit the web site (http://www.rutemoeller. com/mp/ibook/ibook_e.html). Once you are certain you understand the risks and rewards, mount the *.dmg,* and let the installer do the work for you.

HACK 107: Demobilize Your iBook

It happens innocently enough: you leave your kid's iBook on the floor and forget about it for a moment. Suddenly a coterie of four-year-old boys is running rambunctiously through the house with the family dog, and one inadvertently steps on the machine, cracking the screen (see Figure 13-4). Who's to blame? The adult for being careless with the machine? The children for being children? The dog because dogs can't argue? All tempting choices but none are satisfactory; likely the only culprit is fate.

Figure 13-4.
The screen has seen better days

With everyone absolved, the only question is what to do about it. With a MacBook, the cost of replacing the screen is justified; with an iBook the question is murkier. Sinking several hundred dollars into a four year-old computer might not be the wisest idea. On the other hand, it is still a capable machine, so just letting the computing abilities go dormant doesn't seem like a good idea. Why not turn that iBook into a stationary computing station?

As always, there is more than one way to pull this trick off. The first and simplest option is to install a software patch that allows the iBook to run with the lid closed—a nice option but not very hardware hackish (Screen Spanning Doctor will pull the trick off: see **[Hack #106]**). The second way (and probably best, though also the hardest) would be to disassemble the machine completely and remove the bits you don't need. The third way is the dirty hack method. Instead of cracking both the bottom and the top of the iBook, this method saves the internals from possible damage and solves the problem by opening up only the top half of the iBook.

So you've decided to go with the third method, the built-in screen-removing route. The good news is that it can be fun to destroy an integral part of an iBook; the bad news is that there is a lot more going than you probably guessed. The first step is to remove the screws holding the screen to the iBook's lid. There are four of these, and you'll need a hex wrench to remove them. (Be careful here and make sure you use the right size; it is easy to strip the tiny hex bolts of an iBook.) Remove the screws, and hold them carefully in your hand. Then open the window, and fling them with reckless abandon; this is one hack you won't be undoing!

Once the screws are gone, you can slip the plastic shell off. Generally, you would slip the cover off carefully, but the screen is already broken, so just tug and twist at will.

Once the polycarbonate shell is no more, you're left with the bezel on the front and a silver back. Pull the silver backing off, and you'll see the back of the screen. There are a mess of wires and a ribbon cable running around; remove the wires, and unplug the cable. You don't need to concern yourself with the wires just yet. Instead, focus on the ribbon cable attached to the back of the screen. Unplug the ribbon cable and pull the screen out. As you're pulling the screen out, you'll notice one brown and one pink wire attached to the bottom. These wires power the backlight; tug them to release the plug on the keyboard half of the computer. The backlight runs along the bottom of the screen and is reportedly full of nasty stuff like mercury, so keep the assembly together and dispose of properly (see Figure 13-5).

Figure 13-5.
The screen is gone!

Now carefully unhook all the wires from the metal frame running around the area where the screen used to be. With the wires free, it is time to get rid of the metal frame. I used a small hacksaw and cut carefully through the point closest the body of the iBook (see Figure 13-6). The metal is soft and cuts easily, so don't rush it; you don't want to accidentally cut a wire.

Figure 13-6.
The iBook has been unframed

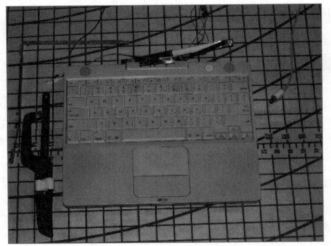

All that's left to deal with is the morass of wires. The thick black wire attaches to the microphone (see Figure 13-7). It is tempting to try and save it, but the connection is very fragile. I decided to lop it off.

Figure 13-7.
The microphone cable, completely optional!

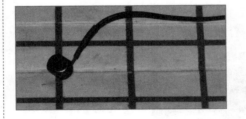

Figure 13-8.
The reed switch

The reed switch (see Figure 13-8) is a tiny magnetically sensitive switch that shuts down the display and puts the iBook to sleep when you close the lid. The default position is open, so I'm just going to clip it off and put the computer to sleep manually when I want that. Be careful though, if you let the ends touch, the computer will sleep. Now, cover the wire ends with electrical tape to prevent them from accidently touching.

Figure 13-9 shows the Airport antenna: don't clip this if you want to use Airport!

Figure 13-10 shows the display data cable. Snip it! Your iBook doesn't have a LCD attached, so this cable is worthless.

Figure 13-9.
You need this for wireless connectivity

Figure 13-10.
Cut this cable

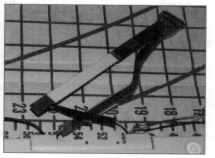

With all the unnecessary cable removed, all that's left to do is to hook your iBook up to a monitor via the video out port. To complete the project, I hooked up a wireless keyboard and mouse, built a small box, and attached the book to the underside of my kid's desk. He won't be able to break the computer (at least not the same way it got broken originally), and it has a lot of mileage left in it (Figure 13-11).

Figure 13-11.
Someone can use this computer again!

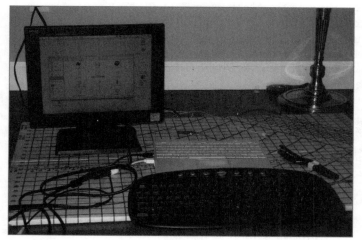

HACK 108: Build a Perfect Laptop Cooler for Your Machine

Laptops get hot, especially when placed under a heavy processor load. Protect your lap with a laptop cooler designed especially for your Mac laptop.

Mac laptops, whatever the flavor, are great machines. They're powerful enough for all but the most strenuous of computing tasks, and you can use one sitting in front of the TV. At least you could if the machine didn't get uncomfortably hot, which happens to be a major complaint of their owners.

It is worth noting that the handiest solution, cramming a pillow between the Mac and your legs, isn't the ideal solution. Apple tells users that such a configuration will restrict airflow and not allow proper cooling thus conceivably shortening the life of your Mac laptop. If you follow the recommendations of Apple, you won't use your Mac laptop on anything but a firm surface like, say, a desktop. A great solution if you don't mind using your machine only on hard surfaces, but it's one most of us would find unacceptable in real-world use.

Damaged machines? Hard surfaces only? Just how hot does a Mac laptop get? In one sense, the question doesn't really matter; if it is warm enough that you find it uncomfortable, then it is too hot. On the other hand, firm numbers are always nice when attempting to quantify a subjective level of discomfort. Additionally, some objective data will allow us to determine if our hack somehow endangers the machine.

Determining Your Laptop's Internal Temperature

If you think your laptop is too hot, you might want to monitor the internal temperature. Turns out that Apple has placed heat sensors at strategic locations throughout the MacBooks but, with the introduction of Intel-based machines, heat management was taken out of the OS, and the burden placed on a system management controller. Because managing the heat isn't part of the OS anymore, getting the correct temperature is trickier if you use an Intel-based machine. There are a couple of solutions.

The first is Temperature Monitor, part of the larger Hardware Monitor suite of applications offered by Marcel Bresink Software System (http://www.bresink.de/osx/HardwareMonitor.html). The software works great (see Figure 13-12), and it will set you back less than $20 per license (the actual price is in Euros so buy the license on a day when the dollar is strong) per license. If you're using an Intel-based machine, you'll have to by a license if you want to monitor the temperature. While there is a free version available from the same site (Temperature Monitor Light), it only works properly on non-Intel hardware—great news for PowerBook owners but not so good for MacBook owners.

Figure 13-12.
Temperature Monitor in action

Building the Custom Cooler

If you've decided you want a more comfortable laptop computing experience, one gratifying solution is building your own custom laptop cooler. Not only can you get the look you desire, you can put the cooling element exactly where it needs to be, and you can choose the appropriate amount of padding for your maximum personal comfort.

Here's the parts list:

- USB Chiller: The Chiller is made by CoolIT, a manufacturer of CPU cooling solutions. As you might have guessed, the Chiller is one of the company's CPU cooling systems repackaged as a pretty spiffy drink cooler. The Chiller uses a Peltier junction cooling scheme and manages to cool the transfer plate to about 45 degrees F, a temperature that will significantly cool down your Mac laptop if properly placed.

- A slab of material of reasonable size to be used as the top of the laptop cooler (in this example ¼-inch plywood is used).

- Comfortable padding (I used foam seat cushions).

- Material to cover the finished device.

Once you have the necessary materials gathered, it is time to do a little research. Where does your portable Mac get uncomfortably warm? "On my legs" is not the answer I was looking for, but thanks for playing. You're looking for optimal placement of the cooling element and, generally speaking, that is directly beneath the processor. You can either research processor placement on the Internet (ifixit.com has great Mac take apart pictures) or use a more direct approach and measure the temperature of your case after the computer has been run under full load for several minutes.

When you've determined the hotspot, you can get to work on your personal customized laptop cooler. (I used multitouch analog temperature monitoring devices called "hands" to identify the warmest spot on my MacBook Pro.) The first step is to create a base for the laptop. In this instance, I simply traced around the MacBook Pro onto a piece of ¼-inch plywood and marked the hotspot (see Figure 13-13).

Figure 13-13.
The general cut lines

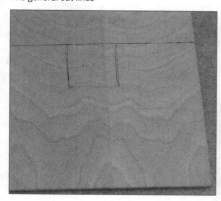

Figure 13-14.
The aluminum heat sink exposed

Now let's look at the Chiller. You're trying to cool down a laptop so the entire Chiller assembly is not necessary; you're only after the parts that do the cooling. A bit of thankfully easy disassembly is called for. The first step is to remove the six Phillips head screws on the bottom. Once removed, the steel back pops off, and the internals of the Chiller are easily extracted (see Figure 13-14 and Figure 13-15).

Figure 13-15.
The inner workings of the Chiller

QUICK TIP ✕

MAX THAT CPU LOAD

Although there are a lot of processor-intensive tasks you can use to truly tax the processors of your machine, there is a quick and simple method to max out the processing load on your Mac. For each physical CPU or core you have, run the following command in the Terminal (use tabs in Leopard, separate windows in Tiger):

```
$ yes
```

The command doesn't do much; it just tells the computer to output "y" as fast as it possibly can. As fast as possible means that the process will take every cycle possible and heat up your computer in a hurry. It's a useful trick for this hack and for cold days when the heater isn't working.

Once the plastic housing is shed, you are left with is an aluminum plate measuring 4 inches by 4 inches that's connected to a large heat sink via four screws. Sandwiched between the heat sink and aluminum plate is the thermoelectric element in which the cooling actually takes place. A small fan ensures a constant supply of moving air. The entire thing is powered by the still-attached, ever useful USB cable.

The size of the aluminum plate (70 mm by 70 mm) makes placement of the cooling element pretty simple. While it would be ideal to have the processor resting in the middle of the cooling element, anywhere on the raised portion of the aluminum plate should provide an adequate temperature differential.

The first step is to ensure the Chiller will make good contact with the MacBook. This is trickier than it sounds: you have to take into account the height of the MacBook feet and the outward circular bulge on the cooling plate. Luckily in this case, the feet and the bulge are both about 1 mm so they cancel each other out. Thus, if the cooling plate edges are level with the top of the laptop pad, there should be good contact between the MacBook Pro and the cooling element.

Which brings us to the tricky part. The cooling plate is 3 mm thick at the edges. To get the plate flush with the plywood, it is necessary to remove 3 mm of plywood—no problem with a router! (No, not a network router, the kind that has a whirling, sharp blade!) In this case, accuracy is not crucial so I eschewed the normal steps of using straight-edge guides and routed the area freehand using a ½-inch straight bit (see Figure 13-16).

Figure 13-16.
The successfully routed area

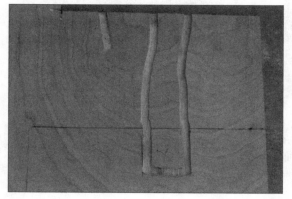

Once the plywood has been routed, it is time to break out the saw. Cutting around the edges marked using the MacBook Pro as a template and the inside of the area routed earlier leaves a rectangle with a square removed for the cooling element. The routed area forms a convenient lip that the Chiller (or what is left of it) will slide right into.

With the basic cooling system ready to go, it is time to pay some attention to personal comfort. Sitting a scratchy bit of plywood on your legs for a period of time is scarcely better than just letting the computer blister the tops of your thighs, so a little padding needs to be added.

For my project, I chose Morning Glory foam seat cushions for no other reason than a seat cushion called "Morning Glory" just seemed funny, and they happened to available at the local mega store for a mere $4. Just slapping the foam on the board isn't an option, because it would cover the cooling element and the fan. A razor knife and a few minutes leaves a piece of foam with a channel cut in to allow adequate airflow (see Figure 13-17). I mounted it temporarily with spray mount (surprisingly still available from art supply stores).

Figure 13-17.
The Chiller, the routed board, and the foam

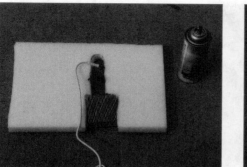

Figure 13-18.
Shortening the cable by coiling

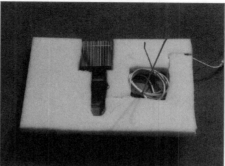

With the foam installed temporarily, I could see that I had way too much USB cable. It wouldn't do to have it flopping around, and making a new card or cutting and splicing the cable would be too much effort. After peeling the Morning Glory foam off the board, I cut channels to route the cable through and took a big chunk of foam right out. In the resulting cavity, I coiled the extraneous length of the USB cable and secured it with zip ties (see Figure 13-18). No extra cable now!

This is a good time to check everything. So I flipped the assembly over, and, for no logical reason at all, applied a coat of paint. I also marked the places where I would drill holes in the top to replace the screw in the Chiller (see Figure 13-19).

Figure 13-19.
Everything seems to be
okay on top

Figure 13-20.
Adding two pieces of foam protects your legs and
leaves a channel for air flow

There was one problem. The foam didn't extend far enough to cover the fan. Add to that the fact the gaping hole holding the coiled USB cable wouldn't be very comfortable, so I decided to add another layer of foam in strategic locations. I used the existing foam as a template, and after a few minutes with a razor knife, I had two foam rectangles attached via spray mount (see Figure 13-20).

After a quick test with the MacBook Pro, I found everything satisfactory (see Figure 13-21).

Figure 13-21.
A quick test, and everything works

Now it's time to make everything a little more permanent. To that end, I glued the conglomeration together with hot glue and replaced the screws to hold the Chiller plate in place. The only problem left now is the unsightly foam. At this point, a great idea would be to get some cool fabric and lovingly upholster the laptop pad. Sadly, the only material I had at my disposal was some outdated stuff my wife had used to make pillows. Careful cutting and tucking yielded something um, passable. Yours will turn out better but my proof-of-concept cooler is still functional (and thankfully usually hidden from view by a MacBook Pro). See Figure 13-22 and Figure 13-23.

Figure 13-22.
The bottom of the cooler

Figure 13-23.
The top of the completed cooler

HACK 109: Dual Drive MacBook Pro

Need more hard drive space on the go and willing to sacrifice the optical drive? Turn your MacBook Pro into a dual internal hard drive machine!

My MacBook Pro's processor is plenty fast for the video and audio I want to work on, but the disks are too slow. I decided to add a second disk to give myself a RAID arrangement to improve the performance.

I installed an MCE OptiBay hard drive (http://www.mcetech.com/optibay)—a second 160 GB 5400 rpm drive—into my MacBook Pro. The directions that came with the drive were simple to follow, and it took about 15 minutes to install (requiring the removal of 20 to 25 screws, plus two ribbon connectors (see Figure 13-24).

Figure 13-24.
The MacBook Pro before the second drive was installed. Installation requires the removal of 25 screws

When I booted back up, Mac OS X recognized the drive immediately (a Samsung HM160JC) and asked me if I wanted to initialize it. Initializing it would prevent me from making a RAID, so instead, I rebooted from an external drive (backed up by the excellent SuperDuper) and created a striped RAID 0 array using my two internal MacBook Pro drives: the original and the one I just installed with Disk Utility (select the disks you want to use and hit the RAID tab).

At this point, I discovered that you can't partition a Mac OS X software RAID volume, so I was stuck with a single, 297.46 GB, volume. I back up my volumes with SuperDuper, and will just have to create scripts that back up a bootable system copy without images or video (and I'll back up images/video separately, which is fine).

I ran Xbench on my system, and the results are pretty impressive. My machine's results are in the first column of the following table, and are compared with the results of comparable configurations pulled out of the Xbench comparison site. The last column features benchmarks from a Mac Pro with a 250 GB, 7,200 rpm, 3.5-inch drive. Note that all reads and writes are uncached.

QUICK TIP ✕

IT DOESN'T HAVE TO BE RAID

In this hack, Eric sets up the hard disks on his MacBook in a RAID array. In case you're wondering, a RAID array is (yay) another acronym. RAID stands for Redundant Array of Inexpensive Disks or Redundant Array of Independent Disks (people start fights over this). It allows you to use two or more disks to maximize performance or reliability, Using RAID for performance gains makes sense if the bottleneck of the machine is the disk I/O. This is commonly the case with disk-heavy tasks such as raw video reading and writing. If you're not throttled by the I/O of your disk, be aware that you can still pull this hack off without setting up your disks in a RAID configuration. You won't get the increased performance benefits, but you will get increased storage.

	Blocks	MacBook Pro Core 2, 2x160 5400 rpm 3 GB RAID 0 (Striped)		MacBook Pro 160 GB 5400 rpm 2 GB RAID 0 (Striped)		MacBook Pro 160 GB 7200 rpm 2 GB		MacPro Quad 250 GB 7200 rpm 4 GB	
		Score	MB/sec	Score	MB/sec	Score	MB/sec	Score	MB/sec
Results		137.52		110.5		118.2		158.46	
Disk Test		67.08		36.37		42.94		69.46	
Sequential		93.51		70.23		77.31		94.80	
Write	4K	163.43	100.34	69.63	42.72	97.99	60.16	70.50	43.28
Write	256K	139.48	78.92	73.79	41.75	86.30	48.83	104.05	58.87
Read	4K	43.68	12.78	57.35	16.78	51.03	14.94	100.62	29.45
Read	256K	151.59	76.19	86.17	43.31	96.58	48.54	118.22	59.41
Random		52.30		24.54		29.73		54.80	
Write	4K	23.24	2.46	8.99	.95	9.68	1.03	21.29	2.25
Write	256K	100.03	32.02	37.83	12.11	83.38	26.69	122.85	39.33
Read	4K	71.24	.50	66.16	.47	85.59	.63	93.7	.66
Read	256K	106.25	19.72	98.17	18.22	123.23	22.87	138.64	25.73

Results

The results are impressive, except that the RAID 0 doesn't seem to like small-block (4K) reads. Both sequential and random reads performed poorly. This should be fine because I'm most often working with large images and video files.

Most 160 GB, 5,400 rpm drives are supposed to become much faster as they fill up. My drives are about 30% full, and I plan to rerun the test as free space decreases. MCE reports that the drive is supposed to shorten battery life on the system by 10% to 15%, but I haven't had a chance to do my own tests.

As for sound, I can hear the second drive now, spinning quietly on the right side of the machine. It's audible but not annoying. The replacement drive chassis doesn't have the same clip receptacles the SuperDrive chassis has, so the keyboard top on my MacBook Pro no longer sits exactly flush on the right side. There's probably a 1-mm gap, which isn't enough to really bother me (see Figure 13-25).

Figure 13-25.
There's a 1-mm gap between keyboard and chassis on the right side

Subjectively, the system feels more snappy, and I'm happy to have made the upgrade. I use up at least 20 to 30 GB per week in the field, and it will be great to be able to work on my laptop without having an external drive chained to it.

Many people don't like using RAID 0 arrays because they double the likelihood of catastrophic failure; I back up my data all the time, even when I'm traveling, so I'm not so worried.

Extended Use Update

This machine is really much faster now. I just booted up Windows XP in Parallels, and it didn't do the usual, take-the-computer-down-for-a-bit routine during XP startup. It just booted and was fast immediately after boot, as it is on my Mac Pro. Normally, the XP load process in Parallels slows my entire machine down as it struggles to pull data from the disk.

My Macbook Pro has always run hotter than my old Thinkpad did. Even when doing simple web surfing or writing emails, I can't use the machine in my lap for long periods of time without putting a book or pillow between it and my crotch "Hack # Build a Perfect Laptop Cooler for Your Machine". It seems to run a bit warmer with the second drive in, but it's hard to remember, in comparison. The left palm area was always much hotter than the right (makes sense, it's where the main drive is); now the right side is also a bit warm but nowhere near the warmth of the main drive area.

The metal strip above the keyboard is always hot now. I don't remember if this was the case before I put in the second drive. It could also be because it has suddenly become warm here in the Bay Area; the temperature in my loft has gone up a lot in the past two days. Extra heat or not, it is worth noting that the internal cooling fans do not run any louder or more often than they used to.

— Eric Cheng

HACK 110: Upgrade a Macbook Pro Hard Drive

Feeling constrained by the size of your MacBook Pro's hard drive? Swap it out for a larger drive!

When you bought your current MacBook Pro (for a MacBook see [Hack #70]), you maxed out the capacity and/or speed of the hard drive based on what was available at the time. A year later, you've just purchased the latest release of Apple Logic Pro, and a full install barely fits. Bigger, faster hard drives are on the market now, but the current generations of laptop internal storage disks weren't designed to be user-serviceable. You've replaced them dozens of times in desktop machines. A laptop can't be that difficult, can it?

Here are some general tips to get this project right:

- Organization is key. Laptops are, by definition, very compact and efficiently designed machines.

- Don't lose any parts.

- Every screw counts.

- Use the right part in the right place.

- If a screw was flush with a surface before you removed it, it should be flush when it goes back in.

- Order and alignment matters.

- Cables folded a certain way should go back folded the same way. Pinch nothing.

- Tolerances are tight so parts don't fall out or apart during regular wear.

- Some pressure is necessary during disassembly and reassembly.

- Circuit boards and connectors are proportionally smaller than in a desktop.

- Don't use too much pressure or you could crack a board and brick your machine.

You'll probably want to do this in one sitting to minimize confusion. So getting all the tools and equipment together you need beforehand is a great idea. To swap out your drive you'll need:

- A clean and static electricity-free work surface

- Small screwdrivers, including a Phillips 00 and/or 000 size

- Torx T6 size

No matter how hard you try, you'll inevitably forget where something went. So grab a digital camera and take lots of pictures, every step of the way. The extra time spent snapping pictures might seem superfluous, but it can be a sanity-saving step when attempting complicated hacks like this.

A special note on screws: you don't want to lose any! Group them in the order you remove them. This will make it a lot easier to reinstall them in reverse order. You're going to be dealing with tiny screws that tend to roll around a lot so remember that sticky surfaces help. Try using double-sided tape, a magnetic tray, anything to keep he screws where you want them.

Here are some personal ingredients for this hack:

- A steady hand

- Patience

- No fear

Process

Start with a new 2.5-inch SATA hard drive matching or exceeding your current drive's specifications. Be sure to match the physical dimensions or use a thinner drive. A thicker drive may or may not fit.

If you want to start from scratch, all you need are your Mac OS X install DVDs. If you want to preserve your old data, you'll need a backup strategy—perhaps Time Machine or one of the methods found in [Hack #1]. Two more items will make this hack easier:

- Printed copy of iFixIt (www.ifixit.com) instructions that match your make and model.

- Pen or pencil to mark up your copy if/when you encounter differences. Watch for such things as different screw counts, types of screws used, etc.

When all that is gathered, you need to spend a moment preparing your workspace. Clean is good; setting out your tools is important; and remember, keep that camera handy (see Figure 13-26)!

Figure 13-26.
A clean, organized space will make the job much easier

Before you can put the new drive in, you've got to take the old drive out.

Start the process with the decidingly unchallenging step of removing the battery (see Figure 13-27).

Figure 13-27.
The battery has to go

Figure 13-28.
You'll need to access the RAM

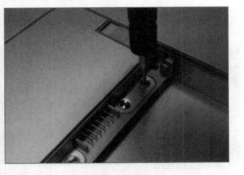

Next to go is the RAM: first remove the Philips head screws that were revealed when you took out the battery (see Figure 13-28).

With the cover gone, the RAM is exposed (see Figure 13-29). Pop out the memory using the instructions printed right on the machine.

Figure 13-29.
The exposed RAM modules

Figure 13-30.
More screws that need to go

Now, remove the Torx screws in the RAM compartment and the Phillips screws on the bottom (see Figure 13-30).

Next, remove the angled Phillips screws from the battery compartment (see Figure 13-31).

Figure 13-31.
Tricky battery compartment screws

There are a lot more screws to get past (see Figure 13-32 through Figure 13-34).

Figure 13-32.
Remove the Phillips screws from the DVI side

Figure 13-33.
And from the Power Socket side

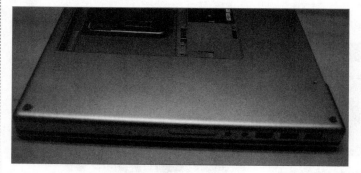

Figure 13-34.
From the rear, remove the Phillips screws at each side of the LCD hinge

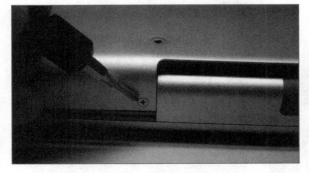

Now, flip the machine right-side up, open the LCD, and *carefully* pry off the top keyboard module from around the edges. The result should look something like Figure 13-35. Note the ribbon connector between the keyboard and the motherboard (see Figure 13-36).

Figure 13-35.
Keyboard free

Figure 13-36.
Careful with the ribbon connector

Next, separate the ribbon connector (see Figure 13-37) from the motherboard socket (see Figure 13-38).

Figure 13-37.
One tiny connector

Figure 13-38.
The motherboard socket for the keyboard ribbon cable

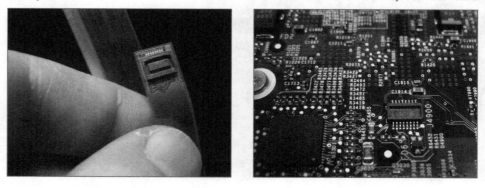

Now, locate the hard drive (see Figure 13-39) and take note (and pictures) of how the cables are routed and taped in place.

Figure 13-39.
The hard drive that is being replaced

Figure 13-40.
Remove the Bluetooth module

Next, slide out and untape the Bluetooth module next to the hard drive (see Figure 13-40).

Unscrew and remove the inner retaining bracket over the hard drive (see Figure 13-41).

Figure 13-41.
Bracket be gone

Gently lift the hard drive out, then untape (possibly both sides, see Figure 13-42) and detach the SATA connector (see Figure 13-43).

Figure 13-42.
Lots of tape

Figure 13-43.
The freed SATA connector

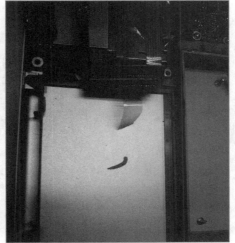

With disassembly complete, it is time to prepare the new drive. Luckily, there are only a few things to keep in mind (see Figure 13-44 through Figure 13-46).

Figure 13-44.
Note the knobs on the lifting edge are rubber

Figure 13-45.
Note the knobs on the hinge edge are metal

Figure 13-46.
Swap the knobs from the old drive to the new drive

Now, with the new drive prepared, it is time to put everything back together.

First, attach the new drive to the SATA connector, reapply the tape (use the tape that came with the laptop: this is no time to see if duct tape really will fix anything), and insert (see Figure 13-47).

Figure 13-47.
The new drive is in place

Next, attach the drive-retaining bracket (see Figure 13-48).

Figure 13-48.
Secure the new drive

Insert the Bluetooth module, and reapply the tape (see Figure 13-49).

Figure 13-49.
Get your Bluetooth back

Next, reattach the keyboard ribbon cable to the motherboard (see Figure 13-50), and carefully close up the top.

> 🪚 The keyboard ribbon cable is one of those parts that you want to press firmly back in place, but not too hard or you risk cracking the motherboard.

Figure 13-50.
The keyboard will live again

You're almost there. Now, reverse the order in which you removed screws. Here's the correct order when reassembling:

1. Rear of the LCD hinge

2. Edge screws

3. Battery compartment screws

4. Screws inside RAM compartment

5. Screws closing RAM compartment and remaining bottom screws

When you reinsert the RAM, make sure they are pushed in all the way so that none of gold pins showing. Figure 13-51 is an example of how *not* to do it; your machine probably won't power on like this.

Figure 13-51.
Do not insert your RAM like this

Finally, reinsert battery.

If you've done everything properly, you should be able to power up your system and begin using your new disk. If that doesn't work, use the troubleshooting tips:

- If it doesn't turn on, check that you inserted the RAM properly.

- Other things to check include the keyboard connector (you didn't flip the cable around, did you?) and the hard drive's SATA connector (pushed in all the way?).

- If all else fails, remove the new drive, reinsert the old drive, and confirm that it still works.

- If the old drive has a 1.5 Gbps SATA interface, check to see that the new drive is configured in 1.5 Gbps interface mode, not a newer 3.0 Gbps interface mode. See the detailed specifications for both drives at the manufacturer(s) web site(s) for more information.

Once everything is working, install from Mac OS X DVD or restore the drive from the backup you made earlier.

If you don't have an immediate use for the old drive, keep it in a safe place. I still haven't dared erase mine. It never hurts to have a spare, just in case.

All it takes is a little time, organization, and a steady hand to service these nonuser-serviceable parts of your MacBook Pro. Plus you've saved a lot of money and haven't given your computer to any third parties exposing it to (possibly) prying eyes.

— Andrew Plumb and Chris Seibold

HACK 111 : SmackBook: The Most Fun You'll
Ever Have Beating Your 'Book

Invoke Expose, Spaces, and others just by smacking your motion sensor-enabled MacBook.

Amit Singh is some kind of Mac genius. When he heard about the motion sensor in the MacBook Pro, he wondered if the sensor could be used as a human interface device. Turns out that it could. So Mr. Singh wrote a nifty program to output the data being collected by the sensor. He followed up by writing a few programs that took advantage of the information gleaned from the motion sensor. The programs were cool but lacked a practical application.

Erling Ellison, another computer whiz, heard about Amit Singh's program to output the data of the sudden motion sensor and had an interesting idea. What if you could change an operating system with a sharp smack to side of your MacBook? Intrigued, he wrote a program to do just that, and the SmackBook was born. By tapping the side of the computer screen, you can switch from OS X to Windows and back again (if you're using virtualization).

Enter the third computer savant. Brian Jepson heard about the SmackBook and thought "Wouldn't it be super keen if you could use the SmackBook idea to invoke Expose?" (For the record, Brian says "super keen" all the time.) Brian modified the software to invoke Expose instead of Windows, and the world suddenly had something that used the motion sensor and was of interest to Mac-only folks.

When I heard about all these clever hacks, I thought, "Hey, I know Brian Jepson...." and pestered him into helping me make the script a bit more flexible.

By now you're probably dying to have your motion-sensor MacBook react to your smacks but before you can get rolling you'll need two programs:

- *amstrack* by Amit Singh; download it from: http://www.osxbook.com/software/sms/amstracker

- *smaxpose* by Brian Jepson is available at: http://www.as220.org/~bjepson/smaxpose2.command

The first step is to make sure you've got everything installed and working properly. Once that is out of the way, you can go about the business of making it fun to hit your MacBook.

To start, open up the DMG disk holding the AMSTracker. You'll see four files. While you should take the time to read the associated text files, the one you are after is the AMSTracker binary. Your goal is to get that file into a folder. No problem: it's a drag-and-drop process. One tip: don't use the Desktop as the repository of the folder; when I tried to do so, the hack refused to work. When I moved the folder to my Applications folder, the hack worked flawlessly.

With the *smaxpose* script, there isn't a download; following the link listed earlier in this example brings you to a page of plain text. But it's plain text that will do neat tricks if you copy it to a text editor (TextEdit will do) and save it into an appropriate file. Once you've cut and pasted the words, save the file as *smaxpose2.command*. You'll get a warning; just hit "Use .command" (see Figure 13-52).

Figure 13-52.
Yes, I want to Use .command

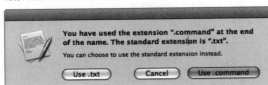

The only trick left is to put the file in the same directory as the AMStracker binary. That's a fancy way of saying that *smaxpose2.command* needs to go in the folder you created to hold AMSTracker so the file can find the binary. Once the file is in the correct folder, double-click it in the Finder, and smack your book. If everything works as expected, Expose will be invoked just as though you had hit the F9 key.

Hacking the Hack

That is great if you like using Expose, but what if you crave something different? What if you'd rather have spaces invoked when you jostle your machine? That change is trivial; first, find the line that says:

```
`osascript -e 'tell application \"System Events\" to key code 101'
```

Now, change **101** to whatever key you want *smaxpose* to magically depress when you smack the computer. Table 13-1 is a quick list of F-key values: insert whichever F-key value you desire.

Table 13-1.
Fkey values

F1 = 122	F2 = 120	F3 = 99
F4 = 118	F5 = 96	F6 = 97
F7 = 98	F8 = 100	F9 = 101
F10= 109	F11= 103	F12=111
F13=105	F14=107	F15=113

But you want more. You want a script where when you smack the right side of the 'Book, it does one thing but smacking the left invokes a different function. Just think of the symmetrical muscle building!

When you're thinking of writing some code, no matter how simple, there is a good chance that someone else has had the same general idea and has already done the work for you. This is the case with the double-sided slap idea. Reading through the responses to Brian Jepson's *smaxpose* post (http://www.jepstone.net/blog/2006/05/25/expose-smackbook-pro-style), you'll discover a response that links to a bit of code the author calls *smackmeuh* (http://morgan.1er.free.fr/divers/smackmeuh.zip).

Download the ZIP file, expand it, and store it in the same folder as AMSTracker. The *smackmeuh* script differs from Brian's script not only in the dual-sided smack, but in the way it is launched. Using the Terminal, navigate to the script's directory and launch it by typing:

```
$ perl smackmeuh.pl
```

The script works by cycling through windows with a right-side tap and invoking Expose with a left-side tap. Perfect if what you want to do is use a right-side tap to cycle Windows and a left-side tap to invoke Expose. That is almost what I want to do, but since now I can cycle through Windows, I don't really need to invoke Expose anymore. Instead I'd rather invoke Dashboard. The change is simple, and you can do it with the same text editor you used earlier:

```
$ foo = $a[0] < 0 ? 'key code 118 using {control down}' : 'key code 101';
```

Replace key code 101 with key code 111. The line should look like:

```
$ foo = $a[0] < 0 ? ' key code 118 using {control down}' ' : 'key code 111';
```

Now you can smack your book and get two different results. Here's a final exercise for the interested: extend the script to accept input for the Y and Z axes as well.

14. MULTIMEDIA HACKS

If you consider the history of the personal computer, you'll note that the device has gone through distinct phases. In the early days of personal computing, machines were woefully underpowered for any but the most mundane tasks, and personal computers were largely restricted to hobbyists. As the computing power increased, so did the number of programs available. The added utility meant computers moved from hobby-oriented machines to spreadsheet number crunchers and graphically challenged game machines. Useful to be sure but not something that would have the masses slavering to grab the newest machine.

Personal computers really went mainstream with the explosion of the Internet. As hard-drive size swelled and bandwidth increased, computers went from flexible but general-purpose devices to a repository for anything that could be digitized. The allure is clear: a one-stop shop for accessing all your personal media and a portal to millions of other multimedia sources. In this chapter, we explore how to master your multimedia-filled life using your Mac.

HACK 112: Let Your TiVo Meet Your Mac

You want your TiVo content to go mobile with you but you don't want to resort to using a Windows machine just to get the benefits of TivoToGo? No problem: you can reach feature parity with your TiVo-owning Windows-using counterparts with this media-expanding hack.

TiVo is similar to Apple in many ways. Both companies owe their success to fantastic user interfaces and attention to detail. For quite some time, there were many rumors that Apple would acquire TiVo but they never panned out. Now, with the introduction of the Apple TV, they can be described as competitors in some respects, but in others they work together quite well.

For a long time, there was no official support for transferring video from a Mac to a TiVo DVR or from a TiVo DVR to a Mac. There were always nifty hacks, but recently TiVo partnered with Roxio to provide Mac users with the TivoToGo functionality that Windows users take for granted. The nifty hacks, however, still prove quite useful.

Most of the recommendations here will apply only to Series 2 TiVo DVRs that are on the same home network as a Mac with Mac OS X 10.4 or higher. You will also need your TiVo Media Access Key, which can be obtained by selecting Messages and Settings followed by Account and System Information on your TiVo DVR. It would also be helpful to have an all-purpose video player, encoder, and decoder such as the free VLC so that you can play and convert multiple video file formats (see **[Hack #113]**).

Share Your Media

The easiest and cheapest thing to do is to make the photographs, music, and videos on your Mac available on your TiVo DVR. In other words: Apple TV without the Apple TV. In order to do this, you need to download and install the official TiVo Desktop software available from TiVo (http://www. tivo.com/mytivo/domore/tivotogo/). As long as your photographs are in your iPhoto library and your music is in your iTunes library, sharing this media with your TiVo DVR is simple. Once TiVo Desktop is installed, it can be configured through System Preferences.

In the TiVo Desktop preferences (see Figure 14-1), you will be able to turn on your TiVo Desktop by clicking the Start button. By default, there are two tabs: Music and Photos. Under the Music tab, you can select which playlists you would like to share with your TiVo DVR and similarly, under the Photos tab, you can select albums to make available.

Figure 14-1.
The TiVo Desktop

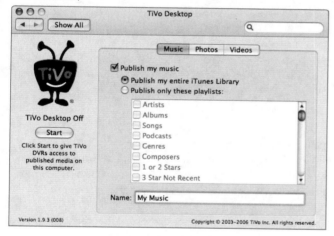

Of course, you can do more with the TiVo Desktop if you know how to unlock the functionality. This time, in System Preferences, hold the Command key while clicking TiVo Desktop. Now you will see a third tab: Videos. This will allow you to transfer videos from your Mac to your TiVo DVR. Under this tab, you can select the directory containing the videos you wish to transfer. You will also be asked for your TiVo Media Access Key.

The reason this functionality is slightly hidden might be that the transfer is not as simple as it seems. There is a nontrivial step that must precede transferring video to a TiVo DVR: converting the video to MPEG-2 format. TiVo Series 2 DVRs can only read this format. and the conversion can be done using a variety of methods. By and large, the free methods are not simple, and the simple methods are not free. I've used FFMPEGX and VLC, and they work, but there are many other solutions are available for this conversion.

Once you have made your photographs and music available, they will be visible on the "Music, Photos, Products & More" screen of your TiVo DVR. You can view your photographs by album or listen to your music by playlist from the comfort of your couch. The video shared through TiVo Desktop (that you converted to MPEG-2 just now) is not actually streamed. It is visible under the Now Playing screen, and the video you select will be transferred to your TiVo DVR.

The real power of the TiVo, however, is in allowing you to take your recorded video with you wherever you go, on the devices of your choice. On Windows, the software to make this possible is provided for free. Mac users, on the other hand, have to buy Roxio's Popcorn or Toast software to get the TiVoToGo functionality. While the Roxio products are fantastic in their own right, it is unfortunate that you have to buy additional software to get the basic TiVo transfer software (see Figure 14-2).

Figure 14-2.
TiVo plus Roxio means portable media

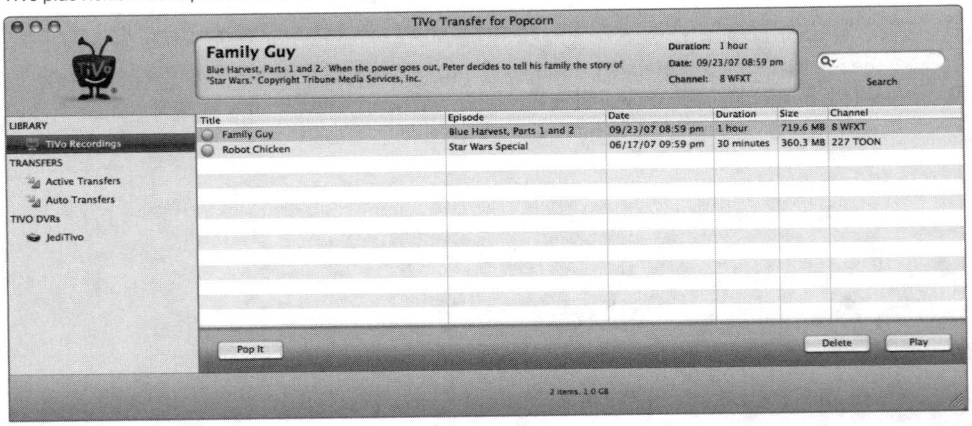

The Roxio software does provide many solid features with great ease of use. With Toast 8, in addition to downloading videos from your TiVo DVR to your Mac, you can also schedule automatic transfers; convert the videos to iPod, PSP, or other formats; or burn the videos on to a DVD. Roxio Popcorn 3 has most of these features (and costs less) and so may be the better choice.

The TiVo DVR stores videos on its own hard drive in an encrypted .tivo format that cannot be played on any computer directly. It needs a key—the Media Access Key—and the right software. It is unfortunate that TiVo chooses to encrypt videos that you have recorded from your own television on a device you own without allowing the same use rights as would be expected from a videotape recorded at home. The officially supported method of decrypting these videos uses the above-mentioned Roxio software, but there are other ways.

There is a free and relatively simple option available to download and decrypt your videos from the TiVo DVR to any Mac on the same network. The software is called TiVoDecode Manager (http://tdm.sourceforge.net), and it has a few useful features, including the queuing of downloads, conversion of videos to MPEG-4 for iPod transfers, and support for Bonjour. The Bonjour protocol from Apple allows machines on the same network to discover each other and advertise services. (It's also called Rendezvous and ZeroConf.) This protocol allows the Mac to find all the TiVo DVRs in your home network (and allows your TiVo DVR to discover all the Macs for the TiVo Desktop functionality).

Using Bonjour, the TiVoDecode Manager automatically detects your TiVo and lists all the videos on it. Once you queue them up, it will download and decode them all as fast as your network and processing power permits. Of course, before embarking on any major video projects, make sure you have the hard disk space, RAM, and processing power to handle it.

Roxio Toast and Popcorn can burn these videos (and videos in many other formats) to DVD with ease. If you use TiVoDecode Manager to convert your TiVo videos to MPEG-2 format, you will have to jump through a few hoops to burn them to DVD using iDVD. The easiest way is just to import them into iMovie or iTunes, which automatically makes them available to iDVD.

Access Your TiVo with Safari

Your TiVo DVR can also be accessed through the browser. In order to access the web server on your TiVo DVR, you will have to find its IP address. You can find this address by going to Messages & Settings→Settings→Phone & Network on your TiVo Series 2. Once you know the IP address of your TiVo DVR (e.g., 192.168.1.10), you can type it in your browser address bar as:

```
https://192.168.1.10/nowplaying/index.html
```

Just replace *192.168.1.10* with your Tivo's IP address). You will be prompted for a username and password. Your username is "tivo", and your password is your Media Access Key. You may also get multiple dialog boxes warning you about unknown certificate authorities and domain name mismatches. These are harmless, as long as the TiVo DVR is yours and operating on your home network.

This page will give you access to all the video on your TiVo DVR. You can download videos or view information about them from this web site. Of course, the videos downloaded from here will still be in the . TiVo-encrypted format that can officially be decrypted using the Roxio software or unofficially using TiVoDecode Manager (see Figure 14-3).

Figure 14-3.
The useful though not officially sanctioned TiVo Decode manager

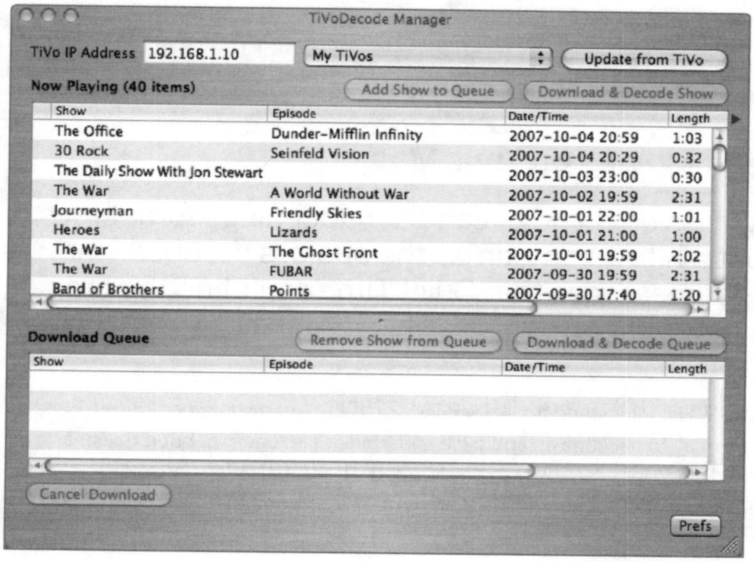

TiVo, DVRs, and Macintosh computers are quite useful machines on their own. Combining their power can take you many steps closer to the ultimate dream of time-shifting and place-shifting your media at will.

— Devanshu Mehta

Hacking the Hack

Devanshu's methods are great if you have a TiVo but what if you have some generic DVR from your cable company? Brian Jepson has the answer.

Ever since I got my first set-top box at the end of last year, I've been itching to connect its FireWire port to my Mac. My friend Emilie called today to alert me to a *CBS Sunday Morning* report on Maker Faire, which I managed to record, and that gave me the push I needed to figure this all out.

There are a few sets of instructions out there on how to do this, but in a nutshell, you connect your Mac to the set-top box, load up a program that can record directly from FireWire set-top boxes (unfortunately, iMovie won't cut it), and do whatever editing you need to the video once you've brought it in.

I found that Ammesset Software's iRecord (http://www.ammesset.com/irecord) did the trick perfectly: I checked its preferences to make sure that my Motorola DCT-6412 was detected, told my set-top box to start playing back the video I had recorded, and selected New Immediate Event from iRecord's File menu. When it was done, I selected Stop Event from File menu.

This left me with an *.m2t* file that I didn't know what to do with at first. Squared 5's MPEG Streamclip (http://www.squared5.com) is a free program that can open and convert all kinds of streams. Using MPEG Streamclip, I was able to trim the clip and export it to one of the many supported codecs. Choosing MPEG-4 allowed me to import the clip to iMovie and edit to my heart's content.

— Brian Jepson

HACK 113: View AVI Movies on Your Mac

Dealing with AVI files on the Mac can be maddening. Sometimes they play without a hitch, sometimes the audio is dropped, and sometime you get messages that QuickTime can't find the proper codec.

Audio Visual Interleave (AVI) is not a standard like MPEG-2 or JPEG, but a *container format*. This means that an AVI file is a way to package an audio file and a video file together, but it doesn't specify how the audio and video information is to be encoded. The actual video and audio can be encoded in any of a variety of codecs. That means there is no one solution to make the Mac play any AVI file. Read on for some options, though.

For One-Off Conversions

Your best bet is to manually convert a single file is with iSquint (http://www.isquint.org/getit.php). iSquint is simple to use: drag and drop the files you want converted onto the iSquint icon, and iSquint will take the files and convert them to the Mac OS X-friendly *.mp4* format.

For More Regular Viewing

If you're watching AVIs on your computer on a regular basis, converting videos manually each time a new one shows up can be an onerous chore. A better method of attack would be to extend QuickTime's abilities. You can add commonly used codecs to QuickTime. Many AVI files use the DivX codec. To play these files, you need a DivX player for the Mac.

Lucky for you just such a codec exists. Point your browser to http://www.divx.com/divx/mac/download/index.php. The resulting *.dmg* file runs an installer (administrator password required), and once installed, you can play DivX AVI files with a simple double-click.

If you don't mind using a separate viewer for videos that are incompatible with QuickTime, check out VLC (http://www.videolan.org/vlc/), which plays almost everything.

For Batch Conversions

If you're downloading video for a destination other than your Mac on a regular basis (say your iPod or Apple TV), adding a DivX player to your computer isn't going to help, because you're not planning to watch the show on the computer anyway. If the destination machine can't handle the files it gets, you'll want to convert them before export. However, manually converting the files can be a big drag. A method that automatically converts the files to a more useful format is necessary.

This is a great time to invoke the power of Automator. Automator is Mac OS X's answer to freeing yourself from repetitive tasks (see **[Hack #22]**). You'll be able to find Automator in your Applications folder, and you might want to spend a few moments playing with it; the program can be very useful. In this case, you won't have to do any playing and very little creating. There is a fairly large Automator community, and it is easy to adapt an existing *workflow* (that's Automator's word for a graphically generated script) to take care of the converting chore. This particular method was developed by Jason Vallery and works well (see Figure 14-4). To pull this off, you'll need to add a few things to your video-watching arsenal:

- QuickTime Pro (http://www.apple.com/quicktime). **You'll have to pay for this one, but it's not horribly expensive.**

- QuickTime Compressions actions and Workflows (http://www.apple.com/downloads/macosx/automator/quicktimecompressionactionsandworkflow.html). **These are the workflows that Automator uses to get the video-conversion job done. When you download one of the workflows you find there, you'll be prompted to install it in Automator. Go ahead, it's safe.**

- The codecs you added earlier in the hack.

Figure 14-4.
Auto install of the new action

The workflow will run fine as is for converting movies but you'll still need to select the movies by hand. That is too much work for the frequent downloader, who just wants the movies ready to play on their platform of choice. Some tweaking is needed. Fire up Automator, select Open Existing Workflow, and open the workflow you downloaded.

Once open, the workflow will look something like Figure 14-5.

Figure 14-5.
The prebuilt workflow

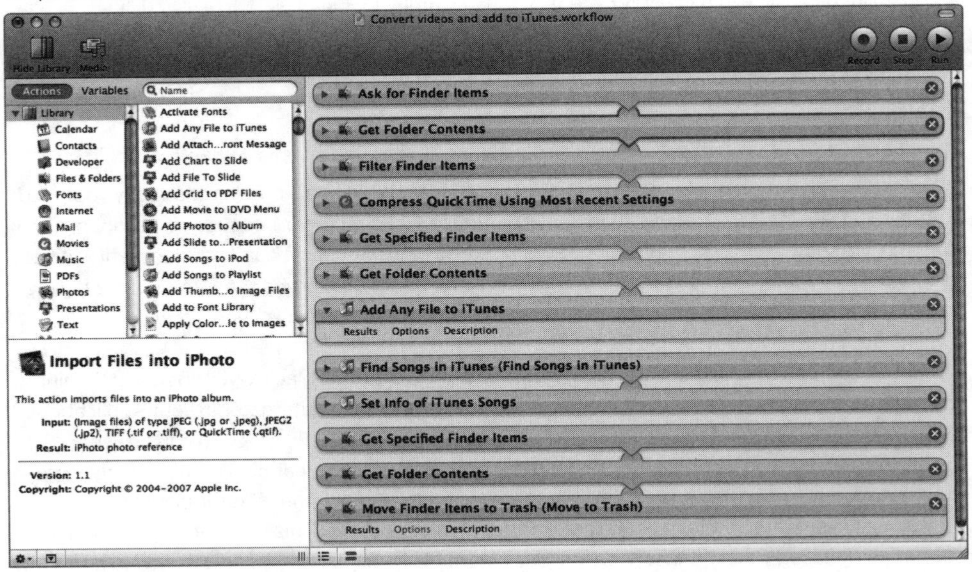

Time to tweak the workflow just a bit. First delete the first action of the workflow (Ask for Finder Items) by clicking on the gray x. Replace the action you just deleted with Get Selected Finder items. You can find the action in the Library under Files & Folders (see Figure 14-6).

Figure 14-6.
Making a good workflow even better

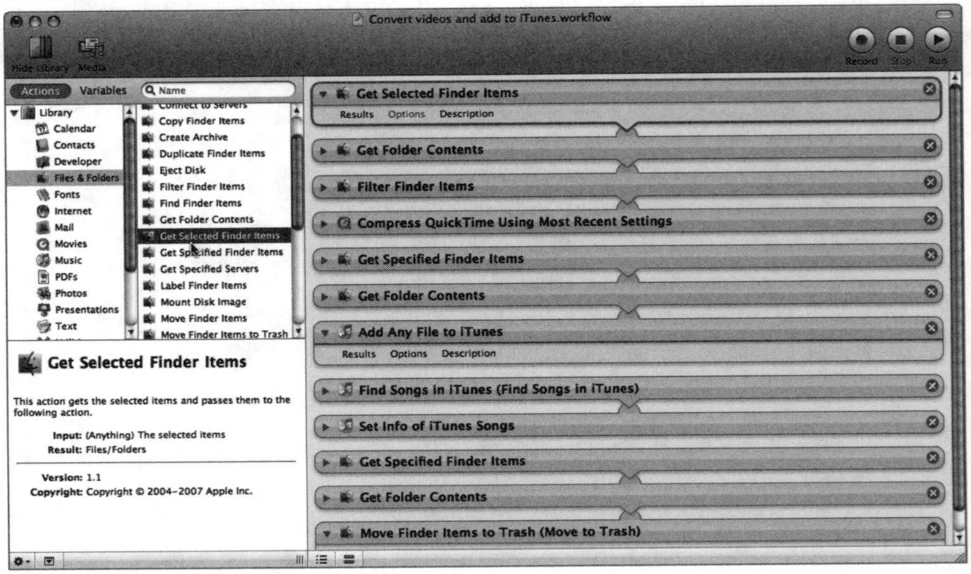

That change will make the workflow run automatically, but you'll need to change a few more things to make the setup complete. Under the action "Compress QuickTime Using Most Recent Settings," it's a good idea to change the directory for the converted files. Create a new folder somewhere you'll remember, and instruct the workflow to use that directory as storage for the converted files.

You'll also need a folder to hold the files you want converted so the Automator workflow can know which files to work on. A folder on the desktop called "Convert this" works just fine, but let your creativity shine.

The last step is to save the modified workflow. Choose "Save As Plug-in..." and associate this action with the folder in which you want to drop files for conversion. Then make sure the Enable Folder Actions box is checked. Once all that is done, fire up QuickTime Pro and choose the settings you want to use when your videos are converted (the plug-in uses whatever settings were last used in QuickTime Pro). Now just drag the files you want converted into the "Convert this" folder and the chore of manually converting files is gone.

HACK 114: Master BitTorrent with Xtorrent

There exists a wealth of media in cyberspace. Everything from videos to the latest Linux distributions are accessible over the Internet. Learn how to efficiently download large files and help others when you master BitTorrent using Xtorrent.

Who can forget Napster, the once ubiquitous file-sharing program that made university servers slow to a crawl and ignited the RIAA lawsuit revolution? Napster has gone corporate, but the program has been replaced by a large number of imitators with equivalent functionality (LimeWire is probably the most popular choice for Mac users).

In the standard peer-to-peer model, you share a folder on your computer with the other users who are sharing files. Once you find a file, you can download it directly from another user. Meanwhile you might have a file you want to share, and some completely unrelated third person can scan your directory, see that file and download it. None of the computers involved in this is a "server" in the traditional sense, but nonetheless each of them is "serving" files to other computers.

The method works fine for relatively small files such as songs but runs into snags for larger files. Imagine someone trying to download a 4 GB Linux distribution from your computer using the standard P2P method. Trying to download a multi gigabyte file from another single computer is problematic for several reasons. First most ISPs cap upload speed, so if you were to choose someone using an ISP with a 512 Kbps upload speed cap, you would expect to spend at least nine hours downloading the file. Were you to download the same file at the maximum speed allowed by your ISP, the transfer time could shrink to two hours or even less, depending on the download speed provided by your ISP.

The solution to this problem is obvious (now that someone has devised it): instead of a single client downloading a file from a single host (the standard manner in which downloads work), what if everyone participated in both the upload and download of the file? Instead of the standard client-host relationship, all parties interested in a file could upload the bits they have on their computer while downloading pieces of the file they are missing.

The concept sounds nifty, but how can you download just part of a file? This is where the Internet comes in. As opposed to the P2P model employed by LimeWire, the torrent model locates easily downloadable bits of the files out there on the Internet. A BitTorrent client can grab these slices of files from different sources and knit them together when the download is complete. The theory works something as follows: a file is split into an arbitrary number of segments. You download segments a, b, and c, stitch them together in a complete file and share (or seed) the file with other downloaders. In this scenario, everyone shares the burden of bandwidth so no one person gets stuck with the overhead.

If the system seems a bit convoluted, that's because it is. The preceding representation is an idealized version, a near communistic "from each according to his abilities, to each according to his needs" deal. The real-world implementation is that BitTorrent has been refined so that the obvious objections ("how can I upload anything if I haven't downloaded anything yet?") are overcome, and the result is a very fast and reliable way to download large files.

The protocol has proved popular, and torrents according to some estimates now comprise 35% to 50% of all web traffic. Which shouldn't be a surprise. Torrents are generally used to transfer large files, so downloading a single movie can easily surpass all the bit count of all your other surfing needs for a single day.

If you're already using torrents, you (obviously) already have a torrent client. If you don't, there are a huge number of choices for Mac OS X, from the official BitTorrent client (http://www.bittorrent. com/download) to the well-done Transmission client (http://transmission.m0k.org/). Both are good choices, with the official BitTorrent client being a little on the sparse side as features go, and Transmission being a more feature-complete yet still lightweight choice for OS X. That noted, neither client has that Mac feel that OS X users demand. And face it, if you're already torrent-savvy you're not reading this hack!

What would be ideal is a torrent program that looks and acts like a program made completely for OS X. Such a client exists: Xtorrent. Xtorrent manages to make downloading and uploading *seeds* (completed files) painless, understandable and controllable. Xtorrent isn't a free program but the cost is minimal for the functionality and usability the program provides. Of course a free trial is available with some features removed, so point your browser to http://www.xtorrentp2p.com/ to get your copy.

Once downloaded, install Xtorrent in your folder of choice (as always, a good place for an application like this is the Applications folder). Fire up Xtorrent, and you'll be downloading and seeding files in no time with just a simple click. Well, after you answer a simple question (see Figure 14-7).

Figure 14-7.
Xtorrent wants to know if you are authorized

Once you've assured Xtorrent you are authorized to download the files, Xtorrent will get busy downloading and seeding the files you desire. But there's more to Xtorrent than just that. Taking a look at the main window (see Figure 14-8), you'll note that Xtorrent reveals more than just the filename and file size. You also get information about the swarm. In torrent-speak, the *swarm* is the number of users transferring the files you're after. It can be any combination of those offering uploads and those downloading the files but, generally, the larger the swarm, the more reliable and faster the download will be.

Xtorrent also allows you to select where your downloads will reside. Want any songs you've downloaded to end up in your Music folder? No problem. Movies should likely go to the Movies folder, and pictures should end up in the Pictures folder right? No problem for Xtorrent. Choose Preferences→Download and check the boxes where you want your newly acquired media to end up (see Figure 14-8).

Figure 14-8.
Set your downloads to end up anywhere you please

Controlling where the files end up is one thing but, depending on your situation, you might really need to control the bandwidth allocated for your torrenting purposes. Xtorrent (and most clients) provide this control. Another trip to Preferences is required followed by a click on the Advanced option. In the Advanced pane, you'll be able to set bandwidth limits for both uploads and downloads, change the port used for "listening" for torrents, and disable sharing at certain times of the day. What you'll most likely want to tweak is the bandwidth limits. The default download limit is 100 Kbps, and the default upload speed is 20 Kbps. Depending on the speed of your ISP, you may want to change the limits. For example, if you get 1 Mbps service, you'll be setting aside 80% of your bandwidth for Xtorrent.

Sharing Torrents

Once you've completed a download, you have the complete file. Most of us would call the process complete, but in the torrent world (as mentioned earlier), a completed file is called a seed. Since someone generously shared portions of the file and their bandwidth with you, it is considered good etiquette to share the completed file with other users for a time. Xtorrent will take care of the sharing part automatically, so no worries, but if you are determined to be a *leech* (torrent speak for nonsharing jerk), Xtorrent will allow you to do that as well. This option is found under Preferences→Sharing.

There's a lot more to discover with Xtorrent. You can, for example, use Xtorrent as a browser or as an RSS reader—particularly nice features for those addicted to torrents. You'll discover a huge number of uses beyond torrents after you use Xtorrent for just a little while.

HACK 115: Legal Online Sources for Music (Besides iTunes!)

The music world may be becoming ever more iTunes-centric, but that doesn't mean you have to join the bandwagon. There are lots of other great places to get legal music. Discover where with this library-filling hack.

The iTunes music store is the world's largest online music store, a fact driven home by sales that have exceeded a billion songs since the store's inception. The store has over three million songs available to purchase and download, but it isn't right for everyone. Fortunately, you can fill your iPod to bursting with music from iTunes alternatives.

Amazon

Amazon has been toying with music downloads for some time, but the company's new beta offering is a serious contender. All the files are in the *.mp3* format, and none are encumbered with pesky digital rights management (DRM) restrictions. The offerings aren't as extensive as iTunes, but the songs, at least the top 100, are a dime cheaper.

The selection is not as extensive (yet) as that of iTunes but, on the bright side, the tracks are encoded at 256 Kbps rate instead of the 128 Kbps generally used by iTunes (see Figure 14-9).

Figure 14-9.
Amazon downloads work with nearly any music player

eMusic

eMusic is an American subscription-based music-download site. Unlike other subscription-based sites such as Napster, once you cancel your subscription, you get to keep all of your music. In other words, what you download is yours to keep forever!

The downside of eMusic is that it lacks the mainstream music iTunes offers. Nonetheless, it's a great resource for downloading lesser artists, and there are thousands of great albums from diverse genres available to download.

They offer three different subscription packages, so be sure to check them all out. If you don't want to take the plunge and subscribe without knowing what you're in for, eMusic offers an excellent free 30-day trial, allowing you to download 125 songs for free. It's one trial you cannot refuse.

MP3Tunes

MP3tunes (http://mp3tunes.com) is more than a site where you can purchase music; it's an MP3 locker, allowing you to store your entire music collection on its servers so you can easily access it anywhere in the world. It also integrates seamlessly with Apple's iTunes—awesome!

On MP3tunes, you can purchase music to add to your locker. Albums cost $8.88, and the site features mostly independent artists like eMusic, but there is some awesome music available if you have some time to explore the catalog.

A year's subscription to use the Locker feature of the site costs $39.95, and a free account is also available with stripped-down features.

A great alternative to an external hard drive to back up and play your music!

Obtaining Free and Legal Music and Video

Don't feel like splashing any cash? Here are a few sites where you can find free and legal music and video available for download.

Download.com

Download.com has thousands of free tracks available for download, with hundreds added weekly, avoid more searching and point your browser directly to http://music.download.com They have a variety of genres to choose from, from classical to hip-hop to blues.

Google Video

Most of you should know about Google Video by now. It's one of the latest Google inventions that makes searching and downloading video a fast and enjoyable process.

Awesome, you say, a video search engine, but how does this have anything to do with getting free content for my iPod?

When playing a video in Google Video, there is an option in the sidebar to download the video in its original form. But wait, there is a drop-down menu that also allows you to select the format you want to download the video in. iPod and PSP are two items in the large list, so you just need to load up a video, click the drop-down list in the sidebar, select iPod, and hit download.

There you have it: fast, free video, ready for your iPod in seconds. Just drop it onto the iTunes icon, and you're all ready to transfer your newfound video content to your video-capable iPhone or iPod.

iTunes podcasts and videocasts

If you've ever explored the iTunes podcast directory, you'll have noticed the growing number of video podcasts available. These can all be downloaded to your iTunes library in iPod format, so there is no hassle. Just download, plug in your iPod, and you're ready to play the shows on the go.

Quick mentions

There are so many great places online to find free, legal, music and videos; we just can't list them all. Here are a few places to start, to help you expand your musical taste and collection:

http://www.epitonic.com/

http://bt.etree.org/

http://www.kahvi.org/

http://creativecommons.org/

http://www.archive.org

Getting your acquisitions into iTunes

Since you now have a bevy of sources for music and other media files, you may want to get them into iTunes. Obviously, if you're buying music from the iTunes music store, the files are automatically added to your iTunes database. The process of adding the files to iTunes is pretty consistent without regard to the source, but for the purposes of this hack, we'll be using eMusic as the source.

Predictably the first thing you'll need to do is acquire the files from the source of your choice (see Figure 14-10).

Figure 14-10.
Downloading music to the eMusic queue

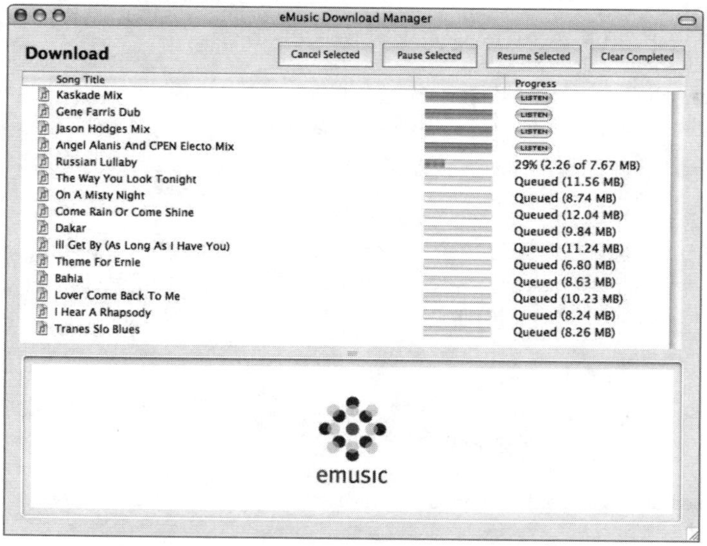

Where the file shows up depends on the source. Common destinations are your chosen downloads folder or the desktop. Amazon is the exception: if you have iTunes installed, the music is added to your iTunes library by default (see Figure 14-11).

Figure 14-11.
The download on the desktop

Once the download is on the Desktop (or anywhere on your computer besides your Music folder), you'll likely want to get the files into your iTunes database. There are a variety of methods to accomplish this task, but the easiest method is completely graphical and just requires the smallest bit of mouse work. Simply drag the downloaded files (or enclosing folder) to the iTunes icon likely residing in your Dock (see Figure 14-12).

Figure 14-12.
Adding new songs to iTunes

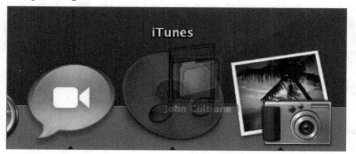

iTunes will then take care of the rest of the work, making sure your newly acquired media is available in the familiar iTunes interface (see Figure 14-13).

Figure 14-13.
New songs in iTunes

Russian Lullaby	John Coltrane	The Best Of John Coltrane
The Way You Look Tonight	John Coltrane	The Best Of John Coltrane
On A Misty Night	John Coltrane	The Best Of John Coltrane
Come Rain Or Come Shine	John Coltrane	The Best Of John Coltrane
Dakar	John Coltrane	The Best Of John Coltrane
I'll Get By (As Long As I Have You)	John Coltrane	The Best Of John Coltrane
Theme For Ernie	John Coltrane	The Best Of John Coltrane
Bahia	John Coltrane	The Best Of John Coltrane
Lover Come Back To Me	John Coltrane	The Best Of John Coltrane
I Hear A Rhapsody	John Coltrane	The Best Of John Coltrane
Trane's Slo Blues	John Coltrane	The Best Of John Coltrane

— Glenn Wolsey

Play Songs Sans iTunes

Sometimes you don't want the visual clutter and processor load of running iTunes, but what other choice do you have if you want to play music purchased from the iTunes store? Discover the joys of playing your tunes from the command line with qtplay.

When spending time hacking about on your Mac, there is every chance that you're spending a lot of time in the Terminal. It might occur to you that it would be very useful (and save some resources) if you could play your music collection from there. `qtplay` is a Unix executable (sometimes referred to as a "binary"), meaning it's a small program accessed via the Terminal. What makes `qtplay` different from all the other binaries is that `qtplay` specializes in handling music files. Using `qtplay`, you can listen to any music file you can play via QuickTime, which includes every type of file iTunes can play.

To use `qtplay`, you'll need to take a few steps away from the likable OS X interface (or a few strides into the land of the Terminal). Once that short journey is complete, you'll be listening to your CDs or music libraries via the resource-light Terminal. You'll also get some familiar functionality: you can play audio CDs, randomize tracks, control the volume, and listen to a play list. Except for fast-forward and rewind (you have to listen to whole songs, even the boring parts), you'll get all the functionality you expect of any decent music player.

Here's what you'll need for this hack:

- Some music files. Anything QuickTime can handle is fine including the protected AAC file format.

- A copy of `qtplay` from Rainbow Flight Software (http://rainbowflight.googlepages.com/#qtplay/)

Getting the Software Installed

Before you can enjoy command-line control of your music, you need to install a copy of `qtplay` (http://rainbowflight.googlepages.com/qtplay1.3.1.tar). This is not hard: just download and mount the *.dmg* file installation. After that, the first thing you have to do is make a choice: Do you want systemwide access, meaning all accounts can use `qtplay`, or do you want to restrict access to specific accounts. Let's take a close look at the systemwide install. (The process is the same for specific users; only the destinations differ.)

Once downloaded, open the *qtplay* folder to find the `qtplay` program icon, shown in Figure 14-14.

Figure 14-14.
The qtplay icon

This is exactly how every other binary looks, so you have to pay attention to the text.

When dragging the files to their final destinations, OS X will tell you that you can't modify the folder. Don't take that kind of guff from your computer. After all, you're running the show. Hit the authenticate option in the dialog box, and type in your password to bend the Mac to your will. You'll need admin privileges, found in the system Preferences panel under Accounts.

Now drag the icon to the *bin* folder. The complete path is as follows: Mac HD (or whatever you've named your hard drive)→*/usr/local/bin*. What's that? You can't find the *usr* folder? It turns out that folder is invisible by default. But you don't have to resort to the command line (though it is easier if you do) to move this file. Under the Go menu in the Finder choose Go to Folder (Shift-Command-G) and type **/usr**. What once invisible now becomes visible. You'll see the contents of the *usr* folder, and you'll be able to drag and drop the file into the required folder.

> If the bin folder does not already exist, you will need to create it. Open a Terminal window, and type:
>
> ```
> sudo mkdir -p /usr/local/bin
> ```
>
> For more information on the sudo command, see [Hack #5].

Once the `qtplay` application is safely ensconced in its new home, you'll want to put the manpage file (short for manual page) where it needs to be. The manpage has yet another generic icon, this one labeled *qtplay.1*.

Once properly installed, this file will allow access to the `qtplay` manual from the terminal (type **man qtplay** for all the `qtplay` information you'll ever need). Follow the same basic installation procedure as with the `qtplay` binary; the only difference is the final destination. In this case it is the *man1* folder. The complete path is as follows: hard drive→*/usr/local/share/man/man1*.

> If this path does not already exist, you will need to create it. Open a Terminal window, and type:
> ```
> sudo mkdir -p /usr/local/share/man/man1
> ```

If you want to give access to this program only to a single user, repeat the procedures described previously, changing the destination to the intended user's Home folder.

Copying the files from the Terminal

Alternatively, you can do all the moving from Terminal. If you're going to be playing music from the Terminal, moving a few files is great practice.

Open up a new shell using Terminal and type **mv** (be sure to add a space after the v) and drag the `qtplay` binary to the $. This auto-completes the path; on my computer, the result looks like this:

```
Last login: Thu Jan 17 15:33:42 on ttys000
$ mv /Users/chris/Desktop/qtplay\ Folder/qtplay
```

Now type the destination, in this case *~/bin/*, for a command line that resembles the following:

```
Last login: Thu Jan 17 15:33:42 on ttys000
$ mv /Users/chris/Desktop/qtplay\ Folder/qtplay ~/bin/
```

Hit return, and you're done.

Repeat the process for the manpage file (*qtplay.1*). The command line should look very nearly identical; when typing, be sure to enter *qtplay.1* (not just *qtplay*), and the destination should be *~/man/* instead of *~/bin/*. (To execute commands in your personal *~/bin* directory, you'll need to make sure that your shell's PATH variable includes that directory. To find manpages in a local *man* directory, you'll have to set a similar MANPATH variable. See [Hack #32] for instructions to set this automatically.)

Listen to the Music

That's it as far as the hard and grungy work goes. The rest is system resource-light music-listening nirvana. Open a new Terminal shell, change to your Music folder with **cd ~/Music**, and run **qtplay** by typing **qtplay —r** at the command prompt. The **qtplay** program will play all the songs in all your subdirectories in alphabetical order. Use Ctrl-C to skip to the next song, and press it twice quickly to stop the program. Nifty.

Of course just playing one song after another lacks a little flexibility so **qtplay** features several commands to adjust the order, play specific files, randomize the entire process, and so on. Listing all these commands would be a little lengthy, and you can always type **qtplay man** in the Terminal to get the full scoop. Still, listing a few of the more often used commands will help get you started: remember that these commands are typed directly into the Terminal:

Play all audio CDs:

    $ qtplay —cd

Play random music files:

    $ qtplay —r —Z ~/Music/

Play a specific song:

    $ qtplay filename

Start playing in the background:

    $ qtplay —r —Z ~/Music/ &

There's more to learn about **qtplay**, but that's plenty of information to get you started listening to your music without the Desktop-cluttering iTunes interface. The added bonus: everyone can use iTunes, but you'll be one of the few who can control the music coming out of your computer using just a few keystrokes.

HACK 117: Play Classic Games on Your Mac with MacMAME

Your Mac has plenty of power to run old arcade games. This hack explores how to get classic games running on your machine so you can relive the good old days without pockets filled with quarters.

All the interest today is in the latest consoles: people are enamored with the Wii, Xbox 360, or Playstation 3. If you're over 30, you remember when home consoles were blocky translations of what you found at the arcade, more of a temporary fix until you got more quarters for the true gaming experience. It turns out that your Mac can play all the arcade games you remember as a youth with a few ROMs and an emulator called MacMAME (for those interested MAME is an acronym for Multiple Arcade Machine Emulator).

To get started on a retro arcade odyssey, point your browser to http://www.macmame.org and download MacMAME. Install, predictably, by dragging *MacMame.app* to the Applications folder. You have the emulator, but without any games, it isn't much fun to have around. Time to find some ROMs.

ROM stands for Read Only Memory. The early Macs had part of the system software stored on ROMs and, as you have guessed, arcade games have relied on ROMs to store the game program.

Game ROMs are copyrighted so you can't just download any ROMs you happen to find with a Google search and remain on the happy side of piracy. In fact, MacMAME will remind you that playing ROMs you don't legally own is a bad idea.

All hope is not lost. There are plenty of ROMs out there you are free to use. A good source for free and legal ROMs is http://mamedev.org/roms, which functions as a repository for a selection of games that have been released or free noncommercial use. Turns out that an old favorite is available—StarFire from Exidy!

If you're hunting for MAME ROMs, don't worry about MacMAME-specific ROMs; the vast majority of ROMs should work with any emulator.

Now for the only tricky part of the installation, getting that ROM to a place where MacMAME can find it. Apparently there has been no small amount of controversy concerning what location should be used as the central repository for MacMAME's ROMs. Controversy aside, the path is ~/Documents/MacMAME User Data/ROMs. Simply drop the .zip file into the folder (if the file unzips automatically, just drop the resulting folder in ROMs folder), fire up MacMAME, and you're ready to play.

MacMAME has been improved greatly over the years but using the keyboard to play games hasn't. To save a little frustration, realize that 5 is "insert coin" and 1 starts the game. To save a lot of frustration, consider purchasing a joystick for dedicated play.

HACK 118: Connect Your Mac to an Xbox 360

You've got media on your Mac and a media-blasting Xbox 360 already hooked up to your home theater. Get your media from the Mac to your Xbox, and you can listen and watch your media with all the fidelity of your media setup.

It came to my attention the other day that many Xbox360 owners (who predominantly use Macintosh computers in their household) aren't aware of a little piece of software that brilliantly links up an Xbox 360 and any form of Mac computer with networking capabilities.

For those who aren't quite sure what I'm talking about, the Xbox 360 allows you to connect to a Windows XP or Media Centre PC (only), giving you the freedom of streaming music, photos, and even movies directly to your console. Unfortunately for us Mac owners, we're not even given a second look by Microsoft on this one.

But that's where Connect 360 comes in.

What Is Connect 360?

Connect 360 was developed by Nullriver Software; the company develops products that enhance connectivity and compatibility between other products not previously supported by their manufacturers to work with the Macintosh platform—for example, PSPWare, which allows a stable connection between your Sony PSP and your iMac.

The idea behind Connect 360 is to trick your Microsoft Xbox 360 into believing that the Macintosh computer connected to it is actually a Windows computer (see Figure 14-15).

Figure 14-15.
The main Connect 360 window

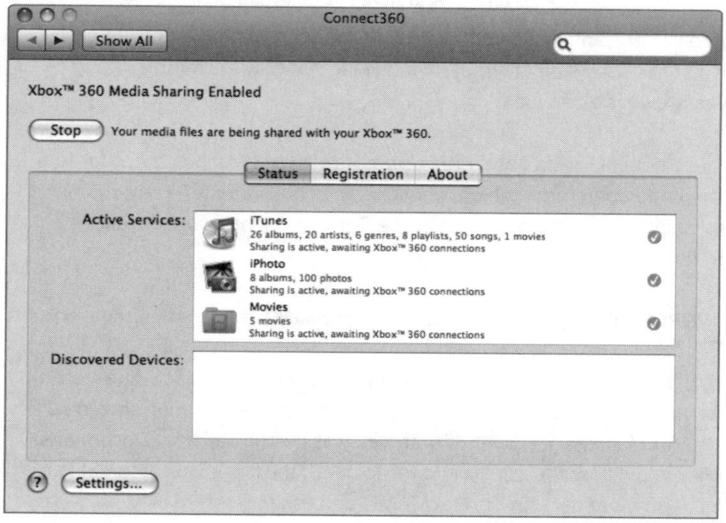

Once connected, you can share your iTunes media library, iPhoto library, and movies from within your Movie folder (provided they are WMV or WMA only) between your Xbox 360 and Macintosh computer. Excellent stuff if you've either got no hard drive with your Xbox 360, preventing you from storing media there, or are running out of room from all the demos you keep downloading from Xbox Live.

How Does It Work?

First you need to make sure you have your Xbox 360 and Macintosh computers connected to a router of some sort (wired or wireless). Once the settings are in place on your console, it's time to install Connect 360 on your Macintosh system.

Configure Xbox 360

Once you've installed Connect 360 to the preference pane in System Preferences, turn on your Xbox 360 and head to the Systems tab, followed by Network Settings and then Test Media Connection. Once everything is connected correctly (you will need to make sure your Xbox 360's IP settings are correctly configured for your network, this won't work until they are), head back to the main Xbox 360 screen and click on the Media tab. In here, select any type of media you wish to stream (for example, Music) and follow the onscreen instructions. The first time you do this you'll be prompted to go to a Microsoft web site and download a program to run on your Windows computer that allows connection to take place. We've already got our little program, so click the relevant button, which should say something along the lines of "I have already downloaded this program."

Configure your Macintosh

The next step is to go back to your Mac and open the Connect 360 preference pane (again, found in System Preferences). In here, make sure Xbox 360 Media Sharing is enabled by clicking on the Start button. You may find at this point that Connect 360 has discovered your Xbox 360 but can't yet connect due to your OS X firewall. It will automatically adjust the firewall for you, but it requires an admin password (if you're not logged in as an admin user, you'll need an admin username as well).

> **QUICK TIP**
>
> **CONVERT VIDEOS TO AN XBOX-FRIENDLY FORMAT**
>
> If you've downloaded TV shows to your Mac, there is a good chance you want to watch shows on your Xbox 360. The bad news is that the Xbox 360 won't play DivX. Fortunately the Xbox 360 will play QuickTime files, so to convert any DivX-encoded shows (or other unplayable content), use a conversion utility such as iSquint (http://www.isquint.org/) to convert the media to something the Xbox 360 will cheerfully play. Supported formats for the Xbox 360 include *.WMA*, *.WMV*, *.mp4*, *.mov*, and *.m4v*, among others. To automate the conversion, see **[Hack #113]**.

After all of this is complete, you should see your Xbox 360 console appear in the Discovered Devices section. Now it's simply a case of streaming your media directly from your Macintosh to your Xbox 360 console. Magic!

Summary

Having used this piece of kit for over some time, I can honestly say it's a joy to have. I've been able to casually browse my music while playing online, and even look at last year's holiday photos on my TV, which is considerably larger than the screen on my iMac. As I've already said, Connect 360 is definitely for someone who either doesn't have much space left on her hard drive or has no hard drive at all (found on the older Xbox 360 Core pack). The only major downfall is the lack of video support (only WMV and WMA allowed), preventing you from streaming a lot of TV shows you may have purchased from the Internet and any movies you may have created with iMovie.

You can give Connect 360 a go by downloading a demo from the official web site (http://www. nullriver.com/index/products/connect360). The demo allows you to stream up to 100 songs and 100 photos, after which you'll need to purchase and register for $20, which seems like a small price to pay if you have an Xbox 360 and a Mac.

— Aaron Wright

HACK 119: Grab and Convert Video from YouTube

You've run across a fantastic video on YouTube, a video so great you want to save it forever, slap it on your iPod, and show it to your coworkers. Unfortunately, YouTube won't let you save the video. Ditch this maddening limitation of YouTube with this workaround.

The Internet is a veritable gushing spring of video goodness; it seems as though you can't open a page without some video playing your browser. Some of these videos are great, good enough that you'd like to save them for manipulation in iMovie or download them to your iPod (or iPhone) and watch them on the go.

The trouble starts when you actually try to download the video; YouTube (purposely) doesn't present an easy way to download a video. The first step is to look for the same video on Google Video, which does allow users to save the video. Alas, not every video that is available on YouTube is available on Google Video, so a more robust solution is needed.

Once you find a video you want to save, the first step is getting the file. As mentioned earlier, YouTube wants you watching files on YouTube, not downloading them, so the process isn't straightforward (see Figure 14-16).

Figure 14-16.
Where's that download button?

You won't find a Download and Save button on YouTube's site, but you can still grab that hilarious/ inspiring/insipid video. It just takes a little work. The information you need to download a YouTube video is hidden in the Embed box. Normally this is the URL and accompanying information you cut and paste to have the video show up in your blog, but in this case, it is the path for saving the video in question to your hard drive. Copy the URL and paste it into a text editor of some sort.

Figure 14-17.
Skip cut and paste, just drag and drop!

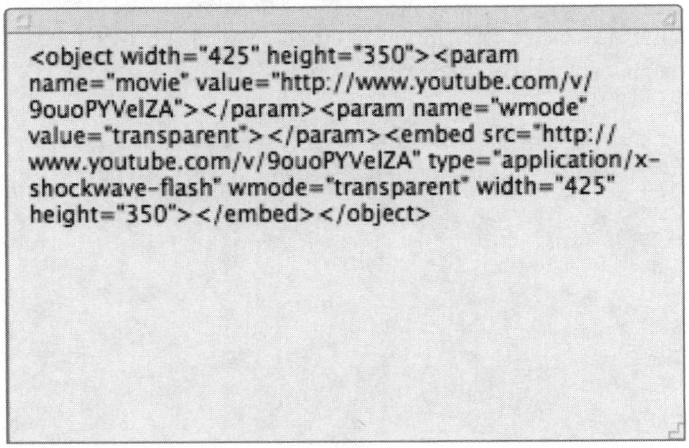

```
<object width="425" height="350"><param
name="movie" value="http://www.youtube.com/v/
9ouoPYVelZA"></param><param name="wmode"
value="transparent"></param><embed src="http://
www.youtube.com/v/9ouoPYVelZA" type="application/x-
shockwave-flash" wmode="transparent" width="425"
height="350"></embed></object>
```

Now you have the text for embedding the video, but you are really only interested in a small snippet of that long line of HTML. Locate the URL of the video following the embed src tag. Here's the complete embed:

```
<object width="425" height="350"><param name="movie" value="http://www.youtube.
com/v/9ouoPYVelZA"></param><param name="wmode" value="transparent"></param><embed
src="http://www.youtube.com/v/9ouoPYVelZA" type="application/x-shockwave-flash"
wmode="transparent" width="425" height="350"></embed></object>
```

The link you want is http://www.youtube.com/v/9ouoPYVelZA.

Paste the newly unearthed URL in your browser and load the page. It looks different than what you might expect (see Figure 14-18).

Figure 14-18.
Full browser window video is the path to download fulfillment

What you have is a full-screen video of the clip you want to save. While the screen looks different, there is a more subtle difference. When you pasted the URL, YouTube changed the URL to something like this:

```
http://www.youtube.com/p.swf?video_id=9ouoPYVelZA&eurl=&iurl=http%3A//img.youtube.
com/vi/9ouoPYVelZA/2.jpg&t=OEgsToPDskKEId0Mp-Xes3klMuK6TlNE
```

Here the text you are interested in consists of p.swf. All that is required is to change p.swf to get_video. Hit return to load the video again, and you've told YouTube you want the file, not just the ability to view it. YouTube will comply. Your download will start automatically, and the video will show up on your desktop. Nifty, now it is yours forever (see Figure 14-19).

Figure 14-19.
Automatic download!

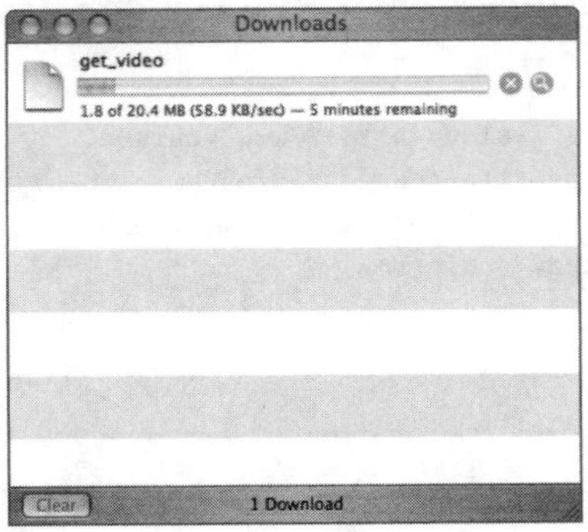

Of course having the video and being able to do something useful with it are two different things. Turns out that YouTube uses the H.263 Flash variant for new videos but for older video, YouTube relies on plain Flash, and neither the iPod nor iMovie can effectively deal with Flash files.

Don't worry: you're not shut out of the fun if you take a moment to download and install iSquint (http://www.isquint.org/). iSquint is an easy-to-use, free program that can convert a variety of video formats to an iTunes- or iMovie-friendly format.

Once iSquint is downloaded and installed, conversion is straightforward. Simply drag the file you downloaded earlier to the iSquint window and let go. iSquint will take care of the rest and save the result by default as a *.mp4* file (see Figure 14-20).

Figure 14-20.
iSquint processing the movie

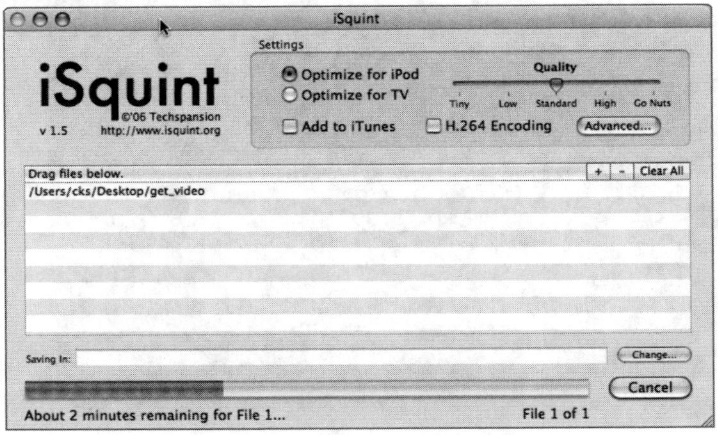

While iSquint will take care of conversion with no user input, you can customize iSquint's ouput. Click on the Advanced button page and tweak away.

Once the video is in the format you desire, you can add it to your iTunes library (or drop it directly on your iPod icon) to get it to your iPod. Additionally, you can edit the video in iMovie, watch it over and over again from your Desktop, or even transfer to your Apple TV and watch it on your main television set. If you're wondering about the quality of the video on larger screens (a 42-inch high-definition screen, for example), the answer is subjective. That said, don't spend all afternoon downloading and setting up a YouTube video for a TV-watching party.

HACK 120: Keep Your iTunes Library on an External Hard Drive

Your hard drive is feeling a bit cramped, and the biggest culprit is the media used by iTunes. Learn how to store your iTunes multimedia files on an external hard drive and save your drive space for the files you have to take with you.

After discussing how I set up my iTunes library with a few readers, I figured this might be a handy tip if you find yourself running out of room to store an expanding iTunes library. My only machine is a MacBook Pro with a 120 GB hard drive, but after installing 40 GB of the entire Final Cut Studio suite and other various software and projects, I don't have room for my 35 GB iTunes library.

I decided to do some experimenting by moving and keeping my library on an external hard drive. There are obvious initial disadvantages to this, but after some tinkering and getting comfortable with iTunes' baked-in library management genius, this can be a pretty useful setup for those who, like me, are cramped for space but aren't willing to trash those albums you're too embarrassed use in a Party Shuffle playlist. This setup also has the inherent, and obvious, advantage of keeping your library on an external hard drive, so it's more or less already backed up. (Though I, with my paranoid data habits, keep a backup of my library on a second hard drive, and I now also use the iTunes backup system to burn my library to DVDs. The lesson from someone who knows: your data can never be too backed up—ever).

If you're ready to make the move to a different drive, read on for a walkthrough (from a very mobile user) of how to move your iTunes library to an external hard drive. I'll include some tips on how iTunes is already one step ahead of this setup, as well as a few habits you might need to adopt when living la vida external-iTunes-library.

The Setup

This isn't very difficult, but for those who aren't familiar with looking under iTunes' hood, I figured I'd lay this out and start from square one to make sure everyone can play along.

The one initial catch with running your iTunes library from an external drive is that you'll need a FireWire or USB 2 drive for best performance; I have no idea how well this setup would perform on older machines with USB 1, or if it would even work at all.

Now, if you're like most iTunes users, your library of music and movies (and now games) is stored locally on your Mac in *~/Music/iTunes/* (where ~ is your Home folder). With the latest iTunes 7 update, there are now (typically) two folders and two files in here (see Figure 14-21).

QUICK HACK ✕

LET ITUNES TAKE THE WORK OUT OF BACKING UP YOUR MEDIA

It isn't the newest feature of iTunes, but it did come along rather late in the game: an iTunes option to back up your library. Fortunately, the process is dead simple and ever so useful. Of course, if you're regularly backing up with Time Machine or a method of your own devising, you might not want or need to back up your music. If you want to back up your iTunes media to DVDs, this is the method for you.

Simply fire up iTunes and point your mouse to File→Backup to Disk... and choose from the options that appear: Back up entire iTunes library and playlists or Back up only iTunes Store purchases (you can also select the option to only back up items added or changed since the last backup).

Depending on the speed of your DVD burner and the size of your library (as well as the option selected, of course) a few minutes or a few hours later, you'll have your iTunes data backed up on a shiny DVD.

Figure 14-21.
The required data

Knowing what you're working with is as important as seeing the pictures:

- Album Artwork folder (new with iTunes 7; missing from iTunes 6 and previous versions).

- iTunes Music folder (this is where all your actual media such as songs, podcasts, movies, and games live).

- iTunes Library (a database file iTunes needs).

- iTunes Music Library (an XML library file iTunes also needs).

Now I'm sure that, as with many hacks like this, there are a number of ways to accomplish the task. I'm simply going to present out the easiest and most hassle-free method I know of because it worked mighty fine for me. As a bonus, there are really only two steps:

1. If iTunes is running, quit it.

2. The only part of your iTunes folder you actually should move to the external hard drive is the iTunes Music folder (the one that holds all your media). Leave the Album Artwork folder, as well as the iTunes Library and iTunes Music Library files in place, locally on your Mac. Of course, if you want to back up your iTunes library for safe keeping (see sidebar "Let iTunes Take the Work Out of Backing up Your Media"), including all your metadata, song ratings, song comments, etc., you should back up these local files in addition to your media

That's it—you've moved your library—you just need to let iTunes know where you moved all its stuff.

Configuring iTunes
Fortunately, telling iTunes where its library now lives is a one-step process.

Go into iTunes' Preferences and locate the Advanced pane, then click on the General tab. At the top of this tab is a record of where your library—your actual media—resides and, as you might guess, you can click the Change... button to tell iTunes it's hopped the pond to external hard-drive pastures. You simply need to browse through the Finder dialog and select your media library, wherever you put it, and click OK. That's it—iTunes writes the necessary changes to those aforementioned local database and XML library files, and you don't have to do any more heavy lifting. As long as your drive is still mounted and running, you can start playing your media just like before.

Unfortunately though, now that you're enjoying external iTunes library bliss, it's time to burst your bubble with a few gotchas to look out for. It's certainly possible to keep on trucking with this kind of setup (otherwise this would be a pretty useless hack), but there are definitely some constraints to consider when going down this road.

The Gotchas

The most significant catch is, of course, the fact that if you ever disconnect your drive—perhaps you're a portable computer user like myself—you obviously can't play any of your media in iTunes. Unless you own an iPod and enable the settings to manage its music yourself, you're pretty much out of luck here.

As you might expect, this also means that managing an iPod with this setup can get quirky too. If you sync your iPod with iTunes, and you connect it while your library is unplugged, iTunes will freak out and, after a few moments, warn you that it can't update your iPod because none of your media is present. However, this doesn't remove any music from your iPod, and your iTunes media will be playable once you connect your drive again. A lot of those "file not found" exclamation points will appear next to your songs in the iTunes media list after a scenario like this, but *don't panic*. Once you reconnect your drive (and/or restart iTunes—that one's up to you), all your media will play and sync just fine again.

If you want to be able to plug in your iPod and exchange files and folders without iTunes automatically starting (and potentially bringing up the aforementioned quirks), uncheck the "Start iTunes automatically when this iPod is connected" option. This way iTunes only starts when you're good and ready to interact with your media and/or your iPod. These might not be easy habits to develop if you're used to iTunes running the show for you, but (as with several hacks) they're most likely necessary if you've read this far into the hack and you're still interested in living the external library lifestyle.

Adding Media to Your New Setup

You're wondering: What happens if I import media, download podcasts, or buy something from the iTunes Store?

This is one of the many areas where I must tip my hat to Apple's engineers, for they really knocked one out of the park when it comes to this situation.

Ever wonder what the Advanced→Consolidate Library menu option does? Well, it was made for just such a setup as your new external iTunes library. If your drive isn't connected when you start iTunes and, for example, you import a CD or download a subscribed podcast, iTunes needs to put it somewhere, and it defaults to placing that media in your local *~/Music/iTunes/iTunes Music/* folder. "But David, this is going to turn my library into a mess!" you exclaim from atop your desk chair. Fear not, intrepid hacker, for the Advanced→Consolidate Library command is to the rescue! This ingenious command tells iTunes to copy any media it's imported from the local default media folder over to your recently customized external folder—once it's reconnected, of course. This is beautiful, because it's a two-click process to move all that new media over with the rest of your library and organize it properly, defusing a potentially complicated library mess.

A fortunate perk of iTunes' ability to have a split library personality is its ability to update an iPod with a new podcast or recently imported album while you're out and about, sans-external library drive. This has the potential to get confusing though, so for the sake of your organizational sanity, I hope you don't need your new podcast episode fix too often while you're on the go.

Finally, as far as reuniting your libraries is concerned, it seems that iTunes copies your new media files over to the drive when consolidating, instead of moving them. Every so often after you run this option, it might be a good idea to dig into your local iTunes Music folder and trash all those files, as they're just dead weight after a consolidation.

Be One with Your External iTunes Library

This should be just about everything you need to cut the cord on your iTunes library if you're looking to save space on your Mac, or if you're simply a nut for using external hard drives. I've been poking around at this setup for about a month now, and I've been pretty happy with it. Aside from the catches I mentioned to watch out for, I was able to save almost 35 GB of space on my MacBook Pro and make way for other projects, with room to spare.

— David Chartier

HACK 121:
Building a Digital Movie Collection from Your DVD Collection

You've got DVDs, and you've got a Mac—why not meld the two together? You'll be able to expand your viewing options, back up the physical DVDs and get rid of the ads the studios force you to watch at the beginning of the DVD.

Media has become a central part of our lives, and as of not very long ago, Apple has made it easy to collect, purchase, organize, and play media through iTunes. They've made it easy to access this content through the Apple TV on your high-definition TV in your living room. One thing they haven't done is give people outside the United States access to the vast number of movies in the iTunes store catalog.

To conquer this lack of digital movies available locally, I've started to encode my entire DVD movie collection to create a digital archive of my movies for quick access on my Mac, or via a HDTV in the future using the Apple TV.

To complete this process, you'll need to arm yourself with your personal DVD collection, plenty of free time, Apple iTunes, and a third-party application called Handbrake. Oh, don't forget a nice large external hard drive to house these movies (typically 1.5 GB each).

What you'll be doing is inserting DVDs into your Mac, ripping them to your hard-drive with Handbrake, importing them into iTunes, and adding metadata.

1. The first step is to move your iTunes Library to an external hard drive; if you don't want too or believe you have enough space on your internal drive, skip this step (see **[Hack #120]** for complete instructions).

2. Now that your collection has a nice storage tank to lie in, you can begin digitizing your DVD collection. The program of choice is Handbrake (see Figure 14-22); it has the advantages of being free and open source, and you can get a copy at: http://handbrake.m0k.org/ ?article=download.

Figure 14-22.
The Handbrake interface

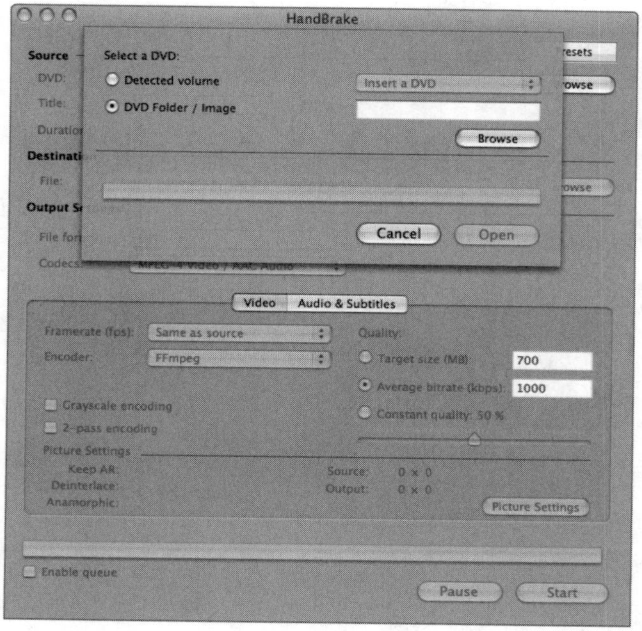

3. Insert a DVD into your Mac, and launch Handbrake. You will then be prompted to select the
    DVD location, which should show automatically. Click OK (see Figure 14-23).

Figure 14-23.
Handbrake finds the DVD!

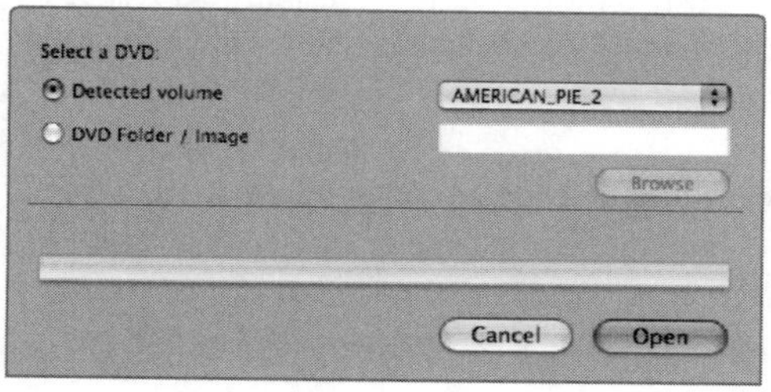

Now it's time to select your ripping (or encoding) settings (see Figure 14-24). My preferred
settings for top quality media are "H.264, 2500KBPS, 2-Pass encoding". The resulting file
will end up around the 1.5 GB mark, and encoding will take a while depending on what Mac
you have. On a 1.83 GHz Core Duo MacBook, this process takes around three hours for an
average length movie. If you want smaller files and a quicker rip time, set up with "MP4, 1-Pass
Encoding, 200MBPS."

Figure 14-24.
The many options of Handbrake

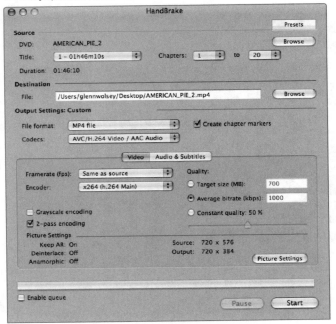

4. Once the encoding is complete, you can eject the DVD and place it back in its case. The movie is now stored digitally.

5. You should see the movie file on your Desktop. Double-clicking this file will open QuickTime and allow you to watch the movie, but we want an organized collection, so open iTunes and drag the movie onto the Movie source pane. Doing this will move the movie into your iTunes Library. Once completed, it's safe to delete the original file from your desktop. That file is now safe inside your iTunes library.

6. The final step is to tag the movie with the correct title, and add any other information to the file you'd like to. Typically, I set the movie genre, and the year it came out in. That's all the information I need on hand. Finally, head over to Google and do an image search for "*insert-movie-name* DVD." You should be presented with a bunch of DVD images, copy one of these and paste it as the artwork on the movie file.

There is no next step; you've successfully imported a movie into your iTunes collection, tagged it, added art, and it's now ready for consumption directly on your Mac, on your iPod, or via your Apple TV.

The following sections describe some steps you can take to conquer a few common questions about ripping and storing movies.

Fun with Your New Files

Who doesn't want to lose the ads DVD manufacturers cram onto a disc? Since you're ripping the DVD, you don't have to rip (and later watch) the ads. To pull this off, you have to plan a little bit because Handbrake doesn't include an option as to where to begin the rip from. However, the program will allow you to choose which chapters to rip, and this usually does the trick. For instance, the ads are typically located on the first chapter of the movie, so with a 20-chapter movie, I'd select chapters 2 through 20 for encoding, leaving all the unnecessary ads out of my finished file.

If you can skip the ads, surely you can just grab the parts of the movie you want, right? Of course you can. Only want movie chapters 12-15? No sweat, simply drop down the boxes, and make this choice. When you hit Start, Handbrake will only extract this section of the movie.

What if you're not ripping the DVD to watch on your Mac? What if you want to watch the movie on your iPhone? Well, then you're in luck. Once your DVD is inside your machine, pop open Handbrake, and hit the presets tab in the top right corner of the Handbrake window. This slides open another window where you should see the option called HB-iPod. Click this, then click rip, and Handbrake automatically changes the settings to output an iPod-friendly file (see Figure 14-25).

Figure 14-25.
The useful presets of Handbrake

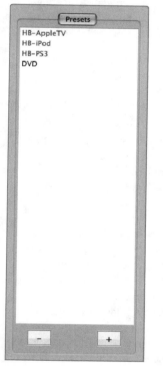

The Payoff

I've currently imported 53 movies into my iTunes collection, totaling 61.05 GB. The hard work I've done in digitizing my collection will shine once my home media setup is completed with a HDTV and Apple TV.

— Glenn Wolsey

Create a Screencast!

You know how to broadcast your voice, your pictures, and your movies. Now discover how to broadcast your screen.

Screencasting, like its older podcasting relative, is gaining in popularity. As the tools to record video and audio from your computer have matured, so have the needs of creators to share their knowledge on virtually any technique, topic, or how-to you can think of. From the latest Photoshop trick to beta software demos and even that handy unsung, time-saving trick in Mac OS X Leopard, screencasters are taking their own growing niche of the Web by storm. Learn how to join the growing legion of screencasters with these tips and tricks.

Just like podcasting, there are plenty of dos and don'ts involved with the actual process of creating a screencast. There are also a number of software and hardware tools that can add a great deal of quality to your production. I had some time to explore this stuff in my experience creating screencasts at my blogging position for The Unofficial Apple Weblog, so here is some software I found to work the best, as well as some tips and techniques on how to add some polish to your show.

The Tools

You'll want to be familiar with the tools for making a screencast.

Recording video

A mainstay of recording video and audio from your Mac is Ambrosia Software, Inc.'s Snapz Pro X (http://www.ambrosiasw.com/utilities/snapzprox). It offers a lot of control over what exactly you record, whether it be your entire screen, a selected region, or even a specific application or window. At $70 for the full version though ($30 just gets you screenshots, not video), I found that I prefer shinywhitebox's iShowU (http://www.shinywhitebox.com) for its more favorable price, better application design, and more control over the things that matter.

For $20, iShowU gives you a simple video and audio recording application preinstalled with a number of customizable recording preferences. You can record to any of QuickTime's built-in formats, customize data and frame rates, specify a specific region to record, and even adjust how audio is recorded, complete with specifying an input source so you can use a custom microphone (more on that later). iShowU also allows you to specify which directory to save the temporary recording files, as well as the finished product, which can come in handy for long recording sessions or when recording on a notebook with a slower hard drive. When recording 20-minute HD screencasts (1280 x 960) on my MacBook Pro that has only a 4200 rpm drive, though, I never ran into any troubles or crashes. Still, when tossing around this much video and audio, it never hurts to use external storage to help take some of the burden off your Mac's internal drive.

Recording audio

Since iShowU can also record audio while you demonstrate and record your video, a crossroads presents itself here. There are a few schools of thought as to how and when to record your audio for a screencast. Some firmly believe that you should pace yourself and act out just the video portion of your screencast, then use something like GarageBand or another audio application to lay down your audio later. This allows you to focus on getting your video right, and you won't have to start everything over if you goof up a line while recording video and audio simultaneously.

The glutton for punishment that I am, I usually prefer the alternative: recording video and audio all at once. With a little preparation and practice, this method can go more smoothly (especially after you do it a few times), and I've always felt that talking your way through a process while recording it on video provides a more coherent and cohesive experience for the viewer.

At the end of the day though, you can chalk this one up to subjectivity. Both paradigms have their pros and cons. My preferred method can certainly be more frustrating when first starting out, and if you aren't one for preparing much ahead of time, but the two-step process of recording video, then playing it back and laying down your audio can be more clunky and time-consuming, depending on how you work. You'll probably just need to play around with both methods and see which suits you best after a few tries.

Say It Loud and Clear

Nothing ruins a podcast like crummy audio, and the same goes for any screencast that needs a voiceover (hint: it helps). It may be tempting to skimp on a microphone and go for that budget $10 headset Best Buy has in this week's ad, but I cannot advise you strongly enough to resist that temptation. Your viewers may put up with YouTube's crummy video compression, but if you aren't using at least halfway decent audio equipment, you might as well be scratching Morse code on a chalkboard with your fingernails.

The good news is that you don't have to spend much more to get at least a decent microphone. Some successful screencasters report getting reasonable audio out of headset and microphone combos in the range of $30 to $50 from sources such as Logitech and Plantronics. If you're willing to step it up a notch, the Snowball microphone from Blue (http://www.bluemic.com/) will give you a crisp, clear sound with a nice balance of bass for around $99. Like many options these days, the Blue Snowball is a USB mic, which means you get more power over it via the audio controls in Mac OS X and most third-party audio-recording applications you'll use.

Getting Their Attention

While your screencasts may involve intuitive applications and lots of moving parts that capture your viewer's attention all on their own, chances are you'll also have plenty of, shall we say, "slow points." Maybe you occasionally have to talk more than show; maybe you're working with intricate buttons or menu items. Whatever the case, many screencasts can benefit from the highlighting tools of Boinx Software's Mouseposé (http://www.boinx.com/mousepose/). This utility is designed for presentations of all kinds, including screencasts. It allows you to invoke a spotlight around your mouse to highlight something you're doing, and it can even display a pop-up notification with any keyboard shortcuts you strike; perfect for showing your viewers the quick way of doing things without having to sound clunky by voicing the specific commands.

Where the Magic Happens

No matter what you're demonstrating in your screencast or how skilled you may be with using the software, most of the magic should happen before you ever hit the record button. The key to a successful, entertaining, and/or educational screencast is preparation and rehearsal. Writing out a script or simply outlining what you want to cover can do wonders for your pacing. It'll help keep you on track and cut down on (or, ideally, eliminate) mistakes. Even if you opt for laying down your audio after you record your video, a smooth voiceover and well-performed video demonstration will inform your viewers and keep them coming back for more much better than something that's put together by the seat of your pants.

— David Chartier

iTunes isn't the only way to encode your CDs. With Mac OS X, you can get to the heart of Unix to rip in alternative encoders such as LAME.

One of the greatest advantages of Apple's OS X operating system is its Unix core. Unix is a flexible environment (once you learn how to use it) that lets you get your hands dirty and solve problems when other applications fall short. While I love iTunes' powerful "jukebox" environment, I wish it allowed more options when it comes to audio encoding. The LAME encoder (it stands for "LAME Ain't an MP3 Encoder"; find it at http://lame.sourceforge.net/) is the Internet standard for quality MP3 encoding.

Amongst those who frequent the Usenet MP3 groups, you will find LAME in much wider use than any other codec, and your ears will hear the difference. Once I realized what I was missing by using the iTunes encoder, I set out to make using LAME easier.

Most command-line audio tools, such as LAME and FLAC—Free Lossless Audio Codec http://flac.sourceforge.net/, are designed to be used on only one file at a time, which makes batch processing tricky. A simple Unix shell script seemed the obvious solution to this problem. All big problems start small, however, and after I had written my batch LAME encoding script, I realized there were lots of little problems that I needed to solve in order to make CD archiving a more pleasant experience.

What began for me as a simple hack for batch encoding CDs and setting ID3 tags turned into a suite of programs aimed at streamlining the handling of MP3 and FLAC files from the command line. I chose the LAME and FLAC encoders, in part because they are both distributed under a version of the GNU General Public License (http://www.gnu.org/licenses/licenses.html), which keeps their development out in the open and ensures that end users are given rights to change the programs if they like. There are many advantages to both of these encoders, but audio quality and openness are chief among them.

Here, then, are eight scripts to make your audio life easier:

`lameit`
Rips CDs to MP3 format using LAME.

`flacit`
Rips CDs to FLAC format.

`id3hack`
Uses the filename to set a track's name and number in its ID3 tag.

`vchack`
Creates a Vorbis comment for a FLAC file using the `id3hack` script.

`vctool`
Borrows the `id3tool` interface to set Vorbis comments in FLAC files.

`vcid3`
Converts Vorbis comments in FLAC files to ID3 tags in MP3 files.

`flacmp3`

Converts FLAC files to MP3 files.

`striptoc`

Reformats a `cdrdao`-generated table of contents file for use with FLAC files.

There are, of course, some binaries that you need in order to make these scripts work. I recommend you install them using Fink or Macports **[Hack #31]** or you can compile them by hand and put them in your directory:

- `cdrdao`: http://cdrdao.sourceforge.net (for `striptoc` only)

- `flac`: http://flac.sourceforge.net (for `flacit` and `flacmp3`)

- `id3tool`: http://nekohako.xware.cx/id3tool (for `id3hack` and `vcid3`)

- `lame`: http://lame.sourceforge.net (for `lameit` and `flacmp3`)

- `metaflac`: http://flac.sourceforge.net (for `flacmp3`, `vchack`, `vctool`, and `vcid3`)

To install each of these using Fink from the command line, simply type:

```
$ fink install <package-name>
```

Some packages might not be available under Fink, or Fink might use an outdated version, and you might need to compile the executable yourself. Instructions for doing this can be found on each program's web site and in the *README* file included with the source archive. Compilation usually involves running a `configure` script, followed by the `make` command. I recommend placing the compiled binaries in either */usr/local/bin* (for systemwide use) or *$HOME/bin* (if you are not the system administrator or don't want to share the utilities with other users).

Rip CDs to MP3 with lameit

The first script uses LAME to rip a CD to the current directory. This process works best if you first set the CD metadata in iTunes. The easiest way to do this is to get the information from the Gracenote CDDB automatically by selecting Get CD Track Names from the Advanced menu in iTunes. If the CDDB information is incorrect, you can then edit it by hand within iTunes. Once you've done that (you might have to eject and reinsert the CD to make sure the information is updated), you're ready to start ripping.

The code

Type the following script and save it to a file called *lameit* in your *$HOME/bin* directory:

```
#!/bin/sh
#
# lameit - rip a cd to lame-encoded mp3s
#
if [ "$1" ]
then
  for file in "$1"/[1-9]\ *.aiff
  do

  if [ -e "$file" ]
  then
    lame -h -m s -b 192 "$file" "0$(basename "$file" .aiff).mp3"
```

```
  else
    echo >&2 "No appropriate files exist in directory: "$1""
    exit 1
  fi
done
for file in "$1"/[1-9][0-9]\ *.aiff
do
  if [ -e "$file" ]
  then
    lame -h -m s -b 192 "$file" "$(basename "$file" .aiff).mp3"
  fi
done
else
  echo >&2 "Usage: "$(basename "$0")" /path/to/cd"
  exit 1
fi
```

The script simply checks for appropriate *.aiff* files (with the track number followed by a space in the filename) and encodes each one using LAME. In this case, the encoding is with a 192K constant bit rate, stereo.

Running the hack

Make the script executable by opening the Terminal and typing the following on the command line:

```
$ chmod +x lameit
```

You can then run the script this way:

```
$ lameit /path/to/cd
```

Replace */path/to/cd* with the path to the CD you're interested in, which can be found in the */Volumes* directory. (Type **ls /Volumes** at the Terminal prompt to see what's there.)

You can modify the LAME command line in the script to suit your needs. Type **lame --help** in the Terminal for some guidelines on encoding options.

Rip CDs to FLAC with flacit

The next script does the same thing, but with FLAC, a lossless encoder, instead of LAME.

The code

Type the following script and save it to a file called *flacit* in your */usr/local/bin* directory:

```
#!/bin/sh
#
# flacit - rip a cd to flac format
#
if [ "$1" ]

then
  for file in "$1"/[1-9]\ *.aiff
  do
    if [ -e "$file" ]
    then
      flac \
        --force-raw-format \
        --endian=little \
        --sign=signed \
```

```
                --channels=2 \
                --sample-rate=44100 \
                --bps=16 \
                --skip=20 \
                --output-name="0$(basename "$file" .aiff).flac" \
                "$file"
        else
          echo >&2 "No appropriate files exist in directory: "$1""
          exit 1
        fi
    done
    for file in "$1"/[1-9][0-9]\ *.aiff
    do
        if [ -e "$file" ]
        then
          flac \
            --force-raw-format \
            --endian=little \
            --sign=signed \
            --channels=2 \
            --sample-rate=44100 \
            --bps=16 \
            --skip=20 \
            --output-name="$(basename "$file" .aiff).flac" \
            "$file"
        fi
    done
else
    echo >&2 "Usage: "$(basename "$0")" /path/to/cd"
    exit 1
fi
```

Running the hack

Make the script executable by opening the Terminal application (*/Applications/Utilities/Terminal*) and typing the following on the command line:

```
$ chmod +x flacit
```

You can then run the script this way:

```
$ flacit /path/to/cd
```

Replace */path/to/cd* with the path to the CD you're interested in, which can be found in the */Volumes* directory.

You can modify the FLAC command line in the script to suit your needs. Type **flac --help** in the Terminal for some guidelines on encoding options.

Label Your Tunes with id3hack

Next comes the question of labeling the files. I use **id3tool** (http://nekohako.xware.cx/id3tool/) to slap together ID3 tags before importing them into iTunes, because otherwise they get lost in my collection. **id3tool** works fine for labeling the artist, album, year, and genre, but setting the track number and song title can become tedious, so I whipped up this little hack.

This hack works only if the files are named with the two-digit track number followed by its name—for example:

- *04 And Here We Test Our Powers of Observation.mp3*

- *01 Moondance.mp3*

- *05 500 Miles.mp3*

You can specify as many files as you want on the command line. I usually just use the **.mp3* wildcard.

The code

Type the following script, and save it to a file called *id3hack* in your */usr/local/bin* directory:

```
#!/bin/sh
#
# id3hack - add track names and numbers to id3 tags
#
if [ "$1" ]
then
  for file
  do
    if [ -e "$file" ]
    then
      id3tool \
        --set-title="$(echo "$file" | sed 's/...\(.*\)\.mp3/\1/')" \
        --set-track="$(echo "$file" | sed 's/\(..\).*/\1/')" \
        "$file"
    else
      echo >&2 "No such file: "$1" -- skipping."
    fi
  done
else
  echo >&2 "Usage: "$(basename "$0")" INPUTFILE [...]"
  exit 1
fi
```

The script uses the Unix utility **sed** to extract the track name and number from the filename and set them as tags with **id3tool**. Of course, the script first checks to make sure that the files that you've given on the command line actually exist.

Running the hack

Make the script executable by opening the Terminal and typing the following on the command line:

```
$ chmod +x id3hack
```

You can then run the script by navigating to the directory containing the files you want to edit and typing:

```
$ id3hack *.mp3
```

I used a wildcard here to apply to every MP3 file in the current directory, but I also could have supplied the filenames for each MP3 file. Either way, make sure the files exist in your current directory.

QUICK TIP

SED'S NOT DEAD

The **sed** utility is a fully functioning editor that edits files according to commands you type at the command line. It's meant for this kind of mass edit exercise, where you don't want to do the same thing over and over again. Type **man sed** at the Terminal prompt to read more, and check out [Hack #32] for an example.

Add Metadata with vchack

This is the same script as `id3hack`, except that it creates Vorbis comments for FLAC files instead of ID3 tags for MP3s. A Vorbis comment is a way to include information such as title and artist in the same file as the music.

This script uses `metaflac`, a tool for editing FLAC metadata that is included with FLAC.

The code

Type the following script and save it to a file called *vchack* in your */usr/local/bin* directory:

```
#!/bin/sh
#
# vchack - add track names and numbers to flac files
#
if [ "$1" ]
then
  for file
  do
    if [ -e "$file" ]
      then
        metaflac \
        --set-vc-field=TITLE="$(echo "$file" |
          sed 's/...\(.*\)\.flac/\1/')" \
        --set-vc-field=TRACKNUMBER="$(echo "$file" |
          sed 's/\(..\).*/\1/' |
          sed 's/0\(.\)/\1/')" \
        "$file"
    else
      echo >&2 "No such file: "$1" -- skipping."
    fi
  done
else
  echo >&2 "Usage: "$(basename "$0")" INPUTFILE [...]"
  exit 1
fi
```

Again, this script is similar to `id3hack`. It uses `sed` and `metaflac` to pick apart the filename and assign pieces of it to metadata tags within the file.

Running the hack

Make the script executable by opening the Terminal and typing the following on the command line:

```
$ chmod +x vchack
```

You can then run the script from the directory containing the files you want to edit by typing the following:

```
$ vchack *.flac
```

I used a wildcard here to apply to every FLAC file in the current directory, but I also could have supplied the filenames for each FLAC file. Either way, make sure the files exist in your current directory.

Fix your Metadata with vctool

Vorbis comments can be tricky to work with. This isn't surprising once you realize that a Vorbis comment isn't just a bit of text, but a metadata container for information like title, track, artist, and so on. And, it's not just a metadata container, it is a metadata container with rules. Out of frustration, I wrote a script that brought the id3tool interface over to the world of Vorbis comments and FLAC. Type **vctool -h** at the command line to get usage information.

The code
Type the following script and save it to a file called *vctool* in your */usr/local/bin*:

```sh
#!/bin/sh
#
# vctool - set vorbis comments in flac files
#
if [ "$1" ]
then
  while getopts t:a:r:y:g:c:h option
  do
    case "$option" in
      t) TITLE="--set-vc-field=TITLE="$OPTARG"";;
      a) ALBUM="--set-vc-field=ALBUM="$OPTARG"";;
      r) ARTIST="--set-vc-field=ARTIST="$OPTARG"";;
      y) DATE="--set-vc-field=DATE="$OPTARG"";;
      g) GENRE="--set-vc-field=GENRE="$OPTARG"";;
      c) TRACKNUMBER="--set-vc-field=TRACKNUMBER="$OPTARG"";;
      h) echo ""$(basename "$0")" <options> <filename>"
         echo " -t WORD Sets the title to WORD"
         echo " -a WORD Sets the album to WORD"
         echo " -r WORD Sets the artist to WORD"
         echo " -y WORD Sets the date to WORD"
         echo " -g WORD Sets the genre to WORD"
         echo " -c WORD Sets the track number to WORD";;
    esac
  done

  shift $((OPTIND - 1))
  for file
  do
      if [ -e "$file" ]
      then
        for var in "$TITLE" "$ALBUM" "$ARTIST" "$DATE" "$GENRE" "$TRACKNUMBER"
        do
          if [ "$var" ]
          then
            metaflac "$var" "$file"
          fi
        done
      else
        echo >&2 "No such file: "$file" -- skipping."
      fi
      done
  else
      echo >&2 "Type "$(basename "$0")" -h for help."
      exit 1
  fi
```

In this script, each argument that you supply invokes a new instance of the program `metaflac` program. I tried to make the script pass the arguments together to each file in one command but couldn't get it to work without **metaflac** assigning blank metadata tags. While the method used here is not ideal, it works just fine; consider it a lazy hack.

Running the hack

Make the script executable by opening the Terminal and typing the following on the command line:

```
$ chmod +x vctool
```

Assigning metadata becomes much easier with *vctool*. Here is an example:

```
$ vctool
```

Type **vctool -h** for help:

```
$ vctool -h
vctool <options> <filename>
  -t WORD Sets the title to WORD
  -a WORD Sets the album to WORD
  -r WORD Sets the artist to WORD
  -y WORD Sets the date to WORD
  -g WORD Sets the genre to WORD
  -c WORD Sets the track number to WORD
$ vctool -r "Archie Shepp" -a "Attica Blues" -y 1972 -g Jazz *.flac
```

Now, we've assigned artist, album, year, and genre metadata to every FLAC file in the current directory. That's a lot easier than typing this:

```
$ metaflac --set-vc-field=ARTIST="Archie Shepp" *.flac
$ metaflac --set-vc-field=ALBUM="Attica Blues" *.flac
$ metaflac --set-vc-field=DATE=1972 *.flac
$ metaflac --set-vc-field=GENRE=Jazz *.flac
```

Convert Metadata to ID3 with vcid3

The *vcid3* script converts Vorbis comments to ID3 tags.

The code

Type the following script and save it to a file called *vcid3* in your */usr/local/bin*:

```
#!/bin/sh
#
# vcid3 - convert vorbis comments to id3 tags
#
if [ -e "$1" ]
then
  if [ -e "$2" ]
  then
    TITLE="$(metaflac --show-vc-field=TITLE "$1" |
      sed 's/TITLE=\(.*\)/\1/')"
    ARTIST="$(metaflac --show-vc-field=ARTIST "$1" |
      sed 's/ARTIST=\(.*\)/\1/')"
    ALBUM="$(metaflac --show-vc-field=ALBUM "$1" |
      sed 's/ALBUM=\(.*\)/\1/')"
    TRACK="$(metaflac --show-vc-field=TRACKNUMBER "$1" |
      sed 's/TRACKNUMBER=\(.*\)/\1/')"
    YEAR="$(metaflac --show-vc-field=DATE "$1" |
      sed 's/DATE=\(.*\)/\1/')"
    GENRE="$(metaflac --show-vc-field=GENRE "$1" |
      sed 's/GENRE=\(.*\)/\1/')"
    if [ "$GENRE" ]
    then
      id3tool --set-genre-word="$GENRE" "$2"
    fi
```

```
        id3tool \
          --set-title="$TITLE" \
          --set-artist="$ARTIST" \
          --set-album="$ALBUM" \
          --set-track="$TRACK" \
          --set-year="$YEAR" \
          "$2"
      else
        echo >&2 "No such file: "$2""
        echo >&2 "Usage: "$(basename "$0")" FLACFILE MP3FILE"
          exit 1
      fi
  else
      echo >&2 "No such file: "$1""
      echo >&2 "Usage: "$(basename "$0")" FLACFILE MP3FILE"
      exit 1
  fi
```

This script avoids the issues of `vctool` because `id3tool` does not assign blank tags. Rather, it simply leaves off tags that contain the empty string.

Running the hack

Make the script executable by opening the Terminal and typing the following on the command line:

```
$ chmod +x vcid3
```

To use the script, navigate to the directory containing the files you want to edit and simply supply the name of the FLAC file (containing the relevant metadata) and the name of the MP3 file (which will have the metadata assigned to it) on the command line:

```
$ vcid3 "02 If You Want Me To Stay.flac" "02 If You Want Me To Stay.mp3"
```

Convert from FLAC to MP3 with flacmp3

Here's the way to get from FLAC to MP3 in one easy step. The script outputs the MP3 files to your current directory, but the FLAC files needn't be in your current directory.

This script performs the metadata conversion (without `id3tool`) side by side with the format conversion, so you won't need to do that separately.

The code

Type the following script and save it to a file called *flacmp3* in your */usr/local/bin* directory:

```
#!/bin/sh
#
# flacmp3 - convert a flac file and its tag data to mp3/id3 format
#
if [ "$1" ]
then
  for file
  do
    if [ -e "$file" ]
      then
        flac -c -d "$file" |
        lame -h -m s -b 192 \
          --tt "$(metaflac --show-vc-field=TITLE "$file" |
            sed 's/^TITLE=\(.*\)/\1/')" \
```

```
        --ta "$(metaflac --show-vc-field=ARTIST "$file" |
          sed 's/^ARTIST=\(.*\)/\1/')" \
        --tl "$(metaflac --show-vc-field=ALBUM "$file" |
          sed 's/^ALBUM=\(.*\)/\1/')" \
        --ty "$(metaflac --show-vc-field=DATE "$file" |
          sed 's/^DATE=\(.*\)/\1/')" \
        --tn "$(metaflac --show-vc-field=TRACKNUMBER "$file" |
          sed 's/^TRACKNUMBER=\(.*\)/\1/')" \
        --tg "$(metaflac --show-vc-field=GENRE "$file" |
          sed 's/^GENRE=\(.*\)/\1/')" \
        -"$(basename "$file" .flac).mp3"
      else
        echo >&2 "No such file: "$file" -- skipping."
      fi
    done
else
    echo >&2 "Usage: "$(basename "$0")" FLACFILE [...]"
    exit 1
fi
```

I love this script. In one step, it performs a complete format conversion, including metadata, and it can do so on any number of files that you specify, even wildcards. Once again, sed to the rescue!

Running the hack

Make the script executable by opening the Terminal and typing the following on the command line:

```
$ chmod +x flacmp3
```

This script takes in FLAC files and spits out MP3 files. If you've assigned metadata to a FLAC file (using *vctool*, for example), it carries that information over to the MP3:

```
$ flacmp3 *.flac
```

That's all it takes to do the job.

Simplify Your Table of Contents with striptoc

This final script takes a cdrdao table of contents (TOC) file and strips away all the unnecessary information in the file. cdrdao (http://cdrdao.sourceforge.net) is used to read and write raw CD data from the command line. Its most useful features are its plain-text TOC files, which can be used to extract pregap information from source CDs. But the TOC files presume a single, huge datafile, which is a really inconvenient way to archive a CD. This awk script takes a listing of FLAC files from the current directory and substitutes them for the track datafile.

You'll have to decompress your FLACs before burning, of course.

The code

Here's an example of the striptoc script in action, using a CD that contains only two tracks:

```
$ ls
01 So Long Eric.flac 02 Praying With Eric.flac Town Hall Concert.toc
$ cat "Town Hall Concert.toc"
CD_DA

// Track 1
TRACK AUDIO
NO COPY
NO PRE_EMPHASIS
```

```
TWO_CHANNEL_AUDIO
FILE "data.wav" 0 17:48:03
// Track 2
TRACK AUDIO
NO COPY
NO PRE_EMPHASIS
TWO_CHANNEL_AUDIO
FILE "data.wav" 17:48:03 27:31:27
START 00:00:49
$ striptoc "Town Hall Concert.toc" > "Town Hall Concert.toc.new"
$ cat "Town Hall Concert.toc.new"
CD_DA
TRACK AUDIO
FILE "01 So Long Eric.wav" 0
TRACK AUDIO
PREGAP 00:00:49
FILE "02 Praying With Eric.wav" 0
$ mv "Town Hall Concert.toc.new" "Town Hall Concert.toc"
$
```

As you can see, the file generated by cdrdao also explicitly states several defaults for each file. This script throws that information out, as well as any ISRC codes and catalog information (which this CD doesn't have). Here's the script that does all the work:

```
#!/usr/bin/awk -f
#
# striptoc - Reformat cdrdao toc files for use with individual track files.
#
BEGIN { print "CD_DA\n" }
{ FS = "\n"; RS = ""
  if ($2 == "TRACK AUDIO") {
    print $2
    if ($NF ~ /^START/) {
      sub(/^START/, "PREGAP", $NF)
      print $NF
    }
    FS = " "; RS = "\n"
    "ls *.flac" | getline file
    sub(/flac$/, "wav", file)
    print "FILE \"" file "\" 0\n"
  }
}
```

Running the hack

This awk script sends its output to standard output, so you need to tell it where to put the newly generated file, and then (optionally) move that file back on top of the old file:

```
$ striptoc Karma.toc > Karma.toc.new
$ mv Karma.toc.new Karma.toc
```

Final Thoughts

I hope you find these scripts useful. I think they really demonstrate the power and flexibility of Unix's programmer-friendly environment. Hopefully, they will inspire you to write scripts of your own to solve your little everyday problems.

— Chris Roose

15 HACK SOME HARDWARE

Hardware hacks are my favorite kind of hack; want to integrate a Mac into the real world? This chapter covers what you need to know, from putting a Mac in your car to turning your Mac into a weather-monitoring beast. Tired of losing the Internet when the power goes out? Run your modem off batteries! You'll find all that and then some in this chapter.

HACK 124: Awesome Mini in a Car Hack!

How cool would it be to have a Mac in your car? Not just a MacBook lying open on the seat next to you, but a complete built-in solution that can run your iTunes or other programs without a hitch. Talk about amazing your friends! Explore one method of installing a Mac mini in your car with this very slick hack.

When the dimensions for the Mac mini were announced, I immediately got to work figuring out what would be the best way to integrate one into my own car. If I was going to put a Mac in my car, I wanted to make sure it had all of the functionality it would have in a home environment while still maintaining an easy-to-operate interface so that distractions could be kept to a minimum. So the researching, planning, sketching and disassembly of my car's interior (to see what would fit where) began.

Choosing the Equipment

After taking the thought process to every extreme imaginable, I decided on the following equipment list:

- 1.42 GHz Mac mini with 512 MB RAM, SuperDrive, Bluetooth, and Airport Extreme

- Xenarc 700 series 7-inch USB touchscreen monitor with VGA and dual composite video inputs (http://www.xenarc.com/)

- Cirque EasyCat USB trackpad (http://www.cirque.com/cpages/?page=24)

- Griffin PowerMate assignable USB control knob (http://www.griffintechnology.com/products/powermate/)

- Lacie 8 in 1 USB flash card reader

- Belkin USB seven-port powered hub (http://catalog.belkin.com/IWCatProductPage.process?Product_Id=158910/)

- Belkin USB four-port bus-powered hub (http://catalog.belkin.com/IWCatProductPage.process?Product_Id=198333)

- Belkin Firewire six-port mini hub (http://catalog.belkin.com/IWCatProductPage. process?Product_Id=196166)

- Alpine PXA-H701 Multimedia processor with RUX-C701 controller

- Female USB, Ethernet, and FireWire ports

- 40 GB iPod dock

- Griffin RadioShark USB FM/AM tuner (http://www.griffintechnology.com/products/ radioshark/)

- Carnetix (http://www.carnetix.com/CNXP1900.htm)

Finding a Home for the Mini

I'm not sure why it seems like such an appealing idea to me, but I have always wanted the dash in my car to have just two A/V devices in it: no radio, no dancing equalizer lights—just a simple interface consisting of a touchscreen and a slot to load CDs and DVDs into. I had a setup like this in my last car (a 1992 16vGTi), minus the touchscreen and really liked how clean it made the dash area look. In that vehicle, I had a Sony head unit buried in the dash that was controlled by the Sony joystick wired remote (for those of you who remember that Sony concept), and a Sony TV tuner that did graphics generation for CD track time, radio station display, and any other pertinent information that the head unit would normally display.

Originally, I planned to have a slot exactly like the one on the front of the Mac mini right above the screen in my dash panel, but then the car fought back. The Mac mini is, as you all know, 6.5 inches square by 2 inches tall. This is slightly smaller than the average in-dash DIN-sized head unit, so I thought my plan would be no problem. However, when you plug all the connectors into the back of the computer, you add roughly an inch and a half to its depth (see Figure 15-1).

Figure 15-1.
Space-hogging connectors

In my case, for the computer to fit in the available subdash area, it would also have to be located behind and slightly above the monitor to give access to the CD/DVD slot while still retaining the original air conditioner control location. If I had the newer Climatronic climate controls in my particular vehicle, I could have simply relocated them, as they are fully electrical, with the A/C flaps and temperature control being operated by servos. However, my car has cable-operated controls, which really never work quite as nicely when you relocate them and extend the cables (I did this in a 1998 Honda Civic Coupe and it worked okay, but the temperature slider was a little stiffer than normal when it was all done). The point of all this is that, when taking into account the connectors and thickness of the screen in this particular install, the computer went from being 6.5 inches deep to 10.25 inches deep. My climate control ductwork (which contains mechanical flaps to control airflow) is about 7.5 inches back from the face of the dash opening. So, short of rebuilding either the complete dash or the entire ductwork system in this car, the Mac mini was going to have to live somewhere else.

I explored locating the Mac mini in the headliner where the sun visor lives (not enough depth) and in the left side of the underdash area (where your left knee is when sitting in the car), and neither were really viable options, so to the glovebox I went. I still wanted the Mac mini to look as if it was a factory-installed option, however, so simply mounting the computer in the glovebox itself or in the glovebox door wasn't really what I wanted to do; that's not the way that I felt Volkswagen would do it. Instead, I chose to modify the internal storage dividers in the glovebox to make an actual compartment that would house the Mac.

I started by building a three-sided housing for the Mac mini using 1/8 abs sheet, cyanoacrylate adhesive and two-part epoxy. This is basically a cradle that the computer fit into snugly. I then used an air-powered pencil die grinder and a right angle grinder to cut out the portion of the original glovebox needed to accomodate this cradle. After that was accomplished, I attached the cradle to the original glovebox again using cyanoacrylate adhesive and two-part epoxy designed for adhering SMC plastics together to make the parts into one complete unit. I finished the process by using black suede flocking (the fuzzy stuff that is inside the glovebox and armrest of my car) to coat the abs plastic cradle for a matching finish with the original glovebox interior. The results speak for themselves (see Figure 15-2).

Figure 15-2.
This looks perfect!

The only issue I ran into with wiring the Mac mini itself after the glovebox was modified was the length of the DVI to VGA adapter when a VGA monitor cable is plugged into it. This connector ends up being ridiculously long when it is all assembled. So, I purchased the Apple DVI to VGA adapter that has an actual cable between the two connectors (Apple part # M8754G/A) to shorten the depth of this connection. I then removed the plastic housing on the adapter's computer side (the DVI side) and heat-shrank it, ending up with a connector about 3/4 inches in depth versus 1.5 inches—a big space savings in this situation.

The full complement of connections was then routed through the subdash of the car, wire-tied along factory harness runs and plugged into the computer. The Mac mini itself slides into the housing from the front to allow access to the back of the computer if service requiring removal of the computer is ever necessary.

The Problem with the Power Switch

The first issue I saw with the Mac mini in a car environment was the fact that Apple located the power button for the computer on the back of the chassis. This makes total sense for them to do because Macs are usually put to sleep instead of being shut down after each use. However, in a car, you really can't let the computer sleep constantly without supplementing the vehicle's electrical system in some way. I considered adding a second battery with a dual battery isolator relay to allow the Mac mini to sleep when not in use without risking the possibility of draining the car's starter battery. That didn't seem to me to fall in line with the inherent simplicity of Apple's computers.

A second idea that was thrown around came from the guy who actually ended up shooting the finished photos of the car. He suggested using a remote shutter-release cable, which has a mechanically driven piston that would be perfect for pressing the power button on the back of the computer. Damn photographers... Pretty slick idea, but I was determined to see if the button could be removed and installed on the dash in a switch blank I had left over from the lack of heated seats in my car. I wanted the button within reach for obvious reasons, but I also really like that little power indicator that Apple screens on their buttons, and wanted it in plain view as well.

After perusing some early posts of people that were taking apart their new Mac minis, I noticed that the power button is a simple two-conductor momentary push-button switch that tells the hardware to fire up. This actually made the process of relocating it (electrically, at least) pretty simple. Cracking open my brand-new computer and getting the button removed without damaging it was a little more difficult—and stressful!

I really didn't want to remove the entire board from the back of the computer (where the connectors are located), so a little gentle persuasion was employed (the button is mounted to a board that is adhered to the back of the case with a removable adhesive) to convince the button to leave its former home. The wiring for the button actually terminates in a connector that plugs into the main board, so I simply unplugged it and cut the original wires, extended them with a Monster Cable two-channel 3 meter RCA cable, and soldered this cable to both ends of the cut switch wires. The Monster Cable has four conductors color-coded and twisted into two distinct pairs (red/black and blue/black), so there would be no confusion on the other end of the cable when I reattached the button to the board. In the same fashion, because the extra twisted pair also uses two conductors and plugs into the main board using an identical connector, I used it to extend the Mac mini's power indicator (see Figure 15-3).

Figure 15-3.
Extending the mini's power button

I then brought the cable through the hole left in the case where the power button originally resided and powered it up. That was a scary moment. I was pretty confident that extending the power button would be no big issue because it either is making contact (on) or isn't (off), but the power indicator LED might respond badly to the extra resistance I was adding by extending its power supply cable by 3 meters. Luckily, Apple didn't give the LED a weak dose of power from the main board, and the extra resistance doesn't seem to have had any effect whatsoever on its brightness (see Figure 15-4).

Figure 15-4.
Perfection

Powering the Mini

Once the scary work was done and the Mac mini was reassembled, it was really just a matter of drilling a couple of really clean holes in the factory switch blank and mounting the button and LED from behind with automotive-grade two-part epoxy. Now that it's done, I really disliked from the outset that I had to use a power inverter to run the Mac mini installed in my 2001 GTi. My thinking is that it was a rather convoluted solution to take an electrical system's output that is 12 to 14v DC, convert it to 110v AC and then step it back down to 18v DC through the Mac mini's power supply brick to make the computer function in an automotive environment.

Aside from my aversion to this aspect of the inverter solution, it also led to simple functionality problems in the car environment, such as the fact that the Monster Cable inverter I used sometimes goes into a protection mode and doesn't allow the Mac to power up normally. Also problems: the lack of ignition-controlled wake and sleep functions, and the quirky workarounds that I had to come up with to allow the computer and inverter to stay on while pumping gas or running in to a store for a quick pickup.

Well, the Carnetix CNX-P1900 dual output 140W intelligent DC-to-DC power regulator solves these problems. Basically, this unit is a direct replacement (with major upgrades!) for the Mac mini's power brick that accepts 7.5 to 18 volts of constant input, has an ignition sense and pulse trigger input, and outputs a stable and consistent 18.5 volts. It also has a secondary 5- or 12-volt output for powering USB hubs or screens, a delayed 12-volt amplifier or accessory turn-on lead, and a pulsed ground output for triggering the Mac mini's power button (this last item allows automated operation of sleep, wake, and startup functions). The wide range of voltage input capability allows the P1900 to never sacrifice its output based on low voltages encountered during engine cranking, where battery voltage can often drop to as low as 7.5v. This unit is precisely what I hoped somebody out there would develop—but I didn't expect it so soon (see Figure 15-5)

Figure 15-5.
The Carnetix CNX-P1900

The installation process—luckily for me—was really very straightforward; detailed instructions for the unit are available (and frequently updated) on the Carnetix web site and are available for download in PDF form. Essentially, you simply open the Mac mini and unplug the power button connector from the board and replace it with the Carnetix-supplied Mac mini power button y-cable that connects to the board, the power button, and the output wire of the P1900 power supply for sleep, wake and startup control. Finally, you connect the power input wires to the P1900 (battery, ignition, ground, and the optional pulse-start input) and the remaining outputs to a USB hub, screen, amplifier, or any other applicable accessory that also needs power. To change the setting that allows the Mac mini's power button to sleep the computer, go to the Energy Preferences pane of System Preferences, and you're pretty much done.

After having this unit in the car for roughly a week, I can absolutely say that I am pleased and impressed by the thought and detail that was put into the design and execution of this little technological wonder. It is smaller than the Apple power supply, the internal fan keeps the regulator cool while remaining quiet, it doesn't induce any audio or video noise, the installation is simple, and it functions exactly like the company says it does. Now, I can use the Mac in my car in exactly the same way as a typical car stereo. When I turn on the car, the computer wakes up, and a simple press of the play button in iTunes (or a press on the Griffin Powermate) gets the music going. When I turn off the car, iTunes pauses, and the computer goes to sleep with no fuss, no crashes, no hard shutdowns. It's really a huge welcome change.

You've probably noticed that in the figures, I did leave the Monster Cable inverter installed. I use it to provide power to the AC outlet installed in my rear side panel. This allows camera and laptop batteries to recharge and runs any other AC device in the car when the need arises.

Housing the Monitor

As mentioned previously, I originally wanted the Mac mini to live in the dash with the monitor and climate controls, but space simply wouldn't allow it. By the same token, I also wanted to leave the OEM cup holder in place (it usually lives above the radio) for the sake of convenience, but this also soon proved to be a problem: time for some fabrication!

Strip things down to the essentials

I'll start at the beginning. The first thing to do when trying to make a large component fit in a small area (like a 7-inch monitor in a double DIN-sized opening) is to take it apart and remove as much stuff as you can that is extraneous or unnecessary to the project at hand. In the case of the Xenarc monitor, this meant opening the monitor case; removing the built-in speaker; reversing the orientation of the power LED to conform to the custom bezel; removing and relocating the infrared receiver for the remote control; and doing away with the front of the case entirely, including the buttons on the front bezel (all these functions are now performed via remote control). This gave me a flat surface to build trim on top of, and it reduced the overall size of the monitor significantly.

Mount the monitor

The next step was to mount the monitor in the opening left me by Volkswagen while still retaining the climate controls and their housing. This is the point at which the cup holders got removed from the equation, sorry to say. There was really no extra material to cut out and still have the climate controls mount securely to the subdash in their original location. So, with the monitor resting on this structure, there simply wasn't enough height to allow the cup holders to still fit. Unfortunately, about half of the opening where they used to reside is now occupied by the last 5/8 inches of monitor. In the end, though, the amount of aluminum that is blank above and below the monitor worked out well stylistically, so I don't miss the cup holders too much.

To mount the screen, I built a back brace out of 1/2-inch acrylic that was predrilled, countersunk, and screwed to the OEM subdash radio mount. It was then two-part epoxied for good measure. The monitor (with its back casing still attached) was then epoxied to this brace as well as to the surrounding subdash area. The 3M Duramix epoxy I used for this and other iPod dock installs is used for factory automotive assembly and is designed to adhere plastics together. It is rather expensive and requires a special "gun" to apply, but it's extremely strong and fast-setting. It is usually available at auto-body supply stores.

Mounting the monitor's case to the subdash in this way allows for easy monitor removal if any issues arise with the screen sometime down the road, although I am happy to say that it has performed flawlessly up to this point. It provides not only a single VGA input for direct connection to the Mac mini, but also two composite video inputs for extras such as a PS2, PSP, PS3 (fingers crossed), or a rearview camera that can be connected and switched to via remote. The rearview camera is definitely coming in the near future; I had one on my last car and really found it useful (and somewhat fun).

As mentioned earlier, I also removed the infrared eye from the monitor's front bezel and relocated it so that I wouldn't have to drill any extra holes in the aluminum dash trim I fabricated. If you look closely in shots of the dash in the figures, you can see where the eye has been located. It's near the top corner of the black trim surrounding the aluminum bezel and behind a small beveled hole I drilled in the factory dash trim. The monitor is signal-sensing for power and auto-detects the Mac mini's resolution. As a result, I hardly ever use the remote, but I wanted access to the screen's menu system, power, and source selection for future upgrades and unexpected occurrences (you might want the screen turned off if you get pulled over, for instance).

Fabricate some parts for finishing

Once the monitor was mounted and wired, I reattached the subdash radio mount to the car's subdash, remounted the climate controls, and began fabricating the aluminum bezel. I started by using double-sided trim tape (3M again) to adhere the factory climate control trim to a piece of ⅜-inch MDF (medium density fiberboard, available at local lumber yards). Using a jigsaw, I rough-cut the places where holes were going to be. I then used an inverted table router with a ¼-inch flush-trim bit to copy the OEM openings and outside dimensions into the ⅜-inch MDF. Next, I unstuck the OEM piece from the MDF and had a copy of the original climate control trim that fit perfectly. I then measured the screen's actual display dimensions with a micrometer and used sticks of ½-inch MDF brad-nailed to a larger piece of ½-inch MDF to create a jig (a custom form that you use for guiding the machine work) for the monitor opening. Again, I rough-cut the opening with a jigsaw and cut it out on the router using a ¼-inch bit to get a solid jig for the opening to be used in making a one-piece jig for the entire dash trim.

Once the monitor-opening jig was cut down to fit perfectly in the dash (with the climate-control jig below it), I used cyanoacrylate adhesive to glue the two together and brad-nailed this two-part jig to another solid piece of ½-inch MDF. After pre-cutting and routing, this gave me a solid jig that had all the climate-control openings as well as the monitor opening and the exact outer dimensions that the final aluminum piece would have. This piece was then detail-sanded by hand (to make sure the openings and corners were perfectly square) and then copied (I used double-sided tape again to adhere the jig to the raw acrylic) using the inverted router into a piece of ½-inch clear acrylic to function as a jig for cutting the aluminum. It would have been possible to cut the aluminum using the MDF jig, but you have to spray lubricant on the router bit while you cut the aluminum, and I have had experience with the MDF softening during this process, resulting in a non-square finished part. So, I always make acrylic jigs for any parts that will ultimately be cut from aluminum (see Figure 15-6).

Figure 15-6.
The acrylic jig

After one more test-fitting and detail sanding to work out any flaws in the jig, I traced the jig's pattern onto a raw piece of ⁵⁄₁₆-inch aluminum plate and precut it (slowly, and wearing safety goggles, I might add) using a jigsaw with a very new and sharp blade. Precutting usually takes about 30 to 45 seconds for a part like this in MDF or acrylic, but precutting the aluminum took 25 minutes. It's not something to do quickly; the jigsaw can easily bounce out of the material and damage the aluminum or any of your many body parts.

I then attached the acrylic jig with double-sided taped to the precut aluminum and, with the inverted router cut a new ¼-inch spiral flush-trim bit while a coworker (thanks, Anthony) sprayed Kent silicone lubricant onto the bit constantly (it took two full spray cans of lubricant to cut this part). It is important to note at this point that the aluminum was initially stuck backwards to the jig to allow for the next bit—a 45-degree chamfer—to cut completely through the aluminum while still having a surface for the bearing to ride on. It finished the machining on this part with a bevel all the way to the inside edge of the monitor opening for cosmetic reasons, as well as to allow full functionality of the touch-screen interface (see Figure 15-7).

Figure 15-7.
The bezel still needs some finishing work

For the next four hours, I hand-sanded the inside of this bevel starting with 80-grit sandpaper and working through 120, 180, 220, 280, 320, 400, 600, and 1,000-grit sandpaper to reach a surface that can be polished. I then used a pneumatic die grinder with a polishing head and a block of blue jeweler's rouge to polish the aluminum bevel to a mirror finish. The last step was to "brush" the surface of the aluminum dash bezel horizontally to mimic Volkswagen's OEM dash trim in the GTI337, 20th Anniversary GTI and R32. This is a slow and tedious process, but it is very important to make sure all the lines left are perfectly parallel and horizontal (see Figure 15-8).

Figure 15-8.
The final product

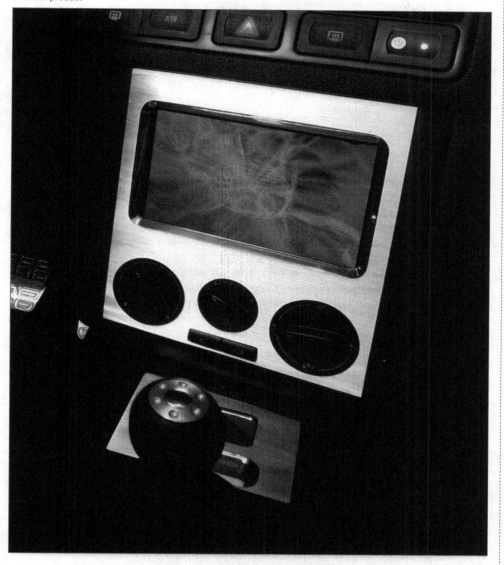

All of the other aluminum parts in my vehicle (the iPod and trackpad plate, the port and flash reader plate. and the ring around the boost gauge) were all made with this same technique of using separate jigs to make a complete one-piece acrylic jig to cut the aluminum parts. They were all then hand-sanded, polished, and brushed in the same manner.

I hope this gives some ideas to those out there looking to do something similar to their vehicles or anyone interested in the process of fabricating one-off parts without needing to take a trip to the local CNC machine-equipped shop for some CAD work and machining fees.

— Matt Turner

HACK 125: Repair Scratched DVDs and CDs

A scratched CD or DVD is just a coaster, and they always seem to get scratched at the worst possible moment. Learn how to repair a nonworking disk in minutes with items you have lying around the house.

> **QUICK HACK**
>
> **CLEAN THAT DISC!**
>
> An unplayable disc isn't necessarily a sign of severe scratches; often the disc is simply dirty. Because it is a lot easier to clean rather than polish a disc, try cleaning it first. There is no secret to this: use a mild soap, plenty of water, and a soft cloth to clean off any dirt, oil, or unidentifiable goo. Make sure the disc is dry and pop it back into your player of choice.

Plastic is a great material from an engineering standpoint. The stuff is cheap, sturdy, easily formed, and readily lends its self to a variety of applications. The positives noted, there are some drawbacks to plastic. Like lacquers and shellacs, the glossier the finish, the more likely visible scratches will appear.

If you're not careful when storing your CD and DVDs or game console discs, scratches are all to easy to inflict on your precious data. No big deal if you've backed up your data (if you *can* back up your data: game consoles use protected discs) but a definite hassle if you're looking forward to watching a DVD only to find that it won't play. Things get worse if you have a four-year-old determined to play Lego Star Wars while just as determined to walk all over the discs.

The solution to shiny-plastic scratch woes? Abrasives. Turns out that the way to get rid of big scratches is by making a whole lot of tiny scratches. The theory is simple: you're removing a bit of the protective plastic to relevel the surface. The easy way to remove plastic in this instance is by slowly scratching it off. If this were a method to make the discs shiny again, you could follow the scratching up with some wax to fill in the very small scratches, but since this is an either/or proposition (the disc either plays or it doesn't), aesthetics aren't very important.

An examination of the anatomy of DVDs and CDs is useful at this point (see Figure 15-9 and Figure 15-10).

Figure 15-9.
Idealized CD cross section

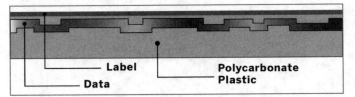

Label
Data
Polycarbonate Plastic

Figure 15-10.
Idealized DVD cross section

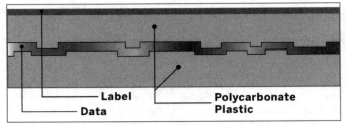

Label
Data
Polycarbonate Plastic

Looking at the illustrations, note some subtle differences between DVDs and CDs. CDs have the data layer next to the label so if you scratch the label of the CD there is a good chance the CD is ruined forever: you can't polish scratches out of the data layer. With a DVD, scratching the label isn't such a big deal; the data layer is sandwiched between a layer of plastic on the top and bottom. In fact, if you hold a DVD up to a light and stare at the side, you'll be able to see the data layer. The upshot of all this anatomy is that you've got a lot of plastic to work with if you're trying to fix a CD and about half as much if you're trying to repair a DVD.

What kind of abrasives will yield the tiny scratches necessary to make surfaces shiny again? Very mild abrasives: I am referring to the type found in Brasso or toothpaste—even a chocolate bar will work. I chose these substances for this hack precisely because there is every chance they are already in your house. If you're planning ahead, there are several specialized formulations for disc polishing; if you've got a young child, it's worth your time to purchase a goodly supply of the stuff.

Repairing CDs and DVDs

When deciding if your disc needs polishing, a visual inspection is always a good idea. Surprisingly, it isn't necessarily the depth of the scratches that render a disc unreadable as much as the direction of said scratches. As the laser reads the disc, it travels in a spiral not unlike the vinyl records of old. This is why a fairly deep scratch that runs in a straight line from the center of a disc to the outer edge isn't as likely to cause failure as a scratch that is parallel to the laser's path. With that in mind, if you examine the disc and note an obvious scratch running along the track taken by the laser, you can polish that scratch out by hand with a soft cloth and one of the abrasives mentioned earlier.

In the real world, the cause of failure isn't always readily apparent. Likely, you'll have plenty of scratches running in a variety of directions and no easy way to determine which one(s) are causing the failure. Polishing scratches out one at a time in this case is possible but not a very efficient use of time. You need something that works a little more quickly. Such a solution exists, and you're likely to already have all the tools needed.

Here's the list of required items (see Figure 15-11):

- Variable-speed keyless chuck drill

- Threaded bolt and nut

- Two metal washers

- Two rubber washers

- Goggles or safety glasses

- Area that can get messy while working

- Toothepaste or other mild abrasive

Figure 15-11.
Tools for making discs shine

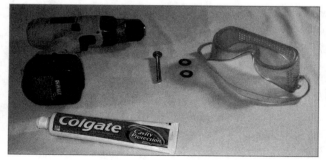

Once you've assembled the required items the setup is obvious (see Figure 15-12).

Figure 15-12.
A diagram of the polishing configuration

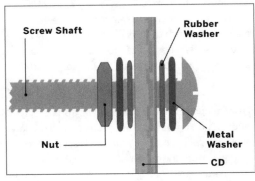

By now you see where this is headed. You're going to place the assembly into a drill and spin the thing at high speed while you polish the disc. I realize that you might be wondering why the rubber washers are there. After several experiments with this method, it turns out that if you neglect the rubber washers, the disc is far more likely to crack (goodbye *Luigi's Mansion* and *Kung Fu Hustle*) while you're polishing the disc.

Once the assembly is complete, place it in the drill's chuck, add a bit of your chosen polishing compound, and fire up the drill. Polish the disc for 30 seconds at a time (or whatever length you feel comfortable with) using a cotton ball or some other reasonably soft bit of cloth. It is necessary to use a light touch, and care should be taken not to remove too much of the plastic. You won't grind a groove into the disc; as long as you keep the polishing cloth moving, the pattern will be randomized enough to resuscitate the disc. Once you've removed the scratches, take the disc out the assembly, remove all traces of polishing compound and try the disc out in the target player. More often than not, you'll find that what was once a plastic coaster has become a useful disc again!

HACK 126: Use Your Mac as a Weather-Monitoring Station

Some people follow the weather like it has a plot, and while there is no shortage of online weather tools, there is nothing more satisfying for weather lovers than precisely monitoring the very, very local weather. Explore methods to turn your Mac into a weather data-gathering powerhouse with this informative guide.

So you want to be a weather person? Good luck. It does seem at times that luck has more to do with weather forecasting than it should. But luck doesn't have anything to do with the amount of interest in the weather.

For example, I maintain a weather website (http://www.richlefko.com) and regularly put up forecasts on my site. It has proved popular enough to attract advertising and a devoted following.

So how is my setup different from the widget that comes with Mac OS X? I don't just glean the data from sources on the Web, I collect my own data from my own instruments. There is infinitely more satisfaction in collecting your own data (and more accuracy) than relying solely on the Web. To monitor your weather, you'll need some hardware.

The good news is that there are a lot of companies making weather stations—some good, some not so good. I have always bought my weather instruments from Davis Instruments (http://www. davisnet.com/weather/index.asp). They've been around for 30 years, and I like their systems. They are well constructed, easy to install, and their phone tech support is very good.

Last year I replaced an older station with the latest top-of-the-line model, the Vantage Pro 2. This station is easy to set up outside and easy to read. The biggest trick is getting it to communicate with your Mac. In addition to the station, you'll need to buy the WeatherLink software for Mac OS X and, because I'm a wireless weather type, I also bought the wireless Weather Envoy.

Before I explain how I set up my Mac, you should understand that there are a multitude of options and ways to set up your Mac. There are wired and wireless systems, add on modules to extend the data your system is picking up, etc. I will be describing just one way—mine (see Figure 15-13). My system is probably a little advanced for someone just starting out, but if you have the weather bug, you'll probably end up in the same place sooner or later.

Figure 15-13.
My outdoor system

This system communicates with the weather console wirelessly (see Figure 15-14).

Figure 15-14.
The info is displayed on the console

The console shows all of the current data and some past happenings. For the purpose of this article, I won't describe what the console can display in depth because you're probably more interested in getting the data into the Mac.

In order to collect and display this information on your Mac, the most direct option is to buy the Mac OS X version of Davis Instruments' WeatherLink software (http://www.davisnet.com/weather/products/weather_product.asp?pnum=06520). There are some third-party developers working on other software options for the Vantage Pro 2, so the WeatherLink software, while useful, is not absolutely needed. What you really need in the box is the data logger that comes with the software; it into the back of the console and provides you with a USB port to plug into your Mac. Then, using the WeatherLink software, you can download the weather data your station is collecting into your Mac.

The biggest issue with this set up is that you have to plug in your console to your Mac to download data or view the current weather conditions. Kind of defeats the whole "wireless" thing in my mind. So I added a Weather Envoy; while it doesn't free a USB port, it does restore the wireless functionality I desired. For example, I can leave the console somewhere convenient for quick viewing while still having the data streamed to my Mac (see Figure 15-15).

Figure 15-15.
You're actually wireless!

The Weather Envoy is a standalone receiver. You plug the data logger into the Weather Envoy, plug the Weather Envoy into your Mac via USB, and you are always connected to your station via your Mac and the WeatherLink software (see Figure 15-16).

Figure 15-16.
Those are some un OSXish icons

Installing the WeatherLink software isn't a standard install. You go about the install as normal but once installed, those drivers must be chosen in the Communication tab of the set-up menu (see Figure 15-17).

Figure 15-17.
Plenty of choices

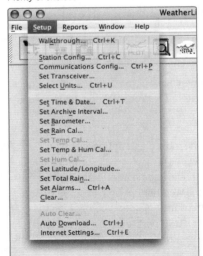

This setup menu has a "Walk through" option that takes you through each step of the station set up. Once this is complete, and the logger has time to collect some data, you can download station data at will and view the Bulletin on your Mac (see Figure 15-18).

Figure 15-18.
A lot of weather data is at your fingertips

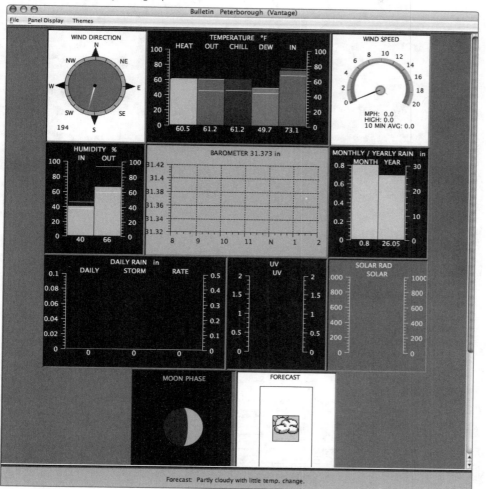

Once you have enough data, you can use the reports menu to construct charts and strip charts; the monthly summary is a great tool (see Figure 15-19 through Figure 15-21).

Figure 15-19.
The Reports menu

Reports	Window	Help

NOAA Setup...
NOAA this Month   F7
NOAA Summarize Month...
NOAA this Year   F8
NOAA Summarize Year...

Yearly Rainfall   Ctrl+R
Degree-Days...   Ctrl+G
Temp Hum Hours...
Soil Temp Hours...
Chilling Requirement...

Sunrise & Sunset...   F2

Figure 15-20.
Every weather hound appreciates charts

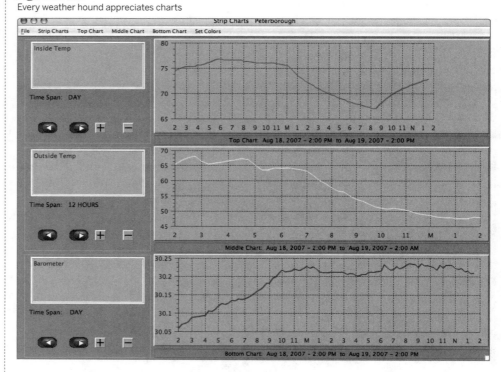

Figure 15-21.
A month's worth of data

NOAA MONTHLY SUMMARY

File

MONTHLY CLIMATOLOGICAL SUMMARY FOR: AUG   2007

NAME: Peterborough CITY: Peterborough STATE: New Hampshire
ELEV: 1020 LAT: 42.87 LONG: 71.95
TEMPERATURE: °F RAIN: in WIND SPEED: MPH

Day	Mean Te...	High	Time	Low	Time	Heat Deg...	Cool Deg...	Rain	Avg Wind...	High	Time	Dom Dir
1	73.5	86.5	2:45 PM	60.5	6:30 AM	0.0	8.5	0.0	0.0	4.0	3:45 PM	WSW
2	75.6	91.2	4:15 PM	59.9	5:30 AM	0.0	10.5	0.0	0.0	4.0	3:45 PM	WSW
3	78.5	90.5	3:00 PM	66.4	12:00 AM	0.0	13.5	0.01	0.3	9.0	8:00 PM	WSW
4	75.8	86.3	2:45 PM	65.2	5:30 AM	0.0	10.8	0.0	0.3	6.0	2:15 AM	WSW
5	65.9	79.2	3:45 PM	52.5	6:15 AM	0.0	0.8	0.0	0.0	4.0	12:45 PM	SSW
6	64.2	75.1	5:30 PM	53.3	3:00 AM	0.8	0.0	0.05	0.3	10.0	12:45 PM	W
7	73.8	84.5	2:30 PM	63.1	5:15 AM	0.0	8.8	0.0	0.0	5.0	12:00 PM	SW
8	75.9	85.3	3:15 PM	66.6	12:00 AM	0.0	10.9	0.61	0.5	12.0	2:30 PM	W
9	67.2	79.0	3:30 PM	55.4	7:00 AM	0.0	2.2	0.0	0.0	4.0	11:45 AM	SW
10	58.0	66.8	2:45 PM	49.2	12:00 AM	7.0	0.0	0.03	0.0	6.0	11:30 AM	W
11	62.5	81.8	2:15 PM	43.2	5:45 AM	2.5	0.0	0.0	0.0	4.0	12:45 PM	NW
12	70.0	84.3	3:30 PM	55.6	6:30 AM	0.0	5.0	0.0	0.0	5.0	5:00 PM	WSW
13	70.2	81.8	1:15 PM	58.6	11:45 PM	0.0	5.2	0.0	0.1	4.0	3:15 AM	SW
14	61.8	74.6	3:00 PM	48.9	6:15 AM	3.3	0.0	0.0	0.0	5.0	12:15 PM	WNW
15	65.4	78.5	4:15 PM	52.3	3:00 AM	0.0	0.4	0.0	0.6	12.0	10:00 AM	W
16	69.9	82.6	3:15 PM	57.2	2:45 AM	0.0	4.9	0.01	0.6	13.0	2:00 PM	W
17	67.9	78.1	2:00 PM	57.8	10:45 PM	0.0	2.9	0.09	0.4	12.0	2:45 PM	W
18	58.4	68.4	2:45 PM	48.3	12:00 AM	6.6	0.0	0.0	0.0	9.0	9:00 AM	W
19	53.3	61.0	1:30 PM	45.5	6:15 AM	11.8	0.0	0.0	0.0	0.0	12:00 AM	-------
20												
21												
22												
23												
24												
25												
26												
27												
28												
29												
30												
31												
MONTH	67.8	91.2	2	43.2	11	32.0	84.4	0.8	0.1	13.0	16	WSW

MAX: >= 90.0: 2.0   MAX: <= 32.0: 0.0   MAX RAIN: 0.61   ON: 8-08-07
MIN: <= 32.0: 0.0   MIN: <= 0.0: 0.0
Days of Rain: (>.01 in) 4.0   (>.1 in) 1.0   (>1 in) 0.0
Heat Base: 65.0 Cool Base: 65.0 Method: (High + Low) / 2

Using the WeatherLink software, you can construct a web page that contains data elements you choose, which you can upload (via FTP) to your ISP for inclusion on your web site. Unfortunately, the WeatherLink Mac OS X version suffers from a lack of parity with the Windows version. This web-page option is buggy, and there is no way to alter the page unless you can dive into the HTML with an editor. In general, WeatherLink for Mac OS X is several versions behind the Windows versions. While the Windows version can do all kinds of upload tricks, the Mac version can't. So, let's hope some enterprising third-party software developer will come to the rescue.

The hardest part of the whole thing isn't the installation or the monitoring; the toughest part is the forecasting. For that part of this hack you are on your own!

HACK 127: No Lights? No Power? Still Got the Net!

No power means no Internet in most cases, and this can be particularly frustrating for those of use who have grown dependent on a 24/7 connection. It doesn't have to be this way: you can power your cable modem with household items and build your own low-voltage power supply.

There is a recurrent, perhaps apocryphal, tale that says nine months after a power outage in major urban areas, there is a sudden spike in the number of births. The reason for the uptick in newborns? Without electricity, there was no TV, and life without television forced people to find less technologically intense methods of entertainment.

While a power outage in the past could have led to amorous adventures, the situation can be absolutely frustrating for those with a monetary dependence on the Internet. Professional bloggers, telecommuters, eBay snipers, or anyone who needs the Internet will find a suddenly unconnected life due to power woes certainly upsetting. It's a situation made worse by the certain knowledge that if only you had a little bit of juice, you could get on the Internet because there is a very good chance that the cable or phone lines are still up and running.

The situation could obviously be rectified if only you could get power flowing to the modem: your laptop runs via battery power after all. The solution? A battery pack for your modem! Building an emergency power supply for your cable/DSL modem will require only a few moments of your time, so you might want to consider placing this book next to a flashlight and completing this hack during the next power outage.

Once you're ready to start, we need to cover a few bases. The typical modem runs off of direct current (DC), whereas the electricity emerging from the wall is alternating current (AC). The process of transforming the varying AC current into the more usable DC current is a task taken care of by the power brick on cable running from the modem to the outlet. It might be the case that some really unusual modem runs off AC current or that the power brick is inside the modem, but these would be an exception. Assure yourself that your modem requires DC by inspecting either the modem or power brick (locations vary) until you find something resembling the sticker in Figure 15-22.

Figure 15-22.
An information packed sticker

What the sticker tells us is that the modem requires a 10 volts at 1.2 amps DC to get the business of transferring data done. The solution seems simple enough: we need to replicate that electrical input using batteries.

The right choice in batteries is crucial; not only is meeting the 10 V specification important, you don't want to blow the modem up by using something that produces far too much amperage. That means the car battery is straight out. There are some choices to be made at this point: what kind of batteries to use and how should said batteries be configured?

It's time to descend in the murky waters of battery pack design for just a moment. Two factors must be considered when designing a battery pack: voltage and amperage. We need 10 VDC and 1.2 amps. You could hit the 10 VDC by coupling a single AA battery with a 9-volt battery. While you would hit the 10 VDC requirement, supplying the necessary amperage would be a short-lived proposition. Batteries are rated first by voltage and then by milliamp hours (mAh). The mAh rating informs us as to the capacity of the battery. Our configuration needs to both hit the voltage requirements and have the ability to power the modem for more than a blink of the eye. Thus, let's settle on eight AA batteries—a configuration that should last about an hour and easily supply the necessary voltage.

Power requirements vary: a suitable configuration for one device will not necessarily work for another. Design your battery pack specifically for your device. For an excellent guide see http://www.rahq.com/images/batteries_101/Batteries_101.htm

To create a battery pack for this particular modem, some supplies are required (see Figure 15-23):

- Eight alkaline batteries

- 1/2-inch PVC pipe

- Rubber band of sufficient length

- Two lengths of hook up wire (preferably different colors)

- Appropriate adaptaplug

Assembly of the battery pack is straightforward. Cut the PVC slightly shorter than the assembled batteries and load the batteries as if the PVC was a flashlight—in series, positive terminal to negative terminal (see Figure 15-24).

QUICK TIP

THE WONDERFUL ADAPTAPLUG

Adaptaplugs in various sizes are available at your local electronics store. They cost only a few dollars and are nothing more than a connection to your device with two leads extending from the back.

Figure 15-23.
Everything you need to create a battery-powered modem

Figure 15-24.
The assembled battery pack

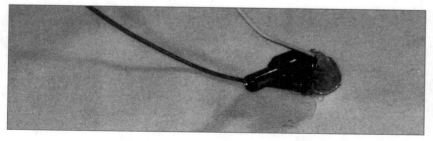

With the battery pack assembled, we can turn our attention to getting the juice from the battery pack to the modem. The trick here is to attach the two lengths of wire to the adaptaplug. If you are a bold, no-turning-back kind of person, feel free to break out the soldering iron and attach the wires thusly. For those lacking the requisite soldering skill (like me), careful connections (twist the wire several times around the terminal) covered with hot glue will do the trick (see Figure 15-25).

Figure 15-25.
The adaptaplug connected

The final step is attaching the adaptaplug assembly to the battery pack and for this, the rubber band is ideal. Not only is the rubber band insulating, the even elasticity means it is self-centering. Complete the assembly by stretching the rubber band around the batteries while using the tension to ensure contact between the positive and negative terminals of your battery pack (see Figure 15-26).

Figure 15-26.
A cable modem running on battery power

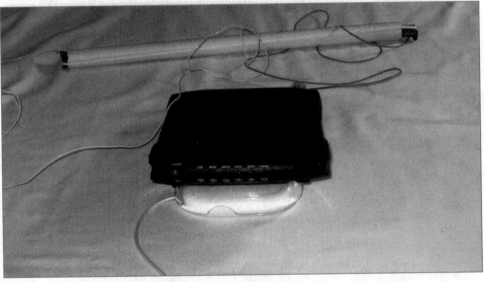

As expected, you can repeat the steps to power wireless routers and other conveniences of modern life by designing battery packs specific to each device. It should be noted however that if you find yourself building more than one or two of these things, you're probably better off investing in an uninterruptible power supply.

HACK 128: Hacks for Smart Homes

If you're like most people, you spend the majority of your time in your house. Everything in your house doesn't have to be controlled manually—you can automate everything from lighting to weather stations with MisterHouse. Check out methods to automate your abode with this engrossing hack.

Of all the grand promises from futurists—the flying car and personal robotic assistants—home automation is one of the few technologies that you can enjoyably, and relatively inexpensively, implement today. In fact, if you're at all technically inclined and enjoy tinkering, it's a fun hobby that you can enjoy and everyone else in your household can benefit from. To get started, you'll need a computer, some X10-based lighting and appliance control modules, and home automation software that you program to manage it all.

While X10 gets a bit of bad rap at times, it's your best all-around choice for automating your home, particularly when you're just getting started. It's a power-line carrier technology, which means it can transmit data over your existing AC electrical system. As a result, you don't have to retrofit your home; most X10 modules simply plug into a wall outlet. Additionally, because X10 has been around for so long (since 1978), modules are easy to find and inexpensive, especially when compared with newer, competing technologies. The basic idea of X10 is that modules "listen" to the power line for commands sent from your computer, remote controls, or other modules such as motion detectors. When a module receives a command that matches its address, it reacts to the command. If the module is connected to a lamp, the command might be "dim to half power." If it's a fan or radio, the command could be "turn off."

While it's possible to somewhat automate your home without using a computer, the methods for doing so are quite limiting. You'll only be able to turn devices on or off at scheduled times, or have simple macros that control a series of devices in an exact sequence. By using a computer to control your system, your home can be much smarter. For example, instead of turning on the porch light every night at 7:00 p.m., your computer can turn on the porch light only if you're not already at home. To accomplish this, you'll need home-automation software.

Get to Know MisterHouse

This section cover the basics of automating your home with MisterHouse, (http://misterhouse. sourceforge.net/) an open source, home-automation application for Linux, Windows, and Mac OS X. MisterHouse was started by Bruce Winter in 1999 and has benefited from other contributors enhancing the program to support a staggering array of options and automation-related hardware. The result is a program that's feature-packed, but more than a little intimidating for a home automation newbie. In this article, I'll sort out the basics and point out some interesting paths to explore once you're ready for some serious spelunking.

Installing MisterHouse

MisterHouse is available for downloading free of cost at the project's web site (http://misterhouse. sourceforge.net/).

Mac OS X uses the basic Unix version, but you'll need to make a few configuration changes in order to avoid having to install several additional libraries and packages to complete the setup. The recommended changes are discussed in the "Getting Connected" section.

There are several ways to interact with MisterHouse: via the command line, over a telnet connection, using a Tk-based interface, using spoken commands and speech recognition, or using a web browser. For the purposes of this article, I'll focus on the browser-based interface. That's not to dismiss Tk or the other interesting methods, but clearly using a web browser to control a server-based application, from any computer on the network, is a familiar and useful approach that's suited to most home automators.

Getting Connected

MisterHouse can adeptly handle home-automation tasks you can throw at it, but to send commands to X10 modules, it needs a power-line interface. MisterHouse works with several controllers, including the commonly used CM11 (http://www.x10.com/automation/x10_ck11a_1.htm). The CM11 relies on a standard serial port; since you're using a Mac, you'll need a USB-to-serial adapter, such as the Keyspan USA-19HS, to make the right connections.

If you're running Mac OS X and using a USB-to-serial adapter, use Terminal to list the devices in /dev, look for the name of your serial adapter, and then use that as the `cm11_port` parameter. On my system, I specify my Keyspan USA19 adapter like this:

```
cm11_port = /dev/tty.USA191822P1.1
```

If you move the serial adapter to another USB port, Mac OS X will reassign the adapter's device name, and you'll have to update the `cm11_port` parameter with the new value.

While you're making configuration changes, you'll probably want to turn off a couple of options. Mac OS X doesn't include Tk, **gd** (a graphics library), or the sound utilities that MisterHouse expects. Turning off these options as shown in this code will prevent MisterHouse from complaining about missing files during startup:

```
gd = 0
Sound_program =
tk = 0
```

Later, after you're up and running and want to go further, you can install the necessary files (or their equivalents) and turn these options back on.

MisterHouse also works with wireless X10 receivers such as the X10 MR26 RF Receiver (http://www.x10.com/products/x10_mr26a.htm) and WGL Design's W800RF32 (http://www.wgldesigns.com/w800.html). These devices are excellent ways to improve the response time and reliability of wireless motion detectors and the like, but wireless X10 is not a replacement for the power-line controllers discussed earlier. If you're just getting started, don't worry about wireless X10 yet. Just know that MisterHouse is ready for it when you're ready to go there.

Now that you've got MisterHouse set up, let's start adding the details it needs to run your home.

Adding X10 Devices

MisterHouse needs to know about the X10 devices you have installed in your home so that it can send commands to them in response to events or your actions. To begin, start MisterHouse running by opening the application (if you downloaded the compiled version) or from the command line:

```
$ ./mh/bin/mh
```

If all goes well, you can then access the main MisterHouse interface by entering **http://localhost:8080** into your favorite web browser. This displays the MisterHouse main menu, as shown in Figure 15-27.

Figure 15-27.
MisterHouse main menu

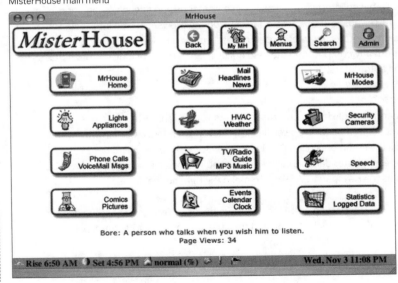

To reach the configuration screens, click the MisterHouse Home button, and then click Setup MisterHouse. Then, in the second row of buttons, as shown in Figure 15-28, click Edit Items.

Figure 15-28.
Setup MisterHouse menu

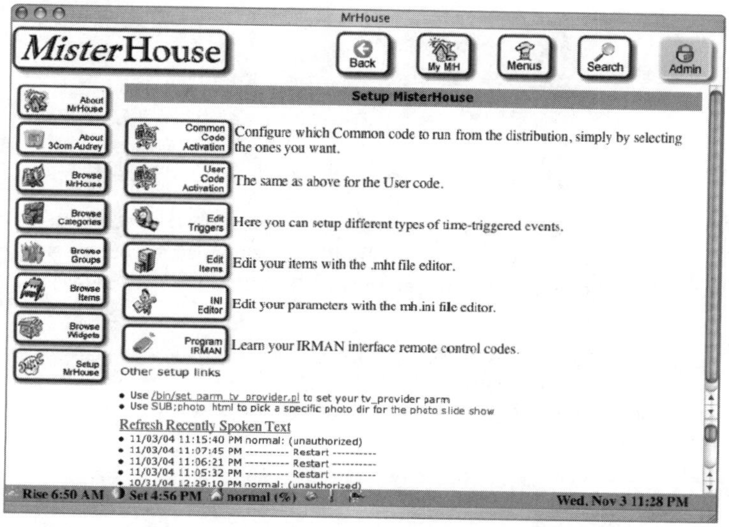

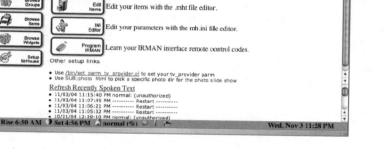

The Items Menu screen allows you to edit an MHT file, which is where MisterHouse keeps track of the devices you have defined. By default, you'll be working with the sample *mh/code/test/test. mht* file that's included with the MisterHouse distribution. Eventually, you'll want to either create your own file or delete all the items from the sample file, but for now let's use it as is, because it illustrates several MisterHouse basics that you'll need to understand before diving into a completely customized setup.

To view the lamp modules that are already defined, click the X10I link in the Item Index to scroll to the section of the page that lists the modules and their addresses, as shown in Figure 15-29. Appliance modules are defined as type X10A.

Figure 15-29.
Listing X10 lamp modules

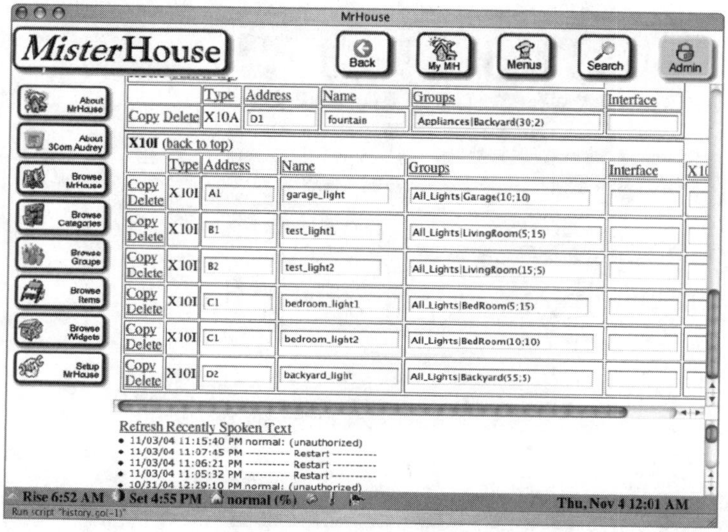

The sample setup has six lamps defined, each with their corresponding X10 address, as shown in Table 15-1.

Table 15-1.
Sample MisterHouse modules

Unit Name	X10 Address
garage_light	A1
Test_light1	B2
Test_light2	B2
bedroom_light1	C1
bedroom_light2	C1

Additionally, each device is assigned to the All_Lights group, and a group appropriate for its location. For example, the bedroom lights are assigned to the BedRoom group. Using groups is a great technique for simplifying your home-automation system and is discussed in more detail later in this hack.

Notice that the two bedroom lights are both assigned to the same address, C1. This is perfectly valid in X10 and is quite useful when you want to control more than one device with a single command. Here, when you have MisterHouse send an off command to the C1 address, both bedroom lights will turn off simultaneously.

✉ While X10 addresses don't have to be unique, each device must have a unique name defined in MisterHouse.

The other fields you see listed on the screen, Interface and X10 Type, are used when you have more than one power-line interface connected to your computer. You can safely ignore these fields for now, and in fact, you might not ever need to utilize them unless you begin to create a particularly sophisticated system.

Let's add a new device; say, a lamp module connected to a light in the office whose X10 address is set to G10. To do this, scroll the web browser window back to the top of the Items Menu screen. Then select X10 Light (X10I) from the pop-up menu that's next to the Create button, as shown in Figure 15-30.

Figure 15-30.
Adding a new device

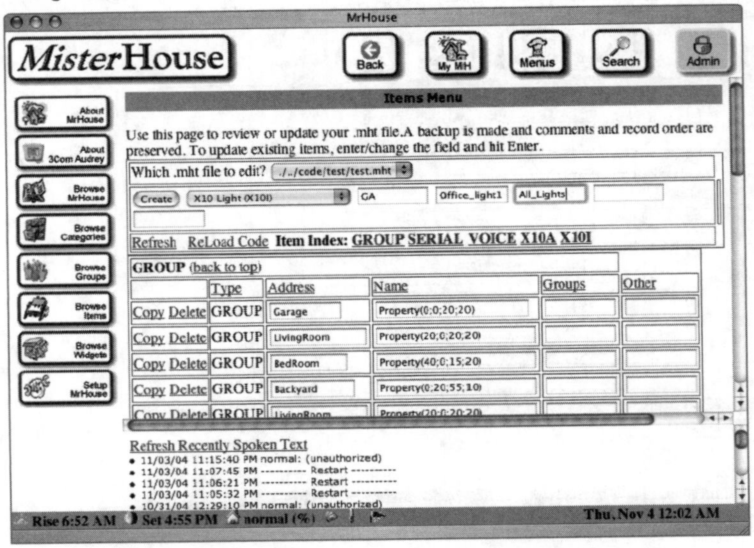

Next, enter a device name of `Office_light1`, the X10 address of the module, which is `GA` (G10 in hexadecimal), and the group that this device belongs to, `All_Lights`. Press Enter to add the new device. If you return to the X10I index listing, as described earlier, you'll see that `Office_light1` has been added to the device list.

If you need to correct or change an entry that you've already made, simply edit the appropriate fields in the index listing and press Enter. If you get confused or want to make sure your changes have been saved, click the Reload link at the top of the page to refresh all of the fields with the last-saved version of the configuration file.

Scheduling Events

If you want something to happen at a specific time in the future, either once or repeatedly, you set up a *scheduled event*. For example, you might want the air cleaner in the office, which is connected to an appliance module, to come on for three hours every other day. Or perhaps you need to get up early tomorrow, and you want the coffeepot to be started at 4:30 a.m.

To create a new scheduled event, click the MrHouse Home button on the main menu, and then click Setup MrHouse. In the Setup MrHouse menu, click Edit Triggers. At the top of the Triggers Menu screen, fill in the fields to add a new trigger event, as shown in Figure 15-31.

Figure 15-31.
Adding a new trigger event

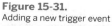

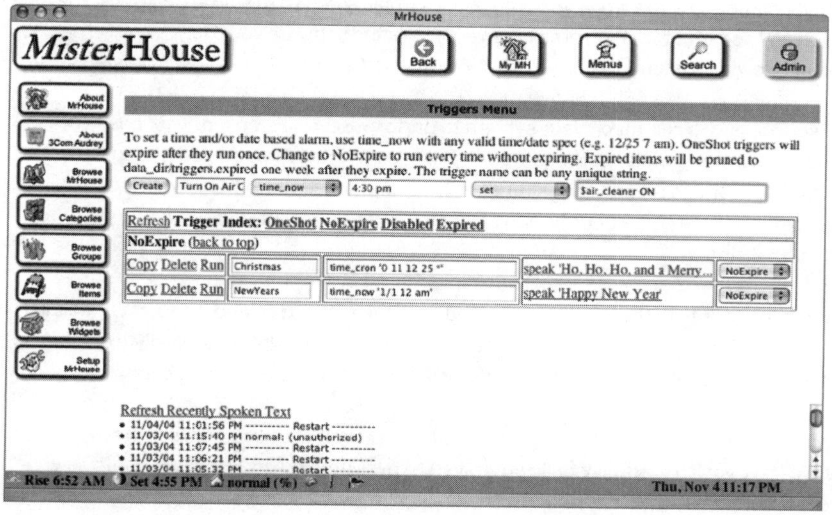

The first field is the name of the trigger, as you want it displayed in the scheduled triggers list that appears in the bottom portion of the window. The pop-up menu next to the name field allows you to choose from several different types of triggers. For a trigger that you want to occur at a specific time, choose `time_now`, then enter a time, and optionally a date, in the next input field, as shown in Figure 15-31. Next, choose an action from the second pop-up menu. To send a power-line command to an X10 device, choose `set`. The contents of the last input field are where you put the parameter for the action that you've selected. In the case of a `set` action, enter the device name and a command, such as `$air_cleaner on`.

Finally, click the Create button to schedule your new trigger event. You'll see it listed in the trigger list in the bottom portion of the window. If you want this event to occur more than once, choose NoExpire from the pop-up menu next to the trigger's action. Otherwise, the trigger will be executed at the specified time and date and then be removed from the list. If you want to temporarily stop a trigger from executing, but don't want to delete it (so you can reactivate it later), choose Disabled from the pop-up menu.

Be sure to read the MisterHouse documentation for information on the event triggers other than `time_now`. You can specify times using `cron` syntax, or define triggers that occur when variables you've created become `true`, and several other options. You might, for example, have a script that downloads the current weather conditions and sets the variable `$is_raining` to `true`, which triggers a spoken reminder to close that oft-forgotten bathroom window.

Responding to Events

Although scheduled events are handy, having your home-automation system respond to stimuli puts the "smart" in "smart home." Like the man behind the curtain in *The Wizard of Oz*, it's MisterHouse responding to events (motion detectors triggering, garage doors opening, etc.) that makes it all happen. And while you can do a lot with scheduled triggers, to really take advantage of MisterHouse's power, you need to write a few scripts.

Every home-automation software package that's sophisticated enough to run a smart home uses some sort of scripting language. With MisterHouse, you use Perl. If you're already familiar with Perl, you'll feel right at home when creating the logic and procedures that send, receive, and schedule events around your house. If you're not already a Perl maven, it's easy enough to pick up the little you need to know to get started. The built-in objects that MisterHouse provides for managing your automation system hides a lot of the scripting complexity from you, but some of the sample scripts can still be overwhelming for beginners. As with any home-automation project, regardless of the software you use, it's always best to start simple and add to your system over time; this approach works particularly well with MisterHouse.

Once you start scripting, you can teach your system to perform several steps for you, based on a variety of conditions. For example, you might push a single X10 button when you're departing for work in the morning, and in response, MisterHouse will turn off all the lights in your home, adjust the thermostat to save some energy, and close the garage door after you leave. It's all accomplished using scripting.

MisterHouse looks for scripts in the location specified with the `code_dir` and `code_dir_common` configuration settings. Drop a Perl script into these locations, and it will be periodically executed. In the default MisterHouse configuration, these locations are *mh/code/test* and *mh/code/common*.

This is where MisterHouse's clever design comes in handy. You can have multiple scripts in the locations, which allows you to gradually build your system over time by adding new scripts as you create or discover them. The *mh/code/public* directory is filled with example scripts for you to explore, modify, and move into your working directory when you're ready to put them into action.

The example script *mh/code/public/text_x10.pl* contains some handy examples to get you started. In the following snippet, MisterHouse responds to an X10 **on** command, sent by address **A2**, by printing a message to the MisterHouse log, speaking the same message aloud using the computer's voice synthesizer, and then turning off the device named `garage_light`:

```
# Respond if the A2 button is pushed ON
$test_button = new Serial_Item('XA2');
if (state_now $test_button eq ON) {
      my $remark = "You just pushed the A2 button";
      print_log "$remark";
      speak $remark;
      set $garage_light OFF;
}
```

Earlier, you learned how to create a trigger event using the MisterHouse browser-based interface. You can also set up triggers via scripting, as shown here:

```
# Turn on air cleaner at 4:30PM
if (time_now ' 4:30 pm') {
        set $air_cleaner ON;
}
# Turn on garden lights at sunset
if (time_now $Time_Sunset){
        set $garden_lights_all ON;
}
```

In the second trigger defined here, the system variable $Time_Sunset is used to determine your local sunset time, which MisterHouse calculates based on the date and location settings of your computer. When the event is triggered, the group named garden_lights_all is turned on. Groups are a particularly handy technique for home automation because they allow you to greatly simplify your scripts. In this example, instead of specifying each light individually in the script, MisterHouse sends the on command to every member of the group for you.

You can define groups with the MisterHouse browser interface (using the Edit Items screen described earlier) while adding X10 units, or you can define groups programmatically with a script. In the following example, the script first defines new X10 units, then creates a group that references each of the units:

```
$garden1 = new X10_Item('C1');
$garden2 = new X10_Item('C2');
$garden3 = new X10_Item('C4');
$garden_lights_all = new Group($garden1, $garden2, $garden3);
```

These have been simple examples, but they demonstrate the essence of home-automation scripting. Your scripts, in response to commands from X10 devices or at scheduled intervals, evaluate current conditions and states and then react in logical, and hopefully helpful, ways. If you're an experienced scripter, you're probably already imagining how you can expand these ideas to incorporate other sources of information about your home, your network, or the outside world. For example, in my book *Smart Home Hacks* (O'Reilly), the "Educate Your Alarm Clock" hack describes how to script a personalized alarm clock that automatically silences itself on weekends, holidays, and when you're out of town.

Using the MisterHouse Logs

MisterHouse keeps an extensive record that enables you to see exactly what's going on with your home-automation system. Not only does the log keep track of everything MisterHouse does, but also, because the application is listening to the power line, you'll see X10 commands that are sent from other sources, too. Learning to interpret the logfiles is essential for debugging your system, particularly when you're developing new scripts and experimenting with new techniques.

MisterHouse logfiles are located, by default, in the *mh/data/logs* directory. You can change this location by setting the data_dir parameter in your *mh.private.ini* file. One of the most useful logs for understanding what's happening with your system is *print.log*. It records the execution of events and triggers, and you can add your own messages to the log by calling the print_log function, as demonstrated in one of the script examples earlier in this article.

The *errors.log* file contains important messages internal to MisterHouse, and the *server_http.log* file keeps track of all of the pages and actions related to the browser-based interface.

Diving In

Now you know enough about MisterHouse to begin building your system, and to begin exploring the samples and documentation that come with the program. You'll definitely want to also visit the archives of the Mister House User Forum (http://www.nabble.com/MisterHouse-f14392.html). You're sure to find helpful advice about add-ons and techniques for creating a smart home that suits you and your family.

— Gordon Meyer

<u>HACK 129</u>: **Twittering Your Home**

Twitter is more flexible than you think; learn how to twitter your home with this hack.

Interest in the messaging service Twitter (http://twitter.com/) is clearly on the rise (so popular, *The Wall Street Journal* has covered it), and while most people are figuring out how to use Twitter for its intended purpose—social networking—I'd like to share a few notes on my more prosaic experiment of using it as part of my home automation system.

Hom-automation enthusiasts, particularly those of the hobbyist bent, have come up with several clever ways to have their systems send notifications of household events when they're away from home. For example, the home-automation system might send a message to their cell phone when the kids arrive home after school or when the UPS delivery person has left a package at the front door. (For more about the usual methods for doing this, and other examples, see my MacDevCenter article: "Macintosh Home Monitoring." at http://www.oreilly.com/pub/a/mac/2006/04/04/automation.html.)

Why Twitter?

I've been experimenting with Twitter to create automated notifications, and so far, I really like the advantages it provides over other techniques.

First, Twitter supports several ways to deliver messages (which are called "tweets" in Twitter-speak). A tweet can be received via SMS to your cell phone, via several instant-messaging services, by visiting a web page, or by using specialized applications such as the terrific Twitterrific.

Another great feature is that the recipient chooses how they want to receive their tweets, and changing this setting is easily done on the fly. The sender of the message doesn't need to know which delivery mechanism is currently active; it's all handled by Twitter. This simplicity is a boon for home notifications that typically either take a shotgun approach and send notifications to several places at once (home, office, and cell phone email); or try to guess (based on time of day or other data) what the best destination might be. Letting the recipient determine where they want to receive messages, at any given moment, makes delivery much simpler and more reliable.

Finally, Twitter has a simple HTTP-based interface for sending messages. Instead of having to script an email program or an SMS utility, sending a tweet is as easy as having your home automation system open a URL.

My First Implementation

Figure 15-32 depicts a notification sent to me from my XTension-based (http://www.shed.com/) home-automation system; it indicates someone has been on my front porch .

Figure 15-32.
Answer the door!

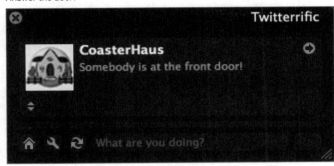

Figure 15-33 shows how the same message appears on my personal Twitter web page.

Figure 15-33.
They're not going away

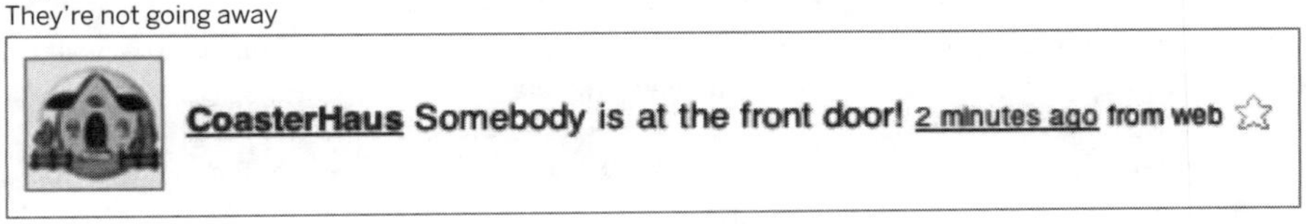

 CoasterHaus Somebody is at the front door! 2 minutes ago from web ☆

When I'm away from a computer, I change my Twitter preferences to send tweets to my phone, instead. Twitter can also relay messages using iChat (AIM), GoogleTalk, LiveJournal, and Jabber but I've found that delivery over IM systems is unreliable, so I don't use those options.

Getting Started

You'll need two Twitter accounts. The first is a personal account that you'll use to receive the messages sent by your home. If you want to receive messages via SMS and IM, you'll have to configure and confirm those details in your Twitter account settings.

Your home automation will use the second Twitter account to send the notifications. When you create this account, you will probably want to select the "protect my updates" option so that your notifications aren't available to the public at large. Then, you can add your personal account as a "friend" of the home's account so that you can receive the messages.

Implementation Details

This section describes how I currently have this working. Some of these details are specific to Xtension (http://www.shed.com/), one of the home automation applications I use, but the concept is adaptable to other systems (see the section "Hacking the Hack".)

When a visitor comes to my front door, XTension receives a signal from a motion detector. (Readers of *Smart Home Hacks* will find the full details about how the visitor is detected in the hack "Who's There?")

The motion-detector activity causes XTension to run a script that constructs a message telling me what happened, and copies the message to the Description field of a unit called "Notify Twitter." (This is one method of passing variables in XTension.)

The following script shows XTension's Master List window; the Description of the Notify Twitter unit has been set by this script to "Somebody is at the front door!"

The motion detector's script sets the value of Notify Twitter to "On," which causes the script attached to the Notify Twitter unit to execute. This script does the following:

- Retrieves the message text from the Description field.

- Formats the message and Twitter login information.

- Sends the message and login information to Twitter's status API.

Here's the script, which borrows some code from Tilman (http://tint.de/mac-os-x-gui/twitunes-applescript) ; it uses `curl` (the command-line HTTP client) to send a Twitter status message:

```
set theMessage to description of me
set TwitterID to "yourID"
set TwitterPassword to "yourPassword"
set TwitterLogin to TwitterID & ":" & TwitterPassword
set TwitterStatus to quoted form of ("status=" & theMessage)
set results to do shell script "curl --user " & TwitterLogin & " --data-binary " &
TwitterStatus & " http://twitter.com/statuses/update.json"
```

You'll need to enter the login and password for your home's Twitter account, as noted in the script.

Shortly after running this script, the message is delivered via Twitter, as illustrated earlier. It's a simple as that.

Hacking the Hack

There are several ways in which this script can be used and adapted. For example, I'm using a variant of it with PhoneValet (http://www.parliant.com/phonevalet/) to send caller ID information when someone calls my office phone (see Growling PhoneValet (http://www.parliant.com/phonevalet/) for a starting point if this interests you).

If I had a security camera on my front porch, it's easy to imagine including a URL, in the tweet, that would lead to a snapshot taken at the time the motion was detected. Although, depending on the length of your URLs, you might need to use something like TinyURL (http://tinyurl.com/) to shorten it before sending. Twitter limits the size of tweets to 140 characters.

If you use Indigo (http://www.perceptiveautomation.com/indigo/index.html), another Mac-based home-automation application, the previous script will work with just a few modifications. Instead of passing the message text using the Description field, use an Indigo global variable.

If you use MisterHouse (http://misterhouse.sourceforge.net/)—an open source home-automation application for Mac, Linux, and Windows—you'll need to adapt this technique only slightly, replacing the AppleScript portions with Perl.

I'm continuing to tweak and adapt the basic idea of this hack to new applications; if you have a suggestion or enhancement, please let me know what you come up with. Thanks, and have fun tweeting!

— Gordon Meyer

HACK 130: Create Custom Video Cables

One way to minimize cable clutter is to minimize cable length. Learn how to be a coaxial-cable-making master with this hack, and make yours just the right size.

Apple has gone out of its way to keep cable use to a minimum. The iMac, for example, can survive with a single cable (the power cable). Other peripherals, your cable modem or the AppleTV, are absolutely dependent on cables, and everyone hates cable clutter. You might not be able to get rid of every cable in house but you can help minimize cable clutter by making your own custom-length cables.

If you buy an Apple TV from the Apple Store, there is a better than even chance that the sales rep, in an effort to be helpful, will inquire as to whether or not you require cables to hook your new purchase to your TV. The obvious answer is "Actually, I was just planning taking the thing out of the box and marvel at the enclosure but thanks for asking." The line should be followed by a quick leap over the counter to pound the sales rep for having the unabashed gall to sell you a $249 device that doesn't come with the required cables.

The truth is that the Apple TV doesn't come with cables for a pretty obvious reason: everyone's requirements are different. You might need four-foot cables while the next guy might require cable runs of eight feet. Of course the cables cost quite a bit of money, and when questions turn to cabling for audio visual purposes, the conversation often turns to assertions stated with utmost certainty that are half tech speak and half voodoo. Someone just looking for a simple cable can end up with monstrously priced cables where the increase in supposed cable quality is of negligible real-world value.

A quick look at the anatomy and theory of a coaxial cable is in order. The typical coaxial cable is a copper wire surround by a dielectric (nonconducting) sheath, which is, in turn, covered in foil and then braided wire. Finally, the entire conglomeration is wrapped in the familiar black coating.

If you're wondering why a silly cable is so complicated, you're not alone. Ask the next person you see why a copper wire needs to be wrapped in nonconducting material and the conducting material, and you'll be met with blank stares. Someone may hazard a guess that the inner wire and the outer conductor are both transporting information, but they would be wrong. Actually, the coaxial cable is a clever piece of design. If you ever find yourself with a free Saturday afternoon, spend it solving the following equation for the case inside a conducting cylinder far from the ends:

$$\oint_S \mathbf{E} \cdot d\mathbf{A}$$

What you undoubtedly found was that the field inside the cylinder was zero. This bit of integral calculus (known as Gauss' Law) is valuable in the design of coaxial cable; it means that electric fields occurring outside the cable won't interfere with the signal conducted by the copper wire in the middle of the cylinder. The idealized version doesn't quite cut it in the real world; gaps will occur in the outer conductor, the outer conductor's ability to whisk away excess charge may be overwhelmed, and perfect conductors are still an unrealized dream in common practice. On the other hand, you can drop some integral calculus the next time you're at Best Buy and talking about cables.

Decide What You Want

If you decide to make your own cables, the first thing you need to decide is what level of quality you hope to achieve with your cable. You can go the super-high-end route and buy solid silver center wire, sheath it with a separately purchased dielectric, wrap that in silver foil and a layer of silver braid, and top the entire thing off with gold-plated connectors. That would be a lot of work. You could also go very low end and throw RCA connectors on the ends of iron-bailing wire and hope for the best. This hack is a middle ground of sorts: the cables we create will be good enough for your Apple TV, hi-definition needs, and cable modems in all but the rarest cases.

The Required Tools

To pull this hack off, you'll need surprisingly few tools. There are a variety of crimp-on or jam-on cable connectors that will work, but these have annoying way of coming loose as time passes. Plus terminating your coaxial cable with a jammed-on end doesn't look very good and cuts down on the times you can reuse the cable. You can also strip the cable with nothing more than a razor knife, ruler, and steady hand, but it soon becomes worth your time to invest in a cable stripper if you're doing more than a one-off cable.

Making a Custom Length Cable for a Cable Modem

This is a thankfully easy process, but you'll likely go through a couple of compression connectors if you don't know the little tricks. First strip the cable. If you're doing it by hand the ideal dimensions of exposed cable are: ⅜-inch inch of pure copper center wire followed by 3/8 inches of the sheathing complete with braided shielding. If you're using the wire strippers, the device will leave the correct amounts of wire and shielding exposed. Simply spin the stripper around the wire until the cable is properly cut (you'll feel the resistance go away). Spin the cable stripper in the opposite direction one complete rotation (to clean up the cuts), and discard the unnecessary bit of outer covering and dielectic (see Figure 15-34).

Figure 15-34.
A stripped cable

Once the cable is stripped, you're ready to add the connector. We're using compression connectors because they produce a solid fit and look tidy. The downside of compression connectors is that they are a one shot deal: get it right or get a new connector (see Figure 15-35).

Figure 15-35.
The cable, the compression fitting, and the compression tool

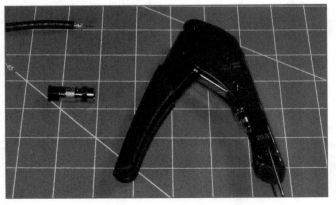

The first step is to peel back the braided sheath and trim the braided wire as close to the outer covering as possible. With the foil exposed, slide the cable into the compression fitting. It might be tempting to think that the compression tool will move the cable to the required position, but that isn't the case, so slide the cable into the connector until the bare center wire barely protrudes past the edge of the connector. Cramming the cable that far in can require considerable force, so don't be shy. Once everything is in place, it is time to use the compression tool. Place the assembly into the tool (see Figure 15-36).

Figure 15-36.
You may feel a slight pressure

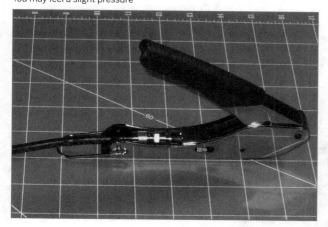

Almost there, grasp the cable firmly so it doesn't get pushed out of what is about to become its new home, and squeeze the handles of the compression tool. One moment later you've got a brand-new custom length cable for all your screw on coaxial cable needs.

Custom Video Cables

If you're looking to run cables between your TV and an Apple TV screw-on coaxial isn't going to cut it, the Apple TV requires RCA cables. You could go to your local home mega store and buy a version of the required plugs that screw on to the coaxial cable you just made, but those have the unfortunate propensity to come loose over time, which can leaving you with a frustrating (though easily fixable) problem. If you want a longer lasting solution, it is time to think about attaching the RCA plugs directly to the cable.

In this hack we're using solder-style RCA plugs not because of any innate superiority, but because the solder-on style plugs were the ones available at my local home store. Manufacturing the cable is a straightforward process. Begin by stripping the cable as described earlier in the hack. Peel back and trim the braided sheath as before, but before you go any further, put the sleeves on the cable. The sleeve is the piece that screws onto the jack, and if you try to put it on after you've attached the jacks, you'll be out of luck. Once the sleeves are on the cable, you can secure the ends (see Figure 15-37).

Figure 15-37.
Ready to be secured

QUICK TIP

RCA PLUGS

When it comes to choosing the actual RCA plug you want to use, you have a bevy of choices. There are, as previously mentioned, simple screw-on models, styles that require soldering, locking mechanisms, and versions that require only crimping. In the different styles, there are also different grades. Choose whichever grade you're comfortable with. In this example, I'm using a generic terminal, but the cable I'm creating only has to go a few feet. If you want a better looking cable or if your cable is going long distances, the RCA plugs made by Calrad (http://www.calrad.com) are highly regarded.

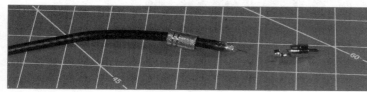

Securing the wire to the RCA jack is a two-step process. First crimp the designated strain relief area over the insulation. Once the jack is crimped to the cable, it is time to solder the center wire to the jack. It is important to do a decent job because this will likely be the weakest link when carrying the signal to its destination. Not everyone is skilled with a soldering iron. While a good soldering job can add strength to the connection, a bad soldering job means you'd probably be better off going with purchased cables or a set of RCA plugs that didn't need soldering. Since the chances of me soldering something properly are about the same as one monkey randomly typing out Shakespeare on the first try, I employed some specialized epoxy I keep around in deference to my lack of soldering skills. Everyone can glue (a small amount will do), so if you want to avoid the solder, pick up some electrically conductive epoxy. The coupling of the solder and the epoxy with the crimp is a surprisingly strong attachment. Screw the sleeve on and your cable is complete (see Figure 15-38).

Figure 15-38.
A few twists of the sleeve and the cable is fully functional

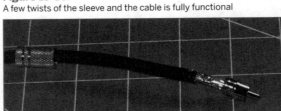

You can stop here is you wish, but AV setups usually require more than one cable. To make the installation of the cables a little easier, most people color-code the tangle of wires. You can use heat-shrink cable covers, but then you'll have to have a heat gun or a willingness to use a butane lighter. I don't like all the colors once the cables are installed, so I employ a multipack of colored electricians tape (see Figure 15-39).

Figure 15-39.
A complete color-coded cable

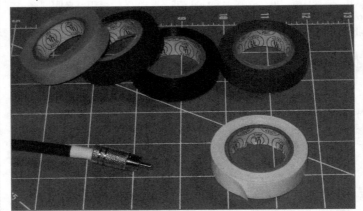

HACK 131: Clean the Mighty Mouse

It is only a matter of time until the scroll ball of your Mighty Mouse stops functioning. Restore the mouse's functionality with one of these methods.

Anyone who has used a mechanical mouse knows that sooner or later the roller ball picks up enough dirt and grime that the internal rollers stop tracking smoothly. In the olden days, this meant twisting off the retaining ring and cleaning everything with a friendly solvent to produce a smooth working mouse. That ceased to be a problem when Apple introduced an optical mouse in 2000.

The days of not having to clean your mouse were comparatively short for Mac users. In 2005, Apple introduced the Mighty Mouse. The mouse kept the optical tracking mechanism. but Apple added a mechanical scroll ball on top of the mouse. The utility of the new scroll ball was appreciated, but the problem of gummed-up tracking mechanism soon became an issue.

The solution to a filthy scroll ball that doesn't scroll should is obvious: a little cleaning. While the answer is obvious, the proper methodology is not; the Mighty Mouse is not made to be easily serviceable, so cleaning its mechanism isn't a straightforward proposition.

Option 1

The method recommended by Apple consists of getting a clean lint free cloth, moistening the cloth with water, and rolling the ball around until clean. If you feel some junky stuff (if the ball isn't moving smoothly), Apple recommends you hold the mouse upside down and repeat the process.

The Apple method has the advantages of being easy to do and safe. The disadvantage of the Apple method is that it doesn't always work. If you've tried the Apple method, and it has failed to resolve the issues with your mouse, it is time to try a different tactic.

Option 2

This is the thermonuclear version of Mighty Mouse repair. It isn't easy, there is a decent chance you'll break part of your mouse or slice your finger open, and it takes a lot of time. On the bright side, if this doesn't work, you know your mouse had something wrong with it bigger than just a little bit of stubborn dirt.

To pull this off, you'll need a razor knife with a thin, sharp blade; small flathead screwdriver; a dab of your favorite glue; and a dollop of intestinal fortitude. The first step is removing the bottom ring. This step is not much of a trick because the ring is soft plastic and is easily freed by prying around the ring with a small-bladed flathead screwdriver (see Figure 15-40).

Figure 15-40.
One ring gone!

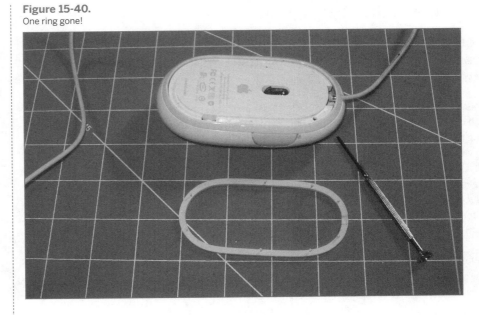

Once the ring is out of the way, it is time for the potentially mouse-breaking finger-slicing part of the hack. What needs to be accomplished next is to remove the retaining ring. Apple has chosen glue to attach the ring to the body of the mouse so prying the thing is out of the question because the ring is almost guaranteed to break. Instead a sharp blade is needed to cut through the glue. Insert the blade in some handy place around the edge of the mouse (the areas immediately below the side buttons are useful), and carefully work the blade through the glue. You'll likely hear the glue crack as you're working your way around the mouse, and the visual cue that you're successful will be the widening gap between the mouse body and the ring (see Figure 15-41).

Figure 15-41.
The hardest part is done, though I went through three blades

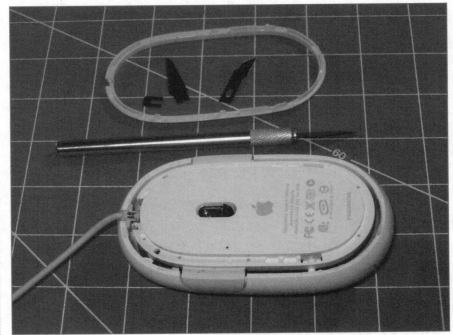

I've done this to several mice, and each one has had a different amount of glue. The mouse used in the figures had been glued in seven places. Work slowly. I found a rocking motion with a largish blade to be the most efficient method, but other methods may work more easily for you. Once the glued-on ring is free, the hard and dangerous work is done. Unfortunately, the tedium is not. The Mighty Mouse opens like a clam with a little pressure applied to the front (see Figure 15-42).

Figure 15-42.
Say "ah" Mighty Mouse

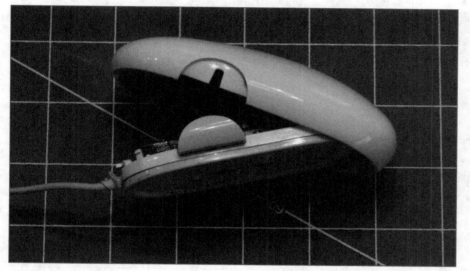

The entire shell will pop off with a twist at the hinges of the clamshell revealing the housing of the troublesome trackball. First, remove the ribbon cable from the mouse housing by pulling straight back on the ribbon cable slightly above the point where the ribbon cable is attached to the lower half of the mouse housing (see Figure 15-43).

Figure 15-43.
Carefully remove the cable ribbon

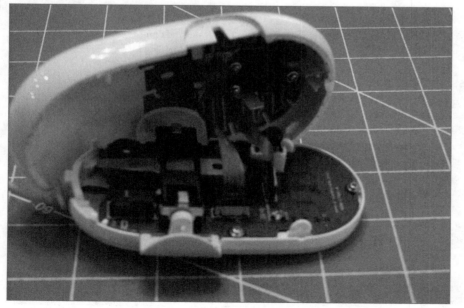

Remove the three screws with an appropriately sized Phillips-head screwdriver and withdraw the mechanism from the upper shell of the mouse (see Figure 15-44).

Figure 15-44.
The problem is in here

You can either clean the trackball and roller in situ or remove all the components. Removing the components allows for easier cleaning, leaving the parts in place makes for easier reassembly.

Reassembling the Mighty Mouse

Putting the Mighty Mouse back together is a simple process of performing the steps you used to disassemble the mouse in reverse order. While it is a simple process, it is also your chance to make sure that the next time you clean your Mighty Mouse, the process is much easier. The easiest thing to use when reassembling the Mighty Mouse is cyanoacrylate (commonly known as Super Glue); after all the thing was hard to take apart, so you better stick it together pretty well right? Well, it turns out that rubber cement is a powerful adhesive when the stresses are up and down but easily defeated with a sharp blade or forces coming it at angles. Thus a little sparingly applied rubber cement (apply to both the ring and the body of the Mighty Mouse and let dry before joining) results in a very usable and sturdy Mighty Mouse but also in a pointing device more easily taken apart when cleaning time inevitably rolls around again.

CREDITS

About the Author

Chris Seibold is an engineer, writer, and cartoonist residing in Knoxville, Tennessee. As an engineer, he has tackled such diverse processes as powder coating and hot dog casing manufacture. As a writer, he has focused on computing and written for a variety of online and traditional media, including serving as senior contributing editor for the Apple Matters web site and contributing hacks to O'Reilly's *iPod and iTunes Hacks*, with a talent for making the complex accessible to the interested but harried user. As a cartoonist, he has produced both cartoon strips and editorials. Chris also managed to spend some time producing radio shows relating to sports. As soon as he hits television, the trifecta will be complete. Chris lives with his wife, young son, and what is quite possibly the world's dimmest canine. He has a degree in physics from the University of Tennessee but has yet to find work involving frictionless inclined planes.

Contributors

The Big Book of Apple Hacks has a big list of contributors. This book wouldn't have been possible without the code, writing, and the patience of the following contributors.

Ari Bader-Natal is currently a Ph.D. candidate in computer science at Brandeis University, where he researches and develops games for peer-driven learning online. You can find more details about his hack—along with some of his other notes on Apple computing and bicycle commuting—on his "Bits and Bikes" blog (http://blog.greaterbayshell.com).

Surya Buchwald, aka Momo the Monster, is an artist-programmer living in Portland, Oregon. He's an audiovisual community evangelist—always looking for ways to support and build this crazy Nerd-Art AV Scene. His professional web/graphics/motion site awaits your perusal at http://momopro.com.

David Chartier, as a recent college graduate specializing in multimedia in Denver, Colorado, Dave Chartier has his hands in the design, Web, and Apple industries. After his first IBM PC in high school got him hooked, Dave hit the ground running—tinkering with just about everything you can do with and to a computer. After getting into design school and catching the Apple bug in 2001, Dave's obsessions focused on what's coming next in the worlds of graphic, video, and web design. On the rare occasion Dave is without his MacBook Pro, you'll probably find him either on his snowboard in Breckenridge or a local bike trail.

Bakari Chavanu is a baby boomer who grew up in Oklahoma City. He was a high-school English teacher for 12 years, and in 2006, he started his professional wedding and event photography business, Lifetime Video and Photography (http://www.lifetimevp.com/). He leads workshops in digital photography, and as a longtime Mac user, he writes articles and blog entries for MyMac.com and O'Reilly Media. If you ask him about his future goals, they include getting into travel photography and writing his own Mac-related book. He resides in Northern California with his lovely wife and two adorable and Apple computer-learning children, Amara and Kobe.

Eric Cheng, a Stanford University graduate (BS '97, MS '98), was a computer scientist and cellist before he took his first underwater photograph in 2001 and fell in love with the beauty of the underwater realm. Since then, Eric has become known around the world for his expertise in underwater imaging. He has meticulously documented his travels around the world and has been published in numerous publications, both in print and on the Web. In 2003, Eric was awarded a prestigious Antibes Festival award for his work with Wetpixel.com, the Antibes underwater imaging web site of the year; and in 2005, he won a category in the prestigious *Nature's Best Magazine* photo competition, which has placed some of his work in the Smithsonian's Natural History Museum. Eric also leads photo expeditions and has given workshops and seminars in locations around the world. He writes a monthly column for *Sport Diver Magazine*, one of the largest scuba-diving magazines in the world. Eric's underwater images can be found on personal web site: http://echeng.com/photo/.

Rael Dornfest is founder and CEO of Values of n, a Portland, Oregon company that is passionate about product, cautiously optimistic about software, and fascinated by the clever ways in which people have adapted technology to fit their needs. Prior to founding Values of n, he was O'Reilly Media's Chief Technical Officer, program chair for the O'Reilly Emerging Technology Conference (which he continues to chair), series editor of the bestselling Hacks book series, and instigator of O'Reilly's Rough Cuts early-access program. He built Meerkat, the first web-based feed aggregator; was champion and coauthor of the RSS 1.0 specification; and has written and contributed to several O'Reilly books. When not programming, Rael can be found writing all-but-illegibly on whiteboards, sketching on reams of butcher paper, or expounding on the virtues of same.

Dave Dribin has been writing software professionally for over 11 years. After five years of programming embedded C in the telecom industry and a brief stint riding the Internet bubble, he decided to venture out on his own. Since 2001, he has been providing independent consulting services, and in 2006, he founded Bit Maki, Inc. Find out more at http://www.dribin.org/dave/.

John Edwards has a B.S. in electrical engineering from the University of Missouri-Rolla and a M.S. in computer science from Colorado State University. As a recent graduate, he is interested in pursuing a consulting/contracting career in the areas of computer security, operating systems, and database design. He is also interested in freelance writing and currently maintains and contributes content to web sites MacSecurityPro.com and OSXEngine.com.

Tanner Godarzi first began his fascination with Apple products during his early school years with a shiny new iMac G3 and has self taught himself the whole way. After a brief stint involving a soul-searching quest and masquerading as a Ninja, Tanner found his one true passion: blogging. To aggregate his nonsense about the Apple world, he joined the crew at Apple Matters and iPhone Matters. When not blogging, Tanner runs an underground-resistance team dedicated to plotting the exact date Skynet will become self aware and jam out to Guitar Hero.

Larry Grinnell has been playing with personal computers since the early 1980s, beginning with a Timex/Sinclair ZX-80, followed by a Commodore 64, and a long string of Apple Macintosh computers (a Windows PC or two may have passed his way, too). After a brief but checkered career in broadcasting and nine years in the U.S. Air Force, Larry began a 25-year career with a major American consumer electronics manufacturer, where he has worked as a radio technician, technical writer, webmaster, printing/publishing technology adviser, systems administrator, and in his free time, obtained an MCSE certification. He shares his knowledge of computers, jazz guitar music, genealogy, and weird German cars of the 1950s through regular blog postings on the MyMac.com web site.

Chris Howard is a senior contributing editor for Apple Matters and was an IT manager in a Windows world until mid-2005 when he was given a welcome reprieve. Liberated from fixing Windows PCs, and with his first first Mac (a PowerBook purchased in 2003) in tow, Chris pursued his creative passions, studying writing and graphic design. Nowadays he provides freelance services and consulting in IT, writing and graphic design. He also writes about these interests and more on his blog, QwertyRash (www.qwertyrash.com).

Brian Jepson (technical editor) is executive editor for O'Reilly's *Make Magazine* Make:Books series, coauthor of *Mac OS X Tiger for Unix Geeks* (O'Reilly), and has written and edited a number of other geeky books. He's also a volunteer system administrator and all-around geek for AS220, a nonprofit arts center that gives Rhode Island artists uncensored and unjuried forums for their work.

Greg Koenig is an industrial designer who lives in Portland, Oregon.

Rich Lefko lives in New Hampshire with his wife and three sons and has been hacking Macs for the last 15+ years. He uses his Macs for video and photo editing as well as web programming. He writes for Mymac.com and is a rabid weather enthusiast. You can find his web site at RichLefko.Com.

Devanshu Mehta is a network research engineer and lives with his wife Shanu in the Boston area. He writes for a variety of online publications including Apple Matters.

Gordon Meyer is a Chicago-based writer and speaker who has authored dozens of software manuals, numerous articles for Macintosh users and technical writers, and O'Reilly's *Smart Home Hacks*, a leading book on do-it-yourself home automation techniques (http://www.gordonmeyer.com/).

Andrew Plumb is an engineer, musician, and parent living in Ottawa, Canada. When not embroiled in the art of analog IC design, he can be found deep in thought shoveling snow off the front drive or uprooting dandelions in the back yard. His scratch pad for sharing works in progress is http://clothbot.com/wiki/.

Chris Roose is a documentary radio producer, jazz/soul/funk DJ, and music-store slave living in Brooklyn, New York. His first encounter with a Unix-like operating system was Linux Slackware 1.0 in 1993. It was Mac OS X, however, that inspired him to explore the full potential of Unix. He can be reached at croose_21@yahoo.com .

Guy Serle is a long-time Mac user (since 1987) who just wants things to work and will go to extraordinarily difficult and time-consuming lengths to keep things simple. He's originally from Florida and a product of that state's educational system, which explains his penchant for having things explained at least twice and veeeerrrryyyyy slowly. He's regular writer for MyMac.com and one of the cohosts of the MyMac.com podcast. He also enjoys talking about himself in the third person and welcomes differences of opinion as long as they're not too dissimilar from his own. He now lives peaceably with his wife Tracey in Virginia and not so peaceably with his two boys Guy Jr. and Peter.

Tom Sgouros is a technical writer, freelance researcher, and performance artist based in Rhode Island. He occupies space at AS220, writes and edits a newsletter about public policy in that fair state, and occasionally hits the road with his good friend Judy, a robot (sgouros.com).

Martin Smit is from Seattle, WA. His web site is www.allbsd.com.

Hadley Stern is a designer and writer residing in Boston. Hadley studied creative writing and western civilization and culture at Concordia University before studying graphic design at the Rhode Island School of Design (RISD). Since graduating from RISD, Hadley has worked as a professional designer at Malcolm Grear Designers, Rykodisc Records, and Razorfish. He has worked on corporate-identity projects, CD packages, web sites, flash banner advertising, and a wide variety of print collateral as well as Internet product development. Hadley has written for *WebMonkey*, *American Photo* magazine, and *PC Magazine*, and is the author of O'Reilly's, *iPod and* *iTunes Hacks*. Hadley is also the founder of AppleMatters.com, a serious yet irreverent look at all things Apple where Chris Seibold also happens to write. That's where they met.

Chris Stone (http://www.oreillynet.com/cs/catalog/view/au/783) is a senior systems administrator (the Mac guy) at O'Reilly Media. He's written several Mac OS X-related articles for the O'Reilly Mac DevCenter (http://www.macdevcenter.com/) and contributed to *Mac OS X: The Missing Manual, Panther Edition* (Pogue Press/O'Reilly). Chris grew up on the San Francisco peninsula, went to Humboldt State University, and spent 10 years hidden away in the Japanese countryside before returning to California and settling in the North Bay area, where he now lives with his wife, Miho, and two sons, Andrew and Jonathan.

Matt Swann lives with his wife Amanda outside of Seattle, WA. When he's not testing web applications, he can be found writing code, tinkering with electronics, or taking photos around the Pacific Northwest.

Chuck Toporek has been a Mac user since 1988, is the author of O'Reilly's *Mac OS X Leopard Pocket Guide*, *Inside .Mac*, *Running Boot Camp*, and is the coauthor of *Hydrocephalus: A Guide for Patients, Families, and Friends*, and *Mac OS X Panther in a Nutshell*. He has written for *MacAddict* and *Macworld* magazines, and pretends to be a photographer in his spare time.

Marco Triverio has been using Apple products since the Mac OS 7 era. He has written articles about Mac OS X security, iPod, Objective-C and Cocoa, Open Firmware, Linux, and electronics. He is a student of computer engineering at Politecnico di Milano (www.polimi.it) and a member of the Arduino User Group (www.openlabs.it). He dreams of working for Apple someday. You can visit Marco's web site at http://trive.110mb.com.

Matt Turner is a professional fabricator and installer of mobile electronics. He has been working in the industry for 14 years and has built numerous award-winning show vehicles for individuals as well as for clients such as NOPI, Car Audio & Electronics, Davin Wheels, HiFi Buys/Tweeter, Microsoft, Boston Acoustics, Kicker, Eclipse, JL Audio, General Motors and Select Products. Matt built the year 2000 IASCA Novice Class First Place vehicle and was an integral part of the four-man team that built the Car Audio Trifecta-winning Chrysler 300m project. His work has been featured in and on the covers of many magazines, including *Car Audio and Electronics*, *Import Tuner*, *Car Sound and Performance*, *Honda Tuning*, *Macworld Magazine*, *MAKE: Magazine*, *Mac Format*, and *Auto Media*. Aside from building show cars, Matt specializes in the seamless integration of new and exciting technologies into automotive interiors. He recently partnered with long-time friend and coworker Randy Lively to form 2point5, a company that specializes in bringing these principles to individuals as well as to the mass market via the spec.dock mobile iPod solution. He has helped bring such innovations to the industry as rearview mirror-mounted radar detectors, docked iPods, and mobile computing.

Glenn Wolsey is a teenage freelance content creator living in New Zealand. His personal technology blog can be found at GlennWolsey.com.

Aaron Wright is a self-employed electrician living in London, England. His fascination with Apple products began after a frustrating decade dealing with Windows computers forced him to look for an alternative. The iPod he owned at the time certainly helped set his sights on a shiny white iMac G5, and since purchasing the machine back in 2005, has not once gone back to his Microsoft counterpart. With a Microsoft Xbox360 playing a vital part in Aaron's home entertainment, it seemed only right that he search for a way to connect his iMac and all the music, film, and photos it possessed to the Xbox360. More of Aaron's writing can be found at www.applematters.com.

INDEX